THE AGE OF
THE CRISIS
OF MAN

THE AGE OF
THE CRISIS
OF MAN

THOUGHT AND
FICTION IN AMERICA, 1933–1973

MARK GREIF

PRINCETON UNIVERSITY PRESS
PRINCETON AND OXFORD

Copyright © 2015 by Princeton University Press

Published by Princeton University Press, 41 William Street, Princeton, New Jersey 08540

In the United Kingdom: Princeton University Press, 6 Oxford Street, Woodstock, Oxfordshire OX20 1TW

press.princeton.edu

Jacket art © Julie Mehretu, *Looking Back to a Bright New Future*, 2003.

Library of Congress Cataloging-in-Publication Data

Greif, Mark, 1975–

The age of the crisis of man : thought and fiction in America, 1933–1973 / Mark Greif.
   pages cm
Includes bibliographical references and index.
ISBN 978-0-691-14639-3 (h : alk. paper)   1. American fiction—20th century—
   History and criticism.   I. Title.
PS379.G73 2014
813'.509—dc23
          2014007905

A portion of chapter 4 was originally published as " 'The Death of the Novel' and Its Afterlives:
Toward a History of the 'Big, Ambitious Novel,' " in *boundary 2*, Vol. 36, issue 2, pp. 11–30.
Copyright © 2009, Duke University Press. All rights reserved. Reprinted by permission of
the present publisher, Duke University Press. www.dukeupress.edu

British Library Cataloging-in-Publication Data is available

This book has been composed in ITC Century Std and Futura

Printed on acid-free paper. ∞

Printed in the United States of America

10 9 8 7 6 5 4 3 2 1

For my parents

CONTENTS

PREFACE

What purpose is served by delineating the core of the human? Or, in an older nomenclature, the "nature" or "condition of Man"? The project recurs in the history of thought. It is not purely continuous. Against a background murmur that may be ceaseless emerge audible moments of conversation and command.

The moments we know well, for example, of the German Enlightenment before 1800 or Athens in the fourth century BC, may inspire a misconception. They encourage us to suppose that in every moment of intensified inspection of the human, a notable mutation occurs, a collective result or definite disagreement emerges, and the idea of humanity is decisively changed.

On the contrary. The more general recurrence may be of episodes in which the imperative to determine the human creates the meaningful effect. This would constitute a form of interrogative rumination that adopts some habits, but not the essential ones, of investigations from a discipline or a science. It would be the questioning of the human that mattered and not the answers.

An impressive number of books (some famous, many forgotten) that appeared in the United States in the period 1933 to 1973 carried a particular kind of title. One knows immediately the era in which American and transatlantic intellectuals produced works like *The Nature and Destiny of Man* (Reinhold Niebuhr), *The Condition of Man* (Lewis Mumford), "The Root is Man" (Dwight Macdonald), *Existentialism Is a Humanism* (Jean-Paul Sartre), *The Human Condition* (Hannah Arendt), and *One-Dimensional Man* (Herbert Marcuse), the same era in which a popular photographic exhibition called *The Family of Man* (Edward Steichen and Carl Sandburg) could bring a quarter million visitors to the Museum of Modern Art in New York before drawing nine million viewers worldwide, and have its title sound not vacuous and naive, as it can today, but stately and exigent.

"The ——— of Man" made a pattern for many of the defining titles of midcentury, not only because of the accident of nomenclature by which "man" stood for "humankind" or "human beings," but because the key instances identified books that shared a fixed and finite constellation of concerns. Similar titles appeared on the covers of more forgettable but equally revealing volumes presenting comparable worries about the human future: *Man the Measure* (Erich Kahler), *Modern Man Is Obsolete* (Norman Cousins), *The Science of Man in the World Crisis* (Ralph Linton), *Education for Modern Man* (Sidney Hook), *Human Nature and the Human Condition* (Joseph Wood Krutch), and *Who Is Man?* (Abraham Joshua Heschel).

These publications left behind the old campaigners that one still finds, bent-spined, on used bookstore shelves, their back covers decorated with appraisals—of the loss of "the dignity of man," of man's fallen "condition," of the need to save man from himself—embalmed in a language that often seems incomprehensible. They are the books, too, that were on the basement shelves of my childhood, in twenty-five-cent or fifty-cent reprints, the worthy and earnest paperbacks that my parents' generation inherited to educate themselves for the responsibilities of their era.

It would be easy to leave the famous books to their individual histories and to ignore the minor books as period pieces from a period few would trouble to define. Having dug through this material, I will argue that the discourse it reveals from the midcentury age of the "crisis of man" is historically indispensable. I will not, however, be arguing that the discourse was wise, or either good or bad. Exhuming history should not require that we venerate it, only understand its constitution and effects. And the discourse was precisely of that peculiar imperative-interrogative type I believe we may often misunderstand or mischaracterize.

The elements of the discourse at its origin can be connected in a straightforward way. In the United States before 1933, pragmatism and progressivism stood as dominant philosophical legacies. John Dewey stood as a figurehead for both. Opponents of Dewey took energy from the overseas rise of fascism and a perceived need to oppose it with certainty, permanence, and transcendent values. The emigration of refugees from Hitler after 1933 deepened this confluence. The émigrés, too, were desperate to mobilize resistance to Nazism, but they contributed new concerns and unfamiliar philosophical lineages. Perhaps the discourse might not have outlasted Allied victory in the war, but after Hiroshima and revelations of the Holocaust, the public reach of the discourse expanded and spread, even as its original rationale weakened. The pressure and purported mortal seriousness of the discourse could be felt in areas far exceeding the narrow philosophical worlds of its origins, as it was adopted by entrepreneurs of ideas for their own small worlds. (Most damaging to the discourse's reputation among intellectuals was its adoption by propagandists for the Cold War, but this can be said to have shaped their further transformations of the discourse, not repelled intellectuals from it.)

From an account of the genesis and early constellations of the discourse—before, during, and in the troubled aftermath of World War II, addressed in early chapters—this study will turn to those surprising transmissions of authority as they affect other intellectual and philosophical positions over the three decades that succeeded the war, or the rest of the period I am identifying as "midcentury," 1933–73.

But this is not meant to be a story of the persistence, changes, or rise and fall of an idea (say, "the Man idea"). The history that matters is how a particular set of collisions and concentrations—which do not rise to the level of "idea," which will come to belong to all political and intellectual orientations (even those initially outside it), and which seemed to participants simultaneously bound to a tiny moment (anti-Nazism) and eternal (what is humanity?)—alters the obligations of intellect and thus what counts as a serious question or answer.

Here we face the level of a transient or anonymous intensification of one inquiry that exerts gravity upon seemingly unrelated questions across the whole public space of thought. We see effects in many specific locations, but cannot later trace them back to the invisible or extinct object that shifted all the legitimate possibilities and positions. For a long period in the mid-twentieth century, fundamental anthropology—the problematic nature of "man"—became a main rhetorical and contemplative current in the streams of thought and writing that shape a public philosophy. It did so in several countries, by the wartime import and export of ideas and thinkers through the United States entrepôt. Thus, this study is meant both to contribute to the history of a single episode in the restructuring of midcentury thought and to theorize an unseen *kind* of principle of determination of historical thought, the common determinant, here, for ideas that scholars treat superbly but separately: totalitarianism, Enlightenment, universalism, existentialism, human rights, relativism, Cold War unity, technology, and critique. It is meant to furnish a new philosophical history of midcentury.

No one will be surprised that the rebirth of modern human rights was one discourse that grounded itself in crisis of man thought after 1945. Nor will it seem unusual that arguments for the recognition and equality of those who might go unconsidered in white America's "unmarked, universal Man"—including women, African Americans, and eventually a wider social movement—lacked standing and were repressed in the early discourse. The more surprising track may be what occurs, and what we can see in retrospect, in literature, in specific manifestations of the "Great American Novel" once major specimens were written under demands and criteria from the overweening, environing discourse. It proved difficult to keep out those counterclaims of racial and gender difference.

———

If this book is a philosophical history, one might reasonably ask why so many of its pages are occupied with literature. The first impetus is a peculiar fact of transmission of authority. Literary critics adapted questions of the nature of man—and affirmation, reconstruction, and revival of "his" will in America—to their demands on future novelists at the same moment that these critics were accomplishing the triumphant installation of past American literature within the university and on an international stage. The standing of this formerly subordinate national art as a source of eternal truth—when read correctly by its scholars—promoted it past mere entertainment and local color and its old dependency on European models. For young writers, however, the demands and invitations to a new literature of man came wrapped in critics' threats of irrelevance and obsolescence should new fiction fail. This was the threatened "death of the novel."

Saul Bellow, Ralph Ellison, Flannery O'Connor, and Thomas Pynchon were intellectuals in their ability and their felt obligation to take up questions of the crisis of man in their early major works. But these authors' grumpy responsiveness yielded answers the early discourse could not have anticipated. *Dangling Man* (Bellow), *Invisible Man* (Ellison), and *A Good Man Is Hard to Find* (O'Connor) are titles that belong to the long list of meditations on the possibility of existence of any unmarked, universal moral core to man in the American midcentury. *V.* (Pynchon), though it names the antithesis of everything animate and the antithesis of man (in a figure of the prosthetic, apocalyptic female), represents an end of this line, and its partial inversion, in the transition to the sixties.

The challenge for all histories of high "ideas" is to find their entryways into vernacular thinking and practice. How does high discourse weigh upon other levels, if it does? How does one know, or prove, that it does? Many inquiries choose not to find out.

Here, fiction becomes key. Certainly Bellow, Ellison, O'Connor, and Pynchon were elites in their thought, influences, reading, and talent for creation. Yet any fiction writer faces a task of thinking *in concreto*. He or she "thinks" through formal instantiations of thinking in vernacular talk and character, in carefully calibrated deviation from verisimilitude and social plausibility, and in artful refiguring of the world as it appears. Since the fiction writers' answers had to take stock of truths of American life that the abstract discourse did not—life as a Jew or an African American, life with an orthodox religious faith or hemmed in by pervasive technology—their accounts frequently undid the hopes of the original questions of man precisely on matters of "difference." Undermining the universal pretensions of the discourse, the writers' work anticipated an opposite turn. This was true even when, in their own views, the writers didn't approve of difference. Life in America provoked it.

I turn to the new social movements of the sixties as a separate and distinct level of vernacular transformations of the discourse of man ("the sixties" for me names a phenomenon and set of thought-complexes rather than a calendar decade). When the sixties intervened, it wrote out in political actions and activism some of the contradictions we will have seen that the novelists had intuited or foundered on, synthesized or papered over. It must be acknowledged that the two routes for access to the vernacular do not touch. I am not claiming influence for the novelists on action or politics but formal and diagnostic depth helpful to retrospection. From the social movement, the study makes a final leap upward, returning to "high" or elite thought and imagination. Vernacular ferment made an upper realm of abstract philosophy effervesce. The future of intellectual life was unexpectedly changed by new modes of post-1968 thinking within the mixed philosophical and literary phenomenon known as "Theory."

This part of the argument could be misunderstood as culminating a chronological passage "from universalism to difference." I hope instead to establish that universalism and difference, as we know them, are two postwar projects drawing on a tertium quid, the discourse of the crisis of man. Contemporary universalism, normativity, and "reason" do not possess an unbroken tradition that goes back before the awful sixties into a magical consensus twilight of the American midcentury. Nor are difference and Theory all that alien to US thought, or all that uniquely distinctive of advances made by Continental masters. Both trace equally long roots into the chaotic and unanswerable ruminations of the crisis of man era—a genuinely transnational chaos.

The sixties make up something like a big bang for the intellectual and literary history of the rest of the twentieth century, and likely for the twenty-first. The years 1968 or 1973 marked the dawning of the period we still live in (1945 did so in a different way; say that it yielded the institutions and materials and the sixties the way we configure and view them). The rhetorical terms many use for this era of ferment and explosion are words like "fracture," "disuniting," and "contradiction." The perception of division may be hard to resist, especially as it draws its strength from hopes and dreams of unity that roiled in the crisis of man. Yet my argument will be that when you approach the individual pieces rocketing apart in the sixties, and sample them, you can see that they are often surprisingly made of the same stuff. Through recovery of the crisis of man, I can offer the prehistory that helps us trace back the trajectories of what now seem different intellectual galaxies, in hopes that others will compass them in a more various future.

—*MG, January 31, 2014*

PART I

GENESIS

CHAPTER 1

INTRODUCTION

The "Crisis of Man" as Obscurity and Re-enlightenment

In the middle decades of the twentieth century, American intellectuals of manifold types, from disparate and even hostile groups, converged on a perception of danger. The world had entered a new crisis by 1933, the implications of which would echo for nearly three decades to follow: not just the crisis of the liberal state, or capitalist economy generally, and not only the imminent paroxysm of the political world system in world war. The threat was now to "man." "Man" was in "crisis." This jeopardy transformed the tone and content of intellectual, political, and literary enterprise, from the late thirties forward, in ways that—because they are so intertwined with panic, piety, and the permanent philosophical questions of human nature—have still not been given an adequate accounting.

To its adherents, the crisis of man specified the danger of the end or barbarization of Western civilization. New conditions seemed destined to snap the long tradition of humanism, the filament of learning, humane confidence, and respect for human capacities that had made intellect modern and progressive since the Renaissance. Thinkers mourned the "end of history" as a forward-moving, progressive stream; it seemed a lonesome terminus in their eyes, and not a fulfillment as in our contemporary "end of history." Their fear, above all, was that human nature was being changed, either in its permanent essence or in its lineaments for the eyes of other men. The change would have the same result in either form: the demolition of those certainties about human nature, which had been pillars for optimistic thinkers for two centuries.

The Rights of Man had been the foundation upon which modern democracies were built. "We hold these truths to be self-evident, that all men . . . are endowed by their Creator with certain unalienable Rights," the Declaration of Independence asserted in 1776. "[T]he only causes of public misfortunes and the corruption of Governments," allowed the Declaration of the Rights of Man and of the Citizen in 1789, are the "ignorance, forgetfulness or contempt of the . . . natural, unalienable and sacred rights of man."[1] After 1939, the unalienable rights of man could not be taken for granted in Europe, as "man" was being alienated and eradicated, altered and undone. These erasures largely occurred at gunpoint, of Nazi, Soviet, or fascist arms, though intellectuals took the threat to be much more general. Perhaps men had been better off in ignorance and naive hopefulness, except that, the intellectuals warned, it was this blindness that had prepared the field for the disasters of Nazism and totalitarianism.

Meditations on fundamental anthropology are as continuous a stream of introspection as one can find in the history of philosophy, alongside questions of the substance of the world and the nature of the heavens; you can reach down and pull up a dipperful of speculations on the human in any year. The distinct return of man as a center of intellectual inquiry, apart from his scientific, practical, or religious nature, marks more definite occurrences within the long philosophical trajectory of the history of the West, and the period of the interwar years and World War II constitutes one such landmark. In this moment, the modern progress of expanded rights and protections for oppressed human groups and ignored subjects—the nonwhite, nonmale, and the nonelite—gave way to a renewed inquiry into the majoritarian, unmarked human subject itself, to change and reground the rationale for human moral status and inviolability.

From the 1930s through the 1950s, intellectuals debated a fundamental abstraction. "Whatever be the line of inquiry, the thread leads back to man. Man is the problem," the Jewish sociologist of religion Will Herberg wrote in 1951, speaking for a perception of the uniqueness of his time.[2] His mentor, the Protestant neoorthodox theologian Reinhold Niebuhr, had stated the discourse's difficulty, however, along with its necessity, a decade earlier, near its inception: "Man has always been his own most vexing problem. How shall he think of himself? Every affirmation which he may make about his stature, virtue, or place in the cosmos becomes involved in contradictions when fully analysed."[3] Interminable analysis itself also became the intellectuals' form of action, a means to pull others into the framework of affirmation and contradiction that their thought created.

"CRISIS" AND "MAN"

"Crisis," in the context of 1939, had been a thundercloud continually forming new shapes since World War I. Eric Hobsbawm has stressed the thirty-one years of continuous war that define the early twentieth century, one year more than the Reformation's bloody thirty-year realignment of Europe from 1618–48.[4] It was a single movement, in a way, of changed political, technological, and philosophical norms for Europe. Hobsbawm observes that those shielded from intervening events, as in England and America, could see it as two discrete wars separated by a bad but recognizable peace; this is how Americans do tend to see it today. In fact, at the time, intellectuals attuned to Continental events could also see it as continuous, from whichever country they looked. From the vantage of England, E. H. Carr, the Cambridge historian, had it as the "Twenty Years' Crisis" in 1939, a continuity of instability from Versailles to the invasion of Poland.[5] Safely in America, the German émigré Hannah Arendt in 1951 described it in this way: "Two World Wars in one generation, separated by an uninterrupted chain of local wars and revolutions, followed by no peace treaty for the vanquished and no respite for the victor," ending "in the anticipation of a third World War between the two remaining world powers."[6] In any country, those with eyes open to the affairs of the world, or ready to listen to such authorities, could sense they were living in a unique and uniquely bad time.

American intellectuals who identified themselves with world politics could recite a continuous list of crises leading up to World War II. They had learned the litany from their newspapers or from networks of political comradeship: 1928, Stalin's expulsion of Trotsky and the old revolutionaries to concentrate his power; 1929, the stock market crash and global depression; 1931, the Japanese militarists' occupation of Manchuria; 1933, Hitler's electoral takeover; 1935, Mussolini's invasion of Abyssinia, raining bombs and poison gas on lightly armed Ethiopian soldiers; 1936, Franco's revolt against the Spanish Republic and the rumbling bloodshed of the first fully ideologized, internationalist war in the midst of Europe; 1939, Hitler's capture of Czechoslovakia, secret nonaggression pact with Stalin, and invasion of Poland to launch World War II. By 1940, France had capitulated, and that signified, in essence, the end of Europe. It was done. From Portugal to Spain to Russia at the furthest meridian of the Continent, democratic forms had expired, either by murder or acquiescent suicide. England stood alone against the ruined Continent, its shapeless island not more than twenty miles separated at Dover from the Normandy coast through which Hitler seemed likely to invade. This meant that those in the United States, who suffered none of these disasters, still knew that the political philosophy of fascism, and its means of controlling populations through terror, complicity, and mobilization (the potent trinity that was very early on called "totalitarianism"), spelled something terrible for the liberal-democratic West and the European tradition with which Americans identified.[7] Serious arguments were proffered that the world was becoming totalitarian because the totalitarian model of the rule of men was more efficient and effective than the liberal state's manner of leaving men on their own, proposals that reinforced the 1930s intellectuals' habitual mistrust of liberalism or fears on its behalf. In the press, too, the world conflict reflected rival models of man. *Time*, in its year in review for 1941, pronounced in its books section, a few years late for the intellectuals, that "The greatest challenge of all" that year "was the triumphant emergence of a new human type, totalitarian man—superbly armed, deliberately destructive and dominant—at the very heart of what had been Europe's cultural sanctuaries."[8]

Visions of the "new man" preceded National Socialism in avant-garde artistic and political utopias of the early century.[9] Yet Hitler's revolution made the rhetoric distinctively its own. Contemporaries could cite Hitler's boast to Hermann Rauschning: "Those who see in National Socialism nothing more than a political movement know scarcely anything of it. It is more even than a religion: it is the will to create mankind anew."[10] Historians of fascism validate the seriousness with which observers in the thirties viewed promises that today seem outlandish, as research has confirmed the centrality of new man theory to propaganda and practice.[11] Joachim Fest has emphasized how "[i]n countless speeches and proclamations Hitler again and again conjured up the image of the 'new man,' and the many people who acclaimed the regime, who applauded every step it made and every point in its programme, celebrated the development of this man as the dawn of 'the truly golden age.' "[12] The cynicism and idealism of the people-shaping program of the Nazi leadership was familiar to Americans who had read the regime's chief scriptures.[13] In *Mein Kampf,* Hitler warned "that by the clever and continuous use of propaganda a people can even be made to mistake heaven for hell, and vice versa, the most miserable life for Paradise."[14] In the other official best seller of Nazi Germany, the Aryan race theory diatribe titled *The Myth of the 20th Century,* Alfred Rosenberg specified that the "measures taken on all social planes to mould a new human type" would define a complementary "task of the twentieth century."[15]

Humanity was divided, said new man theory. The divisions must be accelerated and completed. National Socialists must be taught to identify declining specimens, a subhuman within humanity. This was *Der Untermensch,* eponymous subject of an SS tract from 1935. "For all is not equal which bears a human face! Woe to him who forget[s] this!"[16] Against an Aryan ideal stood the degenerate image specified in the Nazi book *The Counter-Type (Der Gegentyp,* 1938), which "stated clearly what was involved in the sharp distinction."[17] Italian fascism advertised comparable ambitions to divide and transform man. Mussolini's famous 1932 article in *Enciclopedia Italiana,* ghostwritten by Giovanni Gentile, extolled a new "fascist man," while at the "totalitarian leap" (*svolta totalitarian*) later in the decade, "[a]nother activist party secretary, Achille Starace . . . led a campaign to shape the Fascist 'new man' by instituting 'Fascist customs,' 'Fascist language,' and racial legislation."[18]

But Hitler excelled all other totalitarian visionaries in his institutions for reshaping the clay of human life and firing it through violence and crime. "In my great educative work," Hitler said, "I am beginning with the young. . . . In my *Ordensburgen* [the Nazi academies] a youth will grow up before which the world will shrink back. A violently active, dominating, intrepid, brutal youth—that is what I am after. . . . In this way I will eradicate the thousands of years of human domestication. Then I shall have in front of me the pure and noble natural material. With that I can create the new order."[19]

With the US entry into the war after Pearl Harbor, government and mass-market magazines began to take up the language of the new crisis, adding the values of man to those fundamentals that democratic armies defended. *Fortune* magazine produced a major unsigned statement by the editors: "The Heart of the Problem: Without Vision of Deep Purpose We Shall Perish," and turned to professors of philosophy and theologians for "a general meaning."[20] Professor William Ernest Hocking of Harvard, in an article on "What Man Can Make of Man," warned that "In all our doings, and by way of these doings, something is happening to human nature."[21] The French neo-Thomist theologian Jacques Maritain proposed that "the only way of regeneration for the human community is a rediscovery of the true image of man"—in his case, a Catholic image.[22] As a new School of the Humanities was launched at Stanford in 1942, its dean posed, against the outer crisis of the Axis onslaught, the "internal crisis" of the new sense of man, both for evil and good: "Today we see [man] turning the weapons of his brain against himself—groping, amid the noise of a tottering civilization, for some faith in man to which he can cling."[23]

One can detect much in the early discourse of the crisis of man that is desperate and hortatory. But philosophical intellectuals and practical commentators of the true crisis of man discourse alike tried to understand why Europe had gone under and how England and America might not. They asked what man was, in what part of himself he should have a steady faith, and how he had come to this pass. A confusion and difficulty of the philosophical intellectuals' enterprise is that they were claiming to ask anew a question that we know they had always asked. Philosophers had contemplated man's nature for three thousand years. "What is man?" as a discrete phrase is a cliché twice over, and belongs to two different points of origin. One is the Bible: "What is man?" is heard in both Job and Psalms.[24] But "What is man?" held a hallowed place, too, in the philosophy of the Enlightenment. It is remembered from the handbook to Kant's *Logic*, where he says that there are only four true questions of philosophy in its universal sense: "What can I know?," "What ought I to do?," "What may I hope?," and "What is man?"[25]

When the intellectuals took up man in the recognizable language and concepts of midcentury, they created a historically specific configuration.

These intellectuals attempted to wrench the question free of the context of homiletics, invest it with the utmost urgency, and answer it inductively in a single book, sometimes of 300, 600, or 700 pages. Their seriousness was not a hoax. The inquiry was taken up by major thinkers not dealing in clichés or trafficking in old religion. Yet there is always something odd, unnerving, in this tenacious grasping of a question that really might have deserved its neglect as a sermon title or a lecture-room chalkboard scribble. And one is struck by how many significant secular books in the period begin, in their first line, with the cliché, making no attempt to evade the echo. "What is man?" the German émigré philosopher Ernst Cassirer labels his first section of a short summary book of 1944 written for Americans to cover the body of his own thought and the fundamental questions of philosophical anthropology.[26] "What is man?" the native-born historian and urban theorist Lewis Mumford begins another major book of 1944 within his series of researches on civilization and technology.[27] It is in the dissident theologians' work as well, renewed: Martin Buber, for example, used the phrase in a mixed philosophical-theological register (as "Was ist der mensch?") in his inaugural 1938 course of lectures as an émigré to Jerusalem, after years of being monitored and harassed by the Gestapo.[28]

Man became at midcentury the figure everyone insisted must be addressed, recognized, helped, rescued, made the center, the measure, the "root," and released for "what was in" him. But the thinkers who encouraged this were not, themselves, naive. Paragons of erudition, most knew the shape of other answers, the profusion of historical shrubs and undergrowth on this plot of ground that might tempt one to call the query an unanswerable. The more skeptical among them acknowledged that every effort to specify what the quiddity was that defined man seemed doomed. They had to admit to many previous definitions, as the Oxford philosopher R. G. Collingwood noted:

> We know, or at least we have been told, a great deal about Man; that God made him a little lower than the angels; that Nature made him the offspring of apes; that he has an erect posture, to which his circulatory system is ill adapted, and four incisors in each jaw, which are less liable to decay than the rest of his teeth, but more liable to be knocked out; that he is a rational animal, a risible animal, a tool-using animal, an animal uniquely ferocious and malevolent towards his kind; that he is assured of God, freedom, and immortality, and endowed with means of grace, which he prefers to neglect, and the hope of glory, which he prefers to exchange for the fear of hell-fire; and that all his weal and all his woe is a by-product of his Oedipus complex or, alternatively, of his ductless glands.[29]

Still, Collingwood sat down to write his *New Leviathan: Or, Man, Society, Civilization, and Barbarism* in 1942, in the midst of the bombardment of London, as the only way he knew to contribute to the war effort. Knowing already the difficulty or even absurdity of the project, he began his book, too, with those three words that open other books of the period: "What is Man?"[30] And he intended—like the others—to answer.

ANSWERS AND NON-ANSWERS

In one sense, the intense early thinkers of the discourse of man did answer their questions. They said what man was and what he must do. What he must do was, generally, to stay, or become, whatever they said he was already, or to avoid becoming, or not surrender to, whatever he was tempted to be but should not be. The shape of the answers becomes clearer through comparison. They enjoy a limited range of variety.

For Reinhold Niebuhr, man was a being made by God, yet one who sinned in hubristic efforts at self-transcendence (an orthodox theological answer). For Ernst Cassirer, man was naturally made to transcend himself through intellect, his only "essence" his functional ability to frame concepts as symbols and thereby extend his humanity (a neo-Kantian philosophical answer). For Martin Buber, humanity was that which emerged in the semimystical relation between man and man, having reality neither in the individual nor in the collective (a mystical theological answer). For Julian Huxley, man must be measured scientifically by his "welfare, development, and active participation in social processes" and would be defined by a less personal social standard in the new "Age of Social Man" (a utopian technocratic answer). For Collingwood, man would persist only in a civil community, which meant one in which all human relations were purged of the use of force (a liberal philosophical answer). For Erich Fromm, man would indeed be *known* ever more deeply by psychological science, but in his "physico-spiritual" nature, which existed primarily for the better, peaceful realization of a permanent happiness (a humanistic psychological answer). For C. S. Lewis, all men must learn the *tao*, the unity of religious-moral knowledge that underlies all human nature (a conservative amateur-apologetical answer). While for Sartre, "[m]an is nothing else but what he makes of himself" in responsibility and anxiety, inescapably modeling an idea of man for others (an existentialist answer).[31]

In a different sense, these weren't answers at all. They were, rather, elevations or promotions of one value or position to the status of an ultimacy. Or they were stakes, in the sense of commitments, "antes" in a hand at cards—starting points in the guise of endings. Their challenge seems to lie in the status of any single claim within the context of a multiplicity of answers—a multiplicity sure to be expanded, not convergently diminished, by the repetition of the insistence that one must answer. It would be wrong to be disappointed by the closeness of the thinkers' answers to their previous positions, but it might be equally wrong to judge the significance of this particular claim as comparable to other of their claims to truth and argument.

Besides the puzzling status of the underlying discourse and its mode of answers, however—and although in summary of individual positions it can seem as if the thinkers talked past one another entirely—we can in fact notice that constellations of positions emerge in four areas of great importance. Here were the subquestions of that overwhelming question or imperative: What is man and how shall we rediscover him? These areas were passed on, too, to later iterations of the discourse among debaters and writers of the late 1940s, the 1950s, and early 1960s.

The first area of concern was with what man was himself, and whether there existed anything fundamental beneath his facade, a human nature, determinate and accessible, when all else was social and unreliable. I will call this level of concern by its traditional name of philosophical anthropology, the "philosophy of man," or simply the "question" of man and human nature. Was there even such a thing as an abstract, universal man? Was there an individual, freestanding nature that could exist beyond all demands of collectives of men? Should there be such individuality, or was community (of the right kind) a necessary part of human nature?

The second area of preoccupation was with the shape of history. The history question included fears that the twentieth-century cataclysms had shown that the chronology of civilized development was not as people had previously imagined it, that events perhaps had no good order, or that previous fantasies of historical destiny and inevitability had actually led to these violent disasters and therefore needed to be reconceived. Was it possible or desirable to rehabilitate any sense of direction in history?

Third was a concern with faith—a vague word—as a worry about both religion and ideology. What sort of beliefs could and should be maintained in the midst of a world turned upside down? Thinkers wondered whether it was possible or wise to believe in anything abstract, lest it lead to the further abuse of concrete human life, after dogmatic belief—in Germany, Italy, and Russia—had led to the worst disasters. Yet how would they go on without a faith in progress, in God, or simply in a natural supremacy of good rather than evil in the world? It had a concrete political reference, too, in concerns over a "crisis of liberalism," meaning both economy and democracy, and the fear that even if one felt no temptation to totalitarianism, one possessed no reliable historical model for political order under new global conditions.

The fourth area, finally, was a fear about technology, in the sense that human technologies might be outstripping or perverting humane thought and goals. Technology in this debate included material artifacts like machines and bombs, and factory systems to make them, and also human techniques, especially the forms of technique that would organize men and women (whether in collective "planning," usually counted as good by the political left and center, and questioned by voices on the laissez-faire right, or in machine control and the de-individualizing propensity of technical efficiency, which was universally accounted bad).

If the human nature and faith questions seem abstract while the history and technology questions are specific, this mismatch very much belonged to the intellectual texture of the age, in an effort to attach the empirical to the spiritual, to hold together evanescent beliefs with hard facts of destruction, which were much too present. Human nature, in this particular discourse, is not really about physiology or evolution. "History" means the philosophy of history's shape and cycles. "Faith" is less about specific doctrines than the socially binding or undermining function of belief itself. Even technology turns into "technics," an autonomous, world-reordering force.

THE USES OF EMPTINESS

One of the striking features of the discourse of man to modern eyes, in a sense the most striking, is how unreadable it is, how tedious, how unhelpful. The puzzle is why it is unreadable. I don't believe that it's only because the context, or our assumptions, have changed, or because the discourse of man was finished off by different claims—though all of that is true. Rather, the discourse of man was somewhat empty in its own time, even where it was at its best; empty for a reason, or, one could say, meaningful because it was empty.

Because "empty" belongs to an everyday, nontechnical language, it may be misunderstood. I draw a distinction between two very different forms of cultural conversation: empty discourse and cant discourse. The crisis of man had both, usually but not always among different sets of intellectuals and spokesmen. A cant discourse is one in which the words deliberately do not mean anything that can be questioned, argued about, or refined by disagreement. In such a case, the words themselves, as symbols of mystery or profundity, credential the speaker's other utterances without adding discriminable content. Cant represents a default of thought, and likely bad faith. It may originate as shorthand for an original debate that no longer exists in the consciousness of its hearers, or it may be floated in order to evade a discussion that the user was never capable of sustaining. It becomes a counterfeit that drives out the good.

The utility of the discourse of man for cant was something that troubled its intellectuals, especially in the later years. Perhaps "the dignity of man" suffered this collapse at midcentury more than any other formulation.[32] In this strain, the "dignity of man" could be made a name for whatever was good about American democracy and bad about the USSR, since one system (democracy) knew what people were "really like" and the other (authoritarian socialism) betrayed human dignity. Or the "crisis of man" itself could become a name for the existence of people without religion or values, or individuals made lonely by the individualism and anonymity of cities in alienation; in short, a new name for solvent features of the modern, which had been better diagnosed by Durkheim, Weber, or many a sociologist from the turn of the century to its middle.

However, there *was* a useful empty discourse of man, something quite distinct, coherent, and credible, if not necessarily always lovable or redeemable seventy-five years after the fact. The midcentury discourse that, in the face of the massive degradation of the rights of man, tried to rediscover a foundation for man's protection simply said: there must be something that must be protected. The human agency to protect this unknown quantity was absent. And so there was a strong temptation to imagine this protection as self-authorizing, auto-guaranteed. Man must carry his warrant within himself, like his heart or lungs. Any person should have it— whatever it should be, from wherever it came.

The gesture in the best part of the crisis of man that substitutes for grounding, and does the real work of the discourse, was the gesture itself of saying "we must protect." Also: "there must be something to protect." Finally, "there must be something that protects itself." What makes it empty, however, is the consequence when participants successively phrase, answer, rephrase, and reanswer their questions in the service of these imperatives. An empty discourse is one that behaves as if it wishes to be filled with a single inductive or deductive answer—a definitive argument meant to persuade all hearers and end inquiry through complete satisfaction— but in fact generates the continuation of attempts, or tacitly admits to unanswerability.

The value of acknowledging this kind of discourse *as* knowledge might be brought out by a familiar analogy to the therapy of ordinary language philosophy on linguistic analysis. Classic linguistic analysis in philosophy thinks of language most often for its function of description of true or false states of affairs: "Socrates is a man." "The cat is on the mat." Ordinary language philosophy pointed out the significant presence of multiple classes of meaningful statements that do not describe states of affairs. Best remembered are "performatives" (in J. L. Austin's long-ago coinage), including such statements as "I thee wed," "I dub thee knight," "I christen thee *Britannia*," in which the utterance of each of these statements in certain conditions performed an act.[33] Such a speech-act changed a state of affairs in the world through its utterance as a statement, not by itself offering any rival description or proposition.

Say that the form of discourse in the discourse of the crisis of man, too, is not an ordinary truth-describing discourse. It does not cause convergence upon a solution through adversarial arguments and tests. True, each individual participant in the discourse of the crisis of man may give, indeed, is very likely and even duty bound to supply, a single descriptive claim: "Man is X." My concern—quite difficult to resolve at the level of individual participants' psychology, and perhaps only to be decided at the higher level of function and effect—is that it doesn't seem quite right that when each thinker says "Man is X," this is truly being promoted as a single, provable explanation, intended to end all debate. The underlying utterance, say, in all these presentations, remains both collective and imperative: "*We must* give a new or renewed statement of what man is." One does not, in fact, expect to stop others from giving answers; one anticipates ever more answers. The proliferation of answers, not their conclusion, seems to be the underlying point.

GENRES, CHARACTERISTICS, AND SCOPE

Characteristic genres of the discourse of man include collective forms that critics of literature and thought ordinarily hold in ill-repute. One is the series of articles by disparate authorities on a theme or keyword. Another is the anthology. A third is the multiply signed "credo"—more like a monument in front of town hall than a manifesto—combining the prestige of intellectual authorities who but for the present emergency would possess no point of contact. The intellectually arbitrary nature of such formal devices contributes to their force in practice—"here are some geniuses who disagree on all things, but *not this*." When lions lie down with lambs because both fear a bigger beast, humankind must take notice.

As prose objects, instances of these genres can induce the vertigo of hearing a portentous speaker utter completely incompatible statements on fundamentals—like the nameless collective voice in *The City of Man* (1940), tilting between theism and atheism to match its many authors and signatories: "Universal and total democracy is the principle of liberty and life which the dignity of man opposes to the principle of slavery and spiritual death represented by totalitarian autocracy. . . . Democracy is nothing more and nothing less than humanism in theocracy and rational theocracy in universal humanism. . . . Democracy teaches that everything must be within humanity, nothing against humanity, nothing outside humanity."[34] Or it suggests an all-inclusive emptiness and circularity, as in the introduction to an exemplary anthology: "Man is a totality; Man is a unity; and it is irrelevant to a true estimation of his nature to develop an infinite multiplicity of doctrines concerning his nature: a scientific one, a philosophical one, a psychological one, a religious one, a secular or sociological one." For an answer that supplanted others would be in effect totalitarian: "[I]t is productive of tragic consequences to subordinate all other methods to a single approach whether it be a theological, a rationalistic, or an empirical one."[35] In the mass magazine series, the reader can get the impression that it would be preferable to forget the content of each previous month's installment by the arrival of the new one.

The characteristic rhetoric and figures of speech of the discourse of the crisis of man turned to spatial figures, and a simultaneous preoccupation above all with limits and depths. The architectonic was inner, vertical, and spherical—of shells and cores, and Man enclosed by nature and intelligence. Sketched, it would look like Vitruvian Man, whom Leonardo drew touching both the circle and the square. Attachment occurred downward by roots, or upward in aspiration of transcendence. Kinship existed in a family conceived as circular, "nuclear" (for the tiny triad at the nucleus), or tied in a "brotherhood" of individuals who stood to one another in relations simultaneously of identity and fraternity: the human family, alike as paper dolls, linking hands and girdling the earth.

The discourse's intellectual trajectory rose and declined. It gained urgency in the debate over intervention, expanded once the United States entered the war, reached an intellectual peak by 1951, and, at that point, was popularized and banalized. Yet America did not recover "closure" after the war. On the contrary, it expanded its responsibility to the world, at least the "free world." It may be crucial to know even at this stage of our inquiry that intellectuals through the 1950s would declare the crisis not over; it was only being swept of its detritus and obstructions, the twigs the storm had broken, to be seen ever more clearly. Their depression began even before the Cold War took firm hold, and remained as the Cold War renewed the crisis and somewhat altered its meaning again, in the firming up of bipolarity and the fracturing of the world into hostile camps, United States and Soviet.

The literary critic Newton Arvin tried to explain the widespread return to "fundamentals" in 1950: "For one thing, the nerves of even the most imperturbable might, not incomprehensibly, have been deeply shaken in the last thirty-six years and especially in the last four or five."[36] Just to make clear what he is saying: Arvin was proposing that the "four or five" postwar years from 1945–50 might have been more nerve-racking for Americans than the whole rest of the thirty-year crisis since the beginning of World War I. Delmore Schwartz in 1951 described the "mounting and endless crisis" and a "postwar period" that had "quickly assumed the appearance and generated the atmosphere of a new pre-war period."[37]

Large numbers of people may have felt they ought to have something to say, or know something, or do something, about man. While some of this had to do with the emotion of wartime, it was also a function of elites and public spokesmen who felt it their duty to oblige their fellow men to think about man. The discourse of man was not a popular discourse at its origins. It came from the top and settled downward, finding its way into small officials' speeches and, presumably, into the crevices of minds. One runs across publications like this one in 1950 from a charitable lecture group called the "Church Peace Union":

APPENDIX B. SUGGESTIONS FOR ARRANGING
A SEMINAR ON THE NATURE OF MAN

Those who have read this book will realize that a study of human nature is not an academic pastime in our day. We have seen that leaders of thought trace the so-called "crisis in our civilization" to a crisis in man himself. Hence they tell us that if we would understand our age with its problems of crucial importance, we must find a deeper insight into the nature of man. . . .

SPEAKERS
Many communities could arrange a series on the nature of man by using its own leaders in the schools, professional fields and business world. . . .

PROMOTION
The entire series as well as each meeting must be given wide publicity. . . .
   It may also be possible to arrange for programs on the radio—brief addresses by guest speakers or round table discussions on several of the subjects.

And so forth, in "the hope that other communities across the land will arrange series of discussion groups on the nature of man."[38]

THE HISTORIOGRAPHY OF NEGLECT

The 1940s, the initial center of gravity for this study, are often just treated in American intellectual history as interim years of war (as if thought stopped during the largest single cataclysm of the century), or as a divided period, a wishbone that goes half to the "thirties" and half to the "fifties." The thirties, as the remains of the period of "radicalism" and social consciousness, pick up some portions of the war decade, though often in their dimensions of retrenchment and intellectual retreat. The war's massive mobilization, and the period of consumer abundance and yet intellectual anxiety and doubt after the war, get taken up into the Cold War and the "adjustment," "consensus," and "conformity" that define the stereotypes of the decade of the fifties and the presidency of Dwight D. Eisenhower. Even many of the best scholars of the 1940s look for particular impasses or divisions that can break the decade in two.[39]

The crisis of man and its project of re-enlightenment yield a different periodization without such a sharp split: a complete and consistent phase of thought from 1933 to 1951 in which intellectuals looked outward to shared, new threats, and from 1952 to 1973 a still-continuous phase of philosophical demand and rethinking, turning inward toward America while revolving concrete answers, rebukes, and rejoinders to the questions of the earlier period.

It would be odd if scholars had not noted or assessed the discourse of the crisis of man before. They have. Closer to the era itself, in an effort to understand the background to his experience of the 1960s, Edward Purcell wrote a 1972 history of the 1930s and 1940s as part of a "crisis of democratic theory" that is close to my own early account.[40] In political science and jurisprudence, man appeared to translate to the democratic subject or citizen, whom US thinkers questioned in order to seek new grounds for defense. In art history, the scholar of abstract expressionism Michael Leja identified man discourse on the other side of 1945, ably discerning what he termed "the discourse of Modern Man" as a background to Jackson Pollock, Mark Rothko, and their cohort of American painters and their critics.[41] One can piece together a rich and accomplished bibliography on many of the subtopics that the discourse of the crisis of man underwrites in this period: totalitarianism, existentialism, world war, and Cold War propaganda, theological conflicts, human rights, and the United Nations.

The inability to think of the discourse as a generative matrix that subtends these domains and time slices, however, has not just been a matter of chance. The strictures on thought in this area have sometimes had polemical bases, often of the same vintage as the discourse of man itself. We can also write a historiography of neglect. No stricture has been more obtrusive than the thesis of "deradicalization" (also called "depoliticization"). The accusation emerged in the 1940s in internecine fighting on the intellectual left, and only much later migrated from the status of a political attack between former allies to reign as a dominant historiographical thesis. One thus finds a very young Irving Howe, at this point in 1947 associated with one Trotskyist faction, articulating the full thesis in order to criticize another ex-Trotskyist faction with whom he was still friendly. (His immediate target was Dwight Macdonald's *Politics*; Macdonald had used the same charge in 1940 and 1941 to criticize his rivals; a later democratic-socialist Howe, too, as editor of *Dissent*, would find his own place within the crisis of man repositioning):

> The political development of the American "left" intellectuals since the great depression may be charted in four major trends: their attraction to radical politics in the early thirties; their subsequent break from Stalinism and turn to Trotskyism; their retreat from Marxism in the late thirties; and finally their flight from politics in general . . . [in] turns to religion, absolute moralism, psychoanalysis and existentialist philosophy as *substitutes* for politics.[42]

The historical tradition that follows from this polemical chronology dismisses the puzzles and incomprehensibilities of the discourse of man by switching focus to the decline of institutional leftism in the 1930s and 1940s. Historians identify themselves with one or another position of the Old Left. This yields counterfactual speculation on what the discourse of the crisis of man might have substituted for, without trying to reconcile the difficult questions of what it actually was.[43]

The obverse of this mode of neglect is the historiography that constitutes a long progress of progressive-liberal uplift and triumph rather than radical decline. Here, the enigmas and abstractions of the interruption of crisis, and the questionings of man, are not interesting or in need of explanation on their own; they are subsumed within a longer practical project—in the influential work of David Hollinger, for example, "inclusion." On this story, from the turn of the twentieth century through the early 1960s, white American intellectuals fought to include more and more classes of people in progressive, pragmatic, liberal-Protestant unity, in efforts to defuse prejudice and division.[44] This hopeful line, also historically true for its particular protagonists and at its level of chronology, has the consequence that one cannot really treat the sixties, difference, and "multiculturalism" historically except as a betrayal of prior idealism.[45] Other individual accounts do accept that a "crisis" in thought occurred during the midcentury around totalitarianism and the war—often anachronistically attaching it primarily to knowledge of the Holocaust—but seek the triumphant academic reconstructions that overcame it.[46] The most stimulating histories on this side of the evaluative coin understand "unity" to have been a complicated project, or a congeries of discrete projects, without automatically celebrating its solutions.[47] This mode of historical neutrality can be undermined by the fact, however, that the unity, reconstruction, and inclusiveness projects that generated the most unambiguous archives were often those sponsored by the state, or by what we now call "nongovernmental organizations (NGOs)"—sources that quickly look like propaganda, for their effort to convince others to unify rather than wrestling with their own doubts or questionings. And once a historian becomes suspicious that the archive is propaganda, the analytical mood is likely to tip back to the more hostile side of the historiographical divide—regretting deradicalization and false unity, and wishing history had furnished something better.

THE QUESTION OF EXCLUSION

Moreover, to contemporary eyes, the discourse where it is most active and intense neglects some forms of difference that we would think should be acknowledged, if only to be appreciated and included. It was certainly a discourse favorable to "the human family" and "the brotherhood of man," and its rhetoric was useful to antiprejudice campaigns.[48] But one begins to wonder if the delineation of a human core emerged in some way to regulate whom to accept and whom to ignore. In the discourse's midst, one finds encomia to the overcoming of difference in unexpected places, as when Hans Kohn, the rather factual and dry Jewish émigré diplomatic historian, ensconced at Smith College and later Harvard, dedicates one of his series of books about Europe's crisis: "To Those/Who Strove and Fought/For the Dignity of the Human Being/For the Oneness of the Human Kind."[49] Yet this "oneness" vibrated at a very high level of abstraction. A previous dedicatory page in the series quoted Goethe on "humanity," Kant on universal history and the goal of a universal republic, and one bar from the ode of Beethoven's Ninth Symphony.[50] The truth of the high-intellectual discourse of the crisis of man is essentially that it was so assured of its own wishful operation at a level of universality that it could leave basic forms of exclusion and inclusion unthought. It didn't have to actively regulate exclusion, because it was incapable of believing difference to have real meaning for its concerns.

Was there no "crisis of woman"? No "crisis of color" in the country where W.E.B. Du Bois edited *The Crisis* until 1934, on the basis that the biggest American problem of the century was the problem of the color line? Two of the most important exclusions from the early US discourse of the crisis of man were indeed those of women and of African American men and women. These groups' exclusion would matter intrinsically, but also because, from those two perspectives, intellectuals would raise voices later, in the 1960s, to make the most influential and forceful assertions of access to a discourse that they no longer necessarily wanted to join in its original form. Those who did raise their voices in the 1940s were often ignored. Precisely because such positions are excluded, one must look to special events of catalysis and momentary visibility to see their efforts, to recent specialist histories that have documented their repression, and to individual exceptions that broke through to the public culture (seeing these exceptions as latently representative of what others couldn't say).

At the founding of the United Nations, the inscription of human rights into global law and discourse, beyond the boundaries of any single country, was fought for especially hard by organizations representing "minorities." (We will return to the larger filiation of human rights from the discourse of man in chapter 3.) But as the historian Glenda Sluga has written, "Nora Stanton Barney, writing in the feminist periodical *Equal Rights* in 1946, echoed the sentiments of numerous feminist lobbyists of the UN organization when she claimed: 'We all know only too well, and have heard only too often great speeches on human rights by people who have in mind only the rights of men, and never think of the human rights of women.' "[51] Eleanor Roosevelt had been made chairwoman of the Commission on Human Rights, representing the United States. She had been chosen in large part for her enormous prestige as wife of the leader of the Allies, the late Franklin Delano Roosevelt; also because human rights were considered diplomatically minor compared to the Security Council and General Assembly, therefore an appropriate outlet for women's topics and inclinations. Still, only one other woman served as a nation's delegate to the Commission: Hansa Mehta of India, an activist and legislator involved in Indian independence.

According to Kirsten Sellars, "Mehta, and members of the Commission on the Status of Women," objected to a preamble proclaiming "All men are brothers," "and proposed instead 'all people' or 'all human beings.'" Roosevelt quashed the effort to enumerate women as distinct. "American women, she argued, did not feel excluded by the Declaration of Independence's reference to 'all men.'"[52] From other feminists' protests, as Glenda Sluga has written, the Commission on the Status of Women had emerged "out of the fear expressed . . . that women would be forgotten or submerged in the assumption of universality"; then, "once it was created, was effectively marginalized by the Human Rights Commission."[53]

"Man" language, and the thought of superior male standing that it often conveyed, unquestionably remained the lingua franca for philosophical and reformist writing in the 1930s, 1940s, and 1950s. Sometimes, in prose by women participants, the use of "Man," "man," and "he" seems compulsive and disconcerting. Ruth Anshen Nanda, friend and facilitator to "great men," will tell us that "Man alone . . . is free to examine, to know, to criticize and to create. But Man is only Man—and only free—when he is considered as a being complete . . . for to subdivide Man is to execute him." "Honor to those heroic warriors who have preserved for us the priceless heritage of freedom and have kept undefiled the sanctity and divine fire of the essence of Man!"[54] Among Nanda's eighty-five invitees to her three edited volumes of original writings on the crisis of man by the world's most eminent minds—covering the spectrum from Einstein to Bergson and Malinowski to Piaget—stood only one woman, Margaret Mead. In other writers' work, including that of Mead, Ruth Benedict, and Hannah Arendt, one may be able to detect interesting modulations in the way man rhetoric is used. Simone Weil, for example, when she sat to write *The Need for Roots* in London in 1943, interestingly used the masculine language of "a man" and "men" when she generalized in a secular spirit in her first pages, but turned to "the human soul" (*l'âme* or *l'âme humaine*) as she reached for higher spiritual values, and made good ultimate use of the "human being."[55]

Simone de Beauvoir, in Paris, was the truly exceptional figure who broke through and undid the limitations of male language and thought when, in 1949, her *The Second Sex* explicitly announced the inadequacy of a purely male phenomenology of human being. Just three years earlier, as a defender of Sartre but a rising philosopher in her own right, in the orthodox existentialist *The Ethics of Ambiguity*, she had used the familiar encompassing language of "man" and "Man." Indeed, she had internalized it to the extent that in that book, the generic human individual in rebellion is typified as the "young man" ("A young man wills himself free"); wisdom is the young man's mature consciousness of conflict and world-making with other men ("To will that there be being is also to will that there be men by and for whom the world is endowed with human significations").[56] In *The Second Sex*, however, Beauvoir worked out a true alternate language of "Woman" and "women" in a long braid with "female," "feminine," "human," "man," and "men." Claiming a common quandary with the American "Negro" and "the Jew," Beauvoir claimed a common humanity—"The fact that we are human beings is infinitely more important than all the peculiarities that distinguish human beings from one another"—based on mortality and *need*: common nature is "the same essential need for one another."[57] Her final lines in 1949 rise to a pun on the "brotherhood of men," the familiar phrase to which Hansa Mehta had rightly objected at the United Nations. Of course *fraternité*, brotherhood, holds a special resonance in French because of the trinity of values of the Republic: *liberté, egalité, fraternité*. "To gain the supreme victory," Beauvoir wrote, "it is necessary, for one thing, that by and through their natural differentiation *men and women* unequivocally affirm *their brotherhood*."[58] For all this, Beauvoir was ridiculed, vilified, and misunderstood by critics in the United

States and France. Her book's public appreciation wouldn't occur until the late 1960s.

For African Americans, recent scholarship has shown the extraordinary lengths to which the Truman-era State Department went to restrict the forms of black Americans' appeals to human rights possibilities. The state itself worked to make sure that appeals to universality went only in some directions and not others. One direction, acceptable to the Democratic administration and white liberals, led toward civil rights rather than human rights.[59] The other led to a focus on the Jim Crow South as a singular atavism, rather than affirmation of the continent-wide African American presence as an inner nation, comparable to colonial states and the emerging postcolonial nations of Asia, Africa, and the Middle East.[60] African American intellectuals meditated and pursued both routes. Left internationalists with Communist ties, like the singer Paul Robeson and W.E.B. Du Bois, were persecuted and deprived of their passports as betrayers of their citizenship and dangers to America until the Supreme Court ruled in 1958 that this was not within the power of the secretary of state.[61] Apparently more mainstream organizations like the NAACP, under its pragmatic chief Walter White, turned out to have had their own actions and militancy determined by threats and advice from white liberal friends, including Eleanor Roosevelt, to steer clear of appeals that went beyond remedial civil freedoms (which should already have been guaranteed by rule of law) or the integration of government-run institutions.[62] The American discourse of the crisis of man in general was surprisingly oblivious to colonial thinking, and the futures after World War II of the colonial, soon-to-be postcolonial, peoples. Of course, the United States considered itself to have no colonies.

When it comes to other forms of difference that we now consider central but that were, in the 1940s, derided or invisible, instances of self-assertion in terms of the discourse of man can be glimpsed. They adapt its principles to their own needs. The gay poet Robert Duncan advocated in the radical journal *Politics* for "homosexual rights," but only, he said, if they were an aspect of universal "*human* recognition and rights"; for the separatism and difference of even "the most radical, the most enlightened 'queer' circles" make "a second cast-out society as inhumane" as the mainstream "inhumanities of [heterosexual] society." "[T]he growth of a cult of homosexual superiority . . . is loaded with contempt for the human," Duncan wrote. "[O]nly one devotion can be held by a human being . . . and that is a devotion to human freedom, toward the aspiration of human love, human conflicts, human aspirations. To do this one must disown *all* the special groups (nations, religions, sexes, races) that would claim allegiance."[63]

WHAT IS RE-ENLIGHTENMENT?

The discourse of man intellectuals' thoughts were elsewhere—specifically, perhaps surprisingly, on the historical event they called the Enlightenment. It contributed to their most general answers to the questions "Where had the world gone wrong?" and "Where would one start to set it right?"

The crisis was understood by midcentury intellectuals to be a legacy of the Enlightenment, which had failed them and, if fixed, could save them. "The contemporary human crisis has led to a retreat from the hopes and ideas of the Enlightenment," regretted Erich Fromm—but philosophers couldn't simply return to where their kind had been before.[64] Often they called out in anguish for the creation of a new "humanism," which they meant in its loosest sense: a respect for the human being, a measuring of all actions and behaviors by the individual human scale, human mores, humaneness, and humanity. "The idea of man, the counsel of a new humanism, are certainly the very last things to move the present world to a fundamental change" by themselves, wrote Erich Kahler, "[b]ut we may expect this idea to force itself upon men when the course of human events" itself forces it.[65] Their thorough reviews of the modern period to find a flaw or a definite, earlier moment of decision about man's nature—in fairly fixed, endlessly reiterated comparative histories of the eighteenth, nineteenth, and twentieth centuries—spoke insistently to the question of the Enlightenment and their idea of its repair.

Their Enlightenment—as they recalled or reconstructed it—was the era that created a human subject who did not derive his stature from the authority of the Church, or from rulers, or from any state. The political community to which this new man would belong could be constituted only as the expression of his will and consent and that of his equals, his fellow citizens. Man had entered an age in which human inviolability would become self-evident. Man had gained a maturity such that he would not give up his freedom willingly. The era had culminated, without any doubt, in the late eighteenth century, when it wrote the Declaration of Independence and the Declaration of the Rights of Man and of the Citizen. It took the republic as its ideal state form, which seemed at a certain point to have spread to nearly all of Europe as well as America. Though it could invoke the names of Locke, Rousseau, and Voltaire, for these intellectuals, focused on Germany and German philosophy, it had Kant as its final formulator and culminating figure, backed by Herder, Schiller, and Fichte. Where rulers maintained oppression by tradition—in imperial political forms that boiled down to tyranny—they would be undone by a gradually enlightened populace. Where holdouts had not heard the Good News of this Enlightenment, they would be reached by the free circulation of speech and ideas.

That was because the other key aspect of this remembered Enlightenment, besides the change in the stature of man, was its doctrine of progress. Enlightenment was ongoing, teleological, and irreversible. In a first development, man came to have rights and to know the rights of his fellow men by sympathy or sentiment. In a second development, logically and concretely, no one who knew the Rights of Man would be able to justify their violation for others, or would ever will away his own prerogatives. To scholars of the Enlightenment as a historical movement, in its many national variants and philosophical epochs and contradictions, this verges on cartoon. It was the sketch that functioned as a vade mecum for the midcentury intellectuals, however, and so matters to us.

Re-enlightenment differs from a "revival" of the Enlightenment project. Nor did it constitute a "Second Enlightenment." The midcentury re-enlightenment did not attempt a systematic philosophy, and did not produce one or any full self-consciousness of what it was attempting. Nor did it produce individual figures of systematic philosophizing of the stature of Kant, Rousseau, Hume, Voltaire, Locke, or Hobbes.

The midcentury generation's way of addressing the crisis of man represented a consensus that something specific had gone wrong and must be made right. Man must again be made self-protecting. "Autonomous humanism" might be a term for what the practitioners believed they were providing—a respect for humanity that would once again let the human being give the law to itself and all men. But the freedom of man as a self-lawgiver was no longer something they could hope for without reservation, as a consequence of human beings' rational faculty or the ethics that had depended on it. The Nazi jurist and minister of justice Hans Frank, according to Hannah Arendt, wrote in his book *Technik des Staates* (1942) of a new "categorical imperative in the Third Reich . . . 'Act in such a way that the Führer, if he knew your action, would approve it.'"[66] They had thus seen how Kantian rigorist "duty" could be perverted, among the Nazis, into the duty to do wrong. In implying that they wanted only a *re*-enlightenment, it seemed American intellectuals could stand for a humbler effort to restore the project of human liberation, now understood simply as protection and restraint, without the grandiosity or vulnerability of the earlier age's vision.

Perhaps the point of differentiation is that what the midcentury intellectuals really tried to launch (with long-lasting consequences) was not just a new moral autonomy but rather an autochthonous humanism—human respect giving its grounds entirely to itself, without God, natural law, positive fiat, or even anything identifiable about the human person like "rationality." Here is the sunken treasure a historian detects in all the intellectuals' fantasies: a human stature self-born, sprung from its own brain like Zeus from the monstrous Chronos; humanity freestanding, rootless, but nevertheless protected—for it would carry its warrant, without criteria, within itself. It would be humanity without religious sanction, political affiliation, tribal identity, or outside tie, yet still be inviolate: the human as such.

Re-enlightenment at its most thoughtful was chastened, modest. It wanted to know what had gone wrong with the rights of man. It did not insist that it knew how to restore or replace these rights, only that something must be done. It did not often blame the Enlightenment wholesale (though, as we will see, the Frankfurt school émigrés did, and some unexpected American colleagues came close), but neither did it venerate the eighteenth century or insist on its return just as it was. Above all, re-enlightenment represented a questioning of what could be left of the Enlightenment without the idea of progress.

Of course, it took a certain desperation to revive the question of man as the intellectuals did; also a certain hubris. Their grandeur of thought and inclination toward a total project was in its way characteristic of the time. In an era of cataclysm at the largest scale, thinkers were familiar with solutions at the largest scale, through force of arms, planning, and worldwide organization, even when their global solution turned out to be a council of limit. So if there was reason to believe in any new large-scale settlement of the nature of mankind, the passion of re-enlightenment was not only a form of humility but a new kind of ambition.

MAIEUTICS

What shall we call a discourse whose central function has the form "We must ask," "We must think," "We must answer?"—yet does surprisingly little work of disputation, selection, and mutual destruction among the answers? Evidently the discourse is interrogatory, imperative, and ramifying. But these do not capture the whole tenor of the function in its demand to bring ideas to birth as a means, too, of coalition, and interpersonal mobilization. Nor are words for discourses, which are the seeming opposite of what is being undertaken—such as the probative, determinative, or conclusive, the apodictic or assertoric—wholly negated by the practice of the discourse. It does make use of proofs, answers, demonstrations, and assertions, but to a different purpose.

I think we can call a discourse of this form maieutic. The maieutic, by insistent and forceful questioning, seeks to bring into being and bring to birth *in another person* answers that will reward the questioner's own belief in the character of the universal capacity for thinking—and do something to the other person's character, too. In the *Theaetetus*, Plato has Socrates deliver his explanation of his dialectical method of questioning as *technē maieutikē*, "the art of midwifery."[67] Maieutics as it is modeled in that dialogue does require supplying some answers, as well as questions, introducing some arguments, as well as provoking them in others. The dissimilarity between the particular Socratic case and our general discursive category is that with Socrates, a single man—as ironist, dialectician, or adherent of the theory of recollection—delivers others of wisdom while claiming none himself, extinguishing his claim to creativity: "I cannot claim as the child of my own soul any discovery worth the name of wisdom."[68] When we look at our discourse, we have in contrast a transatlantic fellowship of individuals who, claiming to make solitary discoveries, draw others into creation. Maieutics are *shoulds* in discourse or within the intellectual life that help to say what must be addressed or talked about, what stands up as a serious or profound question or contribution, regardless of its ability to solve or determine an inquiry.

What is implied by the discipline of coming up with *an* answer, one single answer, to such a question as "What is man?" It is a straitening of thought. The new imperative seems like the acceptance of an impossibility: How could one wish any one thing to be *the* definitive thing? It is an act of willed restriction. And so it has a dimension of conversion, or consecration of self. After all, what confers the assurance of *depth* in ideas? To some extent, we possess verifiable criteria for depth: complexity, fitness to evidence, originality or unexpectedness, orientation to "first questions," as well as the latest specialized or recondite ones. But there seem to be further criteria, widely shared, that honor corresponding traits not openly avowable: mystery; appeal to unique intuition (and contact with the ineffable); unknownness, even to the edge of incomprehensibility; and orientation to mortal or primeval concepts (death, time, struggle, will, and limit). The sensibility of depth, rewarded by depth effects, is not entirely alien to the life of the mind. We ordinarily step outside of the discursive system, or systems of thought, when we avow these "depth effects" openly. Yet when it comes to topics like "the human," as well as some others (conjecturally: those of "the ethical," "the political," "the philosophical," "the humanities," "God," "science," "the natural"), we will need to acknowledge the role of these purposes as a part, even the principal or defining part, of the production, reception, and dissemination of these eminently respectable discourses and their ideas.

The standpoints of the maieutic are three. In one guise, it makes you work on yourself and your own thought, midwife to something that lies inside you and would be valuable to bring out and articulate even if you are in no wise "correct." From a second standpoint, maieutic stands for the desired effect of your discourse upon others: you supply answers that may or may not be definitive or final but that draw out a comparable process in hearers. Note that here, too, the purpose is not that another will get the right and final answer or that everyone's offerings will improve and converge upon the right answer. The purpose is that another will undertake the task of speaking, thus doing something to himself and to the listening (or reading) public. In its third-person standpoint, however, maieutic is our analytic judgment upon a discourse that all participants see in more familiar and commonplace terms but we, at a distance, can see pursues a different effect. It names the discourse that we can see emerges in furnishing a *should* to a range of speakers, irresolvably, even when they speak only from their own belief that they participate in familiar discourses of human science.

Midcentury thought faced a desire for a protected human-as-such whose existence it could neither immediately "prove" nor "disprove." Yet thinkers knew they needed (for themselves, and their philosophizing) an assumption of that entity's real existence, or knew that they needed it as an active concept (for other people, for present justice, and for future safety), empty though it might sometimes be, to push men gradually to make it real and full.

In the reconstruction of this discourse as it came into being in the 1930s, strengthened in the 1940s, weakened and was transmitted in the 1950s, and metamorphosed and exploded in the 1960s, we will be moving between explanatory levels without foreclosing any. The greater challenge will not be navigating levels of explanation, however, but seeing how and where the consequences of the discourse touch other worlds of actors and participants. The intellectuals' task, after all, was to give their needy assumptions force within their justificatory framework—but, still more, to find other actors who could carry their questions forward into the world. They might need other forces to develop the requisite new forms of knowledge and will for man.

CHAPTER 2

CURRENTS THROUGH THE WAR

The public origins of a crisis of man lie first in the shifting disputes between well-documented thinkers in America at the start of the European war. Intellectual history has dealt extensively with John Dewey and his antagonists over the course of the 1920s and 1930s, studying in detail the rival philosophical, theological, and educational doctrines. Anti-Deweyans, including Reinhold Niebuhr, Robert Maynard Hutchins, and Lewis Mumford, received some of the best biographies and analyses the last generation of intellectual historians produced.[1] Adjutants and followers on both sides, such as Sidney Hook and Mortimer Adler, left testimonies and autobiographies, and their legacies have begun to be reevaluated in turn.[2]

There has been less appreciation of the wider effects of this quarrel—between Deweyan experimentalism and change, and permanence or transcendence as the basis for human thought—on seemingly distant parts of the fabric of intellectual "responsibility" and vocation before and after World War II. The major contributions of Dewey and Hutchins, and even Niebuhr or Hook, are sometimes considered to have diminished by the 1930s. It seems late in their intellectual stories when they turn to crisis writings. It is true that these thinkers' conscious influence on the early crisis of man developed largely from repositionings of their preexisting doctrines at consummating moments of their careers. What they could never have anticipated was the collision of these polemical repetitions with a European influx and the effects of the war.

Though debate over human nature was not new, the stakes of the old debate changed by 1939. With the Nazi threat, and the start of a Nazi war with the invasion of Poland, old antagonists gained renewed energy to flail each other, and other parties joined in. The question of man became a genuinely new debate, however, only when its practitioners interacted with that separate stream of importunate thinkers, the refugees from Hitler, who possessed their own complex Continental tradition. They came to America and England bearing an emergency mood from Germany, meditations on history, and technics that diverged from the American line, and a new questioning of man with practical implications. The question of human malleability was not abstract when thinkers faced the techniques used to alter the behaviors and perhaps the natures of Germans and Italians—and, it was feared, perhaps eventually Englishmen and Americans. Such would be the outcome if the Anglophone countries could not find the will, or the philosophical regrounding, to keep this war on human nature (as well as the rumbling shooting war) from being lost.

THE BATTLE LINES REDRAWN

In 1938, the year before the European war, John Dewey was still the dominant philosopher of pragmatic thought and political progressivism. Insofar as the United States had a major philosopher, and insofar as it cared, Dewey was that man. A scientific pragmatism has been essentially stable as the underlying philosophy of American thought across the twentieth century despite all challenges. It remained in Dewey's hands for the period between William James and Charles Sanders Peirce and the analytic postwar pragmatic naturalism of W.V.O. Quine. Since the early century, Dewey had been articulating a defense of knowledge as practical intelligence. Scientific method was the only appropriate instrument for deciding human projects. Science discovered relations and representations, not things in themselves. Yet practical experiments tied us to the world we inhabit and know; it was the best means to reach truths that "worked." Naturalism was the only philosophy suited to know the natural world, and human beings were natural creatures—equipped with a special ability to study and improve themselves. Dewey was also therefore led to be an educational philosopher: he argued for learning by experiment, a problem-centered curriculum, and action in the classroom rather than a fixed inheritance of old ideas. He was also a social philosopher, an ardent defender of participatory democracy as a way of life. He had made a most influential articulation of the progressive view of human nature: human behavior was an expression of biological inclinations modified by social conditions. In human beings, nature and environment would always stand in balance, but environment could be changed intelligently to teach men new habits of being.[3] The rise of fascism and Nazism troubled him deeply, but disillusionment with his own advocacy of World War I had left him most concerned with the way a European war might lead Americans to alter and undermine their democracy. Neither the fascist threat abroad nor the possible threat at home presented anything to make him change his basic view on human changeability.[4] "Does Human Nature Change?" he asked boldly in a 1938 essay. "[S]o far as the question is a practical one instead of an academic one, I think the proper answer is that human nature *does* change."[5]

Then war came. Germany invaded Poland, bringing it instantly into conflict with England and France. In Scotland, the Protestant theologian Reinhold Niebuhr, one of Dewey's longtime American antagonists, took the opportunity of the University of Edinburgh's 1938–39 Gifford Lectures—an immense honor—to give an entirely different answer about human nature. The modern view of man was wrong, Niebuhr argued, not to accept "[t]he idea that man is sinful in the very centre of his personality, that is in his will."[6] Many others had given the Gifford Lectures over the years, including William James in 1901–2 and John Dewey himself in 1928–29. Niebuhr, reversing Deweyan views, had on his side the urgency of the war and a changed world. Human nature depended on God; it was partial, and always would be. The ease of change was delusory. Indeed, sin was nothing else but man trying to transcend himself without God—mistakenly seeing himself as a creature of nature who could climb above himself purely through natural means (1:140–41). Human nature was divine, it was permanent, it was sinful; for all those reasons, it ought to worry, but worried about the wrong things. "No one expresses modern man's uneasiness about his society and complacency about himself more perfectly than John Dewey" (1:111), Niebuhr added.

Niebuhr was a firm proponent of American involvement in the world war in support of England. In fact, the war for Great Britain began while he talked and delivered *The Nature and Destiny of Man*. The neighboring area was bombed during the third lecture of his second series. The Luftwaffe pounded the Royal Navy base at Rosyth, near Edinburgh, and the audience heard. "Niebuhr was so wrapped up in his message that he heard nothing," his biographer Richard Wightman Fox reports; "he thought they were squirming about something he had said."[7] Niebuhr's anti-Deweyan, permanent-nature message gained from that thunder.

By 1940, France had been invaded, and it surrendered in June. In New York, in September, the intellectuals debated the place of religion and philosophy in their response to the war at a notorious conference sponsored by the Jewish Theological Seminary. The United States was sitting out the war, but fierce battles raged between interventionists and noninterventionists, with President Roosevelt maneuvering to aid the British while still unable to join the war. "A huge tent was erected in the central quadrangle," and five hundred "representatives from all over the nation attended . . . to formulate the basic principles that underlay the democratic ideal."[8] New York was still largely the territory of Dewey—now more than eighty years old and finally retired from the Columbia University faculty. His supporter, Sidney Hook, attended the conference and prepared for a discussion of the European situation and whether the United States should intervene (Hook was staunchly interventionist). Yet here, too, the voices against secular, scientific Deweyism got their platform. As a guest from the University of Chicago—center of anti-Deweyan sentiment and devout belief in the permanence of man—Dewey's onetime student Mortimer Adler took the opportunity of his New York visit and the fall of France to denounce, as the cause of it all, "the Professors," meaning the Deweyans and all "positivists" and "naturalists" who taught human malleability and socialization. Everyone in the audience would make sounds, he said, about "the Present Crisis," but they had only themselves to blame. "Democracy," Adler pronounced, "has much more to fear from the mentality of its teachers than from the nihilism of Hitler. It is the same nihilism in both cases, but Hitler's is more honest and consistent." Lacking God, theology, and a thorough subordination of scientific method to immemorial metaphysical truths, the professors were worse than the Nazis, who were mere "puppets" of the general modern sickness. Adler roused himself to language that sounded a bit like Himmler: "Until the professors and their culture are liquidated," he warned, "the resolution of modern problems—a resolution which history demands should be made—will not even begin again."[9] Hook was predictably furious and denounced Adler in turn. When Adler's speech was syndicated by the Hearst newspapers and Hook published his in the *New Republic*, the battle over human nature between New York and Chicago was thus emphatically renewed under new "crisis" auspices.[10]

The war became an opportunity for thinkers who had previously voiced opposition to progressive and Deweyan attitudes about human nature to restyle themselves as social prophets with a practical and strategic case to make. The force behind Mortimer Adler was Robert Maynard Hutchins, the youthful president of the University of Chicago and Adler's benefactor, superior, and coconspirator. Once the United States entered the war following Pearl Harbor, Hutchins, who had previously been an isolationist, quickly adapted Chicago neo-Thomist beliefs to the business of the United States winning the war. (Indeed, the war-related positions of the different players in these conflicts seem not to have covaried with their philosophies of man: Niebuhr, Adler, and Hook, all philosophical opponents, were interventionist; Hutchins and Dewey, also opponents, more or less isolationist.)[11] When Hutchins was asked by *Fortune* in 1943 how to hold on to the war's gains for "American civilization" and extend them to the world, he impressed upon current strategy the old case for a unitary, unchanging human nature. Hutchins replied, "We want a world civilization. We want this community to endure. If it is to endure, it must be built upon the solid rock of human nature." And *"human nature is, always has been, and always will be the same everywhere."* "World civilization" was a common progressive dream, but Hutchins rewrote it in his own terms: "Unless it is admitted . . . that the natural moral law underlies the diversity of the mores, that the good, the true, and the beautiful are the same for all men, no world civilization is possible."[12]

The wartime reality, however, led to certain new complexities for the sake of point-scoring. Once battle lines had been redrawn between the partisans of permanent human nature and the previously dominant (but vulnerable) theorists of social malleability, their questions became rhetorically loaded and increasingly logically confusing. The hint of illogic was that even the "permanent" camp had to argue a high degree of change in man—having witnessed the totalitarian social control reported overseas during the 1930s—in order to blame the malleability theorists. Permanence advocates could say the Nazis were merely making "surface" or "unnatural" changes, but it was an odd sort of "permanence" that could so easily come into jeopardy, as it did, and a theory of the means of this false but irresistible change would ultimately be necessary. The basic question of philosophical anthropology ("What is man?"), became first a political problem ("Is man being changed?"), then a quick suspicion of the awful reality ("Man is certainly attempting to change man, and, it seems, succeeding"), and finally a polemical bludgeon: "Who is to blame?" (Adler blamed the spirit-sapping positivism of "the professors"; Harvard president James B. Conant blamed "utopians," atheists, and progressives; Hook blamed Adler, repaying him in the same coin: "I do not believe that there is any such thing as a philosophical fifth-column. But if there *were* anything that could possibly be regarded as such, then I believe . . . that it would be not positivism, but the views of Mr. Adler."[13]) If the changes the Nazis made in man's nature seemed social and relativistic, this could demonstrate that a permanent, stable human nature might be something necessary to defend in Americans' own democratic hypotheses. If the changes seemed dogmatic and restrictive, one size fits all and authoritarian, then perhaps they could be turned back upon the permanence theorists themselves, while democracy called for an intelligent cultivation of diverse talents.

The news that both sides should have had to deal with came from the fugitives from Germany, many of them carrying the highest scholarly credentials, who began to emigrate en masse in 1933. Professors, more than almost any other class, were led to depart early and immediately from Nazi Germany if they were Jewish, because Hitler was so precipitate in promulgating the "Restoration of the Professional Civil Service Act" in April 1933, not long after he came to power, removing all Jews from government-paid positions. This included all university teaching. Deprived of their livelihood, academics had good cause to seek employment abroad. The public burnings of politically offensive or inadequately "German" books in May 1933 gave warning to a wider segment of prominent writers and intellectuals, too, extending beyond newly proscribed Jewish authors. By October, it was treasonous to buy all these writers' books.[14] Refugees who were already senior scholars, and who did not simply flee across the borders to

Switzerland or France, very quickly found homes in major institutions of the Anglophone world. The most famous of these places of refuge were the London School of Economics (LSE), the New School in New York, and the Institute for Advanced Study in Princeton, New Jersey. Columbia University and the University of Chicago—antagonistic institutions in the conflicts over human nature—also took in major groups of intellectuals more suited to their individual ideologies, as did other less committed institutions (Harvard, Yale), loosely in the vicinity of New York.

The Hungarian German sociologist Karl Mannheim was one of the first to take a prominent place in England at the LSE, where by the mid-1930s he was revising his German works to try to mobilize an English-speaking audience. In Germany, Mannheim could use concepts of complete collapse and crisis because his compatriots had been witnessing them. In England, after 1933, he encountered a stolid overstability and calm—and he had to seek ways to bridge the gap, to find a cure in his adoptive Anglophone world for the dangers of the Germany he abandoned.[15] Mannheim insisted that readers see a larger pattern in prewar events. "If one looks at the changes in the Western world from the point of view of an observer haunted by a sense of crisis, it is clear that these changes do not consist of a series of disagreeable incidents and isolated disturbances":[16]

> For many of us the problem of human nature and the possibility of changing it has only been raised through the events of the last few years. Two prejudices seem to have collapsed simultaneously: first, the belief in a permanent "national character," secondly, the belief in the "gradual progress of Reason in history."[17]

"National character" here does not have its Scottish Enlightenment or Montesquieuan resonance of international plurality, but the echo of *volksgeist*, a German tradition in which "human nature" could indeed shade into superior national destiny. It drew on the legacy of a certain German Romanticism, which had overlaid the Enlightenment picture of character with "Germanness." Mannheim's linking of the two was a way of registering the horror that Germans could be reorganized under the Nazi banner and told *this* was Germanness, as they had been organized for a different purpose in World War I and told that *this* was Germanness. The myth of national character had proven it could furnish the covering delusion for any sort of baleful "nature." Doubts about the "progress of Reason in history" were immediately recognizable, however, as doubts about passive, progressive enlightenment as the obvious antidote to such dangerous Romanticism—furnishing a central problem of the crisis of man and re-enlightenment for Americans, too.

Mannheim himself was a malleability and "organization" partisan, enough so that he could still, in the early years of Hitler's rise, wish that the West would take up democratic mirror images of the fascist methods of human organization to create a mass counterforce of a successfully mobilized *democratic* citizenry. "This must be done immediately, while the techniques are still flexible and have not been monopolized by any single group."[18] This influenced his slightly oxymoronic slogan of "Planning for Freedom."[19] (Future vindications of democracy tended to reject such means, staking their hopes on the stolid resistance of all free peoples to conditioning or propaganda. One could say, however, that the eventual integration into the US war effort of a spectrum of left-leaning US and overseas social scientists in sociology, anthropology, and psychology was a benign fulfillment of Mannheim's hopes.)[20] The most important, immediate legacy of thinkers like Mannheim may have been simply the data and warnings that these refugees brought to the English-speaking world, whatever their place on the political spectrum.[21] The ultimate problem of human nature wouldn't be solved until one dealt with the immediate changes of men—the result of fascist "organization," or what German thinkers writing in English often called "coordination" (as a translation of the Nazi term *Gleichschaltung*).

Such warnings came, too, from oppositely oriented political actors, like Hermann Rauschning, the conservative nationalist and Danzig senator who had worked with Hitler and then broke with him over the Nazis' dishonesty, their takeover of ordinary civil society, and finally the order they gave him to persecute Catholics and Jews—as Rauschning fled to Switzerland and France and, eventually, to resume a farming life in Oregon.[22] Rauschning, not well remembered today, persistently "warned the West" in terms that were quite influential in the '30s, especially to the specifics of the growing concept of "totalitarianism."[23] In *Hitler Speaks* (1939), cast as the less provocatively titled *The Voice of Destruction* (1940) in its US edition, Rauschning provided the material that was to become most standard on Hitler's promised plans for the transformation of man ("'Creation is not yet at an end,' he [Hitler] said. 'At all events, not so far as the creature Man is concerned'"[24]). Rauschning argued on his own account that the whole German state had become nothing but a system for domination, of anyone and anything—a nihilistic internal-repression machine whose supposed "diplomatic" or "strategic" goals actually fluttered with the wind. The images of ordinary civilians goose-stepping in swastika formation, and the footage of the Nuremberg rallies, combined with reports from insiders like Rauschning of the forced coordination of every part of society with the Nazi Party, changed the picture of what could be done to men. The state was no longer built of multiple elements each devoted to the social good: "Nothing in the whole machinery is there for its own sake."[25] Rather, it had the "aim of forming an all-comprehending instrument of dominion," "the complete 'co-ordination' with the movement of all existing organizations, down to those of the canary breeders and the stamp collectors." These techniques need not have a useful point or objective, a victory or an outcome; they could even be stupid or rudimentary, so long as they retained their ability to give an unsettled, inhuman, and automatized character to the human being:

> [T]he simplest and most elementary, but perhaps most effective and most characteristic method of domination employed by National Social-ism . . . [is] the marching. At first this marching seemed to be a curious whim of the National Socialists. These eternal night marches, this keep-ing of the whole population on the march, seemed to be a senseless waste of time and energy. Only much later was there revealed in it a subtle intention based on a well-judged adjustment of ends and means. . . . Marching is the indispensable magic stroke performed in order to accus-tom the people to a mechanical, quasi-ritualistic activity until it becomes second nature. . . . At the back of all these night marches, marches out, marches back, these mass demonstrations and parades, was the . . . functional integration . . . created and fostered by marching in columns, military drill, military evolutions, the rhythm of a host in step.[26]

"Not increased familiarity with viciousness but a revelation of the vi-ciousness of the familiar was the Nazi contribution towards making Man once more an object of suspicion," wrote Harold Rosenberg in 1944. "That a nation, a whole society—milkmen, mothers, schoolboys, policemen—should have given itself up easily to a community policy of blows and tor-ture, seemed proof that the monster is lurking in the average and every-day."[27] Rauschning's "rhythm of a host in step," rather than the natural gait and easy ramblings of a man, should have been the real terror behind what-ever the permanent human nature partisans had in mind when they launched their renewed attacks on Deweyism and all that they claimed malleability and "conditioning" had wrought.[28] The Nazi molding of man was real. Intellectuals could either wake up to its horror or continue their lofty, cerebral objections. In either case, what one sees is a set of longtime critics of Dewey rising to the Nazi occasion so that their doctrine gained a special resonance (as with Niebuhr), or (like Hutchins and Adler) simply becoming focal points for a debate that would really be moving elsewhere.

NIEBUHR AND THE OPENING WORK OF THE CRISIS OF MAN

Reinhold Niebuhr's *The Nature and Destiny of Man*, finally issued to the American public in two volumes in 1941 and 1943, constitutes the first masterpiece and fundamental work of the midcentury discourse of man.[29] Scribner's published the initial volume of his two books in the year of Pearl Harbor and the US entry to the war. Others had published on this crisis by the time Niebuhr's earlier lectures reached the market, but this gave the thoroughness of his book all the more weight and impact. A moral anthropology based on Christian neoorthodoxy was not the only purpose of the book. It also spoke to a philosophy of history that was among the concerns of the crisis of man. He, too, pointed to the need for a new plan. Niebuhr spoke of original sin; he spoke for "faith"; he spoke of evil; and he demanded a "new synthesis" growing out of modernity's failed optimism since the Renaissance: "We have lived through such centuries of hope and we are now in such a period of disillusionment."[30]

Niebuhr, an energetic forty-nine-year-old public figure in 1941, was a rare specimen even before the war: a theologian reliably read by nonbelievers. Niebuhr's recategorization of man's permanent nature was unique because it explained, at the same time, the impulse to try to change that nature, all within a theological framework. Niebuhr meant to restore limit and prophetic religion to the center of human nature. God had created man as a partial being. His nature was permanent, though he took steps toward transcendence in history, and there a dangerous cycle started. "The fact that man can transcend himself in infinite regression and cannot find the end of life except in God as the mark of his creativity and uniqueness; closely related to this capacity is his inclination to transmute his partial and finite self and finite values into the infinite good. Therein lies his sin" (1:122). The characteristic sin of his transcendence was pride, and a constitutional inability to step outside of the "infinite regression" that looked like progress.

His central discovery was that man rationalized and universalized his every impulse. Niebuhr did not mean this in the way of Kant, whose speculative universalization of the maxim of one's actions would restrain a moral actor from doing anything he could not wish all people to do. Nor was he just speaking of classical hubris. Rather, the sin of pride in universalization for Niebuhr steered perilously close to a religious-political argument against the very unreligious concept of ideology. "[M]an is tempted to deny the limited character of his knowledge, and the finiteness of his perspectives. . . . This is the 'ideological taint' in which all human knowledge is involved and which is always something more than mere human ignorance" (1:182). The way this form of permanence in human nature accorded with the changes occurring under the fascists abroad was thus both dialectical and simple. Man's permanent human nature precisely compelled him to deny his limited nature and try to change and overcome it in line with his temporary interests. Prophets had to remind men that they were overreaching, and put human nature back within limits.

Niebuhr, in *The Nature and Destiny of Man*, consigned to oblivion the belief in a successive improvement of man by his own efforts. "[T]he course of history . . . has proved the earlier identification of growth and progress to be false" (2:206). The Renaissance and the Enlightenment ("which was a less profound second chapter of the Renaissance") produced a philosophy that "assumes that all development means the advancement of the good. It does not recognize that every heightened potency of human existence may also represent a possibility of evil. The symbol for this difference is that in Christian eschatology the *end* of history is both judgment and fulfillment. The modern conception sees the end as only fulfillment" (2:166; emphasis in original).

Niebuhr's was a philosophy of limit for people whose temperament favored limitlessness, grandeur, and top-down solutions. In a way, it was natural to Niebuhr himself; he had, through the 1920s and 1930s, always been a progressive inciter of grand solutions who then recoiled from them, perpetually at odds with his own instinct for violent militancy. Since the turn of the '30s, based at the Union Theological Seminary not far from Columbia, he had been blaming Dewey for a liberal hopefulness about human change that didn't truly seem so far apart from his own aims. In *Moral Man and Immoral Society* (1932) Niebuhr had scored Dewey for being too optimistic about the ability of science to reform social problems by gradual, nonconflictual steps. Niebuhr favored sometimes Marxist, sometimes covert-liberal demands for immediate social change in the distribution of wealth, the treatment of workers, and the order of American society; he wanted to believe he was more hard-edged and realistic, while also more radical. The old impulses show through in *The Nature and Destiny of Man* as a different kind of theological immediacy, calling for human restraint. Sidney Hook, reviewing Niebuhr and meaning to lodge an objection, said "Niebuhr writes as if all men were naturally romantic theologians, victims of a fantastical logic according to which, if God did not exist, *they* must be God."[31] This was exactly on the mark. It might have been what Niebuhr understood about "man's nature," it seemed, by introspection of his own nature.

What makes less obvious sense, but has a profounder import, is how the sense of limitation in *Nature and Destiny*—on true knowledge as well as desire, on even knowing whether one is on the right side in matters of action—shouldn't defeat Niebuhr's militancy about American intervention in the world war. In the finished first book of the lectures, the only explicit mention of "the present European war" comes in a footnote, drawing out the seemingly academic (but politically shocking) point that in a war one may never have a "universal reason" to know which side is in the right—and yet "[t]he very same war . . . may yet concern itself with the very life and death of civilizations and cultures" (1:283–84). Did he not know whether war was "right" against the Nazis? At this very moment, in the months of 1941 before Pearl Harbor in December, Niebuhr was founding the journal *Christianity and Crisis* to insist on intervention and rival other Christian publications with a pacifist or wait-and-see line.[32] In its pages and in other writings, he evolved the famous doctrine of "Christian realism," which linked sinful human pride to progressivism, a movement one might otherwise have associated with humility for its commitment to the downtrodden.[33] The essential place of *Nature and Destiny*, in this sense, in the philosophical path of the discourse of the crisis of man, is that it shows indirectly how imperative rumination—with emphases on depth and responsibility, solemnity and sobriety, impossibility of ambitions but indefatigability of effort, limit and closure—could be made intellectually into grounds for a seemingly contradictory decisionism, activism, and militancy. Limit, defined as Niebuhr does it, facilitates action in imperfect ways and less-than-total knowledge. Crisis curiously ends pragmatics: rather than testing and tweaking in experimentalist gradualism toward an ideal hypothesis, one embraces permanent tragedy and intervenes violently. This was not unique to Niebuhr, though. It is an essential aspect of how the wider discourse could link together crisis response, and mobilization, with man sought in depth and permanently—but perhaps impossibly, unanswerably.

HUTCHINS AND THE POWER OF CHICAGO

Robert Maynard Hutchins, Mortimer Adler, and the University of Chicago—administered with Hutchins as an activist president and Adler as his right-hand man—provided a second, very vocal constituency for "permanent" human nature. The university made up in institutional solidity and energy, plus a wide grouping of like-minded intellectuals, what each of its figures lacked of Niebuhr's argumentative cleverness, moral authority, and charisma. Chicago became famous as a neo-Thomist center, part of a return to the medieval Catholic metaphysics of Saint Thomas Aquinas, who had adapted Aristotelian precepts about the primacy of reason in man. Yet Hutchins's father had been a Presbyterian minister with liberal modernist tendencies, and Adler was New York Jewish and little interested in that faith; neither converted to Catholicism during the years they drew on Catholic philosophy for their thought.[34] Along with Thomism came "natural law" in ethics, and "Great Books" at the level of the curriculum. "Greatness" and "permanence" were truly the Chicago watchwords, drawing from history a conception that human nature *had* no history but the record of discoveries about what was eternally the same—and this led to a long war against Dewey, all doctrines of change, and all education meant to encourage or allow men to follow proximate and experimental, rather than permanent, wisdom.

The oddity of it all was that Hutchins was an energetic democrat and an economic egalitarian. In fact, he shared a common pragmatic background with Dewey's adjutant Hook. In 1927, at the age of twenty-eight, Hutchins had been made dean of the Yale Law School, where he was associated with an intellectual movement for legal realism, a central piece of the progressive relativist assault on permanent truths. Legal realism was the forward-looking doctrine that judges shaped laws by positive acts, not in alignment with universal abstractions. They did so under the influence of conditions in society that they should try to serve and improve, often with help from social science. When Hutchins was appointed to the open seat of the presidency of the University of Chicago at age thirty, in a move that surprised all of higher education, it seemed he would want to keep Chicago, philosophically, what it had been—Dewey's school, a fortress of pragmatist social intelligence. Hutchins set to work immediately in another direction.

One of his first major acts had been to inflict Mortimer Adler, a Columbia PhD whom Hutchins had befriended while at Yale, upon the unsuspecting Deweyan Chicago philosophy department. Adler had become a Thomist, insisting on the absolute superiority of Aquinas's premodern fourteenth-century philosophy, and he was singularly belligerent about it.[35] His was a position basically unique among non-Catholic philosophers. Moreover, Adler's Thomism seemed to arise entirely independent of the ferment then occurring in France among figures of revival like Étienne Gilson and Jacques Maritain. Adler himself had been a deliberately provocative and outlandish undergraduate student of Dewey's at Columbia, pestering the grand old man with long letters proving that Dewey's use of terms in each lecture was inconsistent with their use in previous lectures. At Chicago, Adler was introduced into a department still stocked with pragmatic social scientific philosophers like George Herbert Mead and others of the Chicago school.[36] The department rejected him. Mead and James Tufts resigned in the ensuing contretemps. The ablest younger scholars left, and the department collapsed. Adler could still not be seated there, so Hutchins found a place for him in the Chicago Law School as a minister without portfolio, allegedly at three times the salary of a full professor in the philosophy department.[37]

Part of the cause of Hutchins's loyalty was that Adler had been responsible for Hutchins's education in the Great Books, a sequence of masterpieces beginning with the ancient Greeks and proceeding to the near-present. From this, Hutchins and Adler developed a common project. Adler had learned the idea originally in a different division of Columbia University from the English professor and novelist John Erskine, who also influenced Lionel Trilling, Jacques Barzun, and the middlebrow critic Clifton Fadiman.[38] By the example of these men, it is clear that Erskine's Great Books didn't need to lead in any particular direction—certainly not to the Thomism Adler embraced. But the understanding of the Great Books as it reemerged between Adler and Hutchins in Chicago became increasingly rarified and dogmatic: it held that there was a finite canon of known discoveries in all the ages of man, each revealing another aspect of a human nature that was always the same, such that readers could find the great truths only in particular books as relevant now as when they were written. This was justified by the Thomistic picture of man as an unchanging, reasoning creature, whose reason might be put to greater or lesser uses but did not alter with technique or circumstance. Hutchins, educator and democrat, followed his meritocratic instincts in reorganizing Chicago on its "New Plan"—a more intensive, exam-based higher education, open to anyone qualified, from the age of sixteen. But at the same time, he made the case, on a national stage, for the idea that man's nature was fundamental and unchanging, and education must follow a fixed sequence for all.

The forthright impatience of Hutchins's educational writings will be familiar to anyone who has endured a bad or lazy education at the hands of a supposedly elite institution. He claimed to have suffered such education (at Oberlin, principally), before the rigors of Yale Law School finally taught him to think. Hutchins could blame his early miseducation on a curriculum that was modern, changeable, and ephemeral. His thought lacks the tragic aspect from which Niebuhr got such a shiver of pleasure, but holds a different Protestant sense of virtuous discipline and accumulation. An underlying theme of Hutchins's educational writings is the search for something hoardable or preservable. There is in his writings the Yankee pride of an austere house with the family Bible on the stand and two silver candlesticks on the sideboard. In fact, Hutchins started his presidency at Chicago in November 1929, one month after Black Tuesday had seen the stock market collapse.[39] In the midst of a university in a tumultuous urban population, Hutchins had the wish to make everyone self-reliant—students and outsiders, too (in his programs for adult education)—so that they would discover and enjoy "the good" and know it has nothing to do with material possessions (he inveighed constantly against materialism). His was a democratic wish to equip all aspirants, adults or children, with the same citizens' knowledge.

Incredibly, Hutchins identified "materialism," in all its senses, with Dewey. Though Hutchins mentioned the philosopher nowhere by name in his 1934 *The Higher Learning in America*, he had extemporized a year earlier at Chicago that "the leading anti-intellectuals of our time" were "William James and John Dewey"—an eye-opening thing to tell a group of Chicago faculty and trustees in 1933.[40] It was clear enough in his book that the opposite of "liberal education" was Deweyan "progressive education," and Dewey and Hutchins debated ineffectively in the pages of the journal *Social Frontier*, leaving behind traces of a low-level enmity that persisted through the decade.

RIGHTWARD SHIFTS AND COUNTERATTACKS

In London, Karl Mannheim's program was in many respects Deweyan. The trouble with Deweyans was that they felt no need for change. "[A] book of profound commonplaces," wrote Hook of Mannheim's *Man and Society in an Age of Reconstruction*.[41] Dewey agreed the book "may seem to be saying only what is urged from almost every quarter."[42] Mannheim's natural allies in the United States saw nothing to learn from him.

Hence, Mannheim sought alliance with more conservative forces. The group Mannheim joined was called "The Moot": a tiny roundtable discussion that had been established after a Christian conference at Oxford in 1937. Though few in number, the discussants were elite; one could not say, as Stefan Collini has noted, whether they belonged more "to 'the intellectuals' or to the 'governing class.' "[43] The gathering included heads of Britain's University Grants Committee ("arguably the most influential position in higher education," says Collini), the London Institute of Education, and the University of Glasgow; editors from journals and the BBC; Anglican clerics; John Middleton Murray, the writer and visionary; and, most important, T. S. Eliot, already the best-known poet in the English-speaking world.[44] Mannheim was invited to visit the second meeting and never missed another until his untimely death in 1947.

A Moot participant attested: "I was constantly struck by the sympathy that grew up between T. S. Eliot and Karl Mannheim and by the way they impressed and influenced each other."[45] The men did fill each other's needs, or at least each flattered the other's hopes. In Eliot, Mannheim had a channel to the great public he wished to stiffen for war. In Mannheim, Eliot had a scientist promising a coming new order of English society, insisting that the leadership and advocacy needed were of the kinds Eliot could provide. The gentleman Christian intellectual would link together authority, freedom, order, and survival.

In Chicago, Robert Maynard Hutchins's protoconservative return to permanent traditions analogously slipped away to the right even of Hutchins's seeming inclinations. The long postwar intellectual world would find the

University of Chicago the single most important location in America for the revivals of antistate (or antipublic) and antidemocratic thought, which would come to be called "neoliberalism" and "neoconservatism." Hutchins had created a hospitable US setting for a particular kind of émigré—not just Jacques Maritain (the French Catholic neo-Thomist author of *The Rights of Man and Natural Law* [1943]), a liberalizer of Catholicism, but "dissenting" and unfashionable characters who came centrally to include the extreme antiplanning libertarian Friedrich Hayek and the philosopher Leo Strauss, won over from the New School. Robert Maynard Hutchins engaged Hayek to help his attempt to restructure the Chicago economics department, and took him on as a full professor in 1950.[46] Hutchins encouraged the creation of the Committee on Social Thought—started as a "Committee on Civilization" until its name had to be changed to sneak it past the social sciences—which, under the leadership of John U. Nef, sought to Christianize culture, and gained a reputation as a bastion of elite conservatism in the postwar decades. Straussianism, meanwhile, adapted the themes of Hutchinsian liberal education and democratic "elitism" to an antiliberal doctrine of real elites. The opposition to value-relativism in Hutchins became the virulent antihistoricism and rage against the fact/value distinction in Strauss.[47] The Great Books became Strauss's Great Tradition. "Natural law" might be bunk, but Strauss pled for "natural right." Hutchins's classroom style of reading a tiny canon of works for universally accessible wisdom could be turned by Strauss into the study of a tiny canon of works for esoteric meanings, written between the lines, which only a few could identify.[48] And democracy? Certainly democracy was convenient for Strauss, but it was not the true outcome of philosophy.

In New York, Sidney Hook counterattacked on behalf of Dewey. By the later years of the 1930s and the start of the war, the ablest defender of Dewey's social views was not Dewey himself but Hook, his ally and disciple. On the model of T. H. Huxley (the polemicist for Darwin whom the nineteenth century had called "Darwin's Bulldog"), by 1947 someone had thought to pin the sobriquet "Dewey's Bulldog" on Hook. Hook took it up proudly.[49] In book publications of the late 1930s, Dewey authorized Hook to rewrite passages without Dewey checking them.[50] He was an aggressive arguer, a forceful if single-minded writer, and someone who gloried in debate. Mary McCarthy remembered a public debate in which he "chased Mark Van Doren across the stage and virtually pinned him to the wall."[51] Dewey was not as retiring as Darwin had been at Down House, but he was a colorless writer; Lewis Mumford had been somewhat justified in comparing Dewey's style to lint.[52] In a published eulogy after Dewey's death, Hook confessed only one suspicion of the master, and it was entirely in keeping with their friendship: that Dewey was too good a person.[53]

Hook hit back at Niebuhr in 1943 in an article on "The New Failure of Nerve." He identified Niebuhr's significance as part of something bigger, a new intellectual tone: "the recrudescence of beliefs in the original depravity of human nature; prophecies of doom for western culture, no matter who wins the war or peace . . . the frenzied search for a center of value that transcends human interests . . . the refurbishing of theological and metaphysical dogmas about the infinite as necessary presuppositions of knowledge of the finite."[54] Hook's denunciation had another target, too. Hutchins had made the University of Chicago hospitable to neo-Thomism—and Hook denounced Thomism now as antiquarianism, superstition, dogmatism, conservatism, and irrelevancy.

The debate went back and forth. "The liberal arts are the arts of freedom," Hutchins newly insisted in a series of lectures published in 1943 as *Education for Freedom*; "To be free a man must understand the tradition in which he lives. A great book is one which yields up through the liberal arts a clear and important understanding of our own tradition"—and only his form of education could keep the best of America intact through the war.[55] Hook followed up with *Education for Modern Man*, a book-length rebuke to the new Chicago Scholastics, and a defense of education for the modern child of scientific method. The second chapter was particularly ominously titled (for Hook): "The Nature of Man." "To speak of the nature of man is already a sign that a selective interest is present," he warned. "What is designated by the name 'man' may have many natures."[56] The "selective interest" was, to Hook's mind, nothing less than elitism and class interest. This was deeply unfair to Hutchins, who seems to have genuinely cared about adult education and meritocratic upward movement; though it was not different in kind from Hutchins's earlier insinuations that Deweyism, also radically democratic, supported commercial class interests of a middling materialism and a valueless amoral consumer society.

THE IRRELEVANCE OF FORMAL ANTHROPOLOGY

The other powerful line of thought on the nature of man in America besides Dewey's, which had survived many earlier decades, and which *should* have complemented Dewey's own, was the line of "anthropology" proper, a discipline that had been profoundly shaped in the United States much earlier by the German Jewish émigré Franz Boas, and carried on most devoutly and influentially by his own second-in-command, Ruth Benedict. Yet anthropology, surprisingly, simply didn't become very significant in the battles over human nature in the crisis of man. Boasian anthropology was most associated with two things: antiracism and a robust picture of cultural relativism. Cultural relativism was the doctrine in which different "cultural wholes" could express entirely different aspects of human possibility rather than represent higher or lower stages of human development; they were thus incomparable and equally valuable manifestations of human diversity.[57] This relativism reached an apex in Benedict's best-selling *Patterns of Culture*, probably the most widely read book of anthropology of the time.[58]

Most of Boasian anthropology's stake in the public debates of the '30s, however, was the antiracist one—and the antiracist battle had, in effect, already been won among the intelligentsia by the time of the war. Rival positions on the malleability of men in human cultures, and the permanent unity of all human nature, were doctrines equally easy to square with antiracism. The issue of racism didn't come into the main debates, except perhaps as something each side accused the other of not adequately guarding against. Boas was fiercely set against Nazi racism, as in all his previous antiracist work, and he put Benedict onto the job of publicizing the same claims.

But these professional anthropologists became curiously sidelined in the late 1930s and early 1940s when the "permanent nature of man" partisans pressed their attack. Boas died in 1942, never having strongly favored the war. Many anthropologists performed war work, as the area of "applied anthropology" was born, developing interwar anthropology's ethnographic methods and suppositions for practical intervention rather than worrying about their theoretical defense.[59] When Ralph Linton, Boas's replacement as the head of the Columbia anthropology department since 1937, put together a "symposium" of senior figures in 1944–45 titled *The Science of Man in the World Crisis*, he stressed anthropology's practical applications for the future, and the fact that "younger scientists in the field are engaged in government service, many of them with the armed forces."[60] Benedict herself, after largely sticking to her antiracist public engagement through the '30s, had been shunted out of the Columbia department after Boas's retirement (she and Linton disliked each other intensely, and as a woman she had been passed over for the chair as a matter of course), so she, too, joined the Office of War Information (OWI) in Washington. There, Benedict was able to apply her methods of analyzing cultural and national character patterns to the psychological-anthropological analysis of both allies and foes—for purposes of postwar reconstruction but also perhaps for uses in propaganda or psychological warfare. (Benedict's research on Japanese national character also ultimately led to her influential postwar best seller *The Chrysanthemum and the Sword* [1946].)[61] In the 1943 *Partisan Review* "New Crisis of Nerve" series, after Hook made his strong counterattack on Chicago, Benedict contributed "Human Nature is Not a Trap," a vague and by then old-fashioned defense of human plasticity, difference, and choice. A biological "common nature of humankind," she suggested, in so many different cultural expressions, only "underscores the fact that 'human nature' does not prescribe any one selected kind of human world."[62] This was not urgent enough for the time, when the issue was no longer respect for plural human worlds (like those of the Zuni or the Kwakiutl) but defense and diagnosis of a common human world, which the antifascist "West" hoped it still had.

THE BALANCE SHIFTS

Hook and Dewey possessed, in hindsight, the more comprehensive arguments about human nature, the uses and abuses of scientific method, and democracy, plus fifty years of documentation working them out in every detail. Their pragmatism was socially engaged, interventionist for the war, radically democratic, and as well fitted to the battle against totalitarianism as any of its alternatives. Yet they lost out in the upsurge of nature of man talk.[63] Their view went into public eclipse, as it seemed to contemporaries. The philosopher and historian Morton White, in 1949, looked back on "the submersion of a certain style of thinking which dominated America for almost half a century"; "These are days in which Dewey's ideas are being replaced by Kierkegaard's in places where once Dewey was king."[64] Dewey's biographer, Robert Westbrook, agrees that "At the time of his death [in 1952], Dewey's influence as a philosopher, educator and democrat was approaching its nadir"[65]—but in 1945 it didn't have far to go.

By the time *Partisan Review*, a bastion of irreligion, was obligated by the drift of the times to stage a grudging symposium on "Religion and the Intellectuals" in 1950, and invited Hook back to address his foes, he could only crankily remind the editors that he still held exactly the same now-ignored beliefs about the new dispensation he'd spoken of seven years earlier in 1943 in "The New Failure of Nerve." "I offered an explanation of the revival of religion in terms of the decline of capitalism, the rise of totalitarianism, the outbreak of war, and the simultaneous decay of socialist belief." Those were his incomplete reasons—depression, war, loss of radical faith. Finally, he could only deplore a development that had not gone his way.[66] Yet this does not quite explain why the *question* of a permanent human nature had the new appeal that it did. The human nature ideas took hold not because the permanence position was so appealing but because something other than either malleability or permanence was being sought—a new form of safeguard, in a new climate of worry. To understand where the specifics of *those* worries came from, one cannot look only to American thought as it took notice, often in muddled or imprecise fashion, of disasters overseas. One has to see the energies that were coming back to the Anglophone world from overseas, by direct personal transfer—through the émigrés.

THE ÉMIGRÉS' "MORAL ANTHROPOLOGY"

One sees a convergence immediately, in early English-language publications by those who had formerly worked in German, between the émigrés' fears and the incipient Anglophone discourse of man developing in the battles among Niebuhr, Hutchins, and Hook. The greatest living German philosopher outside of Germany in 1944 may well have been Ernst Cassirer. "[T]he very embodiment of central European liberal culture," defender of the Weimar Republic, the first Jew to have attained the rectorship of a German university, Cassirer was recalled, too, as the grand old man who, in 1929, debated Martin Heidegger at Davos on the nature of humanity, speaking for reason, objectivity, and active intellect, four years before Heidegger embraced Nazism.[67] Cassirer's *Essay on Man* (1944) justified itself in terms of a history of "anthropological philosophy." (Cassirer's answer to "What is man?"—it would turn out in a chapter entitled "The Crisis in Man's Knowledge of Himself"—essentially involved the defense and restatement of his earlier, then-untranslated magnum opus, *The Philosophy of Symbolic Forms*. This is only one more example of how the most common "answer," facing what was evidently a new crisis of man, often became whatever a thinker had thought previously.)[68]

At the New School, around the same time, Erich Kahler was a lesser light than Cassirer, who communicated a much greater sense of urgency, bordering on desperation. Kahler was a historian and literary intellectual who had debated Max Weber and won the praise of Hofmannstahl and Mann. Having just emigrated to the United States in 1938, Kahler delivered a long and nerve-racking series of lectures (in halting, memorized English) to a small audience of undergraduates at the New School in 1941 and 1942; these were quickly collected in his monumental 650-page book *Man the Measure*, published in New York in 1943.[69]

Not unlike Cassirer, Kahler promised what he called a "moral anthropology."[70] Kahler meant to defend "the idea of man" against a crisis conceived with a double character reminiscent of Karl Mannheim's formulations—as Kahler framed it, "The great crisis that began in the nineteenth, and came to a head in the twentieth century, [which] has undermined the concept of mankind as a coherent body, together with the concept of history as the consistent evolution of mankind."[71] In the devolution of mankind into false "national characters," as Mannheim had construed it, and what Mannheim identified as a doubt of "the progress of Reason in history," we see the problems of philosophical anthropology and history in their same stark form. Kahler's mission, too, was nothing less than "to find an answer," one "that makes man, for the first time, the specific and explicit subject of history."[72]

The mantle of philosophy was passing to the émigrés, and it was decreasingly clear who counted as a "great thinker," as status had been determined by German university chairs. The senior rank of philosophers had thinned considerably. Edmund Husserl, the founder of phenomenology, had become a peripatetic lecturer at age seventy-six, banned from Freiburg University for his Jewish heritage; he lectured in Central Europe on the "Philosophy in the Crisis of European Mankind" and "The Crisis of European Sciences and Psychology" before his death in 1938.[73] Sigmund Freud, founder of psychoanalysis, escaped Austria for London in 1938 but died in 1939. Max Weber had died in 1920, Max Scheler in 1928. The Vienna Circle of logical positivism, which would be so central to Anglo-American philosophy over the length of the century, had broken up, and its Jewish members emigrated after its founder, Moritz Schlick, had been assassinated on the stairs of the university by a student in 1936, a deed celebrated by right-wing parties and anti-Semites (though Schlick was not Jewish).[74]

The immediate German crisis the émigré thinkers who made it to US shores had in mind differed, of course, from any known in America. There was the Nazi conundrum itself, since 1933: How could authoritarians be elected and further supported in their dictatorship by Germans who these intellectuals had known and had as their countrymen and neighbors? There was the state-form problem, in the fatal weakness of the interwar Weimar Republic. Was there some fundamental weakness of democracy or parliamentarianism itself that had led to its defeat by forms of fascist organization? German intellectuals could all too easily conceive the crisis in terms of a fundamental flaw of liberal or parliamentary forms, having enjoyed just fourteen years of republican experience under Weimar. But one would not think that freeborn Englishmen, with six hundred years of Parliaments, or their progeny the Americans, with a 163-year-old republic, would be much troubled by this—and, indeed, for the most part they were not, certainly not by the time of the US entry into the war. If anything, for Anglo-Americans the idea of a superstrength of fascist organization against a weak liberalism did metamorphose into an occasional fear about making democratic systems competitive in international rivalries—how to ensure, that is, that democratic and voluntary forms of national cohesion, with all their freedoms, would not be bested in a race for economic or war-making power by totalitarian governments capable of command economy and direct, centralized conditioning of soldiers and civilians without freedom's inefficiencies.

TECHNICS

Instead, the dimension of the German discourse to take deepest root in America was the conflict over "technics." We would only say "technology" today. That word does appear to predominate in America in the 1930s, too, but American technology remained, then and now, primarily industrial or mechanical, in the engine, the drill, the dynamo. Where one finds "technics" as a term in English in the '30s and '40s, there is a good chance it is a sign of penetration from or interchange with the Continental and usually German discourse, from *die Technik* (or, more rarely, *la technique*, the cognate term in French).

Technics meant something more all-embracing than the machine. It could mean anything that was a man-made instrumentality leading to a human goal, consistent with the word's origins in the Greek *technē*. Technics became, first, any of the tools man had developed to master nature. Then, in the German debate before World War II, these tools were understood to have turned to the mastery of human nature. Thus "technics" as a category led from a machine technics to an organizational technics that embraced purely social ways of remaking and regimenting man, what we might call "social technique," organization, or simply government.[75]

Technics, in the manner of other German philosophical concepts (Spirit, dialectic, Being), also had a way of becoming a colossal abstraction, an agency that could unfold on its own. *Technik* became independent, inevitable, a force like humanity or culture. Social reasons for this aggrandization have been traced historically as part of a self-conscious effort in the early decades of the twentieth century, among assorted technical advocates, to merge *Technik* with the more reputable German ideal of *Kultur*. For nationalist modernizers, technics would assure German greatness against foreign, decadent *Zivilisation*. Among professional engineers and technologists, the merging of their work with the familiar ideal of *Kultur* assured them a place among intellectual elites who otherwise would have dismissed their despiritualized physical activity, conceived only as the design and repair of machines.[76] For detractors of technics, on the other hand, a historical explanation for their expansion of the term, too, is a horrified recoil at the shock of rapid industrialism after the turn of the century, and its abuse in the militarist adventure of World War I—the famous "storm of steel" that brutalized both Right and Left. Technics in Germany from the turn of the century through the Nazi period lacked the gradualist, little-c conservative meanings by which technology was assimilated as a tool for the status quo in countries with a longer industrial past—liberal England, principally, and to a lesser extent the United States.[77]

Ambitions for technics had been higher and its possibilities more inno-cent, in Germany as in the United States, before World War I. Hopes swelled for rational management of government on technological lines. Rising technical knowledge and standards of living should exert, it was believed, a cosmopolitan and internationalizing influence upon former peasants and new industrial workers. The German Jewish businessman and statesman Walther Rathenau wrote of the "Degermanizing" influence of the forms of technical interconnection we would today call "globalization," as well as transformations of everyday life by "the machine."[78] When war came, he headed the orderly husbanding and control of raw materials for the Ger-man war effort. Afterward, as a high official in the Weimar Republic, he was assassinated in 1922 by a right-wing paramilitary squad.

Dominating the "quarrel over technology" in Germany in the decade after the war was a "reactionary modernism" (Jeffrey Herf's coinage) that favored technological modernization, not on behalf of science or reason but precisely for forms of violent irrationalism, which, in the hymns of praise this generation wrote to violent technics, often seemed indistin-guishable (to humanists) from the most damning critique.[79] One sees this ambiguity at its extreme in one of the major intellectual figures of the first third of the century—in America as well as in Germany—Oswald Spen-gler, the author of *The Decline of the West*. That Spengler was a reaction-ary, there was no question. His earlier books had cast a doom-laden shadow over a whole generation. But he tried to clarify his immediately relevant views, just before the Nazis' rise, in *Man and Technics* (published in 1931 in Germany, brought out by Alfred A. Knopf in 1932 in the United States). Herf insists that Spengler was *in favor* of the advance of technics in this short book. This has been hard for readers to see, then and since, in the absence of other information from Spengler's biography.[80] Perhaps this is because one must simply reverse one's ordinary presuppositions for this author, who can write that "the genuine human soul" is "a foe to everyone, killing, *hating*, resolute to conquer or die"; that "Every real 'man,' even in the cities of Late periods" (that is, the most decadent places of our deca-dent times) "knows the intoxication of feeling when the knife pierces the hostile body, and the smell of blood and the sense of amazement strike to-gether upon the exultant soul."[81]

Yet Spengler's perhaps glorying conception of violent technics, as a whole, is surprisingly consistent with the critique of technology that would firm up in America during the era of the crisis of man and afterward. As Spengler puts it, technics are the tactics man develops in his perpetual conflict with his own kind, and then with nature. The permanent "tragedy" of Man, which he must play out to the end, is that he will raise his hand against nature, to dominate and destroy her, too, and yet nature will finally win and overcome him.[82] Spengler drew his own conclusion about the end-game: the machine microcosm would revolt against Nordic man, and technics fall into the hands of the dark races, who in their barbarism would attack Nordic man with his own tools but without his noble spirit.[83] This last aspect of the Spenglerian critique did not necessarily cross the ocean.[84]

The philosopher and psychologist Karl Jaspers influentially represented the humanistic antitechnical line. His *Man in the Modern Age* was one of the best of the synoptic accounts from the early '30s to say just what was so epochal in the "world crisis" of the German moment. It went through five editions in Berlin and Leipzig within a year and was translated almost immediately into English in 1933. The former psychiatrist and *Existenz* philosopher warned that in an era of weak state forms and the vacant "de-spiritualization" of the modern, the one objectively new factor, destined "to enwrap the planet in a mesh of apparatus," was "technique."[85]

Jaspers did not purely reject technics. Like others, even at the start of the Nazi period, he was cautiously hopeful that its worst consequences would also reveal new possibilities for man's life—because the human condition would at last be laid bare by artifacts. In truth, Jaspers was uncertain. Man was caught between extremes, and could neither rid himself of technics nor desire its completion: "A paradox results. Man's life has become dependent upon the apparatus which proves ruinous to mankind at one and the same time by its perfectionment and by its breakdown."[86]

As it worked itself out in Anglophone thinking, the question of technics in the discourse of man took up elements of the German discussion, from both left and right, but became very much its own conversation. The essential line of thought went like this: Man had used his tools to master nature, and this was a good thing. He did so in order to liberate human beings from natural necessity. But imperceptibly he was turning his tools from the mastery of outer nature, a task that was nearing completion, to the mastery of human nature—which was closely related, sometimes so closely related that the turn was imperceptible—and this mastery could be unbelievably dangerous.

The more ubiquitous argument was that man's physical technologies would imperceptibly turn back and condition or master him. It had been a cliché already in the American discourse of technology, for example, to say that once upon a time the machine had adapted to man, and now man adapted to the machine. But this need no longer yield merely the tragi-comic result that people now gestured at home with the motion that pulled the hydraulic press at work, or heard their own thoughts with the punctuation of a telegram. It might mean that humans adapted their government to what was calculable by technocrats, fit their dreams to the range of manufactures on the market, and believed only what the gutter press, the loudspeakers, and the wireless could communicate.

The more extreme argument followed from the premise that mastering outer nature led inevitably to mastering human nature. Man had not drawn a necessary line. In a wholly naturalistic order based on Darwin and Newton, which subjected "man the animal" to the mechanical ingenuity of "man the maker," perhaps such restraints were inconceivable. But this would lead to a destructive recursion. Man, in service of the liberation of the human, would modify the nature of the human so that there would no longer be an original humanity to liberate. Technical possibilities of fabrication and modification alone would set the human agenda, as accident or the whim of scientists might dictate. Humanity, too, was becoming an artifact of human technics, until human beings' original purposes became inscrutable—and since there would no longer be a truly human subject left to appreciate and control the process, no standpoint would remain for criticism of the controllers, themselves increasingly dehumanized, whose purpose must become the act of mastery itself. Moreover, the piecemeal replacement of human passions and destinies could occur under wicked tyrannies or under free regimes that simply honored servility, ease, and men's convenience. Leo Strauss, even after the war, hinted at the tyranny of technics that were "slow and gentle":

> In contradistinction to classical tyranny, present-day tyranny has at its disposal "technology"... a particular interpretation, or kind, of science... meant to be applied to "the conquest of nature."... We are now brought face to face with a tyranny which holds out the threat of becoming, thanks to "the conquest of nature" and in particular of human nature, what no earlier tyranny ever became: perpetual and universal. Confronted by the appalling alternative that man, or human thought, must be collectivized either by one stroke and without mercy or else by slow and gentle processes, we are forced to wonder how we could escape from this dilemma.[87]

Likewise, Oxford literature professor C. S. Lewis, in his book *The Abolition of Man*, warned that "the man-moulders of the new age will be armed with the powers of an omnicompetent state and an irresistible scientific technique"—and yet they won't necessarily be "bad men." "They are, rather, not man (in the old sense) at all. They are, if you like, men who have sacrificed their own share in traditional humanity in order to devote themselves to the task of deciding what 'Humanity' shall henceforth mean."[88]

Steering between the ubiquitous and the extreme arguments, some voices put basic physical technics aside and enunciated their uncertainty about the classification of organizational technique. It surely was useful—how else would a good and innocent mankind attain its natural needs? It must partake still of the character of the "innocent" machine, the mill-wheel and the dynamo—yet might it now hide some intentionality of the power-mad "controllers"? American thought, formerly more sanguine about modifying human habits and behaviors for the sake of efficiency, retained its romance of the automobile, combine harvester, and medicinal pill but crept toward the expansive German discourse with increased anxiety about psychological and social organization of men. As Austrian émigré and future US management theorist Peter Drucker put it to American readers in his successful crisis of man book, *The End of Economic Man*, in 1939, "the abracadabra of fascism is the substitution of *organization* for creed and order[,] ... the glorification of organization as an end in itself" (emphasis in original). Insofar as capitalism and socialism alike had depended on *Homo economicus* and his activity to organize society through technical means of organization, by failing to create a separate "new, positive noneconomic concept of Free and Equal Man," both systems had made fascism inevitable.[89]

One sees the darkening of view for technics as it appeared in American thought throughout the period of the discourse of man. Some unanticipated leap forward in the Nazis' crude technicization of man had occurred at the meeting point between the tyrants and the public: in what man, or human nature, would invite and welcome, allowing technology to grind down its surface to release the brutishness inside. The rising giant the Germans and Italians joined was not Hobbes's liberal Leviathan, a single sovereign commonwealth formed of joined consents, but an organizational monstrosity of doubled and trebled mechanisms, tubes and circuits and wheels installed for their own sake, to place the innumerable willing sacrifices made by minds turned into cogs: the figure of the biblical giant and monster returned in Giuseppe Borgese's antifascist portrait, *Goliath*, as it did in Franz Neumann's blueprint of Nazi state form as formless, metastasizing, and irrational, *Behemoth*.[90]

HISTORICISM AND UNIVERSAL HISTORY

Another debate to come with the émigrés from Germany treated conceptions of history. It was quietly influential for the American discourse's manner of drawing out not only the causes of crisis but the historical means to solution.

The historiographical method still associated with Germany in the 1930s, and its great development of the nineteenth and early twentieth centuries, was *Historismus*. Often it was then translated "historism." We now generally call it historicism.[91] The unifying principle of historicism in its different variants is that each era of history should be understood in its own particularity and organic contours. At an extreme, each era might not be measurable in the same terms as another. As a German Romantic reaction against Enlightenment history, historicism could be profoundly conservative. Each instant of history—often the history of a "nation-state" or a "people"—was valuable for its own sake, uncriticizable, holy. (Leopold von Ranke: "Before God, all generations of mankind are equal; and this is the light in which the historian must look at them."[92]) The historian, methodologically, would creatively recapture an era and re-render it for its characteristic savor or essence. But in the hands of social scientists or critical historians, historicism could be materialist and relativist. Indeed, fundamental to all "historicizing" academic work today, which seeks to specify a time and place and social context to disenchanted practices and ideas, is the revolution of *Historismus.*[93] Someone like Karl Mannheim, sympathetic to Marx and advocating a sociology of knowledge, understood historicism as the break with a premodern medieval Weltanschauung and then with the naive universal reason of the Enlightenment to create the precondition for any truly critical philosophy, capable of seeing its own positions, too, as a product of time and history.[94] American historians may have misread (or not read) Ranke, as the historian of the American history profession, Peter Novick, has suggested, and come away with a banal, harmless, and depoliticized version of his philosophy of history "as it really was."[95] But the émigrés who arrived in America in the '30s were still in the midst of a heated conflict over historicism and knew what was at stake.

At the turn of the century in Germany, historicism had temporarily seemed a weapon of Prussian nationalist historians. They went into World War I believing their special historiography supported a separate, triumphant law of development for the German nation, which the war would fulfill. By the postdefeat chaos of the Weimar period, though, and under the influence of modernist currents of thought, historicism could seem synonymous with a form of relativism; if all nations and ages were individual, incomparable, how then should they be criticized by any common law or morality?[96] In German historiography of the interwar period, especially by the tumultuous and violent '20s and '30s, this could be seen as another of the destabilizing discourses of the Versailles Treaty era. Notable figures who identified with the Republic in its liberal center, Ernst Troeltsch and Friedrich Meinecke, tried to stabilize the meaning and practice of historicism, but with difficulty. Troeltsch's contribution of 1922, *Der Historismus und seine Probleme* (Historicism and Its Problems), within ten years had been radicalized into *Die Krisis des Historismus* (Historicism's Crisis) in the religious historian Karl Heussi's book of 1932.[97]

Enlightenment history, in contrast—the phase against which Romantic *Historismus* had originally reacted—had been progressive, critical, and, especially in its late variant in the German Aufklärung, "philosophical."

The basic Enlightenment legacy that offered an alternative to historicism lay in the use of comparative history to criticize irrationality and superstition. As Peter Gay described the original practice of the French Enlightenment, "the philosophes developed a kind of comparative history which they explicitly distinguished from the study of the past for its own sake. . . . [T]hey wrote the history of the human mind as the history of its rise from myth in classical antiquity, its disastrous decline under Christianity, and its glorious rebirth" in secular wisdom.[98] Philosophical history was a further development. It tried to tie accounts of progress in history to progress in human reason, in a chronological development bound by discoverable laws of human nature comparable to the laws of outer nature. The German late Enlightenment ultimately called this project "Universal History" (in Kant, Schiller, and Herder): a history to show that all periods in fact participated in a single line of progress of the species or of the human being regardless of the feints and ruses of historical event.[99] To quote Kant, "[t]he history of the human race as a whole can be regarded as the realisation of a hidden plan of nature to bring about [a] . . . state within which all natural capacities of mankind can be developed completely."[100]

In the American discourse of man through the war years, under the influence of the émigrés (when the émigrés were not writing these books themselves), a particular kind of history emerges—the revival of the Enlightenment's version of a universal critical history, but without a confident faith in progress. This could be called *re-enlightenment history*. It is the basis of many of the classics of the discourse of man, whether or not they are histories in an academic, professional sense. Re-enlightenment writers conceived the whole of Western history as, once again, a long progress, but one in which something had gone wrong; and behaved as if by running through the entire history of the mind, man, faith, or ideas of human nature, developmentally, they might find the flaw and figure out how to repair it. This is part of what gives the crisis of man canon its painfully laborious character for readers. An author will carry a thesis summarizable in a sentence or in five pages through two volumes. "The author has attempted to re-interpret history, not by discussing it, but by re-telling it,"[101] Kahler modestly said of himself—and then retold it for six hundred and fifty pages. To protect civilization at its moment of danger, you, the reader, must hear of it; to find the flaw that endangered this civilization, he, the intellectual, must relive it.

Kahler was the most overheated but also one of the most vulnerably hopeful writers in this mode. He saw the problem of history and the problem of man as linked: the crisis "has undermined the concept of mankind as a coherent body, together with the concept of history as the consistent evolution of mankind. . . . Both ideas, then, the unity of mankind and the unity of history, stand and fall together."[102] Niebuhr's *Nature and Destiny of Man* followed a similar historical pattern tracing an idea of man through successive ages to find the flaw, and Thomas Mann linked the two books in a letter to Kahler: "Contemporary experience has, after all, awakened a certain receptivity to such synoptic and daring books. Niebuhr's *The Nature and Destiny of Man* is . . . a sign of the times."[103] The émigré Hans Kohn in 1944 hid a universal history within his magnum opus on nationalism, paradoxically seeing within a civilization-long trajectory of growing national feeling (now in its darkest hour, subordinated to Nazi purposes), the rising awareness of plural nations and manifold peoples that must inevitably synthesize a higher cosmopolitan internationalism.[104] The most senior cultural critic in America to produce a doorstop re-enlightenment history was Lewis Mumford, who fully met up with the discourse of man in his *The Condition of Man* (1944). Though Mumford was adapting the synthetic historical approach that he had used earlier, and though he meant to be continuing the project begun in his *Technics and Civilization* and *The Culture of Cities*, *The Condition of Man* became much more pessimistic about technics and much more focused on the philosophical history of man himself. Mumford, too, reproved "the present crisis in modern civilization." He claimed that "basic notions as to the nature of man," if discovered, would be the key to its solution.[105] He, too, attempted this in four hundred pages of close type, starting at the beginning of human history and reaching the present.

The sense of civilizational threat also generated a great age for the popularization of intellectual and world history, conceived as a repository of besieged attainments in danger of being lost, which the common man should know. In 1935, Will Durant began publishing his *Story of Civilization*, in its many gift-book volumes, for a mass middle class. The first three volumes of the enormously popular civilization history written by Englishman Arnold Toynbee, important to both intellectuals and the general reading public, was published in 1934, and the next three volumes—including his crucial musings on the collapse of civilizations—arrived in 1939. Against historicist doubt and universal history revival, Toynbee reenlivened cyclical history of countless rises and falls of civilizations on a common scheme. Toynbee's mechanism of history was "challenge and response," which, kept at an equilibrium or happy medium, let civilizations thrive until they tipped one way or another; either overwhelming challenge or enervating ease destroyed each one eventually, of course.[106] Yet Toynbee's moderate pessimism undid the violent pessimism of Oswald Spengler, and his model introduced a voluntarism and heroic resignation he had not necessarily intended. Our civilization "has grown great through its responses," declared *Fortune* in 1943, "and there is no reason (according to the Toynbeean hypothesis) why it should not grow greater if it responds correctly to future challenges."[107]

TWO SCHEMAS OF HISTORY

In the intellectuals' civilization histories, however, the historical story generally settled into one of two precise schematizations. These reappeared with impressive frequency in all sorts of materials and documents beyond the long histories themselves; they furnished a borrowed background and thickening agent for all sorts of meditations on man.

The first one, the three centuries schema, worked entirely within the modern era. The three centuries in question were the eighteenth, nineteenth, and twentieth. The eighteenth century was said to be simply the century of enlightenment, hopeful and essentially intellectual. Men discovered the rights of man and democratic social organization. The nineteenth century was the century of progress, material rather than intellectual: it sowed seeds of trouble. Industrialism, and the technologies to master nature, showed that rights were inadequate to cover exploitation in the economic and social realms. Politically, the new techniques of organization of the nineteenth century were those of the great empires and imperialism. Then came the third and worst century. "The 20th century has betrayed the 18th century's ideas of human freedom and the 19th century's progress towards their achievement," Hans Kohn summarized in a short article for general consumption.[108] The twentieth century was the century of overturning, collapse, disintegration. World War I saw the collapse of the state system in a web of secret alliances. The Depression added the collapse of the capitalist world economy. The techniques used to master human nature exposed the end of man's beneficent mastery over nature with his technology, and thus, perhaps, the collapse of human character itself. The nineteenth century had held two major intellectual forces, nationalism and socialism, and the world had been safe as long as they were opposed; joined together in Russia and Germany, however, they became explosive, creating "totalitarian society with its new type of man: worker and soldier at the same time, the total antithesis of 19th-century man."[109] On this schema, the usual solution had to do with a chastened or improved recovery of the ideals of the eighteenth century by due analysis of the outcomes of the twentieth. The rights of man and hope for human progress would be retained, without the belief that progress was built into nature or history or inevitable. For practical action, hope would come with planning, at the level of the nation, and a world government, at the level of the planet.

The three ages schema, as the major alternative, went back behind the modern and took in the whole of recorded history. It concurred about the crisis of the modern age but sought solutions outside modern life. Its three ages were the ancient (often rendered in two parts: the classical and biblical), the medieval-Christian, and the modern.

The surprise of this schema was that it found its favorite center of gravity in the medieval. This was as true for thinkers who were not theological (like Erich Fromm or Lewis Mumford), as for those who were—whether they were Protestant (like Niebuhr or T. S. Eliot), or Roman Catholic (the only thinkers who truly had a direct tradition linking them through church life to Scholastic philosophy). The medieval period, those dark ages, had been the very center of superstition and obstruction for the Enlightenment.[110] In a recurring theme of the discourse of man in the late '30s and '40s, the medieval seemed the last safe place before the modern undermining that had begun in the Renaissance. Its admirers portrayed it as a time of the whole, undivided, organic—the *integrated*, when the present era was said to be disintegrating. The historian T. J. Jackson Lears has shown how the medieval imagination was a key aspect of modernist antimodernism at the American turn of the century. But discourse-of-man medievalism was different. "Among [the] cast of medieval characters" of the late nineteenth century, Lears writes, "there was one figure missing: the scholastic philosopher . . . Thomas Aquinas, Duns Scotus, and their fellow schoolmen received virtually no attention."[111] In contrast, the intellectualist medievalism of the mid-twentieth-century discourse of man *needed* Aquinas. Catholic Thomists like Jacques Maritain made common cause with non-Catholic Thomists like Adler and Hutchins; the Jewish Adler truly did go back to the fourteenth century for a system of logical thought (as Sidney Hook never stopped accusing him of doing) and metaphysical grounds.

The textbook locus for the discussion of medieval integralism among intellectuals was not always Jacques Maritain's *Integral Humanism* (1936)—an immensely important early title for the discourse of man—or other Catholic works, but yet another work by a German Jewish émigré writing in America, Erich Fromm's *Escape from Freedom* (1941).[112] Fromm was a psychologist, and a reinterpreter of Freud, who had held an association with the Frankfurt school but gradually became estranged from it. His book is remembered as an explanation of authoritarianism. In the modern age, men unmoored from hierarchical and communal societies encounter modern atomized freedom and can't bear it. Deprived of the authentic "corporatism" of the medieval, they escape into the fake corporatism and ersatz belonging of authoritarian obedience, the new authority of the great man in fascism. But Fromm also offered a historical picture of a positive medievalism that preceded modern freedom but was acceptable to those skeptical of Christian nostalgia.[113] (Though it may have been guilty of unhistorical nostalgia of its own: the picture was so well integrated that Fromm's "friend Thomas Merton, the Catholic theologian, cautioned him against an overly positive and one-dimensional picture of the Middle Ages, one shorn of qualification and nuance."[114]) The medieval was a touchstone, though not, this time, something to which the intellectuals could easily wish to return. Instead, they could call for something comparable—not a "corporate" total state like that of fascism but some new human-scaled and human-directed "integration" of society.

RE-ENLIGHTENMENT IN DESPAIR

If one puts together the different modifications and salvational changes the discourse of the crisis of man thought to make to the Enlightenment to reach re-enlightenment, a particular problem appears. The adjustments are overwhelmingly negative. They post a "not" sign after essential positive assertions of the earlier era, seeking to strike out its troubling, dangerous, too hopeful, too unguarded, and self-defeating positive elements.

What remains in re-enlightenment? First is the prospect of enlightenment without just a single path to progress—or perhaps without progress altogether; second, following upon it, a universal history without teleology or inbuilt goal; and third, philosophical anthropology without an a priori, without an essence of man discoverable in the absence of different forms of human life and being—as the refugee novelist Hermann Broch incisively diagnosed Kahler's version, this is a quest "to derive the 'enduring' fundamentals of human nature, what is truly 'human,' from the sober, warranted historical data themselves . . . [so as] to eliminate dogma, metaphysics and ontology from the philosophy of history, and thus from metapolitics."[115] (As an émigré to the United States, perhaps Broch understood so well because he, author of the masterpieces *The Sleepwalkers* [1932] and *The Death of Virgil* [1945], abandoned fiction to undertake his own giant philosophy of human character and mass psychology in pursuit of a saving universality.)[116] Fourth, technics put under the mastery of man, not mastering him. Perhaps the machine could be humanized, as in earlier fantasies, but techniques of organizing men might need to be countermanded, inoculated against by new kinds of education, or banned.

Two books of 1944 accepted the negative path and followed it, taking the critique of technics, and an antiprogressive universal history, to their extremes. Yet they are two books that, as far as I know, have never been placed side by side: Mumford's *Condition of Man* and Max Horkheimer and Theodor Adorno's *Dialectic of Enlightenment*.

Customarily, Mumford and the Frankfurt school theorists would be thought to reside in two different intellectual traditions. Horkheimer and

Adorno returned from Los Angeles to Frankfurt right after the war. Their radically pessimistic book had a small republication in Amsterdam in 1947 and finally a large influence in Germany only in 1969, followed by that of its translation into English in 1972.[117] Thus *Dialectic of Enlightenment* has been assimilated to a New Left moment in Germany. But this was not at all the situation of its composition. Horkheimer and Adorno, two temporary émigrés, wrote it in Los Angeles while living in the sun and verdure that German émigrés liked to describe by analogy to all the wilderness and vacation spots of Europe—Switzerland, the Riviera, the Vienna woods—and listening to NBC radio and watching MGM films.[118] They "published" it in New York in an edition of only five hundred, in German, accessible to the émigré network of thinkers that connected the two coasts.[119] Mumford's *Condition of Man* was published in New York in 1944 by Harcourt in a significant edition, widely reviewed, and couldn't seem more "American": especially with his coda of exhortations to improvement, which the German dialecticians would have scorned. Nevertheless, the two books have a common project—and something of the same thesis, quite unexpectedly.

The year 1944 was extraordinary for the discourse of man because it combined the absolute certainty that the Allies would win with a pessimistic discovery that things would definitely not return to normal when they did. (Everyone knew the Allies would win by the force of US arms, but more particularly by the avalanche of US industrial production.) And yet the two books shared a thesis that should have been incomprehensible to earlier eras: that progress, as proven by a universal history of human development, might contain *within itself* the antiprogressive domination that would undo human liberation. So Horkheimer and Adorno could call enlightenment itself the force of destruction: "[T]he destructive aspect of progress" must be recognized; "Enlightenment," Horkheimer and Adorno suggested in a much-abused phrase, "is totalitarian."[120] Mumford, former technological optimist and folksy universal thinker, met up in his own way with the project of the German dialecticians: "Every gain in power, every mastery of natural forces, every scientific addition to knowledge, has proved potentially dangerous." "Modern man is the victim of the very instruments he values most."[121] If one put down the quotes without the names, one might not know which was whose.

Dialectic of Enlightenment is probably the single most notorious, indeed scandalous, philosophical work to come out of the discourse of man. Jürgen Habermas, inheritor of Horkheimer and Adorno's Frankfurt school of critical theory, calls it their "blackest" book, in the sense of those shattering "'black' writers of the [nineteenth century] bourgeoisie, . . . the Marquis de Sade and Nietzsche."[122] Yet to a degree, *Dialectic of Enlightenment* can be understood, too, as a "re-enlightenment" book. The "critique of enlightenment" was "intended to prepare the way for a positive notion of enlightenment" (xvi). Of course, the critique was total—hence the scandal. Unlike those who believed that modern crisis had demonstrated gaps, weaknesses, or blindnesses within a still-sound Enlightenment, the Frankfurt school authors in wartime turned on the Enlightenment as a single, minor episode within a history of destructive "enlightenment" as long in duration as recorded history itself. "[T]he Enlightenment has always aimed at liberating men from fear and establishing their sovereignty. Yet the fully enlightened earth radiates disaster triumphant" (3). What started as an impulse to liberation, they declare dialectically, invariably became the means of domination. Human power promotes dehumanization. Enlightenment always sought science, instrumentality, reason, and disenchantment, seeking to undo myth, but inevitably hardened into a new myth of rational-instrumental character. Horkheimer and Adorno could see now what others had missed, only because enlightenment was now reaching an absolute stage. They saw the new, final forms of myth not only among the Nazis and fascists but in Hollywood's total administration of American spiritual life. *Dialectic of Enlightenment* is one of the slowest page-turners of all time. It has a riveting quality of shocking revelations. "[W]e . . . set ourselves nothing less than the discovery of why mankind, instead of entering into a truly human condition, is sinking into a new kind of barbarism" (xi). How did it become so? Because "what men want to learn from nature is how to use it in order wholly to dominate it and other men," and this form of learning has a name—"*Technology* is the essence of this knowledge" (4; emphasis added).

Mumford, for his part, blamed "technics" first, then drew out the civilization-level consequences. This was a dramatic change for a writer who in 1934 had anticipated an inevitable *humanization* of technics in the first half of his widely read *Technics and Civilization*, with its blissful fusion of technics with the organic (though careful readers have noted a withdrawal from optimism in the latter half, and sought to trace the rise of Mumford's misgivings).[123] Mumford structured his newer book on the more conventional schema of the discourse of the crisis of man: search every past age for the flaw in the development of human nature, seek to reintegrate man, find that medieval times were the core. But in 1944, he, too, had absorbed the sense of inevitable unfolding that can otherwise, mistakenly, seem so unique in the Frankfurt school. Technics had made a triumph over nature that had become a technicization or "automatism" of man. This eventuality might somehow have been inherent in technics itself, in its permanent way of advancing. In common with Horkheimer and Adorno in their critique of democratic America, Mumford had come to believe that America's now-inevitable victory in the war with the Nazis would not solve man's problem. The first sentence of the following passage surely could have been written by Horkheimer and Adorno; though the second has a characteristic American note of the call to a renewal of human character, which identifies it as Mumford's:

> In the passive barbarism that the United States now boasts under the cover of technical progress, there is no promise whatever of victory or even bare survival. Without a deep regeneration and renewal, the external triumph of American machinery and arms will but hasten the downfall of the Western World.[124]

"Deep regeneration and renewal": this was a distress call, combined with a certain, irrepressible optimism, which never left the American discourse of man. Yet there were things that even these already desperate voices could not know in 1944: that the United States would drop an atomic bomb, burning up 4.4 square miles of the landscape and killing seventy thousand human beings more or less instantaneously—and that the German killing-machine had deliberately put aside rational war aims to round up, transport, and gas or shoot six million Jews to no purpose whatsoever but the purification of Hitler's idea of man. So the next question of the crisis of man is how it spread, rather than ended, with the winning of the war—and how the discourse, established among participants in preexisting debates about human nature, reached new sets of intellectuals without any previous interest in the matter.

CHAPTER 3

THE END OF THE WAR AND AFTER

The historian Paul Boyer, chronicler of the atom bomb's reception in America, has pointed out that the shock of the bomb was much greater than any other tragedy of the war since Pearl Harbor, precisely because of the project's secrecy. Americans had absolutely no preparation for the headlines announcing that a Japanese city had been vaporized with a single unconventional weapon.[1] The mass killing of the Jews, in contrast, had been foreshadowed by mass killings of soldiers, torture of prisoners, and Hitler's hatred and persecution of Jews since 1933. The atom bomb really was unprecedented (except to those members of the bombing command prior to August 6, 1945, who convinced themselves it was just an explosive device like any other). Boyer has also shown that a great deal of pacifying and normalizing influence was subsequently turned upon atomic power in America, linking the bomb to utopias of peace and free energy. Americans thus seemed, ultimately, to find nuclear arms more tolerable, in those weapons' near-magical cool science, than the depraved crudities of gas chambers and crematoria—grotesqueries to which, for years after the initial reception of the camps in 1945 to 1947, they would rarely return in memory.[2]

The intellectuals of the crisis of man dwelt on both events. The Holocaust and the atom bomb certainly did not trigger the crisis of man. Nor, for that matter, did they start grim meditations on World War II. (Those had begun earlier.) Nor would they cause the revival of human rights in the 1940s by themselves, as we will see. Both the Holocaust and the bomb, rather, confirmed for intellectuals what they felt they already knew, and gave all future discussions, highbrow and middlebrow, new reference points for the danger in which man stood.

The bomb and the camps are often taken to have been the absolute starting point for the gloomy, foundational, "existentialist," and human rights turns of the 1940s—in short, for various symptoms of a crisis of man we have already seen in its domestic and émigré origins—and this common intuition has to be taken into account. It seems accurate to say that, on the one hand, fascism, technics, and war could have produced the entire crisis of man by itself. On the other hand, the bomb and the camps completed the intellectuals' already widely articulated logic as they could never have imagined—factually, concretely—and intensified everything, for intellectuals and the populace alike. These events were like an inundation that burst the boundaries of the early discourse, carrying fragments of its rhetoric and questions with them as they flooded American discussion. A factory for the disassembly of men, not long ago just a metaphorical conceit, had been built. It had been warned of, but no one could have known it would happen so practically. A force to destroy the whole physical world, something easy enough to dream up in the "man masters nature, then destroys himself" visions, had genuinely been found—then quantified on graph paper, constructed to engineering specifications, instantiated in a bomb, and used. The effects on thought of these concrete images for Faustian technics and the world's end, in bulldozed bodies and mushroom clouds, really cannot be measured. But images of them turn up, often in surprising places, for the rest of the period (through the 1960s)—often in counterintuitive ways.

The atom bomb first. Commentators like Lewis Mumford, who had been warning of a danger to man, took the new technology of destruction as a final piece of evidence. "[W]e now have to devise, under pressure of the greatest crisis mankind has yet faced"—here he is writing *after* the war had been won—"protective devices that will keep our knowledge, not merely from ruining civilization, but from causing life, in all its organised forms, to disappear from the planet."[3] (Mumford also passed the final bar of extremity in his reaction, prepared to demand the destruction of technics altogether if this was its outcome: "*This means that there is no part of our modern world that we must not be ready to scrap, if the need to scrap it is the price of mankind's safety and continued development. Nothing is sacred but human life. If the dismantling of every factory, if the extirpation of every item of scientific knowledge that has been accumulated since 1600, were the price of mankind's continuance, we must be ready to pay that terrible price*" [emphasis in original].[4])

Others, who were new to apocalyptic criticism, took the shocking event of Hiroshima and Nagasaki as an occasion to join the ongoing search for man's fundamental nature. This was the pivotal moment, for example, for Norman Cousins, who at thirty-three had already been editor of the *Saturday Review of Literature*, a middlebrow-highbrow weekly book review of wide circulation, since the beginning of the war. The bomb spurred him, within a week of Nagasaki, to his editorial entitled "Modern Man Is Obsolete," later expanded into a book with the same title.

The front cover of that Saturday's issue was blank but for a black-bordered quotation from Spengler. Inside, Cousins wasted no time getting to his question: "Where man can find no answer, he will find fear. While the dust was still settling over Hiroshima, he was asking himself questions and finding no answers. The biggest question of these concerns the nature of man."[5]

"Is war in the nature of man?" Cousins wanted to know. If so, then men had to stop and change human nature, because a further war would destroy the human species. If war was not in man's nature, then *conditions* had provoked him to war all this time, so he would have to change his conditions to liberate his real, peaceful human nature. Either way, change was necessary, and it had to come from the reconsideration of man. Modernity, alas, had locked man into a preoccupation with outer things, in the stasis of technology and world history, as he had worked on everything *but* recovering his human nature.

> If this reasoning is correct, then modern man is obsolete, a self-made anachronism becoming more incongruous by the minute. He has exalted change in everything but himself. . . . Man is left, then, with a crisis in decision. The main test before him involves his will to change rather than his ability to change.[6]

Cousins retained a progressive faith in conscious change and planning. He called for science to survey man for "transformation or adjustment." Man must "develop a world conscience." Either he should destroy all science, technology, and knowledge and kill everyone who knew how to fix a car engine or even to read, so that the atom bomb would never be discovered again (Cousins's modest proposal, echoed by many other writers), or modern man should accept "world government" as the only hope for a peaceful future. These sorts of combinations were relatively common as models for the new breed of popular, nonreligious commentators seeking to come to grips with the lessons of the war and the bomb: to retain faith in planning and the highest-level solutions, to call at the same time for the deepest recovery of man, and to promise that the two were compatible, often through an unstable mixture of social science, world-level political planning, and renewed moral faith.

The bomb added certain ideas to the imagination of the postwar years. One was simply that hubristic techniques of mastery, applied once again to outer nature, could actually destroy the entire physical world. At the least, it could make it uninhabitable to man, a gray waste. This was a logical last step to earlier discussions of technics and history. Man had mastered nature. The crisis of man discussions of technics had suggested that he was turning his techniques on human nature. The bomb proved that he could also turn around and destroy all of nature itself. It seemed things could go no further except by man's doing so.

INTELLECTUAL INFLUENCE OF THE CAMPS

The reception of the Holocaust in the United States has recently been reevaluated. Until a few years ago, it was often assumed that perceptions of the genocide have been consistent since the first newsreels and press accounts of the camps reached America. It was assumed to have been understood as it is today: as a shattering event, unique in history, which redefined the real character of Nazism and of World War II from 1945 onward, and gave Jews a special, if horrible, place in that history. This is not quite correct. But where historians have turned up evidence of American indifference to the Nazi murder of the Jews, both before and after 1945, another, equally erroneous view has sometimes taken hold: that the Holocaust was entirely unappreciated when it was revealed; that survivors themselves always kept quiet and did not write memoirs or begin to "tell their stories" until decades later (the notion here was of a trauma that kept them from speaking); and that the Holocaust became relevant only in the later 1960s, primarily to the Jewish community.[7]

In fact, the following occurred: the news of the death camps received significant public notice from 1945 to 1947, as you'd expect of such a tragedy. But it was assimilated into the history of the war and the evil of the Nazis. It was just the sort of things Nazis *would* do. Significant survivors' narratives were indeed published immediately after the war. Although they did make an impact in intellectual and émigré circles, they, too, were assimilated to a more general wartime literature, had no reason to reach a wider readership, and were not canonized in any way as part of a separate literature of Holocaust (a word that did not emerge until the mid- to late 1960s). A period of silence followed the initial interest, from about 1947 through the 1950s, simply because the events were over. There were only scattered hints of anything unique in history, a different moral center of World War II, or something that could teach truths applicable to Americans. The date for Holocaust reemergence, and the reasons for that reemergence, are still contested.[8]

One thought that the camps contributed to the store of postwar ideas, which could never be eradicated or forgiven, was the apprehension that human bodies, once taken apart, could be reused as dead objects. The Nazis left behind, at Birkenau in Auschwitz, a collection from murdered Jews of "348,820 men's suits, 836,255 women's garments, 13,964 carpets, 69,848 dishes, huge quantities of toothbrushes, shaving brushes, glasses, crutches, false teeth, and seven tons of hair."[9] As Dwight Macdonald wrote:

> [T]he crematorium . . . at Maidanek looked like "a big bake shop or a very small blast furnace." . . . [Bodies] were cut up by butchers, loaded onto iron stretchers and slid on rollers into the coke-fed ovens. . . . As in the Chicago stockyards, no by-products were wasted. The clothes and shoes were shipped into Germany to relieve the shortage of consumption goods. . . . No corpse could be burned without a stamp on the chest: "INSPECTED FOR GOLD FILLINGS." The ashes and bones of the burned bodies were used to fertilize cabbage fields around the camps.[10]

One of the most familiar understandings in the midcentury literature of what the Nazis had done with the Jews was turn them into bars of soap. The thought was extended by the Jewish theologian Abraham Joshua Heschel in the mid-1960s, when he delivered his own series of lectures, *Who Is Man?*, to all of the science that had paved the way to the Nazi murder: "In pre-Nazi Germany the following statement of man was frequently quoted: 'The human body contains a sufficient amount of fat to make seven cakes of soap, enough iron to make a medium-sized nail, a sufficient amount of phosphorous to equip two thousand match-heads, enough sulphur to rid oneself of one's fleas.'"[11] The soap idea was not true, but it was somehow symbolically significant. (It appears as a major conceit in literature and outraged commentary, for example, in Herman Wouk's *The Caine Mutiny* [1951], and will turn up again, as we'll see in chapter 8, in the fiction of Thomas Pynchon).[12] What Heschel described of German interwar science was true of interwar biological science generally: if one does research in a US medical library, one finds English-language studies from the period of how much of a given mineral, or given substance, makes up a human corpse. An effect of the camps was to help the later twentieth century be haunted by an industrial-scale turning of human beings into corpses precisely *for* exploitation. The genocide's unforgivability went beyond the fact of mass murder and beyond the murder of a people. It took with blasé good cheer the science that had been meant for human liberation, the satisfaction of human wants, and the repair of the medical body and used it to destroy human beings. It meant Enlightenment know-how truly was amoral. Soap was ostensibly the universal cleanser, affected now by the worst imaginable moral pollution. The reporters at the liberation of the Western concentration camps returned compulsively to the fact that Buchenwald had been situated in Weimar near the home of Goethe. They made a cliché of the rumor that the commandants and their wives had played Bach in their homes after a long day of killing.

NEW YORK AND PARIS: FROM HUMAN NATURE TO THE HUMAN CONDITION

The late stage of the war and then its doubly cataclysmic end show the rhetoric and problems of the crisis of man sweeping through everything and everyone—even the New York Intellectuals, the most studied group in midcentury, and the thinkers you might suppose least susceptible to this kind of thinking.

The New York Intellectuals remained opponents and skeptics of the new currents until the end of the war and, ostensibly, beyond it. The group was made up of Jewish American children of immigrants (or immigrants themselves) schooled in the factional fighting of the socialist Left, and difficult-to-classify non-Jewish literary contrarians like Mary McCarthy and Dwight Macdonald. All were secular and thus unsusceptible to Niebuhrian currents; modernist, and therefore already equipped with a recent canon against Chicago's Great Books; and anti-Stalinist Marxist, and therefore still oriented to society and the class struggle. They lacked metaphysical and traditionalist baggage, and so were initially hostile to talk of an essential man.

When Sidney Hook first made his attacks on Niebuhr and the new "obscurantism," as we have seen, it was in *Partisan Review*, the journal of the New York Intellectual core. (Only in the years after World War II would it ascend to a kind of dominance of high culture in America, as what Richard Hofstadter called a kind of house organ of the American intellectual community.)[13] In the issue prior to Hook's 1943 blast against Niebuhr and Hutchins, the editors at the time, Philip Rahv, William Phillips, George L. K. Morris, Clement Greenberg, and Dwight Macdonald, produced an advertisement for the upcoming salvo. It suggested that they, too, believed in fears of civilization collapse, but from another direction, one in which the crisis of man and human nature talk were at the root of the problem.

> Gilbert Murray once ascribed the collapse of the Roman civilization to a "failure of nerve" in the face of the barbarian threat. There have been of late years many ominous signs in our culture that history may repeat itself.
>
> This special issue of PARTISAN REVIEW will analyze the obscurantist tendencies gathering force in the world today: the revolt against reason and the scientific method; the exaltation of mystery as a mode of knowledge; the recrudescence of reactionary theories about "human nature"; the revival of religiosity and supernaturalism; the abandonment of the historical for the metaphysical approach; the new socioethology of Original Sin.[14]

It is as if Nazism and Niebuhrism (both as "revolt[s] against reason") were in the same boat.[15]

By 1944, as we have seen, it was clear that the United States was going to win the war in Europe. Yet it was then that Mumford, Horkheimer, and Adorno produced their most despairing tomes, and a new tone, vocabulary, and mood become detectable in *Partisan Review*. In the second issue of the year, published in spring 1944, one sees more detailed discussions of man and the nature of man—always referring to someone else's use of the terms, often in book reviews, and universally negative, still seeing in the discourse a form of obscurantism. The terminology just begins to creep in, as a habit of still-hostile speech.

The *Partisan Review* intellectuals were not pleased or confident near the war's end; quite the contrary, they seemed anxious. They began to publish, as well as review, some of the positions with which they disagreed. The turning point might be the 1944 issue in which they reprinted T. S. Eliot's "Notes Towards a Definition of Culture" from an English journal.[16] At first they could only take from Eliot, a modernist genius, what they could not stand from their compatriots. This was his argument against "disintegrated" cultures in the "crisis of the world today." Eliot vaunted the superiority of the medieval world as integrated, traditional, and organic. He announced the failure of all politics and the inability of ordinary people to handle secularization and division without authoritarianism. To round things off, Eliot's essay proposed for his new (Jewish) New York Intellectual confreres that there was only one salvation: universal religion, presumably Christianity, to spread to "all the races of the world." This was a catechism of everything *Partisan Review* thought disreputable and contemptible. Yet, in part as a tribute to Eliot's fame and genius, they published it—and debated it passionately in the next issue, printing statements from a further group of thinkers along Eliot's lines with whom *Partisan Review* disagreed. On and on the double movement goes in that year—criticizing a language and set of ideas about men that the *Partisan Review* writers grow increasingly adept at using. Richard Chase carried on the campaign against obscurantism in a review of Mumford's *Condition of Man*: "The first three words of the Introduction—'What is man?'—do not impress the reader with Mumford's ability to ask fruitful questions."[17] But underneath it on the page was a glowing review of the first novel by Saul Bellow, *Dangling Man*, the *Partisan Review* editors' great hope for a novelist of their own, in an encomium headlined "A Man in His Time." Not yet *man* in his time, but the question of man was a major topic of Bellow's book (as we will see in chapter 5), and it would eventually prove to be an easy enough step to take, both semantically and intellectually.

Partisan Review is too much remembered as aligning itself with patriotic Americanism after the war.[18] This is supposed to betoken a loss of critical power, seen as definite by the early '50s. At the great chasm of 1945, however, when America remained the only Western power not in rubble, and the "American Century" seemed ready to change from a figment of Henry Luce's hectic imagination into concrete prophecy, the New York Intellectuals turned their faces almost exclusively to Europe. There were London letters, Paris letters, even a Rome letter in the magazine, while New York, and for that matter Washington, felt completely absent. Reading the archive of *Partisan Review*, one does not know if the New York Intellectuals cared that the war had ended, or if they had even noticed it. In fact, one knows the victory had occurred only through an allusion made by their American Paris correspondent. He writes, "I went down to my office this morning and read some dispatches about the wild celebrations in New York and San Francisco." Then he drops the matter and instead responds to the editors' request that he explain existentialism to them.[19]

This was oddly appropriate. French existentialism finally became the means by which the discourse of man entered the secular and political core of New York intellect. The romance between the two intellectual groups was short-lived but effected a significant transfer of ideas. When Jean-Paul Sartre visited America in 1946, Phillips and Rahv, bolstered by two fluent French speakers in their orbit, Lionel Abel and Hannah Arendt, took him out to lunch on West Fifty-Sixth Street.[20] Camus visited in 1946, too, in what was by far the most successful face-to-face rendezvous between the new French spirit and the quizzical Americans. Simone de Beauvoir came for a less productive visit in 1947, by which time the mutual personal interest may already have been waning. Later she hurled insults at the New York Intellectuals: "They themselves were sterile . . . they hated life, not only in literature but everywhere they met it."[21] The feeling was mutual; not too long after the visit in 1947, Mary McCarthy ridiculed her as a slumming tourist who could only see America through the violent potboilers she'd read before crossing the ocean.[22] But before things soured, the New York Intellectuals published everything they could get their hands on of the new European spirit, or of things recommended by its leading lights: endless essays on literature by Sartre, a part of his *Nausea*, essays by Beauvoir, and a culmination in the "New French Writing" issue of spring 1946 that contained Camus's "The Myth of Sisyphus," Sartre's "Portrait of an Anti-Semite," Jean Genet, Malraux, Valéry, Julien Gracq, Raymond Queneau, Michel Leiris, and careful, appreciative essays on Sartre and Camus from the editors—even Merleau-Ponty was published a few issues later.[23]

One way to understand why existentialism was so plausible and significant for the secular and skeptical intellectuals of New York—while the native discourse of man had been distasteful—is to mark the difference between "human nature" and the terms of existentialist discourse, "human condition" or "human situation." The "human condition" sought no inner essence. It was nonmetaphysical. It spoke of circumstances that just happened to be reproduced for every single human being, as each person was born mortal in a world of others, a world that furnished certain limits or boundaries within which the individual was free.

"Condition" also conveniently echoed American social-scientific and psychological talk that went with progressive ideas of character formation, whether Marxist or behaviorist. Individuals were conditioned to act and believe by social circumstances. The stress on individual freedom within strong parameters, not themselves rationally explicable but simply given, made for a balance of free will and social conditioning that matched the New Yorkers' (essentially still Deweyan) postwar position. True behaviorist conditioning seemed questionable in light of totalitarian social control. But in a fully mobilized nation, how many choices did one have for one's way of life? The *Partisan Review* crowd didn't feel there were too many. As for "situation," that belonged to Marxism already, in the objective analysis of social conditions as they would or would not lead to revolution. "Situation" had always had a more social and historical feeling than "condition," and it had been a term, too, in the *Existenz* philosophy of prewar Germany, used in common by Jaspers and Heidegger—thus available to German émigrés like Arendt (and of course taken directly from the German line of Husserl and Heidegger by Sartre). Then, helpfully, Sartre, Beauvoir, Camus, and all their comrades agreed that God was dead. This was a relief to the New Yorkers.

Another appeal was political. Intellectuals with non-Communist radical hopes were in a bad position in America at the end of the war. The Communist Party was temporarily resurgent, having rebuilt its membership on the basis that Stalin, "Uncle Joe," was a good American friend in the fight against Hitler. Truman was in office by mere succession—even liberals didn't much like him before his upset reelection in 1948, since they were suspicious both of his competence and his electoral possibilities.[24] He had also used the atom bomb twice, an act that was hard to admire, even if one accepted it. Trotskyists like the *Partisan Review* writers had been split between critical support for the war against fascism (Rahv's and Phillips's position) and a pledge of nonsupport, so as to lead to proletarian revolution within the besieged democratic nations (Macdonald, Greenberg). This division had led to Macdonald's departure, but left no one particularly gleeful, or triumphant, after the war terminated.

Among the few hopeful political possibilities was a share in power for the non-Communist or at least non-Soviet resistance movements in Europe.[25] Europe might be in ruins, but it was still the source of that modernist culture that *Partisan Review* had tried to integrate with radical politics. Sartre, along with Camus, partook of the glamour of the Resistance.

Then, too, the New York Intellectuals, like everyone else, may have obscurely wondered if after the shocks of the long world crisis, and in its evident continuation, all the human horrors that they had described in social, political, and historical terms might really need a description, though still secular, that came down to fundamentals—something better than the Niebuhrians or Chicago Thomists had on offer, but equally profound. This Sartre and his colleagues seemed poised to accomplish, in a pregnant vocabulary that did not make recourse to the usual Anglo-American categories. "Existentialism attempts to construct a theory of man by use of the phenomenological method," announced William Barrett in *Partisan Review*. Existentialism, that is, would be a "theory of man" that would bracket the ultimacies of human nature and focus on the immediately evident. (Barrett, who later became a coeditor of the magazine, was on his way to becoming the most famous interpreter of existentialism in America. He was the author, around this time, of the *Partisan Review* pamphlet *What Is Existentialism?* [1947], and was eventually to become the author of the much more critically minded study *Irrational Man* [1958].) The habitual language of the early framing of the appeal of existentialism to American commentators was drawn straightforwardly from the discourse of man: existentialism was subtitled "A Theory of Man" by one exegete, promoted by another (Marjorie Grene, later a distinguished philosopher) as "a brilliant statement of the tragic dilemma if not of man, at least of man in our time."[26] Particularly valuable for the *Partisan Review* group, however, was the fact that this most abstract philosophy would be explicable by the historical, social, and political practicalities of the French Resistance, the very model of intellectual hope for a semirevolutionary movement apart from the existing ideologies. "As we get close to the state of mind of the Resistance," Barrett wrote admiringly, "Sartre's philosophic categories become remarkably and luminously applicable."[27]

Partisan Review also did something immensely important for the existentialists: it brought existentialism out of literary and avant-garde circles in the United States—where *The Flies, Nausea,* and *The Stranger* (plays and novels) could be hailed and where previous generations of French litterateurs had been received—and into American *intellectual* life.[28]

Indeed, the existentialist moment defined a more significant and longterm change in the position of France in American intellectual life, with important implications. Philosophy before 1945 did not come from France. The exception was Bergson—not much of an influence compared to German philosophy, therefore not much of an exception. Two things came from Paris: fashion and art. This was reflected in the institutional networks that first brought the French existentialists to America, and would have limited the existentialist impact had the message remained in those channels. The long French tradition, not of superior culture but superior couture, led to the odd fact that much of the earliest transfer of Sartre to the United States occurred in *Vogue* and *Harper's Bazaar*. The acquisition of the existentialists as grand-scale celebrities in America was encouraged by this heritage, as in the photos of Camus taken by fashion photographer Cecil Beaton.[29] The immediate predecessor in America to French existentialism was not a philosophical movement but surrealism, especially in the visual and literary arts. André Breton, the surrealist "Pope" and intellectual leader and progenitor, had been in the United States and, like so many others with some celebrity and fluent language skills, had wound up working for the American government's OWI; he had made the migration back to France in 1946, just as the existentialists were arriving. Marcel Duchamp, on the other hand, the clown prince of the old Parisian avant-garde, who had a close association with New York society and artists ever since the 1913 Armory Show, was still living in the metropolis and active in circles there. The biggest lecture of Sartre's American tour in 1946 was at a Carnegie Hall event organized by Charles Henri Ford and his avant-garde art magazine *View*; Marcel Duchamp sat in one of the front rows.[30] When *Partisan Review* took up Sartre's movement, they cast him in a different and ultimately triumphant light. They printed *intellectual* and *critical* statements by Sartre and others, and reviewed and alluded to such untranslated works as *L'Être et le néant* (Being and Nothingness). They knew well enough that Sartre was essentially a translation or transposition, in key ways, of Husserl and Heidegger. They knew, too, that Heidegger was both a major thinker and morally unacceptable—a Nazi of the vilest type, who had assumed a leadership role to Nazify his university, backed out eventually, but remained unrepentant. It is not true that Heidegger's Nazi past waited to "come out" for the revelations of Victor Farias in the late 1980s; this was a case, as so often in history, of material that is known in the contemporary moment, then forgotten or discounted only to be discovered again. Hannah Arendt told readers of *Partisan Review* in 1946 a bit of what Heidegger had done (though she later apologized for Heidegger's speeches and actions as rector of Freiburg, once the teacher and student, and ex-lovers, had reestablished correspondence and contact): "As is well known, he entered the Nazi Party in a very sensational way in 1933—an act which made him stand out pretty much by himself among colleagues of the same caliber. Further, in his capacity as Rector of Freiburg University, he forbade Husserl, his teacher and friend, whose lecture chair he had inherited, to enter the faculty, because Husserl was a Jew," though she already somewhat apologetically "attributed" his "complete irresponsibility partly to the delusion of genius, partly to desperation."[31] Even more starkly, when Heidegger was praised briefly in the pages of *Partisan Review* for his philosophy by a young American admirer, the magazine ran a long correcting letter from an émigré professor who had been personally dismissed by the Nazis, detailing Heidegger's rectorial address, his SS guard, and his eager collaboration with Nazi racism and anti-intellectualism: "In the name of all decency and honor, in the name of all who were sacrificed to the Nazi-Moloch, in the name of all men of 'good will,' I accuse Martin Heidegger of treason against Humanity[,] of the blackest treason possible."[32] But the Nazi monster Heidegger and the Jewish victim Husserl (dead since 1938) could both be recovered through the French. Sartre had studied phenomenology in Berlin before the war and reoriented the philosophy to make a major statement against anti-Semitism as unexistential (*Anti-Semite and Jew* was among the earliest of Sartre's properly philosophical essays to reach a broad American public). *Partisan Review* writers also went back to the nineteenth century and stressed the existentialist heritage from Nietzsche, and especially from the Danish writer Kierkegaard, whose major revival in the United States had been ongoing since the 1930s.

It is important to remember that Sartre, and the French, were not necessarily *misread* when they were transferred to America—even if they were indeed taken up because they could answer American needs. By invoking humanism in France, too, Sartre was changing the character of existentialism to split the difference between more doctrinaire philosophical poles—the Catholics and the Communists—who wished to understand human nature in either religiously fundamentalist or Marxist progressivist terms.[33] Sartre was provocatively making good a concept—"humanism"—which for an elite audience seemed retrograde, soft, and outdated; meanwhile, for a popular audience, he was softening the alleged pessimism and nihilism of his doctrine.[34] Here is the sort of thing that he said in his most influential lecture, which Americans were soon to read:

> What is meant here by saying that existence precedes essence? It means that, first of all, man exists, turns up, appears on the scene, and, only afterwards, defines himself. . . . Thus, there is no human nature, since there is no God to conceive it. . . . Man is nothing else but what he makes of himself. Such is the first principle of existentialism. It is also what is called subjectivity, the name we are labeled with when charges are brought against us. . . . But if existence really does precede essence, man is responsible for what he is. . . . In fact, in creating the man that we want to be, there is not a single one of our acts which does not at the same time create an image of man as we think he ought to be.
>
> If existence really does precede essence, there is no explaining things away by reference to a fixed and given human nature. In other words, there is no determinism, man is free, man is freedom. . . . That is the idea I shall try to convey when I say that man is condemned to be free. . . . [M]an, with no support and no aid, is condemned every moment to invent man.[35]

This invention of man, this creation "in every action" by an individual "of an image of man such as he ought to be," turned existentialism in its public presentation away from the Heideggerian mysteries of Being (which had much more occupied Sartre's *L'Être et le néant*) and toward a moral responsibility represented in the figure of Man and the vexing relations between each individual specimen and an abstract ideal. "Existentialism is a

Humanism" proved to be the programmatic text of Sartre's that was quickly translated and published in the United States—simply titled *Existentialism*, brought out by the Philosophical Library in 1947. Thus, this humanistic existentialism, delivered in short form for a general audience, was the only properly philosophical statement most Americans had of Sartre's position. *Being and Nothingness* (1943), his magnum opus, was not translated until 1956.

The existentialist period of New York intellect portended a reframing of opposition to crisis of man thinking in terms of the language and habits of the crisis of man. Rahv could still call for "a struggle against the new religiosity" along with all those who "refuse to abandon the progressive and secular outlook"—but now he and his allies, too, had their own analysis of man, which went to the core.[36] The powerful New York skeptics would not give in to a failure of nerve, but they now accepted that fundamental analysis of the human was a central task. This development meant a completion of the reorientation of the field of left intellect in America, apart from two groups increasingly marginalized: Deweyans and strict Communists. Dewey himself pointedly called a book *Problems of Men* in 1946—it was *not* "the problem of *Man*," after all, and he refused to give up his "scientific instrumentalism," which helped living men. The Communist Party itself was about to lose its last, best attempt to stay in tune with the mainstream of liberal culture in America, though, with the loyalty investigations for federal employees that Truman initiated in 1947, the second Red Scare, and the defeated Progressive Party candidacy of Henry Wallace in 1948, which the Communists had backed. Opposition and argument would henceforth occur in nearly all US intellectual life *within* the language of man and not outside it. This meant also that all serious differences were now to reemerge within the discourse. This total success first led to certain interesting extremes of the discourse, and then ultimately encouraged the discourse's banalization.

"WE, TOO, ARE GUILTY" AND THE RESPONSIBILITY QUESTION

One of the peculiarities of intellectual history is that the most extreme positions taken after a particular conjunction of surprising events, outliers in their own times, periodically turn out to be lasting or, at least, recurring positions for subsequent years. Perhaps it is a consequence of the willingness by an extreme thinker to break out of commentators' natural tendency to assimilate events to whatever has been happening already. Perhaps it is simply that extreme ideas have a different kind of salience, marking out peaks (absurd peaks, sometimes, to be sure) against a flatter intellectual history, which have a greater usefulness by their newness, their breaking of routine, or the ability to attribute them to single figures rather than the zeitgeist or conventional wisdom.

The new mood of a return to "Man" as linguistic generator and lodestar was carried to an extreme that many of the other New York Intellectuals would never approach in the work of a semi-apostate member, Dwight Macdonald. Macdonald is one of the more enigmatic intellectuals of mid-century. A Yale graduate, non-Jewish and somewhat aristocratic by temperament, he went from nonpolitical success at *Fortune* magazine in the 1930s to a new, contrarian life in the anti-Stalinist and heavily Jewish world of *Partisan Review*. As a Trotskyist, he held a strong line against US involvement in World War II when *Partisan Review*'s main editors offered critical support to military intervention; yet as a follower of Trotsky, he gave rise to the Old Man's famous (and perhaps fabricated) quip that "Every man has a right to be stupid on occasion but comrade Macdonald abuses it."[37] After his departure from *Partisan Review*, Macdonald founded the magazine *Politics*, where, in a grand tradition of the Left, he watched one after another of the left-wing independent forces in Europe fail—culminating in the failure of the French Resistance to seize power in Paris and the return of Charles de Gaulle at the liberation in 1944 and his acquisition of a provisional government. (An organized French left coalition subsequently recovered ground in national elections.) Since it was in Macdonald's character to be antidoctrinaire and uninhibited to an unusual degree, not to mention impulsive, Macdonald made a full turn away from Trotskyist hopes—to a doctrine of Man. He drew on his previous hero's own words: Trotsky had once said that if the worldwide revolution did not come (believing, though, of course, that it *would* come) then a new minimum program would have to be drawn up to save whatever could be saved. Macdonald decided the time had come, and thus tried to draw up his own such program in a controversial two-part article, baldly declaring the conclusion the new principle of action he believed true radicals would have to admit: "The Root is Man."

Specifically, Man could be made the root of a new resistance—recovered in all his individual strength, antiauthoritarianism, and remaining socialist hope—only if capital-H "History," as a process with a direction, and technology, as a tool of mastery, were alike repudiated, and left to those milquetoasts Macdonald disparagingly called "progressive." The old kinds of history and technology shouldn't be counterbalanced or reformed but rejected outright. "Radicals" must push back immediately. Macdonald admitted that in turning to "the nature of man himself," as he wrote, he was lining up with many others not known as "radicals": "I am not particularly original of course: a similar shift of interest may be observed among most Western intellectuals, the most recent example being the vogue of existentialism."[38] But Macdonald drew from the long story of technics the extreme lesson of immediate de-technologization ("large masses of people may . . . conclude that they don't want electric iceboxes if the industrial system required to produce them also produces World War III" [204]), and from the recent, bad direction of progressive history, he drew the lesson of anti-History and small-scale, face-to-face, anarchistic communities. "We must begin way at the bottom again, with small groups of individuals" (209), with the new political values of "(1) Negativism (2) Unrealism (3) Moderation (4) Smallness (5) Selfishness" (210); "group action against The Enemy is most effective when it is most spontaneous and loosest in organization. . . . What seems necessary is thus to encourage attitudes of disrespect, scepticism, ridicule towards the State and all authority, rather than to build up a competing authority. . . . We must emphasize the emotions, the imagination, the moral feelings, the primacy of the individual human being once more. . . . The root is man, here and not there, now and not then" (214–15).

In the industrial success of the end-of-wartime US economy, with Right and Left maneuvering to gain the spoils of swollen productivity, and top-down government mastery of one form or another—the Right pushing for managerial control, the Left for full employment—Macdonald's antiorganizing approach was a drastic position. He is sometimes said to have been, with Paul Goodman, Wilhelm Reich, and other '40s bohemians and contrarians, a man before his time, a displaced father of the liberationist '60s. I think it is more important to note that Macdonald, in his slight apostasy, was able in the '40s to put together pieces necessary for a radical '60s future from *inside* the early discourse of man. The point is that the key elements that the future could cherry-pick emerged with the discourse itself at the end of the war, ministering, however, to a smaller public of intellectuals with a very un-'60s cultural tone and affect: immensely serious, somber, haunted, and preoccupied with different kinds of safeguards and reconstruction.

Central among the surprising conjunctions that Macdonald made was his anger at *both* the atom bomb and the Nazi death camps in which six million Jews of Europe were murdered. Macdonald is sometimes praised as one of the only American commentators to link the two in detail rather than pursuing them on separate tracks.[39]

Part of the reason for his prescience was the peculiar personnel of *Politics*. Exiled by *Partisan Review*, needing writers from a non-Communist Left not already engrossed by *Partisan Review*'s Phillips and Rahv, and perhaps temperamentally drawn to those thwarted and exiled, Macdonald made his magazine, quite deliberately, a vehicle for émigrés who were not already prominent. This included an unofficial coeditorship of sorts with the Italian exile Nicola Chiaromonte, as well as contacts with German professors and anti-Nazi refugees of lesser status than superstars like Cassirer, Mannheim, or Mann. In fact, Macdonald drew on a German émigré circle from one of the more remarkable passages of intellectual history—the staffing by Weimar-era intellectuals and leftists of a particular section of the federal government's OWI devoted to translating German propaganda and Continental news.[40] One of *Politics*'s pseudonymous features was a column by the émigré Lewis Coser, later a sociologist and cofounder of the journal *Dissent*, detailing whatever he had read and translated at the OWI that month.[41] The émigrés' information, or just their talk and worries, let Macdonald see the importance of the camps and know that Auschwitz and Majdanek (death camps liberated by the Soviets, therefore underreported in the United States) were more significant than Buchenwald and Dachau (prison camps liberated by the Americans and British).[42] He published, in a *Politics* article of March 1945, a bibliography on Auschwitz that one could have found in few other places at that time. Perhaps partly under the influence of these writers who were so close to the European catastrophe, and who were suspicious of America's glib refusal of its own authoritarian tendencies, Macdonald joined Mumford in the suspicion of American responsibility and dehumanization that was to blossom so fulsomely in later years. "We, Too, Are Guilty," ran one of his headings—though what he meant by that is not perfectly transparent.[43] He quoted a US bombardier interviewed by the *New Yorker*: "Whatever I tell you," he said to the interviewer, "boils down to this: I'm a cog in one hell of a big machine. The more I think about it . . . the more it looks as if I'd been a cog in one thing after another since the day I was born."[44]

One of the mysteries of the moral history of the postwar decades is the overwhelming, free-floating "responsibility" even ordinary people seem to have felt, or at least declared they felt. Macdonald's "extreme" position came to be less and less extreme, more familiar. The intellectual historian Thomas Haskell has suggested that there are conditions for the feeling of moral responsibility for distant situations. You must have some kind of causal or technical mechanism that links you to an evil situation at least hypothetically. You must also have means that *could* let you intervene (as with an airplane to fly you there, a market in which your dollar will buy products from there, citizenship in a government that sends soldiers to such places). Then there must be a relative ease to the intervention (so that, for example, you might be more likely to petition your government, or withhold your dollar, than to fly to the trouble-spot—unless you were a diplomat or a trader or traveler already).[45] Haskell called the relevant knowledge on how to intervene "recipe knowledge," since you must be able to imagine a recipe for how intervention *might* occur, and have those ingredients of circumstance that would make it sufficiently easy to obligate you to do so.

The effects of the full mobilization of World War II, its public rhetoric of responsibility ("I'm Counting on You" [on a poster of a somber Uncle Sam]; "Give it Your Best!" [beneath the American flag]; "For our own—for our allies"; "Are you doing all that you can?"[46]), its massive government interventions abroad—not to mention the communications revolution in ultravivid representations (by radio and newsreel) of suffering in places it would be hard to reach—can be said to have fulfilled the first of Haskell's criteria, the causal and technical linkage. The second criterion of personal action, however, is more confusing. Did Americans feel they could act? The fully connected globe of their time still came with a sense that all real solutions were accomplished by organizers at the top level, by armies of millions, invasion forces, Manhattan Projects, and Marshall Plans. "People have been badgered half out of their minds by the sense of a sort of 'global' responsibility," James Agee wrote despairingly in 1950, "the relentless daily obligation to stay aware of, hep to, worked-up over, guilty towards, active about, the sufferings of people at a great distance for whom one can do nothing whatever; a sort of playing-at-God (since He is in exile) over every sparrow that falls, with the sense of virtue increasing in ratio to the distance."[47] What *could* they do?[48]

It is significant that the responsibility question was partly solved, and partly intensified, by one aspect of French existentialism—its rhetoric of the moral dilemma, the free choice, the grounding of vast responsibility in the individual's experience of guilt and sometimes paralyzing deliberation. Achieving a stance *itself* could seem like action. These aspects met in the work and person of Albert Camus. Perhaps it should be no surprise that in the period Macdonald was writing his somewhat singular "The Root is Man," he met with Camus in person, and by all appearances was deeply influenced, taking steps to collaborate with him in unfulfilled plans for French American discussion groups. Camus was making his own triumphal tour of New York after emerging at the liberation as a Resistance hero, *Combat* editorial writer, and playwright in Paris. Nicola Chiaromonte, Macdonald's Italian collaborator, happened to know him well from his own earlier exile in Oran, Algeria, where he had met a young Camus and his friends. The brave Resistance editorialist was not a systematic thinker, but then he was not a mandarin as Sartre was, and he came to be beloved by the New York Intellectuals in a way that more philosophically demanding rivals were not. Hannah Arendt wrote to Karl Jaspers: "He is one of those young men from the Resistance . . . absolutely honest and has great political insight."[49] Camus's mixed literary and philosophical books *The Stranger, The Plague, The Myth of Sisyphus, The Rebel*, plus the play

Caligula took their place in America as powerful, popular, and accessible vehicles for existentialist ideas and for a particular ethos of responsibility. Chiaromonte was correct, a few years later, in his assessment of Camus's particular genius: "not cogent demonstration so much as an artful mobilization of the emotional power contained in the western concepts of the 'human' and of the 'individual.'"[50] One can see this emotional power, directed to the "We, Too, Are Guilty" thesis, in a speech that Camus gave at Columbia in 1946, calling for an attitude of resistance to "The Human Crisis." The lines are astonishing, though sincere, and clarify how *thought* could become a form of action and a taking responsibility even for crimes unrelated to oneself. It became a kind of resistance:

> We must call things by their right names and realize that we kill millions of men each time we permit ourselves to think certain thoughts. One does not reason badly because one is a murderer. One is a murderer if one reasons badly. It is thus that one can be a murderer without having actually killed anyone. And so it is we are all murderers to one degree or another.[51]

It would be wrong to underestimate the impact of such statements, even when they seem contrary to sense. The American scholar Justin O'Brien, who moderated the event at Columbia, dreamily recollected the effect on the twelve hundred hungry listeners in attendance: "When he told us that, as human beings of the twentieth century, we were all of us responsible for the war, and even for the horrors we had just been fighting . . . all of us in the huge hall were convinced, I think, of our common culpability. Then Camus . . . told us how we could contribute, even in the humblest way, to re-establishing the honesty and dignity of men."[52] Camus's answer? "[I]t is necessary to understand that this attitude requires that a universalism be created through which all men of good will may find themselves in touch with one another."[53]

This was not a universalism of identity or recognition but responsibility. And this "universalism" was pitched at the personal level, rooted in the individual, connecting with other individuals, as in the planned Macdonald-Camus Europe-America Groups, which, as Gregory Sumner writes, "never really got off the ground," but also Camus's own French-based groups, which fared about as well.[54] Yet in the New York speech, Camus also alluded, in passing, to something else occurring at the very moment he was speaking, "in this very city"—that men and women were "holding an important session" of the United Nations.[55]

The United Nations offered a major *public* solution to the crisis of man immediately after the war, or at least its underlying rationale did, in a "world government" movement that briefly united a surprising number of our previous players in the discourse of man upon a single stage.

WORLD GOVERNMENT AND HUMAN RIGHTS

Human rights, reborn in the 1940s, a major element of our twenty-first-century versions of international activism and social hope, must be understood historically as the result of a massive historical failure to attain what was truly wanted at the end of World War II by a vast range of different commentators, but also by significant popular movements and average opinion. It was the also-ran that became a point of hope—lamed and stunted though it seemed—when the favorite was disqualified.

Many intellectuals' primary practical hope throughout the war had been for "world government," even among the figures we've already seen. Kahler had demanded a postwar "worldwide planned economy."[56] Norman Cousins, he of "Modern Man is Obsolete," took it for granted as the necessity of the time. Mumford said he wanted more "world government" than the United Nations would ever be able to provide: *Today unconditional cooperation is the price of man's survival.*[57] Robert Maynard Hutchins, habitual organizer and founder of grand projects, launched the Committee to Form a World Constitution—in which he and others, like the Continental Congress, would actually sit down and write a single document by which to govern the globe. In a series of twelve two- or three-day meetings, "alternating between Chicago and New York," he put together his group of well-known thinkers to write the new constitution between February and April 1947.[58] The participants included Reinhold Niebuhr, Erich Kahler, Mortimer Adler, and Hutchins's dean of the Humanities Division at University of Chicago, Richard McKeon (best remembered today for a standard edition of Aristotle). Niebuhr had been making gnomic statements on world community since 1944 ("the final possibility and impossibility of human life," "mankind's final possibility and impossibility"[59]). He participated in Hutchins's hubristic project and then pulled out at the last minute. (McKeon, too, ultimately refused to sign.) But Norman Cousins stepped in and published the Chicago–New York group's completed constitution of "the Federal Republic of the World" in the *Saturday Review of Literature*. "[T]he age of nations must end, and the era of humanity begin," it intoned.[60] The movement went to France, too. Garry Davis, a twenty-six-year-old former American bomber pilot and Broadway actor, tore up his passport in Paris in May 1948 to renounce his citizenship in any nation and start a movement for world citizenship. In the publicity, demonstrations, and petitions that followed, Camus (among others) endorsed his aim.[61]

Yet world government as a dream expired by the end of the '40s; its closest practical realization, the United Nations, was a painful disappointment to everyone but Great Power diplomatists from its start, too much a means for existing nation-state diplomacy and too clearly and cynically dominated by the countries that made up the Security Council and retained the famous veto.[62] (Hutchins & Co. wrote their constitution, notably, *after* the UN Charter.)

The more apparently impractical movement, and yet the one to survive and thrive, was the organized legal development of postwar human rights. This was also the movement that more immediately matched and reflected the intellectuals' concerns in the crisis of man, and came into contact with them in its initial project of self-legitimation.

According to the diplomatic and legal historian Elizabeth Borgwardt, the phrase "human rights" shifted in the 1940s to acquire its present meaning in the United States:

> Before the war, the phrase occasionally appeared as a somewhat disfavored variation of the older locution, "rights of man." Human rights also sometimes served as a synonym for the narrower legal term "civil rights," as part of interwar era controversies relating to the Bill of Rights or specialized fields, such as labor rights. By the end of the war, however, the term "human rights" was consistently serving as a caption for those so-called "fundamental freedoms" that differentiated the Allies from their totalitarian rivals. . . . These fundamental freedoms included a subset of traditional civil rights, such as freedom of speech and religion, to which all individuals were entitled "simply by virtue of being human."[63]

Human rights, in a diplomatic context, had been on the agenda of Franklin Roosevelt from very early in the 1940s as a way of globalizing and moralizing the meaning of the '30s world crisis. Isolationist Americans wanted to see two crises as separate events: an economic recovery from the Depression at home and a Continental war across the ocean that the United States should leave alone. FDR began speaking of human rights before Pearl Harbor as a way of linking human needs on both sides of the ocean. In his Annual Message to Congress of January 1941, maneuvering against isolationist opponents of Lend-Lease and the US backing of Britain against Germany, he enunciated his "Four Freedoms."[64] Indeed, Roosevelt dictated the Four Freedoms himself while his speechwriters looked on.[65] Because of Norman Rockwell's paintings of these basic goals of FDR's American democracy during the war, in their use to boost morale, they are often remembered as having a domestic purpose.[66] But FDR's significant refrain, adding to and expanding beyond familiar domestic demands, pointed relentlessly to his internationalist purpose—"everywhere in the world":

[F]reedom of speech and expression—everywhere in the world. . . . [F]reedom of every person to worship God in his own way—everywhere in the world. . . . [F]reedom from want—which, translated into world terms, means economic understandings . . . everywhere in the world. . . .

[F]reedom from fear—which, translated into international terms, means a world-wide reduction of armaments . . . [so] that no nation will be in a position to commit an act of physical aggression against any neighbor—anywhere in the world.[67]

"Freedom means the supremacy of human rights everywhere," FDR flatly said in that speech. He kept repeating this unusual phrase "human rights"—and put it into the Atlantic Charter, which he signed with Churchill on a ship at sea. Both the Atlantic Charter and the Four Freedoms were publicized globally by the US government and the armed forces during the war.[68] The Italian intellectual Niccolo Tucci reported that his countrymen had received the Four Freedoms dropped by Allied airplanes, and desperately believed in them.[69] The promise of individual, inviolable rights became part of a conscious policy to win even the citizens of fascist countries to the Allies. Roosevelt put human rights into each of the documents in the public-diplomatic trail of declarations by which he broadcast the expansion of the alliance against Hitler. A scholarly observer, looking back from 1945, could rattle off the sequence: in the " 'Four Freedoms' . . . the Atlantic Charter of August 14, 1941, and the Declaration of the United Nations of January 1, 1942, [human rights] became a part of the common covenant of the States aligned against the Axis . . . [in] the Teheran declaration of December 1, 1943 . . . the Dumbarton Oaks text of October 9, 1944, up to the Charter of the United Nations . . . the line of progression is clear."[70]

FDR died two weeks before the conference that met to develop the UN Charter. This was the United Nations Conference on International Organization, better known as the San Francisco conference, held in that city's Opera House, though much of the diplomacy occurred in the Fairmont Hotel, where the US secretary of state and his delegation were staying. The outline for the new world organization had already been written by four powers—China, the Soviet Union, the United States, and the United Kingdom—at Dumbarton Oaks, and then reaffirmed without China's participation at Yalta, much to the consternation of smaller countries and world government advocates. According to the human rights scholar Paul Lauren, at the start of the San Francisco conference, the "briefing book . . . of the U.S. delegation did not contain a single agenda item for human rights."[71] Boilerplate rhetoric of man, however, pervaded statements on what the new order must achieve. The new president, Harry Truman, told the conference at its opening: "We must build a new world—a far better world—one in which the eternal dignity of man is respected."[72]

What this could mean in practice, however, was still unclear. Beyond the power-politics delegations from the Big Four powers, San Francisco hosted three hundred delegates from forty-six nations, thousands of delegate advisers, and, according to Paul Lauren, more than two thousand print and radio journalists, including representatives from all the major US news organizations, who kept their eyes on the proceedings and criticized lapses.[73] In one of the most unusual inclusions, the US State Department also invited forty-two nongovernmental groups to attend in an advisory capacity. Among that number were the American Jewish Committee, the League of Women Voters, the NAACP, the CIO, some more short-lived groups specifically agitating for international cooperation, and even fraternal organizations like the Rotary Club, Lions, and Kiwanis.[74] The role of the nongovernmental organizations (NGOs, as they would later be called) was supposed to be to publicize the event for their constituencies across the country, in a sort of goodwill campaign. Instead, they have gone down in history as the pivotal and unexpected actors in the assertion of human rights for the legal structure of the emergent United Nations—and thus the bearers of the discourse of man into the practical future of the world body.

The inaugural moment of an institutional framework for modern human rights is taken to be a heated meeting on May 2, 1945, in a conference room of the Fairmont Hotel. In this encounter, a group of US NGOs and their most persistent spokesman, Joseph Proskauer, president of the American Jewish Committee, insisted to US secretary of state Edward Stettinius that human rights *had* to be addressed in the charter, though they had thus far been ignored. Stettinius yielded, either willingly or reluctantly—the histories disagree. It is important to address, on any account, how little the US government thought of the importance of the question. This episode is retold many times in the still semi-amateur literature on the history of human rights, with predictably many variations. Disputes center on exactly *why* the US State Department agreed so readily to what had seemingly not been on their agenda, and subsequently pushed the other Great Powers to support human rights proposals, often against those countries' inclinations.[75] The explanations encompass two major alternatives: idealism abetted by assumed triviality or publicity efforts and international propaganda. (A third is a horrified reaction to the Nazis—undoubtedly real, but it did not dictate the specifics of response.) Mark Mazower has put the question of adequate explanations most pointedly in an article in diplomatic history entitled "The Strange Triumph of Human Rights," where, while fleshing out the true details of the diplomatic context, he notes the importance of "wartime intellectual ferment within the Anglophone world"

and a "wartime thought . . . [in which] 'the claims of the individual '
stretched . . . across the political spectrum."[76] He cannot himself recover
their details. It would be my argument that crisis of man discourse is precisely the ferment, cutting across conventional political lines, that backgrounds human rights.

The UN Charter, in the end, was a hodgepodge. It includes many noble
statements on human rights, and absurdly weak provisions for their enforcement.[77] A Commission on Human Rights was established under the
purview of the Economic and Social Council. Eventually headed by Eleanor Roosevelt, it had much greater public appeal than, perhaps, it had any
significance at first within the UN organization. Human rights captured
the attention of the press. It was widely, and somewhat misleadingly, believed that the commission would soon draw up an international "Bill of
Rights" like the one that state ratifying conventions of clamorous Americans in 1789 had added to the US Constitution. Truman himself had as
good as promised such a document in his final remarks to the San Francisco conference in June 1945.[78]

"CRISIS OF THE INDIVIDUAL"

But what was the stake of the discourse of man in human rights at its modern inception? How far were these institutional initiatives embedded in
intellectual and philosophical concerns? To see the strands come together,
one can look at a journal founded in New York in 1945 and explicitly created to address the new contours of the postwar world: *Commentary*. It
was a Jewish but mainstream publication—not an oxymoron during the
flowering of New York Jewish intellect at midcentury, when ethnic pride
went hand in hand with an assimilationist patriotism and healthy internationalism. *Commentary* had an extraordinary pool of talent to draw on,
not only the New York Intellectuals, overlapping in personnel with *Partisan Review* but free of its political line, but also the émigrés from Hitler,
and an impressive range of Catholic, Protestant, and secular-scientific intellectuals who published in its pages in its early years. Social scientists
had a larger place in its pages than in other mainstream journals then or
since, as did jurists and historians, all writing for the general public. It
really was a great journal in its early years. The American Jewish Committee funded it as a successor to its more parochial *Menorah Journal*, hiring
as editor a talented veteran of the earlier enterprise, Elliot Cohen. *Commentary* had an extreme editorial independence, as long as it treated
"Jewish" topics, but the war and the Nazi murder of Europe's Jews had expanded the definition of what those might be. "The movement for the development of effective international machinery for the protection of minori-

ties and of human beings generally will be a continuing concern of COMMENTARY," the editors promised in the first issue, and so it was.[79] And *Commentary*, from the first, integrated the practical demands of the United Nations, the intellectuals' broader world government hopes, and intellectuals' analyses of new "human rights," into a comprehensive, though rarely consistent, set of topics for postwar intellectuals, making a truly unique conversation and archive.

The editors of the new journal immediately inaugurated a major philosophical series entitled "The Crisis of the Individual," that went on issue after issue for nearly one and a half years. (Already, in the slip of nomenclature from "Man" to "the individual," one may detect either inclusiveness of women from a journal committed to antiprejudice, or, more likely, the beginnings of the Cold War change in which it is US individualism against Soviet collectivism that helps define the core of "Man.") In the editors' note to the first of the series (Reinhold Niebuhr on "Will Civilization Survive Technics?"), they wrote:

> In our time, the individual human being has been more violently debased than in many centuries. Every aspect of the human personality— his civil rights, his individuality, his status, the regard in which he is held, the dignity accorded him—all have been violated. We have seen living human beings used as beasts of burden and guinea pigs, and their dead bodies treated as natural resources.[80]

The series constituted a kind of state of the art of what different figures made of this crisis of man after the war. Before the second in the series (this one by Leo Lowenthal, an émigré of the Frankfurt school of Horkheimer and Adorno, covering "Terror's Atomization of Man"), the editors further explained their purpose:

> The series seeks answers to questions such as these: "Why is this happening to us?" "Where did our Western civilization go wrong?" "Is this merely a transition to a new society with better values?" "Is the contemporary crisis due to technology and large-scale planning, or their present day misuse; or to a distortion of basic ideals which would require a renascence of religious belief or some other inner revaluation of values?"[81]

The long line of respondents of every type and school—John Dewey, Hannah Arendt, the novelist Pearl Buck, the economist William Orton, the social critic Waldo Frank, the psychoanalyst Abram Kardiner, the economic historian Karl Polanyi, and others—constitutes a kind of time capsule of the explanations of the deformation of man that had been caused by the war and must set the agenda for the coming decade. The respondents agreed that neither individualism nor collectivism was adequate. They fought endlessly over the ground of common topics: planning, organization, religion, technics, nature, and history. Sounding increasingly desperate, the editors cut down the options to some common themes, and wrote in the introduction to the eighth in the series: "Is the crisis of our time due to the abuse of technology, the failure of religion, the debasement of culture, the bureaucratization of politics—or what?"[82] This suggested the gathering trends of the answers, and also the series' drift away from overseas fascist evils to a fear of organization and conformism at home—a change that would come to define the crisis of man through the postwar decades. One sees the beginnings of the anticonformist rhetoric of "facelessness" in one of editor Elliot Cohen's rare articles, near the end of the war decade: "[the intellectual] wonders whether the faceless administrator and the faceless citizen are not reverse sides of the same coin—an administrative society in which fitness consists solely in 'fitting in,' and the one is lost in the all."[83]

The inconspicuousness of *race* in this intellectual discourse of man, however, is one of its major surprises. In a Jewish journal, when Judaism was still often read as a racial identity like African American identity, there was a great deal of use of the discourse of man to justify why racial categories shouldn't limit or imprison individuals, but very little breakup of "the human as such" or "man" into a racialized perspective or racial dimension. The "universalist" ethos of the 1940s and 1950s is sometimes overplayed. It was also, after all, the age of antiprejudice, which, in service of a universalist ethos, emphasized racial division and autonomy, Gunnar Myrdal's *An American Dilemma*, the desegregation of the armed forces, and the campaigns to end anti-Jewish quotas in higher education. But in this area of the discourse of man, the elision of race for the "universal" rings true.

THE PHILOSOPHERS' COMMITTEE

Meanwhile, an international mechanism for disseminating and consecrating the intellectuals' views was being developed—one that was to become a central "official" avenue for the rhetoric of crisis of man discourse. The founding of the United Nations Educational, Scientific, and Cultural Organization (UNESCO) created a world institution entirely devoted, at its start, to a substantive view of human nature that was antiracial and universalist. Though an educational organization, it framed its mission as encouraging education in the nonracial unity of all mankind and stimulating an international culture that must become single and universal. According to UNESCO's originating document in 1945, the "terrible war" had been "made possible by the denial of . . . the dignity, equality and mutual respect of men, and by the propagation, in their place . . . of the doctrine of the inequality of men and races."[84] The organization planned to do something about this. The USSR did not participate in UNESCO before 1954, so the Western powers' intellectuals had a freer hand. The job of director general went to Julian Huxley, an optimistic English biologist and popularizer who believed in a unified scientific human nature open to continuous, improving progress. He had made his own earlier minor contribution to the discourse of man in books like *The Uniqueness of Man* (1941) and *On Living in a Revolution* (1944).[85] (Another candidate for the director general job may have been Robert Maynard Hutchins, according to Hutchins's biographer; he certainly would have suited the early UNESCO.)[86] The new organization moved into a symbolic residence on the Avenue Kléber in Paris: "formerly the Hotel Majestic, then headquarters of the Gestapo, then headquarters of the United States Army, now headquarters of the Unesco Secretariat."[87] From fascist militarism, to liberation, to culture, this was their upward progress. "The more united man's tradition becomes, the more rapid will be the possibility of progress," Huxley wrote soon after he took office, in a pamphlet that was somewhat controversial because of its tendentious claims for the meaning of the whole organization (and especially because of his robust defense of eugenics!): "several separate or competing or even mutually hostile pools of tradition cannot possibly be so efficient as a single pool common to all mankind." Therefore, "[t]he task laid upon [UNESCO] of promoting peace and security can never be wholly realised through the means assigned to it—education, science and culture. It must envisage some form of world political unity, whether through a single world government or otherwise, as the only means of avoiding war."[88]

While UNESCO was gaining its intellectual footing, the more practical Human Rights Commission, under the leadership of Eleanor Roosevelt, began meeting in the UN's temporary headquarters in the former Sperry Gyroscope factory in Lake Success, Long Island, in January and February 1947, to work out its Universal Declaration of Human Rights. At one of its earliest sessions, the group encountered its first major disagreement as soon as the philosophical basis of human rights came up. "When we speak of human rights," declaimed Charles Malik, the delegate from Lebanon, "we are raising the fundamental question, what is man? . . . Is man merely a social being? Is he merely an animal? Is he merely an economic being?" Malik, a neo-Thomist, spoke against collectivism and for the inviolability of man. Vladislav Ribnikar, a left liberal delegate from Yugoslavia, stood up to assert the Marxist position: collective values must necessarily come before atomized individuals. Other delegates leaped in to split the difference: man was individual, yet a social creature. Eleanor Roosevelt tried to cool down the combatants. Such debates on reasons had to be put aside for the commission to accomplish its work—they simply had to figure out *what* to protect, leaving the why to others.[89]

UNESCO in Paris got wind of the Lake Success drafting process and, apparently unasked, decided to canvass the world's philosophers to help the Human Rights Commission with its work. Huxley dispatched the poet Archibald MacLeish to Lake Success in January 1947 to say that they wanted to be "as useful as possible," though it is not evident that the jurists and diplomatists of the Human Rights Commission cared.[90] Meanwhile, Huxley assembled a team including Jacques Maritain, Chicago's Richard McKeon, and Cambridge's E. H. Carr, who together developed a questionnaire by March and mailed it out to 150 "thinkers and writers" of the UNESCO member states.[91] Recipients included Benedetto Croce, Mohandas Gandhi, Aldous Huxley (Julian's brother and author of *Brave New World*), Pierre Teilhard de Chardin, and the omnipresent Lewis Mumford.

The accompanying many-page "Memorandum . . . on the Theoretical Basis of the Rights of Man" gives a learned and remarkably lucid statement of the re-enlightenment position and its obligations for the philosophers of the world. Obscure as it has been in intellectual history, I believe this can be counted as the institutionalization of the full historical crisis of man argument in the international process. It employed the familiar three centuries schema and admitted the dangers of progress, while striking a new note of a world divided between Western and Soviet spheres—justifying a turn to a new primary dimension, in its philosophical anthropology, in a debate between the human as an individual and the human as a collective being.

Only one group solicited for philosophical advice dissented from the whole project of a declaration of rights undertaken to be written in this fashion. This was Boasian anthropology, which still formed the dominant core of the "cultural" sides of their profession: ethnography and linguistics, as opposed to the bones and fossils of physical anthropology and archaeology. UNESCO had gone to Melville Herskovits, Boas's distinguished student, who had contributed much to Boas's antiracism campaigns, and during the war had published his *Myth of the Negro Past* (1941), arguing for the unacknowledged continuity of West African cultures with African American culture. (He is remembered today as a white pioneer of Africana and Afro-American studies programs in the US university.) Herskovits drafted and redrafted a stinging response that called into question the whole program of unity, which the Human Rights Commission was using as its basis for the protection of human rights. When UNESCO seemed to reject the response—it was never printed in their collections of replies—

Herskovits submitted it for publication under the name of the Executive Committee of the American Anthropological Association itself, after consultation with other members and the editorial staff at the AAA's official journal.[92]

Their statement acknowledged that the familiar purpose of any "Declaration of the Rights of Man" was to defend the individual against the tyranny of his or her society. In an international context, however, the anthropologists insisted that a thoughtful statement must defend different human "cultures." All human beings possessed an identical biological capacity for intelligence and identical biological needs: "[A]ny normal individual can learn any part of any culture other than his own, provided only he is afforded the opportunity to do so."[93] This was the Boasian doctrine of human psychological unity, which countered racism and imputations of inferiority. But every individual was then embedded in a "human group" that determined the way he or she expressed that capacity. And "human groups," "modes of life," and "cultures" gave entirely differing criteria for freedom, meaning, and success—each within their own evolved ways—for achieving basic human ends. "All peoples do achieve these ends. No two of them, however, do so in exactly the same way." It was not up to a roomful of international sages or diplomatists—or a worldwide mailing list of philosophers either—to say what counted for protected human values and what didn't.

This was the Boasian doctrine of pluralism and cultural relativism. Peoples needed their own rights and freedoms to defend against the tyranny of "rights conceived only in terms of the values prevalent in the countries of Western Europe and America"—who had spent centuries absolutizing their own values at gunpoint through "economic expansion, control of armaments, and an evangelical religious tradition."[94] Although the words are not said, the background of the anthropologists' plea is clearly the old colonialism and the new cultural imperialism: the closest the document comes is in its reminder that the "noble . . . American Declaration of Independence" accompanied American slaveholding, and that the most truly "revolutionary . . . struggles" in the French Revolution were the attempts at "extending it to the French slave-owning colonies," as in the suppressed revolution in Haiti. Groups of people needed self-determination before they were told how their individual members would henceforth be "free." And those groups must be determined, not by state form, sitting government, or national borders dictated by international law but through individuals' own identifications with or against local practices. "There can be no individual freedom, that is, when the group with which the individual identifies himself is not free."[95]

This statement seems prescient now, and its conception of respect for human diversity will return toward the end of our study, but it is a sign of the marginalization of Boasian sentiment in the wider intellectual world of the late 1940s—and the success of human rights as a ruling concept of the decades that followed—that, for several generations of anthropologists looking back on the statement, "the term 'embarrassment' is continually used."[96] It is remembered as a bad mistake—reputationally, mostly. "[A]nthropology got off on the wrong foot with human rights" is how even one recent defender of the AAA statement puts it.[97] In fact, American anthropologists' distance from the statement historically has not come from any naive embrace of universalism in their own profession, but from the way this open statement of Boasian principles made them marginal thereafter to government consultation and international reform movements based on human rights.[98] Others would have soft-pedaled it.

Acceptable responses in hand, UNESCO convened a "Committee on the Philosophic Principles of the Rights of Man" in early summer 1947.[99] It delivered its formal report to the Human Rights Commission, now meeting in Geneva, which, according to scholars of the commission's deliberations, probably ignored it.[100] The Universal Declaration of Human Rights was ratified at the Palais de Chaillot in Paris in December 1948, without an explicit philosophical justification, but containing language that pointed to various different traditions and justifications all at once. Let me point these out in parentheses: "Whereas recognition of the inherent dignity and of the equal and inalienable rights of all members of the human family is the foundation of freedom, justice, and peace in the world" (*dignity, equality, inalienability*, and *human family*, as well as the utilitarian virtues of a human rights regime for peace), looking toward "the advent of a world in which human beings shall enjoy freedom of speech and belief and freedom from fear and want" (FDR's Four Freedoms, including both civil and social rights), "Now, Therefore, The General Assembly Proclaims . . . All human beings are born free and equal in dignity and rights. They are endowed with reason and conscience and should act towards one another in a spirit of brotherhood" (Rousseauian natural freedom, *dignity* again, *reason* of the *animal rational*, the puzzling *conscience*, plus a normative call to *brotherhood* in the family vein).[101] Had they left anything out? In his introduction to the proceedings of the UNESCO philosophers' committee, as they were published in 1949, Jacques Maritain alluded to the problem that bedeviled all political deliberations on human rights, which had not been solved by the declaration, and one can see why not. "It is related that at one of the meetings of a UNESCO national commission . . . someone expressed astonishment that certain champions of violently opposed ideologies had agreed on a list of [human] rights. 'Yes,' they said, 'we agree about the rights *but on condition that no one asks us why.*'"[102]

HANNAH ARENDT: MASTER OF THE DISCOURSE OF MAN

For reasons of these confusions over underlying foundations, and the shifting winds of the "individual" versus the "collective," the West versus the East, it is revealing that the one true masterpiece and culminating work of the early period of the discourse of man is not remembered as concerned with man himself but, misleadingly and significantly, with one of the discourses man would collapse into in the later period—that of totalitarianism. It was a learned and intellectual book that was surprisingly critical of *both* the corrupt will to change man's nature and the supposed international goodwill to protect it. It was a book concerned to identify the emptiness at the heart of the rights of man in their modern history, pursuing an assertive gesture of a new protection without ever taking its eyes off the long-standing absence of protection even among the best-intended regimes, or the chance that such protection was impossible. The book is Hannah Arendt's *The Origins of Totalitarianism* (1951).

Hannah Arendt was one of the younger intellectual émigrés at the time of Hitler's ascent to power and had no academic position to buoy her to university protection. Arrested for anti–Nazi Zionist activity, she escaped to France, where in 1940 she was interned as an enemy alien in the French concentration camp at Gurs. Conditions were not comparable to the concentration camps of Germany but were still gruesome, as the historian Anthony Heilbut has suggested based on interviews with other internees.[103] She made it to America in 1941, where she worked for Jewish relief agencies and at Schocken Books, the German Jewish publishing house, and composed *The Origins of Totalitarianism* between 1945 and 1949.[104]

Arendt was master of the discourse of man at this stage, because she was the only one able to simultaneously give the direst practical critique of the pretensions of the rights of man and to speak of the necessity for their new or renewed basis. It was not a matter of talking out of both sides of her mouth. Arendt undertook historical research to show how Europe had moved to national policies that made the abrogation of the rights of man their raison d'être. From this empirical-interpretive position, she then wrote a different kind of history, fragmented, prismatic, and even out of order, because her history was essentially philosophical. She showed how recent history had dealt with the rights of man and what sort of assertions would need to be maintained and affirmed to correct them, and also why this could not be done easily by philosophers or jurists from the top down. Arendt kept both exigencies in mind: that there must be a new order of humanity for the "human as such," and that the "human as such," it had been historically proven, could not be defended on its own.

Her book was famously poorly titled.[105] In the United Kingdom, its title on publication was *The Burden of Our Time*. In its contemporaneity and prophetic timbre, *The Burden of Our Time* framed the forward-looking half of her project, just as *The Origins of Totalitarianism* reflected her historical story. An equally good descriptive title for her book might have been *The Origins of Why Modern Men Would Want to Change Human Nature, and How the Worst of Them Have Tried, with Hints on What to Do Now*. According to Arendt, the purpose and end point of totalitarianism was nothing other than to change the nature of man, in the process usually destroying it. "What totalitarian ideologies . . . aim at is not the transformation of the outside world or the revolutionizing transmutation of society, but the transformation of human nature itself" (1st, 432).[106] Totalitarianism wishes to change the nature of man, or destroy it, partly because it *can*, possessing also the technics to do so. Yet it does so fundamentally in the interest of consistency, which is its general goal—to make worldly reality conform to its ideology. Totalitarianism develops existing or new technics of domination to change the status of living men to something other than life: "[T]otal domination" lets "the change of the nature of man begin in earnest," by a "calculated attack on human nature, on humanity, and on history through the erection of a world of living dead" (1st, 433). At times, Arendt can seem pitiless, because it is not ordinary cruelty, torture, or barbarism she really cares about, nor the ravages of war, but this particular assault on human nature: "Suffering, of which there has been always too much on earth, is not the issue, nor is the number of victims. Human nature as such is at stake" (1st, 433)—retaining the present tense though the world war was over. Arendt suggests it is better that people be killed as men than reduced, as in the concentration camps, to living non-men. She frequently points out the ironic legal advantages of a person arrested and jailed for a crime, who at least has a law to punish him as a criminal (with his human nature intact), over the non-criminal who is deprived of law and exposed to a state of inhuman rootlessness and rightlessness. Wherever totalitarianism "has ruled, it has begun to destroy the essence of man" (New, viii).

Her historical story of how such a state of affairs had arisen was extremely complex. Arendt makes clear that totalitarianism, though historically unique, could exist only because it solved other, longer-lasting conflicts of modernity: "totalitarianism became this century's curse only because it so terrifyingly took care of its problems" (1st, 430). Imperialism had started the process that created the elements that could fuse together to create totalitarian disaster. Surplus capital in the accounts of the European bourgeoisie had led them to manipulate the nation-state into becoming an instrument of economic expansion in the Middle East and in Africa, against the laws and the communal interests of the limited territorial nation. The techniques of lawless government in the new imperial holdings—bureaucracy and administration, secrecy and "shadow government"—got reimported to Europe after the late-imperial scramble. The idea of "race" as a tool of domination was also reimported to Europe, where it became attached to a new anti-Semitism with its own distinct modern political history.[107]

This meant that Arendt, too, used the re-enlightenment three centuries schema, but with her own peculiar understanding. To her, the eighteenth century had, when it declared the Rights of Man, released itself from history. By this she meant that it overthrew an authority built on the long tradition of the Church and another compounded of monarchy and the rights by legacy of sovereign subjects. But it deceptively assured itself of its solid foundations by turning away from God and from man, too, to *nature*—at once the natural progress of economy and civilization, which would assure the best development for mankind, and a "human nature," which should supposedly assure each individual man inherent rights. When in later centuries human nature proved to be no protection, when it proved to contain the willful submission to ideology and the techniques to make other people *only* naturally human and no longer men in the concentration camps, when finally technology extended the mastery of nature to the possible destruction of the whole world and human life thereon, then, Arendt thought, in the twentieth century, human beings had been dangerously freed from nature, too. "Man of the twentieth century has become just as emancipated from nature as eighteenth-century man was from history. History and nature have become equally alien to us, namely, in the sense that the essence of man can no longer be comprehended in terms of either category" (New, 298).

Arendt, both so like and unlike the others of her time, saw in this twentieth-century outrunning of traditional bases for guidance an unavoidable, immense responsibility, which she linked in its positive possibilities not to a sentimental picture of the "family of man" or a unity of a spurious human nature, but to the actual economic, physical, and military unification of the globe, such that any action ramified globally:

The most immediate political consequence of this new historical situation . . . is that some of the factual responsibility shared by the members of every national community for all the deeds and misdeeds committed in their name has now expanded to the sphere of international life. The peoples of the world have a vague foreboding of this new burden and try to escape from it. . . . They know that they will be "punished" for sins committed at the other end of the globe, and they have not yet had much opportunity to learn that they may also benefit from every step in the right direction that is taken elsewhere. (1st, 436)

Shades of Camus; shades, too, of Jaspers and a world-embracing technics. The Rights of Man failed in the twentieth century, Arendt argued, because they really existed solely in the context of the national state, even while they pretended to exist independently, "inalienably" in individuals who were subject to the law of nature. The nation-state itself, meanwhile, was construed doubly: as a state of laws and a nation of "the people"—a natural body politic separate from the abstract equality of law. As soon as groups emerged in the twentieth century that were cut off from the organic body of the "people" or nation, and who lost the positive rights of the state citizen, they turned out to have no rights at all. The famous chapter in which she outlined her conclusions with all the power of a deductive proof was chapter 9, "The Decline of the Nation-State and the End of the Rights of Man," still today a touchstone for the philosophical debate on human rights.[108] "The Rights of Man, supposedly inalienable, proved to be unenforceable—even in countries whose constitutions were based upon them—whenever people appeared who were no longer citizens of any sovereign state" (New, 293). Arendt turned from the language of the rights of man to the then-renewed language of human rights, of which she was suspicious, to make her point that the horrible disillusioning discoveries of the long world crisis had still not been learned, or were being corrected in equally unsound delusions: "The conception of human rights, based upon the assumed existence of a human being as such, broke down at the very moment when those who professed to believe in it were for the first time confronted with people who had indeed lost all other qualities and specific relationships—except that they were still human. The world found nothing sacred in the abstract nakedness of being human" (New, 299).

A NEW GUARANTEE—WHICH MAY NOT BE POSSIBLE

The *human being as such*—at the very moment that others called for one, to discover, to protect, to exalt in the late 1940s—seemed unstable to Arendt. Alas, the human being as such had already been made most completely in the concentration camps, as others did not yet quite recognize; it was no use to remake him as the subject of utopian hope. "It seems," she warned, "that a man who is nothing but a man has lost the very qualities which make it possible for other people to treat him as a fellow-man" (New, 300). Truly human qualities must be public and political. But to belong to politics, to engage in it, Arendt argued, one had to be part of a political community, rooted—never susceptible to being expelled or reduced to the merely human.

Here she made her discovery of the only extranational and extrapolitical value that was absolutely necessary to the maintenance of man and the preservation of a (political) civilization: the "right to have rights." "For man as man has only one right that transcends his various rights as a citizen: the right never to be excluded from the rights granted by his community, an exclusion which occurs not when he is put into jail, but when he is sent to a concentration camp. Only then is he excluded from that whole sphere of legality" (1st, 436–37). This, for Arendt, was the sane path—not groundless human rights, but one single "human right" to recreate a new kind of citizenship: "Corresponding to the one crime against humanity is the one human right. Like all other rights, it can exist only through mutual agreement and guarantee" (1st, 437). And this led to a practical correction of all world-governmental and human rights schemes put forward in her time:

> The concept of human rights can again be meaningful only if they are redefined to mean a right to the human condition itself, which depends upon belonging to some human community, the right never to be dependent upon some inborn human dignity which *de facto*, aside from its guarantee by fellow-men, not only does not exist but is the last and possibly most arrogant myth we have created in our long history. (1st, 439)

In practice, Arendt's sketching of this one undeniable right proved strong enough to affect Supreme Court opinion in the 1950s, when in 1958 in *Trop v. Dulles* Chief Justice Earl Warren made use of "the right to have rights" to rule with the majority for the unconstitutionality of the denationalization of citizens as a judicial punishment.[109] In her larger practical-philosophical aim, though, one can see that Arendt faced an insoluble problem—or, say, a problem not soluble in philosophy but only in history, which would change the fundamental terms of political philosophy and thus avoid a vicious circle. The right to have rights must be guaranteed to men and women regardless of the actions of individual nations. So it would seem to require a supernational, planetary, or species-level guarantee, some sort of overlaw, as that of a total world government. But Arendt rejected any such permanent guarantee as, on the one hand, historically nonfunctional (she had shown supergovernment dreams to have failed before), and on the other hand, part of a fantasy of escape from the human condition—which is marked by plurality, localism, and the opinions and actions necessary for politics. Whenever only a single person was thought to be needed to guarantee his own standing, Arendt was sure philosophy had lapsed into delusion and the impulse to the totalitarian—the fantasized end point at which the whole could be resolved into a single position and all contradictions of different persons annulled.[110] She called for something bridging the suprapolitical and the political: "human dignity needs a new guarantee which can be found only in a new political principle, in a new law on earth, whose validity this time must comprehend the whole of humanity while its power must remain strictly limited, rooted in and controlled by newly defined territorial entities" (New, ix). This sounds as "empty" as what others had offered, in both the disappointing and productive sense. Her "new political principle" could not proceed on the model of a restoration or shoring up or protection of old forms, as others counseled: "For man, in the sense of the nature of man, is no longer the measure, despite what the new humanists would have us believe. Politically, this means that before drawing up the constitution of a new body politic, we shall have to create—not merely discover—a new foundation for human community as such" (1st, 436).[111] No small task, but a horizon for hope: "In historical terms this would not mean the end of history, but its first consciously planned beginning, together with the bitter realization that nothing has been promised us" (1st, 436).

"Humanity," as an idea, spoke of that new beginning. It was "empty" in the effective sense—aware of what was missing and that only human conviction could point at the absence and convince others to make something of it. Arendt, drawing on Kant, was right to recognize that there might be something beyond positive, man-made law, but that it was still a consequence of human action and human thought, always contingent and always subject to human backsliding and misjudgment—that is, a "regulative idea," in this case the regulative idea of "humanity"—a unified, civilized idea of a common status of all men, a belief *attainable* to all men, but not inevitable from nature, not assured by history. Arendt felt at last, as we have seen, that there was a purely factual and empirical basis for the regulative idea of commonality, because imperialism and war had been the dark side of a technical process that had, literally, made every community in the world dependent on the others and on the world system. Yet the form "humanity" must take, paradoxically, was not a globally individualist universalism but the universalizing claim that every individual be inexpugnable from local particularity. To put this in its most paradoxical form: "Humanity" must be developed within local communities as part of a shared value common to *all* local communities in order to guarantee universally a human "right to have rights," experienced only locally. "It is by no means certain whether this is possible" (New, 298), Arendt admitted.

THE LEVELING OF THE PHILOSOPHICAL DISCOURSE AND
ITS ENTRY INTO RIVAL FIELDS OF REPRESENTATION

As a set of philosophical questions, the crisis of man could only ever work practically on the world through other discourses. But other discourses could also co-opt and diminish it. After the masterpiece of *The Origins of Totalitarianism*, strictly intellectual addresses to the general problem of man show a decline. *Commentary*, publisher of the earlier, important series of essays after World War II, which seemed to sum up the mature questions of the 1940s discourse, went on reviewing crisis of man books through the 1950s with increasing disillusion and sarcasm. The newer works, only a few years after Arendt's summary masterpiece, represented an intellectual undermining of their serious earlier discourse. First, *Commentary* just faced benign cliché: in 1954, they hit Joseph Wood Krutch's *The Measure of Man* as a book of "familiar . . . predicament of modern man" claptrap in which "democratic man is on the way to becoming like totalitarian man."[112] Then they encountered more cynical misunderstandings: in 1955, they attacked *The Dignity of Man*, a book by Russell W. Davenport, former editor of *Fortune*, editorial page writer for *Life*, worker for *Time*, and general Luce publications pooh-bah. Davenport reduced the significance of the antitotalitarian questioning of man's nature to an "us" versus "them" philosophy of anti-Soviet jingoism. "[Davenport] had decided that Russia could not be opposed with any hope of final success unless a definition of man or an agreement to search for one could be found."[113] *Commentary* was not impressed with his new "philosophical" resolution.

In other hands, the universality of man continued to function as a sentimental antidote to the worries of a nuclear-armed world of US-USSR bipolarity. In 1955, during the first half of the year, a photographic exhibit of *The Family of Man* went on display at the Museum of Modern Art in New York City. Curated by Edward Steichen, with inspirational texts by his elderly brother-in-law, the poet Carl Sandburg, the collection of 503 pictures was one of the most successful art exhibits of its time. It was a thoroughgoing popularization of the earlier discourse of the crisis of man, and yet perfectly sensible and honorable within its own terms. All men (or, rather, men, women, and children), were born, ate, played, worked, made love, lived in families, and died, to be succeeded by others. These most minimal but touching arrangements formed the basis for collages of photographs. Pictures showed individuals from many nations, of different skin colors and body types and climates, doing everyday activities, often set side by side in similar poses or arrangements, all to express, in Steichen's words, "a mirror of the universal elements and emotions in the everydayness of life—as a mirror of the essential oneness of mankind throughout the world."[114] "Steichen consciously chose to generalize the human condition through *The Family of Man*," the art historian Erik Sandeen has written, in his careful investigation of the exhibit in its original incarnation and its subsequent international travels; "[t]he collection was built of a rhetoric of unity."[115] When the viewer climbed the stairs to reach the *Family of Man*, from its first days of opening in January, he was confronted with a stanza composed by Sandburg:

> There is only one man in the world
> and his name is All Men.
> There is only one woman in the world
> and her name is All Women.
> There is only one child in the world
> and the child's name is All Children.[116]

By October, when the then twenty-seven-year-old art critic Hilton Kramer went to see it for *Commentary*, *The Family of Man* had set all sorts of attendance records: six thousand people in a single day for the Museum of Modern Art (a twenty-five-year record), a quarter of a million visitors overall, and a quarter million copies of the paperback edition sold by July 15, only two months after publication.[117]

Hilton Kramer savaged it. He objected to the title *The Family of Man* because it denied the political differences of mankind. It effaced conflictual politics altogether. He imagined it ought to be doing the work of the earlier discourse—it ought to aim at real meaning and lessons for action—or put man into practical terms, recognizing real distinctions in details of American and global life or the realities of a Cold War world. In 1956, when the touring exhibit of *The Family of Man* reached Paris under the name *The Great Family of Man*, another critic who would later make a significant mark in the United States, Roland Barthes, wrote a short critique of his own. He hit the same notes that American critics like Kramer had, that the exhibit was antipolitical and antihistorical, while adding some anticolonial and antiracist skepticism (well into France's decolonizing wars in Indochina and now Algeria, and after the start of the new US civil rights movement) about man's display of "unity." "[W]hy not ask the parents of Emmet Till, the young Negro assassinated by the Whites what *they* think of *The Great Family of Man*?" . . . [L]et us also ask the North African workers of the Goutte d'Or district in Paris what they think of *The Great Family of Man*."[118] The anticolonial context had come home to the French in 1956 even as it was largely repressed in America.

In the widely read book version of the exhibit, Steichen was perfectly explicit about the deliberate de-intellectualizing impulse of his mid-'50s show. He wanted this: "Photographs concerned with the religious rather than religions. With basic human consciousness rather than social consciousness. Photographs concerned with man's dreams and aspirations and photographs of the flaming creative forces of love and truth and the corrosive evil inherent in the lie."[119] This wasn't naïveté—it was a purposeful targeting of the widest resonances and the broadest audience possible. As Sandeen has crucially discovered in his reconstructions of the original exhibition arrangement, when the viewer reached the end of the exhibit, he or she encountered something that was not preserved in the bestselling paperback and hardcover collections of the exhibit: a gigantic "six-by-eight foot color transparency of a hydrogen bomb explosion," positioned to draw the viewer into its cloud, along with a wall-sized photograph of a meeting of the General Assembly of the United Nations as the alternative to destruction. So Steichen did have a point, a point that dated back to the "Modern Man Is Obsolete" and world government discourses of a decade earlier, and it was the only one that could be supported by a collection of this kind: that all of the world's peoples were fundamentally the same and united as "Man" by their familial and intimate bonds and not their political differences—and that this greater nonpolitical unity would be the only means to avoid a common and total atomic destruction. Minimal commonality *did* have significance, if what one wanted was to appeal to all the peoples of the earth not to annihilate themselves in a thermonuclear war. "One left the exhibition through a roomful of [pictures of] children at play," finally, as the symbol of a more hopeful future.[120]

It was one of Steichen's proudest achievements that the exhibit went, on its world tour, not so much to France (to be seen by Roland Barthes) but to Moscow, where the citizens of the globe's other nuclear-armed nation could be reminded of worldwide commonality.[121] Yet arrangements for the world tour, under the US Information Agency auspices (the government's arm of "public diplomacy" after 1953 and an instrument of the Cold War), always raised the question of an America-centered or propaganda purpose for the exhibit, just as discussion of man in the '50s risked lapsing into a propaganda debate about Americanism versus Sovietism.

Again, there is the danger here of worrying about—or witnessing accusations of—ideological "junk" when, in fact, one has simply left the thread of the philosophical discourse altogether, and, indeed, gotten ahead of the real intellectual chronology of the discourse of man. Already by 1951, and in fact for a few years before that date, pressures from the discourse of man had been transferred to other spheres of representation—including the demand that artists answer the problems of the age. One such mode of representation would be, specifically, *the novel.* What a generation of American thinkers could not do only with philosophy or international organization, the critics among them sought to do with the aesthetics of their dominant literary form, fiction, and this is the more meaningful intellectual trajectory of the crisis of man in the 1950s—as part of the continuing American search for a "Great American Novel" and a new classical literature.

PART II

TRANSMISSION

PART II

CHAPTER 4

CRITICISM AND THE LITERARY CRISIS OF MAN

Humanism has always been animated by texts. The fifteenth-century *umanisti* projected their philosophical focus onto man to escape supernaturalism and Christianity, and develop Renaissance learning. They were capable of doing so because they had inherited and plumbed a particular trove of books: the manuscripts of classical antiquity.

Since that time, "humanism," partly by its sound, has worn other, looser meanings, of something like a love for *Homo sapiens*, respect for mankind. Malcolm Cowley praised this commonsense humanism very eloquently, a few years before the crisis of man, in 1930: "Partly it is an emphasis on the qualities it considers to be essentially human. Partly it is a defense of human dignity, of human possibilities; partly it is an opposition to all the forces that threaten them."[1] Others in his time who made humanism a positive doctrine insisted they could read empirical truths from man's persistence, in some traditional or natural form, to rival more idealistic "-isms" (communism, socialism, fascism, Nazism, capitalism) as a source of normative judgment, and make "man the measure of all things," adopting a dictum of the pre-Socratic philosopher Protagoras, much quoted and abused from the 1930s to the 1960s.

But the concern of humanism with the book constantly recurs, and as Peter Sloterdijk has argued, humanism is rarely just about the benign education of man for his responsibilities of live and let live. It is also always *against* something, because it is always trying to pull man out of a barbarism.[2] One sees a hidden strife of books against books: pagan classics against Scholasticism and canon law or, at midcentury, battles over the creation of a *new* canon of texts that could be at once "humanizing" and value-laden. Even Malcolm Cowley, in his formulation of humanism for 1930, was opposing his common sense to the so-called New Humanism, the conservatism of Irving Babbitt and Paul Elmer More, a literary-critical philosophy of turn-of-the-century restraint and decorum.[3]

When, after 1939, certain formulations of the restoration of man against his recent degradations turned back to humanism, they again developed it also in the narrower sense of a concern with the book. The sort of text thinkers turned to, however, was the *novel*—not the tract, not the poem, not the sermon, not the academic report. The novel had the obligation to humanize a fallen mankind.

This was odder, and more time-bound, than we may be prone to recognize. The novel—as a vault of cultural knowledge, a tool for culturing people, and a work of art rather than an entertainment—may really have attained its one permanent high-water mark in the years of midcentury. I think it achieved a cultural authority, and for a period of time sustained obligations of national and moral import (for adults, and not just schoolchildren), which it no longer holds today, except tinctured with nostalgia, and may never bear again. The novel became an agent of a certain kind of humanism associated with the restoration of man, reconceived by some important critics as a nationalist or American humanism.

BASIS OF THE TRANSFER: FROM CRISIS
OF MAN TO DEATH OF THE NOVEL

The forceful and enterprising critic who transposed the intellectuals' arguments about the crisis of man into the terms of the novel was Lionel Trilling. Various deaths of the novel had been proposed in literary culture since the early days of modernism, often to announce that some new literary rival had already arrived. T. S. Eliot and José Ortega y Gasset had been forerunners in pronouncing an end to the novel in the 1920s; one could also point to Paul Valéry and the European avant-gardes from futurists to surrealists. In the Eliot-dominated midcentury, educated readers of 1948 would have known well "*Ulysses*, Order, and Myth" (first published in the *Dial* in 1923) and its flat statement that "[t]he novel ended with Flaubert and with James."[4] However, that end came because, for Eliot, the novel began again with Joyce's discoveries—like "the discoveries of an Einstein." The distinction between the death of the novel in the '40s and its end in the '20s is that the earlier statement came generally as a deck-clearing cannonade, a declaration of the irrelevance or imminent demolition of an old form in favor of some *particular* alternative within sight. These earlier inhuming gestures preceded announcements of an immediate and evident rebirth. Trilling's did not.

"This opinion is now heard from all sides," Trilling wrote. "It is heard in conversation rather than read in formal discourse, for to insist on the death or moribundity of a great genre is an unhappy task which the critic will naturally avoid if he can, yet the opinion is now an established one and has a very considerable authority."[5] He then listed three theses, though, that he thought *could* justify his claim that the novel might be dead. In each, we can see implied a particular philosophical view of literature's relation to the world, and, in two of them, a connection back to the crisis of man.

He first offered the possibility that the novel might be "exhausted," simply used up, all of its major possibilities explored, "worked out in the way that a lode of ore is worked out" (1272). Trilling explicitly drew this idea from Ortega y Gasset, the Spanish thinker whose 1925 essay "Notes on the Novel" (which elaborated this idea) had just appeared in English.[6]

The exhaustion idea was a formal and aesthetic view, implying a life history of artistic forms and a purely internal story of the development of art. To Trilling, it wasn't very convincing, and he quickly disposed of it.[7] Second, much more promising, was the likelihood "that the novel was developed in response to certain cultural circumstances which now no longer exist" (1272). Drawing on familiar sociological explanations of the rise of the novel as a result of European social conditions, with changes in class structure and the rise of a petty bourgeois and domestic servant-class readership, the turn to secular values, individualism, and romantic love, Trilling could find easy understanding among his readers for a suggestion that if the novel was no longer meaningfully being written, it was because the world and its values had changed drastically yet again.[8] This was the historical view.

The third possibility was that values and circumstances hadn't changed but rather had become so intense—sped up, proliferated, distracting, and excessive—that modern people no longer knew how to use the wisdom of novels, nor would know how to write them in the future. Call this a hybrid technological-anthropological view.

A mixture of the historical and the technological-anthropological worried Trilling far beyond literature: "It is not . . . unreasonable to suppose that we are at the close of a cultural cycle, that the historical circumstances which called forth the particular effort in which we once lived and moved and had our being is now at an end" (1278). Twentieth-century American social class was simply not like nineteenth-century social class; for that reason alone, there would certainly have to have been a historical change in the work of the novel. But then, too, there had been a more indefinable change: a "great . . . falling-off in the energy of mind."

The deep problem was that after World War II, as Trilling spelled it out, we *knew* things, even had seen things, horrors and realities, that the deepest enlightened and skeptical minds of earlier times might intuit but could never confirm, nor convince all men of. Trilling described our knowledge explicitly as a new vision of man. Montaigne, Shakespeare, Swift, and Freud had all detected the depravity in human beings. They worked "to diminish man's pride," and the greatest writers' "demonstration of man's depravity, has been one of the chief works of the human mind for some four hundred years" (1280). Yet a saving grace of this literature, in the past, was that the reader witnessed such great minds as Shakespeare's making these baleful discoveries and representing them in rhetorical art. "[T]he activity of the mind was a kind of fortitude" (1278) in these cases. Plus, as long as the bulk of society remained optimistic, worshipped Progress, and believed "in human and social goodness" (ibid.), Montaigne, Shakespeare, Swift, and Freud could never *prove* their case against man (while in their own demonstrations of greatness, they supported man), and thus they did him only good in warning him of his bad excesses.

After World War II, though, too many defenses were gone. "[T]he old margin no longer exists; the façade is down; society's resistance to the discovery of depravity has ceased; now everyone knows. . . . The simple eye of the camera shows us, at Belsen and Buchenwald, horrors that quite surpass Swift's powers" (1279). How could the novel help us, when a mindless camera could do all the unmasking itself?

> At this point we are in the full tide of those desperate perceptions of our life which are current nowadays among thinking and talking people, which, even when we are not thinking and talking, haunt and control our minds with visions of losses worse than that of existence—losses of culture, personality, humanness. (1280)

The loss of "humanness" became Trilling's keyword. Paraphrasing Ortega, he admitted that a difficulty of previous modern art had been its "dislike of holding in the mind the human fact and the human condition" (1279). Trilling insisted that the novel would now have to do the work of the *restoration* of the human—the novel, above all other art forms and media. This is because "[t]he novel . . . has been, of all literary forms, the most devoted to the celebration and investigation of the human will; and the will of our society is dying of its own excess" (1280). From unmasking to revival, from negation to affirmation, "[s]urely the great work of our time is the restoration and reconstitution of the will" (ibid.), Trilling wrote. Later, he calls this task "reconstituting the great former will of humanism" (1281). He gives a recipe, in fact, for what he thinks the new novels will be like. They'll still tell stories, against Sartre's new, more austere, avant-garde, individualist, existentialist theories of fiction in *What Is Literature?*[9] They won't be concerned with form. The new novels will, rather, have an explicit relation to *ideas*. They will be novels, in effect, *of* and *for* intellectuals. And, stuck on ideas, they might just find in the "organization of society into ideological groups" (1288) a subject matter commensurate with the older organization of European society into classes.

Trilling was at once highly individual and uniquely positioned to influence an uncommon range of intellectual groups and readers. I suspect he is to this day probably the best-remembered literary critic of midcentury America, at least by reputation—yet if he was, then and now, the most emblematic and authoritative, he was in other ways anomalous or individualistic. He did not produce a large body of criticism of actual literature. Instead he wrote primarily a series of programmatic essays and occasional statements that stood as idiosyncratic benchmarks for his peers and emulators. As a teacher, then a professor at Columbia from 1931 forward (tenured in 1939), he had the authority of the academy—yet he was famously the first Jewish member of the English department, appointed after a historic struggle with its genteel anti-Semitic faculty, and so he was free of its pipe-tobacco staleness.[10] Trilling kept an Arnoldian tone but published his most important essays in literary quarterlies like *Partisan Review* and *Kenyon Review*. He is associated with the world of the New York Intellectuals, yet managed to stay above the fray, insulated as the cerebral older sibling whom they failed to turn on—in part because the heights of his achievements reflected well on them. Trilling represented ascent into the highest culture, even though he could quite conspicuously make it his job to translate the highbrow for "the people"; from 1951 to 1963, for example, he wrote introductions and enticements for the Reader's Subscription Book Club and its newsletter, *The Griffin*, purveyor of quality literature (his collaborators were the poet W. H. Auden and the historian Jacques Barzun).[11]

"Art and Fortune" is not a purely representative essay of the time; if I had to make a list of the most influential single essays in criticism of that era, however, I would put it near the top. "[O]ne of the dreams of a younger America, continuing up to recently, was of *The* Great American Novel" (1290), Trilling declares at one point, as if an older America had grown wiser. Yet the effect of the Trillingesque recipe—much as he tried to disown it—really was to help revive the dream of "the Great American Novel," a phrase (and a dream) that had first appeared after the wounding division of the Civil War.[12] For Trilling's diagnosis was taken seriously, I think, not only among critics but, grudgingly, miserably, in the quarter where it most mattered—among novelists. His ideas were too much the inevitable, though best, expression of a whole mood of the late 1940s, and the intrusion of the crisis of man into the progress of the novel, to ignore.

PRESSURE ON WRITERS: THE CALL FOR AN AFFIRMATIVE LITERATURE

A suspicion one could hold about Trilling's essay, of course, is that his "opinion . . . heard from all sides" (1271) was really just his own. In fact, it wasn't. Many of the other "death of the novel" critiques in the 1940s pursued the technological-anthropological argument that events were changing too quickly for "man the novelist" to master them or for "man the reader" to understand them through fictional art. Hannah Arendt, who in addition to her masterpieces of political philosophy was also a gifted occasional literary critic—writing analyses of Rilke, Kafka, Broch, and Camus—explained at the high intellectual end that in an age of depersonalized "happenings," novelists "have been supplanted by the reporter."[13] Clifton Fadiman, the *New Yorker* book reviewer and radio personality (host of *Information Please*), and a former student of Mortimer Adler, warned middlebrow audiences, in his major essay of the 1940s, "The Decline of Attention," of the dehumanizing, because antiliterate, bias of technology: "It seems fairly clear that in our time the attrition of one kind of attention—the ability to read prose and poetry of meaning and substance—is becoming more and more widespread: and that the faculty of attention in general is undergoing a wholesale displacement away from ideas and abstractions towards things and techniques."[14]

The *Saturday Review of Literature*, on the other hand, more closely followed Trilling's historical-change explanation. Human beings had formerly believed in the usefulness of reasoned progress, and thought that if they showed depravity in fiction, then good people would ameliorate it in real life—as after the exposés of Dickens and Zola. Matters had since changed. "Toward the end of the nineteenth century Western man began to lose the certainty that humanity might someday live in a state of grace."[15] Unless this human hope for "Western man" could be recovered by the novel, it could not fulfill its former office. It must return to hope and values. The Luce magazines (*Time, Life,* and *Fortune*) were the only cultural source unembarrassed enough to demand affirmation from new American writers that would be not only redeeming but patriotically American. In the same season with Trilling's complex essay, *Life* ran an editorial briskly titled "Fiction in the U.S.: We Need a Novelist to Re-Create American Values Instead of Wallowing in the Literary Slums."[16]

It is significant that it was the *novel*, not the poem, religious work, or treatise, that had become for all parties the agent of moral, quasi-spiritual uplift. If Trilling warned in "Art and Fortune" that "we have come to overvalue" the novel, he worried about it precisely because he, and others, did in fact now value the novel more highly than any form of art or even intellect. (He meant by "overvaluation" only that he feared that critics had made the mistake of letting novelists know their own magnitude, so that the novel had become self-conscious, therefore self-defeating.) Trilling could say elsewhere, that same year:

For our time the most effective agent of the moral imagination has been the novel of the last two hundred years. . . . It taught us, as no other genre ever did, the extent of human variety and the value of this variety. . . . Yet there never was a time when its particular activity was so much needed, was of so much practical, political, and social use—so much so that if its impulse does not respond to the need, we shall have reason to be sad not only over a waning form of art but also over our waning freedom.[17]

No novel, no freedom! This was quite a burden to place on a cultural form best known, for centuries, as a not-always-respectable (but sometimes socially reforming) entertainment.

AMERICAN LITERATURE AND THE DOUBLE CANON

Yet there was another source of the potential "overvaluation" of the novel beyond anything Trilling had in mind—and this represented the culmination of a decades-long enterprise of the twentieth century, coinciding with a sudden university-based demographic shift after World War II and the unexpected spring tide of US geopolitical supremacy.

The years of the 1940s were the era of the final consolidation of American literature as an object of criticism. A small set of works displayed the American genius in a way that could be crated up for cultural export and laid out on butcher paper for internal university cultivation. The case for the greatness of this literature was made not just on its literary achievement but, very often, its national character. The opuses included would show the nation's individualism, its energy, its religious darkness, its democracy, its philosophical depth to rival Europe, and its fecundity.

The unusual quality of the consolidation was that it didn't entrench a simple canon, one list of masterpieces proceeding chronologically in a single stream. It crystallized a double canon, the outflow of two currents of privileged achievement, each one lasting not much longer than a decade. These two periods of superior expression stood in parallel to reflect and illuminate each other, forming almost a closed interpretive system through which one could trace the dye of "Americanness" old and new. The two periods were the "American Renaissance," newly given a name, taking up just a few years in the 1850s, and an unnamed period we would now call American modernism, centering on the decade of the 1920s, though overlapping its numerical limits.

University professors had only begun to teach modern fiction in the later nineteenth century. This supplement to the traditional college curriculum of classical texts had gained a firm establishment by 1890, restricted to English writing (and, separately, "modern" foreign languages).[18] The first college-level course in American literature seems to have been offered as an oddity at Princeton in 1872. Little else followed before 1900, but a self-consciously modernizing ferment had begun, and by the 1920s, as Kermit Vanderbilt's research has shown, American fiction and poetry was taught "at the more adventurous universities."[19] "[I]t remained a distinctly minor part of the curriculum until after World War II," David Shumway has confirmed, only to become a truly central part of the disciplinary curriculum with the massive influx of new classes and categories of Americans into universities under the postwar GI Bill, who needed a course of study that was secular and morally authoritative but did not require elite "prep" school background in the classical languages.[20]

The 1940s did the defining work that made this curricular transition possible. At one end of the decade, in 1941, the left-wing Harvard critic F. O. Matthiessen enshrined the nineteenth-century American writers definitively and gave the first canonical period its name in his *American Renaissance*, perhaps the most important book in the literary criticism of America during midcentury (and very likely the most influential book of literary criticism of America, ever), a volume released at just the moment the United States was entering the war against fascism. Matthiessen made the case that the single most fruitful and characteristic period of American literature had been the middle decade of the nineteenth century. His list of master authors ran to Emerson, Thoreau, Whitman, Hawthorne, and Melville. With a bit of gerrymandering (especially with Emerson's career), Matthiessen managed to narrow the explosive rebirth of American genius to just a five-year period, with the election to the canon of *Representative Men* (1850), *The Scarlet Letter* (1850), *The House of the Seven Gables* (1851), *Moby-Dick* (1851), *Pierre* (1852), *Walden* (1854), and the first edition of *Leaves of Grass* (1855).[21] Despite our reservations that nowadays we would prefer the Emerson of the *Essays: First Series* to that of *Representative Men*, and have favored Melville's shorter works (*Billy Budd*, "Benito Cereno," "Bartleby, the Scrivener") as the best accompaniments to his novel about the whale (though there is always some scholar to champion a reclamation of *Pierre*), this is exactly the canon of books, unchanged, that we still possess as the main American nineteenth-century reading list. It forms the core of any college syllabus.[22]

At the other end of the 1940s—in the year when Trilling mooted the possible death of the novel henceforward, and issued his call for the restoration of human will—the landmark scholarly publication of 1948 was a collective, summary work, offering conclusion to a long search for renewed American literary origins: Robert E. Spiller, Willard Thorp, Thomas H. Johnson, and Henry Seidel Canby's *Literary History of the United States*.[23] The two oversized volumes of this history, compiled by a distinguished roster of literary critics, communicated the wisdom of the interwar and wartime generations of scholarship and replaced the last synoptic attempt, *The Cambridge History of American Literature* (1917), which dated to the end of the Great War. The contemporary literary historians Evan Carton and Gerald Graff have correctly seen Spiller as both the symbolic final incarnation of the effort of American literature to constitute itself as an academic field in the two decades leading up to World War II and as a declaration of US dominance in the postwar era:

> [T]o the editors of *Literary History of the United States* fell the unfinished task of legitimating American literature as a subject befitting America's new international prestige. That meant circumscribing American literature as a distinctive whole, isolating the works that constituted the field, identifying what was distinctively American about these works, and, finally demonstrating their parity with the established English classics.[24]

The archaeological work of reclamation and circumscription had mostly been done earlier. Herman Melville had needed to be rediscovered and redeveloped as a great American author almost from scratch, in work done by scholars at Columbia in the 1920s. *Billy Budd*, a key document in his revival, was only discovered and published for the first time in 1924.[25] The key field-workers at Columbia were Carl Van Doren, who had written up Melville for *The Cambridge History* (1917), and his energetic disciple Raymond M. Weaver, who wrote the first biography of Melville, transcribed and published *Billy Budd*, and introduced the first Modern Library edition of *Moby-Dick* (1926) and the landmark publication of Melville's *Shorter Novels* (1928). Lewis Mumford himself contributed to the revival in 1929 with a biography, *Herman Melville*, which reached a bigger audience through the Literary Guild book club, making the case for Melville as comparable in depth to Dostoevsky and Dante.[26] D. H. Lawrence, meanwhile, had outlined an influential myth of raw individualism and an incipient canon in *Studies in Classic American Literature* in 1923; Van Wyck Brooks had begun his essential series reviving American literature in 1915 with *America's Coming of Age*, but was still at it in 1947 (*The Times of Melville and Whitman*). It can be easy to forget now how much of literary enterprise and writing in the literary quarterlies, well into the 1930s and 1940s, was devoted to the rediscovery of figures specifically like Melville and Whitman, who were then treated as much newer and more mysterious than the versions of them we possess now.

The Spiller volumes picked up where that broad-field archaeology had left off, not unlike the report from the museum offices assembling all that the various excavations had uncovered, deliberately making a longer, completist's survey in contrast to Matthiessen's microscopic delectation. Chapters covered everything from early American literature to American folk humor and tall tales. Yet they left no doubt about the universal agreement that the supreme achievement—the Valley of the Kings, by whose monuments and furnishings daily appliances could be measured—was located in the 1850s. Those years earned a whole division of the book filled with individual chapter-length author studies—in order—of Emerson, Thoreau, Hawthorne, Melville, and Whitman, in a period the book named, not quite for rebirth after intellectual darkness (like Matthiessen's "Renaissance"), but for completion of an unacknowledged project: "Literary Fulfillment."

If the final section of the book, devoted to the American modernist decades, did not give Hemingway, Faulkner, and the other recent novelists it discussed quite comparable treatment, it still surprisingly suggested that their achievement ought to be viewed in comparable terms: "It can scarcely be doubted, . . . on the evidence of the foregoing chapters, that a literary movement of power and character existed in the United States after about 1910. . . . Nothing like it had occurred in our literature since the mid-years of the past century, when Emerson, Melville, and Whitman were in their prime."[27] Again, in the final words of the second volume, remarking how observers in the 1940s acknowledged the triumph of American literature worldwide, this second coming was the US modernist moment: "Europeans were not slow to recognize that there had been a literary revival here after 1910; and they showed the same hospitality to the new writers of the interwar period that they had shown, a century before, to the writers of the New York and New England renaissance."[28]

Elsewhere in popular literary culture, critics were more explicit. Speaking of "[t]he writers of the Twenties," the *Saturday Review of Literature* claimed that "[t]he only period in American literature that can be compared with this efflorescence of creative talent is the Forties and Fifties of the nineteenth century," the days of "Thoreau, Emerson, or Hawthorne."[29] And American modernism, too, in the 1940s, was acquiring its twenties triumphant canon. The crucial works could be compressed, if not into five years, then into ten: Eliot's *The Waste Land* (1922), Hemingway's *In Our Time* (1924), *The Sun Also Rises* (1926) and *A Farewell to Arms* (1929), and Faulkner's *The Sound and the Fury* (1929), *As I Lay Dying* (1930), and *Light in August* (1932). The outlier most associated with this group, in the American modernist lineage, was Henry James. (A "James revival," as it was called then, constituted a huge center of literary-critical energy well into the 1950s. James's prefaces had been republished together for the first time in *The Art of the Novel* in 1934, and both Eliot and Hemingway, two impressively different American modernist writers, claimed him as an essential forerunner.) Faulkner was the last writer to be revived and brought in, rather as Melville had come in last for revival from the earlier period, and he proved to be a surprising lynchpin. Individual critics could also choose to flavor the odd canonical foursome of Eliot, Hemingway, Faulkner, and their predecessor Henry James, with a range of additional modernist works in poetry: Ezra Pound's early *Cantos* or Hart Crane's *The Bridge* (1930) (Wallace Stevens does not yet seem to be much mentioned as at all canonical, despite *Harmonium* [1923]—his enshrining would come significantly later); while in the novel, John Dos Passos and F. Scott Fitzgerald might be tacked on to the essential foursome, as critics' temperaments or biographical commitments inspired them. (Both Malcolm Cowley and Edmund Wilson maintained a personal commitment to dead Fitzgerald, and Trilling also championed him, adding up to "the Fitzgerald revival.")[30] But the core remained solid.[31]

At this dual fulfillment, academics and critics had thus assembled old and new testaments of the US novel, which engrossed much of their attention at the time of the proposed death of the novel. Our much-used contemporary word "canon"—meaning a corpus of literary texts taught in any given subfield of a university discipline—has its original meaning in the determination by ecclesiastical authorities of the books that make up Holy Scripture. But there's something especially appropriate in employing it for the collation of midcentury writings of Hawthorne and Melville or Eliot and Faulkner, because the proud, reverent, symbol-seeking investigations of that moment did, in fact, treat these works as something in the family of national scripture. Indeed, there may be occasion here to introduce a more forgotten word of Christian hermeneutics—typology.[32] Typology was an exegetical practice that linked events and characters of the Old Testament to the elements of the New Testament they prefigured, as "type" to "antitype." Typological interpretation became a matter of discovering the former elements in the latter, often uprooting Old Testament events from their original significance to find their fulfillment in the coming of Jesus Christ and his transformation of history and law.

Something in the creation of *two* parallel sets of masterworks, not one, does change the nature of criticism, and midcentury criticism of American literature, I want to suggest, became mildly typological in ways that still determine the field today. Any given figure of the modernist generation could be an antitype to a type of the American Renaissance. The double canon made it possible for critics in the late 1940s to have the usable US past they needed, and new toys to play with, while leaving contemporary novels the unfortunate obligation to vie for a place in the apocrypha. It would be particularly hard for any new work to enter this system, and gain recognition as high literature, unless it tried to do so via techniques, themes, and with a certain kind of grandeur and ambition that recognizably echoed the heritage of the American Renaissance or American modernism. Yet the wide knowledge and esteem of the two canons put any new, echoic text into increased jeopardy of being found derivative, lackluster, or superfluous. One of the most perceptive of the younger writers of the 1940s and 1950s, Gore Vidal, made an eloquent protest:

> One senses . . . in academic dialogues and explications the unstated burden of the discussion that, at last, all the novels are in. The term is over, the canon assembled if not ordered, the door to the library firmly shut to the irrelevance of new attempts.
>
> It is agreed, for instance, that there are among us no novelists of sufficient importance to act as touchstones for useful judgement. There is Faulkner, but . . . and there is Hemingway, but . . .[33] (ellipses in original)

And Vidal has his imaginary critic's list trail off there.

THE RAGE OF DISAPPOINTMENT

The atmosphere dictated that even as a whole new generation of postwar writers was emerging, and new authors were rising to prominence, the defining (and quite surprising) feature of the criticism of contemporary American novels through the whole of the late 1940s and early 1950s was how bad a shape nearly all critics, both major and minor, believed the novel to be in, even as they sometimes cheered individual books. There was something hysterical about this criticism, which can be traced also to expectations for the novel—as a restoration of the will, as a true and even premeditated meditation on man—that could not yet be met. It was an era of excitement and almost desperate expectations for individual novelists (with the near-religious belief in the novel's office), coupled with unremitting pessimism about new novels as a group.

In 1944, William Phillips deplored "the low state of writing today," feeling that its poor quality had not been much acknowledged in criticism. Yet he still had "some hope, too, that a generation of young writers will return from the war with a fresh image of its realities."[34] That hope was quickly dashed as the criticism, following the new novels, came pouring in. Louis Bromfield in 1947 warned "[t]he old, established writers aren't producing [novels] in sufficient numbers and there aren't any signs among the younger writers of another Hemingway, another Fitzgerald, another Sinclair Lewis, or much of anything."[35] John Crowe Ransom wrote in reply to a query from *Partisan Review* in 1948: "One is tempted to say of the creative effort of our decade: It is largely abortive."[36] John Berryman, in reply to a similar query: "The question apparently wants me to say that [earlier] novelists are being revived mainly because we have no fiction of our own; so I will; but it's obvious."[37]

By 1948, the date of Trilling's essay, a number of well-praised and even best-selling young writers of individual promise were emerging: Norman Mailer, Carson McCullers, and Truman Capote, plus Gore Vidal and Jean Stafford, to whom would soon be added James Jones, Paul Bowles, William Styron, and others. Meanwhile, the tone of disappointment about the total import or significance of these writers' work became unanimous among the same high- and middlebrow critics who might praise them singly, and ever more widespread across the range of publications with different pretensions. The usually cheery and publicity-minded *Saturday Review of Literature* said at the end of the decade: "American literature so far has failed to live up to its promise at the end of World War II."[38] *Harper's* editorialized: "These days a good novelist, like a good man, is apparently hard to find."[39] It was "an arid period" (Hartley Grattan).[40] The beating-up went on and on, even after books emerged in the early '50s that *did* begin to satisfy the demands, as we will see, of critical exponents of the death of the novel and the crisis of man.

A landmark of this moment of disappointment was the publication in 1951 of John Aldridge's *After the Lost Generation*. His book was one of the last ambitious treatments of an entire literary age, his own, by a talented young critic evaluating a generation of fellow writers with whom he ought to have everything in common. It was a project in line with famous synoptic books of the '20s and '30s, Wilson's *Axel's Castle* and Cowley's *Exile's Return*. Aldridge himself was only twenty-nine. But Aldridge's book is not similarly remembered today, probably for one major reason. He went through the new writers of his time and found that, in essence, none of them could be assigned the importance he wished to give them; above all, they simply did not measure up to the '20s novelists of the Lost Generation, his standard of accomplishment.

Aldridge's literary concern, too, had become "the overt affirmation of values" in the context of a crisis, and whether such an affirmation could be made by the new writers.[41] Post–World War II writers "have come through a war even more profoundly disturbing than the first; but the illusions and causes of war, having once been lost, cannot be relost."[42] His conclusion was that no one had yet found a way of reconstructing positive values through the materials of present-day life. If a writer wrote without such values, he was insignificant. If he just claimed values by vigorous gestures, it yielded either compulsive copying of the twenties or rootless, meaningless phrases.

> If . . . [writers] have insight into values that seem worthy of affirmation and point the way out of the chaos of loss, they can [only] superimpose them upon the old material which is still available. They can, in other

words, assert the need for belief even though it is upon a background in which belief is impossible and in which the symbols are lacking for a genuine affirmation in dramatic terms.[43]

A "rage of disappointment" was the *Partisan Review* writer and philosopher William Barrett's summation of the mood behind Aldridge's total denunciation of his contemporaries (whom Aldridge said he had initially hoped to praise and champion). This phrase served just as well for Barrett himself and the gathering host of critics of the immediate postwar era—attached not only to a humanism of the Trillingesque variety but a subtle underlying Americanism or nationalism that, curiously, echoed the déclassé views of the publicists of *Life*. "[A] rage of disappointment," Barrett explained further, "that a large, vital, and industrious country like the United States is not now producing the great literature that, from all purely rational considerations, we should expect of it."[44]

THE TEMPORARY ALTERNATIVE: A HUMANIST LOST GENERATION?

One solution was to go back to the Lost Generation writers themselves and find ways to refashion them to meet the needs of the crisis of man—and, in the most notable case, to *rediscover* a neglected one of them and make, in essence, a new figure. This was the case with the transformation of William Faulkner.

A superb study of Faulkner's late rise has been written by the literary historian Lawrence Schwartz, entitled *Creating Faulkner's Reputation*, in which Schwartz argues that "[t]he sudden inflation of William Faulkner's literary reputation after World War II is at once the most dramatic and obvious aspect of his writing career." "I wondered how it was possible," Schwartz writes, "for a writer, out of print and generally ignored in the early 1940s, to be proclaimed in 1950 a literary genius, perhaps the best American novelist of the century?"[45] The mechanics of Faulkner's rise are associated with a single tenacious critic and publicist: Malcolm Cowley. As late as 1944, Cowley later claimed, at the time he began his exertions on the novelist's behalf, that Faulkner simply didn't exist as a literary commodity. "His seventeen books were effectively out of print and seemed likely to remain in that condition, since there was no public demand for them. How could one speak of Faulkner's value on the literary stock exchange? In 1944 his name wasn't even listed there."[46]

In fact, Cowley's claim—along with some of Schwartz's more hyperbolic formulations—exaggerates for effect. Faulkner had neither been all that unknown nor, for that matter, particularly unsuccessful. His short stories continued to appear in the *Saturday Evening Post*, a large-circulation bastion of Middle America, throughout the thirties and early forties—also in *Scribner's*, *Harper's*, and the *American Mercury*. This was not oblivion. Impressively, he made the cover of *Time* magazine in 1939—at age forty-one—which was accompanied by a generous article including a thorough biography of his life and work; but this was all conceived to coincide with publication of *The Wild Palms* (a book later minimized in the "canonical" Faulkner).[47] Internationally, he was of great interest in the 1930s to writers like Sartre, who wrote on Faulkner, Erskine Caldwell, and hard-boiled crime writers together, to find in American violence and darkness some of the roots of a literary existentialism. The problem was that everyone valued this Faulkner for what would later be seen as all the wrong things. Gothic horror, excitement, degeneracy, disintegration, Southern violence—such were the hallmarks of the Faulkner who had a European coterie reputation but was fast on his way to being forgotten by the intelligentsia in America. He hadn't been uplifting, full of values, a defender of the "human spirit," or necessarily always published as high art. His Hollywood period, in which he contributed to the screenplay of *The Big Sleep* among others, was, from this upended perspective, not a tragic exile for a misunderstood modernist (as we tend to think today), but the natural place for a macabre commercial entertainer to end up (who had, it was true, flirted with Joycean experimental techniques, retarded by a decade, in early books). Schwartz is then absolutely correct to point out that Faulkner had been valued, at home and abroad, for elements in the prewar period (Southern decay and nihilism) that were magically changed in the postwar period to signs of indomitable human spirit and American tradition. The most popular of the earlier books, including the most violent and potboilerish, like *Sanctuary* (1931), would simply, ultimately, be set aside.

And Malcolm Cowley was indeed the principal agent of the change, but his impulse, and his swift success, cannot be explained except by the fact that he had a weight of historical need on his side. He published a series of essays on Faulkner in major journals near the end of World War II, all done in preparation for his editing of Faulkner's oeuvre for Viking, published as *The Portable Faulkner* (1946). Equally important, for the *Portable*, Cowley got permission from Faulkner to let him sift through all of the novelist's books and mosaic them. He reordered the bits and pieces as an epic of fictional Yoknapatawpha County, now running *chronologically* from Native American times to the end of World War II. Cowley then convinced Faulkner to write a new, concluding chronology to support this. Often entertainingly fanciful, this timeline covered all the generations of the Compson family (protagonists of *The Sound and the Fury*) from 1699 to 1945, with denouements to their lives that had not appeared in the books—registering a contemporary freight of meaning, and as if the forces acting on their stories shaped Faulkner's sense of their destinies beyond any given novel.

The mosaic and chronology served Cowley's purpose of insisting on a single underlying pattern and legend that made Faulkner's work a vast historical and social mediation on the values of the South and, ultimately (he suggested), on the values of America. Cowley specifically identified a change in tone in Faulkner's writings dealing with "Modern Times," making the books of the '20s, in his view, into meditations on the loss of humanistic values in the interwar decades, the loss of a "code." "With the old families had vanished the code they tried to observe in their human relations; almost the only code followed by their successors was that of grab-and-git. This was the age of machines, and of persons who reacted like machines, in spastic patterns of stimulus and response."[48]

Following the *Portable*, other critics picked out for themselves aspects of Faulkner's books that were (and still are) recognizably great—even if they were becoming great now for their *humanism* and tradition, rather than their nihilism and fragmentation. One follower who aided this change in focus was Robert Penn Warren, helpfully a Southern critic (and novelist and poet) rather than a Northern carpetbagger like Cowley. It proved essential to Faulkner's success that Faulkner was reclaimed by the South as an honorable son, not a gutter-minded embarrassment. Yet explicitly disagreeing with Cowley's social and Southern framing of the "code" and the deep "pattern," under the guise of dissent, Warren—the true Southerner—managed to shift Faulkner even further into the universally human and the rhetoric of modern human crisis. "It is sometimes said that Faulkner's theme is the disintegration of the Southern traditional life. For instance, [by] Malcolm Cowley, in his fine introduction to the *Portable Faulkner* . . . . I should put the emphasis not in terms of South and North, but in terms of issues common to our modern world."[49] Starting in the *New Republic* in 1946 and continuing through writings of 1950, Warren gave his own evolving diagnosis of Faulkner in terms of the crisis of tradition, the loss of the individual's right relation to society and the state, and, again, the "abstraction" of man, and his modification by mechanization: "The modern world . . . in which the individual has lost his relation to society . . . is a world in which man is the victim of abstraction and mechanism," unlike earlier eras of coherent order. Warren admitted, somewhat tortuously, that Faulkner had never actually *thought* in his books that the earlier, traditional order was good or just. But Warren countered that Faulkner showed there had been at least an *idea* of justice that was not being met today. For "Faulkner's world is" still "full of 'good' people . . . probably a longer list [of them] from Faulkner than from any other modern writer. 'There are good

men everywhere, at all times,' Ike McCaslin says in 'Delta Autumn.'"[50] Here
was affirmation from pessimism, water squeezed from rock:

> That is the central fact in Faulkner's work, the recognition of the com-
> mon human bond, a profound respect for the human. . . .
>
> If respect for the human is the central fact of Faulkner's work, what
> makes that fact significant is that he realizes and dramatizes the difficulty
> of respecting the human. Everything is against it. . . . His hatred of "mod-
> ernism"—and we must quote the word to give it his special meaning—
> arises because he sees it as the enemy of the human, as abstraction, as
> mechanism.[51]

Thus the Faulkner of the '20s was reread through something like Trilling's "reconstitution of the will of man" in the postwar years. Lawrence
Schwartz puts it in the following way, while dating the change precisely to
the same year of Trilling's essay on the obligations of novels, 1948: "[T]he
ideological shift prompted by the war converted Faulkner into the postwar
moralist and symbol of solitary literary genius."[52] But Faulkner, still living,
was able to *participate* in the rereading. Unlike other writers spruced up
for new purposes of criticism, he was available to join in this recasting and
act out the role of grand old gentleman and house writer for the crisis of
man. It is fascinating to see the greater writer converting himself, too,
quite apart from Cowley or Warren's good offices, and with talent. The signal document is his Nobel Prize speech of 1950.

Faulkner's speech bore the title, "I Decline to Accept the End of Man." By
the 1960s it had come to be included in late editions of the *Portable Faulkner* alongside that book's other unique materials, and thus has been read
by generations of students as part of Faulkner's "meaning."[53] First reading
it myself as a high school and college student at the turn of the twenty-first
century (without benefit of suspicion of the crisis of man), I had always
found the speech pretty close to meaningless. Faulkner's short statement
is, of course, very simple, to the point of cliché. He thanks the Swedes for
his award: "I feel that this award was not made to me as a man, but to my
work," Faulkner began, "a life's work in the agony and sweat of the human
spirit." Faulkner warns concretely of the atom bomb and tells younger
writers not to let the new fears undermine their work but to keep the old
truths alive. This language he uses about the old truths is both vaporous
and actually quite particular:

> Until he [the young writer] relearns these things, he will write as though
> he stood among and watched the end of man. I decline to accept the end
> of man. It is easy enough to say that man is immortal simply because he
> will endure. . . . I refuse to accept this. I believe that man will not merely

endure: he will prevail. He is immortal, not because he alone among creatures has an inexhaustible voice, but because he has a soul, a spirit capable of compassion and sacrifice and endurance. . . . The poet's voice need not merely be the record of man, it can be one of the props, the pillars to help him endure and prevail.[54]

Speaking for myself, when in the past I had read "endure," "prevail," "immortal," "inexhaustible," a "soul," "a spirit," "compassion and sacrifice and endurance," counterpoised as if critical distinctions were being made (*not* endure but prevail; *not* a voice but a soul, a spirit), I rolled my eyes, finding the terms empty, and more than empty—hortatory boilerplate, junk. Yet it becomes clear with research that the speech was extremely meaningful to those who encountered it in 1950. It was reprinted in the *New York Herald Tribune Book Review*—then one of the country's major book supplements—and in the *Saturday Review of Literature*, where it was called "magnificent."[55]

The Nobel speech was also made the centerpiece of a special publication meant to link America and Europe, which involved almost the whole spectrum of contemporary highbrow intellectuals of the late 1940s: one forgotten, but very revealing, journal called *Perspectives USA*. If you encounter it in the library, you are immediately put on your guard; even sixty years later, the paper is far too velvety, thick, and unyellowed to be within the means of any legitimate literary magazine. *Perspectives USA* is justifiably forgotten because it was not a "real" domestic journal but an export-ready compilation intended for European readership during postwar reconstruction, a tool in the anti-Soviet "war of ideas." Funded by the Ford Foundation, it reprinted the best of American literary and critical work, to convince European intellectuals of the seriousness of contemporary American civilization, lest they be tempted by Soviet blandishments.[56] In hindsight, the impressive thing about this organ of propaganda is that it really *was* reprinting what history would record as much of the best work of the time, at least the best work then being credentialed by New York: James Baldwin's "Everybody's Protest Novel," Ben Shahn's art (in color), and a section from Saul Bellow's forthcoming *The Adventures of Augie March*. You can view this as a troubling warning of how reputations are made by power or take it as a sunnier lesson on propaganda: sometimes propaganda need only be art. Its publisher was James Laughlin of *New Directions*, then the premier publisher of avant-garde writing in the United States. Lionel Trilling and Malcolm Cowley served as guest editors for whole issues. The journal also possessed representatives on its editorial board from many of the warring groups we have seen in earlier chapters— there is Mortimer Adler, on behalf of Chicago and the Great Books—brought together to present America to the world through its literature.[57] And this publication used the Faulkner Nobel speech not once but twice. As the inaugural statement of the journal's prototype, then the first item of the first issue, it became the premonitory, or, by now, *encoded* message in the bottle that intellectuals and critics floated across the Atlantic—that man would not just endure but prevail.[58]

Next came Hemingway. Ernest Hemingway, formerly a much more titanic and intellectually deified figure than Faulkner, now viewed in the 1940s as a washed-up monument of a previous age, came to be redirected, again with his own active participation, to crisis of man–style humanism.

By the end of World War II, when Hemingway was only in his late forties, his new work seemed entirely played out. In 1947, writes biographer Michael Reynolds, "Hemingway had not published a book in six years and would not for another three. In 1940, he was a lion among writers; in 1947, he was becoming an historical artifact, a relic from the Lost Generation whose early work was entering the academic literary canon."[59] In truth, his reputation as a writer of new works had been on the decline in highbrow circles since the masterpieces of the 1920s, when he had had the support of Gertrude Stein on the Rue de Fleurus. *For Whom the Bell Tolls*, his commercially successful production of 1940, when he was supposedly still a "lion," had received mixed assessments among highbrow critics. *Across the River and Into the Trees* (1950) then was mercilessly attacked. It seemed the final proof that Hemingway's brain had been hopelessly ravaged by his celebrity-fed myth of himself as "Papa." "This novel reads like a parody by the author of his own manner," *Partisan Review*'s Philip Rahv wrote, "a parody so biting that it virtually destroys the mixed social and literary legend of Hemingway that has now endured for nearly three decades."[60] His early works alone survived—those works of disillusion with war, disgust with brave words, rejection of nationalistic deceptions—as gilded classics, part of a fixed 1920s canon to be taught alongside the 1850s canon of the American Renaissance. *A Farewell to Arms*, the best of his '20s novels, was being introduced in a "college edition"—with an introduction, no less, by that same busy scholar-writer, Robert Penn Warren.[61]

It was in this climate that Hemingway produced his own "man" book, *The Old Man and the Sea*. There is tantalizing biographical evidence to suggest that Faulkner's Nobel speech may in fact have been at the origins of Hemingway's writing of the book. "It may have been only coincidence, but [Hemingway] started to write *The Old Man and the Sea* hard on the heels of Faulkner's much publicized Nobel Prize acceptance speech," notes biographer Michael Reynolds—a prize of which Hemingway was deeply covetous. Later, when *The Old Man and the Sea* was complete, the *New York Times* journalist Harvey Breit solicited an innocuous comment on

Hemingway's book from Faulkner for an article, and then passed the comment on to the author. Hemingway sent Breit this scathing response: "He [Faulkner] made a speech, very good. I knew he could never, now, or ever again write up to his speech. I also knew I could write a book better and straighter than his speech and without tricks or rhetoric."[62]

The resulting slim volume pitted a lone fisherman against elemental nature and adversity—expressed in the form of a giant marlin and trailing sharks. This was the discourse of man at its most reduced: old man faces nature, old man will endure. (It may also have been a parable of Hemingway's relation to his own writing, like pulling up a marlin, and to the critics, the sharks who destroyed it with scores of cowardly bites.)[63] *Life* magazine, known for its denunciations of novelists who failed to affirm American successes (which it often phrased as "human" successes), took the unprecedented step of printing the entire *Old Man and the Sea*, without advertising interruption, in their first fall issue, September 1, 1952. The editors said of the book, "It is a tragedy, but it tells of the nobility of man. Hemingway's work may be disaster-haunted, but his heroes face up to disaster nobly." Unable to resist a dig at the younger generation, they went on: "If he has influenced any of the twisted young men now writing fiction, he hasn't influenced them enough in this respect."[64]

Hemingway himself was turned into a kind of incarnation of the old fisherman. "Old Man Hemingway has produced a masterpiece and won back the championship," James Michener declared in a blurb: "He's still the pappy of us all."[65] The issue featuring the novel was *Life*'s largest print run in history, according to Reynolds—five *million* copies were said to have sold out. This feat was followed six days later by *The Old Man and the Sea*'s book publication, a Book-of-the-Month Club edition, and twenty-six weeks on the *New York Times* best-seller list.[66] The success of the short fable is often credited with finally helping Hemingway earn the Nobel Prize in 1954.

FORMAL CUL DE SACS, EXPERIMENTS WITH MAN: *THE OLD MAN AND THE SEA* AND *A FABLE* AS NOVELS OF MAN

In fairness, however, both of the actual new *books* that Hemingway and Faulkner produced to meet the challenge of a literature about the "will of man" are quite a bit more interesting and significant, at least to my mind, than their publicity and reception indicate. Both writers, as it turned out, really could "write a book better" than any single speech, even a speech as celebrated as Faulkner's. But both also chose immediately obvious or logical forms for how, within the parameters of the novel, a writer might try to render an abstract, universal man, and then celebrate the best parts of his permanent nature; and both proved, by a kind of exhaustion of these logical possibilities, simply within the duration of their single texts, that neither method, fish-tale and parable, was really going to work or provide a wider model. The books, in formal terms, discovered dead ends.

I'd like to take a moment to look at these books. As uncomprehending as the reception of *The Old Man and the Sea* could be—along with its subsequent assimilation to the canon of juvenile literature (in the category of adult books with short words and apparently uplifting messages)— Hemingway's boasts for his work were mostly justified. It is frequently brilliant.

The Old Man and the Sea manifested one way of attacking the "question of man"—the "man alone" route, or a purely subtractive plot. To get to the essence of man, it instructed removing one specimen from humankind and testing him, as if in a laboratory or, perhaps more pertinent, as man was tested in the book of Job.

Hemingway's book does not abstract man initially, but that is its end goal. We learn at the beginning that the protagonist is an old fisherman with many specific traits: he is named Santiago, is Spanish-speaking, Cuban, a baseball fan, and a sailor who once saw the coast of Africa in his younger years as a crewman on a big boat. He has been eighty-four days on the ocean without catching a fish. On his tiny skiff, his mast is "patched with flour sacks and, furled, it looked like the flag of permanent defeat."[67] But the old man wants to let his banner fly once more: "Everything about him was old except his eyes and they were the same color as the sea and were cheerful and undefeated" (10). At first, this feels like a novella of human rights, if such a thing can be imagined from Hemingway: a noble old man who can barely feed himself, who lives a subsistence life from the unreliable sea, in the midst of an advanced world and in a tourist town in Cuba, which could easily feed him. He sets sail from under the shadow of the Terrace where famous celebrities drink, and where he can occasionally see the vacationing managers from the baseball leagues and listen to the rich American mainland on the radio. As he debates baseball with his young devotee Manolin, in Hemingway's semicomic, grandiose transcription of Spanish, he seems like an anthropological subject ready for first world largesse:

"The Yankees cannot lose."
"But I fear the Indians of Cleveland."
"Have faith in the Yankees my son. Think of the great DiMaggio."
"I fear both the Tigers of Detroit and the Indians of Cleveland."
"Be careful or you will fear even the Reds of Cincinnati and the White Sox of Chicago." (17)

Surely such a man could use the benefits of the rest of the first world—freedom from want in his old age, freedom from fear, the benefits of a post-subsistence civilization. But Hemingway turns out not to be interested in any help for Santiago. The man, or "man," is just fine as he is. Hemingway puts the old man out on the water, alone, in his skiff. The sailor rows out to where the sea is deep, far beyond all other boats. Hemingway might equally have put a character on the moon; he seems to be in complete isolation. Then commences an incredible tour de force of natural description, as the fisherman watches flying fish, waterbirds, weather, signs of dolphins, and hints of prey fish, in a sort of descriptive argument that isolated man's true pairing is not with other men but with nature: "He looked across the sea and knew how alone he was. . . . The clouds were building up now for the trade wind and he looked ahead and saw a flight of wild ducks etching themselves against the sky over the water, then blurring, then etching again and he knew no man was ever alone on the sea" (60–61).

From this pairing of man and nature, however, the book strips down to a reduced pairing of man and his own body. A marlin strikes the old man's line, and it is so enormous that it carries his boat far out to sea and leads him to fight it for days. Hemingway's novel begins to ring changes on that key word "endure" from Faulkner's Nobel speech and from Faulkner's earlier writing (most famously, the last line of *The Sound and the Fury*), first as the old man "tried not to think but only to endure" (47), but later, in the fight, "I will show him [the fish] what a man can do and what a man endures" (66). The book becomes a rare depiction of physical pain in work, and the work that the body, rather than the mind, can do. "'Don't think, old man,' he said to himself" (66); instead, he deals with the cramp in his hand, the cuts on his palms, the lashing and pulling on his back from the fishing line, his eating sickening raw fish flesh to gain strength, the "treachery of one's own body" (61) in its risk of cramps, "diarrhoea," vomiting, up through his near blackouts in the final battle with the fish. Man alone turns out to be a creature of work and pain, as the fish is a creature of hunting and pain—man has a few more tricks but is no different. "I must hold his pain where it is, he thought. Mine does not matter. I can control mine. But his pain could drive him mad" (88). When the old man has won, of course, he learns that there are evil parasites in the world who don't understand man's solitude and its code of brotherly killing. Riding home with the beautiful catch lashed alongside, the marlin is attacked by schools of sharks and, though the old man kills as many sharks as he can, the fish is picked to its bones by the mass in the night.

Man as a creature of nature; man as a bearer of pain; man utterly alone, doing what he was "born to do." This is one way of dramatizing or even solving the questions of man, by insisting that anyone out of touch with basic nature—understood as the struggle to honorably kill and subdue its wildness and perhaps be killed in turn—has lost real humanity. The book ends with a sudden turn to two idiot tourists who see the fish skeleton: they can't even tell it was a marlin (honorable nature) and not a shark (dishonorable nature). Hemingway's is one way of abstracting the "human condition," writing a book of maximum isolation in which a minimal natural "code" is adumbrated. But this leaves the question of the rest of the world. "Man" can't lead his whole existence out of sight of land. Hemingway also, irresistibly and puzzlingly, generates a Christian allegory in the final pages while the old man sails home. When the sharks come, it is for the man as if he were "feeling the nail go through his hands and into the wood" (107). From the rocks of the harbor, "he shouldered the mast and started to climb," and "at the top he fell and lay for some time with the mast across his shoulder"; "he had to sit down five times before he reached his shack" (121); "[t]hen he lay [and] . . . slept face down on the newspapers with his arms out straight and the palms of his hands up" (121–22). Here in Cuba is a mini-Calvary. Santiago is made Christlike. Are all men, then, Christ? Or is "man himself," if he gives in to his suffering and holds on to his will to suffer, Christ, dying for the rest of us fallen tourists of existence? Or did writers as good as Hemingway (on their home ground) ultimately not feel confident to give a meaning to the pure stripping-down of man himself without resorting to an ambiguous religious faith?

William Faulkner went on in the years after his Nobel speech to publish the long novel *A Fable* and the play *Requiem for a Nun* (the latter a pious follow-up to the famously scandalous *Sanctuary*). The "question that is raised by Faulkner's much-quoted Nobel speech, by the moralistic sequel to *Sanctuary* and by *A Fable*," Maxwell Geismar noted at the time, "is of course that of his return to 'faith.' "[68] This isn't quite right—though a question one might wish to ask both of these great Lost Generation writers, Hemingway and Faulkner, who tried to produce books of man, is why they each had to turn one of their central characters into an imitation of Christ. For *A Fable* also presents that problem—indeed, it has been most frequently analyzed for its overpowering Christian allegory, which is, however, I think, just one aspect of its plot. The other part is connected, again, to the formal problem of whether a novel can ever deal with a strictly abstract, universalized man.

In a simple comparison of method, where Hemingway's fable was subtractive, Faulkner's *A Fable* is proliferative. The book's initial question is whether man as an unknown, natural quantity, could stop a war despite all the layers of social authority sustaining the conflict and urging men to it.[69] The opening conceit is that in 1916, on the German western front of World War I, a regiment of French troops sits still in its dugouts and does not move when ordered to attack, following two years of bloody stalemate. Their German opposition, facing the undefended opening, fails to counter-attack. An inexplicable stillness spreads down both lines until, inertly, inarticulately, this natural human refusal stops the whole mechanism of war. "[N]o sign nor signal from man to man, but the entire three thousand spread one-man deep across a whole regimental front, acting without intercommunication *as one man*"—because the collective essence simply wills it.[70] *A Fable* tries to grasp abstract man first by treating him in the mass, in groups and crowds—neither completely personified as a simple creature of the whole nor highlighted through single exemplars pulled out of the crowd—which will represent the mystery of whatever sort of will man has in common. Huge crowds gather in the opening chapter, filling a town, emptying a region, to wail and moan as they watch the magical original regiment, now made prisoners by their officers, pour into a prison camp. The depictions of de-individualized and speechless (though not soundless) human beings, exerting will unconsciously, grow out of Faulkner's older techniques of "the town's" way of knowing collectively in *Absalom, Absalom* or *Light in August*. There they were background to characters; here, man, in this mass, is the foreground of the novel.

Yet the temptation to add witnesses, speakers, individuals, and novelistic centers quickly overpowers the oddity of the first conceit and generates a different kind of book. *A Fable* adds plot upon plot and layer upon layer—of generals, bureaucrats, observers; investigators (like "the runner," the flyer, the "quartermaster general")—and, in the only element that is usually remembered about the book, a second Christ, to make a detailed "fable"-like Christian allegory out of what would otherwise be just abstract questioning. The suspense turns on whether the truth of the cessation of the war can be rightfully identified with man or whether the generals will propagandize it as a temporary cease-fire of their own making—after which they can wait a week and restart the violence. The telling of this drama, however, cannot come from man himself, in the mass, but comes instead entirely from those *opposed* to this life of man. *A Fable*'s life stories come to be those of the generals and officers, each of whom "had sold his birthright in the race of man" (10). Their stories are fascinating but clearly their effort is on the wrong side: "Let the whole vast moil and seethe of man confederate in stopping wars if they wish, so long as we can prevent them from learning that they have done so" (54). The book starts to seem like a machine that can't stop creating these rootless speeches about man by his enemies—it is the only way the author can characterize his real target. The kind of speechless but willful man in-the-mass that Faulkner is aiming at proves to be, fictionally, formally unrepresentable.

Faulkner tries assorted specimen-observers and spokesmen for man in-the-mass, then kills them off like failed prototypes. There is the "runner," an ex-officer who returns to the ranks to be with the men and learn about them. There is an old Negro preacher from the Deep South whom Faulkner, in a seeming act of desperation, imports to France as if from an earlier book, making him a witness for 'man.'" The runner and the preacher band together in a late plan to *prove* that man, not the generals, stopped the war ("Don't you see . . . they can't afford to . . . let us stop it. . . . If they ever let us find out that we can stop a war as simply as men tired of digging a ditch decide calmly and quietly to stop digging the ditch—" [311]). The two run out to No Man's Land to embrace the enemy and are obliterated by both sides' artillery. With these proxies in smithereens, the plot turns from such relatively realistic surrogates for man toward its second Christ, Faulkner's alternative.

The story of the second Christ is staged as a conflict between the old generalissimo of France, who seems to represent omnipotent fate, and the Christ-figure, the corporal, who apparently organized the mass resistance just by moving among the men. This corporal has twelve disciples. He is followed by three women, Marthe, Marya, and an unnamed Magdalen. During a last supper in the prison, one of his disciples has betrayed him, and another denies him. By a complicated set of discoveries, the corporal proves to be the biological son of the omniscient old general—a cruel God the Father type. Or is he a Satan? In lengthy philosophical conversations, the old general tries to convince (or tempt?) the corporal to stick with the earthly order and *not* sacrifice himself in the name of man. "[W]e are two articulations," the old general says of the two of them, lapsing into synopsis, "postulated, not so much to defend as to test two inimical conditions. . . . I champion of this mundane earth . . . ; you champion of an esoteric realm of man's baseless hopes and his infinite capacity—no: passion—for unfact" (348). The son of man refuses to accept the old general's "fact" against man's "hope," so he is tied to a wooden post between two criminals and shot. His corpse is carried home by the three women and placed in a tomb, only to disappear, inevitably, in a blast when the war resumes upon his burial ground.

The clever denouement of the book, which was Faulkner's original germ of the story in 1944, is rendered perfunctorily in the last chapters: the strangely intact body of the Christ-figure, through a series of further coincidences, comes to be entombed by France as the Unknown Soldier, which is to say, perhaps, symbolically, that Christ remains within the unknown, unspecifiable everyman, who the nation wrongly believes it possesses for its own glory; and those who suffer in war die for us all. Yet in the very last pages, the book ends with the triumphant burial of the general within the Invalides, God the father, who indeed kept the war going to the end he had already decreed—"(six months after the false armistice in May, that curious week's holiday which the war had taken which had been so false that they remembered it only as phenomenon)"—while the actions of man, not to mention the son of man, seem forgotten. A half-blown-apart amputee, apparently the "runner" (not dead yet!), evidently there to represent the memory of man, interrupts the funeral, is beaten by a mob of ordinary people, and ends the book vowing "I'm not going to die. Never"—as, in his disfigured person, the memory of man goes on (437).

"[T]he book is unlikely to interest readers except as an indication of where Faulkner's imagination wandered in the decade 1944–1954," drily writes Faulkner's most recent biographer, Jay Parini.[71] That may be so. For our purposes, though, it holds interest as the book that occupied Faulkner in the period of the public rise of the discourse of the crisis of man, his Nobel success, the "I Decline to Accept the End of Man" speech, and all the rereadings of him as a redemptive humanist. Its composition neatly covers the metamorphosis begun by Cowley's first labors to rework Faulkner's legacy for the *Portable* (their correspondence started in 1944) and ended by Hemingway's acquisition of the Nobel Prize (1954).[72] *A Fable* is equally interesting, as a formal object, for its proof of the insufficiency and failure of another set of logical strategies by which to write into the novel a vision of the will of abstract, universal man.[73] Like Hemingway, Faulkner turned to a literary expression of the "enduring" quality of man at a maximum of pain and suffering: in the stasis of trench warfare. He did it with a hope to answer some of the most obvious questions of his time—Norman Cousins's query (from 1945, after the bomb dropped) of whether it was in the nature of man to make wars or in the nature of man to stop them; whether something in man could forestall mass death regardless of officers and politicians; and what precisely it *was* in man that had control of events, in the form of will. Faulkner tried to do the rendering in the mass, but had to turn to surrogates, including the devils themselves (the generals) who deny man, or else the Christ, incredibly lifeless and fleshless as a character, who is to redeem them but gets (mostly) forgotten.

The extreme darkness of the later parts of *A Fable* and its seeming knowledge that it is a failure as a novel about man are captured in one of the most astonishing passages of the book: the culmination of the interview between the general and his son, which it is important to read in its proper context. Here, Faulkner explicitly rewrites his Nobel Prize speech, using almost exactly the same words, but with perspectives reversed, so that the old general declares that only man's *folly* will endure. One must have in one's ear the echoes of Faulkner's hopeful speech to hear the gruesome, parodic self-repudiation in *A Fable*. (That speech again: "I believe that man will not merely endure: he will prevail. He is immortal, not because he alone among creatures has an inexhaustible voice, but because he has a soul, a spirit capable of compassion and sacrifice and endurance.") The old general has been predicting instead a future of monstrous tanks, jet aircraft, metal shells for men, leaving man a worm inside them, a technics out of his control, "his own frankenstein which roasts him alive with heat, asphyxiates him with speed, wrenches loose his still-living entrails in the ferocity of its prey-seeking stoop" (353–54), until man

"crawls out of his cooling burrow to crouch . . . beneath a clangorous rain of dials and meters and switches and bloodless fragments of metal epidermis, to watch the final two of them [i.e., his metal war-monsters] engaged in the last gigantic wrestling against the final and dying sky robbed even of darkness and filled with the inflectionless uproar of the two mechanical voices bellowing at each other polysyllabic and verbless patriotic nonsense. Oh yes, [man] will survive it because he has that in him which will endure . . . because already the next star in the blue immensity of space will be already clamorous with the uproar of his debarkation, his puny and inexhaustible voice still talking, still planning . . . his voice, planning still to build something higher and faster and louder; more efficient and louder and faster than ever before, yet it too inherent with the same old primordial fault since it too in the end will fail to eradicate him from the earth. I don't fear man. I do better: I respect and admire him. And pride: I am ten times prouder of that immortality which he does possess than ever he of that heavenly one of his delusion. Because man and his folly—"

"Will endure," the corporal said.

"They will do more," the old general said proudly. "They will prevail." (354)

It was his American critics and admirers who returned Faulkner to simple man and faith—and he was ready to go along, up to a point, though not always when one read him carefully (as in this passage of *A Fable*), or when he seemed to lose that simple faith himself. Faulkner had become, for Americans, the representative of a badly needed native tradition, a Southern history, ancient wounds, fused with avant-garde technique and redeemed by apparent piety. Despite mediocre or uncomprehending reviews, committees awarded *A Fable* both the National Book Award and the Pulitzer Prize.

OTHER CANDIDATES

Richard Wright, too, wrote his own novel of the crisis of man while an expatriate in France, a book usually simply classified as "existentialist." This was *The Outsider* (1953).[74] Wright's protagonist, Cross Damon ("To think I named you Cross after the cross of Jesus!" says his mother [391]), a failed philosophy major at the University of Chicago, is trapped between his angry wife and pregnant lover and has just taken out a crippling loan from his bosses at the post office. Thanks to a lucky subway accident, he is assumed dead, sheds all ties, and moves with pockets full of money to New York City where, except for his African Americannness (which gives him privileged lucidity as an "outsider"), he stands as unmarked "modern man" in total freedom—man himself. He uses his freedom to deliver an impressive number of soliloquies. "The question summed itself up: What's a man? He had unknowingly set himself a project of no less magnitude than contained in that awful question" (460–61). "'Maybe man is nothing in particular,' Cross said gropingly. 'Maybe that's the terror of it. Man may be just anything at all'" (507). "He was without a name, a past, a future; no promises or pledges bound him to those about him. He had to become human . . . Dimly he realized that his dilemma, though personal, bore the mark of the general" (509). The plot resumes once Cross gets involved with the Communist Party, and Wright falls into concerns that had plagued him personally since his split with Stalinism. Finding the Communists corrupt, Cross begins playing God, killing off local racist fascists and Communist commissars alike—which allows the book to enter into meditations on "totalitarianism" juxtaposed with the cursed freedom of man the existentialist, in the "dilemma of the ethical criminal" (743) committed to actes gratuites in the midst of a historical crisis of human will: "Today we are in the midst of that crisis . . . The real world stands at last before our eyes and we don't want to look at it, don't know how to live in it; it terrifies us" (755).

Finally Cross is betrayed and murdered by the Communists, though not before having read "Nietzsche, Hegel, Jaspers, Heidegger, Husserl, Kierkegaard, [and] Dostoevsky" (820), as is revealed by the detective who also invites him to deliver a muddled, deathbed prophecy: "'Is there anything, Damon, you want me to tell anybody?' . . . 'I wish I had some way to give the meaning of my life to others . . . To make a bridge from man to man . . . Starting from scratch every time is . . . is no good. . . . Man is all we've got . . . Man is returning to the earth . . . The real men, the last men are coming . . .'" (840).

The only major figure the new publicists had not gotten to was the longest-standing hero of Lost Generation American modernism, a more recalcitrant, less commercially minded writer and a poet—T. S. Eliot. Eliot, as we have seen in chapter 2, was unique among these writers for having genuinely participated, as a thinker, poet, and public figure, in the earlier crisis of man discourse. He had already received his Nobel in 1948. He would continue in the '50s to present an incipient Christian orthodoxy and high-art apolitical formalism to those who wanted it, but he had nothing to prove.

So it is comic, and instructive, to note an attempt made in the postwar years to publicize Eliot in line with a more simpleminded humanist (and US nationalist) dispensation. *Time* magazine gave Eliot its cover in 1950, and a long biographical article, on the occasion of one of his verse plays, *The Cocktail Party*, opening in New York. The poet who had rejected America, its values, and its unchurchy religion would be championed on the grounds of his defense of civilization, man, and of religion generally. *Time:* "Why should anybody want to meet Mr. Eliot—even halfway? More particularly, why should Americans bother about this Missouri-born American who talks like an Englishman, has not lived in the U.S. for the past 36 years, and gave up his U.S. citizenship to become a British subject? . . . Perhaps the simplest answer is: Because T. S. Eliot is a civilized man." *Time* was equally interested in his "faith," which they praised: "Eliot is a Christian and therefore in a sense a 'pessimist' about the nature of man. Yet in his 'pessimism' Eliot is far more hopeful about man's future than most of the more secular prophets." Annoying though it might be that the St. Louis native now had to be shared with England, was High Church, and wanted a king, it was useful that he formed a contemporary bridge of American hope, faith, and culture to European civilization.[75]

In short, the Lost Generation writers were briefly reconstructed for a humanistic modernism. The new works this spawned were not lastingly convincing, but they didn't need to be. Critics found enough depth in the *longue durée* of these writers' careers, and enough fodder in new perspectives on their '20s masterpieces, to have a humanistic purchase on living writers who could definitely be looked to for answers about the nature of man. By the mid-1950s—specifically, during the years 1954–57—the latest arriving entrant, Faulkner, became the subject of a greater number of books, articles, and monographs in the *Modern Language Association* bibliographies, the standard record of all literary criticism in America, than any other living writer in English, followed next by Eliot and Hemingway.[76] Critics of the contemporary novel at midcentury had some extra room to be disappointed in new works, because they had writers in place already who could be reinterpreted and even redirected to speak simply and stolidly to the need for "values"—leaving younger writers more annoyed and rivalrous than ever.

THE YOUNG WRITERS' IMPASSE: FRUSTRATION AND DEPENDENCE

The "death of the novel" and the extended humanist canon of prewar modernists had thus set up an awkward and unprecedented situation for young American writers. Esteem for the novel and the novelist, in the abstract, was at a peak. Critics said they wanted new novels. They felt, from the impulses of the crisis of man, that they needed the novel to do more than entertain or even reflect the tenor of the times; they needed a revitalization of the will of man. Yet their intellectual concepts told them man and his conditions might have changed. The successful culmination of decades of Americanist literary excavation in a closed canon of greats, from Hawthorne to Faulkner—with the living, second half of that canon willing to tailor itself to suit the new demands—didn't very desperately require, or even leave much room for, the work of new, young writers. Thus the "death of the novel" thesis, which had behind it essentially intellectual or philosophical assumptions drawn from the crisis of man, became implicated in practical matters of hope and disappointment, expectation and opportunity, and competition and resentment within the literary field. The young Norman Mailer, always the most rivalrous and the most mischievous, took the high tone of all the discussions of the heroes of the '20s down to a bass note: "Dare one mention that their work since World War II has been singularly barren and flatulent?"[77]

Such anger will bubble up again later for this book's central writers, principally when they enjoy periods of individual triumph in the 1950s (and cheer one another's triumphs), rather than earlier in the '40s when they are still more reliant on critics and therefore couldn't always afford to speak their mind. As we will see in successive chapters, it was Bellow who crowed, upon Ralph Ellison's success with *Invisible Man*, that the novel was not so dead after all: "So many hands have been busy at the interment of the novel . . . that I can't help feeling elated when a resurrection occurs."[78] Indeed, in 1957, five years later, after Bellow's own comparable triumph with *The Adventures of Augie March*, the first three of our study's central fiction writers—Saul Bellow, Ralph Ellison, and Flannery O'Connor—all contributed to a volume edited by the reformed Marxist critic Granville Hicks, which he titled *The Living Novel*.

This book was specifically a rebuke to the now nearly decade-old renewed "death of the novel" thesis. "The idea that there should be such a book grew out of the distress I felt on reading one more pronouncement— it doesn't matter whose—on the death of the novel," Hicks wrote. "How . . . could I explain this solemn assertion, repeated every few weeks by somebody or other, that the novel was dying if not quite dead?"[79] Hicks's book included only working novelists, letting them answer back. In Saul Bellow's contribution, he returned to the original 1948 provocation and finally had a forum to attack Lionel Trilling, if not by name then by university affiliation, with "Morningside Heights" standing in for Columbia:

> Finished! We have heard this from Valéry and from T. S. Eliot, from Ortega and Oswald Spengler, and most recently from the summit of Morningside Heights. We are supposed to be done for.... For every poet now there are a hundred custodians and doctors of literature, and dozens of undertakers measuring away at coffins.
>
> The novelist has been trained to take words seriously, and he thinks he is hearing words of high seriousness. He believes it is the voice of high seriousness saying, "Obsolete. Finished." But what if it were to prove the voice of low seriousness instead?[80]

Hicks was correct to say that the writers were being pestered from two sides: "Our novelists, it becomes clear, are not altogether happy about their present situation. They are disturbed both by the talk in highbrow circles about the death of the novel and by the middlebrow demands for affirmative fiction useful for propaganda purposes."[81] O'Connor, for her part, contributed her essay "The Fiction Writer and His Country" to his book. The essay famously opens with her particular and quite public annoyance with *Life* and its "slick" affirmative demands for "spiritual purpose," though not spiritual purpose of *her* kind.[82] Ellison delivered the calmest and most learned essay in the book in "Society, Morality, and the Novel," but still took issue with Trilling at length for his reduction of the American novel to the novel of manners, gently rebuked Cowley for his "reduction of the meaning of Faulkner's" stories in the *Portable* (while praising Cowley's resurrection of Faulkner's reputation), and even-handedly probed the differences of obligation between critics and writers to explain "something of why the novelists keep writing despite the current attempts to legislate to the novel a quiet death."[83]

Ultimately, the adoption by creative writers of the problems of the crisis of man brought to them through this intervening discourse of the death of the novel (which it was their obligation to prove wrong), was confounded with an intense status conflict with the new cadres of intellectually powerful critics who praised the novel as a privileged medium but still seemed to set their own pronouncements above its concrete products. Who would get to speak for man, or the novel? Who got to choose who would say what, and what must the chosen people say? The critics dominated the choice of new fiction that mattered, but they couldn't produce that fiction themselves. The novelists who came to matter were often closely connected to critics and intellectuals with a standing reputation (Bellow and Ellison were connected to Alfred Kazin, Delmore Schwartz, Kenneth Burke, and even Lionel Trilling; O'Connor to the translators and writers Robert and Sally Fitzgerald, poet Robert Lowell, and critic Elizabeth Hardwick, and a whole circle around the literary colony at Yaddo). Yet the novelists had to find ways to differentiate themselves from the critics, even if only to fulfill the critics' continued expectations for the writer as a solitary genius—independent, freedom-loving, and somewhat primitive—who would stand for America and independent human values, not for criticism. This was the double or triple bind of the fiction writer at the apex of the novel's twentieth-century cultural power (as storyteller, thinker, and inspired oracle). It is no accident that when those writers emerged who best pleased critics in their demands about the crisis of man (Ellison, Bellow, and in other ways O'Connor and Pynchon), their books—read closely—are often much more troubling about that discourse's possibilities than the contemporary critics who praised them ever really came to understand.

EVERYBODY'S ALTERNATIVE: THE KAFKA CULT AND AN ANTINATURALISTIC HUMANISM

I can't move on to those authors' works without one major caveat, however. It's not the case that *no* new literature besides the revived modernists immediately fulfilled the demands for expression of the crisis of man from the period of the war forward (until figures like Bellow and Ellison were able to break through and satisfy those demands). It's just that one key exemplar who did is not included in histories of *American* literature in the twentieth century, though he probably should be. Starting at the end of the 1930s and the dawn of the war, and intensifying at the end of World War II and in the early postwar period, something truly unexpected occurred: the discovery and enshrining of Franz Kafka, a Czech Jewish writer of German prose who belonged to no clique or obvious tradition, as a master equal to the familiar Western European and American modernists.

Kafka became one of the single most important hidden influences on American fiction, as great as Hemingway and Faulkner, in the postwar years and even up to the present day. He also helped break the impasse between writers and critics by his example or mere existence, rather than by any particular literary school he gave rise to. He became an inspiration by showing what was possible, and a free-floating resource because he really belonged to no one (despite everyone's attempts to claim him). He, too, wrote "fables," but with a different and liberating character.

Figures best known as intellectuals were deeply involved in Kafka's initial rise in America. Hannah Arendt personally oversaw English publication of his writing at Schocken, especially his *Diaries*, while she was editor there from 1946 to 1948 (she even assisted in translation). Clement

Greenberg, the most important art critic of the American midcentury—
theorist and publicist of abstract expressionism—translated Kafka on several occasions, as did his brother, Martin Greenberg, of the journal *Commentary*. James Burnham, the social theorist who had predicted "the
managerial revolution" in which bureaucracy would come to dominate
both the Communist East and capitalist West, hailed Kafka as a literary
genius of the times.[84] The much more utopian radical Paul Goodman (a
literary, social, and educational critic) wrote a fine early book entirely on
Kafka.[85]

These names would suggest that Kafka was purely a New York Intellectual possession. Yet Kafka was also accessible to other groups—especially
as material for Christian theology. By 1940, the *Southern Review*, a journal at Vanderbilt edited by Charles W. Pipkin with Cleanth Brooks and
Robert Penn Warren, had already picked up an essay called "'The Trial'
and the Theology of Crisis," whose author determined that Kafka had produced "[a]n eschatological novel—an allegory of man's relations with God
in terms of a Calvinistic theology," "an elaborate parable [of] the basic principles of a modern system of theology, erected on the startling teachings" of Kierkegaard and best understood through the great neoorthodox
theologian Karl Barth.[86] Indeed, a series of such Christianizing efforts
written both in England and America made up a large part of a 1946 anthology of the then-extant critical writing on Kafka, Angel Flores's *The Kafka
Problem*.[87]

By all parties, Jewish and Christian, religious and secular, Kafka's works
were understood to be parables of "modern man." Some took Kafka as a
theologian, others as a social analyst. For Hannah Arendt, he captured the
evils of an administered world: "The generation of the forties, and especially those who have the doubtful advantage of having lived under the
most terrible regime history has so far produced, know that the terror
of Kafka is adequate to the true nature of the thing called bureaucracy—
the replacing of government by administration and of laws by arbitrary
decrees. . . . Kafka's so-called prophecies were but a sober analysis of underlying structures which today have come into the open."[88] For James
Burnham, "[T]he condition of Kafka's hero is not in the least fantastic or
peculiar. It is exactly and literally the human condition."[89]

Kafka's work naturally seemed to contemporaries to prefigure the Holocaust ("the catastrophe . . . which Kafka foresaw here and there in his
work with startling exactitude of detail," wrote Heinz Politzer[90]), especially in its mood of persecution and hyperrational insanity. Indeed, his
sisters and their families were murdered in Auschwitz, a fate Kafka was
spared only by dying young of tuberculosis. He seemed to show the condition of the individual under a continuous line of totalitarians—first Hitler

in Western Europe, now Stalin in the East—with Kafka usefully, geographically, in Prague, Czechoslovakia, on the border between them. As readers looked around America, Kafka's work gave a picture of alienation and loneliness under technology or without God. The name most consistently given to the puzzle Kafka depicted was that peculiar catchphrase of the era, already quoted from Burnham: the contemporary, crisis-ridden "human condition."

This moment of attachment of Kafka to the crisis of man can be seen in fine relief against a slightly earlier moment of the interwar period when he was completely irrelevant to Americans. Kafka died in 1924. His friend and publicist, Max Brod, energetically promoted Kafka's work as a new contribution to the avant-garde. Kafka's first appearances in English were events of zero consequence. The transatlantic modernist journal *transition*, a pillar of Paris–New York avant-gardism in the twenties, known for its early publication of Joyce's *Work in Progress* (later *Finnegan's Wake*), Gertrude Stein's *Tender Buttons*, and Hemingway's "Hills Like White Elephants," translated some short stories of Kafka's without fanfare—the first in 1928, the second in 1932. They seem not to have stood out beyond work of other avant-gardists. Kafka's *The Castle* was brought out in New York by Alfred A. Knopf in 1930, a sign that he was moving through high-level, but likely purely writerly, channels. It made no discernable impact.

In 1937, a different phase of Kafka reception erupted. Knopf published a second novel, *The Trial*, which would become the mainstay of all critical discussions and explanations of Kafka's significance for the next twenty years. The *Partisan Review*, then just restarting as an independent publication (after its break with the Communist Party), took up Kafka as one of its central discoveries and a centerpiece of its worldview. In the very first issue after the 1937 relaunch, the assigned reviewer, F. W. Dupee, admitted he was still puzzled by *The Trial*, but the editors assigned increasing importance to its author. Within a few months, they were advertising new publications of biographical information on Kafka ("specially translated for *Partisan Review*"), and could speak of "the characteristic Kafkian art" (though they weren't yet quite ready to describe it in words).[91] A few months after that, now apparently in a heated competition with *transition* for new publications of Kafka, they advertised his work as their lead coming attraction: "BLUMFELD, AN ELDERLY BACHELOR a hitherto untranslated long story by FRANZ KAFKA."[92]

It's not entirely evident at first *what* had happened in 1937, and the years near the start of World War II, to make Kafka erupt, but something surely had.[93] The practical means of transfer has to have been German intellectuals who found something in Kafka in the late '30s that spoke initially to their own situation, which the émigrés were able to impress upon the

Americans—who then responded on their own, for their own reasons, and all the more vividly during the war. For Kafka's work took on an American life quite quickly, and by the end of the 1940s had become absolutely central.[94] Journalists and critics then spoke of the "Kafka cult" (Irving Howe), "the amazing cults of Kafka and Kierkegaard" (John Berryman), "the present Kafka boom" (Heinz Politzer), or the "vogue for Kafka" (Elliot Cohen, the editor of *Commentary*).[95] *Kafka Was the Rage* is the title the bohemian bookseller and later book reviewer Anatole Broyard gave to his memoir of the era.[96]

Contemporary critics spoke of the "cult" without surprise, as if it were familiar and acknowledged, even when they were unsympathetic to it. Edmund Wilson identified himself with an earlier generation in producing the only specimen I've seen of backlash against "the cultists of Kafka." His article of 1947 noted the suddenness and depth of the consensus on the Czech author, as well as suggesting some explanations for its puzzling occurrence. In "A Dissenting Opinion on Kafka," Wilson wrote, "Since the publication in English of *The Trial* in 1937 (*The Castle* came out in 1930 but did not attract much attention), Kafka's reputation and influence have been growing till his figure has been projected on the consciousness of our literary reviews on a scale which gives the illusion that he is a writer of towering stature."[97] "Some of his short stories are absolutely first-rate, comparable to Gogol's and Poe's," Wilson admitted, "[a]nd Kafka's novels have exploited a vein of the comedy and pathos of futile effort which is likely to make 'Kafka-esque' a permanent word."[98] (Wilson was right in his expectation.) But this older champion of American modernism could not accept the overinvestment that intellectuals of all kinds were making in Kafka as someone *more* than a writer. "One realizes that [for them] it is not merely a question of appreciating Kafka as a poet who gives expression for the intellectuals to their emotions of helplessness and self-contempt but of building him up as a theologian and saint."[99] "[M]ust we really, as his admirers pretend, accept the plights of Kafka's abject heroes as parables of the human condition?"[100]

Wilson was surprisingly alone in his objections, but correct, in some sense, in his instinctive suspicions. It's hard to think of another author who was accepted so unequivocally as Kafka, so quickly, and yet who, himself, in his work, was so unique, peculiar, and deeply, satisfyingly un-American—at least on the surface of things. (For analogues, one would have to look to Gabriel García Márquez in the 1980s or Roberto Bolaño in the 2000s.) Surely this, too, was a part of his appeal in the 1940s. Kafka provided a way to move out of conventional categories and literary cliques while answering immediate problems. His works showed individuals menaced or terrified by something absurd—symbolic, rootless, and all-encompassing—

that undid them as human beings (in the famous *The Metamorphosis*, when Gregor Samsa wakes up as a bug), or as whole, unviolated bodies ("In the Penal Colony," "The Hunger Artist"), or as citizens subject to comprehensible laws and rights (*The Trial*). Yet these fragmentary stories, inexplicable transformations, bureaucratic persecutions, and ominous surrealisms, rendered ultrarealistically, offered a modernism that was *not* like the usual Western European version but was clearly new (even if it dated to several decades earlier), and clearly, somehow, relevant and freeing. It did not portray old melodrama in altered style, as did Hemingway or Faulkner. It did not richly portray the inner flow of subjectivity, as did Faulkner or Joyce. It was not encompassing, cerebral, and allusive, as were Joyce or Eliot or Mann. It was impersonal, comic, and slightly terrifying but flattened and without shock, filled with sentimental figures (animals, sufferers) without sentimentality. Above all, it was an alternative to "naturalism," both as a matter of style and as a literary school. "Naturalistic" action is often deranged in Kafka, violating the verisimilitude of ordinary occurrences, allowing things to happen that could not happen in the real world. "Naturalism" as a literary school had captivated a certain mainstream of American fiction from the 1890s through the 1930s, in writing about individuals threatened by the determining forces of environment (judged scientifically) and an orderly society (judged sociologically). Kafka wrote of threatened individuals, too, but the threats were no longer environmental, scientific, or orderly—except as order and technology itself had become irrational and inexplicable. These were threats more in line with intellectuals' ultimate descriptions of the crisis of man.

Philip Rahv pointed to Kafka as a central inspiration for writers' contemporary (postwar) revolt against naturalism in his "Notes on the Decline of Naturalism." Without guessing the shapes this nonnaturalism would take in the different surrealisms of Ellison, O'Connor, or Pynchon, and even in the cartoonish "bounciness" of Bellow in *Augie March* (the most conventional naturalist writer of the group), Rahv intuited that Kafka could stand as an inspiration for formal change, even if it was not always Kafkaesque change—that Kafka would be available to writers in ways more fecund than mere imitation. "After all, what impressed us most in Kafka is precisely this power of his to achieve simultaneity of contrary effects, to fit the known into the unknown, the actual into the mythic and vice versa, to combine within one framework a conscientiously empirical account of the visibly real with a dreamlike and magic dissolution of it. In this paradox lies the pathos of his approach to human existence."[101] Kafka, in this somewhat blurry description of a union of the empirical and metaphysical, does suggest a formal analogue in fiction to the regulative discourse of man as it appeared in 1940s philosophy. But Kafka still furnished genuine *form*, which is a core resource for literature as it is not always for philosophizing; he supplied technical means that suggested ways, in stories and novels, out of the vagueness of the critics' demands and the near-mathematical logic of "individual" or mass that had led to aesthetic dead ends in Hemingway and Faulkner.

It may indeed be hard for any young writer to read Kafka for the first time and not want to sit down to write a story in which animals act like frustrated people, people turn into animals, and the world is subject to distant and contradictory statutes. The ease of imitation of Kafka was a problem from the start. In 1941, Randall Jarrell saw Kafka's influence mismanaged in the *New Directions* annual of avant-garde writing: "Half the stories are heavily influenced by Kafka, who by now has become a non-naturalistic convention at everyone's disposal; used badly enough, it is as dreary and unimaginative as naturalism."[102] Philip Rahv felt "one can criticize the imitators of Kafka that have been turning up of late as being one-sided and even inept. . . . [I]t is easy to see where his imitators go wrong. It is necessary to say to them: To know how to take apart the recognizable world is not enough, is in fact merely a way of letting oneself go."[103] The accusations of Kafka imitation tended to fly against rival groups rather than against one's own friends, who might be imitating Kafka themselves. English imitators of Kafka were named with special scorn, as if Kafka were now essentially an American possession. These English followers included the today forgotten writers Rex Warner and William Sansom, the latter of whom, wrote Isaac Rosenfeld (Saul Bellow's close friend and schoolmate, and a critic-novelist himself), "belonged to the group of young British writers who work in the Kafka tradition, . . . the structure that can be turned any way to fit modern life, the analogues of experience, the philosophical tone." But "[o]nly for Kafka was the manner the man," Rosenfeld insisted; "[f]or the rest it is something like a magician's trick, presto—it works!"[104]

The closest comparable inspiration in fiction was Dostoevsky; but there was a particular Dostoevsky, too, who was made to emerge in the '40s and who lasted into the 1950s, and who sheds some light on the Kafka arrival. This was the Dostoevsky of the Underground Man. Dostoevsky's writing was not a new quantity—all of his work had been translated by Constance Garnett in the 1910s. *Notes from Underground* would, in most eras, probably not have seemed the prime achievement of a novelist who had given the world *Crime and Punishment, The Brothers Karamazov,* and *The Possessed.* Yet many "stresses of Dostoevsky's thinking are embodied in the 'underground man,'" William Phillips argued in 1946, "the new human type created by Dostoevsky, and undoubtedly his prime achievement."[105] *This* 1940s Underground Man, not just "sick" and "spiteful" like Dostoevsky's original, but increasingly positive and heroic, could also be assimilated to the idea of a Resistance, in a peculiar concrescence of terminology that drew in the "underground," which had emerged in France and other countries to fight the Nazis.

In the era of a search for the distortions of human nature that had been wrought by the modern world crisis, and ways to undo them, it was the depiction of the "new human type" that mattered. A year later, in evaluating Kafka and Dostoevsky together, Phillips would suggest that Kafka himself was not the author of writing *like* Dostoevsky's, but actually had been a living specimen of the underground man, whom Dostoevsky had created only as a literary conceit. "Perhaps the closest analogue [to Kafka] in modern writing is Dostoevski's *Notes from Underground*; but where Dostoevski felt the need to objectify and to be self-conscious, Kafka simply projects his own being."[106] Kafka equaled this figure of "underground man," and underground man, suitably generalized, was proffered as the inner being of man in crisis in a "modern society." "We are all the Underground Man," William Barrett declared in 1951—exactly the same year, as we have seen, that he exhorted the United States (and by implication its writers) to the "great literature that, from all purely rational considerations, we should expect of it."[107]

The American fiction writers who occupy the rest of this study *did* in fact take the crisis of man questions of philosophical anthropology, history, faith, and technology head-on, to a very large degree. The "underground man" mood makes its way into their works (and figures of literal underground men recur in Ellison's *Invisible Man* and Pynchon's *V.*). Likewise, one finds in them a kind of Kafkan *freedom*, if not a Kafka feeling. It is not apparent to me, when I read their work, that they were Kafka followers in the way that many more minor American writers were and continue to be obvious Kafka followers. (Kafka following and imitation might furnish a long study in itself, from Shirley Jackson's "The Lottery" [1948] to the present, drawing in a fair percentage of all the short stories published in the *Best American Short Story* volumes in every year from 1945 to today.) But with Saul Bellow, Ralph Ellison, Flannery O'Connor, and Thomas Pynchon, readers have indeed occasionally been tempted to allude to a Kafka inheritance, correctly understood as a particular new start in approach rather than a bequest of formal methods. Caroline Gordon, writing to a young Flannery O'Connor after reading her first book manuscript (*Wise Blood*), invoked the comparison:

> I know a good many young writers who think they are like Kafka. You are the only one I know who succeeds in doing a certain thing that he does. . . . I do not mean that it is in any way derivative of Kafka. In fact,

this book seems to me the most original book I have read in a long time. But you are like Kafka in providing a firm Naturalistic ground-work for your symbolism.[108]

Gordon's passage is remarkably astute at capturing what the addition of Kafka's example to the American setting could mean for writers' work: a firm naturalistic groundwork for symbolism, but with symbolism itself freed from the overgrand Christ allegories that trapped even Hemingway and Faulkner. It provided a new ground of understanding and comparison that didn't require direct influence or imitation, a deeply personal way out that had proven it would still be recognized as writing about man. Ralph Ellison's biographer Lawrence Jackson likewise titles one of his chapters on Ellison's road leading up to *Invisible Man* "The Black Kafka and the Fight against Reality."[109] *Invisible Man*, which self-consciously activates so many literary traditions for its own purposes (including so many modernist techniques and pastiches, with an especially extensive pastiche of Faulkner), does not really use Kafka overtly at all; and yet there is something truly revealing in thinking of the two writers together, because of the freedom Ellison found for psychological autobiography, generalized to a wider condition, rendered in modes of surrealism—again, as Gordon put it so well about O'Connor, in "a firm Naturalistic groundwork" for his "symbolism."

Saul Bellow's early European influences came more directly, and quite self-consciously, from Dostoevsky. Yet through all these writers, down to Pynchon (whose truly drastic surrealism seems to have come, in its stylistics, directly from French writers of the 1920s, as he himself has suggested in one of his rare statements),[110] one feels the elaborations of a postwar half century freed up for a kind of antinaturalistic realism—partly freed up, I will say just one last time, by the existence and respectability of an obscure Czech German Jewish outlier modernist named Franz Kafka, who nobody owned and who stands over postwar American fiction as, from one vantage point, its most significant "new" author.

The intellectuals and critics who demanded so much of their young American writers, and partly trapped them in those demands, thus also, by choosing the closest thing to their ideal literature in a dead non-American obscurity, accidentally gave the rest of the century some breathing room and air for a new flowering. We turn now to what the writers did with this freedom.

PART III

STUDIES IN FICTION

CHAPTER 5

SAUL BELLOW AND RALPH ELLISON

Man and History, the Questions

Saul Bellow and Ralph Ellison took walks together in Riverside Park. New York had made each of them famous, and a particular metropolitan milieu introduced them to each other and to the literary world. This was the circle of the New York Intellectuals, who managed the journals, like *Partisan Review* and *Commentary*, in which Bellow and Ellison could read each other's work and who helped determine what was then outstanding as an intellectual problem, and what a writer at midcentury was obliged to do.

At that time, these obligations included addressing the problem of man. Both writers' first novels were to some degree named for the investigation: *Dangling Man* (1944) and *Invisible Man* (1952). Each book fits the pattern. The two men's novels were among the most prominent to answer Trilling's challenge to writers, that "the great work of our time is the restoration and reconstitution of the will . . . reconstituting the great former will of humanism." Their triumphs were well rewarded. Ellison and Bellow won sequential National Book Awards in 1953 and 1954. Ellison's great single novel, *Invisible Man*, came quickly to stand out as the best-regarded novel of the entire postwar period (1945–89), a stature that has never seriously been challenged through the beginning of the twenty-first century. In his lifetime, Ellison won unprecedented rewards on the basis of one work of fiction. In a journalistic profile in the 1990s, David Remnick compactly noted that Ellison had "won the National Book Award, the Presidential Medal of Freedom, the Chevalier de l'Ordre des Arts et [des] Lettres, a place in the American Academy of Arts and Letters, and a position at New York University as Albert Schweitzer Professor of Humanities" based on *Invisible Man*.[1] His contemporary Bellow, more prolific, was similarly prizeworthy. Bellow received the crowning honor for any American writer, last given to Hemingway, Faulkner, and Eliot (and Steinbeck) in the modernist generation, a Nobel Prize in Literature, the only one awarded to an Anglophone American writer of the postwar generation.[2] (The unusual non-Anglophone American Nobelist was Isaac Bashevis Singer, who had come to the United States in 1935 at age thirty-one, and been naturalized in 1943, but always wrote in Yiddish. It is a mark of Bellow's centrality that even this other US Nobel winner of his era had seen his American career midwifed by Bellow, who crafted the exceptional translation of the introductory story that became Singer's American calling card—"Gimpel the Fool"—during the time he was coming out with his own *The Adventures of Augie March*, a book influenced by Bellow's childhood fluency in Yiddish; this helped the émigré author's story to be published and admired in *Partisan Review* as part of Bellow's own intellectual world.)[3]

Here is what Bellow said about the connection with Ellison. "We had known each other in Manhattan. I had reviewed *Invisible Man* for *Commentary.* . . . Both of us at one time had lived on Riverside Drive. We met often and walked together in the park, along the Hudson. There we discussed all kinds of questions and exchanged personal histories."[4] This would most likely have been in 1953, after Ralph and Fanny Ellison moved to their apartment at 730 Riverside Drive. Nothing tells us definitively how long Ellison and Bellow had been reading each other or how long they had known each other personally. The earliest possible meeting is evidenced by a reminiscence in James Atlas's biography of Bellow, from the novelist Wallace Markfield, that the writer Isaac Rosenfeld's apartment on Barrow Street had played host a decade earlier both to Bellow, as a frequent guest (he stayed there whenever he visited from Chicago), and to Ellison. This could have been at any point from 1943 onward.[5] More reliably, in 1944, Ellison became a client of the literary agent Henry Volkening of Volkening and Russell, and Bellow seems to have become Volkening's client in the same year; so this would have been another point to have knowledge of each other.[6] Bellow had read Ellison's "Battle Royal" sequence in 1947, published in *Horizon*, or so he testified in his *Commentary* review of *Invisible Man* in 1952; Ellison, in turn, was likely to have read Bellow's earlier stories and excerpts in *Partisan Review*.[7] In a published letter he wrote to his friend Albert Murray, dated January 8, 1952, Ellison said, "I was talking with Bellow and he told me about you in Paris. He was both amazed and amused about your ease of operation."[8] The easy familiarity and sharing of news recounted would have thus taken place before the release of *Invisible Man*, before Bellow's review of it, before even the publication of the prologue to Ellison's book in *Partisan Review*, not to mention well before *The Adventures of Augie March*—so we do know they were personal acquaintances before either was publicly famous, before their walks, and before Ellison had published a book. For that matter, both were part of the small cenacle that attended the Christian Gauss seminars at Princeton in 1952, where Edmund Wilson was outlining the material that would become *Patriotic Gore*. "Ralph Ellison came down regularly [from New York] to attend our parties," Bellow told an interviewer about that year, during which he himself was guest teaching at Princeton.[9]

A peculiarity of both postwar writers' massive success is that Ellison and Bellow are remembered as exemplars of schools of writing identified with race or ethnicity.[10] By critical consensus, the tradition of African American writing is continued and transformed in Ellison. He makes a bridge from Richard Wright to James Baldwin, and a foil for Toni Morrison in the next generation. Jewish American writing likewise begins a new postwar phase with Bellow. He shapes the transition from prewar immigrant writers (like Anzia Yezierska and Henry Roth) to those complexly at home in America in the mode of Philip Roth. Biographers and still-living friends of the two writers point out, as a partial corrective to the racial classification, that Bellow and Ellison did not want to be considered only, or even primarily, as Jewish or black writers. "Neither he nor I could accept the categories prepared for us by literary journalists," Bellow wrote decades later, recalling, fairly or unfairly, the substance of his discussions with Ellison while they walked along the urban reaches of the Hudson. "He was an American writer who was black. I was a Jew and an American and a writer."[11] Ellison's stated position was actually more detailed: refusing to call himself an "American Negro," Ellison referred to himself for decades as a "Negro American," arguing that there was no white American culture without its black involvement, and no black culture in America apart from white involvement. The "Negro American" belonged to a national history that was mixed in its essence, as all "Americans" were so mixed.

The two men's personal positions on race and writing are sometimes taken simply to express the fact that they were "universalists." Universalism in this context evokes a doctrine that all men "are the same under the skin," all therefore should get equal treatment, and (often a hidden corollary) that in a universalist vision of social reform, people from any background and circumstance may feel and behave the same, if only they are treated alike. Such universalism tends to be viewed as a default intellectual position of the 1940s and 1950s when it comes to race (as color blindness, the Brotherhood of Man), without much detailed accounting of its nuances. Either it is praised as an Old Left antidote to today's identity politics or disparaged as unquestioned and old-fashioned assimilationist baggage that made Bellow and Ellison disclaim their heritage. For opponents of a nonracial view of their work, it is easy enough to stress their individual books' real "particularism," the novels' ability to make arguments, stage scenes, or be understood only through facts of the authors' racial identities and experiences. It is an unfortunate either-or.

The way to untangle what the two writers actually did accomplish in their early work, I think, is to go more carefully into the details of what they attempted, and determined, in their treatments of the problem of man.

One reward is that it points the way out of the impasse of a pair of opposites, universalism and particularism, which simply aren't really very useful, literarily, for identifying what Bellow and Ellison thought, cared about, and wrote. The other is that it helps us see how the crisis of man ran into complexities, and required different solutions philosophically and historically, when it encountered the daily experience of race in the postwar era—when the forties and fifties are still somewhat mangled in our memory, and intellectually oversimplified. These writers of the turn of the 1950s urgently wanted to know whether there was any such thing as a human being outside of social types, and, if so, what that abstraction would mean for them. Was the "human"—live category of the time—to be a new state of freedom? (And freedom for what?) Or was it to be an eternal determination of what man permanently and irresistibly was? (And what was he?) To discover this abstract man, they had to know first whether the identity as Jew or black or, indeed, any subset of men, any category by which men would be recognized, was a hindrance or an aid to reaching the purely human state. Thus Ellison and Bellow became concerned with a philosophical anthropology. If there was a human being as such, what did it have to do with always being marked as something besides the generic "person," being named, being already, as it were, outlined by the ways others will recognize you?

Investigating this properly does require acknowledging both writers' positions as intellectuals. Even today, Bellow is frequently condescended to for his university pretensions, his attachment to formal intellect, his "deep thoughts" in novels cluttered with the names of Heidegger and ancient authors, and his career at the Committee on Social Thought at the University of Chicago and in numerous universities elsewhere. Bellow's own biographer, James Atlas, writes, surprisingly, "Bellow was not a complex thinker."[12] With Ellison, critics can't understand or forgive why one of the greatest novelists of his time should spend the rest of his published career on essays. Yet a compelling alternative way of thinking of the shape of Ellison's career is that he was an intellectual first, as his true, lifelong career, who happened to write his ideas once as a novel—because that was then the form of literary authority most in demand—which itself happened to be one of the best novels of his time. Though he felt haunted by his inability to publish a second such novel, he didn't need to do it again. One fiction masterpiece at *Invisible Man*'s level might be enough, and certainly it authorized him to argue thereafter as a thinker, unmasked.[13]

Writers make a different kind of intellectual history—even the most intellectual of writers. The intellectuals and critics who preceded Bellow and Ellison could say in outline what man had been and project a silhouette of what he was becoming. But they did not have to portray him *in concreto*, vivify character, set their ideas against a backdrop of worldly objects, planks and driven nails, hot sidewalks, and empty bottles. Novelists have to test abstractions on the world. And the primary obstruction they had to meet or shape was indeed race—a matter of flesh and personality but also an abstraction, a work of intellect, itself.

Yet the main influences on their solutions, the way they answered the question of man (rather than in the ubiquitous impulse to phrase it), did not, in truth, come from the New York Intellectuals who introduced them to each other and to the world. This made them iconoclastic answerers within the fixed, more familiar institutional situation that helped assure their careers. Bellow had been educated in the Midwest classicism of Chicago. He had first faced Robert Maynard Hutchins's Great Books program as an undergraduate, then later took paid employment with Hutchins and Mortimer Adler as a researcher on Adler's *Synopticon* to the Great Books of the Western World series. Ellison had reached intellectual maturity on the edges of the black Communist world of Harlem, around the party headquarters on 125th Street and the newspaper *New Masses*. He learned amid such conflicted Communists as his mentor Richard Wright, who combined African American nationalism with hope-filled support of the Soviet Union. These were the real influences, rather than that of the New York Intellectuals, that brought Bellow and Ellison to the core of their meditations on the second of the first and second central topics of crisis of man discourse—philosophical anthropology, projected through the prisms of race and the concrete factuality of fiction and the shape of history, this time in its influence on the imagined individual lives of their protagonists. Their solutions are pursued in this chapter and the next.

DANGLING MAN AND THE QUESTION OF RECOGNITION

Not many readers today start with *Dangling Man* (1944), Bellow's first book, in part because it is a novel unsure, in its first pages, whether it would prefer to be an essay in *Partisan Review*. It opens with this diary entry:

DECEMBER 15, 1942

There was a time when people were in the habit of addressing themselves frequently and felt no shame at making a record of their inward transactions. But to keep a journal nowadays is considered a kind of self-indulgence, a weakness, and in poor taste. For this is an era of hardboiled-dom. Today, the code of the athlete, of the tough boy—an American inheritance, I believe, from the English gentleman—that curious mixture of striving, asceticism, and rigor, the origins of which some trace back to Alexander the Great—is stronger than ever. Do you have feelings? There are correct and incorrect ways of indicating them. Do you have an inner life? It is nobody's business but your own. Do you have emotions? Strangle them. . . . Most serious matters are closed to the hard-boiled. They are unpracticed in introspection, and therefore badly equipped to deal with opponents whom they cannot shoot like big game or outdo in daring.[14]

As with so much of Bellow at his best, the strength of this is tied up with a linguistic schizophrenia. Up to a point, this really *ought* to be an essay. You hear the accents of 1940s highbrow intellect. There is the compulsive history making from a fear of decline ("There was a time when," "But . . . nowadays"; "this is an era of"). There are the spurious intellectual derivations from uncited scholarly chitchat: "an American inheritance, I believe, from the English gentleman," "the origins of which some trace back to Alexander the Great." It is the Trilling mode well echoed, with Trilling's circle of "thinking and talking people," his "opinion[s] . . . now heard from all sides."[15] *Dangling Man*'s "unpracticed in introspection" is the sort of pyrrhic overphrasing that infects expository, not novelistic, prose. The passage is not a parody, though out of context it reads like one.

The true note of the novel, which makes this not a candidate for essay or exposition, is the violence or bursting surplus of emotion that always breaks in: "Do you have feelings? . . . Do you have emotions? Strangle them." The passage establishes the novel's mood—a will to intellectual exposition, helplessly punctuated by sudden resentments—as well as its main themes. The narrator will take stock of his inner life, but "[h]ard-boiledness," the enemy and alternative, is also present. Hemingway is identified as the representative of the hard-boiled attitude: here the hard-boiled "shoot big game"; a page later they will "fight bulls or catch tarpon," which is explicit enough to pick out 1930s Papa (especially after *Death in the Afternoon* and his Key West sport fishing).

The idea of a dangling man is someone up in the air, a do-nothing or dreamer, known in Yiddish as a *luftmensch*, but also a person who holds possibilities in suspense, and therefore perhaps can be free. The book's progress follows the modulation of this emotion back and forth into violence, fury, and the temptation to make a scene, to fall into fixity—to be all one thing, "hard-boiled." The fear is that an absence of clear identity can make one a condemned man, much as being sentenced to be hanged would. The narrator, when unseen and socially unimportant, is not just a man at the end of his rope, but figuratively a man at the end of *a* rope. "There is nothing to do but wait, or dangle, and grow more and more dispirited. . . . I sometimes think of it as the background against which I can be seen swinging. . . . Before I can properly estimate the damage it has done me I shall have to be cut down" (12).

Bellow's *Partisan Review*–like book was, in fact, excerpted in *Partisan Review* in late 1943.[16] At this point, it still carried the title *"Notes* of a Dangling Man"—making clear the connection to Dostoevsky, whose *Notes from Underground* the book would call to mind in any case.[17] ("I am deteriorating, storing bitterness and spite which eat like acids at my endowment of generosity and good will" [12].) What is certain, for echo and allusion, are the deliberate accents of mid-European rooming-house/boarding-house misery: "I have reversed the summer and made myself shiver in the heat. . . . When Marie [the charwoman] comes to make the bed, I shall get to my feet, button on my coat, and go to the store" (13). The formality of some of this makes it seem one is reading a European novel in translation: "The streets at this time of year are forbidding, and then, too, I have no overshoes" (14).

Bellow's narrator, only named "Joseph," explains that he is in an environment where all men either work or are in the army, but he is neither employed nor inducted. He quit his job anticipating military service, which has been delayed for half a year because, born in Canada, he is a resident alien—all in "a sort of bureaucratic comedy trimmed out in red tape." The natural order has been reversed; his wife supports him while he is "like any housewife" (16) dangling at home. The action in the *Partisan Review* excerpt occurs in just a few episodes, which also make up most of the early action of the published book. First Joseph explains his predicament: he has no job and feels he should be able to do without one, but can't. "I have thought of going to work but I am unwilling to admit that I do not know how to use my freedom and have to embrace the flunkeydom of a job because I have no resources, in a word, no character" (12). He visits the home of his successful in-laws, the Almstadts, and can't understand how his father-in-law tolerates the domination of his wife. The mood is one of disgust: "She powders herself thickly, and her lips are painted in the shape that has become the universal device of sensuality for all women, from the barely mature to the very old" (19). The old woman pours Joseph a glass of juice with a brown chicken feather floating in it.

Next Joseph takes steps toward the world of men and work, as he meets an old friend for lunch. Myron thinks he can get Joseph a temporary job. But elsewhere in the restaurant is a fellow, Comrade Jimmy, who Joseph used to know in Communist Party days. "I said hello to him, and he acted as if I simply wasn't there" (32)—because Joseph had left the party ten years earlier. Joseph can't stand the snub; he compromises his chance at a job to confront his political invisibility, no matter how little it means (while Myron is shouting, "Why, you're a madman! Come back here!").[18] Joseph has to force Comrade Jimmy to recognize him:

> "Don't you know me? It seems to me that I know you very well. Answer me, don't you know who I am?"
> "Yes, I know you," Burns said in a low voice.
> "That's what I wanted to hear." (36)

If this sounds like a certain, particular kind of '30s dialogue, it should: this sequence leads toward a transformation of a person who *tries* to keep himself suspended, who *tries* to search for the "whole man," into the dreaded alternative—someone hard-boiled, and all in the pursuit of a simple recognition of himself by a political order he doesn't even care about. The climax comes at the end of the *Partisan Review* excerpt (it is one of several similar such climaxes in the published book). We've heard of Joseph's humiliations at the hands of a sacrificed job and careless bureaucratic army, in his grotesque family home and in the business-lunch terrain of old friends and political organization. Now he receives the same humiliation—for his indefinite identity—from the young, and a consumer mass culture he loathes, and he finally strikes back. Joseph and his wife are dining at the home of his brother, sister-in-law, and little niece Etta—a niece who, we're pointedly told, happens to look exactly like Joseph, his juvenile female double. This fifteen-year-old Etta is spoiled and vain. More than anything, though, she's attuned to "unimportance." Anyone poor is by nature unimportant to her, anyone without an identity—therefore Joseph. When dinner and the family are too frustrating, Joseph goes upstairs to use the attic phonograph. Putting on "a Haydn divertimento for the cello, played by Piatigorsky" ("It was the first movement, the adagio, that I cared most about"—this careful connoisseur's note is either touching or insufferable), Joseph falls into a reverie about pain, art, and mankind, a rare indulgence in the otherwise dramatically direct *Partisan Review* excerpt:

> Its sober opening notes . . . showed me that I was still an apprentice in suffering and humiliation. . . . Surely no one could plead for exception; that was not a human privilege. . . . I recognized its rightness and was vehemently moved by it. Not until I was a whole man could it be my answer, too. . . . I was too weak for it, I did not command the will. (67–68)

In the midst of this intellectual rhapsody—with its notes of anxiety that the "whole man" must be reached but "the will" is still lacking, of dependent "human privilege" and its grounding in suffering—Etta bursts in: "I want to play these Cugat records Mama gave me." Xavier Cugat, the ersatz musician and film-score composer, versus Joseph Haydn, classical master of the Age of Enlightenment? Joseph tries to reason with her. Etta sasses back with what he denounces as "movie talk." Soon Joseph is at it, too, and the scene turns into a titillating confrontation straight out of a certain kind of hard-boiled *roman noir*:

> "Oh!" she gasped. "You dirty . . . dirty no-account. You crook!" I caught her wrist and wrenched her toward me.
> "Damn you, Joseph, let go! Let me go!" The album went crashing. With the fingers of her free hand she tried to reach my face. Seizing her by the hair fiercely, I snapped her head back; her outcry never left her throat; her nails missed me narrowly
> "Here's something from a beggar you won't forget in a hurry," I muttered. I dragged her to the piano bench. (70–71)

Joseph spanks her until the rest of the adults burst in to witness the scene: "She no longer fought against me but, with her long hair reaching nearly to the floor and her round, nubile thighs bare, lay in my lap." Even James M. Cain might have handled this less crudely in *Double Indemnity* or *The Postman Always Rings Twice* a few years earlier; it is deliberately sub-Hemingway hard-boileddom, on the way to Mickey Spillane, and all about an unrecognized person being *seen* at last, in the worst possible way. Joseph defends the quasi-erotic violation by reminding us of the niece-uncle doubling: "I wonder if any of them were capable of observing how exactly alike we looked at that moment." The point of the doubling, however, is only that Joseph becomes worst when, floating on Haydn, he had tried to become his best; evidently one needn't be a tough guy to become hard-boiled. For a character concerned with preserving inwardness, there turn out to be two ways of having no inside: by being empty, which is what he tries consciously to avoid, or by hardening, being boiled like an egg, all the way through, in the fire of caring too much how people see you—or *that* people see you. Joseph tries not to be the first—empty—with his many deep thoughts about his true human freedom. But it is the second possibility that creeps up and gets him, in the heat of outrage and amour propre, in the act of asserting his importance and the demand that his glorious inwardness be seen, and *recognized* by others. The irony is that it is seen in the wrong way.

WILL CHICAGO SPEAK FOR MAN?

Dangling Man thus starts with man's nature, in abstract reason and freedom, with a humanity unencumbered by any gravity but that of weightless thoughts. It turns out to be about the desperate need to get recognized, to be seen *as* something, even though this falsifies, demolishes, or denies the hope for a free abstract man.

The gloomy morbidity of the book is that Joseph absolutely does not believe the interior realm of "humanity" can or should collapse into jobs, commerce, respect, and struggle. Neither, it often seems, does Bellow, the authorial consciousness, who paints the problem but does not seem to stand apart from it except by a kind of hellish irony. Joseph fails abstract man over and over again. In the midst of the pseudo-European gloom, one major early passage of philosophical musing has Joseph surveying the city of Chicago. His forehead pressed to the cold window, he sees "poor dwellings, warehouses, billboards, culverts, electric signs blankly burning, parked cars and moving cars." It leads to what Joseph calls the "invariable question" (notable that *this* should be the invariable question!): "Where was there a particle of what, elsewhere, or in the past, had spoken in man's favor?"

> There could be no doubt that these billboards, streets, tracks, houses, ugly and blind, were related to interior life. And yet, I told myself, there had to be a doubt. . . . In their businesses and politics, their taverns, movies, assaults, divorces, murders, I tried continually to find clear signs of . . . common humanity.
>
> It was undeniably in my interest to do this. Because I was involved with them; because, whether I liked it or not, they were my generation. . . . And if, as was often said, this part of the century was approaching the nether curve in a cycle, then I, too, would remain on the bottom and there, extinct, merely add my body, my life, to the base of a coming time. This would probably be a condemned age. But . . . it might be a mistake to think of it that way. . . . How did we know that it was? In all principal ways the human spirit must have been the same.[19]

This language calls out to fears and abstract responses we have seen already. Here you have the Spenglerian cycles of civilizations, the condemned ages on which a new cycle might be built. ("I brooded over Spengler in college," Bellow later reported.[20]) You have the fear of an extinguished or Alexandrian culture and an apocalyptic fear of a spiritless urban morass ("billboards, streets . . . ugly and blind"). Then comes the hope for solace in the idea that "in all principal ways the human spirit must have been the same," a topic, phrased as a question, that was on many writers' minds at just this moment (Lionel Trilling, in his essay "The Sense of the Past" from 1942: "One question we ought to raise is whether, and in what way, human nature is always the same"[21]).

"Where was there a particle of what, elsewhere, or in the past, had spoken in man's favor?," though, is a particularly *Chicago* question in a different way, and "in all principal ways the human spirit must have been the same," flat and definitive, is a very Chicago answer—we should say, a University of Chicago answer, of the sort we have seen in chapter 2.

This Chicago marked Bellow both when he was young and in much of his later life. Bellow had started at the University of Chicago in fall 1933 and stayed until winter 1935, when family troubles caused him to withdraw. He transferred to Northwestern University, from which he graduated in 1937. Bellow remembered Robert Maynard Hutchins and the "U. of C.," though, as an intellectual underpinning of his later sense of himself. He and Tuley High classmate Isaac Rosenfeld carried the same Chicago ethos along in their migration to the New York Intellectuals: "'For some reason neither Isaac nor I could think of ourselves as provincials in New York,' Bellow wrote to Alfred Kazin years later, after reading an excerpt from one of Kazin's memoirs: 'Possibly the pride of R. M. Hutchins shielded us. For him the U. of C. didn't have to compete with the Ivy League, it was obviously superior. It never entered our minds that we had lost anything in being deprived of Eastern advantages. So we came armored in self-confidence, and came to conquer.'"[22]

The Chicago Great Books idea, of course, required as its essence that men were the same in all ages, and the "human spirit" the same—that was why the same canon of books could be read with profit by all. ("[H]uman nature is, always has been, and always will be the same everywhere," as we have heard Hutchins say in chapter 2.[23]) Bellow, in his searching early novels, kept this dogma open as a question. But he continued to exist in a milieu where it was *not* a question but the starting point of all inquiry. Bellow went back to the University of Chicago to earn his daily bread between 1943 and 1945, in the period when *Dangling Man* had been accepted by Vanguard Press but not yet published, and held an editorial job under Mortimer Adler on the *Synopticon*, a massive effort under the direction of Adler and Hutchins, to index the published edition of Great Books that Hutchins was arranging through the *Encyclopaedia Britannica*. This *Synopticon* (officially, *The Great Ideas: A Synopticon of Great Books of the Western World*) was also meant to stand alone as a two-volume index and summary of all the most significant ideas found to be permanent in the history of the world, including entries on such topics as "Necessity and Contingency," "Liberty," and "Man."

Dangling Man thus faces the questions that were habitually asked in a certain intellectual world of Chicago, but it does not yet accept the habitual answer—unable to reconcile it with the present American conditions.

THE LEASH OR THE NOOSE

The self-conscious argument of the different elements of *Dangling Man* can gradually be fitted together. Joseph is a student of the Enlightenment ("About a year ago, I ambitiously began several essays, mainly biographical, on the philosophers of the Enlightenment" [11]), and he's a man of Reason—or this, at least, is what he wants to be. Certain phrases haunt him. One is "the whole man," the Renaissance humanist ideal that a united person can best understand life; another is "the craters of the spirit," a coinage of his own—at once a vision of the battlefield he's on and something as distant and glorious as the mountains of the moon. Joseph, in his brave moments, wants to "return the verdict for reason," in a trial that is partly his endless waiting without a job (as another Joseph, Kafka's Josef K., once had his own bureaucratic trial) and partly his pitiless observation of his friends and contemporaries.

But there seem to be too many advantages to unreason in the wartime home-front climate. With an imaginary interlocutor, *Tu As Raison Aussi* or "The Spirit of Alternatives"—no clanking chains, or white sheets, but another himself, an alter ego—Joseph stages a debate of reason against happiness. His genial debater encourages him to ease up, be happy, but Joseph refuses, wanting at the very least to find in himself the "capacities" (138) of "Those who proved it possible to be human" (136)—those, that is, who chose Reason over malleability and surrender. "*Tu as raison aussi*" (you're right, too; "But on the other hand" [135]) is a caricature of the liberal idea. Instead of alternatives, understanding, laxity, and ease, Joseph feels an insistence has to be made on some larger truth that has no single front. Everyone else chooses a single way to be—"An ideal construction, an obsessive device"; Joseph wants the higher truth (140–41).

More unreasoning alternatives appear in acquaintances who reflect other heroic or degraded forms of will. One such figure is Jefferson Forman, "listed as having crashed in the Pacific" (82). Joseph knew Jeff in college—now he's a casualty of the war. But Forman turns out to have been a particular kind of person, an exemplar of pure will or just kicks, "in love with excitement." He had been arrested in Genoa for shouting "*a basso* in a public place. No name, simply *a basso*." As pure will, revolutionary energy without object, crashed in a military plane, he offers a different way to achieve what Joseph longs for—to come down out of the air. It's hard not to read the dead flyer's name as *for man*, one alternative of human personality in an American vein, in a novel musing on what would speak in man's favor; or, wishfully, as *foreman*, the front-runner in action or, say, the lead juror who could "return the verdict" Joseph seeks, but too hastily and at too high a cost. Man on this model would be will without forethought. As

Joseph says of Foreman's pure over-will, "I always suspected of him that he had in some fashion discovered there were some ways in which to be human was unutterably dismal, and that all his life was given over to avoiding these ways" (83).

Joseph's neighbor Vanaker is another alternative. He is like the man of the boardinghouse from nineteenth-century fiction: mysterious, unkempt, harboring a secret life. No Père Goriot or Vautrin himself, however, he proves to have no inner secret but only the slovenliness and surrender of boundaries that symbolize yet another kind of troubled human freedom. Stealing from his neighbors, he wears Ida's perfume and Joseph's socks; male and female are mixed up in him. He keeps "picture magazines with photos of nudes" and the maid insists he is no gentleman. Worst of all to Joseph, who is driven to distraction by it, he urinates in the hall bathroom *with the door open*. (This is a sort of freedom, too.)

These are the schematic sections of *Dangling Man*'s debate about man; yet these parts, novelistically, are lifeless. The novelistically interesting part of the book is the dramatic rage of giving in or wishing to give in or watching others who have a stable identity. Joseph hates his friends. In truth, of all the things Bellow contributed to the American novel, one of the most striking must be his basic novelistic structure of a friend, or friends, whom the first-person narrative will observe and attempt to overcome and outdo with an amazing forensic clarity and raging lover's intensity. It also structures such books as *Henderson the Rain King*, *Herzog*, *Humboldt's Gift*, and *Ravelstein*, but it begins in *Dangling Man*. Joseph identifies in his friends the fallings-down from freedom he should suspect in himself. Etta's spanking shades into a scene where his friend Clark Abt hypnotizes a drunken hostess at a party, then pinches and humiliates her; Joseph sees it as a sign of Abt's inferiority: "Yes, I thought, he *likes* this" (53). Myron Adler, who tries to get Joseph a job, is conventional and simpering. John Pearl left Chicago for New York to be an artist but instead draws junk for an advertising agency. "For months I have been angry with my friends. I have thought of them as 'failing' me" (38), Joseph says in a moment of lucidity.

These crimes of his friends and failures of himself are truly vivid because wrapped up with a particular way of "making scenes," both for Joseph and for Bellow's way of plotting the book. Joseph is depended on to do the wrong thing, socially, by demanding he be *seen* as something *other than* what people take him for. Making a scene comes down to being seen—and recognized—though it's not clear what ultimately Joseph wants to be recognized *as*. He must get recognition as a man, as a jobholder, or would-be jobholder, as anything, finally, but a dangler. Further vindictive scenes repeatedly expose women, as in the Etta episode (and the episode of the party hostess, and, later, of Joseph's mistress Kitty); it is women, after all, who know how to paint, and silk, and bedizen themselves, to show a face to the world too easily while men are left unrecognized.

It's thus perfectly natural that all these strands should come together, at the book's finale, in an action that otherwise seems ludicrous. Joseph rushes down the hall while the despicable Vanaker is urinating, sets his foot in the door, and pushes back when Vanaker tries to close the door—to expose the old guy, as he's previously only exposed women, and catch him in the act. "When he turned, hearing me, my foot was already in the door. He had neglected to turn on the light, but I could see perfectly clearly by the small bulb outside." Vanaker doesn't get to fasten his fly until Joseph is done shouting at him, upbraiding him for a grotesque form of laxity—the wrong kind of freedom. Vanaker, to spell out the crude joke, is now the one "dangling," not Joseph. In sexually exposing a man rather than a painted woman, Joseph somehow makes a triumphant refusal of freedom where it looks like license; then Joseph heads straight to the draft board and demands his military induction. "The leash," he whispers to himself—relieved at his surrender; at least it is the leash rather than the noose.

BEING SEEN, MAKING SCENES

Recognition rather than *freedom*—identity rather than that abstract or total figure, the "whole man." When Bellow's Dangling Man looks for the abstract man in himself (an effort, by an ordinary person, to figure out what in his life would support the larger abstractions of Reason or Enlightenment), he winds up landing on a jobholder's identity and trying to refuse it; lapsing into the hard-boiled man who rules over women rather than the chaste, icy intellectual who exists in a realm of free will; landing finally in the army, when, in 1942 or 1944, there might be no more reliable way of gaining a job or manhood. He winds up, in short, in immediate and unintellectual forms of being recognized. He wants a bank manager to cash his check without question for once, because he *looks like* a man of parts. He wants an ex-friend to say hello to him.

This is one way of dealing with the essential emptiness that has already been a feature of the existence of any abstract Man or human being—the Man who is the subject of the Rights of Man, the person who mattered for intellectuals of the era and whom they sought to defend. But *Dangling Man* is about this project's unwitting failure. The novel had the power to remind readers that the abstraction "man," worked out in practice, wound up dependent on other kinds of activities that had a specific life in America, down to the banal workaday things of the office, the household, or the bedroom.

As I've said, a main tradition of criticism has supposed, not unreasonably, that the great topic of recognition for authors like Bellow and Ellison ought to be identity or race: black and Jew. This is what first and foremost would have kept them from being just abstract human beings in the great morass of Man; or what, since these authors would indeed often be considered as writers on "the human condition," might have been a doorway to the supernal regions—to let them, through Jewish or black specificity, declare for the universal qualities of human life despite it all. Yet Judaism is missing in *Dangling Man*, deliberately so. When Joseph goes to visit his brother's family, they're celebrating Christmas, though the holiday itself is scarcely marked, and requires rereading to identify—it is memorable only as the occasion on which Etta receives her Cugat records (58).

Bellow did turn to a deliberately "Jewish" take on what makes a man a man in *The Victim* (1947), though again it was a matter of how one is seen from the outside, against the sort of blankness one feels within. The earlier Bellovian preoccupations recur. The protagonist, Asa Leventhal, a Jew, has gotten a job after a period of grave anxiety about finding anything. Because he once made a scene, an outburst, when he was unemployed, a Gentile blames him for losing him his job. The mood is again from Dostoevsky, this time *The Double* instead of *Notes from Underground*. The doubled peer or colleague comes in as the anti-Semite, Kirby Albee. In *The Victim*, it is as if the protagonist is, from the start, holding on desperately, positively, to the forms of recognition that had been accepted only as nihilistic solutions in the earlier book—his job, for example. Yet now the group belonging of Jewishness is forced on him as a rival identification, when, in fact, he feels it is the job and fitting in and avoiding the freedom of his emotions that are at issue in a human universalism. What terrifies him is being pushed by the anti-Semite's recognition of him as a Jew to the freedom of rage, which he associates with madness and unreason. Leventhal takes care of his brother's wife and child, where previously he could reject that *bürgerlich* existence. He tries to keep himself from making scenes, and is embarrassed in public for one of the few times he let himself go. It is, in a sense, *Dangling Man* from a reverse perspective, with freedom no longer the ambition but the dangerous thing that one might happen into if subject to an unwanted recognition, as Judaism is pressed on Asa by a demonic double, to make him assert himself, to resist.

The Victim was a dead end, too, I think it's fair to say, both for Bellow's philosophical meditations and his ambitions as a novelist of grand effects. This was not a means to get back to the essential unfinished problem— how you *could* restore the human as something more than the particular, faced with all the temptations and obstacles of the particular. Bellow came a step closer when he turned away from his own ambiguous particularization of racial identity to the question of an opaque identity beyond his own, that of the African American—when Bellow turned, interestingly, to *black* recognition.

BLACKS AND JEWS: "LOOKING FOR MR. GREEN"

In a 1998 book, Emily Budick argued, controversially, that the idea of long-standing black and Jewish alliance didn't really exist before the late 1950s or early 1960s. The idea of a personal solidarity and natural affinity between blacks and Jews, she believes, belongs only to the civil rights movement of that period, or, more cynically, to a certain nostalgia or too-rosy past conjured in the wake of unexpected black-Jewish tensions after the end of the civil rights movement.[24]

What is not controversial is that blacks and Jews after World War II *could* find in common that each was discriminated against in American society—the degree to which they chose to do so is, of course, the historian's problem. The simplest common denominator was that each could still be discussed under the rubric of race, and Jewish and black restrictions could be equally considered a matter of "race prejudice" and part of America's "race problem." The Jews had not yet, in the coinage of Karen Brodkin, entirely "become white," though that process was under way.[25]

A real consideration for black and Jewish intellectuals in this period seems sometimes to have been whether, in fact, there *was* any deeper connection to accompany this semantic or ideological shared fate. *Commentary* was the most prominent Jewish intellectual organ of the period from its inception in 1945. In chapter 3, we have seen its deep concern with the crisis of man after 1945. From about 1948 it also had an ongoing, intense, but always slightly distanced fascination with black life. The journal published young black writers on the subject of black life and culture seemingly more frequently than any of the other "white" literary quarterlies. It matched these publications by black writers with neutrally reported articles by white, usually Jewish, writers trying to communicate knowledge—often in the tone of ethnography—about the blacks who peopled the lives of the journal's Jewish readers and coexisted or interacted with them.[26]

Thus, in *Commentary*, in 1948, readers saw James Baldwin's essay on "The Harlem Ghetto" and his first major-market short story, "Previous Condition."[27] Having excerpted Sartre's *Anti-Semite and Jew* in three issues in 1948, the journal impressively published, in 1950, the black critic Anatole Broyard's reapplication of the same analysis to blacks, "Portrait of the Inauthentic Negro: How Prejudice Distorts the Victim's Personality," where Broyard used the language of "the victim," which was very much also applied to Jews in the metaphysics of anti-Semitism (as it was in the title of Bellow's second book).[28] From one of its Jewish contributors, in 1951, it published an article called "The Bergmans' Queenie," an essentially sociological report on the life of a black maid to a Central Park West Jewish family. The title could make you think the article is from the perspective of the maid's Jewish employers; in fact, it was ironic. The Bergmans are invisible. One finds out instead how "Queenie" lives when she isn't working, which you feel the Bergmans ought to have known or cared to find out, and how meaningless her work identity of domestic service is to home life in Harlem, her family structure, household, religion, leisure activities, and property.[29]

And *Commentary* also furnished the context for "Looking for Mr. Green," the masterful short story that Bellow published in March 1951. Mr. Grebe, the story's protagonist, isn't a sociologist, but he does have to go into unknown houses on official business. Grebe's tale seems to be the next explicit step and triumph in the Bellovian drama of man and recognition—connecting the problem of recognition to black separateness. This time he asks whether the black situation is similar or different, and what precisely the alienness of groups has to do with the chance to grasp "man" in his higher abstractness.

Bellow's story once again also adds *work* relations as the grounds for a kind of minimal abstract humanity. "Looking for Mr. Green" is set two decades before the year of publication, during the Depression, on Grebe's first day on his new job delivering relief checks to the unemployed in the "Negro district" of Chicago.[30] "Hard work?" the story opens. "No"—it's not the work itself that's hard, but a "peculiar difficulty" of which Grebe begins to "grow aware." The frustration of the story is that, stripped of all familiar resources in the unknown neighborhood, Grebe can't find a man named Green on this one wintry day, when evening is coming early and the wind is cold. No one in Green's tenement will help Grebe, because the man from the relief is white—he could be a cop, a bill collector, or a summons deliverer. So Grebe embarks on a set of interviews.

This is a story about the minimum conditions for *finding* an individual man (in Green), as well as for *staying* an individual man (in Grebe). The brilliance of the early part of the story is in its communication of the incredible discomfort felt by a character who's out to keep up the basic dignities through a simple task. Plunged into darkness, he burns match after match, trying to find the numbers in the tenement obscurity. "[A] young Negress answered" at his knock on one door; "She had a dream-bound, dream-blind face, very soft and black, shut off" (253). Each new door he tries reveals the same "somnambulistic," hallucinated mood; he is ushered into a room of silent people, "sitting on benches like a parliament" (253). They put him to a sort of trial. Odd gaps come into the narrative and a hint of unrealism: words are "impossible to catch" (253) and the black residents laugh for no reason.

Why are these residents black? Certainly there's a touch of old literary-metaphysical blackness, from Poe to Conrad, which makes characters of African extraction the repository of spiritual unknownness—a crowd of unrecognizable "enormous" men and women, "in the earthen, musky human gloom" (254). But Bellow also conjures up a historically specific problem, in a story about the search to identify a single person—that to be black in America is to be so pejoratively overrecognizable for being black that one can learn, defensively, not to let oneself be seen individually by whites. To name a character "Green" is to reduce him by his name to a color, and the first resonance of his name is that he is *all* color, he is the man whom "Grebe" (a diving bird, incidentally) cannot find because of his color, and knows about him *only* his color.

The essential quality of these black rooms and hallways, as it emerges from the narrative, is that the residents are intelligible and recognizable to one another but not to Grebe. They possess furnishings and property from the white Chicago world Grebe knows, but in arrangements and settings that puzzle him. Their graffiti are like those in any impenetrable civilization: "So the sealed rooms of pyramids were also decorated, and the caves of human dawn" (253). If Grebe is out of his element, lost, vulnerable, and without a clue, it's because he is an unmarked man—uncolored, unrecognized—who's reached a culture more tight-knit, less visible, apparently bigger, and perhaps more living than his own.

At this stage of the story, the narrative suddenly goes to a flashback. We witness an interview that Grebe's playful young supervisor Raynor made of *him*, earlier in the day. It turns out that Grebe is, in fact, "a man of culture" (255)—a former classics instructor and fellow at the University of Chicago! Grebe the classicist has been reduced by the economic disaster of 1929 to selling canned meat and window shades. At the back of his dogged will to break through the protective affiliation of "Negroes" in the tenement, we begin to have an inkling of his own form of affiliation. Raynor calls it "[t]he attractive power of civilization," joking that it pulls equally on men like them and on "office boys in China and braves in Tanganyika" (255). This civilization in Raynor's view is, say, a community like that of race, but beyond race, a civilization one is not necessarily born into, but can enter; Raynor and Grebe know each other by exchanging Latin quotations, to the puzzlement of the office boys all around them.

Here Raynor makes a mistake, assuming that Grebe must, like him, have been born into this higher civilization, unlike the Chinese office boy and the "brave," and raised by rich parents who transmitted it and assured Grebe's freedom—"with permission," Raynor jokes, "to go out and find out what were the last things that everything else stands for while everybody else labored in the fallen world of appearances" (256). In fact, Grebe comes from another race of servants (though not the Jews): "My father was the last genuine English butler in Chicago" (256). He stands identified with those who work for others, not for themselves. Still, Raynor's mistaken semijoke ("to go out and find out what were the last things that everything else stands for") pointedly describes the philosophical kernel of the rest of the story: Grebe *is* a man trained to look for "last things," aware of the Platonic distinction between the real ideas or forms and mere "appearances"—when it is a distinction, we begin to see, that stands in some confusion or some danger.

For the story begins to intimate more insistently a threat to a higher civilization, as the colloquy between Grebe and Raynor is interrupted by a commotion outside. It is Mrs. Staika, a corpulent Polish woman, who makes false scenes at the relief office for more money. Beneath the show she puts on, Grebe feels a base reality, "the war of flesh and blood . . . intensely ugly . . . on place and condition" (257).

Eyes opened to "flesh and blood" ugliness, Grebe reawakens from the flashback to the present moment and the story resumes chronology; he searches for Green, delays, delivers an easier check. Continuing to stew over possibilities—whether civilization existed only "by agreement and when things collapsed the agreement became visible" (259), therefore revocable, whether underneath it there was "*something* that is dismal and permanently ugly" (260)—he finally "sighed and gave it up, and thought it was enough for the present moment that he had a real check in his pocket for a Mr. Green who must be real beyond question. If only his neighbors didn't think they had to conceal him" (260). Still, if this is the real quest and hope—to prove the existence of just one man—then Grebe performs it equivocally. He thinks he finds Green's house. He runs to his door, rings, and enters. He waits expectantly at the foot of a long stairway and finds, instead of Green, a Negro version of Mrs. Staika—a foul-mouthed, naked black woman, flesh and blood, descending the stairs, who might be Green's wife or his mistress. Grebe hands the check to her, even though the woman's evasive answers never admit explicitly that the man upstairs is even Green, or that the man will receive the check. "Though she might not be Mrs. Green, he was convinced that Mr. Green was upstairs. Whoever she was, the woman stood for Green, whom this time he was not to see" (261). Balked by raw energy and a figure of the "ugly" will—incarnated once again as a woman—Grebe defers the meeting while believing he's held out and done his job, found his "man." If one were to make a particularly schematic reading of the story, in alignment with literary concerns of the 1940s, one would have to say that just as God seems absent but anticipated in the familiar interpretations of other works of midcentury—from Kafka's earlier *The Castle* to the contemporary *Waiting for Godot* (composed in the late '40s and performed in Paris in 1953 and New York in 1956)—so the ending of "Looking for Mr. Green" seems to say: one can do one's best to find a man, but not yet really find "man." It is enough to have tried, and the meaning is in the search. (This deferral of the outcome to the task would then be another way of coping with the crisis of man and restoring the "will.")

One thing has always bothered me about the story, after encountering the original in *Commentary*. At this stage, Bellow was more often publishing in glossy magazines, when he wasn't in *Partisan Review*—and this story, given to a Jewish intellectual journal, is one of his absolutely best works of the period. It was the very first to be collected, a few years later, when his stories were compiled to fill out the first publication of the novella *Seize the Day*. I find myself asking: Is there any reason it was published, unusually, in a *Jewish* journal, and why, in that circumstance, is there no Jewish presence in the story?

"Green," as I've said, is a name for a man defined entirely by his color. Bellow's early best friend Isaac Rosenfeld once wrote in a passage on "the differences... between men" in his novel *Passage from Home* (1946): "[W]hy was he a Negro and I a Jew? Why not the other way around?... Everything would remind me of it: ... any color named, or the word, 'color' spoken, ... a black dog, or a white dog ... I should constantly be thinking, 'I am a Negro, I am black.'"[31] Green is the one color name that is also by common agreement a "Jewish name"—as people casually say that certain surnames historically belong to groups. Popular culture contained Shecky Greene, the Jewish Catskills comedian (but also, importantly, Al Green, the black soul singer). Green remains a way that assimilating Jews shortened Greenberg or Greenstein; indeed, *Commentary*'s business manager on the issue's masthead was Frances Green. Seeing the title in the *Commentary* table of contents, you would have felt "Looking for Mr. Green" was another Jewish article in a range of them (in the same issue with another piece called "Papa, Mama, and Grandfather Florance"). So one is tempted to the reading that the mysterious figure Bellow's Gentile Grebe is pursuing is also a Jew—or, say, a trace of the Jewish inside a story about blacks by a Jew in a Jewish publication interested in blacks. I take it that the principal Jewish question in the story is really: Are *we* in this story? If so, where? Are we like Grebe, who's recognized by his boss for the attainment of a superior high culture, though he was the son of servants? Or are we like "Green," and might finding an individual man behind the ethnic opacity of a black community be like trying to find "man" within the obscurity of the Jewish community? Or is Grebe himself finally a middle ground and a solution—a man who comes from servants but *chooses* a devotion to the classics and, today, one single man who knows an abstract higher civilization (of Latin quotations) and chooses to improve a more immediate civilization (in the organized forms of politeness and effort that can restrain the underlying raw human disorder)?

Dangling Man, I've tried to say, wants to be about human freedom but abandons the attempt. It winds up showing the compulsion to grasp any immediate and petty kind of recognition, giving up on abstract man for the sake of fitting in and having a place to be recognized. It has no context of Jewishness or racial identity, no a priori form of recognition that could interfere with freedom or preempt and liberate one from the need for recognition of other kinds. "Looking for Mr. Green," on the other hand, understands that there's a more significant obstacle within forms of recognition that already exist—like race—and is equivocal about whether one can break through those rigid forms in the quest for man. It posits higher culture—of the University of Chicago kind, knowledge of the ancients, and so forth—as a perhaps favorable form of community, but turns its back on it, too, in the face of chaos and "need." Instead, it pursues a chastened vision of what a minimal picture of man would be like—aligning the will with a form of thankless but noble work more than just holding a job ("Hard work? No"). It proffers a provisional agreement, to a provisional civilization, as a way to find a shared man, knowing that people can just as easily consent to ugliness and sensing there might be something inside us that is permanently ugly.

At this point, Bellow's progress on the abstraction "man" must come to a pause—because it was about to be vastly outdone, from the "Negro" side, by a novel directly from the perspective of the questioning black consciousness, which had so far managed to stay invisible.

INVISIBLE MAN AS A BOOK OF COMPLETION

As I have said, Ralph Ellison's *Invisible Man* came to be regarded, within a few years of its publication in 1952, as incontestably the best novel of the postwar period, even of the second half of the twentieth century. To sense the unusual quality of this, it is necessary to recall that this "best book of the half century" was published only two years into the half century, which various awards and polls would prove it dominated, only seven years into the postwar period. "The greatest American novel in the second half of the twentieth century," R.W.B. Lewis flatly called it.[32] In 1965, Ellison's book was chosen as the most distinguished novel since World War II by a collection of "200 authors, critics, and editors" for *Book Week* magazine.[33] In 1978, when *Wilson Quarterly* surveyed professors of American literature on the most important novels published in the United States since World War II, it was confirmed at number one by a wide margin.[34] In 1987, when Raymond Mazurek repeated the experiment, it remained the "most taught" postwar American novel in the English departments he surveyed, and there is no reason to believe it has lost any stature since.[35]

From the moment of its publication, *Invisible Man* stopped people in their tracks. Seymour Krim, then a young writer making his reputation with "whither the novel?" essays in the early '50s, had just come to the end of a follow-up letter in *Partisan Review* in May 1952 on how bad the short story and novel had become—when he had to append an unusual, stop-the-presses postscript to announce a sudden change in the novel's fortunes. He had just read Ellison's *Invisible Man*—and "it is the only recent U.S. novel trying to pioneer in the direction we've been discussing."[36]

Why did the lastingly best novel of this period appear at the period's beginning rather than closer to the end, once critics had seen what others had done? Because *Invisible Man* answered *all* the demands for the novel that then existed, in ways critics didn't even quite see, yet responded to. Ellison's book was, in a sense, not really an early entrant into the postwar novel or the young book of a new formation. *Invisible Man* does not originate literary styles and themes, but solves and caps them, making one of the best finishing literary works of an earlier tradition, that of prewar modernism. Yet Ellison manages to use the perfection of modernist techniques, and their logical evolution, to answer a set of questions that are distinctly of the postwar moment. What is remarkable in Ellison is how much he perfected of the modernist past (call it quotation, voice, myth, or pastiche), how delicately he handled the addition of the "non-naturalistic basis for realism" we have seen in the Kafka legacy (call this his surrealism or comic estrangement)—and how he was able to turn all this to the new questions of man.

Ellison begins his novel from behind the bar of a seemingly unbreakable identity, an inevitable recognition, to ask: How inevitable is it? *Invisible Man*'s philosophical prologue takes the form of a riddle of a traditional descriptive kind, like the riddle of the Sphinx, offering attributes—I am "invisible," I am "not a spook," I "play" "invisible music," "I am an orator, a rabble rouser," I am "black and blue"—the sort of riddle that traditionally ends with the question "What am I?" Ellison's riddle will evidently have the same answer as the Sphinx's—I am Man. That fixed answer is the easy part; the hard part, the work of the novel, is figuring out which are the real attributes that could make this answer meaningful. In *Dangling Man* and "Looking for Mr. Green," Bellow had shown the difficulties of holding on to a vision of an abstract, free humanity but relied on conventions and social codes. Ellison, in *Invisible Man*, would ask whether *any* of the requests for such a humanity were honest, made sense, and weren't humiliated by the real racial facts of American social life.

Much criticism of *Invisible Man* concentrates on the first half of the novel—up to the point where the narrator-protagonist joins "the Brotherhood," a movement loosely modeled on prewar New York Communism. I'm more interested in addressing the second half of the book. The episodic, brilliant, memorable early chapters of *Invisible Man* are well understood, I think, by readers, and have been well treated by criticism. They provide an exposé of the obstacles, hindrances, and injustices that face the narrator before he has come to any sort of "consciousness" (one of the book's keywords), or even knows that such consciousness is his aspiration. They show the paradox of his invisibility: whites don't see him, and blacks, seeing black, don't see *him*. They also provide early, simpler alternatives to the different theory or solution in the second half of the book—which I think has not been as well understood or well treated—especially in the later parts where the chapters are more continuous, less episodic, and both headlong, and, at times, puzzling. In the early part of the book, one knows just what Ellison is "saying" and showing us, generally through a kind of allegorizing or dramatization of ideas in nonnaturalistic figures. In the second part—especially in the musings of the protagonist when major action is not occurring—there is a temptation, I think, not to track Ellison's open philosophizing to its conclusions, and to let the extreme violence and uncertainty of the end unfold for its own sake, experiencing it as an apocalypse without a theory. But *theory* is where the book gradually goes.

That doesn't mean the early part of the book can be ignored. Bellow's work (and the work of the intellectuals) had thus far tried to answer the crisis of man from the point of view of sophistication and disillusion, trying to recover what had been lost. Ellison starts from zero. *Invisible Man* begins with a naive narrator, not an intellectual. The recognition question is already solved—in the sense of being a permanent burden. Behind the opacity of color, everybody recognizes Ellison's black protagonist already as *something*.

The early portion of the book thus asks a simple question: What do whites want from blackness, and what do blacks want from whiteness? The answers appear in discrete episodes, each with its own now-customary name: the "Battle Royal," "Trueblood," the "Paint Factory," and the "Factory Hospital." The underlying exposé that motivates each episode can be stated starkly. "Battle Royal," in which a white stripper is tossed in the air and little black boys are forced to beat each other bloody, transpires because the white chamber of commerce needs black proxies to express the stunted sexuality it can't unleash in any other way. In "Trueblood," Mr.

Norton, the rich philanthropist, listens to a black sharecropper who had sex with his daughter because, it turns out, Mr. Norton seems to have wanted to have intercourse with his own dead daughter ("'You have survived . . . You did it and are unharmed!' he shouted, his blue eyes blazing into the black face with something like envy and indignation").[37] But the rich white benefactor sublimated the desire for incest *within* his line by becoming a Great White Father to *un*desirable children, in a college for Negroes, making them his proxies and "destiny."

So blacks, early on, are the instruments for whites' intertwined impulses of sex and domination. The narrator doesn't encounter a single white friend who isn't up to some kind of erotic monkey business; the early episodes rest on some very serious dirty jokes. It's as if, by offering up the single most reductive sex-and-power theory of racism right away, Ellison is telling a partial and necessary, insulting truth, but then clearing the decks for something new. His critique begins to metamorphose. By the time we reach the white supremacist paint factory ("Optic White is the Right White!"), with its black dope added to sickly gray paint base to bleach it to a perfect whiteness—and a tiny black engineer in the basement boiler room who once built this whole empire—we learn that government white, and all surface white, is built on an invisible admixture of black. The African American is not just the instrument but the hidden builder *and* the hidden substance of whiteness. "What was I, a man or a natural resource?" (303), asks the narrator in a great Ellisonian question, one of the magnificent aphorisms of *Invisible Man*. In the factory hospital, where the injured protagonist is tortured with electricity to make him docile, he learns that technical power, used against him, can be converted into something neutral: "I discovered that I could contain the electricity—a contradiction, but it works" (27). This is the turning point that summarizes and closes the beginning: every effort coming from whites to help blacks is a need to get sexy through them, fight through them, experiment on them. The only defense might be to abstract or neutralize those impulses into something else: to "contain" and reuse them rather than pushing them away. The theory of the book will become twofold: theorizing how to locate a self that isn't worked through, made a marionette, over- or underrecognized; and how to restructure power as neutral, or cast it in a register accessible to all and colorless—sometimes by learning its history to find the black within the white, sometimes by *leaving* that history, opting out.

INVISIBLE MAN AS A BOOK OF REOPENING

The Brotherhood's arrival marks the eruption of overt theorizing in *Invisible Man*. The book to this point had been developing a theory without putting a name to it. Although no one had told the protagonist previously that there was a theoretical meaning to all his experiences, now someone does. "[W]e stand at a terminal point in history, at a moment of supreme world crisis," says Brother Jack at the party in the building called the Chthonian. (The "Chthonian": that is, an infernal or underworld high-rise; no one can say there aren't clues that the Brotherhood isn't all it's cracked up to be.) "[T]he enemies of man are dispossessing the world! . . . There is a scientific explanation for this phenomenon . . . but whatever you call it the reality of the world crisis is a fact" (309).

> "To the Brotherhood of Man . . . to History and to Change," he said, touching my glass.
> "To History," we all said.

The Brotherhood invokes the Communists both in their prewar, Popular Front folksiness and in postwar intimations of creepy Soviet control and ghoulishness (as when Brother Jack, after losing his fake eye, is unmasked and begins "spluttering and lapsing into a foreign language," presumably Russian) (473). But there are reasons not to think of Ellison's Brotherhood as simply the Communists. The name Brotherhood—and Ellison's decision himself to mask and generalize the movement—picks out the postwar language of facile "universal brotherhood," which was much on offer in all liberal circles into the 1950s. The Brotherhood presents a generalized progressivism, as well as a straight Communism. For that matter, it also picks up the language of automatic fraternity in an African American community, where *Invisible Man* suggests it's common to "see black" rather than see black people—from the greeting of "hey, brother," or "what's happening, brother," to the white and black Brotherhood habit of calling everybody "brother"—Ellison toys with this kind of formalized, clearly spurious political Brotherhood, against the real individual relations of one black person to another: "Good evening, Brothers" . . . "Shit, he goddam ain't no kin of mine!" (423–24).

Ellison did have close inside knowledge of life in black Communist circles. His intellectual education came, more than any other source, from Communism, and then disillusionment with the party and its abandonment of black causes in the war years. Lawrence Jackson's superb biography of Ellison traces his leftist education in Harlem and notes the small contingencies and temperamental inclinations that kept Ellison from joining the party officially, though he gained an education in Marxist theory, which he then modified for a black American purpose.[38]

Ellison assiduously read Marx and Lenin and the daily Communist press, and he drew his own conclusions from progressive "theory and practice." His protagonist in *Invisible Man* is sent to study theory specifically with Brother Hambro, in one of the rare marked gaps in a book of continuous action. A chapter ends with the education about to start; the next begins, "Four months later . . ." Ellison himself studied for much longer than this; it took years of his life.

From his first arrival in New York after his third year of college—when he encountered Langston Hughes and was taken under his wing after just two days in the city—Ellison perceived metropolitan intellect as synonymous with left politics. Within a matter of months, Hughes had him proclaiming himself "decidedly interested in the left" and reading John Strachey's "Literature and Dialectical Materialism."[39] The Harlem Renaissance figure Louise Thompson first took him to the Communist Party and its headquarters at Lenox Avenue and 125th Street. Ellison read *New Masses* regularly for years, and published his own early work there, staying with the paper even when many intellectuals left for Trotskyism or liberalism, both because it afforded better writing opportunities to him and because Communism retained the strongest position on the rights of African Americans.

But Ellison's greatest influence was Richard Wright, his close friend and mentor, an important party member and the head, for a time, of the Harlem bureau of the *Daily Worker*, who finally broke with the Communists in 1944. Lawrence Jackson argues that Wright's travails positioned Ellison to stay out of the party officially. Because he witnessed how a much more famous writer, and friend, could be subject to so much party infighting and censorship, he had a clearer-eyed perception of the party's defects as well as its beneficences.[40]

Ellison gradually works out his own theory in *Invisible Man*. It's part of a black tradition, to be sure. It offers an original reading of American race relations from the black perspective: assuming black normalcy, black perspicacity, intelligence, complexity, and ambiguity, and then white simplicity and unself-consciousness. But it also—like the Brotherhood ideology Ellison's protagonist is reading, and like the Left intellect Ellison studied and knew—comes from Hegel and the tradition of Western philosophy.

One must pause for a minute to talk about Hegel. Specifically, we have to renavigate some familiar waters in the best-known part of Hegel's historical dialectic of consciousness, the dialectic of lordship and bondage. The material takes up fewer than ten pages in *The Phenomenology of Spirit*.[41] Hegel's project is a philosophical account of how consciousness evolves upward, into self-consciousness, and, higher, toward Spirit. This stage tells of the moment when two self-consciousnesses confront and acknowledge each other, in what came into English as "the process of Recognition" (111). Each self-consciousness discovers itself as an "*other*" (ibid.). Then comes a mysterious violence in Hegel, which is surely the most notorious thing about this stage in the dialectic. Each self-consciousness "stakes its life"; each "seeks the death of the other" (113). In this struggle, self-consciousness discovers that it exists in two aspects—as that which is "pure self-consciousness," purely for itself, and that which finds physical life essential to it, and becomes only a "consciousness in the form of *thinghood.*"

Here Hegel makes his eventful leap in nomenclature: the former part comes to be called "the lord," or master, and the latter "the bondsman," or slave. At this stage the dialectic slips from a pure description of consciousness—in which master and bondsman are obviously metaphors—into the temptation to feel that we are dealing with two personal consciousnesses, like two men, and a real struggle. "The lord is the power over this thing, for he proved in the struggle that it is something merely negative . . . [H]e holds the other in subjection" (115). Other commentators (most famously, the early twentieth-century French Hegelian, Alexandre Kojève) did not read master and bondsman as a division between two aspects of consciousness, but as the separation of two sorts of consciousnesses. In memory, it becomes almost irresistible that the dialectic is recalled as occurring between an actual master, and an actual slave, in the battle to the death of recognition.[42]

Later in Hegel, the bondsman will turn out to be the means of further developments in consciousness. Forced back upon himself, having no slave to recognize and satisfy him, the bondsman becomes "truly independent." He invents *work* on thingness and the world of things; he undoes the primitive attachment to natural existence, transforming it by work (118). Hence the central significance of this part of the dialectic for the Left, for Marx, and for all forms of historical dialectics that believe that progress comes out of labor or the developing consciousness of subjected people.

This way of slipping to master and bondsman as separate figures, however, and explaining how they were produced as victor and vanquished in a struggle, draws on and recapitulates a much older tradition in liberal philosophy, going back to Hobbes and Locke, which explains how slaves come into being and why it is justifiable that they do so. If we misread Hegel, we do so in line with our tradition. Slaves, the story goes, are people who, in a life-or-death struggle (specifically, in war) are about to be killed but choose a life in subjection rather than death. In Hobbes's *Leviathan*, the fear of death is so strong that one cannot do anything to will death or to avoid wishing to remain alive; so one hardly even *chooses* subjection, it is just the natural response to loss in this struggle. Still, one's life has been given away, in a sense, as justly as the subject's life is owed to the state. (Hobbes thus models the master-slave relation on his form of social compact, as David Brion Davis has pointed out.) Locke's view of slavery was worse in its indifference to rights, viewing slavery as a forfeiture of life in a state of suspended death, entirely outside the social contract—when the slave wished, he could resume the state of war and receive from his master the death he had postponed. Hegel, beyond the liberal philosophers, at least framed the relation between slave and bondsman as the outcome of contingent events, let them encounter each other as consciousnesses, and made the outcome of their confrontation an engine of history.[43]

Ellison had begun reading Hegel in the early 1940s. The interest came from his reading of Marx, but as Lawrence Jackson has shown, Ellison gravitated naturally from "the theories of dialectical materialism and class struggle" to "the evolution of the individual consciousness."[44] During the period of controversy in Harlem after the publication of Richard Wright's *Native Son*, Ellison made public appearances defending the content of his friend's book on theoretical grounds in New York's black Communist community. He asked Wright specifically for a copy of Hegel's *Phenomenology of Spirit* to bolster his arguments but seems to have known it already in profile, or as myth, since it was Hegel to whom Ellison turned in diagnosing Wright's novel on theoretical lines:

> He, Bigger, has what Hegel called the "indignant consciousness" and because of this he is more human than those who sent him to his death; for it was they, not he who fostered the dehumanizing conditions which shaped his personality. When the "indignant consciousness" becomes the "theoretical consciousness" indignant man is aware of his historical destiny and fights to achieve it.[45]

It's not too much to say that Ellison's own protagonist, and his "achievement," would be directed to reaching this later stage of "theoretical consciousness" by the boomeranging and disillusioning in the book *Invisible Man*. Such was Ellison's advance over Wright, his novelistic teacher and mentor, the man who had started him writing fiction. Ellison's triumph was to deal with Hegel by fully literalizing him, acting him out, and thus making him newly useful. Half against Marx, too, Ellison reads dialectics not economically but racially. Susan Buck-Morss has speculated that Hegel himself might have come to the master-slave dialectic by news of slave revolt and independence in Haiti under Toussaint L'Ouverture.[46] We know that Hegel was inspired to other ideas in the *Phenomenology* by the career of Napoleon; his famous declaration avers that philosophy "is its own time apprehended in thoughts."[47] So Ellison puts black and white relations back into the Hegelian account; he then, in a sense, turns back the clock, or sets the dialectic to rewind. And to integrate the changing theory of *Invisible Man* into its action, Ellison wrote, as a final step, the prologue and epilogue, which wrap the philosophical problems (of invisibility, recognition, responsibility) to enclose the book at either end. ("The prologue was written afterwards, really. . . . I wanted a foreshadowing through which I hope[d] the reader would view the actions which took place in the main body of the book."[48]) Here is the very first piece of action in that prologue to *Invisible Man* (it is the third paragraph of the book as a whole):

> One night I accidentally bumped into a man, and perhaps because of the near darkness he saw me and called me an insulting name. I sprang at him, seized his coat lapels and demanded that he apologize. He was a tall blond man, and as my face came close to his he looked insolently out of his blue eyes and cursed me, his breath hot in my face as he struggled. I pulled his chin down sharp upon the crown of my head, butting him as I had seen the West Indians do, and I felt his flesh tear and the blood gush out, and I yelled, "Apologize! Apologize!" . . . Oh yes, I kicked him! And in my outrage I got out my knife and prepared to slit his throat, right there beneath the lamplight in the deserted street, holding him in the collar with one hand, and opening the knife with my teeth—when it occurred to me that the man had not *seen* me, actually; that he, as far as he knew, was in the midst of a walking nightmare! . . . Then I was amused: something in this thick man's head had beaten him within an inch of his life. I began to laugh at this crazy discovery. Would he have awakened at the point of death? . . . Poor fool, poor blind fool, I thought with sincere compassion, mugged by an invisible man! (4–5)

Invisible Man is prefaced, I think, with an attempt to return to the Hegelian, dialectical original situation of "recognition," not now between two parts of consciousness, or two consciousnesses—or master and bondsman, result of the life or death struggle—but as the battle between white and black. It is specifically the "blue-eyed" "blond" beast who appears, insulting and then nearly killed by a protagonist who has *not yet identified himself in the book as black* (only "invisible")—we stand wholly in the narrator's consciousness, looking out. It is as if the original division could yet be undone. (The book stands equally inside the literary tradition, it should be noted, replaying *it* just as the protagonist refights this social battle, for stakes of *literary* repossession. "Apologize! Apologize!"—a reasonable thing to ask of any white person, historically—recalls the opening pages of Joyce's *A Portrait of the Artist as a Young Man*, "Pull out his eyes, /Apologise," in one of the most important of *Invisible Man*'s many modernist allusions.)

Thus, in a myth-centered book, the myth that *Invisible Man* replays in its overture isn't Brer Rabbit or Jack the Bear—it's Hegel. It is a replay of the original struggle, in which the hereditary bondsman discovers that he gets no second try. The long absurdity of the philosophical thought on slavery was that the original struggle, so arbitrary and unannounced, could never be fought again—no matter the circumstance, no matter the change in the balance of forces. In the fairy-story version of Hegel's dialectic, one always wondered: Through all those years and centuries in captivity, doing the lord's work, improving on the natural environment, as the lord sat around dumb and happy and useless in his being recognized, why doesn't the bondsman creep up on the lord and finally slit his throat? The Hegelian, and Ellisonian, answer is simply because it can do nothing for him; it is too late; he can't get the lord to *see* him, or bestow the gift of real recognition that had been the prize in the first place, and is still the prize. It's a cause to "laugh," all right, if it doesn't make you turn to the blues, which make their appearance a little later in the prologue. No wonder the bondsman will have to seek his independent consciousness by other means.

But this Ellisonian way of thinking about a violent struggle at the core of recognition is not *just* Hegel, not at all—it has its roots in a specific African American line, as in Frederick Douglass, and his theory of what "becoming a man" meant for American blacks. (One should remember the portrait of Frederick Douglass that comes to hang on the protagonist's Brotherhood office wall in *Invisible Man*, a reminder from an ex-slave who passes on his burden of hope to the protagonist.) These roots go back to Douglass's original picture of his transformation, while still a slave, from a slave's dependence into real independence, when he fights back against the overseer Covey:

> The fighting madness had come upon me, and I found my strong fingers firmly attached to the throat of my cowardly tormentor; as heedless of consequences, at that moment, as if we stood as equals before the law. . . . He was frightened, and stood puffing and blowing, seemingly unable to command words or blows. . . . I was a changed being after that fight. I was *nothing* before; I WAS A MAN NOW. . . . A man, without force, is without the essential dignity of humanity. . . . I had reached the point, at which I was *not afraid to die*. This spirit made me a freeman in *fact*, while I remained a slave in *form*.[49]

Douglass points intuitively to the problem in the philosophical history of the West, which Ellison understood analytically.[50] In later exegetes of Hegel (including Kojève and his followers among the students of Leo Strauss), it is the greater fear of violent death that furnishes the explanation for why one of the consciousnesses should arbitrarily submit rather than the other (as well as, perhaps, Kojève hints, a greater unconscious creativity, or unwillingness to be fixed as a master).[51] The question for a black thinker then becomes: What would it take to go back to that original situation and *not* give up through fear or despair when you know that sheer violence may no longer do any good? For Douglass, it is the deprivation of his tormentor of "words or blows" alike because the slave himself has returned to the fundamental battle but, this time, "I was *not afraid to die*" (emphasis in the original). In Ellison, it is expressed as a wrenching ambivalence about violence, but also captured in the alternative way out that Douglass himself found he could use, too: a truly superior power of speech.[52]

Invisible Man's prologue ends in confusion about how a synthetic consciousness, beyond master and bondsman, could be sought. It introduces a new, un-Hegelian term, riffing on "responsibility," as what the protagonist will seek in the drama to come; his current "irresponsibility," which he believes would be the accusation from whites; and what it would take to affirm anything, to get to that Hegelian word "recognition," rather than remain in violence and denial:

> Irresponsibility is part of my invisibility; any way you face it, it is a denial. But to whom can I be responsible, and why should I be, when you refused to see me? Responsibility rests upon recognition, and recognition is a form of agreement. (14)

In "responsibility" and "irresponsibility" we should also hear "response," "responsiveness"—Ellisonian tones keyed to an art of relations and intervals, an aesthetic of the already-built. The book's question becomes: How do you begin to prepare the grounds for a synthesis, for *recognition*, not through a new original struggle, and without new conventions and agreement, and still without partners with whom one already knows what one shares—how, in all this trouble and ignorance, can you begin to prepare the ground yourself?

ELLISON AND THE "HUMAN"

The task of such a novel, as we can see, for the black writer and for the universal intellectual of the '40s, will finally be wrapped up in his protagonist's journey and attempt to become, *by speech* (and, in Ellison's own practice, by writing), something given one of the most puzzling but highly valued names in the book (much as it was debased coinage everywhere else): "human."

The plot of the human in Ellison is made explicit through four speeches the narrator delivers, each of which we hear at length. The first speech, during the Battle Royal, exists in what I called the plot of "exposé" in the first half of the book. The other three speak more directly, I think, to the "theory" of the second half. Alternating these moments of public action in speech with public events of violence (the riot at the eviction, the battles with Ras, the death of Tod Clifton, and the final riot in Harlem), the novel calls attention to the steps toward an answer to his original puzzle, "What am I?"

The second speech—the one that begins the theorizing of a positive solution, a picture of what a man can or could become in public—comes at the eviction. Up until now, the narrator has been a sufferer and an observer, a rabbit for people in authority to "keep running," and a mechanical man for the authorities to juice up. He has just had his "I am what I am" revelation in the yam scene. He has learned to accept the things he likes, even when they're associated with a "Negro" identity, and has renounced his shame of what he thinks people will dislike in the things he likes.

Then the protagonist stumbles on an event, the crowded eviction of an old man and wife. The evictees had known slavery, and we see their free papers, Bible, knickknacks, and furniture put out on the sidewalk, dispossessed. The narrator stands in the doorway to speak and head off the crowd's violence. He winds up stirring it and focusing it—so that volunteers carry all the furniture and belongings back into the house, knocking down the white marshals, as the protagonist flees across the roofs.

The easy thing to forget about this speech is that the discovery that carries him through isn't indignation and expression but a renewal of shame at what *can be seen*—after he had just renounced shame at what he *was*. As the crowd breaks the law to put the tenants' evicted possessions back into their house, his code for this is that they're "law-abiding":

> "[T]ake everything. Take it all, hide that junk! Put it back where it came from. It's blocking the street and the sidewalk, and that's against the law. We're law-abiding, so clear the street of the debris. Put it out of sight! Hide it, hide their shame! Hide *our* shame!" (281)

This speech is counterintuitively about humanity in the renewal of shame, about not having yourself be seen when you don't will it—maintaining shame, in its right place, as privacy and the closed circle of a home. Just because you are *invisible* as a black person doesn't mean you should be subject to every kind of way of being seen. This establishes a pattern in the speeches, where one kind of self-assertion is expected ("we are who we are!," or "the brotherhood is the way!," or "we must band together to make sure Tod Clifton did not die in vain!") while another insistence—on something like a private or personal boundary, as an *abstract* discovery—comes through instead.

The next speech is in the arena. The protagonist is now a speaker for the Brotherhood. He comes into the spotlight to deliver his address. Light, we've heard at the beginning, is the element that makes his form. But here onstage he is seen, but cannot see. Thinking he has achieved visibility at last, he's struck blind. He speaks first for the program of the Brotherhood on behalf of the "dispossessed," then in response to the voices in the audience; only at the very end does he feel and say something entirely unexpected, previously unknown to himself, as to everyone:

> "And now, at this moment, with your white and black eyes upon me, I feel . . . I feel . . . I feel suddenly that I have become *more human*. Do you understand? More human. Not that I have become a man, for I was born a man. But that I am more human." (345–46; emphasis in original)

He asks if the audience understands; but he himself doesn't understand. Rather than an answer to the question of how one becomes more human, this sudden flash of insight at the very end of a more orthodox speech becomes the mystery of the rest of the novel: What precisely was it that provided the assurance of being "human," not just "a man"? The narrator meditates on his perplexity later that night:

> What had I meant by saying that I had become "more human"? Was it a phrase that I had picked up from some preceding speaker, or a slip of the tongue? For a moment I thought of my grandfather [who had been a slave] and quickly dismissed him. What had an old slave to do with humanity? Perhaps it was something that Woodridge had said in the literature class back at college. I could see him vividly . . . before the blackboard chalked with quotations from Joyce. . . . "Stephen's problem, like ours, was not actually one of creating the uncreated conscience of his race, but of creating the *uncreated features of his face*. Our task is that of making ourselves individuals. The conscience of a race is the gift of its individuals who see, evaluate, record. . . . We create the race by creating ourselves and then . . . we will have created something far more important: We will have created a culture." (354; emphasis in original)

In the voice of Woodridge, the college professor, Ellison makes a declaration about one possible meaning of "humanity," transmitted, very appropriately, as a bit of literary criticism—which is, after all, a part of what he is doing with *Invisible Man* in its appropriation of the literary tradition. Joyce's intention to forge "the uncreated conscience of my race" at the end of *A Portrait of the Artist* is often interpreted as the call for a new consciousness for the Irish. Ellison's character Woodridge's rereading insists instead on the priority of distinct and individual persons, before any group consciousness or its greater manifestation, a "culture."

What does it mean for a man to create "the uncreated features of his face"? An old thought of theologians was that God had given men faces, one of the great divine gifts, so they could be told apart. Without the face, human culture would collapse too much into homogeneity; one person would not know he was distinct from others. If Hegel's form of recognition described the two parties to a combat, or two aspects of a consciousness, discovering themselves as the same sort of thing and then struggling to become dominant and subordinate, Ellison, at this stage, veers away. It would be better if they were to discover themselves as distinct. His words take his protagonist away, too, without his knowing it, from the Brotherhood line. The effort to recognize each single face is quite different from any generic encounter with the other, whether historical-materialist dialectical or just the commonplace American encounter between groups, "black" and "white." We begin to understand how it is different in the climactic fourth and final speech that is made over the coffin of Clifton.

> "What are you waiting for me to tell you? . . . All right, you do the listening in the sun and I'll try to tell you in the sun. . . . His name was Clifton and they shot him down. His name was Clifton and he was tall and some folks thought him handsome. . . . His name was Clifton and his face was black and his hair was thick with tight-rolled curls. . . . Can you see him? . . . His lips were thick with an upward curve at the corners. He often smiled. He had good eyes. . . . His name was Clifton, Tod Clifton, and, like any man, he was born of woman to live awhile and fall and die. . . . His name was Clifton, and for a while he lived among us . . . His name was Clifton and he was young . . . His name was Clifton and he was black and they shot him. . . . His name was Clifton, Tod Clifton, he was unarmed and his death was as senseless as his life was futile. He had struggled for Brotherhood on a hundred street corners and he thought it would make him more human, but he died like any dog in a road. . . . He thought he was a man when he was only Tod Clifton." (455–57)

The name and the face, the face and the name. Names have a peculiar role in *Invisible Man*. Figures who have wisdom, or a real chance to get it, possess no proper name: not the "vet," not the "grandfather," not the protagonist himself. (He receives several false names throughout the book, none of which we ever hear.) The proper names in the book are mostly ciphers: generic names for white forefathers, like Emerson or Norton; jokes, like Brother Tobitt and Brother Wrestrum ("two-bit" and "restroom"); an honorific, like Ras (a generic term for an African king, which Ellison used playfully in his letters); or a rebus like Rinehart (rind and heart—asking what link there is between surface and interior of the hipster-hustler, who seems all surface). It's as if these names were pasted over their real names. They are the verbal equivalent of the mask that covers a face. Even Tod is a pidgin-German allegorical name—he's the character marked for sacrificial death ("Tod Clifton [Tod, Tod]" [441]) but *Clifton* is a real name, and that's what the protagonist is discovering, and repeating, over and over in his funeral speech.

The form of illumination here is finally the sun, not a blinding spotlight or a streetlight. It lights everyone evenly from above, and the protagonist, making his speech, can see his listeners as they can see him. Under the sun, all see each other (in the protagonist's repossession of all literature, the allusions here are to Shakespearean funerals; to the "heat o' the sun" funeral song ["Fear no more the heat o' the sun/Nor the furious winter's rages"; *Cymbeline*, 5.2]; and to the name-refrain, like Antony's "Caesar" in the funeral oration against Brutus [*Julius Caesar*, 3.2]). The incantatory speech on the face (lovingly described) and the name (thuddingly repeated) works a change in the crowd, which lasts only a moment and is forgotten but seems a key part of the sense of the human at the end of the book. "The crowd sweated and throbbed, and though it was silent, there were many things directed toward me through its eyes. . . . And as I took one last look I saw not a crowd but the set faces of individual men and women" (459).

This is no longer dialectics, but *nominalism*. Categories and abstractions have no real existence. One tries to apply universal names to people and clasps the air. Only individuals exist—and the categories that would cover more than one of them are illusory. I take it that in "Looking for Mr. Green," but also, much more drastically, here in *Invisible Man*, the sense of covering names—names that link characters to each other or call to categories in the world but fail adequately to pick out each person himself—leads to an awareness of the difficulty of calling someone by his *real* name, which would not be the one given by society (or, in the case of blacks, inherited from a slave-master ancestor) but one that fit his face, the purely unique appearance of him, communicating his inner uniqueness.

Ellison and Bellow are often called individualists, correctly enough—but then many people can be "individualists," and of different types. It can be a term for the understanding of growth from the inside. In the tradition of that other Emerson (not *Invisible Man*'s gay Mr. Emerson), it is a term for self-fashioning. They seem to aspire to something else, to an acknowledgment of the difficult conditions that ordinary "individualism" treats as transparent. Ellison's and Bellow's suspicion is that between the philosophical or, say, ideological tradition of claiming to be wholly individual and wholly free—and the hostile or embracing tradition of being hidden in the group and calling for recognition as a member of that group (as, say, a black or a Jew), but also as a jobholder, a man rather than a woman, and so forth—any single person may very well fail to be recognized correctly at all.

Ellison may be more conscious of the difficulties than Bellow at this stage. Certainly he goes much further with it toward this nominalism of the human. And Ellison possesses, at bottom, a term that I think does not carry much real weight, if any, in early Bellow; as I've already noted, this term is "responsibility." Paradoxically, the writer whose protagonist is rejected, reviled, and ignored—"to whom can I be responsible, and why should I be, when you refuse to see me?"—makes that protagonist, especially at the book's end, painfully aware of his responsibility: he was supposed to save Harlem, he was supposed to save universal Man. Instead, he became a tool used to fan the fires, to try to make black Harlem into rubble and ash in the final deadly riot—in search of universal humanity in universal history, which only makes ruined buildings, and dead men. His nominalism both will and won't work, as Bellow's needs for recognition and commitment to convention or duty worked in some situations and not in others. As we'll see in chapter 6, it will be a new reading of history that breaks the deadlock both for Ellison and for Bellow. The solution or way out of dilemmas of man will depend on some unusual reimaginings of history, which take us forward, also, to Bellow's *The Adventures of Augie March*.

CHAPTER 6

RALPH ELLISON AND SAUL BELLOW

History and Man, the Answers

Harlem goes up in flames in the last chapter of *Invisible Man*. Black people are killed fighting the police. Why does it happen? The book offers multiple possibilities: because Ras the Exhorter, the nationalist, who refuses the white man's present-day planes and guns, along with his society, tries to lead Harlem forward to its historical destiny by leading it backward, on horseback with a spear—a form of history-drunk suicide? Because the Brotherhood pulled its support for Harlem at the crucial moment, anticipating a race riot as a cause célèbre, spilling black blood on history's canvas, to make a tableau it can display worldwide—a history-motivated homicide, then? The protagonist takes the weight of it on himself, with the nagging key term of "responsibility." By believing in a teleological history, "I had helped, had been a tool," he thinks, "had made myself responsible for that huddled form lighted by flame and gunfire in the street, and all the others whom now the night was making ripe for death."[1]

History, Ellison's protagonist discovers, for those like the Brotherhood who cling to it and crave it—who separate it from the lives inside it, who see in it a pattern but divorce it from the past (so that their "history" is always a code for the future)—leads to Apocalypse. And just as nominalism takes you outside the evaluation of "man" as a type, so, after Tod Clifton has plunged into death, the protagonist, caught between the history-tales of Ras and the Brotherhood, becomes preoccupied with a vision that takes one outside of history—by the recognition of all who "plunge" outside, whose faces go unseen and voices unheard. "Why did [Tod] choose to plunge into nothingness, into the void of faceless faces, of soundless voices, lying outside history?" (439). History, he begins to think, is recorded only for a few—"only those . . . that the recorder regards as important . . . [by] those lies his keepers keep their power by" (439). Not yet an original thought: this could sound like the truism that history is written by the victors. Rather, the originality in the protagonist's turn to look outside of history, for those "faceless faces" and "soundless voices," lies in whom he finds waiting there for him. First of all, he finds . . . hipsters. Hipster youth in zoot suits, "hips in trousers that ballooned upward from cuffs fitting snug about their ankles"; hipster youth who talk in jive; hipster youth with "conked hair" and wide hat brims to snap; hipster youth who read "comic book[s]," not Joyce. As the protagonist moves amazed, eyes newly opened, up from the subway entrance "through the crowds along 125th Street," he finds a whole new invisible population, "other men dressed like the boys, and . . . girls in dark exotic-colored stockings, their costumes surreal variations of downtown styles. They'd been there all along, but somehow I'd missed them. . . . They were outside the groove of history" (440–43).

As the Brotherhood fades from significance in the novel's last stages (except for its final implication in the riot), two alternatives for black people's future history rise to the top, and these turn out to be the nationalist and the hipster. The protagonist learns to name and symbolize them as Ras and Rinehart. He thinks he understands Ras, the antitechnological, antiwhite, friend-or-foe, "African" firebrand. Ras would lynch the protagonist as a betrayer, borne into a violent history that is no longer rooted in time; he attains his apotheosis in an insane horseback charge against the police. But Rinehart, and the hipster culture he represents, remains an enigma and a guaranteed, terrestrial survivor. The protagonist discovers that by miming the hipster, in dark glasses and a snap-brim hat of his own, he enters a distinctive form of *deliberate* invisibility, and a uniquely pure community of recognition, stripped of thought, in which only outward signs and masks are recognized, only code words heard, where "knowledge" exists only as the face of being already in the know. *Style* becomes the absolute mark of a person, though it is, necessarily, no longer individual style but at most individuation of a subcultural identity (the one hat you prefer of all the similar hats or the one comic-book hero you favor in all the similar comic books). Nor does hip any longer take part in the deep historical communities in which the protagonist has achieved humanizing recognitions of himself—no more yams or folktales from the South, and no more literary history to aspire or allude to, when what you read is *Superman* and *Weird Tales*.

This might seem to steer us away from the problem of man, but Ellison was right, in a certain way, about where the problem of man was headed in history—into an era of a bifurcation of the treatment of history and humanness. He knew, very presciently, what would come to intervene and help undo any concern with an abstract will to be human: Ras-style nationalism on the one hand (called "identity," whether racial or ethnic), and Rinehart-style "identity" of pure mass-cultural taste affinities, sometimes blandly called "pop culture," on the other. One does not have to be human, perhaps, if one is just black, Jewish, or Asian. But one also does not need to care about being human as a primary characteristic if one is a hipster, beatnik, freak, or hippie, or, much later, a B-boy, gangsta, Rasta, Oreo, preppie, or wigga; a Goth, punk, skater, and so forth—belonging to any of the small subcultural classes through which recognition would be sought and personal identity established among the young by synchronic style distinction and repetition, not diachronic culture. These really *were* the two alternatives that triumphed, not just in black culture, but in all of America, in the second half of the twentieth century.

Ellison's protagonist is held between the options, appalled by each. "I have also been called one thing and then another while no one really wished to hear what I called myself," the protagonist orates in the epilogue. "But what do *I* really want, I've asked myself. Certainly not the freedom of a Rinehart or the power of a Jack [the doctrinaire Communist], nor simply the freedom not to run. No, but the next step I couldn't make, so I've remained in the hole" (575). He ends the book waiting underground—inside, famously, a kingdom of lightbulbs, a room of full illumination for who he is, which, still, *no one else can see.* The significance of those lightbulbs and the power that illuminates them, I want to say, is the reregistration of hierarchical power as pure neutrality. And yet he can't yet take that neutrality outside, to a world that isn't ready for his reemergence. Although the character—in his self-styled Plato's cave, with the sun of enlightenment now rigged up by him, ingeniously, *inside* this place of protection—seems to wind up in the classic position of aporia (that newly enlightened perplexity, knowing what one doesn't know, which tended to end Platonic rather than Hegelian dialectic), the book *Invisible Man* as a whole bequeaths an argument for how the outside could, over time, be reconstructed or reconceived to make America a place worth living in. The book adds up to a plan for a particular view of American history as an absolute synthesis of black work with white representation, until it could *all* be reregistered as part of a common heritage, and thus—like power turned into sharable electricity—neutralized.

THE ELLISON–FIEDLER–MORRISON THESIS, OR UN-MONOPOLATED LIGHT AND POWER

Invisible Man's ultimate historical contention, in the broadest sense, is that the philosophical and world-historical West is as much the possession of blacks as whites, and perhaps—if one takes seriously the bondsman's creativity and independence as the one who does the actual *work* of civilization—more African Americans' possession than anyone else's.[2] The synthesis that could restore some common ground of "agreement" to the black and white tradition is that which registers white and black in other sets of terms. The paean to light in the prologue is a first step in this re-creation of vocabulary. White, which is the color of domination and of whitewashing, covering, and coating (as we learned in the paint factory), becomes *light*, which stands neutrally between what is seen and what there is to see: it is an instrument, or tool, that can belong to no one in advance of its use. Hierarchical power, likewise, is recast as electricity, a form of energy, the temporary possession of "Monopolated Light & Power," which the narrator taps with hidden lines—because power in electric form can be used by anyone; it is color-blind. With the same logic, blackness can be removed from substantive existence, even from its sometime identification as a lack, the absence of color or illumination, to be made invisibility in its positive form, the inability *yet* to be seen (which is someone else's loss rather than your own), or the invisibility of drawing into deliberate darkness (or total illumination), of passing through dangerous situations under a cloak of invisibility to those without eyes to see neutrally, or equitably.

The interdependence and synthesis of white and black traditions is, of course, acted out in *Invisible Man* at the level of style and allusion. The opening of chapter 5, about the college, is a pastiche of Faulkner. The young Mr. Emerson episode rather arbitrarily conjures one of the great names of the American Renaissance and invokes another figure, Whitman, in the bohemian (presumably, gay) bar called Club Calamus (185). The great name Ellison evokes, "Emerson," was also his own implied last name—he was, on his birth certificate, Ralph Waldo Ellison—a peculiar birthright that could give anyone a strong personal sense of the overlap of the black and white traditions. Ellison makes good on these precursors without being overwhelmed by them because he sticks to *allusion* and quotation rather than pervasive influence, and piles up the material rather than get caught in any single groove. Reading *Invisible Man*, one hears direct allusions also to Joyce, Yeats, and lesser figures—even to a then-famous, now-forgotten short story called "The Girls in their Summer Dresses," by Irwin Shaw, the author of the *The Young Lions*—in short, to anything and everything promiscuously. It is the *fact* of the allusions rather than any specific referential content that does his work for Ellison. The more compulsive, ubiquitous, and lightly tossed-off the allusions, the more they seem embedded in every part of his *African* American saga. The daring of this would have been even clearer at the time: the last high modernists were not then just the antique references that everyone must allude to; many were still contemporary and active. And Ellison was alluding to, responding to, and segmenting figures in canons that a scholarly effort was just trying to settle at that moment. He was laying claim, in other words, to a presence within the deed or will of American literature before the ink had entirely dried.

I would link this to what I'd call the Fiedler-Ellison-Morrison thesis. This is a repeated but far from pervasive idea—captured by three key proponents in the second half of the twentieth century—that classic American literature was from its inception built on the presence of African Americans, both where it seems obvious and where it was unacknowledged.

It was the Jewish critic Leslie Fiedler, in 1948, who initiated the line with the publication of "Come Back to the Raft Ag'in, Huck Honey!" and later *Love and Death in the American Novel,* in which he identified a central pattern in American literature of "boys' books" built on a homosexual love between a white hero and his "colored" friend—surpassing the love of men and women and serving a "sociological significance" in a nation riven by racial division.[3] Lawrence Jackson, who has studied Ellison's notes, drafts, and unpublished essay materials, as well as the genesis of *Invisible Man,* believes that by the mid-1940s Ellison had already developed versions of the theses that Fiedler brought to the public eye. "Ellison theorized that white fiction writers, far from rejecting the Negro, had long been obsessed by Negroes, whose blackness they had consciously and deliberately connected with sin in order to rationalize the injustice and cruelty of slavery. By condemning the Africans to the paradoxically powerful cultural role as the antithesis of right and good, the ruling elites . . . found some means of excising their rampaging guilt."[4] When Fiedler's first publication on the subject appeared in *Partisan Review,* Jackson reports, Ellison read it with annoyance, but took Fiedler seriously enough—in the critic's connecting of guilty white interest in blacks to a homosexual love—to return to reading Whitman following Fiedler's lead. Ellison, I think, then in effect wrote a parody of Fiedler's thesis into *Invisible Man,* in the scene with the younger Emerson and his gay offers of friendship and invitation to Club Calamus. Jackson interprets the homosexual Emerson generously as "a character who would move outside of at least some of the textures and patterns of normative behavior to help the Invisible Man."[5] This is quite reasonable, but I'm inclined to see it as less 1990s-progressive: the young Mr. Emerson scene contains an acknowledgment of the Fiedler thesis while having fun at the white critic's expense, recasting Emerson in fay gay stereotype as yet another white "friend of the Negro" who only wants to get at him sexually. (This, in turn, is complicated by the sense that Ellison as a person may have been less motivated in his annoyance by homophobia than by frustration at white intellectual exploitation, finding new ways to make the black presence subordinate—for the newest research on the original manuscripts of *Invisible Man* in the Library of Congress has identified an extensive deleted sequence with a black gay professor at the college who is as wise an outsider figure as any in the book.[6] In fact—why be coy?—it is Woodridge, who the protagonist goes back to when he finds he "had become 'more human'").

In more recent decades, the principle that allusions to whiteness and blackness in white American literature should be attributed to actual white-black relations reached a post-Fiedler-and-Ellison completion and canonization in Toni Morrison's plainspoken *Playing in the Dark* (1992): "There is no romance free of what Herman Melville called 'the power of blackness,' especially not in a country in which there was a resident population, already black, upon which the imagination could play; through which historical, moral, metaphysical, and social fears, problems, and dichotomies could be articulated."[7] Readers know explicitly that Melville's "Benito Cereno" is about a slave-ship revolt (it is quoted in one of *Invisible Man*'s epigraphs); but to begin to make the "whiteness of the whale" in *Moby-Dick* about actual devilish whiteness is the brave step taken by the Fiedler-Ellison-Morrison idea. Some will connect the black "apes" in Poe's "The System of Dr. Tarr and Professor Feather" to a distortion of fears of black insurrection in the South, but to make the final supernal whiteness in *The Narrative of Arthur Gordon Pym* an aspect of an American fantasy to purge blacks is a still further step. The African American presence is *everywhere*. To see in *The Adventures of Huckleberry Finn* and Cooper's *The Deerslayer* alike not just a plot that includes blacks and Indians but an effort to rest white adventure on a fantasized homosocial love affair with nonwhite sidekicks—who love whites in return, despite enslavement and genocide, forgiving them for their crimes—is a further step (though it was Fiedler's original, earliest contribution; some points only gain credence with slow repetition).[8] If these have all now become familiar readings of these canonical American works, it is because of the Fiedler-Ellison-Morrison line.

The implication of all this in *Invisible Man* is that just as any African American has a place already made for him in the history of the West that he helped build—which he has to fight to reclaim by *literalizing* it, making it immediate, putting it into action, even by words and blows, or by something beyond them (like "theory")—so the black American writer already has a place in literature, too. It, too, simply must be literalized and brought into action, through allusion, overcoming, and practice—here in the writing of a *new* work of great American literature, a Great American Novel, that reactivates elements of the old. Our end is in our beginning—and in closing we can turn back from the epilogue to the previously most riddling passage in the prologue, which stays in one's mind like a rebus throughout one's reading:

My hole is warm and full of light. Yes, *full* of light. I doubt if there is a brighter spot in all New York than this hole of mine, and I do not exclude Broadway. Or the Empire State Building . . . Those two spots are among the darkest of our whole civilization—pardon me, our whole *culture* (an important distinction, I've heard)—which might sound like a hoax, or a contradiction, but that (by contradiction, I mean) is how the world moves: Not like an arrow, but a boomerang. (Beware of those who speak of the *spiral* of history; they are preparing a boomerang. . . .) I know; I have been boomeranged across my head so much that I now can see the darkness of lightness. And I love light. . . . Light confirms my reality, gives birth to my form. . . . That is why I fight my battle with Monopolated Light & Power. (6; italics in original)

How are Broadway and the Empire State Building "the darkest" places "of our whole civilization"? They are dark first morally because they are the triumph of a civilization that keeps a good part of its people, if no longer in bondage then still, so to speak, invisible. Then dark again racially, because black music and black dancing, termed "popular" music and movement, formed the basis of the modern entertainments of the "Great White Way." Dark, too, because the Empire State Building was built, like all the great edifices of America, on girders laid by black hands. The protagonist knows different learned theories on these matters ("civilization" vs. "culture," whether the allusion is to sweetly lit Matthew Arnold or twilit Oswald Spengler), but doesn't much care—not now that he's learned that history is, first, Hegelian (it "moves" by "contradiction") and, then, that this Hegelianism is victimizing (the "boomerang" comes back to knock the bondsman, for example, upside the head). Such realizations, worked out in the book the prologue is preparing us for, have freed him to repossess and turn the "white" achievements into new registers. One is literature. ("Darkness of lightness" here is a pun and revenge on Poe's "blackness of darkness," pulling out its racial overtones, as well as a kind of rhyming code for Ellison's real thesis about the *blackness* of *whiteness*.) The other is *power*, refigured as light and electricity, available to help *make* a man, give him his own form and face, not dominate him.

If Ellison's ignored voices are finally to "plunge" into anything—if there is a normative account that connects Ellison's history to his vision of man—they should plunge out of capital-H History but into this hybrid history, in the fight for a culture, technics, and "power" that are already their own, and not turn against it, since it is theirs, too; not assuming that any path will bring it easily to them, because of the danger of the "boomerang." Hence style—as treated shallowly by those hipsters—*does*, or could, touch a culture with a purchase on whiteness, too, but a culture broader and deeper than the hipsters know. And hence "history" will let you make your-self "human," but only if you continually reregister the terms in which the dominating world would prefer to give your humanity to you.

THE INDIVIDUAL WAY TO "MAN—HIMSELF"

Ellison had written a new Great American Novel. He had broken through. Readers who had been looking for a new definitive entry into the effort to bring respect to the postwar novel knew, upon *Invisible Man*'s appearance in 1952, that Ellison had won their case for them. They sensed he had even answered the question of man—and yet they couldn't all quite say yet, exactly, how.

Some followed the "human" reading to the utmost, like Delmore Schwartz, who wrote the official review for *Partisan Review*: "Ellison's hero . . . has never been seen as a human being and a unique individual. . . . *Invisible Man* . . . is truly about being a human being, any human being and all human beings," he wrote. It "is not merely a story about being a Negro, and not a protest novel, unless we are willing to call it everybody's protest novel, to use James Baldwin's phrase."[9]

The absolute valedictory came in *Commentary*, the explicitly Jewish organ of the Jewish intellectuals, and it came, significantly, from Saul Bellow. Bellow was, at this stage, looking toward *The Adventures of Augie March*. He had published portions of his novel well in advance of Ellison's novel; in fact, large swathes of the book had appeared in a variety of journals (the *New Yorker*, *Harper's Bazaar*, and the *Partisan*, *Hudson*, and *Sewanee Reviews* among them). He praises Ellison, but also takes him as a model of "the writer," the "truly heroic" figure who can still exist when others feel "there is no strength to match the strength of those powers which attack and cripple modern mankind"—a role into which other writers will fit, as, for example, Bellow. He hails the "independence" of Ellison's writing from particularity: "For there is a 'way' for Negro novelists to go at their problems, just as there are Jewish or Italian 'ways.' Mr. Ellison has not adopted a minority tone." He gives a wrong reading of the book's meaning: it shows the fundamental battle between instinct and civilization, the real individual and the social Man. But Bellow, in a certain way, also gets Ellison right:

> In our society Man—Himself—is idolized and publicly worshipped, but the single individual must hide himself underground and try to save his desires, his thoughts, his soul, in invisibility. *He must return to himself,* learning self-acceptance and rejecting all that threatens to deprive him of his manhood. This is what I make of *Invisible Man*.[10]

"He must return to himself"—but with "Himself" a capital-letter entity, sliding back and forth between an individual instance and a repeated, or stable, historical type—in this, Bellow subtly sounds a note that could recast *Invisible Man* in connection with *Augie March*. And what one begins to see, from this point, is a kind of interfiling between the careers and possibly even the work of two major writers, and between black and Jew, at the time of their two major works, in an atmosphere that understood the challenges of "the human condition" and "Man—Himself" (plus the "individual—himself") as the grounds on which these authors would make their breakthrough achievements. Bellow was part of the committee of five that voted to award Ellison the National Book Award in 1953.[11] Ellison's novel beat out Hemingway's *The Old Man and the Sea*, and thus reflected a partial changing of the guard, at least among highbrows (Hemingway got the more middlebrow Pulitzer). In his acceptance speech, Ellison called for a fiction that "can arrive at the truth about the human condition, here and now." He wrote to Richard Wright privately about the not-yet-published *The Adventures of Augie March*: "Watch out for Bellow's novel, by the way. It is the first real novel by an American Jew."[12] In 1954, in turn, Bellow's *The Adventures of Augie March* won the National Book Award. *Augie March* finally solved Bellow's earlier questioning of man in a way that corresponded to, but differed from, Ellison's—because *Augie March*, too, finally integrated the man question with a particular theory of history, this time fully influenced, at last, I'll argue, by philosophies floating around the University of Chicago.

RECOGNITION COMMUNITIES AND THE JEWISHNESS OF *AUGIE MARCH*

The Adventures of Augie March must be one of the most forced-feeling great novels of modern literature. Trotsky quipped that Céline entered great literature the way other people enter their houses.[13] In *Augie March*, Bellow, you feel, had to batter the lock until it gave. Nevertheless, it is a major novel and had a significant influence on American postwar writing. It made its own answer, of sorts, to the crisis of man—and Bellow, more than Ellison or anyone else, attained fame as a laureate of the crisis. Scholarly books about him carry such titles as *Saul Bellow: In Defense of Man* and *Saul Bellow and the Decline of Humanism*.

It is well known that Bellow often described his overwhelming ease in composing the immensely long *Augie March*—he said repeatedly that it was like catching the writing with buckets.[14] The contrast between the forced texture of the prose and this biographical fact of effortlessness is, I think, explained by the truth that what readers are witnessing in *The Ad-*

ventures of Augie March is a colossal work of disinhibition, which comes out also in the book's meaning or implicit argument. The greatness of the book, let's say, has to do with its ability to take a put-on mood, a forced boisterousness and energy, and run through it for hundreds of pages until it takes root and seems natural, while hanging on to the philosophical obstacle course of worries that had given such a fettered and lugubrious character to earlier works. Trilling had called for a reconstitution of the will of humanism. What Bellow produced is one of the great reviving achievements of *willed* will, or willfulness, with its own forceful answer to the critics.

Following *The Victim*, "Looking for Mr. Green," and, for that matter, *Invisible Man*, we might expect that the novel *Augie March* should first confront the problem of racial identity and communities of recognition, and over- or underrecognition, if indeed it is to try to solve the same problems. *Augie March* does start with the problem of recognition, but in a peculiar way; it treats it as a certain kind of forgettable fact, not a problem. This can be seen by posing a question whose answer (in the affirmative) is often taken for granted, in 1953 and today: the puzzling question of whether *Augie March* is or is not a "Jewish" book.

Certainly, we know the title character and narrator, young Augie March, is Jewish—or rather, when asked, he "guesses" he is, in his words. In effect, he'll come to mean by this that those who already know don't think of it; those who can guess correctly won't care; and those who *would* guess—and dislike his race—can't guess. His interview with the employer Renling, the first boss who takes him out of Chicago, goes like this: " 'Jew?' . . . 'Yes. I guess.' . . . 'Well, out there on the North Shore they don't like Jews. But,' he said . . . 'they'll probably never know.' "[15] The recognition of a hard kernel of Jewish difference from the outside world occurs only one other place in the book, in its allusion to anti-Semitism among children, and Augie's narration neatly takes care of it: "And sometimes we were chased, stoned, bitten, and beat up for Christ-killers, all of us . . . articled, whether we liked it or not, to this mysterious trade. But I never had any special grief from it, or brooded, being by and large too larky and boisterous to take it to heart" (12).

The book has none of the internal content of Judaism. There's not a synagogue in sight, no rabbis, no Passover seder (like the seder that opened Rosenfeld's *Passage from Home*), no annual holidays, no Jewish ritual even at the wedding of Simon to Charlotte Magnus. Looking closely at the wedding scene—the rare ritual in the book where some liturgy would seem to *have* to be present, otherwise how has the pair been married?—it becomes evident by the exclusion how religion as such has been purged, even while Cousin Anna calls Simon "*meshuggah*" (241). There can certainly be Yiddish, the old creole language of negotiation of multiple worlds, but there's no Hebrew. Nor is it any surprise when Clem Tambow, out of the blue, orders sweet-and-sour pork (433). This is a point at which a conspicuously historical book (portraying the Depression, the war, etc., as turning points in the lives of its individual characters—Einhorn is ruined in the crash, Augie joins the merchant marine) is choosing a particular track of historical material about the *roots* of movement and human diversity. The book isn't forgetting, but doing something deliberate and profound. Surely a Jewish wedding included a wedding ceremony. Surely there was a synagogue in Jewish Chicago between 1915 and 1945. Surely not all first- or second-generation Jewish Americans were atheists and freethinkers?

Yet the whole point of *Augie March* is, in fact, to maintain Jewishness at first as an absolute *bounding* concept for the beginning world of the book, which still does not seem to influence the *contents or range* of its characters. Everyone in the early part of the book is Jewish as a matter of course. Usually you can tell this by last names and occasional bits of dialogue with nearly Yiddish dialect rhythms. Yet the collection also exists to reproduce all the different parts of American society within a purely Jewish world. Thus, the tough boxing hopeful is "Nails" Nagel. The creepy cousin who sells out Augie to the Magnuses is Kelly Weintraub—as if even the Irish hoods were Jewish in this book. The reason you don't need to hear about *religious* Jewishness is that it's the enclosing, credentialing wall; it's the boundary, common to all, that has no dogmatic place in the internal distinctions of the mobile community.

That "recognition community," as I'd call it, of Jewishness is only the first of several such concentric worlds. The initial one hundred pages or so of *Augie March*—which includes many of the chapters Bellow serialized in journals, and the part most everyone reads before a certain percentage then give up on the book—are incredibly static, precisely because the gravity of these first households is so great. Maxwell Geismar was right to call the chapters on Augie's early households a series of "daguerreotypes."[16] Only when households break down (with George's and Grandma Lausch's successive institutionalizations and Einhorn's financial collapse in the Depression), and the book starts to experience a kind of centripetal overload, does the novel develop a narrative drive. There begins a series of breakaways from slum Chicago and fallings-back. It's as if the book's question was, what quantum of energy is needed to make a person change levels? What will send Augie out of his narrow orbit into the next orbit higher? He leaps up to Evanston, to Buffalo, to the university district, to Mexico—each time returning to his starting point.

The remarkable thing about the book is how easy all translation between one language and another, one class and another, and then one racial or national location and another proves to be. Augie functions in all neighborhoods and flourishes at all levels of wealth and poverty, in Mexico and France as well, and as naturally, as in Chicago. *Augie March* does not acknowledge the meaning of the phrase "language barrier."

If *Augie March* were an African American novel, it might be called a novel of passing, when a person manages to be taken for whatever racial character he needs to be to wind up on the right side of the American order. The absence that makes that assessment false here is that Augie doesn't feel the anxiety of passing. His way of moving between levels is quite different. It's worth noticing how often Augie is dressed up in new clothes by different characters, and how little it seems to express anything either worrisome (they're changing my character) or exciting (they're going to disguise me). He can't be disguised, because the easy recognition of clothes never functions as an obstacle or a compromise. The need for a deeper recognition doesn't matter, either, because Augie feels no solid core that he wishes could be recognized. He has instead an *energy* that is to be expressed. He functions equally well in all places. Hollowness, in effect, doesn't trouble him. It makes him buoyant.

Recognition communities in *Augie March* then, I think, are not opaque or obstructive but congruent and superimposed. Repetition is the mode of demonstration of the book. Episodes that would furnish the material of one whole novel are each played over at least two or three times by the end of *Augie March*, driven by characters who become variations on fundamental types. The oversized male teacher resurfaces in Einhorn and Mintouchian; the domineering female teacher in Grandma Lausch and Mrs. Renling; and the professing madman in Robey and Bateshaw. All take Augie through isomorphic communities that could be named "Jewish Chicago," "America," or "humanity," if their levels were cleanly divided; instead, the levels reproduce themselves in multiple locations. This way of construing the "civilizations" formed by those who recognize each other— in a novel apparently so indifferent to something as highfalutin as civilizations, so insouciant about these kinds of recognition—lies at the root of *Augie March*'s way of solving Bellow's previous problems with the idea of man.

CHICAGO REDUX: MAN AND REPETITION

Central to the crisis of man was the fear that the history and inheritance of civilization would no longer be continuous, or that something in man had been lost. The claim of *The Adventures of Augie March* is that you find the same fixed possibilities of human character in each category of people, each community, each microcivilization—and that the larger civilization carries on its "history," with perfect continuity, because of it.

The individuals whose characters repeat don't just echo one another; they also map onto the great figures of recorded history. They are tagged with other names—Cornwallis (5), Danton, Napoleon, Bayard, Cincinnatus (29), Castiglione (58), Pope Alexander VI (67) or formulas, such as "Fouché got as far as Talleyrand" (58)—to illuminate Simon's anger, Grandma Lausch's ambitions for Augie, or Einhorn's manners, and the local luminaries, themselves, study the ancient great ones, too: Grandma Lausch reads Tolstoy, Einhorn interprets Shakespeare.

Education turns out to be the process of learning how to find the common characters in each part of one's experience, through each repeated, isomorphic community. It's true that there is no description of a book more uninteresting, on the face of it, than that it is a "novel of education." The term "bildungsroman" has just been too successful as our one technical term for the novel of any individual's education into sensibility or experience. (Maybe the phrase would be less evacuated of significance if we had single terms for a wider range of types of books—as, say, if *entwicklungsroman* or *kunstlerroman* had made better showings in English, too.) But *Augie March* truly is an education novel, of a rare sort that rebukes the bildungsroman as we commonly know it. It thematizes different, indeed formal, models of education. It contains scholarly learning—specifically, from the canon of "liberal education" or the Great Books. It proffers teacher after teacher, in the form of Grandma Lausch and Einhorn, and later Robey and Mintouchian. These are professors in the simplest etymological sense—having doctrines to profess. And they are understood in the light of the great thinkers of the past, as relatives of Machiavelli, Solon, or Shakespeare ("I'd ask myself, 'What would Caesar suffer . . . What would Machiavelli advise or Ulysses do . . . What would Einhorn think?'" [60]).

Bellow's professors teach their theories, however, and demonstrate their practice without institutional affiliation or tenure, often from the kitchen or den or even the toilet. The book declares itself for the tradition of liberal education but suggests the tradition's real teachings take place entirely outside the university, which Augie moves near but does not attend. In this sense it is a rebuke, too, to the campus novel, famous instances of which chronologically bookend Bellow's 1953 success—Mary McCarthy's *The Groves of Academe* (1952) and Randall Jarrell's *Pictures from an Institution* (1954). The physical location of historical learning in the novel is a much-abused but treasured set of the Harvard Classics, the Five-Foot Shelf of Books. This original is Charles William Eliot's fifty-volume 1909–10 publishing effort, intended to include all the books a man should read for his education. The set comes to Augie from Einhorn after they're damaged in the fire that Einhorn set in his own house for the insurance money. "I had only a few things left. However, there was Einhorn's fire-damaged set of classics in a box under the bed, and I . . . was lying in my socks reading" (252). I find it hard to read of the Five-Foot Shelf in *Augie March* and not think of the Chicago Great Books. The one seems a representative of, or surrogate for, the other. It certainly takes us back to what Bellow had been doing for employment between 1943 and 1945. Indeed, the results of that work had just appeared: in 1952, Hutchins and Adler released all fifty-one non-*Synopticon*-and-introduction volumes of the Great Books of the Western World—exactly one more volume than the Harvard Classics. Saul Bellow's name can be found opposite the copyright page of the *Synopticon*, included alphabetically near the top of the list of "editorial staff."[17]

In *Augie March*, there is a passage at the start of chapter 7 that compares Einhorn at length to Croesus. It retells the classical "old tale of Croesus" in a mixture of high and demotic language, taking in his dealings with Solon, Cyrus, and Cambyses. And, crucially, it is essentially unintelligible, completely opaque even to a normally educated reader, unless he or she already knows the outline of this history in detail. If one doesn't know that Solon said to Croesus, "Count no man happy until he's dead," or that Croesus was first put in chains and then redeemed and made a counselor, and so forth, it makes no sense. How would one know—how would one have heard this "tale" that is rendered like a folk story or a bit of slang street legend? Only from Herodotus—in volume 6 of the Great Books, and one of the volumes that Bellow was specifically responsible for indexing for the *Synopticon*.[18] For that matter, the retelling isn't easy to parse even if you *do* know your Herodotus. In a sense, the point of *Augie March* is that only *living* the Great Books gives one access to them of the right kind. If Bellow must be opaque to prove that point, he will.

The nobility of the Great Books was always synonymous with an idea of liberal education, advancing a simple position: men were the same in all times. Every age could produce great thinkers who examined the same human problems from their own vantage points and recorded the results. Even though the material conditions of life might change, the answers human beings had given would always be relevant. We, today, will best learn to be excellent, free men once we consider all the best results from the past as the basis for answering the questions of our own times. Hutchins resummarized this in the year before *Augie March*, as he had been doing since the '30s:

There is something called man on this earth. He wrestles with his problems and tries to solve them. These problems change from epoch to epoch in certain respects; they remain the same in others. What is the good life? What is a good state? Is there a God? What is the nature and destiny of man? Such questions and a host of others persist because man persists, and they will persist as long as he does. Through the ages great men have written down their discussion of these persistent questions. Are we to disdain the light they offer us on the ground that they lived in primitive, far-off times?[19]

Had Bellow, by the time of *Augie March*, finally accepted the Hutchins and University of Chicago answer? The principle that every person was equally capable of reading the Great Books, and that therefore the intellect's capacity (if not training) was in every healthy person the same, was meant to be an expression of democracy. The meanest fatherless urchin—Augie March, say—would find that Tacitus might make his life more worthwhile than that life lived without Tacitus. But Hutchins did not necessarily have a theory that always put such knowledge into action, "to work." This might have smacked of the experiential, experimental attitude of Dewey. It was an article of faith that liberal education would be more useful to the urchin than any learning that started from the idea of "difference." But how would one submit it to proof?

According to James Atlas, in letters Bellow wrote to his publisher James Henle in 1943, Bellow himself claimed that when he first took the *Synopticon* job, he was not a Hutchins-Adler man himself but a naturalist, a follower of George Herbert Mead and John Dewey.[20] Dewey's educational theory (like Mead's sociology) had also been associated with the University of Chicago, before Hutchins's arrival, as we have seen in chapter 2. And the Laboratory School that Dewey had founded still stood as a reminder of the development of his educational theory of "learning through occupations," his idea that a sequence of self-guided, experimental pursuits of varied lines of tasks under the gentle direction of a supervisor would best lead students to the skills they needed for life.

Augie March can seem a merger of the two opposing theories: Hutchins plus Dewey, or, say, Dewey as a Great Books–trained thinker might like to imagine him. Augie has vocation after vocation, each of which leads him back to using his "Five-Foot Shelf of Classics," his Great Books—not as part of school, but for the discovery of the stable, repeating nature of the personalities around him in the world.

Jobs structure the forward motion of the book. They link the household to the community. It takes full lungs to list all the vocations Augie undertakes during the course of the book: handbill distributor, assistant newspaper deliverer (to Coblin), Woolworth's packing clerk, train station kiosk clerk, street-corner salesman, department store shopboy, flower shop as-

sistant, man Friday to Einhorn, thief of handbags, women's shoes salesman, sporting-goods salesman (for Renling), rubberized paint salesman,
driver for illegal immigrant smuggling, dog kennel assistant, thief of books,
coal sales manager (for his brother Simon), CIO organizer, Eagle trainer (un-
paid), man Friday to Robey, apprentice teacher, merchant marine sailor,
and semilicit middleman-importer in postwar Europe. Yet the ruminative
interest and emotion of the book tends to revolve around ad hoc households: first those made by families, that of the Marches and Grandma
Lausch, the Coblins, Kleins, Einhorns, Renlings, Magnuses, and so forth,
then those defined by Mimi, Thea, and Stella, or each woman he winds up
with—each with an apartment or home and habits that give a stopping
point to the ceaseless transit and forward motion from one job to the next.
Employments are tools; households are persistent dwellings; in trials by
each, character discloses itself.

The permanent lesson of this education is that the great ones are already around you. Are they as great as Machiavelli and Hobbes? No, probably not; but they are great in their line as Machiavelli and Hobbes were in
theirs (to use *Augie March*'s language), and have certain common qualities
and family resemblances with their better-known predecessors. Can we
always find people in our immediate neighborhood who are the same as
those in remote antiquity, as written down in books? *Augie March* seems
to say, basically, yes. There may not be a single human nature, but there is
indeed a fixed set of human characters, or ranges of development, that repeat. *Education* is then a name for the expression of energy by which a few
of those people rise above absorption in the immediate to discover this
truth of the world. Einhorn did it, Simon did it, and Grandma Lausch did it.
Augie may not add up to much, or have any sure superiority beyond this:
that he has learned it, too, in fact, beyond any of them, and keeps striving
toward higher levels of this discovery and movement, and attaining them,
moving through one "recognition community" after another, orienting
himself by the repetition of character and his fluid movement within this
gridded picture of man.

The first recognition level, I've said, is Jewish, where disparate characters are linked by last name or Yiddishisms or kinship (I think of the book's
undertaker, Kinsman, as if, at death, they're all kinsmen under the skin).
The second level is Chicagoan and American. Here disparate people can be
recognized by their common language, slang, and mores. The third level is
human, known by "love." We learn of it in the late pages of the book, and
see that Augie's greatness is as a privileged discoverer of the rare thing in
every one: "Why, I am a sort of Columbus of those near-at-hand and believe
you can come to them in this immediate *terra incognita* that spreads out
in every gaze" (536). Even abstract humanity, then, is not quite something

you have to discover in or by yourself, as it is in Ellison. It exists in the permanent repetition of the concrete within natural parameters—something more dependable than Bellow's earlier worries about mere convention and commitment, linking disparate people by "work," in "Looking for Mr. Green," and more knowable (if complex) than the impossible single abstraction sought in *Dangling Man*.

This isn't quite a universalism. It may be a form of successive universalisms, or education in universals. Bellow's new stance is not the grand universalism that would say that man survives because there is a common, bright thread running through all men, that some simple common attribute makes them the same. Neither is it a pluralism that would value diversity for its own sake or believe in an undetermined and malleable range. It is a way of representing a finite spectrum of differences, always within some prior general category (Jews, Chicagoans, Americans, wise men of all times, and "wise guys," too) for an essential family feeling, a mutual recognition, that can be established at each level. The meaning of true education is a moving-up through those levels of family-feeling. So the moral aspiration might be to learn by a true education that one's family extends, ultimately, so to speak, to man. It also proposes an ontological principle: that in every milieu and generation, certain human types will always be found, once one knows how to look for them and engage them, and this ensures the continuity of man against many contemporary worries about decline.

Trilling's demand for new "will" may be solved—but still will be available only to those with Trilling's certain "energy of mind." Though all men are the same (and human), without the initiation into the life of education, one remains only the same as inferior persons and does not join the common realm of the superior ones—therefore, in a different sense of the word, the uneducated man stays "subhuman" (a word Hutchins himself was not afraid to use). Another way of putting this doctrine of democratic elitism, as it works out in *Augie March*, is that education is the process by which you distinguish yourself in discovering that other people are the same as you—thus discovering that you are the same as some others on a higher, more capacious level. Because it posits forms of human character that get copied in individual men, the nearest diagnostic terms for this might be "characterological Platonism," or even "type idealism" (for it is not the case that there is *one* right ideal form of man, but a limited, finite set of forms that appear in men).

TYPE IDEALISM AND THE PROBLEM OF BIRTH

Of course, again, with Bellow, once you have reached this far into his answer to the crisis of man, you discover another moment of aporia. For this

Platonism about human types meets the openness and newness that are supposed to be characteristics of America, and causes a grave conflict. The purely new, absent a prior type, has *no way* to come into the world. There is none of what Hannah Arendt called "natality," the power of birth and change that counters "mortality" and the eventuality of death.[21]

This consequence of Bellow's philosophical logic in *Augie March* deposits a hidden structuring problem in the book. It helps to explain the feature of the novel I had never been able to explain, as a reader, to my satisfaction: why the book's moments of emotional climax, in love, fear, comedy, and disgust, relentlessly but mysteriously revolve around the wish for children, combined with the obstruction of pregnancy and birth.

To me, the single best, most powerful, and formally coherent part of the book—the portion that can assure you that *Augie March* does have some qualities of a world-level masterpiece—has always been chapter 12, in which Augie helps Mimi Villars attempt abortion, through one means after another. First Mimi drinks an inadequately effective abortifacient. Then she goes for two surgical procedures—one official, achieved by lying to hospital doctors—the other dangerous and illegal. Finally, Augie has to bring her to the hospital to save her life from an infection after the illegal procedure.

Idling near the maternity ward, Augie witnesses one of the most dramatic pictures of pain or violence in the generally buoyant book:

> I passed through to another division where the labor rooms were, separate cubicles, and in them saw women struggling, outlandish pain and huge-bellied distortion, one powerful face that bore down into its creases and issued a voice great and songlike in which she cursed her husband obscenely for his pleasure that had got her into this; and others, calling on saints and mothers, incontinent, dragging at the bars of their beds, weeping, or with faces of terror or narcotized eyes. . . . And just then, in the elevator shaft nearby, there were screams. . . . The door opened; a woman sat before me in a wheel chair, and in her lap, just born in a cab or paddy wagon or in the lobby of the hospital, covered with blood and screaming so you could see sinews, square of chest and shoulders from the strain, this bald kid, red and covering her with the red. She, too, with lost nerve, was sobbing, each hand squeezing up on itself, eyes wildly frightened; and she and the baby appeared like enemies forced to have each other, like figures of a war. (282)

An abortion—near maternal mortality—then a vision of live birth, as war, and terror, and a baby covered with blood. At the end of this sequence of abortion and parturition, Anna Coblin takes Augie in on New Year's Day and cries out for the husband and children she wishes her own daughter would have: "'And children.' 'And children—,'" Augie repeats inconclusively (284).

Augie's brother Simon and his wife Charlotte, at the end of the book, can't have a baby, though their terror—as the specter of disorder threatening all that Simon has achieved—is that Simon's mistress Renée is pregnant. No one who wants a child in the book will have one normally; only those who fear them face the horror of being saddled with the obligation of giving birth. Even when Augie winds up in a lifeboat near the book's end, with the psychopathic Bateshaw, this companion's maniacal dream is that he's solved the problem, and found a way to make life from nothing: "'You didn't create life!' 'In all humility, that's exactly what I did. Six universities have thrown me out for claiming it'" (505).

It's not children, per se, that are the problem. Children are much wanted, not least by Augie himself, because they are needed as the right subjects for *education*. It is the *making* of them that is the problem, the creating of new life through ordinary means or by Bateshaw-like mad stratagems. Augie, too, in his own fantasized future, retains a dream once made real by the Shakers, who adopted children to educate but held a theology strictly opposed to procreation, and therefore produced none themselves:

> "I aim to get myself a piece of property and settle down on it. Right here in Illinois would suit me fine, though I wouldn't object to Indiana or Wisconsin. . . . [W]hat I'd like most is to get married and set up a kind of home and teach school. . . ."
>
> "But where are you going to get kids for your school?"
>
> "I thought maybe I could get accredited with the state or county, or whoever does it, as a foster-parent, and get kids from institutions. This way the board and keep would be taken care of, and we'd have these kids."
>
> "Plus children of your own?"
>
> "Of course. I'd love to have my own little children. I long for little children. And these kids from institutions who have had it rough—" (456)

Even when Clem Tambow raises that question "Plus children of your own?," Augie doesn't quite take it in. And Augie March himself, the fatherless protagonist, is the rare literary bastard who has no interest in looking for his father. Perhaps the danger of a child newly made, of a real fathering rather than the surrogate fathering of Great Books culture, is the threat that the child might fall *positively* outside as an eruption of the non-same, a threat to the book's philosophy of permanence in history. Newness entering the world is a point of threat, and terror, as well as hope and recurrence—a moment of uncontainment. If the children are adopted as wards of the state, or made in a test tube, or just already imagined, then new or future life is something that is always had already, safely. "I wonder if it's a phase, or what," Augie admits puzzlingly in the final pages, "but sometimes I feel I already am a father"; and, propositioned by an Italian whore, a lie slips out: "'I have children. *Io ho bambini*' . . . I imagined I already had the *bambini*" (529–30).

There shouldn't be utter newness in the world, potentially blank or hostile for Bellow. There can be no such thing as an eruption of the purely new and individual at the level of persons. Rather, there is the spirit-affirming discovery that exposes a superior sameness at a higher level. Certainly this is a way of making sense of the fear that the nature of man might be in jeopardy, or broken, or undiscoverable—the conflict that Ellison took up, too. But this view is not compatible with Ellison's view, which I've called a nominalism, in which no one can rely on an abstraction called "man," and every individual must make himself worthy of possessing his own face and his own name. Some in Ellison will have to plunge outside history to do it. A plunge outside history, for *Augie March*, is inconceivable—though you might escape it by mere ignorance, by the failure of self-education. Superior people are those more equipped with energy, better able to reach the standpoint where they can see similarities and repetitions and recognize them, thus able to love a wider breadth of mankind. "Will" will be willing "will," and "freedom" going at things "freestyle," unencumbered by history because one is always acknowledged within it, if one knows where to look.

For Ellison, so many people have been always outside the flow of official "history," of what's recorded, that it's mad to restrict them to what has already been known and achieved. Who's to say that there isn't something bubbling up in the darkness that the world has never, but never, seen before? A black future, children, an African American legacy are what the white world does not want but which, paradoxically, have been the whole source of life and new fertility for the white world, too. In a dream at the end of *Invisible Man*, the narrator is castrated, his "parts" hung from a bridge, and he suddenly sees "[t]hat there hang not only my generations wasting upon the water . . . But . . . your universe, and all that drip-drop upon the water is all the history you've made, and all you're going to make" (570). This history was not perennial and repeating but modern and miscegenated. Communities were fused between different, mutually unrecognizing factions, as part of a long process in which the hidden and excluded counted as much as the recorded. In his way, Ellison, too, generated hope for man through the picture of a superior individual, and a process of self-education. But this superior mind would be one who could step out and down, into darkness and suspension; one who avoided the brief temptations of new counterrecognitions (nationalism, hipsterism), as well as the exclusive primary recognitions of white and black.

THE HOUSE OF AMERICAN LITERATURE AND THE BLACK DOG

Ellison and Bellow moved in together after 1958. It was in a house in Tivoli, New York, that Bellow owned and maintained, and where he had lived at different times with his second wife before she left him. Ellison had occupied the house before, when the Bellows were absent, and he now joined Bellow there alone when Ellison taught at Bard College, away from the apartment in New York he shared with his wife, Fanny. Fanny came up to Tivoli for weekends, apparently, though Bellow edited her out when, forty years later, he wrote his most striking account of the two writers' time together.[22]

Bellow wrote about the cohabitation at least twice. The difference in those accounts is striking—not a difference in facts, which, after all, may be a matter of fluctuating memory, but the way one of the two versions becomes a story with something to communicate. "Ralph Ellison in Tivoli" is this literary retelling, published in 1998, four years after Ellison's death. It is a remarkable little fable.

The opening of the remembrance starts with the house, a term Bellow quickly corrects: "'House' is not the word for it; it was, or once had been, a Hudson River mansion."[23] He makes it over once as a home of "aristocrats" whose dwelling he and Ellison had moved into together, taking over from "great names . . . the Livingstones, the Chapmans and the Roosevelts" (524)—just as, in metaphorical terms, these "two literary squatters," a black and a Jew, by their mammoth successes in the early '50s, moved in to inhabit the house of American literature. In further descriptions, Bellow makes it over a second time as one of the ruined mansions well known from the heart of that same American literature, of the great nineteenth-century American Renaissance, and its predecessor Poe—for "the two years we spent together in what I called the House of Usher" (527).

This mansion of theirs is the place for a proper idyll. Bellow writes *Henderson the Rain King* upstairs. Ellison types away in the ballroom downstairs. The typewriter's "long rhythms made me feel that we were on a cruise ship moving through the woods" (525), says Bellow—another of those boats or rafts of the American fraternal relationship. They go fishing together and discuss American history and literature. Ellison cultivates African violets, knows how to hunt, how to make superior drip coffee, and how to fix anything. He comes to breakfast in "his Moorish dressing gown" (528) and "slippers with a large oriental curve at the toe" (526).

I think it's not too much to say that Bellow may be giving us Ellison as the black king, Othello the Moor. Bellow intimates that during this time of writing, the farmer mowing next door, Chanler Chapman, "before I could be aware of it, became Henderson the Rain King," in the book Bellow was getting under way—raising the tantalizing and discomfiting suggestion that the black aristocrat downstairs, Ellison himself, was contributing something, in Bellow's mental alchemy, to Henderson's blood brother and teacher, the African king Dahfu. Not so far-fetched when we know how Bellow worked, and one considers that other friend-characters in Bellow's major books have all been quite easily and overtly identified by readers or critics: Delmore Schwartz as Humboldt, Jack Ludwig as Gersbach, Allan Bloom as Ravelstein, and so forth. I take it, anyway, that in this little portrait, Bellow is trying out roles for Ellison in their companionship: Huck's Jim, the great-souled Othello, maybe Dahfu.

Like all idylls, this one must come to an end. The "main cause of trouble," Bellow explains, was a black dog. Ellison had brought the dog with him. It was a purebred black Labrador, and bounded out of the black writer's Chrysler at the moment of arrival, like his familiar spirit.

The trouble between Ellison and Bellow is that Bellow only treats the dog like a dog. He blames the cur for fouling in the garden, and swipes at it with a broom. This "offended Ralph greatly." Bellow explains Ellison's outrage thus: "I was incapable of understanding, I had no feeling for pedigrees and breeds and . . . I knew only mongrels and had treated his *chien de race* like a mongrel."

Once in a while, a critic has to overread. Facing this text dating to forty years after the novels of Ellison and Bellow's major triumph, I can't help but feel that Bellow, in this literary reflection, produces a parable of each writer's significance—and each writer's limitations—on his view. He and Ellison were indeed perfect partners in a certain enterprise: that of reinhabiting American literature. Though they refused to think of themselves as Jew and black only, those were the identities that made their inhabitancy notable, and it couldn't have been otherwise. This is how "recognition" came to them. They had much to teach each other, and their literary interconnection may have been "Arcadian or Utopian," as Bellow says. But, of course, there was a certain presence that accompanied Ellison ("He did not come alone")—a black dog, or, in the insistent and odd phrasing Bellow keeps repeating, *un chien de race.* By this phrase, Bellow may just mean a thoroughbred; but then, of course, if that was all Bellow meant, he could speak English. We are facing, rather, a race-dog, the racial fact that dogged Ellison but not Bellow, who found a way to boost himself above this.

What I take Bellow to be saying is that, while Bellow could let go of the racial problem of being a Jew, and did so in *Augie March* and beyond, Ellison could not let go of his racial problem of being black. There are overtones in this encomium of what Bellow did in his writings with so many friends—to declare them superior, in order then to show how a Bellow surrogate would still outlast, outshine, or outlive them. (Henderson in the book Bellow was then writing, of course, lives to see the death of Dahfu, unhappily becomes king himself, and then flees with a yellow baby lion—not unlike a recoloring of the black dog—by which Henderson takes home, possesses, and patronizes the spirit of his dead friend. I wonder what Ellison thought when he read it.) In all fairness, though, Bellow is just plain right about a particular social fact of the years around the two writers' triumphs in 1952 and 1953—that Jews slipped progressively into the white mainstream, while African Americans remained black.

What does this have to do with the problem of man? Certainly it shows how it was right that their solutions to the crisis of man, as worked out in their novels, should be so different, because the recognition problem arrayed different possibilities for blacks and Jews. African American Ellison found "man" in an individual's interior quest to find the features of his own "face," looking for true faces in the unacknowledged uniqueness of immediate neighbors, or plunging out of "history," as long as was necessary, to find his own, to become "human." Jewish Bellow found man in a communal jumping-up of levels in which *longue durée* historical repetition justified the superior student's claim to belong in any milieu and be comfortable there. Bellow had no face to discover; his own, like that of all the illustrious predecessors, was judged white.

"[I]n situations such as this many Negroes, like myself, make a positive distinction between 'whites' and 'Jews,'" Ellison wrote in an exchange with Irving Howe. "Speaking personally, both as a writer and a Negro American, I would like to see the more positive distinctions between whites and Jewish Americans maintained."[24] Ellison was not to have his wish.

But neither was the problem of man so easily able to dispose of these "positive distinctions" that America had retained between some of its citizens and others—not even when a further writer came along, Flannery O'Connor, who attacked the "universal" problem from other grounds—those of faith. As we will see in chapter 7, she tried to answer the questions of man by denying, for religious reasons, that man could ever be anything but partial. She took man again out of history—only to be brought back, complicatedly, by further exigencies of race.

CHAPTER 7

FLANNERY O'CONNOR AND FAITH

One of the outstanding problems in the moral and intellectual history of the twentieth century and of modernity as a whole is the persistence of religion alongside social secularization. The general secularization of our collective life seems undeniable, yet it does not stop individuals from thanking Jesus for personal successes or beseeching him for relief from affliction. A medicalization of bodily experience has meant that one is not reliant on divinity to allay disease. The physician, his tamed microbes, and his stainless machines determine which natural plagues will persist (based on the latest state of his expanding knowledge) and which are cured. Yet God is still given the credit for an individual's recovery.

The return to a fascination with man was often yoked to religion in the mid-twentieth century. "What is man?" was, as we have seen, originally a scriptural question. The discourse of man unrolled a welcome for the last great era in which theologians (Reinhold Niebuhr, Jacques Maritain, Paul Tillich, and Pierre Teilhard de Chardin) would be taken seriously as intellectuals by intellectuals in general. The first postwar decade understood itself, and has been recorded by historians, as a period of religious revival, unmistakable but of oblique and indecipherable character. Among the New York Intellectuals, *Partisan Review* held its symposium on a return to religion; while in the general population, America "witnessed" a "spectacular growth in public piety . . . between 1950 and 1955. . . . [M]embership in churches grew at more than twice the rate of the nation's population growth during this period. In 1953 the figure stood at 59.5 percent, easily the highest rate in American history."[1]

This did not straighten out the convolutions of belief. In scripture, unlike its place in the midcentury revival, the question "What is man?" had been rhetorical. The believer knows that he is a creature belonging to God and made in his image. Man's wonder at "What is man?" (in the Psalms, in Job) is that God would bother to pay attention to him. Man's scriptural fear, likewise, is that he will mistakenly exalt himself above his mortal worth. Revealed religion knows what man is. The discourse of man did not know— it was the thing that had been elected for questioning. The postwar religious revival in the intellectual sphere was not a revival of confidence but of *interest*, that weak passion of a secularization that regrets its default of stability. The texture of the return of "faith" in the discourse of man lies in hall-of-mirrors glimmerings, questioning what, among what one believes, one is really entitled to believe in, exposing in flashes the perversities of certainty in a plural age.

The importance of Flannery O'Connor is that her absolute resistance to secular answers—confronting, mocking, refusing them—and yet her four-square dependence on the discourse of man and the questions it assigned to fiction writers, made her etch an incomparably lucid tracing of what was and was not possible for "faith" in the era. The outcome attains to generality despite the singular elements that make her so illuminating. These are her will to insist on Catholic orthodoxy, dogma, and "mystery" in her public thought and as the true basis for her stories, and her intense and flexible literary talent—channeled into a New Critical realist art of writing she learned at the university. O'Connor exemplifies the complications of a return of religion to midcentury meditations on man's "nature and destiny" precisely because multiple, seemingly incompatible programs of thought exist in her work—running, so to speak, all at once. The statements of theologians cannot be equally clarifying, because they don't face the same formal and intellectual challenges internal to their accustomed forms (sermon, lecture, op-ed, treatise). Other voices who anticipated that a crisis of man could find answers or dissolution in orthodox religion (as O'Connor explicitly did, whenever she could bring herself to speak unsarcastically about the discourse of man, most often in private letters, though also in lectures and essays) faced no truly comparable obstacles in how complicated their cultural form and audience would make such attempts. O'Connor, through a fiction writer's necessities and an individual mind's effort to militate publicly for religious faith in the postwar era, *displays* the complexity.

It emerges in several strands. O'Connor's fiction evinces a turn from concern over man's spirit to fascination with the taking apart of his body. The dissolution of the body into its parts is a religious event for her—yet it is evidently a medical and practical, even technological, event in her culture. She juxtaposes her explanatory insistence on an orthodox religious fiction of symbolism and near-allegory, drawn from real theology and dogma, with her fiction's practical uses of forms of psychological explanation, which are thoroughly *liberal*—liberal in the progressive and post–New Deal sense, defending progress toward the perfection of reasoned goals of equality and freedom, feeling compassion for outcasts because of their sociological circumstance and demographics and situation; liberal too in the sense of church doctrine, both on the Protestant side (which surrounded her in the South) and on the Catholic side (her minority religion by birth and lifelong commitment). O'Connor means to rebuke all these liberal leanings—but couldn't structure her stories or have them make sense without a kind of adherence to them.

IS "MAN" HARD TO FIND?

One can locate how the preoccupation with "man" comes into O'Connor, even though she resents and satirizes it. Here is a grandfather, trying to intimidate his grandson with wisdom, catechizing him in a peculiar way:

> A huge coffee-colored man was coming slowly forward. He had on a light suit and a yellow satin tie with a ruby pin in it. . . .
> Mr. Head's grip was tightening insistently on Nelson's arm. . . . "What was that?" he asked.
> "A man," the boy answered and gave him an indignant look . . .
> "What kind of a man?" Mr. Head persisted . . .
> "A fat man," Nelson said. . . .
> "You don't know what kind?" Mr. Head said in a final tone.
> "An old man," the boy said . . .
> "That was a nigger," Mr. Head said. ("The Artificial Nigger")[2]

Thus, Mr. Head is trying to specify what a man is by separating out a separate ontological category from man, "the Negro"—which isn't really right. (Yet O'Connor's lesson, as we'll see, is *not* that men are all the same and "Negro" is not a meaningful category nor skin color a meaningful difference. This will be the liberal case she does not so much reject as bypass.)

Again, here is Mr. Shiftlet, the one-armed man in "The Life You Save May Be Your Own," trying to explain why he's as good as anybody else to the old lady he's trying to hustle—why he's not any different for being handicapped, as we'd say in modern liberal terms, but just a man. "'[O]ne-arm jackleg or not. I'm a man,' he said with a sullen dignity, 'even if I ain't a whole one. I got,' he said, tapping his knuckles on the floor to emphasize the immensity of what he was going to say, 'a moral intelligence!'" But his listener, the old woman, is "not impressed"—and neither is O'Connor.

O'Connor overtly starts to make certain kinds of habitual fun of pompous intellectuals who think in terms of "Man" or "Woman," and can say the word with a straight face. When she has one of her overeducated young intellectual or writer protagonists locked in a struggle with an innocent or Pollyannaish mother, the intellectual will burst out, "Woman! Do you ever look inside? Do you ever look inside and see what you are *not*?" (268). This, to her innocent mom, as if she herself were an existentialist prophet. (The daughter Hulga, formerly known as Joy, is holder of a philosophy PhD. A page later, her mother reads a passage of Heidegger from one of Hulga's books and is horrified.) O'Connor has some similar fun in the monologue of the self-centered Kafka-emulator Asbury in "The Enduring Chill": " 'I came here to escape the slave's atmosphere of home,' he had written, 'to find freedom . . . Woman, why did you pinion me?' " (554). *Woman* is not the right address because it locates the unknown truth of the person in the wrong place—in status as a man or a woman, a "whole" being, indeed, the "whole man" that the re-enlightenment of midcentury liked to invoke and cultivate. In O'Connor's story "Revelation," the lunatic college girl who attacks the protagonist and throttles her in a fit of apoplexy is reading a "Wellesley College" textbook with the ironic title *Human Development* (643, 635).

O'Connor faces down a great question of midcentury, "What is man?," and then supersedes and ignores it, because, religiously, she already knows well enough what man is. What matters is that everybody who goes around *declaring* what man is in her stories, especially about him- or herself, is deluded or else trying to put one over on somebody. Rather than deal with these man-theorizers in their own terms, she mocks them and goes around them, to a completely separate understanding of human characteristics. The title of her book, *A Good Man Is Hard to Find*, puts it in the tradition of concern with man that snuck into the titles of *Dangling Man* or *Invisible Man*. O'Connor might say, in contrast to this Southern truism (which we saw Robert Penn Warren paraphrasing, a propos of Faulkner, in chapter 4), that *man* is hard to find, and why would you want to look if you don't know the right place to find him? A "good" "man" is hard to find in any secular perspective, because, first, people think "good" is a secular judgment, when it's not; and, second, they think a "man" can take his own measure, without God, which he can't.

Of course, it is not just intellectuals she chides for getting caught up in the wrong sorts of faith, the wrong abstract beliefs, as they are expressed in this language of man. In the early masterpiece "A Good Man Is Hard to Find," the play of wills between an old-fashioned grandmother, her modern spoiled family, and the gas station owner who idly shares the grandmother's values—and then the murderer who rebukes them by shooting her and her whole family dead—depends on a misplaced faith in the wrong kind of "good," the wrong nature of "man," and the wrong sense of history among ordinary people. "People are certainly not nice like they used to be," the grandmother begins to tell the gas station owner. This leads the owner to wonder why he foolishly let two men buy gas on credit a week earlier.

"Because you're a good man!" the grandmother said at once.

"Yes'm, I suppose so," Red Sam said as if he were struck with this answer. . . . "A good man is hard to find," Red Sammy said. "Everything is getting terrible." (142)

A "man" is not "good" or bad for trustingly selling gasoline. "Everything is getting terrible" is a nonsense thought for O'Connor, the worst caricature of stories of crisis or decline. Time doesn't change things. It has *always* been terrible, and is terrible at every instant, in the sense of fearsome and awe-inspiring, because the fact of Christ's Incarnation, two thousand years ago, makes all progressive accounts of history trivial.

It is worth reproducing a passage from O'Connor's most important critical essay that states her public position about the "whole man" and then the partial people she insisted on depicting as her characters.

> Whenever I'm asked why Southern writers particularly have a penchant for writing about freaks, I say it is because we are still able to recognize one. To be able to recognize a freak, you have to have some conception of the whole man, and in the South the general conception of man is still, in the main, theological. . . . I think it is safe to say that while the South is hardly Christ-centered, it is most certainly Christ-haunted. The Southerner who isn't convinced of it, is very much afraid that he may have been formed in the image and likeness of God. Ghosts can be very fierce and instructive. They cast strange shadows, particularly in our literature. In any case, it is when the freak can be sensed as a figure for our essential displacement that he attains some depth in literature. ("Some Aspects of the Grotesque in Southern Fiction," 817–18)

FAITH AS RELIGION, FAITH AS LIBERALISM

As an intellectual and reader, O'Connor consumed the French and German theologians and religious philosophers of the crisis of man era. Her letters document her reading of Jacques Maritain, François Mauriac, Gabriel Marcel, Étienne Gilson (the exegete of Thomas Aquinas), and Teilhard de Chardin—all Catholic figures, but all of the crossover era when these figures counted as "public" thinkers and general philosophers. In 1952, the young O'Connor said she was a Thomist.[3] In 1955, she made a more self-deprecating remark on her relation to Saint Thomas: "I couldn't make any judgment on the *Summa* [*Theologica*], except to say this: I read it for about twenty minutes every night before I go to bed."[4] Her fiction's emphasis on faith alone as the means to grace and the limits of human nature and mind makes it Augustinian not Thomistic. She knew Mauriac's "Christian humanism" and seemed sympathetic to it as a solution for one of her correspondent's difficulties, though "[t]he times do seem a bit apocalyptic for anything so sane."[5] O'Connor defined herself as a "Catholic with a modern consciousness," which did not mean in any way a " 'modern Catholic,' which doesn't make sense": it meant, rather, that "I am conscious in a general way of the world's present historical situation, which according to Jung is unhistorical. I am afraid I got this concept from his book, *Modern Man in Search of a Soul*—and am applying it in a different way."[6] She was not above joking in 1958 that while "crisis theology" was in the air, she would be happy if people would just have a sense of ordinary theology.[7] Yet a month later, to her most trusted correspondent, A., she had special praise for the significance of crisis theology, the neoorthodox movement that had begun in the 1920s in Germany among those other Weimar crisis philosophies we have seen:

> I am surprised you don't know anything about the crisis theologians. . . . They are the greatest of the Protestant theologians writing today and it is to our misfortune that they are much more alert and creative than their Catholic counterparts. We have very few thinkers to equal Barth and Tillich, perhaps none. This is not an age of great Catholic theology. . . . What St. Thomas did for the new learning of the 13th century we are in bad need of someone to do for the 20th. Crisis means something different of course for the Catholic than for the Protestant. For them it is the dissolution of their churches; for us it is losing the world.[8]

O'Connor so frequently painted herself as a savage and an outsider that it is worth insisting on the sophistication of her knowledge as an intellectual. She had absorbed Heidegger by the mid-1950s, at least the limited writing that was available in English, and praised his essay on Hölderlin and his concept of "the holy."[9] She would have been almost uniquely early in receiving Heidegger among US writers and intellects. Heidegger had in fact been born into the German Catholic minority and received an education when young for the priesthood. His appearance in America came first through theological channels.[10] The volume O'Connor must have been reading (and the one that makes Hulga's mother's eyes pop in "Good Country People") was the first postwar English translation of Heidegger's writing, released by the Chicago religious publisher Henry Regnery, later a key conduit for the revival of right-wing political thought in the United States (in the postwar period a close associate of Robert Maynard Hutchins, who used Regnery to publish Great Books Foundation study editions).[11] The edition included an impressive summary of the untranslated *Sein und Zeit*.[12]

"My audience are the people who think God is dead. At least these are the people I am conscious of writing for," O'Connor said.[13] "[I]f you live today you breathe in nihilism."[14] Nietzsche had called those who would live in the atmosphere of nihilism "last men" (in *Thus Spake Zarathustra*). C. S. Lewis, in his discourse of man book *The Abolition of Man*, had warned that they would be "men without chests." O'Connor now put the figure into her comic language of birds: "[T]he moral sense has been bred out of certain sections of the population, like the wings have been bred off certain chickens to produce more white meat on them. This is a generation of wingless chickens, which I suppose is what Nietzsche meant when he said that God is dead."[15]

A central part of her rejection of this secularism was her hatred of "social science" as a supreme liberal vanity of rational improvement. She shared this critique with a strong strain of conservative revival, which we have encountered already: with Friedrich von Hayek and Karl Popper, for example, in their attacks on Karl Mannheim; Leo Strauss, who reprobated social science in the person of Max Weber; and, in effect, the whole cluster around the University of Chicago after the Hutchins and Adler era, whom we have seen vilifying John Dewey.[16] "In college I read works of social-science, so-called. The only thing that kept me from being a social-scientist was the grace of God and the fact that I couldn't remember the stuff."[17] When in 1955 the publicist Russell Kirk, an essential figure in the maintenance of a conservative "intellectual tradition" in the United States in the years before the arrival of William F. Buckley, visited Georgia, "he and I were visiting the same people for the weekend so I saw plenty of him. . . . He is non-conversational and so am I," but the two managed to bond in a "spurt of successful uncharitable conversation" over their shared glee at the death of John Dewey—three years earlier, in 1952. "'John Dewey's dead too, isn't he?' . . . 'Yes, thank God. Gone to his reward. Ha ha.'"[18]

INCARNATION AND ARTIFICIAL BODIES

Yet rejecting the idea that there *is* either a secular-sociological or secular-philosophical question to be answered in the question "What is man?" (for we have the answers of Catholicism), O'Connor was able to pose a question that wouldn't have occurred to previous writers: "What is a body for?" One significance of O'Connor in a social history of American literature is that, in fact, she reached a very timely and modern question of the twentieth century by a supposedly untimely, off-kilter, and traditional means and rationale: the taking apart and putting back together of the body, a feature of postwar life that would come to matter more and more once totalitarianism became an academic and not an immediate fear in its power to change human nature at home and in Western Europe. (We will see this in a more technological line with Thomas Pynchon in chapter 8; O'Connor and Pynchon, as successors to the earlier generation of explicit crisis of man writers like Bellow and Ellison, share some surprising affinities in their concerns.)

The replacement of body parts with artifacts was a persistent interest for O'Connor; man *was not* inviolable in his body, and never had been, she could answer the discourse of man novices. Plus, medicine made the dreams of simply "helping" man more complicated than secularists knew. Medicine appears in O'Connor as a central topic, especially as her short stories enter the 1960s. It extends from stories set in doctors' waiting rooms, to prostheses (including a whole store full of them in "The Lame Shall Enter First"), to a parable involving a satiric reworking of the old Henry James plot of the person invested with profundity because he is mysteriously dying ("The Enduring Chill"). But Jamesian mortal profundity just isn't possible anymore—"Nowadays doctors don't *let* young people die. They give them some of these new medicines. . . . People just don't die like they used to" (562), the not-dying man's mother insists. And it turns out she's right.

O'Connor probably would have denied that these concerns were especially of her time, or that they reflected a different way of going at truly secular problems of man, which she thought she had disposed of. Certainly, the various missing limbs and colossal accidents belong to her stories from the first. She ascribed to them a simple payload of significance of individual religious character. Interpreting her own story "Good Country People," she writes, "[W]e're presented with the fact that the Ph.D. [Hulga] is spiritually as well as physically crippled. . . . [W]e perceive that there is a wooden part of her soul that corresponds to her wooden leg."[19] But one senses that O'Connor is getting the significance wrong, or simply underplaying it. I think it's important, first, to see that characters are literally able to pick up each other's legs, put them in a suitcase, and walk off with them (as the Bible salesman does to Hulga), not a familiar thought in most writing about human beings; or that a person can happen to have an artificial leg and live with it with impunity, not mind it, not believe that bodily disassembly was essential to the new state of man, but gradually grow pride in this artifact that replaced the human part and let the artificial limb substitute for a soul. "As a child she had sometimes been subject to feelings of shame but education had removed the last traces of that as a good surgeon scrapes for cancer . . . But she was as sensitive about the artificial leg as a peacock about his tail. . . . She took care of it as someone else would his soul, in private and almost with her own eyes turned away" (281). This imagination of the surgeon scraping for cancer and the "artificial leg" make up something quite different from O'Connor's explanation, for didactic consumption, of the "crippled" person and a "wooden leg." Hulga is, rather, *un*crippled in the way that O'Connor feels she shouldn't be (finally she is rendered legless, in punishment, at the end). And the so-called wooden leg in the story is an *artificial limb*—that word, "artificial," is an absolutely crucial one for O'Connor—it's not a peg like a pirate's: "The artificial limb, in a white sock and a brown flat shoe, was bound in a heavy material like canvas and ended in an ugly jointure where it was attached to the stump." It may be ugly, but it's a shod foot and clad leg; I think it points to a different kind of order of the body.

O'Connor works out a peculiar calculation, too, of the baleful affinity of human beings for automobiles and tractors, and of cars and tractors for men. They come to be automata making idols of human will and human spirit, and they return at the ends of stories as agencies of fate. Mr. Shiftlet is O'Connor's great theorist of the automobile. "The body, lady, is like a house: it don't go anywhere; but the spirit, lady, is like an automobile: always on the move" (179). But he scants his soul for the sake of an automobile, abandoning "an angel of god," whom he has married, and making off with her mama's car, and earns, from the heavens, the derisive laughter of damnation. The tractor in "The Displaced Person" becomes a cross, to make a martyr of a Polish immigrant so that the Americans around him will learn they are sinners. The bull in "Greenleaf" is perhaps the final incarnation of the assimilation of all sorts of alternatives to man—the bull becomes nearly a bulldozer in Mrs. Greenleaf's dreams (with its "rhythmic chewing," it would be "eating the house and calmly with the same steady rhythm would continue through the house" [501])—and fuses finally with the automobile, organic and artificial as all these machines are made into deadly fates. The black bull is drawn to the automobile too—"he got loose and run his head into their pickup truck. He don't like cars and trucks. They had a time getting his horn out of the fender" (512)—and the next chance he gets, he drives his horns into the hood of a car with Mrs. Greenleaf sitting on it and puts one horn through her heart.

What do all the artificial body parts, and automotive substitutes, add up to? From one perspective, they are simply a reworking with modern means of a Catholic doctrine of the virtue of bodily suffering. The religious historian Robert Orsi has shown how a cult of the "cripple" was a feature of local American Catholic life around midcentury, in a fascination with children on crutches and bad legs that looks odd to contemporary secular eyes but fit Catholic theology as it was understood in America.[20] O'Connor's own disease, lupus, and her swollen face in photographs from cortisone injections, and her movement on crutches, links her to her characters, too—and is a reminder that it is no shameful thing, automatically, to be subject to mortifications of the flesh. O'Connor does seem to communicate a pure sense that only an opened body can let a Holy Spirit enter. The central mystery of the Eucharist, for her, seems to be the sheer materiality of the transubstantiation, that the bread and wine really are the body and blood of Christ. She seems to add, in her fiction, that this transubstantiation reoccurs everywhere in the physical world—as the hermaphrodite in "A Temple of the Holy Ghost" really is at once a physical body with parts that signify "man and woman both," and a temple of God ("God made me thisaway and I don't dispute hit" [207]). All natural facts begin to teach the same truth, up to the last lines of that story: "The sun was a huge red ball like an elevated Host drenched in blood" (209).

Yet O'Connor's preoccupation with artificial extensions of the body, and with their losses, thefts, and creations of illusions, from another perspective, is a rebuke to the crisis of man perspective that anyone *could* come to grips with the progress of technology or the divided and broken-up nature of modern life by thinking it through, or using human means to restore a "whole man." O'Connor's attachment to the spirit reached through the body, her interest in disfigurement, and a certain violent cruelty done to her characters' bodies goes beyond any usual theological rationales or ways of thinking humanity through. She is attacking what one might think of as the "liberal" view of man, in intellect as in religion. It becomes an effort to confront a picture of the human being that belonged to all parties in her era: a picture that believed man's reality is all in his mental character and not his incarnation, and the liberal attitude that finds the various extensions of the physical into the artificial either benign or something to be worried about and fixed—not themselves routes to realization of divinity and partiality. O'Connor feels differently about physical incarnation, including its being broken up and integrated with the artificial. Artificial changes make more than one type of person in the world—a vaster menagerie created by God.

"THE ARTIFICIAL NIGGER" AND THE QUESTION OF LIBERAL READING

Yet the further complication is that if you must accept the body in which you are incarnated for the sake of the spirit, which is all that matters, there is the sense in O'Connor that a different skin color may make you a different sort of person, since physical incarnation divides human beings, making more than one type of "man"—a fraught subject in the age of antiprejudice and the "brotherhood of man."

O'Connor has been defended in the past against racism—most famously by the African American novelist Alice Walker—and I agree that it doesn't make sense to think of O'Connor in these terms.[21] The minimal defense is fairly straightforward: O'Connor certainly does not suggest in her mature prose that actual black people are worse than whites or deficient in any way. She is unusual, and more admirable than some "compassionate" white liberal writers, because she goes out of her way *not* to suggest that she has any idea what her black characters' inner lives and interior consciousnesses are like. She portrays them entirely from the outside, and lets her white characters talk about them without the black characters assenting, and gives her black characters autonomy, while still letting them seem human, not ciphers or symbols.

Compatible with this defense, however, is the possibility that O'Connor's stories really do suggest that blackness is relevant to one's existence as a human, and produces a somewhat separate class of beings, neither worse nor better than any other. This is part of the reason *why* she cannot and will not enter into their world except to describe them from the outside. Rather than it being true just of her black characters, it's consistent with the fact that O'Connor's fiction portrays a wider spread of classes of beings than most of us probably entertain in life, since outward aspect does represent a different inner existence. So, for example, there seem to be certain people in O'Connor's story who are more or less angels, like Lucynell in "The Life You Save May Be Your Own."

This is where O'Connor, as a writer of *religious* faith, gives a challenge to what I have called "faith" as a general topic of the crisis of man—by which I mean the debate over fundamental beliefs one could still be justified in holding, after witnessing the horrors of the '30s and '40s, that would help to shore up man. Central to that kind of faith in man is the idea that man is essentially one. The unity of man, in each consciousness and each body, identical to every other, is a liberal article of faith that grounds many of the approaches to man's crisis, whether religious or secular.

O'Connor's stories can't be correctly read, or interpreted, without the liberal expectations foremost in one's mind (in her midcentury readers' minds, and in ours)—of psychological explanation for motivation, and the basic psychic commonality of all people. But one is hard-pressed to know when she is relying on them for fictional purposes, when she believes them, and when she is rebuking them. Her work creates an interpretive problem, as well as insight into alternative possibilities, before the sixties, for the "liberal" faith in a unity of man.

"The Artificial Nigger" is one of O'Connor's best and most troubling stories at the crossroads of the different lines of her vision. It contains within it a liberal story of how young whites are taught to hate and fear—how, as we would say today, racism is "socially reproduced." A certain amount of the humor is based on its country-bumpkin protagonists' ignorance, both of city ways and of what "we" (a superior, implied readership) know of racial equality and the "unity of mankind." In one vein it is comic when the country grandfather and grandson bend down to drink from a suburban lawn sprinkler as if it were the town pump—that is local color humor. It is comic in a different way when the two country people, wandering into an all-black neighborhood, are astonished and terrified to find that "Colored children played" by "rows of stores with colored customers in them," "Black eyes in black faces were watching them from every direction," "Negroes . . . going about their business as if they had been white" (221, 223). As if, that is, there were a basic distinction between black and white such that blacks ought not to play, or have eyes, or faces, or have "business" to go about, except as imitations or doublings of white existence. We think, at the start of the story, that we as readers (not bumpkins) know much better than this.

And one expects the rest of the story, I think, to be made essentially comic, too, with the two narrow protagonists disabused of their racial illusions, perhaps on the O'Connor pattern of "pride humbled, grace enters," and in the style of the antiracist 1950s (or today). There should be a dignified and humane black character who will let them see that all men are brothers. However, it's the source of energy of "The Artificial Nigger" that no disillusionment of *that* sort occurs. Whatever liberal lessons the reader wants to take from the story, he will have to complete himself—though O'Connor lards the prose with enough hints and exits to let them be constructed. Her interest lies in getting to a different kind of disillusioning— the breaking-down of Mr. Head and Nelson's senses of self by means of the black terror of the black city. The two influences who stand behind this story—two of O'Connor's favorite writers, as she often announced—are, I suppose, Joseph Conrad and Edgar Allan Poe, who showed how racial blackness could be tied to moral darkness and made to function for psychological illumination. Conrad's *The Nigger of the "Narcissus"* (1897), for that matter, is the only precedent I can think of for the use of this racial epithet in a title in the white canon of English literature. John Crowe Ransom, according to Sally Fitzgerald, objected to the title of O'Connor's story before accepting it for the *Kenyon Review* in 1955, but O'Connor insisted on it.[22]

Mr. Head is a grandfather, Nelson his grandson. Each has his familiar point of pride, introduced right at the start so that we know it will be humbled. Mr. Head is proud that "age was a choice blessing . . . that calm understanding of life that makes [a man] a suitable guide for the young" (210). Nelson is proud that he was born in Atlanta, the big city he has never seen, to which, on this day, his grandfather is taking him, promising to show him around and prove it's no good. "'Have you ever,' Mr. Head had asked, 'seen me lost?'" (211). By this statement, habitual readers of O'Connor will know from the first pages of the story that they will get lost.

Mr. Head's fundamental threat to Nelson's pride, however, has to do with knowing what a "nigger" is. "'You ain't ever seen a nigger,' Mr. Head repeated. 'There hasn't been a nigger in this county since we run that one out twelve years ago and that was before you were born'" (212). This is something more than comic ignorance; this is racism of the lynching and exiling kind, which Nelson will have to be taught over the course of the story. I have already quoted the passage in which they see a rich black man pass on the train, and Nelson has to be informed that the "kind of a man" he is, is a "nigger." That, I take it, sounds in its way, at first, like a bit of didactic fiction meant to show Mr. Head's primitiveness and to remind us that all men are the same. When the pair gets to the dining car and Mr. Head has a confrontation with a black waiter, getting the better of him with an insult about the kitchen, which makes "[a]ll the travelers" laugh—all the white travelers, that is—we're less sure that the Heads are getting an education in liberal virtue. Once in town, Mr. Head has Nelson put his face into the sewer grate and explains how men get sucked into it "down endless pitch-black tunnels" (220), a darkness underlying the entire city, which Nelson connects "with the entrance to hell" (220). This begins the metaphorical figure by which the two characters come to imagine that a single threat links the "Negroes" to the city sewer. Despite this, Nelson still insists the city is where he comes from—as if he could own up to a common origin with this place, too—until, that is, they do get lost.

At this point Mr. Head commits his sin. It certainly isn't racism. Nelson falls asleep from exhaustion. To teach him a lesson that will make him hate the city, Mr. Head leaves and hides; when Nelson awakens, he panics and causes an accident, and Mr. Head, afraid of the police, denies his grandson, as Peter denied Jesus. They walk away in an agony of mutual hatred, each in touch with the rising blackness: Mr. Head "knew now he was wandering into a black strange place"; Nelson "felt, from some remote place inside himself, a black mysterious form reach up as if it would melt his frozen vision"; while "The old man felt that if he saw a sewer entrance he would drop down into it and let himself be carried away" (228). Now he *knows* he's lost: "Oh Gawd I'm lost! Oh hep me Gawd I'm lost!" In the meantime they have wandered into a rich white suburban neighborhood, whiter and whiter, like the hyperborean whiteness at the end of Poe's *The Narrative of Arthur Gordon Pym*, where "The big white houses were like partially submerged icebergs in the distance" (228). In this land of frozen whiteness, knowing now by his sin what "time would be like without seasons and what heat would be like without light and what man would be like without salvation" (229), Mr. Head sees a vision ahead of him that transforms them both:

> The plaster figure of a Negro sitting bent over on a low yellow brick fence. . . . The Negro was about Nelson's size. . . . One of his eyes was entirely white and he held a piece of brown watermelon. . . .
>
> Then as the two of them stood there, Mr. Head breathed: "An artificial nigger!"

It was not possible to tell if the artificial Negro were meant to be young or old; he looked too miserable to be either. He was meant to look happy because his mouth was stretched up at the corners but the chipped eye and the angle he was cocked at gave him a wild look of misery instead. (229)

This vision brings grandfather and grandson back together, standing identically, hands "trembling identically," "gazing at the artificial Negro as if they were faced with some great mystery, some monument to another's victory that brought them together in their common defeat" (230). It becomes, suddenly, the purely religious moment of revelation that, in the O'Connor story, we have been waiting for from the beginning, once their pride has been wiped away. O'Connor is unusually explicit about it here, in bald theological language: "They could both feel it dissolving their differences like an action of mercy." "Mr. Head stood very still and felt the action of mercy touch him." Soon thereafter he is reflecting on all sin since "the sin of Adam" and yet how "God loved in proportion as He forgave" (231). Before the religious moment runs its course, Mr. Head delivers himself of an explanation of the meaning of the artificial Negro, which is at the crux of the story, and which is, in fact, hard to make sense of, to the point of its meaning being undecidable. Here is that epigram, on the order of the Misfit's famous "She would have been a good woman if there had been someone there to kill her every day of her life" (in "A Good Man Is Hard to Find"): "Mr. Head opened his lips to make a lofty statement and heard himself say, 'They ain't got enough real ones here. They got to have an artificial one.'"

What does the climactic epigram mean? To start with, this really is comic—that is to say, inane; it is the worst possible explanation of the existence of a black lawn jockey in a white neighborhood, from our enlightened perspective. That is, a superwhite neighborhood has too few blacks (to dominate, to scare bumpkins), so they have to make a dummy one.

What one wants O'Connor to mean by it—to be making a liberal sociological point, a point simply consistent with the struggle in the story, or just the same religious ritual of humbled pride and entering grace O'Connor produces everywhere—will clarify what one wants from O'Connor perhaps more than what O'Connor wants from us. The liberal meaning would work as follows. When Mr. Head identifies "They," he is speaking of the rich white residents of the neighborhood, an order of people they do not see but know exist. In the lawn jockey, rich whites have made a mockery or idol of the black from above, as previously Mr. Head and Nelson did from below. This is as much as to say that blackness, we are to realize, is really a psychological projection of white status worries or conflict. If whites don't have a "real" subjugated Negro, a scapegoat and so forth (to draw on the language of midcentury), they have to invent one. But if rich whites project a picture of the Negro to assert dominance, these poor whites, who have tried to do the same, now, lost in order to find themselves, realize their own subordination in the larger order, alongside the poor lawn jockey who, we're told, is just about the size of Nelson. Then the "monument to another's victory" commemorates the original erection of the system of power by the most powerful. And the "wild look of misery" on the lawn jockey's face would depict how blacks have been made miserable for white fun—a secular discovery. If Mr. Head and Nelson are not expected to understand all this themselves, well, we progressive readers are getting an additional lesson from their reaction—coming back together in their fear of the black idol—as we see again, shamefully, how any confrontation with blackness serves to restore the solidarity and fellow-feeling of whites.

I am sympathetic to this reading, wishing it were justifiable (how easy and progressive O'Connor would be then!), and yet not much compelled by it. That is, I do think O'Connor has built this reading into the story by offering elements that conduce to it—but she still means to condemn anybody who falls for it. There is a degree of base-covering going on; if she did not write stories that bore these midcentury antiracist liberal possibilities, she would not have been tolerable to midcentury readers—nor, probably, would she be tolerable now.

The likely meaning of the epigram in the story, more neutrally, is simply that the black presence in the city, increasingly removed from real African Americans and associated with a force of sin or evil in the world (the sewer underneath the street, the cowardly denial waiting behind prideful wisdom) has foiled the Heads even here, so that an idol awaits them even where the reality has momentarily disappeared. Only this realization of the inescapability of fear sends them, perhaps, away from the prideful intellectualism of their "heads" to the knowledge of the heart. "They ain't got enough real ones here. They got to have an artificial one." The "they" is then a general force outside of the Heads—or a useless pronoun substitute for forces beyond persons. The misery of the lawn jockey is the sadness of a simulation passing for life itself, when life too is a kind of imprisonment. Mr. Head's pronouncement is still being made fun of, but it's a mistake that is useful for him to suffer. Anybody else could tell you why the lawn jockey's on the lawn—for casual racists to welcome other racists to their driveway. But to him it's like a Golden Calf, pure pagan mystery, made by people so wicked that his own wickedness, without an outlet, shines out to him more clearly.

I think it should be no surprise that O'Connor is aiming at a religious reading here. The *religious* content, or what O'Connor would call the "anagogical" content (linking the material to the divine), is in the artificiality of the Negro, too. There really is, the story proclaims, a mystery to be found in man-made representations and tools that double and incarnate, and now, in 1955, *supplant* natural and spiritual dangers. The sewer *really is* the gates of hell; mankind has made it this time, materializing the filth he has forgotten within him. The idol of the black, the artificial Negro, *really is a picture of a Negro*, and Negroes should help teach whites their place within the cosmos—because there are different beings on the earth, many radically different beings. (For that matter, the Heads are, as O'Connor's characters might call their stratum in other stories, "white trash"— something they may not be able to see, but which their humiliation in a rich white neighborhood helps to make clear to us.) Those differences are still nothing to be proud of, because we will shed them before God; and yet those differences can't be forgotten, or one forgets everything else mysterious and God-given—as liberalism forgets all mysteries in a great deceptive mush. Because men cannot see the reality truly, they carelessly or compulsively reproduce the reality in artificial forms; then they can't see the shock of their artificial substitutes—until finally someone like Mr. Head does. The artificial Negro is like the "guffawing" tin can top raindrops that flail Mr. Shiftlet's ill-gotten car, or the tattoos the godless Parker must compulsively have drawn on his skin in "Parker's Back"—other sideways movements between nature and artifice. The power of God to mock people for their vanities, with their vanities, lies in the human aptitude for recreating human problems in the artificial. There are then two different vanities in men to be mocked: that of taking themselves too seriously with too much pride, and that of failing to see that material incarnations and physical objects never escape, but only advance, divine truths. The "victory" to which the lawn jockey is a monument is also a divine victory, restoring the real force to man's action of artifice substituting for life. The sad and nearly tortured features of the lawn jockey may be a way out, liberally, for O'Connor (she certainly doesn't believe that blacks *ought* to be represented as lawn jockeys as a sociological or white supremacist statement). But she doesn't care about him. "There is nothing that screams out the tragedy of the South like what my uncle calls 'nigger statuary,'" O'Connor confided to a correspondent.[23] The tragedy was of a white population that could feel exalted by such plaster idols; it was not, say, the existence of evil as slavery or Jim Crow.

O'Connor was always aware of the liberal reading of reality and liberal readings of her stories—so hyperaware, I have suggested, as to build the stories to make these readings available and then to try to humiliate them, too. She plays a hostile and disillusioning game everywhere with liberal readers and liberal critics. She had trained in their schools (at the Iowa Writers Workshop), knew how they thought, and would prepare what would otherwise be a symbol, a doubling, to lead down the wrong track.

PERMANENCE AGAINST HISTORY

The trouble with this vision of irrelevance for contemporary, progressive history—juxtaposed to the timelessness of Christian mystery—emerged once new historical change became conspicuous. Worse, the change threatened to combine a "liberal" view of social order with a distinctly religious vision of justice. This threat, or promise, came from the civil rights movement.

In stories that O'Connor wrote after 1960, it seems that history may have restarted, at least nearby in the South, or that something new entered O'Connor's menagerie of beings. By and large, O'Connor went along with the norms of her society. She possessed some measure of whatever would have been the "right" racial attitudes for a progressive liberal intellectual when in the North, but in the South she followed the right attitudes for a surprisingly "traditional" Southerner—even while she religiously, theologically removed herself from all such transient norms. Southern society had kept a difference between men under Jim Crow, preserved by law. O'Connor's first collection of stories appeared just after the Supreme Court declared school segregation unconstitutional, but its stories really belonged to the earlier period. *Everything That Rises Must Converge*, her second collection of stories, appeared posthumously, in 1965, and belonged to a later period. In the first paragraph of the first page of the book, however, we learn, in passing, that she had been watching things change: "the buses . . . had been integrated" (485). Other fundamental presumptions were being called into question, and not happily.

The problem went deeper than O'Connor's own racial feelings or values, to the uniqueness and forcefulness of her prophecy. One might call it, only partly facetiously, O'Connor's "James Baldwin problem." The African American writer Baldwin emerged as a youthful prodigy in the New York Intellectuals' magazines, as O'Connor had. Like her, he offered entry to a different world exotic to the circle of the *Partisan Review* and *Commentary*. O'Connor's friend Maryat Lee seems to have suggested that she either meet or see James Baldwin when he visited the South in 1959. Even at that date, O'Connor writes, "No I can't see James Baldwin in Georgia. It would cause the greatest trouble and disturbance and disunion. In New York it would be nice to meet him; here it would not. I observe the traditions of the society I feed on—it's only fair. Might as well expect a mule to fly as me to see James Baldwin in Georgia. I have read one of his stories and it was a good one."[24] "Disunion" is a bit much, as if a white writer meeting a black writer in the South would cause a sectional crisis all over again, but O'Connor softens her refusal with blandishments. By 1964, however, she had well established that she didn't like Baldwin, and her positioning of herself then—after the most famous successes of the civil rights movement, including the March on Washington, and during the year of the Civil Rights Act and legally enforced desegregation—are revealing.

> About the Negroes, the kind I don't like is the philosophising prophesying pontificating kind, the James Baldwin kind. Very ignorant but never silent. Baldwin can tell us what it feels like to be a Negro in Harlam [*sic*] but he tries to tell us everything else too. M. L. King I don't think is the ages [*sic*] great saint but he's at least doing what he can do & has to do. . . . My question is usually would this person be endurable if white. If Baldwin were white nobody would stand him a minute. I prefer Cassius Clay. "If a tiger move into the room with you" says Cassius, "and you leave, that don't mean you hate the tiger. Just means you know you and him can't make out. Too much talk about hate."[25]

We might note that Baldwin had positioned himself, with *The Fire Next Time* (1963), as something like O'Connor's deepest imaginings come to life—and winning the argument against her. Both of O'Connor's full-length novels *Wise Blood* (1952) and *The Violent Bear It Away* (1960) take as their protagonist a very young man, a poor white, who rebels against Christianity and a future of becoming a preacher or prophet, only to wind up testifying to the inescapability of Christian destiny no matter what he does. Well, in the memoir portion of *The Fire Next Time*, Baldwin actually *was* that very young man, scrawny and pugnacious in the way of O'Connor's characters, but a poor black, who himself became a child preacher, deduced that it was a con game, and began preaching (and never stopped) that Church and Cross were impositions but that true spiritual force existed—and could be incarnated only in racial justice, the passion of love, and this-worldly American historical change. Not only was Baldwin not punished and corrected by God as he should have been, he was adopted by the *New Yorker*. So O'Connor's venom against "the philosophising prophesying pontificating kind" of Negro, "[v]ery ignorant but never silent," has a special animus.

In some ways, I think, O'Connor was caught off guard by quick social changes, though she was enough of a sensitive seismograph of the culture to register the changes and to try to see what they meant for her worldview and her characteristic way of producing stories. "Everything That Rises

Must Converge," the story concerned with bus desegregation, is the more direct and familiar story for O'Connor. Her fundamental plot is in place. Just as, at the very beginning of O'Connor's career, the grandmother in "A Good Man Is Hard to Find" "did not want to go to Florida," idly warns of the Misfit on the loose and is, in the end, shot dead by him, so Julian does not want to escort his mother to her "reducing class," is idly warned of her high blood pressure, and sees her drop dead of it. His mother is disconcerted that blacks are allowed to ride the buses and no longer know their place. Julian, in contrast, is proud that he is "free of prejudice." He cherishes his own better reactions: "When he got on a bus by himself, he made it a point to sit down beside a Negro, in reparation as it were for his mother's sins" (489). But this makes him an incompetent reader of the events that are unfolding around him and furnish the drama of the story. When a black man gets on their bus, "He would have liked to get in conversation with the Negro and to talk with him about art or politics or any subject that would be above the comprehension of those around them" (493), but the man isn't interested. This neglect of immediate surroundings and material facts, by intellectualism, will always be punished in an O'Connor story. When a black woman and child mount the bus steps and sit down on opposite sides of the aisle, upsetting Julian's mother, he is equipped with the symbol-sniffing nose of the incompetent, liberal literary critic to get the wrong explanation: "Julian saw that" his mother was upset "because she and the woman had, in a sense, swapped sons. Though his mother would not realize the symbolic significance of this, she would feel it" (496). (In fact, Julian's mother is upset because she and the woman are wearing the same hat.)

> He imagined his mother lying desperately ill and his being able to secure only a Negro doctor for her. He toyed with that idea ... then dropped it for a momentary vision of himself participating as a sympathizer in a sit-in demonstration. . . . Instead, he approached the ultimate horror. He brought home a beautiful suspiciously Negroid woman. . . . Now persecute us, go ahead and persecute us. (494)

Normally, Julian's *vanity* should somehow lead to his mother's death. But really, when the mother dies, it isn't just because Julian denied her or patronized her, and thus set in motion the usual Rube Goldberg machine that should cause a fatality in an O'Connor story. It's because she tried to give a penny to a black child, and the black mother beat her with a pocketbook, shouting, "He don't take nobody's pennies!" (498). That shock of the new social order kills the mother, as she has a stroke or heart attack.

Everything That Rises Must Converge is the book in which violence by blacks erupts as it has not done before in O'Connor's work. It happens again in "Judgment Day," a rewriting of one of her earliest student stories, "The Geranium." In the original story, an old Southern man living in New York is humiliated when he has to be helped up the stairs by a genteel and well-spoken black man who observes no social differences between the two of them. The Southerner is then further punished (perhaps for his racism) when the geranium he likes is dropped out of a window and smashed by the evil white man across the alley. It is a straightforward, liberal antiracist story of sorts, a very early effort from the 1940s.

In O'Connor's final version, "Judgment Day," the old Southern man in question tries to make *friends* with the black man next door, thinking that the neighbor's race puts him in a connection to the South—reminding the old man of his black best companion at home. But instead of helping the old man up the stairs, this black next-door neighbor, now with "a large surly mouth and sullen eyes," grabs the front of the old man's shirt, mocks him, and does some kind of unspecified act of violence to him that helps lead to his death: "His daughter found him . . . His hat had been pulled down over his face and his head and arms thrust between the spokes of the banister; his feet dangled over the stairwell like those of a man in the stocks. . . . [The police] cut him out with a saw and said he had been dead about an hour" (695).

"Revelation," written in 1963, the last purely original story O'Connor wrote on her deathbed, really is a final masterpiece, and it shows how the somewhat different explorations of contemporary social order—and race—in *Everything That Rises Must Converge* could be brought to mature fruition, with her religious concerns intact. The story is set mostly in a doctor's waiting room, one that makes it clear that the bus in "Everything That Rises" was also a kind of waiting room, a place where characters would spell out a range of possible positions on the changes then going on in society. "Revelation," in fact, creates nearly the same cast of characters of "Everything That Rises," but switches them around in a way that yields an unusual result. The middling good-natured woman is now the center of consciousness—in Mrs. Turpin. One of the two other women, barely fleshed out on the bus, is now "the lady," perhaps of a slightly higher class than Mrs. Turpin herself, with whom she feels entirely in sympathy. The other is "white-trash" (637), low class, "[w]orse than niggers any day" (635). The intellectual figure, who had held the center of the earlier story in Julian, is now a college girl who seems to hate Mrs. Turpin for no reason, to take offense at all of her complacencies, vanities, and prejudices, and finally becomes crazed enough to attack her physically. It's clear that the missing, defining figures through all their discriminations of class are blacks, who appear in the flesh only in the character of a delivery boy—neither smart, nor dumb, nor demonstrative, nor sullen—who goes about his business while everyone watches, and then leaves.

Black people help imaginatively to let Mrs. Turpin make the fine-grained decisions about who she is and who she isn't, who she'd like to be and who she wouldn't. She dwells on what she would have done if Jesus had sent her back to Earth with only two choices, to be either white trash or black—"'All right, make me a nigger then—but that don't mean a trashy one.' And he would have made her a clean respectable Negro woman, herself but black" (636).

The distinctions get finer and finer (another woman "was not white-trash, just common" [636]), but it turns out that the "white-trash" woman thinks more highly of herself than of Mrs. Turpin, because Mrs. Turpin works with black labor. Under the pressure of early '60s social equality and a need to entice workers, Mrs. Turpin complains of how she has indeed learned to smile and wave and "run out with a bucket of icewater" for black itinerant farmhands. And Mrs. Turpin also keeps pigs. "'One thang I know,' the white-trash woman said. 'Two thangs I ain't going to do: love no niggers or scoot down no hog with no hose.' And she let out a bark of contempt" (639). The addition of animals to the mix of beings who signify status (the most elite animals, we're told, are "registered white-face cattle" [636]) leads to the one joke that unites the white waiting room in laughter: "You know what comes of" racial mixing, Mrs. Turpin's husband says, "White-faced niggers" (641). (Only "the white-trash" woman and the intellectual girl don't laugh.) The intellectual girl, instead, is chosen to attack Mrs. Turpin and then deliver her a holy message, which, as a sign of Mrs. Turpin's general acuity, she knows is a true "revelation": "Go back to hell where you came from, you old wart hog," the girl proclaims.

Mrs. Turpin is, in a sense, at last the perfect reader of an O'Connor story. She is smart enough to take the pronouncement perfectly seriously—joke though it is to us. This condemnation leads her to review and analyze the different parts of her life, well ordered in every way, and, in fact, morally upright and decent—it seems so even to us readers. "'I am not,' she said tearfully, 'a wart hog. From hell'" (647). She goes to her beloved husband to ask him if she's a wart hog from hell. This gives us our one picture in any of O'Connor's stories of fulfilled romantic love. She goes, even, to the black laborers, while bringing them ice water, and can't help but ask them, too, about the accusation that she's "an old wart hog from hell." Though all the black laborers' previous talk had been fake praise of workers for an employer, their outrage here seems genuine. For once, we seem to have a character who, for her faults, is not to be undone in an O'Connor story by any vanity that others can see right through. But all these people are still "like the comforters of Job, reasonable-seeming but wrong" (648).

So Mrs. Turpin does just what she should do, and, brought low herself, goes, in effect, to ask the most material, the basest—the hogs—about her spiritual condition, as she angrily washes them down. Then she just watches them: "A red glow suffused them. They appeared to pant with a secret life"—and from them she absorbs "some abysmal life-giving knowledge" (653). She looks up to the sky and is given a vision, a second revelation in the story and the reward for taking the first seriously.

> She saw . . . a vast swinging bridge extending upward from the earth through a field of living fire. Upon it a vast horde of souls were rumbling toward heaven. There were whole companies of white-trash, clean for the first time in their lives, and bands of black niggers in white robes, and battalions of freaks and lunatics shouting and clapping and leaping like frogs. And bringing up the end of the procession was a tribe of people whom she recognized at once as those who, like herself . . . had always had a little of everything and the God-given wit to use it right. . . . They were marching behind the others with great dignity, accountable as they had always been for good order and common sense and respectable behavior. They alone were on key. Yet she could see by their shocked and altered faces that even their virtues were being burned away. (654)

Now, one can read this as the usual O'Connor moment of grace or action of mercy. Even the just will have "their virtues . . . burned away" in the last judgment. I think, rather, the change here is that there *are* just people, unillusioned, dignified to the end. And even up to the last, order is maintained. "[A]ccountable as they had always been for good order" is simply not ironic; where other inversions obtain ("white-trash . . . clean," "black niggers in white robes"), the ordinary righteous whites are straightforward and "on key."

From the option to turn readers away from the worry about man, O'Connor's last major work turns *back* to a vision of social order that matters more in the climax of the story than the moment in which human vanity is burned away. O'Connor's work had lasted from the clichés of an age of the crisis of man into an era of new leveling in civil rights and then the first events of the sixties. She lived, just barely, into an age of renewed equality and complexity among men. And this created a new problem from a new discovery: that her ability to teach her characters their partiality and primitive equality before God—*this* nature of man—might depend on the stability of a social order of different classes and races, which civil rights sought to undermine in the name of the same God and divinity.

Thomas Pynchon, however—our next and last writer about man in the era of crisis—started publishing just as O'Connor was finishing. For him, the chaos of disordered energies would be just the element in which to work; and we find some of O'Connor's oddest topics, like the taking apart of the human body, and a more plentiful order of semihuman beings, returning again under the mantle of the 1960s and the ultimate rubric of *technology*.

CHAPTER 8

THOMAS PYNCHON AND TECHNOLOGY

At the beginning of this study, for the world crisis with its bull's-eye centered on the early 1940s, concentric rings spilling outward, I identified four areas of concern for the intellectuals of the crisis of man: *philosophy, history, faith,* and *technology.* Each generated its own set of complex questions.

The last area in a way seems the simplest in its afterlife. Does technology change human nature by altering man's habits, his body, by conditioning him, by fitting him to the machine? Or does it even make man obsolete by superseding his puny strengths or threatening to vaporize him from the earth, as a bomb-wielding species? The question of the consequence of technological growth remains the one we have most actively on our agenda today. It is a question no one will fail to understand if you ask it. No one will ask for qualifications or think your inquiries pretentious or out of the ordinary.

In part, it remains so obvious because there seems little difficulty about knowing what technology *is,* while definitional complications arise when one asks what human nature is. After midcentury, technology included factory presses and assembly lines, dynamos and centrifuges, automobiles and bombs—all tangible, all still slightly disconcerting. In earlier chapters on the intellectual discourse of man, especially in discussing the German discourse on technology, it has been clear that technology had been considered in another way, too: as existing also in techniques of human organization, reaching their nadir in fascist and totalitarian coordination. This organizational critique, too, had survived, albeit in altered form.

By the cusp of the 1960s, the technological discourse had changed both in its mechanical and organizational dimensions. In America, high technology had come home from the factory and been domesticated. The dishwasher, laundry machine, electric refrigerator, and countertop appliances gave the kitchen or back pantry the hands-free mechanical processes of the factory. Broadcast technology, after the rise of TV to ubiquity and the proliferation of portable transistor radios, confirmed a sense of thralldom to electronics that now followed Americans wherever they went. Meanwhile, in the real factory, automation had replaced mechanization or industrialization as the great looming threat or herald of liberation for the

American worker. Industrial robot arms would replace sinewy human arms. Self-regulating machines, taking their own temperature, calculating and adjusting their own readiness, would obviate the need for human monitors. The new computers could do calculations that far outran human cognition. When automated systems and complex electronics performed the most difficult tasks (but also, perhaps, narrowed the channels of the worker's initiative), such new autonomy might free men, might make them obsolete, or might—to the most foresighted prognosticators—redirect Americans into a new evanescent labor, of managing, marketing, broadcasting, and advertising the fruits of these self-running factories, before going home to enjoy the private technologies awaiting them on the Formica of their suburban homes.

This caricature belonged to both the exuberant futurists and Cassandras of the time. The technology-as-organization narrative of the discourse of man, meanwhile, became through the 1950s an increasingly domestic fear that Americans were being overorganized and underautonomized within industry and the manager-driven corporation, not to mention the overdeveloped home sphere of "quality of living" comforts. At this point, the discourse of man on its technological side merged or collapsed into one of the best-studied and most familiar aspects of "the fifties"—the fear of organized conformity and tepid lifelessness amid a new managerial middle class. The major best-selling titles that contained "man" now became *The Man in the Gray Flannel Suit* (1955) and *The Organization Man* (1956). It is enough for our purposes, I think, to invoke this well-known historical phenomenon rather than fall into it, for the most interesting carryover of technological contemplations from the earlier discourse of man lies elsewhere.

PYNCHON AND THE TECHNOLOGICAL MUNDANE

Thomas Pynchon is known and remembered as a writer on technology. Most often he is discussed as a wielder of high-technological, scientific, or engineering concepts. The concept of entropy, drawn from the laws of thermodynamics, predominates in Pynchon criticism, the fault of his own early short story "Entropy" and its appearance in his books; he can also be singled out for complex metaphors of rocketry, warfare, and the history of invention. This is a high-technological Pynchon I would like to step away from momentarily—noticing, instead, the primacy in his two major early books, *V.* (1963) and *The Crying of Lot 49* (1966), of the technologies of mundane, ordinary life. Rather than consider the V2 rocket, I think it is more important, first, as in *The Crying of Lot 49*, to consider those new planned developments in Southern California that mesh with the radio in a

'60s reader's breast pocket: "a vast sprawl of houses which had grown up all together, like a well-tended crop . . . [Oedipa Maas] thought of the time she'd opened a transistor radio to replace a battery and seen her first printed circuit."[1] Entropy may matter, and such comic inventions as the antientropic Nefastis Machine will appear, but first it matters to notice that Pynchon is putting a TV set in every room of his fiction—often to drive the action. One is "stared at by the greenish dead eye of the TV tube" (*CL49*, 9); there is always now "the TV in the corner" (*CL49*, 28) or the buzzing "car radio" (bringing Oedipa and her lover the voice of her cuckolded husband as they drive) (*CL49*, 80). In *V.* we hear that someone truly human would be "somebody for once on the right or real side of the TV screen."[2] But one can no longer know with bygone certainty on which side one appears. The puzzling new corporations also appear, but cut down to size, with high technologies that rest first on mundane technologies. Yoyodyne Inc., the enormous defense contractor in Pynchon's fictional world, is a titan of bomb making and an anchor of the new conspiratorial and paranoid right-wing culture of the greater Los Angeles area's Orange County, where aerospace development and libertarian Republicanism grew side by side.[3] Yoyodyne itself, however, has a corporate history that shows how toy gyroscopes (not unlike yo-yos, hence the name) led to gyrocompasses, which led to missile guidance systems; and so from the most mundane simple machine, one gets to the most destructive high-tech—and, perhaps, back again, as it hops from *V.* to the childish ambitions of its uncannily young engineers in *Lot 49*.[4] Automation fears, too, and the computation era, are woven in as domestic burlesque, like that of the Yoyodyne executive "automated out of a job" who commits to killing himself, and is trumped there, too, by the computer: "'Nearly three weeks it takes him,' marvelled the efficiency expert, 'to decide. You know how long it would've taken the IBM 7094? Twelve microseconds'" (*CL49*, 113 and 115).

Pynchon's way of conceiving the problems took up the intellectual torch of the 1940s and 1950s. Previous critics have documented his continuity with intellectual books of the discourse of man, including Marshall McLuhan's *Understanding Media: The Extensions of Man* (1964) or Norbert Wiener's *The Human Use of Human Beings: Cybernetics and Society* (1950, revised 1954). Pynchon avowed Wiener's influence himself.[5] One can certainly find in Wiener the necessary discussions of entropy, information science, human beings as machines (but warnings that machines must be dehumanized), and even such relevant suggestions (for *The Crying of Lot 49*) as that the United States has mastered the "art of waste."[6] Yet I find the direct technological transfer largely beside the point. "Man" as a being and a concept is put into jeopardy for Pynchon, not first by high-technological machines or weapons but by the use of ordinary materials and the creation of mundane objects—the changing status of the *parts* of men, and the insertion of inanimate *things* into their bodies and daily habits. The trouble with things, furthermore, is not that they are produced ephemerally and vanish in their use (as it was sometimes common to say in critiques of consumer society and consumer production from Pynchon's era). The trouble, rather, is that material objects *persist*, transferring neutrally from one time and place to another, while all values and intentions get stripped from them. Human values are sloughed off the material, while things themselves survive and circulate with their own recalcitrant residues of value—inanimate things, neutral themselves, which can become an offense or a danger to whatever is characteristic or deliberately cherished about self-willed humans.

In other words, it is no longer the objects produced, nor uses and ways of consumption, nor organizing forms that matter about technology but "cycling" and recirculation. As communications technologies grow in significance, alongside material leftovers and remnants, something unnerving happens—the immaterial circulation of signs crosses over with material circulation, until one witnesses a further denudation of values. Stories and personal relations mix with leftover or forgotten objects, and are leveled down to the same neutral status, out of human control. This collapsing together of the material and immaterial is a step that his shorter tour de force *The Crying of Lot 49* takes beyond the early magnum opus, *V.*—which had introduced Pynchon's characteristic approach to technology in the 1960s, in an opposition between the "animate" and "inanimate," and a "decadence" conceived both as a triumph of objects and a capitulation to aestheticizing stories about people.

Inanimate material, *not* high technology; the insertion of material into men, *not* a threat to man from outside bombs and devices; persistence, *not* ephemerality; recycling, *not* production; a leveling commensurability denuded of values, *not* power hierarchies—these are the concerns one has to draw out in Pynchon, to see, I think, his true position, and his important innovations and completions of a part of the crisis of man. (The book I will not consider is Pynchon's *Gravity's Rainbow* [1973], since it belongs, in effect, to the end of this study's period. It could only prove how intellectual life had been drastically reordered *after* the cataclysms of the sixties, with the questions of man devitalized. I will go with Pynchon as far as to leave us on the edge of that devitalization—at a real entry point, finally, to the sixties.)

There is also the question of what kind of writer Pynchon is, more generally. My approach to his work depends on a few hypotheses that are not guaranteed to be generally held. One is my belief that Pynchon is the major

American author most affected by World War II, apart from the immediate postwar novelists like Norman Mailer and James Jones. This is true even though he is a generation younger. Pynchon was able to take on a particular line of concern with the Holocaust—concerning the uses and abuses of human bodies as a template for the depredations of that war—in a way that has been hard to acknowledge. Part of the reason it has been hard to acknowledge is that it differs from other usual foci of Holocaust interest by offering no particular attention or solemnity to the fate of the murdered Jews as Jews rather than as simple human bodies.

As Michael Bérubé has intelligently identified, becoming an admiring Pynchon critic is not like being a critic of just any major writer. It has become conventional that becoming a critic of Pynchon requires an acknowledgment, on entry, that you will never match the omniscience of Pynchon himself—you will always fail his puzzle-construction, you cannot live up to his efforts, you will wrongly co-opt him by drawing him into literary criticism.[7] I'd prefer to try to put aside the games and arcana, on the hypothesis that Pynchon's work exists not primarily to be deciphered but to be experienced and, if anything, *situated*. He is not a puzzle writer with clear solutions. He is a theme writer with moods. By a "theme writer" I mean an author whose method is to choose a particular set of thematic concerns and central terms ("animate" and "inanimate" in *V.*, communication in *Lot 49*), and gradually accrete material around them. By a writer with moods, I mean that he builds up his themes within a certain climate of affect, which makes you lend value to some elements, and less to others, but which is not strictly determined by plot or character. Pynchon is also a research writer, who looks up history and technical methods—of plastic surgery, or life in 1920s Montmartre, or the 1898 Fashoda Incident—and works the material into his books, dropping in, for example, a lengthy clinical description of a nose job when necessary. One therefore wants to know, as a critic, *what* in the culture Pynchon was drawing from or sensing, without getting caught in puzzles to solve—and then to follow an itinerary through the moods of the work.

A final hypothesis is that it doesn't pay to decide what Pynchon is, finally, for or against—whether he is a "humanist" or just includes some humanist characters, and whether he is fearful or unfearful of technology. It becomes impossible to declare Pynchon's ultimate "values" without exposing yourself to the embarrassing admission that you may just want Pynchon to share your values, and thus settle for one or another of his alternatives on that basis. I tend to think of Pynchon as essentially humane—but this, again, is a matter of mood. Literally, his declarations on behalf of humane values of any kind are almost always masked and ironized. "[I]f you were going to be humanistic about it" (*V.*, 103), he will interject facetiously into a moment of a narrator's direct evaluation. The ironizing habit comes into, for example, the closest thing the first novel *V.* has to a humane slogan: Keep Cool but Care. The black jazz musician, McClintic Sphere (sharing Thelonious Monk's middle name, but more like Charlie Parker) has been trying to decide how to live between indifference and craziness, and reaches a banal but, in context, touching solution. "Love with your mouth shut, help without breaking your ass or publicizing it: keep cool, but care" (*V.*, 366). But a few pages later, it's SHROUD, the simulated human mannequin who hints at the triumph of the inanimate, who (telepathically, inexplicably) tells *V.*'s protagonist, Benny Profane, the new slogan: "Keep cool. Keep cool but care. It's a watchword, Profane, for your side of the morning" (*V.*, 369). No logical link could have taken the phrase from Sphere to the mannequin. It moved only through the narrative medium of the book—which ought, you would think, to support its claim to authorial utterance—a reminder that the book itself is a set of patterned representations from a central intelligence (Pynchon) who is communicating with us through nonautonomous characters. And yet that central intelligence, by handing the line to a figure who seems to mock and oppose it, knows he's putting into question, as always, whether "Pynchon" believes any of his characters' positions—or which of them. "I'll bet under that cynical butyrate hide is a . . . sentimentalist," says Benny to SHROUD, speaking just as well for the reader's challenge to the author behind his masks. The response: "There's nothing under here. Who are we kidding?" (*V.*, 369).

BECOMING INANIMATE; OR, THE MEANINGLESSNESS OF UNIVERSAL MAN

Benny Profane's last job in New York in *V.* is as a night watchman for a scientific company called Anthroresearch Associates. Anthroresearch doesn't mean getting to the bottom of the nature of man in this setting. It means subjecting humanlike mechanical bodies to all the atrocities inanimate objects can inflict on living beings—radiation as in an atom bomb blast, crashes in test cars—to estimate the human damage. The mannequin SHROUD, or "synthetic human, radiation output determined," like the other model SHOCK, "synthetic human object, casualty kinematics," is himself inanimate, doesn't have a real human body part, though he has "lungs, sex organs, kidneys, thyroid, liver, spleen and other internal organs" of "clear plastic" (*V.*, 284). Yet SHROUD soon starts talking with Benny. He boasts that no one should mistake him for humanlike; rather, humans are on their way to becoming something else.

Me and SHOCK are what you and everybody will be someday. . . .

"What do you mean, we'll be like you and SHOCK someday? You mean dead?"

Am I dead? If I am then that's what I mean.

"If you aren't then what are you?"

Nearly what you are. None of you have very far to go. (*V.*, 284)

This is one riddle, like the riddle of the Sphinx that opened *Invisible Man*. The riddle this time does not point to man but what man will become. The answer SHROUD seems to be hinting at, for his puzzle of the eventual fate of man, is—in the terms of the book—inanimacy. Man will become inanimate. But SHROUD gets much more explicit:

Remember, Profane, how it is on Route 14, south, outside Elmira, New York? . . . Acres of old cars, piled up ten high in rusting tiers. A graveyard for cars. . . . Now remember, right after the war, the Nuremberg war trials? Remember the photographs of Auschwitz? Thousands of Jewish corpses, stacked up like those poor car-bodies. Schlemihl: It's already started.

"Hitler did that. He was crazy." . . .

Fifteen years ago. Has it occurred to you there may be no more standards for crazy or sane, now that it's started? (*V.*, 284, 295)

But *what* exactly has started? *V.* doesn't so much answer this later riddle as fill it out with its own unique and reiterated nomenclature. The first set of terms the book adopts is "animate" and "inanimate." "Schlemihl" is another term, a Yiddish word made over with a technical definition: it means, in *V.*, someone, like Benny Profane, who cannot get along with objects. Objects are always slipping from his hands, hitting him in the face, failing to work. Alarm clocks won't ring on time, spades will turn, electronics won't run. "Everybody else was at peace with some machine or other" (*V.*, 215). Profane muses—but not him. A real man would be "Master of the inanimate. But a schlemihl, that was hardly a man: somebody who lies back and takes it from objects, like any passive woman" (*V.*, 288). *V.*'s other major technical term is "decadence," which recurs most frequently in the book's second, historical plot. As a phenomenon in history (in the words of a minor character, Itague), "A decadence . . . is a falling-away from what is human, and the further we fall the less human we become. Because we are less human, we foist off the humanity we have lost on inanimate objects and abstract theories" (*V.*, 405).

Profane stands at an angle to the dominance of inanimate objects in one way—disqualified by his schlemihlhood, his incompetence. Herbert Stencil, the second protagonist, is set to the side of inanimacy in another way, as an investigator or scribe. He has vowed to trace the pattern in history of the mysterious woman V.—a human being, or force of nature in the shape of a woman, who seems to have willingly given herself over to the force of the inanimate. (And Stencil's search is the only way to "sustain" for himself his own "acquired sense of animateness" [V., 55].)

It is worth being a bit simpleminded, initially, about the two genre books, filed together, that make up V.—in large part because Pynchon's profligacy of approach can unhelpfully disguise them. Generically, one half of V. would have been a 1950s road novel or satire on New York bohemia. This Beat novel (if it had been simply that) is centered on the wanderer Benny Profane, his beloved Rachel Owlglass, and secondary figures of painters, partiers, record producers, jazz musicians, and ersatz thinkers who make up the "Whole Sick Crew." There are passages of customary satirical sociology of a fifties postcollegiate art underground: "Once I will say it, is all: that Crew does not live, it experiences," says Rachel. "It does not create, it talks about people who do. Varèse, Ionesco, de Kooning, Wittgenstein, I could puke. It satirizes itself and doesn't mean it. Time magazine takes it seriously and does mean it" (V., 380). The other book within V. would have been popular historical fiction in the spy-thriller vein. It skips through settings and eras—imperial spy intrigue, World War II memoir, Grand Guignol–era Paris, Weimar Germany transposed to colonial Africa. In both these halves of V. books, the somewhat familiar genre is undertaken from a remove of suspicion. A different aim substitutes for the usual prurient exposé (of bohemia) or adventurous thrills (of the historical spy novel): the development of a perspective, analyzing the contemporary moment and the past, on how *something* unexpected has happened in our century to change the status of human beings.

If this is a late formation of the discourse of the crisis of man, it is interesting to see how quickly, and self-consciously, V. disposes of equally plausible, and equally contemporary, formulations of the problem. V. starts to undo abstract man, first of all, by reintroducing the problem of the two sexes in a book that has passages of mildly pornographic comedy (Esther's erotic nose job, Fina's "gangbang")—introducing expectations for what a female desires, and what a male desires, as necessary specifics that corrupt the universal. Stencil's quest, too, is wrongly diagnosed, we are told, in the Whole Sick Crew's bohemian talk, as "contemporary man in search of an identity" (V., 226) (there are frequent gibes against Sartre and the popular philosophy of the time—Benny is suffering through a Western called *Existentialist Sheriff* when SHROUD starts telling him what's really going on). The "Problem" for Stencil is not a problem of the individual or any "abstract man," but how to see a pattern, not above but underneath all the different identities in his history of the woman V.—fusing a few single personalities with many material things. Then, too, *V.* gets past the problem of race or religion in its own unusual way. It makes "identity" not something to be resolved or overcome but something undecidable. Benny Profane is Jewish on his mother's side, Catholic on his father's. This means that each religion (matrilineal and patrilineal) would claim him. Therefore, there's no way to know just what he is—nor does it make any difference. The chance of having multiple identities, and whether it can ever move one beyond particularist identity to "universality," is mocked explicitly with "Fergus Mixolydian, the Irish Armenian Jew and universal man"—where Fergus's real innovation, it turns out, is his way of "watching the TV." "He'd developed an ingenious sleep-switch, receiving its signal from two electrodes placed on the inner skin of his forearm. . . . [T]he skin resistance increased over a preset value to operate the switch. Fergus thus became an extension of the TV set" (*V.*, 56). Technological advance, the mixing of the material and the bodily, supersede all questions of racial or ethnic particularity and universality.

Such images of what technologists used to call "man-machine interface" recur all through the present-day portions of *V.* They seem to set the initial tone for *V.*'s worries about the inanimate. At times, it seems as if machines really are still the main issue, in a slight updating of old technological fears: besides such throwaways as Fergus Mixolydian's television, the major character Rachel Owlglass is first seen sexually caressing her MG automobile—"Young Rachel . . . half an MG" (*V.*, 288)—a vision that haunts Benny until late in the book.

Yet this, too, is ultimately—partially—set aside, as we come to be taught that the "inanimate" objects turn out to be not just machines but the latent possibilities in all sorts of daily objects and practices. We see the new possibilities hinted at in the helping professions and medicine, for example, which come in for a very serious sort of satire. Instead of lifesaving surgery, *V.* the novel is interested in plastic surgery; instead of psychotherapy, the made-up field of psychodentistry, or "psychodontics." Stencil, the second protagonist who will trace the history behind the contemporary moment, considers himself "the century's child" (*V.*, 52) (born in 1901)—this is part of his claim on the ability to incarnate some force behind the twentieth century. But it turns out that Schoenmaker, the plastic surgeon, is also "coeval with the century" (born 1900). Rather than trace the century's impetus like Stencil, Schoenmaker represents the century by participating in it, cutting and grafting and filling human bodies with surgical changes. In World War I, Schoenmaker took up his craft originally to undo the damage done to humans by machines: "Others—politicians and machines—carried on wars . . . others—on the highways, in the factories—undid the work of nature with automobiles, milling machines" (*V.*, 101). But the early days of experimentation with plastic surgery introduced a kind of symbolic mistake, withdrawn but never quite repudiated: "allografts: the introduction of inert substances into the living face" (*V.*, 99). This spirit of surgically adding the inanimate to the human body, we sense, never really went away. And by the time he is working in New York, Schoenmaker is no longer trying to undo the damage of machines but making new artificialities of his own; he would like to redo all of Rachel's friend Esther, make her over as an ideal object, a purely fantasized man-made woman.

Thus, even the humane will to help, like Schoenmaker's, leads to "a deterioration of purpose; a decay" (*V.*, 101)—this is an aspect of the "decadence" that haunts the book, which *V.* suggests makes parts of the human body no longer distinguishable from the inanimate. Likewise, Eigenvalue, the avant-garde dentist, is the minor character who introduces "psychodontia" (*V.*, 153): the replacement of the postwar American search for a therapeutic soul, psychoanalysis, with soul as read through the *teeth*—dead objects in the head that outlast the living being even when buried in the ground. (This is what teeth seem to signify generally for Pynchon—it's remarkable that he should care about them—though they also allow him to make the bad joke that they too introduce a form of "decay" to the century: tooth decay.)

THE CENTURY'S HISTORY: INANIMACY, GENOCIDE, FANTASY

Herbert Stencil's quest for the meaning of the previous half century, meanwhile, takes up a fundamental narrative of the discourse of the crisis of man and reframes it with a concern for an extended vision of technology. This is the crisis of man's history story. Pynchon's history, too, is about progressive dehumanization through wars and politics. However, it is not this time the dehumanization of men by other men in cruelty and organization but dehumanization by the increasing confusion of human beings (and parts of human beings) with inanimate objects, in service of pleasure as well as torture.

Stencil, we know, begins his researches in 1945, occasioned by the end of World War II (*V.*, 54). His history narration, included in the book's inset historical chapters, goes back immediately, however, to the 1890s and various imperial misadventures of what Kipling had called "the Great Game." This could be a puzzling juxtaposition for many readers, I think. But it will probably not be puzzling to those who have read Arendt's *The Origins of Totalitarianism*—and therefore have a sense of the arguments, fifteen years before *V.*, that rooted the rise of totalitarianism in the mind-set of imperialism, and imperialism's production of World War I.

V. herself, we learn near the end, is directly associated with Mussolini and the Italian fascists—but by this stage it seems redundant or beside the point (*V.*, 473), because we have also learned that her mission is much broader, associated with a wider evil. V.'s death on Malta in 1943, and the culmination of the book on that obscure island, is set in context, for example, in a curious way, if one goes back to read Dwight Macdonald's 1945 essay "The Responsibility of Peoples" (quoted in my chapter 3). Macdonald's essay was about how the Nazi murder of the Jews signified a larger disaster for the respect for human life. Macdonald's essay also found its way, curiously, to Malta. "Perhaps the most heavily bombed community in this war is the strategic British-held island of Malta, which in a 28-month period had 2,315 air-raid alerts, or an average of three a day. One in 200 of the civilian population died during these raids."[8] According to Macdonald, the tragedy was that the Maltese disliked their British imperial masters even as they hated the Italians, then Germans, who relentlessly bombed them—and so Malta represented the continuity between the instrumental view of human life held by the great empires and the homicidal view of human life of the multiple fascist regimes. Through a roundabout circuit of imperial power, late imperial holdings, bombing from the air, and inanimacy on the ground, Pynchon is following out a line of thought, implicit in aspects of the earlier crisis of man, that its analysts could not carry much further—both because they did not know what was coming and because they were not imaginative writers of Pynchon's caliber.

In searching for the origins of the concentration camps in Germany, Arendt emphasized that the first camps were not created in Germany but in Africa during the Boer War. Pynchon, bringing the strands together, gives us an imperial story in Southwest Africa among German holdings, told by a "young engineering student" from Munich, Kurt Mondaugen (who would later work for the Nazis on the destructive airborne V1 and V2 rocket bombs) about his early scientific researches, and how they get absorbed into the memory of German imperialists' 1904 genocide of Herero and Hottentot. This was not yet the Holocaust but a version of it: "Allowing for natural causes . . . von Trotha . . . is reckoned to have done away with about 60,000 people. This is only 1 per cent of six million, but still pretty good" (*V.*, 245). Pynchon gives us the "natural concentration camps" (*V.*, 267) of African geography before the unnatural ones that follow.

But he also reimagines this early genocide as a manifestation of fantasies, of decadent aesthetic pleasures rather than of unmixed political policy. Lothar von Trotha's mass murder comes into the book as it is remembered (and hallucinated) in a closed Gothic house in 1922, impregnated with the '20s spirit of Weimar Germany—that is, of cabarets, libertinage, and sexual violence: "Vera Meroving and her lieutenant in profile, she striking at his chest with what appeared to be a small riding crop, he twisting a gloved hand into her hair" (*V.*, 238), which somehow becomes connected to the murders outside. The change World War I had wrought, one character says, was that it "committed" people to "work out . . . political hallucinations on a live mass, a real human population" (*V.*, 248). Pynchon reminds us that the hallucinations were not all properly political. In Southwest Africa, the murderous wielders of the *sjambok*, the whip, begin to hallucinate that their victims—"Sarah," "Abraham"—want the pain and death, and love it; the German *génocidaire*'s only fear is that if a "season" like this "ever came . . . again" (as in the later Holocaust), it would no longer be "furious and nostalgic; but rather with a logic that chilled the comfortable perversity of the heart" (*V.*, 273). The impulse to make people inanimate is not just for industrial efficiency (as the "factories of death" thinkers worried) but for *pleasure*, specifically, the pleasure of certain kinds of aesthetic decadence.

Thus, Pynchon moves from his imperial stories to an initially unaccountable chapter on 1920s Montmartre, in which a young dancer, Mélanie l'Heuremaudit, falls so much in love with herself as a living mannequin (as she is loved in this guise, too, by the ubiquitous V.)—in a modernist ballet staffed with automata built by "[a] German engineer" (*V.*, 396)—that she impales herself on a pike and dies. Here, again, the sense seems to be that commonplace nostalgic fantasies of something like Grand Guignol theater or Weimar decadence will become implicated in the inanimacy and dehumanization of the present, as *aesthetic* and historical-nostalgic "hallucinations," too, will be worked out on a "live mass." People come to take an attitude toward people that one can sometimes take toward objects for play, as well as objects for use—that these objects *want* to be used, that the tree wants to become a canoe or the punching bag wants to be hit. (This leads back to what is surely Pynchon's strangest near-allegory of genocide, in a comic register: the black-armbanded Alligator Patrol that Benny joins in the sewers under the street. Baby alligators were sold as toys to children, then flushed down the toilet when they began to grow. The animate was taken for the inanimate, and the alligators' only desire now, it begins to seem to Benny, is to be exterminated and released. This produces a very equivocal image: that even Benny, kindest and most hapless of protagonists, armbanded and set to work against his inclinations, will be brought into the emotional logic of extermination, on the side of the *génocidaires*.)

Once an inset chapter takes us into World War II itself, these historical meditations become explicit, as if a treatise were being written on the subject at last (though never quite directly—still behind another Pynchonian narrative mask). In "The Confessions of Fausto Maijstral," Maijstral recalls Malta in 1943 under the burden of bombing, and reflects directly on his understanding of the absence of humanism in his time: "I know of machines that are more complex than people. . . . To have humanism, we must first be convinced of our humanity. As we move further into decadence this becomes more difficult" (*V.*, 322). Maijstral introduces us to his concept of "non-humanity. Not 'inhumanity,' which means bestiality; beasts are still animate" (*V.*, 307). The people of Malta, with the bombs falling, move under the street—where Benny sought the alligators, and where he hid in the subway among all the other "human yo-yos" who can't make their way aboveground (where Ellison's Invisible Man had to retreat, too, a literary decade earlier)—since, aboveground, the kingdom of the inanimate is establishing itself. It is human beings who take on the character of "debris, crushed stone, broken masonry" (*V.*, 307) beneath the falling bombs, while the bombs no longer seem to have human beings behind them. We hear this thought in a poem:

> If I told the truth
> You would not believe me.
> If I said: no fellow soul
> Drops death from the air, no conscious plot
> Drove us underground. (*V.*, 326)

Even the humans who helped the transition, who made the inanimate objects and dreams that will take over from man, are disappearing or disassembling. Maijstral finally witnesses the death, by "disassembly," of V. herself.[9] Pinned under a beam by the war's bombs, she is found by a gang of children in the ruins—as in newsreel images of the kids playing in the cellars of the Blitz. They are, of course, the holders of the future. What do they do? Stripping off her clothes, they remove "a foot—an artificial foot," "[a]t her navel . . . a star sapphire" (echoing the comic tale earlier in the book of the man with a screw for a navel, whose bottom fell off when it was removed), "false teeth," "a glass eye" (*V.*, 342–43). Each of the children carries a piece of her inanimacy off into the future—and something fundamental has transpired in this instant of World War II, which is, of course, where V.'s history ends.

WORLD WAR II AND THE TAKING APART AND REUSE OF BODIES

For the intellectual as for the layman, there are, I suppose, as many ways to be horrified by the Holocaust, the Nazi murder of the Jews, as there are different people to read the accounts of the genocide. Historically, though, certain responses have gathered consistency, emphasizing different elements of the crime. One horror is that so *many* human beings could be murdered, the horror of the "six million." Another is that they could be murdered so mechanically and with so much organization, the horror of the "factories of death." An intellectual variant upon this is a particular horror that all the advances of modernity, meant to help and liberate mankind, could seem to culminate in a progress of extermination. (This is a still-active idea, in a tradition running from contemporary thinkers like Giorgio Agamben and Zygmunt Bauman back to the wartime theses of Horkheimer and Adorno.)

A rarer and less visible source of horror might be that the bodies of the murdered victims could be *reused*. Yet I think this has been a particularly strong current in American imaginative work, rather than intellectual musing, because it often seemed too vile a fact, too much a profanation, to discuss in other discourses. This is the horror that came out in the apocryphal but once-widespread myths of soap made out of people, which I have discussed in chapter 3. (Pynchon hadn't forgotten: "I guess on the rare occasions you bathe you wouldn't mind using Nazi soap made from one of those six million Jews" [*V.*, 354], Rachel says to Benny in a lover's quarrel, when he seems inadequately committed to human life.) We have also seen Dwight Macdonald's fury in the 1940s at what else the Nazis had used Jews' bodies for: "The ashes and bones of the burned bodies were used to fertilize cabbage fields around the camps."[10]

What if, though, a thinker began to feel that what had been done in World War II, though apparently a one-off atrocity, lingered in all sorts of behaviors decades later? Or if the *material* that had been harvested hadn't simply disappeared? What if the writer let himself follow out the thought that there will always be some ash left, and that the cabbages themselves, part of the food chain, carry on?

This is a part of the transition that Pynchon made in his thoughts on the inanimate and the fate of the technological side of the crisis of man, as he moved on to *The Crying of Lot 49* (1966). Dwelling in California in the mid-'60s, the book's heroine, Oedipa Maas, can't help noticing on her TV the "deafening ad for Beaconsfield Cigarettes, whose attractiveness lay in their filter's use of bone charcoal, the very best kind." "'Bones of what?' wondered Oedipa" (*CL49*, 34). Assigned to execute the last will and testament of her former lover, real estate oligarch Pierce Inverarity, Oedipa finds out the answer soon enough. They are human bones, of course—but human bones with a piquant provenance. Lago di Pietà was one of the lost American battles of World War II, "now ignored (in 1943 tragic)," in which a company of GIs were massacred, to the last man, as they defended their dug-in position for weeks against German planes and machine-gun fire. The Nazi killers dumped the bodies into the lake. An American mobster dredged the bones up in the "early '50s" in hopes that patriotic Americans "would somehow refocus attention on the fallen of WWII" (*CL49*, 63)—but that acknowledgment of history didn't happen, and when it didn't, the dead Americans' bones simply entered the American commercial system of raw materials: sold for fertilizer first, warehoused for a time in Fort Wayne, Indiana, and then bought by Beaconsfield Cigarettes in the end. So good contemporary Americans, instead of remembering the soldiers who died in a forgotten tragedy, in what was supposedly a "good" war, now were smoking them, with luxurious, oblivious pleasure. There was no single crime but a whole system of negligences. (The only small quantity of bones to escape got shunted to the lake bed of one of Inverarity's Southern California housing developments, Fangoso Lagoons, where Oedipa unravels the tale; they join Disneyesque ersatz history, a shipwreck in this inland lake, for the amusement of scuba-diving tourists.)

Lago di Pietà represents a kind of paradigm story for the fate of human materials after World War II in *The Crying of Lot 49*. Pynchon had worried earlier, in *V.*, that a confusion was emerging between the inanimate and the human, with a division of human beings into replaceable, insertable parts. In the later book, he starts to show how the *removed* parts could be reused, and how they persisted, by themselves, without any context of values.

When Oedipa visits the philatelist, Genghis Cohen, who appraises Pierce's stamp collection, she finds that in drinking his homemade dandelion wine, she drinks the forgotten and dishonored dead in the same way that the Beaconsfield customers have been smoking them. "I picked the dandelions in a cemetery, two years ago," Cohen explains. "Now the cemetery is gone. They took it out for the East San Narciso Freeway" (*CL49*, 95). Here, the material transformation of human remains seems to push some of its old incarnation into the new form. Cohen thinks the froth is the *dandelions* awakening: "You see, in spring, when the dandelions begin to bloom again, the wine goes through a fermentation. As if they [the plants] remembered" (*CL49*, 98). Oedipa takes the darker view that it is, in fact, the dead human beings, who fertilized those dandelions, who pass on a residue of consciousness and bitter regret: "As if their home cemetery in some way still did exist, in a land where you could somehow walk . . . no one to plow them up. . . . As if the dead really do persist, even in a bottle of wine" (*CL49*, 99).

Thus Pynchon comes to ask whether some inner meaning or memory remains stored in waste objects, too, and whether this will gradually make contemporary human beings, with their belief in thought-out and chosen values (for those who still believe in them), feel unreal or left out of the truth of "what's really going on"—as the inanimate objects fill up the human world, carrying with them confused histories of bits of all the broken human values and traces they had held previously. New bits, too, are generated constantly, and lose their original meanings—their genealogies—just as quickly.

As a book, *Lot 49* is especially interested in rendering the ephemera of a broadcast and commercial culture. Part of the feeling of prescience in Pynchon ("how did he know that was important?," one is always asking in hindsight) is that he goes out of his way to notice technologically and socially novel things—or things that *feel* novel—and to work them in, so that they pattern the satire in his fiction. The first pages of *Lot 49* submit us to mentions of a Tupperware party (Tupperware, invented in 1945; the unique parties, early 1950s), Muzak (expanded in the 1940s), LSD tests (Timothy Leary started his in 1961), *Perry Mason* (aired beginning in 1957), and relentless Beatlemania in the form of "Sick Dick and the Volkswagens" (instead of "I Want to Hold Your Hand"—song of the British Invasion in 1964—they sing "I Want to Kiss Your Feet" [*CL49*, 23]). (*Lot 49*'s house band, the Paranoids, is made up of sixteen-year-olds, each "with a Beatle haircut" he can't see through.) These contemporary references appear as the setups for endless jokes ("too much kirsch in the fondue" [*CL49*, 9] for the drunken matrons of Tupperware, the goofy "Vivaldi Kazoo Concerto" [*CL49*, 10] for the Muzak).[11]

The last moment that Oedipa is certain that human values were clearer, and not a joke, was during World War II. For Mucho, she thinks, "Maybe, God help her, he should have been in a war, Japs in trees, Krauts in Tiger tanks"—it would have been less traumatic to him than "the lot" where he formerly sold used cars (*CL49*, 15). Yet the material traces of World War II, carried into the present, *don't* protect anybody from rearrangement, despair, and loss of meaning, as the book is ready to tell us. When the Yoyodyne executive is about to kill himself (by self-immolation, like the protesting Buddhist priests he now sees on early Vietnam-era TV), it is a cruel irony that he plans to use his "faithful Zippo, which had seen him through the Normandy hedgerows, the Ardennes, Germany, and postwar America" (*CL49*, 114–15). The same lighter has *not* seen him through postwar America, we should say.

But the artifacts of the wrong side, the Nazis, also found their way to postwar America as surely as that Zippo survived the war (and may survive its owner). Oedipa, as she understands more and more of the fabric of Orange County in the mid-1960s and its dark underweave, becomes furious with the Volkswagen Beetles she sees everywhere on the state's freeways and cloverleafs: "She drove savagely along the freeway, hunting for Volkswagens" (*CL49*, 150). The Nazi "people's car" had survived the war—a neutral machine artifact—and now cruised up and down American highways as a chic object, cut off from the values that invented it in 1937. She soon meets Winthrop Tremaine, the very embodiment of the Puritan founding (something like John Winthrop, first governor of the Massachusetts Bay Colony, crossed with Johnny Tremain, hero of Esther Forbes's famous

1944 children's book about the American Revolution). Winthrop Tremaine, a "government surplus" seller, is now vending swastika armbands to adults and SS uniforms to kids in a "back-to school campaign, lot of 37 longs, you know, teenage kids sizes" (*CL49*, 149). For even remembering the war, Oedipa seems a joykill to the other characters: "Some people today," Metzger rebukes her (he likens her to the "bleeding heart" protesters who "March on Washington"), "can drive VW's, carry a Sony radio in their shirt pocket. Not this one, folks, she wants to right wrongs, 20 years after it's all over" (*CL49*, 75–76).

THE HIDDEN HISTORY OF WASTE: TRADE-INS, RERUNS, AND RECYCLING

The bone cigarettes and bone wine are extreme transformations, metaphors. Pynchon is prepared, however, to make more practical claims for the horror behind the exchange of material despite the loss of its meanings. As with *V.*'s junked car lot in Elmira, New York, in *V.*, like Auschwitz with its piled corpses, Oedipa's husband Mucho's trauma in *Lot 49* comes, too, from a used-car lot—one he put his misplaced, humane hopes in and thus could never get over. Mucho "believed in the cars," wanting to give forgotten people a new start: "how could he not, seeing people poorer than him come in, Negro, Mexican, cracker" (*CL49*, 13)? All they produce, though, is a "residue" and loss. All they gain—under cover of some exit from the system, something new and better—is more of the same, in ominous "trade-ins":

> trade-ins: motorized, metal extensions of themselves, of their families and what their whole lives must be like . . . and when the cars were swept out you had to look at the actual residue of these lives, and there was no way of telling what things had been truly refused . . . and what had simply (perhaps tragically) been lost.
>
> [In] the endless rituals of trade-in, week after week . . . each owner, each shadow, filed in only to exchange a dented, malfunctioning version of himself for another, just as futureless, automotive projection of somebody else's life. . . . To Mucho it was horrible. (*CL49*, 13–14)

Trade-in is a more pivotal term in the apparatus of *The Crying of Lot 49* than one might think. It signifies less on its own than it does in a constellation of allied concepts: *rerun*, for television shows (called "endless repetition" [*CL49*, 34] in the book), and *cycling* (*CL49*, 105) for communication and energy. In modern terms, we would say that a problem Pynchon intuits is the problem of *recycling*—paired always with the novelty that motivated it, the exponential growth in postindustrial America of consumer waste and trash.[12] This intuition links Pynchon's unusual sensitivity to the survival and persistence of forgotten materials, to new technologies of ephemeral production and unmoored signs and simulations.

In part because the single most frequently discussed scientific concept in all of Pynchon's work is "entropy," the most discussed pseudotechnological artifact in *The Crying of Lot 49* has been the Nefastis Machine.[13] This is a box invented by the loony Berkeley scientist John Nefastis that is supposed to incarnate the real nineteenth-century scientist Clerk Maxwell's hypothetical sorting "demon"—an agency that, without adding work to a system, can organize molecules by their heat to overcome a natural tendency to energy-dissipating disorganization. Nefastis thinks his box works if the right kind of sensitive person stares at it long enough. "Communication is the key," he cries, "To keep it all cycling" (*CL49*, 105), as he tries to talk Oedipa through his insane mechanism. Oedipa is, however, not all that impressed with Nefastis's explanation of his antientropy box. If communication is the key, it isn't working with her: "you're not reaching me" (*CL49*, 106), she complains, even in words, despite the technological bunkum. So Nefastis has to admit a basic truth that Pynchon admits, too: " 'Entropy is a figure of speech, then,' sighed Nefastis, 'a metaphor. It connects the world of thermodynamics to the world of information flow'" (*CL49*, 106). Or, to put it even more simply—a propos of Pynchon's own plotting in the book—it metaphorically links states of material to states of immaterial information.

The function of this metaphor in *Lot 49* is to situate a last, central concern. How can it become the case with this "cycling" that information seems to be crossing over with the world of real molecules and heat energy—how, in other words, has there been a confusion and blending of two kinds of cycling, material and immaterial? It has become possible, most obviously, because of new technologies that represent the material as the informational, and broadcast it: not at all Nefastis's box with its "photo of Clerk Maxwell" (*CL49*, 86) to stare at but the television box with its photos of countless living and dead people to watch. (Indeed, a joke of the Nefastis sequence seems to be that while Oedipa pours her soul into watching one box with a picture, desperate to make something happen, she is in effect doing the same thing as Nefastis watching the boob tube in the next room.) This crossover may exist, too, on the telephone full of known and unknown disembodied voices, and the radio with its disc jockeys and songs penetrating everywhere.

The allegory that the book puts at its center for this kind of constant circulation of material stuff and immaterial messages is the mail—more specifically, an alternative to the US mail, the hand-carried correspondence system, alternately known as W.A.S.T.E or WASTE, which Oedipa discovers is somehow tenuously connected with a centuries-old postal conspiracy called the Tristero. The Tristero, it emerges, was a rival mail service in the welter of modern European and nineteenth-century American private services—Thurn und Taxis, the Pony Express. But it may have turned to violence and opposition, rather than peaceful circulation, at some point in its history, and it may survive today. At the least, the Tristero's sign, the muted post horn, survives in an unknown connection with the secret mails of WASTE.

In part, the meaning of all this is that in such a world of circulation and communication technologies, one begins to wonder if the slag material signifies—and starts to make (or fake)—messages of its own. (Or, for that matter, whether all the circulation of supposedly significant messages by broadcast is just a new form of things produced in order to be thrown out—a whole new field of deliberate waste.) Ordinarily, waste is just waste, leftovers. Waste becomes W.A.S.T.E. in the book, a signifying system, by a simple addition of periods. Up all night in search of the secret message system, Oedipa finally locates one of its mailboxes underneath the freeway. It looks suspiciously like a trash can. In fact, it's marked "W.A.S.T.E." "She had to look closely to see the periods between the letters" (*CL49*, 130)—not waste but W.A.S.T.E. communication.

The reverse process obtains though, too—in which associations and signs, meant to communicate, fall into the blankness of the material, just stuff, and seem either warped or wiped out. In his nightmares of the used-car lot, Mucho remembers gaping at the sign announcing the lot's affiliation with the National Auto Dealers Association—well-known publishers of prices and valuations for used cars, even today (and since the 1930s, when they started). For Mucho—unlike Oedipa, who can find the periods in WASTE and thus make it signify—the periods slip away. "Just this creaking metal sign that said nada, nada, against the blue sky. I used to wake up hollering" (*CL49*, 144). This organization for concrete valuation turns out to also be a name for material and its absence, what is, or is worth, *nada*, *nada*, nothing, under the aspect of eternity.

At the level of supposedly enfranchised men and women, who try to work within the systems of convention, the new regime of communication and circulation is clearly somehow incompatible with human personality. *It* is now the feature of the world that jeopardizes the human product, that threatens man in his daily existence. The men Oedipa is close to, who disappear from her sight, or "dissipate," are caught up in the vacancy and equal value or valuelessness of mere cycling. Pierce Inverarity speaks to Oedipa only once in the book, sometime before his death. He reaches her by phone, speaks to her in five different voices, communicates nothing but that he has communicated, and attains a last voice of "The Shadow" from the old radio serial—as if talking through the phone had become a form of broadcasting, too, and he was only a darkened projection, the shadow of the light his body blocked. (Even the different forms of communication themselves become commensurable and indistinguishable, forms of rerun.) Metzger, the child actor turned lawyer, has his old films rebroadcast, interrupting his current life; has a pilot television show made *about* his life, starring someone else; and all these media can be broadcast whether he is young or old, alive or dead, surviving as both material and projection when he is just dirt in a graveyard—"The film is in an air-conditioned vault at one of the Hollywood studios, light can't fatigue it, it can be repeated endlessly" (*CL49*, 33). The ex–child actor elopes with a girl child, finally, and disappears, as if his own life has begun to cycle. (The obsession of so many of Oedipa's men in the book with "young stuff" [*CL49*, 105], as the book terms it, points to a collapse in time or history, a coincidence and depthlessness of generations, as if the terminal quest would be to copulate with the very child who is the result of a coupling. This "[e]ndless, convoluted incest," in Mucho's phrase for his horror of trade-ins, bespeaks another crossing-over from trading-in objects to trading-in persons [for younger models], and another Oedipal echo for our heroine's name. Oedipa herself is marooned in a world almost entirely made of dissolving and regressing men; female characters scarcely exist.) Mucho is most tragic of all, because through LSD he finds his old desire for human connection—like his wish to help the poor, the forgotten, on the car lot—only in a discovery that all voices, when broadcast on his radio station, become essentially the same in their "power spectra," no matter what they're saying or singing. Thus, all people can be connected with him. "Man" as a concept becomes the totality of his own spread voice. And Mucho makes the fatal mistake (or insight?) of becoming convinced that mere communications have turned back into the material he has lost: "The songs, it's not just that they say something, they *are* something" (*CL49*, 144). From code alone, from the magnetic recording of a few notes played by a particular violinist on a string tuned "a few cycles sharp," he fantasizes the actual person could be made physical: "Do you think somebody could do the dinosaur bone bit with that one string, Oed? With just his set of notes on that cut. Figure out what his ear is like, and then the musculature of his hands and arms, and eventually the entire man" (*CL49*, 141). (Similar fantasies of the informational's commensurability with—and overtaking of—the physical have marked the half century since, in cognitive science and bioinformatics, erupting most publicly in the sequencing of the human genome a decade ago.) The question *Lot 49* investigates but does not answer is whether there are other ways to use the systems of circulation, for those who have *already* been "disinherited," cut out of the hopes of man—or, for someone like Oedipa, where to turn when you are overincorporated within society and feel its unreality, and start to escape it. Is there anywhere to escape to ("What was left to inherit?" [*CL49*, 180])? The problem of answering has everything to do with the way in which the mood of *Lot 49*, besides its sophomoric comedy, is one of unremitting anxiety—and why the unofficial systems of mere circulation seem malevolent at every turn. Why does Oedipa perceive the Tristero system, even as she knows more and more about it, as "sinister," "malign" (*CL49*, 54), no matter who makes use of it or how comic the purpose? It doesn't otherwise seem that bad. Why does a historical mail service with violence in its past (less than was practiced by the US government, as its antigovernment, libertarian, and Barry Goldwater–supporting characters keep reminding Oedipa), but no proof of violence in the present, come to seem to her like "The Adversary" (*CL49*, 80)? For recycling, rerunning, reusing could be benign. In this realm of more ephemeral communications, the ability of underground subcultures to communicate without government interference might even be a good thing, what the book has termed a "miracle," the intrusion of another world's order into this one, "a kiss of cosmic pool balls":

> For here were God knew how many citizens, deliberately choosing not to communicate by U.S. Mail. It was not an act of treason, nor possibly even of defiance. But it was a calculated withdrawal, from the life of the Republic, from its machinery. Whatever else was being denied them out of hate, indifference to the power of their vote, loopholes, simple ignorance, this withdrawal was their own, unpublicized, private. Since they could not have withdrawn into a vacuum (could they?), there had to exist the separate, silent, unsuspected world. (*CL49*, 124–25)

This has the populist flavor of a passage from Mario Savio, orating at Berkeley at the start of its free speech movement in 1964, on behalf of people tired of the "odious operation" of "the machine," and all those forgotten by American progress. Indeed, the book pushes Oedipa through Sather Gate on the Berkeley university campus to flounder in the protesting sixties, "a plaza teeming with corduroy, denim, bare legs, blonde hair, hornrims, bicycle spokes in the sun, bookbags, swaying card tables, long paper petitions dangling to earth, posters for indecipherable FSM's [free speech movement], YAF's [Young Americans for Freedom], VDC's [Vietnam Day Committee], suds in the fountain, students in nose-to-nose dialogue" (*CL49*, 103). Oedipa's activism is distinct but not entirely unrelated. She has discovered, trying to work out the legacy of Pierce Inverarity, real estate developer, the world outside the suburbs. Introduced to us as a housewife stereotype rusticating in the fastnesses of "Kinneret-Among-The-Pines" on the Bay Area Peninsula, a benumbed and insulated twenty-eight-year-old

"Mrs.," with nothing occupying her but Tupperware parties, her therapist, gourmet "ricotta," "marjoram and sweet basil" from her "herb garden," "days ... more or less identical" (*CL49*, 10–11), she breaks out of "her ... tower," "a captive maiden" (*CL49*, 21), into a world of flophouse derelicts, criminal businessmen, injustice, and opposition. Formerly "insulated," "unable to feel much of anything" (*CL49*, 19), upholstered by her garments and possessions like "a beach ball with feet" (*CL49*, 36), she is stripped, her nerves and intuition touching the world again.

Yet I take it that the anxiety and malignity remain in *Lot 49* because there is no proof that the human efforts at an exit from hierarchical "encapsulation," through countercirculation, really do work; no proof there's anywhere to go, once you're down and out. Where *is* the other world? In *V.* it was called "under the street," which was also Ralph Ellison's place of discovery, on the subway, for the people who plunged out of history; in *Lot 49* the airwaves and telephone wires seem to have supplanted it as a place where one can no longer be safely down and out but up and circulated. *Lot 49* has many "undergrounds," in the book's terminology, merely circulating messages but no true safety. Oedipa finds no proof that material stuff does *not* simply dominate in the end, along with whatever meanings were attached to it by its earliest possessors, destined to perpetuate what has already been done to it by earlier exploiters. Thus, matter, which was inanimate to start, became even more malignly inanimate once it had been put into human circulation with some humanization but beyond the control of human values. One's conclusion about the outcome of *Lot 49*, whether optimistic or pessimistic, becomes increasingly arbitrary in the final pages because the final pages of *Lot 49* don't really depend on the rest of the book. The last chapter, and particularly its rhapsodic last pages, seems to stand alone, as a wrap-up that doesn't necessarily wrap up anything.

The Tristero, we learn at last, began with a man named Tristero—a single man like Pierce Inverarity, the California "founding father" (*CL49*, 26), or like each of America's own Founding Fathers whom one learns about in storybooks. Tristero claimed to be heir to (and thus in control of) the legitimate European postal service, and began a career of terrorism to avenge his central grievance of "disinheritance" (*CL49*, 160). It is never known, and can never be known, if Tristero was an heir, a pretender, or a thoroughgoing madman. Oedipa realizes that his system has been taken up, in America, by those who truly *are* disinherited—in an America that has become so locked in its ways that there are no longer new means to overcome earlier misallocations of material. But she doesn't know what this development means, and neither, it seems, does Pynchon. In a near-final rhapsody of the book, *Lot 49* reaches out to other books, to a whole tradition that goes back through elements we have seen in Saul Bellow, Ralph Ellison, even Flannery O'Connor, and then earlier, to the proletarian 1930s, which the discourse of man was accused of effacing. It gives a picture of the people who are too poor or ethnic to be "recognized" (as in Bellow), who had to plunge outside of history when it didn't include them (as in Ellison), who find religious revelation (the "Word") in broken-up bodies, artifacts, and prostheses, and not in any sanctioned church (as in O'Connor)—then, too, it sweeps up a kind of writing that connects to Steinbeck and to Kerouac—and masses everything together in the reconnection between universal "man" and "America." Here is Oedipa, transforming the old 1930s images gradually into new pictures of squatters in the American life *Lot 49* now knows—in the automobile junkyard, the lines of communication, or mere voices on a wire or in a broadcast:

> Were the squatters there in touch with others, through Tristero; were they helping carry forward that 300 years of the house's disinheritance? Surely they'd forgotten by now what it was the Tristero were to have inherited . . . What was left to inherit? That America coded in Inverarity's testament, where was that? She thought of other, immobilized freight cars, where the kids sat . . . or slept in junkyards in the shells of wrecked Plymouths, or even, daring, spent the night up some pole in a lineman's tent like caterpillars, swung among a web of telephone wires, living in the very copper rigging and secular miracle of communication. . . . And the voices . . . that had phoned at random during the darkest, slowest hours, searching ceaseless among the dial's ten million possibilities for that magical Other who would reveal herself . . . the recognition, the Word. (*CL49*, 180)

Oedipa recovers the lives of hidden and forgotten people, in passages recalling *On the Road*, now mixed with Steinbeck and the WPA writers' project or Farm Bureau hard-luck photos of the thirties: "[O]ld Pullman cars, left where the money'd run out or the customers vanished, amid green farm flatnesses where clothes hung, smoke lazed out of jointed pipes. Were the squatters there in touch with others, through Tristero; were they helping carry forward that 300 years of the house's disinheritance?" (*CL49*, 179–80). "She had dedicated herself . . . to making sense of what Inverarity had left behind, never suspecting that the legacy was America" (*CL49*, 178). And *still* she never does get over her sense that behind W.A.S.T.E. is the Tristero, and the Tristero is malign. *Lot 49* may seem affectionate toward its many fringe groups and underground elements, but they don't make up a world in the end. That is because the book worries about something beyond them—its question of whether remains are transmitted beyond each individual communication, buried in the material facts of the *founding* of the system of communication, and whether this residue may shadow and smudge the prospect of those who join such a system, without them even knowing it. The mad picture of hobos up in the air in hammocks strung of copper wires of telephone trunk lines and relays, cocooned in electricity but "untroubled by the dumb voltages flickering their miles," slips in to darken the Dorothea Lange or Walker Evans slideshow, as if this deafness to the real, surrounding messages might be one more piece of the underground American myth of the "common man." Rather than simply having been disinherited once again, the forgotten people are being further defrauded by their own efforts and assent. They believe each of their hapless peripheral circles is a center. They sleep within the chrysalis of communication but are no closer to interpreting or influencing the nation's messages.

It's often asked what, precisely, the odd title *The Crying of Lot 49* names. Most evidently, to any reader patient enough to postpone his curiosity to the end, the title reproduces the last five words of the last sentences in the book—"The auctioneer cleared his throat. Oedipa settled back, to await the crying of lot 49" (*CL49*, 183). This is the first appearance in the text of explicit allusion to the title. Literally, Oedipa ends the book anticipating the auction-calling, or "crying," of that part of Pierce's stamp collection that contains forgeries from the Tristero, and hopes (or suspects) that a Tristero representative may show up in person to recover them. She'll then be able to put a human face, a human person, to the system she's stumbled on. Yet it feels as if Pynchon were adapting the convention by which untitled poems are named for their first lines, their initial impulses, here to point out the significance in *his* prose of the moment the circulation of words and ideas breaks off, the telephone line goes dead; as if Pynchon were titling his book by an arbitrary break in a system of circulation that has no proper beginning (inaugurated for Oedipa by Inverarity's assorted voices as whispers on the phone); as if the false quest for an ending, its ultimate arbitrariness and impossibility in a period of endless cycling, were meant to infect the book itself. Or else Pynchon has indulged, at our expense, the comic convention of the "shaggy dog story," that form of American joke defined by its interminability, and then the frustration of a punch line; in such jokes, the convolutions of the route taken to arrive at the non sequitur and anticlimactic punch line—originally, "That dog's not so shaggy"—is all that makes it funny. So one could say that Pynchon is alerting us that the course of the story, and not a solution to its mystery, is the matter to attend to. Symbolically, it's only fair to acknowledge that religious critics have associated its numerology with the 49 days leading up to Pentecost.[14] Though "49," insofar as the number has been spoken in the book before this, was, explicitly, 1849, the year that Tristero's ethos of eternal opposition began in America, fleeing the thwarted revolutions of 1848 in Europe—a curious beginning in defeat, insofar as Pynchon thinks of his California sixties as dreaming of a new moral revolution. Also, the year 1849, in the context of California, can only remind one of its myth of its own European American repopulation—with the Gold Rush, and that year's influx of fortune seekers, the "49ers," leading to statehood in 1850 (and the name of San Francisco's football franchise).

If there is one word in the title that *does* belong to the whole book, however, it's that word "lot"—as one of many accumulations of material stuff in the book, or as a measure, or even a parcel of earth.[15] That one word keeps recurring in the book: with the stamps, with "the lot" of used cars that first drove Mucho into crazed anxiety, then in the real estate lots (*CL49*, 51) that developers like Pierce Inverarity fixed and speculated in to build their unholy cities. The "lot" becomes an already conditioned and imprisoned piece of the brute "earth" of California emphasized, in the book's very last pages, as the resistant and dead material that is ruled off as the substrate of so many hallucinations of "transcendent meaning" (*CL49*, 181). This material, once it has been originally possessed, pummeled into shape, and passed down, is "America," too, in the book's terms. Oedipa "had dedicated herself . . . to make sense of what Inverarity had left behind," we're told flatly, "never suspecting that the legacy was America" (*CL49*, 178). So Pynchon asks, in line with the national meanings, which spread beyond man, technology, and history, whether America, too, specifically, has any room left for new values and undetermined meanings in its already founded and ruled regime of objects, waste, and cycling. Thus "lot" in its last sense becomes the disposition, or fate, or humbled fatalistic destiny of persons and things and dreams that once began with the greatest hopes. It might be no longer plenty and jumble, out of which you can project a world; it might be a register of states made either-or, on-off, in the new digital computation: "[H]ow had it ever happened here, with the chances once so good for diversity? For it was now like walking among matrices of a great digital computer, the zeroes and ones twinned above, hanging like balanced mobiles left and right, ahead, thick, maybe endless" (*CL49*, 181). What's left? "[W]aiting above all; if not for another set of possibilities to replace those that had conditioned the land . . . then at least, at the very least, waiting for a symmetry of choices to break down, to go skew" (ibid.). Waiting for the sixties, its social movements, to blow things open? Or waiting interminably, paranoiacally, or mystically?

Pynchon's ending, as the door is opened to the later 1960s and in many ways shut on the old concerns of man, is really up to the reader's inclinations to sound out. It is populist as the crisis of man's search for universal man was not—looking to the "disinherited." It is enmeshed in the details of mundane technologies, wasted artifacts, daily communication, as the crisis of man's grandiose discourse of technics was not. The end of the book seems so steeped in dread because it feels that something must be done but holds the suspicion that *this*, the new communication, the new circulation, *isn't it*. Nor has the long story of a crisis of man, which Pynchon knows and in some way completes, solved its problems in time, and the time has now become too late.

So far we have spoken of the problem of man, and each worrier who faced the problem at least believed that there was a unified subject to be troubled or jeopardized. Of Mucho Maas, after his dissolution into radio broadcasts, someone finally says in *Lot 49*, "He's a walking assembly of man" (*CL49*, 140). Pynchon has many affinities with the old crisis of man when he is showing how we have gotten to this point. But he knows that an "assembly of man" is no longer the man of which midcentury nervous re-enlightenment had spoken. He winds up making a claim in answer to the old question "What is man?" by saying that the subject in question is no longer the same.

The problem will not be one of man misorganized (as in totalitarianism) or simply overmechanized (as in old industrial fears) but man too much confused with material that does not belong to him; and man, through material-immaterial circulation, becoming *too many men* at once, as each person, encountering communications but still dominated by material relations, gains too many implausible incarnations of himself with too little control of each.

It is the sense of multiplicity, then division, breaking apart the idea of abstract man itself, that became an aspect of the breaking apart of the discourse of man in the 1960s—as well as the turn back to "America" as the place of forgotten people and continuing threats, which Pynchon registers so well. These divisions put us finally across the threshold into the era for which a crisis of *man* would come to seem archaic: tyrannical, purblind, and finally not making adequate sense. However the precise years are dated, one must turn for a conclusion to that era and social phenomenon called "the sixties."

PART IV

TRANSMUTATION

CHAPTER 9

THE SIXTIES AS BIG BANG

This study has taken many chapters to chart the rise, migrations, and complications of the crisis of man. I have hinted throughout this study that the period that eventually ended the discourse of the crisis of man is the time, or set of events, or change of mood that we call "the sixties." Part of this ending was intellectual and drew on culminating insights from pure philosophers who had taken part in the earlier creation of the discourse of man. The discourse of man transformed and undid itself, among some of its best practitioners, in iterations in the later years between 1951 and 1966, as in works by Hannah Arendt and Herbert Marcuse, as this chapter will detail. Part of the ending was practical-intellectual, as the artistic representations of the novelists and writers, like those of Bellow, Ellison, O'Connor, and Pynchon, reflected and dwelled upon the daily realities of American life. The fiction writers had taken the abstract discourse of man into the realm of practicality and discovered its missing portions, then had drawn answers that went far beyond its original exponents' suppositions. The novelists' earlier discoveries have, vis-à-vis the social history of the 1960s, a quality both meditative and predictive. To unmarked human nature, the novelists added the problem of race and tried to understand where it fit (or didn't). To debates in the philosophy of history, they brought awareness of those who go unrecorded and don't count, and those who, still unrecorded, find an identity, salutary or spurious, from the annals of history. To a worry about faith, the novelists drew up accounts of those who tried ideology, held to orthodoxy, put belief in idols, or failed to believe in anything, without lapsing into the abstract discourse's occasional belief in belief for its own sake, or an alternative, tepid skepticism about all dogmas. To the exclusive focus on high technology and rational organization of men, the writers added mundane technologies of everyday materials; they noticed the difficulty of defending bodily inviolability when people voluntarily, for medical, therapeutic, or cosmetic reasons, would have their bodies taken apart and parts replaced.

But then there is the fact of fatigue, cliché, and overuse, which is harder to measure. One has to look for scattered indications by the way. The Spanish philosopher José Ortega y Gasset published his book *En torno a Galileo* in 1942. The title could be *About Galileo*, or even *Around Galileo*, in a pun on the Galilean discovery that the earth turns around the sun. When it saw translation and publication by the publisher W. W. Norton in 1958, it became simply *Man and Crisis*.[1] In his autobiographical satire of scholars at the library of the British Museum in the early sixties, the British literary critic and novelist David Lodge has his characters reminisce about the more fortunate days of 1956: "[E]veryone was writing books on the Human Condition and publishers were fighting under the desks for the options."[2] The literary scholar Wallace Douglas published a cruel diagnosis of the literary critical style of the early 1950s in the *American Scholar*. He identified every pomposity, tic, and pretension by which critics made their interpretations falsely serious. The apex, however, was this: "[T]o be really perfect, they . . . need at least an overtone or two of the plight of man."[3]

The Cold War continuation of fears of the "new man" and totalitarian man could not command the same authority as those backed by Hitler's own promises and boasts. Arthur Schlesinger Jr.'s *The Vital Center* of 1949 was a "serious" book, in part thanks to its ballast of crisis of man talk. But one feels the leak of air from the warnings against the current Soviet totalitarian man—pictured now just as a functionary or apparatchik, whose trouble is that he doesn't feel healthy existential anxiety as an American, in 1949 at least, should:

> The final triumph of totalitarianism has been the creation of man without anxiety—of "totalitarian man." . . . The totalitarian man denies the testimony of his private nerves and conscience until they wither away before the authority of the Party and of history. . . . We know well the visages of these new men in the Gestapo or the MVD, in the Politburo or in the Assembly of the United Nations—the tight-lipped, cold-eyed, unfeeling, uncommunicative men, as if badly carved from wood, without humor, without tenderness, without spontaneity, without nerves.[4]

If totalitarianism threatens man, and the Soviet state is totalitarian; if the United States fights the Soviets, and the United States is not totalitarian; then the United States, fighting a totalitarian power, must be fighting for man. In the years following the glacial clarity of Cold War, from 1950, the term becomes a summary of goods and ills into which different elements may be swapped. Man—whoever or whatever he may be, which had been so centrally in question earlier—is what *we* defend (as he is naturally) and *they* endanger (as they shape him unnaturally).

One can begin to feel even a sentimentalism of man, plucking at the string of mobilizing pity customarily felt for children, the family, and the hearth. Debates about philosophical anthropology, the shape of history, the justification for any faith, and the distortions of technology could be flattened in favor of man's characteristics as inflected by publicists for Cold Warriors: *natural* individualism, *natural* freedom, even natural American-style capitalism. Picking up the question "What is man?," the jingo view often favored the answer *Homo economicus.*

The key feature that unites these frustrations from the decline and ina-nition of the discourse of man with its transformation in the sixties is the discourse's *domestication.* Through the 1950s and into the early 1960s, forms of jeopardy to man, which seemed ultimately to come from outside the United States or the West—or from US capitulation to streams of evil running elsewhere, or from inside man himself in all his incarnations, and so forth—radically changed character whenever they newly came to seem *particularly* the products of the United States or the West. This began with new works by some of the major thinkers of the original crisis of man, who radically changed their analysis at the tail end of the period in ways that were genuinely reorienting. They, too, turned from the global to the domestic.

LATE DISCOURSE: THE CRISIS OF MAN TURNS UPON AMERICA

In 1958, Hannah Arendt released *The Human Condition.*[5] The great anat-omist and master of the early discourse of man in *The Origins of Totali-tarianism* had, within a decade of her original summary statement, made a turn toward a new understanding of the crisis of humanity. Arendt had come to look around her, in the United States and Western Europe and the modern postwar world, to see a change in human nature that *did not* de-pend on totalitarian society per se. Rather, it had reached all "societies" as such—and might be rooted in America and the West.

Looking back to a Greek classical tradition, Arendt believed that the permanent human condition includes only three types of activity in the world: *action, work,* and *labor. Action,* for her, was the interaction that goes on among free men in speech and politics, deciding in common what their life and world will be like. It does nothing tangible, makes no perma-nent product, and does nothing to sustain daily bodily life—yet it is the highest form of human activity, because it creates a shared world. *Work* is a step down, but still useful. It is the action of creating permanent objects, in the manner of an artisan's work, which makes up a lasting, common, physical world between men. The worker makes a table that is handed down through generations, and he has made part of the world. *Labor* is, however, in ancient tradition, the lowest form of action, because it re-sponds to mere bodily necessity, set by mortal nature and not by reason. Labor betokens the effort that has to be invested to keep the body happy: fed, clothed, and maintained. It keeps the body "not dead," essentially, rather than vividly alive.

Arendt argues that the antihuman effect of modern societies is to have made this labor the *central* category of human activity. And what country had truly made "labor" in this sense the pinnacle of modern life? Not the supposedly Marxist USSR, which was hampered by terror and wartime destruction, but the mid-twentieth-century United States. In this most advanced country, where basic necessity had finally been abolished (there was now enough food, shelter, and clothing for everyone, mankind's dream since the dawn of time), instead of turning back to a political world of action or an artisanal world of work, a continuous surplus labor was developed in which everyone would labor only for *more* and *more* instant consumption in their own bodily health, grooming, self-maintenance, "standard of living," and waste—forms of fake necessity not dictated by nature and totally hostile to traditional hopes for philosophical liberation into higher human values. Man was not freed for better things; he freed himself for more of the worst. "One hundred years after Marx we know the fallacy of [his] reasoning; the spare time of the *animal laborans* is never spent in anything but consumption, and the more time left to him, the greedier and more craving his appetites" (133). The "human condition," as she used it in her title, was something *Americans* now were trying to evade or destroy.

In 1964, Herbert Marcuse published *One-Dimensional Man*. Marcuse was less suspicious than Arendt of bodily necessity, more sympathetic to the bodily goods of food, shelter, and life maintenance. As far as he was concerned, the very first principle of liberation was the assurance to everyone in society of these goods as a public matter. If technical achievements could produce those goods and end all natural necessity, so much the better. His problem, too, however, was that technical rationality had brought necessity to an end in a way that didn't release people for different, higher, oppositional thought and life. Rather, it created new, false "necessities" as products of technical evolution itself, renewing the antiliberatory control by organized authority, which Marcuse called "repression." "The people recognize themselves in their commodities; they find their soul in their automobile, hi-fi set, split-level home, kitchen equipment. The very mechanism which ties the individual to his society has changed, and social control is anchored in the new needs which it has produced."[6]

Both of these major books, *The Human Condition* and *One-Dimensional Man*, had a great deal in common with other works of more popular social criticism of the late 1950s and early 1960s. Marcuse credited them happily: "I should like to emphasize the vital importance . . . of studies which are frequently frowned upon because of simplification, overstatement, or journalistic ease—Vance Packard's *The Hidden Persuaders*, *The Status Seekers*, and *The Waste Makers*, [and] William H. Whyte's *The Organization Man*."[7] These were domestic critiques that fell into categories by their particular worries: conformity, consumerism, managerial overorganization, the control of individuality by big business and Madison Avenue. One could say that they were to different degrees in line with earlier, world-embracing portions of the discourse of man—but Arendt and Marcuse *proved* that their domestic worries could again be enlarged to complete those philosophical, world-embracing worries of that earlier moment, logically carried forward in time.

Curiously, both books also seem to have arisen spontaneously from a common provocation. Arendt and Marcuse were each funded, separately, to add a study of Marxism to their previous body of knowledge. The purpose in each case was critical study, in the sense of a hostile or condemnatory account. The Guggenheim Foundation awarded Arendt a fellowship in 1952 to research "Totalitarian Elements in Karl Marx." It inaugurated a project she would continue for several years.[8] The Rockefeller Foundation gave Marcuse a grant in 1952 to study Marxism.[9] In addition to being himself a critical theorist and philosopher of Marxist orientation, Marcuse had a separate realm of professional expertise to draw upon. From the time the United States had entered the anti-Nazi war in 1941, Marcuse had been embedded in the Office of Strategic Services (OSS), the newly founded World War II agency that prosecuted the Allied espionage war in Europe. This position gave him incomparable access to documents of Nazi Germany, as well as Stalin's Soviet Union, and he led a sort of double life as an official policy analyst and a private philosopher. At the war's end, he transferred to the State Department, staying there until 1951, when he was able to return to university research and teaching. In a sense, then, this powerful element of transformation of the discourse of the crisis of man came from a Cold War propaganda effort backfiring—both Arendt and Marcuse had no trouble detecting the latently totalitarian elements in Karl Marx and the tyrannical total administration of the Soviet Union, as they were funded to do, but both also came to the undesired conclusion that those same dangers to humanity were achieving their greatest extension, in disguise, in America.

The Human Condition was, in its origins, very directly a further step in the earlier discourse of man. Critics of the *Origins of Totalitarianism* had chastised Arendt for failing to focus adequately on Soviet totalitarianism, modeling too much of her threat to man on Nazism. Always philosophically minded, she wound up focusing her attention, not on the USSR but on Marx. As she reread the supposed philosopher of Soviet Russia, she found a portrait instead of the inner tendency of America, the true vanguard country of capitalist modernity, with its life of ephemeral jobholding labor turned to waste in the life of ceaseless consumption. "Marx . . . only summed up, conceptualized, and transformed into a program the underlying assumptions of two hundred years of modernity."[10] To her, his "revolution" was truly in favor of labor and consumption as the values that were successfully destroying the human condition throughout the first world.

One-Dimensional Man, similarly, was the contemporary follow-up to an earlier line of crisis thinking—a new conclusion, as it were, for works like Horkheimer and Adorno's *Dialectic of Enlightenment*, a book Marcuse may have been originally scheduled to cowrite with Horkheimer before Adorno took his place.[11] The émigré Marcuse had been engaged in the criticism of "totalitarianism" as early as the mid-1930s, and was the first member of the Frankfurt school group of thinkers to use it as a concept of analysis.[12] Like Arendt, Marcuse was a Jewish escapee from Hitler's rule; like Arendt, he was one of the émigrés who chose not to return to Germany, and truly embraced his new country while remaining critical of its ways beyond anything conceivable by his new countrymen. He published his critique of the actually existing structure of the USSR, the fruit of his Rockefeller money, as *Soviet Marxism* in 1958. But Marcuse had also now been inspired to return to the concept of totalitarianism, notoriously, for a critique of America, in its new unmaking of man through repressive false happiness:

> By virtue of the way it has organized its technological base, contemporary industrial society tends to be totalitarian. For "totalitarian" is not only a terroristic political coordination of society, but also a non-terroristic economic-technical coordination which operates through the manipulation of needs by vested interests. (3)

The essential point Marcuse wished to make in 1964 was again about man, but it no longer took the human being to be in jeopardy for the same reasons as before. His title, *One-Dimensional Man*, seemed prepared to make a diagnosis in the old vein. Yet what he found in men's lives in America was a "total administration" that was no longer the terroristic administration of fascism. It was a conquest of consciousness that did not produce happiness but "euphoria in unhappiness" (5), and a "standard of living" that became the enemy because it gave social hope a wrong direction or blocked it: "Under the conditions of a rising standard of living, nonconformity with the system itself appears to be socially useless" (2). Society becomes "one-dimensional" because it has learned to contain all opposition in its pleasant commodities and gentle encouragement to fun. Thought becomes "one-dimensional" because it cares only about technical operations and empirical results, fooled because so many techniques seem to point to the liberating end of need, even while new, false needs are continually being produced by the same means. Man becomes one-dimensional because he has lost all grounds to wish to become anything other than what he is, while this "what he is" is being altered by the demands of a technical-economic system he no longer chooses or even notices. In this last stage of the discourse of man, the televised smiley face, rather than George Orwell's 1949 "boot stamping on a man's face—for ever" had become a symbol of the danger to man's future.[13]

RACE: HUMANISM OR WHITE-ISM?

The essential flaw in the American discourse of man had always been race. (We could have known this from the novelists already.) The discourse of man turned out not to be capacious enough to contain the divisions of racial identity and racial inequality. This constriction highlighted the first place of disunity. The rhetoric of a universal man and human stature proved inadequate to the complexity of African American existence in the postwar period, the violence of Southern response to the start of the civil rights movement at the end of the 1950s, and, looking globally, the stimulus of struggles for independence by Europe's "colored" colonies throughout the postwar decade and through the turn of the '60s.

Flannery O'Connor had given us a short story set on a newly integrated bus—then spiritualized it into an allegory of human vanity and misunderstanding. James Baldwin, in 1961, could give the reportorial view of the fracture that had occurred, as a matter of mood, not abstractions, which confirmed desegregation did not show anything about man but something about the suspicion between particular groups of people, black and white:

> I took a bus ride . . . solely in order to observe the situation of the busses. . . . Negroes sat where they pleased, none very far back; one large woman, carrying packages, seated herself directly behind the driver. And the whites sat there, ignoring them, in a huffy, offended silence.
>
> This silence made me think of nothing so much as the silence which follows a really serious lovers' quarrel: the whites, beneath their cold hostility, were mystified and deeply hurt. They had been betrayed by the Negroes, not merely because the Negroes had declined to remain in their "place," but because the Negroes had refused to be controlled by the town's image of them. And, without this image, it seemed to me, the whites were abruptly and totally lost. The very foundations of their private and public worlds were being destroyed.[14]

Reading Ralph Ellison's *Invisible Man* a decade after its creation, in context of the developments of the early '60s, I find it hard not to feel that Ellison produced a prefiguration of Malcolm X. The real historical figure seems too much a brilliant and charismatic combination of Ellison's disciplined nationalist Ras, the West Indian street-corner politician, with Ellison's comic-book reading hoodlums, hipsters, and zoot-suiters—brethren of the vocation-shifting hustler, Rinehart—who fall outside conventional divisions of politics. Malcolm X had been one of those Rinehartian hustlers, according to his posthumous *Autobiography*, ghostwritten by Alex Haley, and Malcolm proved later, as a spokesman for Elijah Muhammad's black nationalist Nation of Islam, to be an orator of astounding power, in the vein of Ellison's unnamed, socially "invisible" narrator. More than Martin Luther King Jr., who might use the language of "man" and make the case for the "Negro" within it, Malcolm X represented philosophically the taking apart of the "comparable minorities" model—Negroes, Jews, Chinese—to create a new division of "black" and "white," a new kind of once-divided universality that made the "unity of man" incoherent.

Malcolm had uses for the discourse of man, but they were selective uses, ironic adaptation of its rhetoric in opposition to its blindnesses, which blew it apart. In an era when African Americans were called "Negro," then invited into or excluded from the "brotherhood of man," he created a different kind of unity, the "black man." "[V]ery few of our people really look upon themselves as being black," Malcolm preached. "And no matter how dark one of our people may be, you rarely hear him call himself black. But now that The Honorable Elijah Muhammad has been teaching among the so-called Negroes, you find our people of all complexions going around bragging that 'I'm a black man.' This shows you that a new teaching is taking place and there is new thinking among the so-called Negroes." This made visible the marking that was held against those who weren't "white," to undo the basis for a "man" who could exist as unmarked: there was no background colorless universal, only different colors. Even though the possessors of this color knew they didn't possess it ("very few of our people really look upon themselves as being black"), they would take up its differentiating function in the interest of a new, rival universality. For—and here was the revolutionary part—as Malcolm averred, by "black man we mean . . . all those who are nonwhite."[15]

Similarly, in a speech of 1963, Malcolm could use the then-unfashionable crisis of man begotten notion of "human rights"—in substitution for and passing beyond the "civil rights" being fought for in the civil rights movement—to make clear the extent of what whites in America were truly violating in their treatment of blacks: violations "not only of civil rights but even of human rights." But this was in effect because "human rights," rather than civil rights, were what the poor parts of the rest of the world possessed, and Malcolm, in his strategy of black against white, was pursuing an internationalist black nationalism. Recalling the Bandung Conference of 1955, he saw the "black, brown, red, and yellow man" now as one, and declared "the black, brown, red, and yellow man agreed to submerge their differences and come together against the common enemy, the thing that all of them had in common: . . . they were all being oppressed by the white man. They called him European, but actually he was a white man."[16] In place of a generalized humanism, Malcolm cast his spotlight on a new term, "white-ism." "Our present generation is witnessing the end of colonialism, Europeanism, Westernism, or 'White-ism' . . . the end of white supremacy, the end of the evil white man's unjust rule."[17] Human rights proved susceptible to an ironic splitting that posed it *against* civil rights awarded by a white, putatively universal American order. This wider universalism proved the parochialism and hidden particularity of American white brotherhood, which was not in a position to give or award "colored" people anything. "White-ism" was the source of division. "Civil rights means you're asking Uncle Sam to treat you right. Human rights are something you were born with."[18]

Martin Luther King Jr., from his rise to national prominence as a spokesman in the Montgomery Bus Boycott forward, had stayed much more within an older formulation of the appeal to man. In Montgomery in 1955, he launched radical claims in the safe language of the brotherhood of man—but with greater force, perhaps, because it was reabsorbed into a prophetic Christian rhetoric, and a language with a rich philosophical picture of human nature behind it. "[A]ll life is interrelated. All humanity is involved in a single process, and all men are brothers." "Because men are brothers[,] . . . [i]f you harm me you harm yourself."[19]

King used universalist rhetoric to argue for the equality, sameness in humanity, and civil rights of a recognized minority, the Negro. Yet with King's moral appeals, one does not feel the ordinary perils of fatigue and cliché of a language depleted by the late 1950s. At least in part, this seems to arise from the tension between King's optimism about the possibilities for perfection and improvement in the human person and a moral anthropology he had learned and accepted—as a kind of anchor to his own buoyancy—drawn from Reinhold Niebuhr in the earlier discourse of crisis. In King's situation, the Niebuhrian awareness of evil within man didn't exist only for preaching to Americans of the reality of darkness, pride, and hubris inside themselves. Though this was not King's overt or explicit purpose, it could furnish a realism and a sort of fortitude in confrontation with the depths of depravity of black Americans' segregationist opponents. Even though it speaks of universal human nature, the following sort of language drawn from Niebuhr changes value, I believe, when it comes from King, the righteous man who speaks for the sufferers of "brutality": "I think that Niebuhr's anthropology is the necessary corrective of a kind of liberalism that too easily capitulated to modern culture. . . . [O]ptimism has been discredited by the brutal logic of events. Instead of assured progress in wisdom and decency, man faces the ever present possibility of swift relapse not merely to animalism but into such calculated cruelty as no other animal can practice. Niebuhr reminds us of this on every hand."[20] Insofar as King himself remains optimistic for social improvement, this caution helps to frame *white* culture.

Fredrik Sunnemark, in his careful analysis of King's rhetoric, has specified "the identity of man" as a "central feature of King's civil rights movement discourse." Of course, Niebuhrian darkness did not exhaust the topic's significance for King. Equally important was man's fashioning in God's image, and the theology of human connection and brotherly responsibility. Man as such still has the old anchoring function. "[I]n King's rhetoric we find an almost constant attempt to formulate and stabilize the identity of man; a meaning of 'man' that is fixed so that it becomes an integral element in the identity and purpose of the struggle."[21] This man, in Sunnemark's analysis, is repositioned alternately in primary relationship to God; to the collectivity of man in society; or to man's ideal nature and obligations, as it became variously necessary to make King's liberatory points before different audiences. King presented sermons on multiple occasions under the traditional title "What is Man?," with a strongly Niebuhrian answer that man "is in nature, yet above nature," biological at the same time that "Man is a being of spirit."[22] A stronger sense of King's ability to use man for civil rights work comes through in quotations from "The American Dream" as late as 1965:

> [E]very man has a capacity to have a fellowship with God. And that gives him a uniqueness, it gives him worth, it gives him dignity. And we must never forget this as a nation: There are no gradations in the image of God. Every man from treble white to bass black is significant on God's keyboard, precisely because every man is made in the image of God.[23]

Only when King made his turn to Northern and international racism and poverty in 1966 and 1967, and "turned to place civil rights in a global frame in the last year of his life, at the price of heavy stigmatization," did he, like Malcolm X, have to make use of that different strain of universalist argumentation that had come out of the '40s crisis of man discourse—human rights, different and separate from civil rights, valuable in a framework of new frustrations and proofs of white power.[24]

ARE WOMEN INCLUDED IN "MAN"?

Among white reformers, the recognition of a tyrannizing uniformity and concealment of differences in the rhetoric of man moved slightly more slowly. The New Left, up through the early 1960s, still centrally used the language of man as universalistic, morally unimpeachable, and the ultimate reference of political and moral improvement. Their major authorities spoke within the discourse of the crisis of man, still. In the "Port Huron Statement" of Students for a Democratic Society, the 1962 inaugural gesture of the philosophy of the major New Left organization, this talk forms the core of the section the document entitles "Values":

> We regard *men* as infinitely precious and possessed of unfulfilled capacities for reason, freedom, and love. In affirming these principles we are aware of countering perhaps the dominant conceptions of man in the twentieth century: that he is a thing to be manipulated, and that he is inherently incapable of directing his own affairs. We oppose the depersonalization that reduces human beings to the status of things. . . .
> Nor do we deify man—we merely have faith in his potential.[25]

The writings of the sociologist C. Wright Mills, often hailed as the most direct inspiration to the New Left, are soaked in the discourse of man.[26] Mills had called the innovation of new kinds of movements toward a more democratic society "the central goal of Western humanism"—which he spelled out further as "the audacious control by reason of man's fate."[27]

The white American thinkers who acknowledged their most conspicuous exclusion from the language of man were women. A powerful disuniting incipience of the discourse of man was the nomenclature itself. It didn't leave obvious room for the word or thought "woman," as a name for half of the human beings it was supposed to include. We have learned to recognize "man" as gender-specific language, therefore exclusionary; we may think we know that the revival of a powerful women's movement after 1963 brought attention to "woman" in a way that further hastened the demise of the rhetoric of unity. This misses the subtlety of the moment. In a book on the tradition of French feminist appeals to universalism, Joan Wallach Scott has pointed out the paradox for the position of a female speaker who must say "we are equal, we are unmarked, we are the same, we are universal" while making this appeal *as* a woman, thus pushing difference forward in the act of disclaiming it.[28] One noticeable thing about a close look at second-wave feminist discourse in the American 1960s is how it cannily reverses this paradox whenever it chooses to retain, not abandon, pieces of the discourse of man: it speaks of and for women, first, and then—dipping into the common language of man often without comment—lets that universalism announce its own thoughtlessness or grammatical incoherence, falling apart by itself.

When Betty Friedan administered the shock of her book *The Feminine Mystique* in 1963, she stamped an inaugural date on the intellectual and associational surge subsequently labeled the "second wave" of American feminism. (By convention, the first wave was suffragism in the 1910s, though in fact US feminist thought and organized activism goes back to antislavery abolitionism, evangelicalism, and international reformism circa 1848.) The framework of Friedan's argument, one must remember, is that in the interwar years and the mobilization for World War II, America had already begun engaging the vital energies and self-realization of women as well as men; she allied the adventurous "new woman" of earlier decades with a successful civic humanism. For Friedan, the destructive and insinuating "feminine mystique"—"the fulfillment [for women] of their own femininity"—was a new intrusion, bred in the 1950s, and specifically counterpoised to wise recognition of "the nature of man" in recent broad views of "Western Culture."[29] In part, she adopts "man" and "human" rhetoric in the book as a benevolent communal value that America already recognized as an ideal around which it could rally against the cynical partiality of commercial culture and its "sexual sell." This is the genius of Friedan's accommodation of universalizing discourse. The production of feminine difference is registered as the culture's sexualizing of the unmarked human person—a new assault on the human core. At other moments, in an even more interesting rhetoric throughout her book, Friedan evinces an ironic savoir faire analogous to that of Malcolm X; she similarly splits cliché language against itself. Her extremely subtle shifting of the use of the term "man," for mankind and humanity, and then for "men" as distinguished from women, brings forward the contradictions. "Down through the ages man has known that he was set apart from other animals by his mind's power to have an idea, a vision, and shape the future to it," she intones, here clearly writing in the tradition of man as mankind, yet immediately adds that "American women" have been cut out of man's "discover[y] [that] ... he is a man, a human being"; especially, she charges (adopting the live discourse of technological transformation of humanity, so central to Arendtian and Marcusean analyses), as "the very nature of human reality has become increasingly free from biological and material necessity."[30] When Friedan adopts the language of depth psychology— "There have been identity crises for man at all the crucial turning points in human history"—meaning, here, identity crises for everybody, she turns again quickly to the elision of one-half of psychology's subjects: "But it [identity crisis] is considered a man's problem."[31] One experiences a useful whiplash in her prose. The shadings of these usages, intelligible but incompatible, pull into relief the failures of common principle without requiring Friedan to stand aside and plead from the point of view of "woman."

To a surprising degree, this complex rhetorical method of feminist assertion, which both preserves and dissects the universalizing rhetoric of man, turns out to persist into the period of radical feminism in the late 1960s and early 1970s when one studies its texts carefully. The discourse of man remains a resource beyond the "liberal" feminist moment, so-called for its search for rights-based integration in the workplace and representative government, which remains associated with Friedan and the National Organization of Women (NOW), the organization she founded in 1966. Sometimes the resource is used with greater irony, sometimes less. But the memory of a strong linguistic and ideological rejection of the old universalism, though it possesses more reality than the stereotype of "bra-burning" (which seems never to have occurred, even at the 1968 Miss America protest in Atlantic City where it was supposed to have started) should be slightly revised.[32] In Shulamith Firestone's seminal and confrontational *The Dialectic of Sex* (1970), universality has to be purged of its taint of male-only thoughtlessness. Yet feminists must avoid thinking of themselves as "*only* women," giving up the center of discussion, in a division of horizon that would make them see themselves "as defective men: women's issues seemed to them 'special,' 'sectarian,' while issues that concerned men were 'human,' 'universal.' "[33] The "strictly female reality" must be "integrated . . . into our worldview" as a manifestation of whole and universal experience before "we can begin to talk seriously of universal culture."[34] Thus Firestone puns on the language of the discourse of man in even more complex, occasionally mind-bending ways: as in her chapter "Racism: The Sexism of the Family of Man," which argues the origin of race hatred in the patriarchal family with its primary oppression of women and children.[35] (Only now, it might be added, in this phase of white radical feminism, did the legacy of Simone de Beauvoir's *The Second Sex* truly come into its own. Firestone's book is dedicated to Beauvoir.)

In the anthology that Robin Morgan edited at the end of the 1960s, the first neologisms that would point out man's linguistic bankruptcy, when used as a synecdoche for all humankind, were already on display: "The Women's Liberation Movement . . . is creating history, or rather, *herstory*."[36] A feminist journal called *Womankind*, punning on mankind, would publish by 1971.[37] An alternative pursuit researched the extent and consequences of gendered language, and new means of genuinely universalizing English usage, so that it neither favored men nor women, or, even better, could be without gender (as English, unlike the romance languages, ostensibly is). The linguist Robin Lakoff published her "Language and Woman's Place" in 1973.[38]

Linguistic imbalances are worthy of study because they bring into sharper focus real-world imbalances and inequities. . . . A good example, which troubles me a lot at present, is that of pronominal neutralization. In English, as indeed in the great majority of the world's languages, when reference is made individually to members of a sexually mixed group, the normal solution is to resolve the indecision as to pronoun choice in favor of the masculine: masculine, then, is "unmarked" or "neutral," and therefore will be found referring to men and women both . . . An analogous situation occurs in many languages with the words for *human being*: in English, we find *man* and *mankind*, which of course refers to women members of the species as well. This of course permits us innumerable jokes about "man-eating sharks," and the widespread existence of these jokes perhaps points up the problem that these forms create for a woman who speaks a language like English.

I feel that the emphasis upon this point, to the exclusion of many other linguistic points, by writers within the women's movement is misguided. . . . But many nonlinguists disagree. I have read and heard dissenting views from too many anguished women to suppose that this use of *he* is really a triviality. The claim is that the use of the neutral *he* with such frequency makes women feel shut out, not a part of what is being described, an inferior species, or a nonexistent one.[39]

In an article in *Ms.* in 1973, Alma Graham described the steps she and her fellow male and female lexicographers had taken when working on a children's dictionary, *The American Heritage School Dictionary*. A computer study of word frequencies in books for children had proven to them a masculine bias in language. She wittily summarized "the fault . . . of a language in which the same word denotes both the human species as a whole and those of its members who are male":

If a woman is swept off a ship into the water, the cry is "Man overboard!" If she is killed by a hit-and-run driver, the charge is "manslaughter." If she is injured on the job, the coverage is "workmen's compensation." But if she arrives at a threshold marked "Men Only," she knows the admonition is not intended to bar animals or plants or inanimate objects. It is meant for her.[40]

But she and her colleagues worked toward solutions.

In order to avoid sexism in language that has come to sound "natural," we devised logical sex-blind substitutes. When referring to the human species, the dictionary employs the term *human beings*, not *man* or *men* . . . . In our efforts to reduce the superabundance of words referring to the male, we found it was possible to use the word *person* or a more specific substitute instead of *man*. The best man for the job is the best person or candidate; a 12-man jury is a 12-member jury; a real-estate man is a real-estate agent; and machines are used for work formerly done by people or by human beings—not by men. To avoid unnecessary use of the pronoun *he*, we frequently shifted from the singular to the plural. Instead of saying "insofar as he can, the scientist excludes bias from his thinking," is it easy to change to *they, scientists*, and *their*. Plural pronouns desex themselves. The use of *one* is also convenient. A breadwinner, for example, can be "one who supports a family or household by his or her earnings."[41]

The inspiration from women's liberation to gay liberation added a very different turn to the discussion. Now "man," as a name for the unmarked, universal subject, could be turned this way and that to display a surplus, tyrant *manliness*, a confining masculinity and domination, which added its iron weight to the balance, as in Mike Silverstein's call to liberation in the pages of the queer periodical *Gay Sunshine*:

> I must lose in a world where only the winner is a Man, a human being. I was not a real Man. I was a queer, a half-Man, a pseudo-Man, like a woman. . . . Men fought and won, they fought other Men for the ownership of the rest of creation, lesser peoples, the losers, women, the Third World, as well as the natural environment. I could never be a real Man.
>
> We must not give up our humanity to become like the Man. We must not seek to conquer, to become the master. Our gayness, our ability to love one another, is our humanity, and it must not be sold for the Man's mastery over others. And if the straight Man's revolution is based on mastery and conquest we will have no part in it. But we are going to make a gay revolution, a revolution that will be an assertion of humanity. And remembering what you taught us of our humanity, we gay men, together with women, and all the other victims, those who don't seek to be masters, can create it.[42]

"MAN" BECOMES "THE MAN"

A most interesting, but also most challenging, aspect of the story is how a consciousness of difference emerged at the heart of the self-conception of "white people," those US citizens who were unmarked, unitary, and in whose name the universalistic language of man would seem formerly to have spoken. Invocation of "Man" had assumed them as its constituency. Yet a fissure seemed to yawn open within their ideas of themselves—at least within the young sons and daughters of the 1960s.

The challenge is to find measures of the breadth of this disaffiliation, and how the production of internal color-consciousness, among white activists who had encountered civil rights, led to the lasting embedding of a feeling of critical difference—an exclusion from the tyrannical universal, as an attribute of the mainstream or unitary culture itself. The universal and unmarked, as such, loses its appeal. But how can one trace this?

One marker of white disaffiliation from universalism in the 1960s, particularly useful for our purposes, was a simple but powerful mutation in nomenclature: capital-M "Man," unitary reference of an accepted human nature, moral improvement, and social hope, turned linguistically into a new capital-M enemy, "the Man." The locution was borrowed from African American usage, but migrated so powerfully into white countercultural slang that its African American origins were ultimately effaced. Who was keeping you down? The Man was keeping you down. How were you going to fight back? You would find a way to stick it to the Man. This seems slightly absurd in hindsight, but The Man would be a linguistic and conceptual figure of increasingly wide diffusion for everything in American culture that was frozen, monumental, petrified, lethal, or sealed off to inner difference or change. The linguistic coincidence (and rivalry) between two monolithic usages ("man" and "the Man") lets us measure the spread of consciousness of "difference" into white milieus that might otherwise lose themselves within "the mainstream."

"The Man" had been African American slang for a policeman, a boss, or simply for white people as a whole for some length of time before it ever came to the attention of white lexicographers. It is usually assigned Southern roots. An unusual black-authored compilation of slang from 1970, the International Publishers *Dictionary of Afro-American Slang* by Clarence Major, provides an in-culture definition. I add two other definitions for key terms designating the master and mistress of the white family, "Miss Ann" and "Mister Charlie":

> The Man—policeman, and white authority figure; one's white boss
>
> . . .
>
> Miss Ann: a white woman—carry-over from Southern terminology, but now used with a good-natured sneer or with outright maliciousness
> Mister Charlie: a white man—carry-over from Southern use, with no friendly over- or under-tones; see *Charlie*[43]

A 1960 white lexicon, the Crowell *Dictionary of American Slang*, suggests the sort of crossover that must have been occurring for decades in laboring and subcultural circles before any wholesale transfer. It has "Man, the" simply as "*n.* 1: The law; a law enforcement officer; a private detective," drawing its usage example from a 1957 exposé in the *Saturday Evening Post*: "The drug trade's slang for a law enforcer was, indicatively, 'The Man.'"[44]

A more politicized use stands out with increasing visibility in sources from the early 1960s. Whites began to hear it as African American writers became more open in describing their own experiences of resistance. James Baldwin, in 1963, in *The Fire Next Time*—previewed for white America in the *New Yorker* issue of November 17, 1962—introduced the term without capitalization as part of the language of ghetto despair spoken during his Harlem childhood. "My friends were now 'downtown,' busy, as they put it, 'fighting the man,'" Baldwin wrote, "lost, and unable to say what it was that oppressed them, except that they knew it was 'the man'— the white man."[45] In further literary efforts, Baldwin continued to publicize the unknown terms that black Americans used to demarcate oppressive whites, from the play *Blues for Mr. Charlie*, performed by the Actors' Studio Theatre in 1964, to his short story "Going to Meet the Man" of 1965, psychosexual inner monologue of a racist Southern sheriff, which supplied the title to a collection in the same year.

The bitter phrase "the Man" came to greet white America more directly in a rising rhetoric of militant opposition to racism from 1964 forward, articulated especially by organizers active on the new Northern fronts of the black freedom struggle. The historians of the long-standing militantly nonviolent civil rights organization, the Congress on Racial Equality (CORE), note that in 1964 individual Northern chapters, starting with Cleveland, began forming gun clubs to defend themselves. When, a few months later, in Harlem, three New York CORE chapters rallied to demand an arrest in the police murder of a black teenager, organizers spoke a new language of opposition. "Among the speakers was Chris Sprowal, chairman of Downtown CORE, who in a rhetoric now used by a number of CORE chapter chairmen announced, 'It is time to let "the man" know that if he does something to us we are going to do something back. . . . I belong to a nonviolent organization, but I'm not nonviolent. When a cop shoots me, I will shoot him back.'"[46]

Sprowal's remark—reported in *Newsweek* at the time, in their issue of August 3, 1964—becomes the first citation given in the *Historical Dictionary of American Slang* (1997) to the use of "the Man" as a black term for oppression. That dictionary's citation for "the Man" as *white* slang, for white oppression, then comes from just five years later, now from the Yippies, the quasi-prankster, quasi-militant Youth International Party, founded by Abbie Hoffman and Jerry Rubin on New York's Lower East Side. The Yippies contributed memorably to protests at the Pentagon in 1967 and at the Democratic National Convention in Chicago in 1968. Rubin and Hoffman numbered among the defendants at the Chicago 8 trial in 1969 on charges of incitement to riot for the demonstrations at the previous year's convention. The *Historical Dictionary of American Slang* citation comes from a *US News and World Report* of May 19, 1969, which told readers that the Yippies had the "avowed aim . . . to destroy 'The Man,' their term for the present system of government."[47]

This makes one laugh—it is too "square." *US News and World Report* had not yet mastered the new language. But parts of the white counterculture had. By the later sixties, the historic development of "the Man," to put it even more starkly, is one in which the hateful figures of "white people" generally did a remarkable double-duty rhetorically, as an enemy for blacks *and* an enemy for young white people themselves. There had to have been a significant road to travel to the new usage of "the Man"—and a considerable introduction of threat and violence to let white children learn that they could stand in the same relation to the universal tyrant Man as the African American descendants of those he had enslaved.

VIETNAM AND THE RETURN NORTH

An instance of that threat and one place of crossing over was Vietnam. A military draft had remained in effect since 1948. Once Lyndon Johnson began committing American ground troops to warfare against the North Vietnamese Army and the guerillas of the Viet Cong in 1965, young men of all backgrounds lived under threat of conscription and passage to Indochina to fight and possibly die in a profoundly unpopular war. Though racial integration of the armed forces had been mandated in 1948, Vietnam was the first major US conflict since the Civil War fought without any segregated units. Insofar as war against anticolonial peasant forces on the other side of the world became something that both white and black young men (and soldiers) could oppose, the new evaluation of the generic "White Man" who was behind it emerged as something blacks and whites could share in rejecting.

The African American reporter Thomas A. Johnson went to Da Nang and Saigon to write "The US Negro in Vietnam" for the *New York Times*, published in April 1968. Johnson took an optimistic attitude toward race relations in the army, but revealed some curious details of the solidarity he saw. "The term 'soul session' is often used here to describe Negro efforts to 'get away from "the man,"' to luxuriate amidst blacks or to 'get the black view.' These sessions occur in front-line bunkers and in Saigon villas, and quite often they include some 'for real' whites," he wrote.[48] Where everyone's life was at risk in an integrated but hated army, stereotypes of whites could be told to whites themselves. The most extraordinary exchange Johnson reports comes when "a rear-echelon Negro private first class, sitting in a bar in Saigon's Khanh Hoi with a white friend" from the Deep South "started to discuss why Negroes separate themselves":

> "White people are dull," he said. "They have no style and they don't know how to relax."
>
> "What do you mean?" the white youth interrupted.
>
> "Shut up," the Negro said. "I'm not talking about you, nigger. I'm talking about white people." (358)

The deeper crossing over and inspiration of solidarity of young whites with African American culture had been the civil rights movement. But white involvement in Southern civil rights had reached a pivot point in just the years that the Vietnam conflict truly escalated, in 1965 and 1966. Following the federal Civil Rights Act of 1964, formal freedoms had been won in the Jim Crow South. Organizations like King's Southern Christian Leadership Conference (SCLC), the Congress on Racial Equality (CORE), and especially the youth leadership of the Student Nonviolent Coordinating Committee (SNCC) turned their efforts to black poverty and economic and power inequality in the urban North as well as the South. They would attack racism de facto as well as de jure, striking also at its capitalist roots. As part of the new campaign against de facto white supremacy, and looking to augment habits of black self-determination and independence without white distraction, in 1966 SNCC changed policy in the South. It sent home its white workers and allies, and became exclusively African American in leadership. The change was sometimes controversial. SNCC spokesman Stokely Carmichael, explaining the new policy, wrote of the organization's white allies,

> If they are liberals, they complain, "What about me?—don't you want my help anymore?" These are people supposedly concerned about black Americans, but today they think first of themselves, of their feelings of rejection. . . . The need for psychological equality is the reason why SNCC today believes that blacks must organize in the black community. . . . In the past, white allies have furthered white supremacy without the whites realizing it—or wanting it, I think.[49]

Black organizers released their white workers with explicit instructions, though, in line with the new Northern strategy. They should go home to their communities of origin and identify racism among their fellow whites. The most valuable thing they could now do for the black freedom struggle was to fight it from within. The charge was neither implausible nor vindictive. It had a paradoxical but perhaps not unforeseeable consequence, however, especially as energy had begun going to other struggles in the national culture, especially the movement against the Vietnam War and its draft, to which white youths as well as people of color were subject. White activists who tried to fight antiblack oppression in the urban North, and met with frustration and hatred, could come to feel, or realize, that they themselves were stigmatized and oppressed by white order—and thus come to think of themselves, though lightly pigmented, as silently repeating, in attenuated form, the struggle in the South; they, too, were now excluded, on other bases, from the "universal" dominant community. In some ways this might reinforce racial solidarity. In others, it encouraged a shift away from antiracism to more amorphous personal opposition, in the shape-shifting "movement" increasingly oriented toward ending the war in Vietnam, or in developing "counterculture."[50]

Style became a marker for opposition to the dominant order. To speak of these shifts, however, is to risk entering into a kingdom of cliché. The look of the face, the length of hair, bodily carriage, and the debris of language communicated political meanings and yet could neuter or sham the political. In the style choices that drew from African American, Native American, or a more generic "native" or natural or primitivist culture, it is also difficult to disentangle solidarity and affiliation from pantomime and theft. African American writers and speakers had themselves articulated part of the political and philosophical appeal of black identity for America as the opportunity to slip away from the white community that enforced racial terrorism as part of the web of its other rigors, rules, stiffness, and dogmatism. In James Baldwin's address to the white jailer who had become his prisoner's prisoner: "The only way he can be released from the Negro's too radical power over him is to consent, in effect, to become black himself, to become a part of that suffering and dancing country that he now watches wistfully from the heights of his lonely power."[51] He could rejoin peaceful and "sensual" life, Baldwin promised: "The word 'sensual' is not intended to bring to mind quivering dusky maidens or priapic black studs. To be sensual, I think, is to respect and rejoice in the force of life, of life itself, and to be present in all that one does, from the effort of loving to the breaking of bread."[52] In white hands this would shade into "slumming" and exoticism. In black hands it feels, at the very least, legitimate, whether or not this compensatory representation was in any way true. One hears a trace of comparable pride in the words of the "Negro private first class" who knows why it's worth escaping white culture: "White people . . . have no style and they don't know how to relax." This charge became a part, in ways still hard to trace, of what people who would record themselves in the census as white, too, could agree they disliked about white people, when they wanted to renounce their culture's violence and racism; what they disliked about themselves. It clearly became a part of the "informalization" that became a feature of advanced manners in the 1960s and up to the present day.[53] (The historical sociologist Sam Binkley has documented the end state once "soul" and "telling it like it is" were recoded as 1970s colorless lifestyle attainments rather than possibilities of African American culture, in the neutralized decorative ethic of "hanging loose": "loose, formless beanbag chairs flopped onto lush shag carpets and creative natural fabric wall hangings and macramé compositions adorned living room walls . . . while at the office ties were loosened or disappeared entirely, top buttons came undone, hair was allowed to hang down to shoulders, mustaches drooped, sideburns crept, chest hairs peeked and first names began to replace formal modes of address."[54]) Yet one wants to recover the moment when it was not just decor, as another essential step in the production of "difference" as of positive personal value.

Baldwin's "breaking of bread," for example, turned out to be a figure of speech with profounder resonances: "It will be a great day for America, incidentally, when we begin to eat bread again, instead of the blasphemous and tasteless foam rubber that we have substituted for it. And I'm not being frivolous now, either."[55] The bread in question is "white bread"—bleached and processed bread, trademarked Wonder Bread—a most powerful and strangely long-lasting metonymy for all that ignorant white people will accept of brutishness in unitary, homogenized whiteness bleached of inner difference or visible grain.[56] On this metaphor, Baldwin and Norman Mailer had a meeting of the minds—at least intertextually—fulfilled on the other side of that turning point of 1966. Here Mailer, in *The Armies of the Night*, recorded as reportage the full imaginative density of one split-second gesture made by an African American activist in the company of predominantly white anti–Vietnam War organizers, before the 1967 March on the Pentagon:

> The thirty or forty young men there in Washington to represent the twenty-four Resistance groups in the country were sitting in a group on the lawn talking among themselves. Their leader (whose name [Mailer] subsequently learned was Dickie Harris) turned out to be a Negro with a goatee and horn-rimmed glasses, not very tall, slim, wearing dungarees and a shirt open at the neck. . . . Harris, the Negro, had the dash, the panache (as an English journalist had once described it) of the old cadres in SNCC who used to drive all day from one Deep South town to another, rallying, organizing. . . .
>
> A few loaves of bread, a jar of peanut butter, and a couple of quarts of milk were being passed around. . . . The neat remains eventually came back to Harris's feet. . . . [H]e now stared out at the listening onlookers, picked up the bread and said, "Anyone like some food? It's . . . uh . . ." he

pretended to look at it, "it's . . . uh . . . *white* bread." The sliced loaf half-collapsed in its wax wrapper was the comic embodiment now of a dozen little ideas, of corporation-land which took the taste and crust out of bread and wrapped the remains in wax paper, and was, at the far extension of this same process, the same mentality which was out in Asia escalating, defoliating, orientating; yeah . . . the white bread was the infiltrated enemy who had a grip on them everywhere, forced them to collaborate if only by imbibing the bread (and substance) of that enemy with his food processing, enriched flours, vitamin supplements, added nutrients; finally, and this probably was why Harris chuckled when he said it, the bread was *white* bread, not black bread—a way to remind them all that he was one of very few Negroes here.[57]

The most discussed physical object of taste in the politics of the 1960s would be hair—the natural style for African Americans, and the lengthened, unruly, and unshaved style for whites.[58] Hippie chic and a Broadway musical might trivialize it. But figures like the Yippies theorized and publicized the aesthetic manifestations of a white disaffiliation from "White" on the grandest scale for TV and the press while still insisting on political implications. "Long hair, beards, no bras and freaky clothes represent a break from Prison Amerika, a rejection of the God is White Milk, cleanliness-is-godliness values and the birth of us as a new nation of freaky artists," Jerry Rubin wrote from jail during the Chicago 8 trial. "Rebellion begins on your face."[59] One can think also of David Crosby earnestly singing "Guess I feel/Like I owe it/To someone," for why he must muster the courage not to cut his long hair; presumably, the "someone" is the oppressed, and it's his moral obligation to keep "letting my freak flag fly."[60] To judge by the lyrics of late '60s rock in general, even at its most popular and banal (the Five Man Electrical Band's "Signs" [1970], even Bob Seger's "Turn the Page" [1972], as he suffers—"all the same old clichés, is that a woman or a man"),[61] this new experience, for young heterosexual white men, of being baited, mocked, and fought in public because of a minor feature of their appearance tough to hide—their hair—was shattering, or galvanizing; it may have echoed the daily experience of women and people of color in only the most marginal fashion, but these young men had never known anything like it.

Yippie founder Abbie Hoffman had originally become politically active as one of the white volunteers in the South for the SNCC, who was sent back North in 1966. He returned to New York to work on the SNCC cooperatives that were being developed in the urban environment, before finding a new purpose in "free stores" modeled on hippie efforts in San Francisco.[62]

In his 1968 book *Revolution for the Hell of It*, Hoffman emphasized that white urban radicals like himself had to find ways to develop a common consciousness with Latino street kids and African Americans in his neighborhood of the Lower East Side, and that style could help—not to blend in, but for comparable victimization, since the fastest way to understand the experience of people of color was to be harassed, arrested, and jailed yourself, as a "white" person, for long hair, countercultural clothes, and marijuana possession.

Hoffman's book chapter beginning with a long open letter to Stokely Carmichael, whom he had known in the South, is admiringly titled "The New Niggers." A later chapter, strategizing how hippie life can finally bring down police repression on whites, which will properly radicalize them, is titled "The White Niggers." This figure of speech became epidemic at the end of the sixties. Gloria Steinem, depressed by the candidacy of Richard Nixon in 1968, avowed, "We're all Niggers now."[63] Jerry Farber published *Student as Nigger* in 1969. John Lennon recast Yoko Ono's declaration in a 1969 interview that "Woman is the Nigger of the World" as a single in 1972. In the same year, the Democratic National Convention is often seen as the origin point for multiculturalism and plural racial and ethnic identities as an essential value of the Democratic Party. At that convention, Ron Dellums, the African American congressman from California, spoke ardently for the enfranchisement and power of "America's Niggers," by which he meant "the Young, the Black, the Brown, the Women, the Poor— all the people who feel left out of the political process."[64]

In the transfer of feeling from practical solidarity to style, however, something could get lost. Politicization is always a challenge when it comes to style, however, because of the ambiguities of the mobilization of taste. The white person who evinces taste for black music and black culture can initially be paying a compliment, with no pretense to origination or conquest—as long as he or she is "authentic," that challenging but essential criterion of the late sixties. Yet taste, as a blended faculty between the immediately sensual and latently intellectual, satisfies its owner experientially that it is not *merely* learned or acquired. It assures its possessor that he or she is an inner aristocrat, holder of superior intuitive judgment. The stance of dependency on another, of obligation and nonindependence, accords poorly with taste, while those who don't share such tastes become disgusting, charged with the crudeness of those who find savor in the insipid and spit out the truffles we know to be most precious.

As Andrew Ross has written in his history of white hipsters and "hip": "By the end of the 60s, to be white and hip no longer meant a wholesale identification with black culture although it still included a ritual quotient of references to black music. By then, it had become the distinctive possession of an ideological community—the predominantly white counterculture—bound together by a set of 'alternative' taste codes fashioned in opposition to the straight world."[65] At the same time, it cemented the advantages, to these apolitical people, of dispensing with the idea of a unitary culture, or a "universal" category to which they belonged—one that, when it had been taken seriously, had also sometimes contained a strong payload of the multiracial or interracial, the famous (or infamous) "brotherhood of man." They were ridding themselves of cant and cliché but also disarming formerly potent instruments of solidarity. With these contradictory effects, "Man," formerly a name for an ideal, had been discredited for forward-looking whites. And "the Man" became all that was uncool. The *New Yorker* journalist Renata Adler had been covering the civil rights movement in the South. After mid-decade, she was alarmed to hear "the Man" transferred from Southern sharecroppers to ordinary white teens who liked to dance at night on the Sunset Strip to Buffalo Springfield and Love, and didn't want to be hassled by hippie-baiting police:

> A young man, fairly conventionally dressed and coiffed, crossed the patio towards the group [of teenage counterculturists]. "Has the Man been here tonight?" he asked, speaking low and rapidly.
> "No," Zak said.
> The young man immediately removed his jacket and tie, and brushed what proved to be an astonishing amount of hair forward from behind his ears.[66]

It wasn't long before Columbia Records, corporate distributor of music to the millions, label of the New York Philharmonic and Frank Sinatra, was advertising its new roster of rock artists with the slogan: "But the Man Can't Bust Our Music."[67]

BEYOND HUMANISM

When *Partisan Review* did one of its late symposia in 1967—recalling the great and important ones of the 1930s, 1940s, and 1950s, but now with a tone of lostness and dissipation—it featured Susan Sontag railing against the United States for creating a new genocide "in Vietnam, where each evening [President Lyndon Johnson] personally chooses the bombing targets for the next day's missions." "America was founded on a genocide, on the unquestioned assumption of the right of white Europeans to exterminate a resident, technologically backward, colored population in order to take over the continent. . . . Today American hegemony menaces the lives not of three million but of countless millions who, like the Indians, have never even *heard* of the 'United States of America,' much less of its mythical empire, the 'free world.'"[68]

This was a new kind of disunity beyond the internal disunity of black and white relations, of which many of the other symposium contributors warned. An external enmity between Vietnam and America mirrored the inner conflict of race, which was now being taken over by "advanced" whites like Sontag, especially those primed in other ways for disaffiliation (avant-garde, Jewish, female, and lesbian). This was the disuniting of the world, along with the country. "Americans know their backs are against the wall: 'they' want to take all that away from 'us,'" Sontag wrote. "And, I think, America deserves to have it taken away."[69]

Sontag meant to be an exemplar of "the new sensibility" in much of her work, and she does give a sense of the changes wrought by the sixties in several dimensions.[70] In art, Sontag ultimately championed the "decidedly impersonal character" of "serious works" while advocating an unprogrammatic, "erotic" reception of them; "[t]he work of art . . . as 'object' . . . rather than as 'individual personal expression'"—to be received in its immediate sensuous form but not in its humanistic message or content.[71]

Back in 1956, Roland Barthes, whom Sontag helped publicize in the United States, had written that short critique we have already seen (in chapter 3) of the touring exhibit of *The Family of Man*, which reached Paris under the name *The Great Family of Man*. In 1973, in an essay integrated into her later book *On Photography* (1977), Sontag went back once again to flay *The Family of Man*, still in much the same terms as her predecessor. "By purporting to show that individuals are born, work, laugh, and die everywhere in the same way, 'The Family of Man' denies the determining weight of history—of genuine and historically embedded differences, injustices, and conflicts," she wrote.[72] And yet this was no longer really her main problem; the denigration came only in passing; it was old, familiar. This time, what really worried her was a Diane Arbus retrospective of 1972, the other subject of her essay, which showed, she believed, the ignorant side of post-'60s *antihumanist* triumph, just as *The Family of Man* had done for pre-'60s ignorant humanism. *The Family of Man*, she said, "assumes a 'human condition' or a 'human nature' shared by everybody." The comparably popular Arbus exhibit, to her eyes, expelled all "representative folk doing their human thing" and instead showed difference as monstrosity to frame a new apothegm: "Humanity is not one." By 1972, it had become popular conventional wisdom, Sontag explained, to presume a new "anti-humanist message which people of good will in the 1970s are eager to be troubled by, just as they wished, in the 1950s, to be consoled and distracted by a sentimental humanism."[73] How did they get there?

In truth, by the early 1970s high intellectuals in the United States had access to a line of "antihumanism" in thought that undid man entirely, and ran much deeper than the mood of any Diane Arbus exhibit or Sontag's belletristic field notes on the changing American mind. This is the odd chimera that decades of late-century students learned to call "theory."

CHAPTER 10

UNIVERSAL PHILOSOPHY AND ANTIHUMANIST THEORY

From social history, we return to high intellect. As universal man came into doubt throughout the 1960s, existing resources in America for philosophizing the practical situation did not seem satisfactory. New sorts of tracings must be made of the social system. In 1965, standing before the assembled demonstrators at an April anti–Vietnam War rally in Washington, DC, Paul Potter, president of Students for a Democratic Society (SDS), made his often-quoted declaration: "We must name the system. We must name it, describe it, analyze it, understand it and change it."[1] Theorizations of structure acquired new urgency. Not only must the organization and mind-set of the Pentagon, the corporations, the welfare state, the electoral machine, the media, and an acquiescent electorate be described and analyzed but a counterstructure should be assembled to push back on every weak point.

One might well ask why the social movement, and changes in daily practice within oppositional culture or counterculture, would want reconstruction in the high intellectual realm at all. Why does praxis seek new theorists? Yet it always does. At the least, for sixties radicals, a whole must be conceived that would allow conceptualization of the linkages between the parts, on the side of established power and among the struggling grass roots. As historian Jeremy Varon has summarized this double necessity for the wider conceptualization of system: "[Paul] Potter posited a unified structure of domination responsible for discrete forms of oppression, whose elimination required changing the whole. Consistent with this premise, New Leftists increasingly used 'the system' as a label for the complex entity they opposed and focused their protest on the structures that elites served. . . . To the system, they counterposed 'the movement,' a capacious term that referred to everyone from student and antiwar activists to black militants and politically engaged hippies," configured into new assemblages.[2]

For the sake of all of those disparate actors linked through new identities and affiliations, sixties thinkers would need to acquire philosophical tools that could clarify the role and power of each individual consciousness after the rejection of Man as thought's ultimate reference. The prophet of changing thought with whom we ended the last chapter, Susan Sontag, proves to be one of the most emblematic figures of this search. Sontag was sometimes mocked, during her lifetime, for her preservation of gravitas in a turn to pop. In hindsight, she was instrumental in selecting, importing, and building the resources that allowed the flow of new sensibilities back up to traditions continuous with the strata of philosophy and theory with which this study began.

Sontag gives a personal cast, too, to the options in a search for new high intellect in the sixties. Born in 1933, Sontag was a true child of the crisis as an established feature of the intellectual world. Arriving too late to hold any stake in the circumstances of the discourse's origins, she acquired its underlying seriousness and mission while changing the polarity of essential elements. Committed as Sontag was from an early age to the glamour of thought, pieces of the crisis of man appear throughout her intellectual formation in broken, uprooted form. She came upon the Holocaust, she recalled later, only when she saw "photographs of Bergen-Belsen and Dachau which I came across by chance in a bookstore in Santa Monica in July 1945 . . . (I was twelve)."[3] At age fourteen, she sought out Thomas Mann in his exile in California—and spent an afternoon with the representative of the German emigration. It did not change her life. Its significance was just that European genius, broken into single exemplars, had been dropped into America for use and adoption whenever one needed.

At sixteen, having completed high school and a semester at Berkeley, Sontag gained a scholarship to Robert Maynard Hutchins's unique college at the University of Chicago. This would not offer the first glimpse of knowledge to a neophyte. An earlier era might have seen someone in Sontag's position worrying, perhaps, about her Jewishness, whether she would encounter prejudice. Before leaving for Chicago, instead, Sontag overcame "the incipient guilt I have always felt about my lesbianism" with experiences in the underground gay world of San Francisco. "I know how good and right it is to love" women as well as men, she told her diary, writing down study lists of gay slang and the names of lesbian bars on both coasts.[4] "Bisexuality [is] the expression of fullness of an individual," she wrote; the real "perversion" would be what "limits sexual experience."[5] Her identity as an inheritor and iconoclast would include many facets: precocious youth; easy adopter of mature erudition; native West Coaster, adoptive New Yorker; avant-garde novelist; university intellectual; Jew, woman, and lesbian or bisexual—not necessarily in that order.

SONTAG, HEIR AND APOSTATE

By the time she began graduate work at Harvard in 1954, Sontag possessed the thorough historical grounding in Great Books and permanent culture that a degree from Hutchins's college afforded. Unlike her classmate Allan Bloom, who followed the line of their Chicago teacher Leo Strauss into tradition and conservatism (and lifelong closeting of his homosexuality), she recruited her command of the tradition to avoid subordination to great men.[6] Her literary instinct (in years when the novel stood supreme as a means to truth) took her to the Harvard English Department; when she sought to enroll for the PhD, professor Harry Levin told her he did not "'believe' in women graduate students." So following the other royal road to wisdom and authority, she "ask[ed] the philosopher Morton White to allow her to enter the graduate program in philosophy" instead. Two years later, master's degree in hand, she began studying philosophy on the customary Harvard philosopher's sojourn at Oxford, pursuing the Anglo-American "analytic" tradition under the supervision of A. J. Ayer, and writing the beginning of "a PhD dissertation on 'metaphysical presuppositions of ethics.'"[7]

From the library atmosphere of Oxford, 1957, however, Sontag bolted for Paris. French thought inspired her as the Anglo-American mode, ultimately, did not. She heard Simone de Beauvoir speak (and encountered rumors that Beauvoir was homosexual, which made her wonder what the implications of this fact would be for "feminism" as such).[8] Subsequently, she returned to New York and easily settled into the remains of postwar Jewish intellectual life, never quite believing in it ("Are the Jews played out?"[9]), where she took up a temporary job at *Commentary* and began contributing to *Partisan Review*.

This can all seem merely biographical, or unique. Sontag was not ordinary. She was, however, a bellwether in fundamental ways. To see the alternatives she was choosing between, and the choices she then made, is to see the roads available to ordinary thought, as well as extraordinary ambition and talent. Literature or philosophy marked one choice. This study's chapters on how the novel confronted philosophical demands in the 1950s and early 1960s will, I hope, have clarified some meanings of that division. The choice between Harvard-Oxford philosophy, what we would call analytic or Anglo-American philosophy, however, and the things she glimpsed in Paris, reflects another divergence of the profoundest importance—one that we will see extended beyond the biographical.

By the time Sontag began publishing the essays that made her famous, beginning with "Notes on Camp" in 1964, she was the best successor the New York Intellectuals could have—they saw her comprehensive erudition, formality of style, and intellectual seriousness—yet, almost without them noticing, she was digging up the piles their intellectual edifice rested upon. In "Notes on Camp," for one thing, she began substituting for the authority of "the Jew"—exemplary victim of the Nazis, bearer of liberal values and intellect—the homosexual or bisexual as the source of value for a new era, a "new sensibility":

> The peculiar relation between Camp taste and homosexuality has to be explained. . . . Jews and homosexuals are the outstanding creative minorities in contemporary urban culture . . . they are creators of sensibilities. The two pioneering forces of modern sensibility are Jewish moral seriousness and homosexual aestheticism and irony. . . . The Jews pinned their hopes for integrating into modern society on promoting the moral sense. Homosexuals have pinned their integration into society on promoting the aesthetic sense. Camp is a solvent of morality. It neutralizes moral indignation, sponsors playfulness.[10]

Sontag's sexuality became an open secret by the later sixties, and she frequently published remarks in favor of bisexuality, though she never joined gay liberation openly. She did not join feminist groups formally, but she also rejected the previous generation of exceptional female intellectuals' temptation to exempt themselves from victimization and the need for feminism as its antidote. She defended the radical feminist analysis that "All women live in an 'imperialist' situation in which men are colonialists and women are natives. . . . Anything less than a change in who has power and what power is, is not liberation but pacification. . . . A radical, as opposed to a liberal, change in the status of women will abolish the mystique of 'nature.' . . . I have always been a feminist."[11] Sontag embraced white disaffiliation from whiteness, preferring to side with African Americans, Native Americans, and colonized peoples than with the part of Western Enlightenment that had "civilized" the savage with its advanced ways. ("If America is the culmination of Western white civilization, as everyone from the Left to the Right declares, then there must be something terribly wrong with Western white civilization."[12])

Yet the systematic philosophy and philosophical resources that Sontag began to gather to suit these political and immediate inclinations did not really come from American radical milieu. They came in large measure from the international currents she so admired and had tasted in the freedom of Paris rather than Oxford. It is not altogether surprising to find Sontag as one of the first American commentators to begin systematically declaring for and importing figures of what would become the entry of "French theory" into American thought. She was among the first champions of Claude Lévi-Strauss in the 1960s and wrote a review of his work that appeared in one of the first numbers of the newly founded *New York Review of Books* in 1963, and found its way into her *Against Interpretation* (1966).[13] She was part of a larger circle in New York that kept abreast of French developments. The *Review of Books'* young editor, Robert Silvers, gave her Lévi-Strauss's *Structural Anthropology* to review because he had been impressed by the anthropologist's *Tristes Tropiques* during a previous sojourn in Paris.[14] Their friend Richard Howard, even more ardently pursuing literary communication between New York and Paris, translated some of the earliest US publications of then little-known French thinkers Roland Barthes and Michel Foucault.[15]

THE NEW THEORY

The history of theory in America has not yet been written convincingly. We know loosely what happened, which figures and ideas held sway in changing formations, but not where it began and why.[16] Yet the rise of theory is another of the things that the history of the crisis of man can clarify.

Theory had two centers for our purposes and in its historical role for those who first solicited it to America. One was the critique of the subject. For "subject," we might say individual, self, or sovereign consciousness. The other was the use of difference as a basic, activating principle in the construction of complex systems operating at levels far removed from individual consciousness. Difference, as we have seen, was a matter for social identity in America. One might be marked in one way or another that removed one from the universal, as female, black, Jewish, or gay. The concept controlled deeper and more multiple locations in French theory. Difference stood as a kind of operator within structuralism. It dwelled in the differential signifiers in the Saussurian structural linguistics drawn upon by Claude Lévi-Strauss, Jacques Lacan, or Roland Barthes. It became *différance* in the deconstructive philosophy of Jacques Derrida. But it was the size and impersonal complication of the systems in which this difference became meaningful—as big as language itself, myth, or discourse, structures that determined the thoughts and actions human beings could conceive within them, rather than leaving the field free to the willfulness or rational interests of the individual actor—that made theory appealing.

The best name for the unifying philosophical impulse behind theory is antihumanism. Yet sympathizers and even neutral observers in America rarely use it.[17] In English the word can hardly avoid the sound of something like "hatred of the human"—an inspiration somewhere between misanthropy and cannibalism. One truth to remember is that antihumanism nearly always has a normative or therapeutic motive we would identify as humane. That motive may be liberation, emancipation, and opposition to tyranny in intellect or politics. It may be scholarly, in the improvement of explanation and the extension of thought. The simplest vindication is that the name "antihumanism" refers to a principled removal of the level of explanation of phenomena from single rational human actors and their explicit self-understandings to sub- and superpersonal aggregations. It denotes an explanatory antipathy to humanism understood as the doctrine that "man is the measure of all things" and that individual consciousness is the arbiter and best explainer of its own behavior, social practices, and beliefs.

Nonetheless, it is undeniable that antihumanism possesses a creeping moral hostility, too, in its distaste for the complacency of humanism when humanism assumes its own social centrality, homogeneity, and transparency. Thus, antihumanist thinkers stand in reaction against the postwar enshrinement of a discourse of man in France, and later in the United States.[18] Michel Foucault alluded to his impatience with the old humanist discourse to an interviewer in 1981, in explanation of his role in the French "death of man": "You can't imagine into what kind of moralizing pool of humanistic sermons we were plunged after the war. Everyone was a humanist. Camus, Sartre, Garaudy were humanists. Stalin too was a humanist."[19] (Roger Garaudy was a philosopher of the French Communist Party and author in the 1950s of the book *Marxist Humanism*, also a target of Louis Althusser's.) Pierre Bourdieu, four years younger, testified to something similar in 1985: "Many of the intellectual leanings that I share with the 'structuralist' generation (especially Althusser and Foucault) . . . can be explained by the need to react against what existentialism had represented for them: the flabby 'humanism' that was in the air, the complacent appeal to 'lived experience' and that sort of political moralism."[20]

The turn to a new French antihumanism in America isn't fully meaningful unless one understands how philosophy in the United States, partly inspired by one particular tributary of 1930s crisis discourse, had set off on a course of its own that led to separation from large-scale grids or systems rooted in social analysis. After all, the "critique of the subject" could easily have been found in Freud or Marx, Durkheim, or even American pragmatist thinkers including James and Dewey. The superpersonal explanation of social effects by structure rather than individual agency is at the core of all classical social theory, and almost a basic principle of social science as such. The thing that must be identified is a great divergence in principles of thought—such that the alienating world of the "behavioral sciences" in the post-1945 university could engross traditional fields of wisdom for self-making and social action—which emerged contingently from the wartime interchange between America and Europe.

ANALYTIC–CONTINENTAL DIVIDE

To understand the turn in the late 1960s to a new French philosophy, one must understand what had happened especially to American academic philosophy since World War II. As one of its postwar exponents and chroniclers, Morton White (the admirable nonsexist philosopher who welcomed Susan Sontag into the Harvard philosophy department), would put it in 1972:

> Anyone familiar with American philosophy after the days of Dewey knows that it abandoned the grand manner. The ablest American philosophers continued to be interested in the nature and scope of science; but their motivation ceased to be as obviously religious, political, legal, or educational as it had been for their predecessors. They did not invest the problem of knowledge with the significance it had for Dewey, who felt—as Locke and Mill and James had—that the fate of a whole society might depend on the correct analysis of scientific method. This narrowing of philosophical vision was accompanied by a predictable decline of philosophical influence in American society.[21]

The philosophy that took the place of older, pre–World War II lines—Dewey included—belonged to the style known as "analytic." The analytic tradition has often been castigated for being apolitical or quietist by people elsewhere in the humanities. But this charge was not fair for the new philosophy in its origins.

It helps to note the social and political commitments of its inspirers. The original prime movers of the new methods—Bertrand Russell, Ludwig Wittgenstein, and then the Vienna Circle thinkers in interwar Austria, Rudolf Carnap and Otto Neurath chief among them—included one of the English-speaking world's best-known pacifists, atheists, and antinomians, Russell; the odd pacifistic Wittgenstein; the militant socialist and utopian Neurath; and the more moderate leftist internationalist and socialist Carnap. (The logician Gottlob Frege, generally counted as the progenitor of analytic philosophy, belonged essentially to an earlier era and was relatively isolated intellectually; his work was important because Russell, Wittgenstein, and Carnap developed it.) The Vienna Circle has often been maligned as cold, scientistic, and formalistic. Yet it is obvious in hindsight that its often Jewish and socialist or liberal leading lights embraced scientific experiment and logical truth to confront unreason, blood, nation, *völkisch* prejudice, and the metaphysical. An eliminative reconstruction of language to identify irrationality and euphemism seems a reasonable response to the sinister, calumnious atmosphere of Austria and Germany between the wars. An ideal of international cooperation between researchers who share a transparent, rule-bound universal language of logic and mathematics represents a noble cosmopolitanism—as long as one sees the background of fascist cobwebs they wished to fumigate.

From Frege and Russell, the Vienna Circle, joined by an allied group in Berlin, gained the tool of the new mathematical logic to rehabilitate language for what made sense in a material, provable world of observation and verification—and what did not. Hence, the names for the resulting philosophy of empirical observation and logical formulation: "logical empiricism" or "logical positivism." ("Analysis" came from the more basic and earlier Russellian project of logical atomism in linguistic analysis; via Cambridge and Oxford, it reached America at the same time that Wittgenstein forged a communicating link between Vienna and Cambridge.) A chief philosophical antagonist became the same antagonist that so many anti-Nazi philosophical figures in the German-speaking countries had discovered: Martin Heidegger. Carnap took up "The Nothing itself nothings," from Heidegger's inaugural lecture upon replacing Husserl at Freiburg, as a celebrated example sentence of the sort of sententiousness that would not be expressible in a language freed of unscientific, unverifiable metaphysics.[22]

As the philosopher Michael Friedman has recently shown, Carnap knew Heidegger's work and standpoints well, and had read him quite seriously. He attended the debate between Heidegger and Cassirer at Davos in 1929 and took a walk with Heidegger and conversed with him in a café. He studied *Sein und Zeit* (*Being and Time*) and expounded its philosophical purpose to the Vienna Circle around Moritz Schlick as an entrée to the group.[23] Heidegger represented a rival means and approach to "overcoming metaphysics," the task that this magician of the Black Forest promised to accomplish by going back to a more primordial, prerational sense of human existence, its elementary Dasein, which stood as the opposite of the progress of science and cosmopolitan modernity. Once Heidegger had turned Nazi, Schlick had been murdered, and Carnap, Neurath, and Philipp Frank—along with their allies Hans Reichenbach and Carl Hempel in Berlin—began to migrate West, away from anti-Semitic repression, their political conflict with the forces of the xenophobic Right filled out and extended the terms of the methodological conflict.

This was the original "linguistic turn."[24] Recent biographies have strongly humanized Rudolf Carnap away from the image of a stern logician and into a true man of enlightenment and a utopian of international cooperation.[25] Carnap favored the construction of "ideal languages" both in logic and in reality, artificial languages that could overcome the errors and historical demerits of natural language, not from any disapproval of human history but because he maintained the cosmopolitan Enlightenment ethos of Kant's "Perpetual Peace," as in his love of Esperanto. Friedman has pointed out the touching rhapsody in Carnap's intellectual autobiography when he recounts teaching himself the language at the age of fourteen and attending a performance of Goethe's noble *Iphigenia* performed in the rationalized international language.[26] "It was a stirring and uplifting experience for me to hear this drama, inspired by the ideal of one humanity, expressed in the new medium which made it possible for thousands of spectators from many countries to understand it." After the tragedy of World War I, young man Carnap hiked through Finland, Estonia, Latvia, and Lithuania with a Bulgarian friend: "We stayed with hospitable Esperantists and made contact with many people in these countries. We talked about all kinds of problems in public and in personal life, always, of course, in Esperanto."[27]

The public project of the Vienna Circle was their Unity of Science movement, championed most strongly by Neurath. Carnap also left the fields of sociology and theory of history to Neurath, whose own commitment to international communication ran to visual communication and design (in his ISOTOPE system for symbolization of data) and whose radical sympathies led him to temporary work in the Soviet Union. Deweyans in America, pragmatists, and scientific instrumentalists, themselves practitioners and defenders of logic and empiricism, welcomed this side of the logical empiricists in the 1930s. The Vienna Circle found an early home at the University of Chicago, thanks to the sponsorship of Dewey's follower Charles Morris.[28] The New York that formed the center of pragmatist Deweyan philosophy in the 1930s was likewise sympathetic to their project. Dewey, Sidney Hook, Ernst Nagel, and Horace Kallen all favored such comprehensive scientific cooperation and unity in Neurath's spirit. Dewey didn't share the Europeans' will to eliminate the irrational or metaphysical (though Hook may have)—just to gradually naturalize it, as he thought was occurring in the ever-more religiously tolerant United States. In fact, Dewey contributed a monograph, his *Theory of Valuation*, to Neurath's *Foundations of the Unity of Science* encyclopedia project. At the 1939 Congress of the Unity of Science movement, held in Cambridge, Massachusetts, a raft of New York pragmatists attended, where they would have encountered a young acolyte of Carnap's from a wholly different orientation—a young logician named Willard Van Ormon Quine.

W.V.O. Quine had been part of a historically momentous coincidence that occurred in 1932, the last year in which young apprentice philosophers could make the customary pilgrimage to the German-speaking countries before National Socialism took power. Two twenty-something Anglophone graduate students unknown to each other—Quine was one, the Englishman A. J. Ayer the other—separately traveled to Vienna and were sent on to Prague in search of Rudolf Carnap, and each became a wholehearted disciple. The midwesterner-turned-Harvard-man Quine and the Oxbridge-cultured Ayer would triumph in their respective countries and national traditions as the public faces of an importation of the Vienna Circle's most stringent eliminativist project in the philosophy of language. As Jeffrey Isaac has shown, Quine was a science and technology–focused logician, an admirer of engineering and know-how, who found the eliminative uses of mathematical logic sympathetic—in part as a tool to counter those other, softer currents in the famous Harvard philosophy department, native ground of William James, George Santayana, and C. I. Lewis, which he found uncongenial.[29] Quine became a central exponent and patron of Carnap in rivalry to Charles Morris in Chicago, and by extension a helper of the larger networks of the Vienna Circle. Archie Ayer rephrased Carnap's early doctrines in an influential small book, *Language, Truth and Logic*, published in England when Ayer was just twenty-six—a small academic success in 1936, but a best seller when it was reprinted after World War II, when it seemed a sign of modernizing, antitraditional values to read it, and courage to subscribe to its demotion of all sorts of metaphysical, religious, and moral beliefs as unscientific and nonsensical when put into logical format.[30]

But neither of these two exponents of the doctrines of "logical positivism" (Ayer's preferred term, which stuck) pursued the sociological, historical, socialist, and Enlightenment values of the Vienna Circle as a whole. Otto Neurath, who might have expanded Americans' sense of the Vienna Circle project, never moved to the United States and died prematurely in 1945. Carnap drew a line between his political activities and the outcomes of his philosophical work. Both Quine and Ayer took over Carnap's 1932 antipathy to Heidegger, but not Carnap's historical learning, knowledge of Heidegger's context, or sympathy with a wide German humanist tradition. (In his original article, Carnap's explication of Heidegger's words was actually quite extensive; the article ended with an encomium to music and a distinction between the emotional power of art and the necessary rationality of philosophy, all culminating in praise of Friedrich Nietzsche.)[31]

Quine rose to full professorship and primary authority in Harvard's philosophy department after World War II—as Harvard extended its prestige in philosophy, thanks to its new turn and a continuing partnership with Oxford—and became famous postwar for such dogmatic utterances as "Philosophy of science is philosophy enough," and his hatred for the history of philosophy prior to the present.[32] (He even despised his brief obligation at Harvard to teach the doctrines of his empiricist predecessor David Hume: "Determining what Hume thought and imparting it to students was less appealing than determining the truth and imparting that."[33]) In England, Ayer published the 1947 manifesto "The Claims of Philosophy," which divided philosophers into bad "pontiffs" and good "journeymen." Pontiffs follow "their own 'philosophical' brand of irrationality," "have recourse to metaphysics," and "think it within the province of philosophy to compete with natural science"; "few men, indeed, have ever reasoned worse than Hegel," the last century's pontiff, while "the leading pontiff of our times" is Heidegger. Ayer's slighting reference to Heidegger, however, seems to be only to the words he knows from Carnap's article. The proper task of journeymen is to solve logical puzzles and do linguistic analyses to help science as well as they can while making no claims about values, which, after all, can't be deduced from fact and belong to an active life, not to philosophy.[34] As late as 1960, in *Word and Object*, Quine was still flogging Heidegger's same *Das Nichts nichtet* with citation to Carnap.[35]

Logical positivism came to be pilloried near universally by humanists after World War II, in a C. P. Snow "Two Cultures" world where logic and mathematical notation seemed an alienating way to pursue questions of general import. The second generation of New York pragmatists and Deweyans after Dewey's death turned against logical positivism as antisocial and dogmatic, "totalitarian" in its intolerance and scientism; but it was Columbia, the New School, and City College that consequently faded from the scene, ceasing to be significant philosophical centers.[36] One is hard-pressed to find anyone who spoke well of the "analytic" program outside professional philosophy, and yet within philosophy its core project was considered to have been largely repudiated by the end of the 1950s.[37] Indeed, Quine made his true reputation, after years of championing Carnap and soliciting honors for him, by gradually rebuking the tenets of the old analytic project of logical empiricism, as in his seminal rejection of the analytic/synthetic distinction in "Two Dogmas of Empiricism" (1951). We face the surprise of a transformation of Anglo-American philosophy in the name of contentful doctrines almost immediately repudiated postwar juxtaposed with the retention of those doctrines' methodology and style.

The exact date at which the analytic style and approach achieved dominance in American philosophy departments seems to have come no earlier than the mid-1950s, the very moment when strict logical positivism was dismissed.[38] The style was laconic, logic-driven, scientistic, apolitical, masculine, presentist, and Anglo-liberal. Large numbers of philosophically significant thinkers in these departments learned to conceive themselves as outliers and odd ducks (Richard Rorty, Stanley Cavell, Arthur Danto, Hubert Dreyfus, even Hilary Putnam).

Meanwhile, the postwar agenda of the social sciences in America had turned away from theories of rival classes, social forces, and ideologies to doctrines of consensus, structural-functional stabilization, methodological individualism, and a quest for unification of the many different studies of man through a science of "behavior" reduced to identifiable variables and simple causal mechanisms. Suitably reconceptualized on the model of simple problems in engineering or laboratory science, human action in society should furnish a wealth of commensurable data. With computerization—whose initial uses outside the university were associated with armaments and Cold War defense—many postwar students and thinkers had some sense (not incorrectly) that the arrangement of circuits used to store binary information depended on a computation theory developed by mathematicians and logicians in overlapping circles with the logicist philosophers, and were politically repelled. Quine, during the student disturbances at Harvard in 1969, proclaimed himself part of the "conservative caucus" of the faculty; in his autobiography he sniffs at the supposed intimidation of the faculty by "shabby black undergraduates," and excoriates the creation of a "program of Black Studies . . . [to] accommodate the new racism"—by "racism" he means African American particularism.[39] (The autobiography is a curious document, mostly stories of tourism mixed with a lifetime of philosophical snobbery and prizes. Rarely can any philosopher have thought himself more cosmopolitan or have been more parochial.) No less an authority of the Left than Marcuse read Quine and witheringly quoted the Harvard philosopher's attempted witticisms on the rationale for a restrictive philosophical ontology (from "On What There Is"): an "overpopulated universe is in many ways unlovely. It offends the aesthetic sense of those of us who have a taste for desert landscapes, but this is not the worst of it. [Such a] slum of possibles is a breeding ground for disorderly elements." Marcuse noted the echo of a police mind-set in Quine's metaphors, from "the authorities of Investigation and Information," while elsewhere he detected the "manipulative-technological elements" at the core of Quine's sense of science.[40]

When the sixties came, the only portion of mainstream American philosophy capable of responding to the social tumult was its largely disvalued component of ethics and political theory. The sudden return to "applied ethics" and to normative political theorizing from metaethics is often portrayed as an act of courage and disciplinary renewal. For some of the more activist ethicists and political theorists this was true. In effect, however, the general drift of the public-minded portion of analytic philosophy departments under the pressure of 1960s events was to make common cause with the law school, and tack analytic styles of logical reasoning onto legal reasoning. Professional philosophy, at a moment of social insurgency and social movement, preferred normative mediation, appointing itself the faculty of judges or referees for the "should" of those who would determine what is ethically proscribed, what is permissible, and what is obligatory, for all rational agents. John Rawls published *A Theory of Justice* (1971) while a professor at Harvard, a book considered foundational to political philosophy as it has been practiced in analytic departments for the more than forty years since; while the journal *Philosophy and Public Affairs* (started by a group that originally called itself the Society for Philosophy and Public Policy) began its prestigious run in 1971 from a publishing base in Princeton as the premier organ for the new turn in analytic ethics to "practical ethics."[41] "Rights" came almost inevitably to the fore as the framework for all arguments on social matters; historical study had been so extensively expunged from philosophy departments that rights were not seen as historical appendages to liberalism or just one among competing traditions, as they would be viewed in departments of history or political science. John Rawls's reconstruction of mild Franklin Delano–Rooseveltian political liberalism and welfare capitalism, eliminating political contestation, proposed that its substantive prescriptions might be inevitably chosen from a hypothetical position in which a group of randomly selected citizens reasoned, reflected, and reached consensus on arrangements of inevitable inequality and hierarchy together, as long as none knew where he or she would eventually fall within that hierarchy. Rawls acknowledged that no such universal, unmarked, and undifferentiated position—the "original position," as he called it—could exist for any real person, which was a gain of sorts over naive universalism. But he didn't see why it still couldn't be, as it was imagined in this thought experiment, the basis for a normative social order. One simply had to imagine what subjects would choose if they were temporarily denied all knowledge of their eventual particularity of identity or social position. This arrangement would be enough to bind them to the emergent order once they recovered from their amnesia (officially, their "veil of ignorance") and had to live within their real identities, within the imagined case; and the imagined case should be enough to serve for us as legitimation of the principles of social organization and governance, for our world, that Rawls argued the imaginary deliberators would choose.

THE TRANSATLANTIC CIRCUIT OF LÉVI-STRAUSS

Where *would* true philosophy come from for those affected by the sixties? It couldn't just speak for individual prohibition or obligation. It couldn't just go to law. In a sense, it came from America—from a French émigré mold, this time, in one of the most complicated and slow-growing mixtures of all the intellectual alloys compounded by the émigré flight from Europe.

Three years younger than Jean-Paul Sartre, Claude Lévi-Strauss belonged to the academic cohort of Simone de Beauvoir and Maurice Merleau-Ponty. In preparation for his *agrégation* in 1931, the comprehensive test that allowed elevation to the academic ranks, he completed his practice teaching at one of the Parisian lycées alongside both of them. He sat the test in the company of Simone Weil. In 1934, Brazil's wish to inaugurate the new University of São Paulo with French leadership led him to accept a place for a professorship in sociology in the next departing group, along-side a similarly little-known Fernand Braudel. Braudel would help trans-form the history profession, as Lévi-Strauss would anthropology, in the direction of impersonality and grand systems integrating nature and culture.[42]

According to the tradition inaugurated by Durkheim and Mauss, French sociology contained ethnology. Lévi-Strauss used his school vacations during five years of South American employment to perform ethnographic fieldwork among the Bororo, Caduveo, and Nambikwara. Returning to France to resume a metropolitan career in 1939, his timing was inauspi-cious. As a Jew, Lévi-Strauss was banned from teaching under Vichy in 1940, and quickly faced greater dangers than unemployment. He escaped deportation to a concentration camp by shipping from the port of Marseille to America in 1941. The agency of his visas for emigration to New York was the New School, the same institution that had rescued German scholars through its University in Exile. Now it had begun hosting a new initiative, the École Libre des Hautes Études, chartered independently but closely allied with the Free French forces of Charles de Gaulle and anti-Vichy net-works springing up globally after the fall of France.[43]

But Lévi-Strauss was able to get out of France also because of his ties to US anthropology. Franz Boas's disciple Robert Lowie, as well as the South Americanist Alfred Métraux, sponsored him for the New School with sup-port from the Rockefeller Foundation.[44] On arrival in New York, Lévi-Strauss met Boas in person, visited him at home, and became acquainted with the Boasians and their occasional rivals. He tightened his ties to Lowie, Mead, Benedict, Karl Kroeber, and Ralph Linton.

Despite the proximity of the German emigration, the École Libre kept to itself among the German scholars.[45] Within the French-speaking com-munity in those tiny, overused classrooms and offices, however, Lévi-Strauss sought out a stranger whom he had heard could aid his research: Russo-Jewish émigré polymath, Roman Jakobson. Jakobson had taken refuge at the École and was delivering lectures in French (one of many languages he spoke). He was a linguist who had distinguished himself as a founding participant in both a so-called Moscow school and the Prague school of linguistics. He narrowly escaped the Nazi conquest of Czecho-slovakia by fleeing to a series of Scandinavian teaching posts. His best-known innovations in linguistics concerned the reduction of the morphol-ogy of speech to phonemes, its smallest differentiable units. Jakobson rooted their significance in one wing of the larger theoretical apparatus of structural linguistics derived from the lectures of the Swiss linguist Fer-dinand de Saussure in the 1910s. Analysis should be capable of reducing all languages to structures of fundamental elements that would hold relations to one another but held no preordained connection to the worldly objects they signified.

The essential goad to Lévi-Strauss from Jakobson's thought was analytic rather than substantive. His linguistics proffered language as a template of universal reducible structure, making the babel of tongues susceptible to the same kinds of diagnostic operations across countless specific instances, and implying the primacy of language-like cognition for other of *Homo sapiens*' ways of adapting the world to human uses.[46] In the mess of descriptive ethnographic facts that Lévi-Strauss had begun to make himself churn through each morning from nine till noon, in the decades of field-workers' collections on deposit in the American room of the New York Public Library, such clarifying rigor was precisely what was needed.[47] Ethnography had piled up unruly positive data. It needed to be submitted to an operation that could cut through the proliferation of facts and terms. Lévi-Strauss's earliest intellectual formation derived from musing upon the "unconscious structures" of the human mind and human history discoverable in his first masters, Freud and Marx.[48] Structural reduction should offer a model of universal analysis with even greater scientific and mathematical perspicuity than theirs, if the right minimal elements were identified. Lévi-Strauss followed his Jakobsonian insight into language to ask what other sorts of human data could be similarly processed by systematic arrangements of distinctions, and he began coming up with elements at the heart of the ethnographic tradition, with enormous moment for the broader study of culture and society as such: kinship, totem systems, myth, and art. Structural linguistics as Lévi-Strauss interpreted them promised rigor and universalistic scientific analysis that would put the human sciences on a footing with natural sciences.

IRONIES OF INTERNATIONAL THOUGHT

This, too, was a "linguistic turn." And the step that would produce structuralist, and later poststructuralist theory for France and for all American devotees of this continental line, happened in the United States, in a stew of influences available in New York by 1945, linguistic, anthropological, sociological, and philosophical.

It probably makes very little sense to attempt to distinguish national contributions when the defining feature of these wartime transformations is cross-pollination and unanticipated fructification—beyond national borders—though within a world riven by ideological conflict and still conceiving itself on national lines. Christopher Johnson has acutely noted the "complication of a *bilingual* formulation of theory": "it is a fact not frequently commented upon that a number of Lévi-Strauss's important early texts were originally written in English"—including his "monograph on the Nambikwara Indians" of 1941, which he then had to translate into French as his complementary thesis (a requisite of French professorial credentialing) in 1948. Similarly, Lévi-Strauss wrote "seminal essays on linguistics and anthropology and the structural analysis of myth" first in English well into the early 1950s, after he had already returned to France.[49] It is a commonplace that Lévi-Strauss was chided in France for "Anglo-Saxon" dimensions of his thought, but he may not have been chided for the right ones.[50] Boasianism, of course, was already its own curious mixed formation of liberal nineteenth-century German *Bildung* and a new American ecumenical thrust shaped by sympathy with pluralism and pragmatism and recoil from racism and cultural imperialism. Lévi-Strauss refused to return to France at the liberation, preferring to complete his research at the library. He had hardly spent a year in France in a decade. He reaped the benefits of the Free French recovery of France after the Allied reinvasion, however, as he was rewarded with the sinecure of "cultural attaché" in New York and established in a mansion uptown, with his off-hours free for scholarship. Instructions came from the French government to wind down the École Libre, and introductions given to cultural and diplomatic circles as the new postwar order was established.[51] When the existentialists Sartre, Beauvoir, and Camus made US tours, Lévi-Strauss hosted them. When French education undertook negotiations with the Rockefeller Foundation to support the awakening of postwar social science in France, the young anthropologist took part in devising the famous Sixth Section of the École Pratique des Hautes Études—later to be associated with Braudel and Lévi-Strauss himself.[52] For Lévi-Strauss did return, of course, before the 1940s were out, and published *The Elementary Structures of Kinship* in Paris in 1949, an intellectual bombshell.

This book, whose title announced a rivalry or filial relation with founder Durkheim's *The Elementary Forms of Religious Life*, applied structural analysis to the seemingly mysterious or arbitrary and given diversity of that most basic system that ethnographers try to diagram upon arrival: family structure, who is related to whom, especially across clans and by marriage. What rules determine who should ally and who should not? Working with a vast range of examples, Lévi-Strauss worked transformations by simpler structures of differentiation, ranging famously over theses from the transfer of women for intergroup solidarity to the necessity of the incest taboo to produce communication and alliance. He included in this tour de force an appendix by the mathematician André Weil—Simone Weil's brother, then at the University of Chicago—interpreting Lévi-Strauss's model through algebra.

There is thus an enormous irony to the later charges, after 1968, from departments of philosophy in America and England, that the wave of French theory, for which Lévi-Strauss created the basis, was altogether irrationalist, unrigorous, or rhetorical. If you look objectively at the structuralist project of generating a purified form of language analysis to cut back the overgrowth in the human sciences in quest of a universal systematic method to unify human and natural science, then Lévi-Strauss (inspired by Roman Jakobson's linguistics) starts to look a lot like Carnap. Structuralism gains a true likeness to the analytic project in philosophy. This new "linguistic turn," occurring in Europe from 1949 to 1966, in fields unfamiliar to Anglo-American philosophy, rather closely tracks that other "linguistic turn" taken by the Vienna Circle's conquest of America. These are two comparable linguistic turns in twentieth-century intellect, and they occur at comparable times.[53] It is an oddity of history—but perhaps expresses the closeness of the development of ideas, whose implications then went in different directions—that Quine and Ayer, pilgrims to Prague in 1932, could in the same year and city have skipped over Carnap and apprenticed instead with Jakobson and the Prague linguists. Going back a generation further, Carnap's extension and theoretical transformation of the logic lectures of Gottlob Frege, which he had witnessed at Jena between 1910 and 1914, is not altogether unlike Jakobson's discovery and rigorization of Saussure's lectures collected posthumously in the *Cours de linguistique générale* (1916).[54]

This was a new rigorism for French thought, in contrast to the phenomenological tradition represented by Sartre. Carl Schorske has written perceptively of the "new rigorism" that changed various human sciences in America in the decades after World War II. It led to formal systems for the modeling of qualitative phenomena (like game theory or rational choice), mathematization of philosophical principles (in "analytic philosophy" or the removal from economics of the older, moralistic "political economy"), and the elevation of quantitative and statistical methods in a variety of disciplines, from sociology to political science.[55] The structuralism that Lévi-Strauss brought to France was a slightly different kind of interpretive rigorism suited to the different French context. As Lévi-Strauss's biographer Patrick Wilcken puts it, Lévi-Strauss "heralded a belated modernist turn in the social sciences" in France.[56] Lévi-Strauss worked with underlying structures of the mind as they expressed themselves and negotiated local circumstances through social forms. Comparable projects could and should have been seen in other postwar US disciplines, including some dimensions of Anglo-American philosophy. (The word structuralism, at midcentury, already had a meaning for US sociologists: the understanding of society as an interlocking functional order of institutional structures that adjust to assure stability and reproduction. This structuralism is most strongly associated in the postwar era with the systems theory of Talcott Parsons.)[57] Lévi-Strauss did not attend the Macy Conferences on cybernetics, often used as the landmark for the rise of information theory in the 1940s and its entwinement with the human sciences. Roman Jakobson did, though, and he took care to send Lévi-Strauss the new literature of computational approaches to "cultural" fields.[58] Lévi-Strauss integrated both Claude Shannon and Warren Weaver's *The Mathematical Theory of Communication* (1950) and Norbert Wiener's *Cybernetics* (1948) into his work at the start of the 1950s, and his hopes for a thorough convergence of these multiple formalisms on a comprehensive science of human expression and mind. Jakobson himself became a central arbiter for the Rockefeller Foundation of their research agenda on communication, and held professorships after the war at Columbia, Harvard, and MIT.[59] On one side, he was the inspirer of Lévi-Strauss; that is how most intellectual history remembers him. But he was tied to Anglo-American linguistics and philosophy, too. When Quine wrote his major work on the philosophy of language, *Word and Object*, the book was solicited by Jakobson (in 1951), who also found Rockefeller funding for it.[60]

LÉVI-STRAUSS AND CULTURAL DIFFERENCE

Such similarities and connections return us to the question, however, of why such philosophy would be appealing to American avatars of "the new sensibility," rebels against "the System," participants in the movement to stop the war in Vietnam and bring social justice home to all the forces repressed by the Establishment. Americans questing for a public philosophy suitable to the sixties surely didn't need more scientism for its own sake.

But there is another dimension to Lévi-Strauss that was *very* different. It was almost an alternative track to his structuralism, and yet it took a place at the center of the movement of French structuralism that radiated outward from his linguistic science. This was his anticolonialism, antiethnocentrism, and fundamental philosophical, moral, and political commitment to difference. In 1952, the anthropologist was called to give a lecture on race at UNESCO. This would be part of a series, distributed worldwide in multiple languages, containing authoritative statements on race by scientific experts. Earlier in this study, we saw the founding of UNESCO as an educational appendage of the United Nations. The thwarted ambitions for the United Nations to pursue true international cooperation and mutual understanding found one home in this "Educational, Scientific, and Cultural" organization, which represented the "soft" side of the United

Nations, closely linked to the Commission for Human Rights and its eventual declaration and convention. We have also seen how the closest thing to an enshrinement of the universalist discourse of the crisis of man occurred in UNESCO's survey of philosophers for the use of the Human Rights Commission; seen, too, that the one dissenting and cautionary voice about the possible imperialistic and difference-destroying capacities of human rights in 1945 belonged to the American Anthropological Association and its Boasians—and that their contribution was ignored and left unpublished. In the aftermath of UNESCO's successful collation of universalizing authority for human rights, the thrust of the organization turned to the extirpation of the concept of "race" worldwide. Its UN directorate, as the historian Anthony Hazard has written, "followed the 1948 Universal Declaration of Human Rights by assigning UNESCO the task of defining 'race' in order to support the idea that racism was morally unacceptable and unsupported by science."[61]

The progressive definition of "race" was expected to proclaim that it was a fiction that falsely divided a humanity everywhere fundamentally the same. Lévi-Strauss, as we know, believed mentality and the cognitive power of structuring experience were universal to the human species, as species-level biological and cognitive equipment; he was antiracist in this Boasian way. But his lecture (and small book) *Race and History* came as a shock, and scandal, to the UNESCO model. He began by putting aside the biological difference between races: that was nonsense. But he then seemed to admit the very thing that universalism existed to dispute, namely, that no sane, intelligent person could deny *difference* without doing damage to his own knowledge and senses. To deny difference would disarm the antiracist, too, when he faced the very obvious presence of societal differences that seemed to be at the base of naive racism:

> It seems to us, however, that the very effort made in this series of booklets to prove [the nonexistence of race] involved a risk of pushing into the background another very important aspect of the life of man—the fact that the development of human life is not everywhere the same but rather takes form in an extraordinary diversity of societies and civilizations. . . .
>
> It would be useless to argue the man in the street out of attaching an intellectual or moral significance to the fact of having a black or white skin, straight or frizzy hair, unless we had an answer to another question which, as experience proves[,] he will immediately ask: if there are no innate racial aptitudes, how can we explain the fact that the white man's civilization has made the tremendous advantages with which we are all familiar while the civilizations of the coloured peoples have lagged behind, some of them having come only half way along the road, and others

being still thousands or tens of thousands of years behind the times? We cannot therefore claim to have formulated a convincing denial of the human *races*, so long as we fail to consider the problem of the inequality—or diversity—of human cultures, which is in fact—however unjustifiably—closely associated with it in the public mind.[62]

Lévi-Strauss takes the problem at its most difficult point. But the word "diversity" is key (*diversité*—the word is the same in French and English, two central languages of UNESCO presentation). Difference between the modern West and many indigenous cultures is undeniable. But this does not come from the West advancing historically while other cultures remained stationary. On the contrary, every culture that exists at this point in time is the product of the same length of dynamic development and changes since the origin of species. There is no such thing as a people without history (as the anthropologist Eric Wolf would phrase it later); all cultures have histories. The ones that can't point out those histories to us, as we can point out ours, are cultures that don't have *writing*. In this sense, Lévi-Strauss says, one can easily identify the mechanism of what we see as a greater development: some cultures, like that of the modern West, are self-consciously and visibly "cumulative." But more cumulativeness—pointing yourself in a single direction to maximally enhance one trait, with all its consequences—does not betoken superiority to cumulative cultures heading in some other direction, or less cumulative cultures whose dynamism is not as unidirectional.

Difference, yes—no one can fail to notice that it exists. But superiority and inferiority—and a universalism that believes your own values to be more advanced or more developed—well, such attitudes exist for all cultures, and they are perfectly right if your purpose is to dwell, unenlightened, unscientific, within your own narrow range. This is, Lévi-Strauss says, "the paradox inherent in cultural relativism":

> [T]he more we claim to discriminate between cultures and customs as good and bad, the more completely do we identify ourselves with those we would condemn. By refusing to consider as human those who seem to us to be the most "savage" or "barbarous" of their representatives, we merely adopt one of their own characteristic attitudes. The barbarian is, first and foremost, the man who believes in barbarism. (*R&H*, 12)

The betrayer of enlightenment turns out to be the universalist.[63] "Faced with the two temptations of condemning things which are offensive to him emotionally or of denying differences which are beyond his intellectual grasp, modern man" tries "to account for the diversity of all cultures while seeking, at the same time, to eradicate what still shocks and offends him in that diversity" (*R&H*, 13). Universalism, Lévi-Strauss suggests, creates a new order of highest and lowest *cultures*—instead of civilizations—which is only the old "false evolutionism" again, which the struggle of anthropological antiracism (and Franz Boas) overthrew once before. Now it has returned. Universalism is evolutionism without race; really, it is what we think of as "racism" but with the "race concept" abandoned. "It is really an attempt to wipe out the diversity of cultures while pretending to accord it full recognition" (ibid.).

Lévi-Strauss has a fateful name for this racism without the race concept. In French, it is *L'Ethnocentrisme*, the title of his third chapter; in English translation, "The Ethnocentric Attitude."[64] Western "progress" needs to reconsider its certainty that itself, as it stands, is the only right and true progress there could be. We possess science. But all cultures, Lévi-Strauss says, have their science, their equal cognitive contribution to confrontation with their changing circumstances in time and space, their means of differentiation from or convergence with their human neighbors, their record in sensible form of observation of the sensible world. "The societies we describe as 'primitive' have as many Pasteurs and Palissys as the others" (*R&H*, 36). (The proper recognition of the science of indigenous systems—of myth and rite, as a "science of the concrete" but a science nonetheless—is explicated in the later *La Pensée Sauvage*.[65] Our science is progressive if what you want is "to equip man with increasingly powerful mechanical resources" (*R&H*, 26–27). If it proves its superiority because "underdeveloped" peoples clamor for it, one must consider the exact "inequality of force" created by the particular cumulative direction of our culture toward those same mechanical resources that dominate others physically and economically. "[W]e may note that the acceptance of the Western way of life, or certain aspects of it, is by no means as spontaneous as Westerners would like to believe. It is less the result of free choice than of the absence of any alternative. Western civilization has stationed its soldiers, trading posts, plantations and missionaries throughout the world. . . . When the balance of power is not so unequal, societies do not so easily surrender" (*R&H*, 30). Other societies will prove most superior, most advanced, and most developed if you attend to the development of other resources—kinship complexity, say, or interior bodily and psychic awareness—but the majority will not have become so lopsided in any one direction. Therefore, perhaps it is not advance we should be prioritizing—which suddenly seems like hypertrophy and excess, once we have discovered the plurality of cultures—but rather diversity itself: "[T]he true contribution of a culture consists, not in the list of inventions which it has personally produced, but in its difference from others. The sense of gratitude and respect which each single member of a given culture can and should feel towards all others can only be based on the conviction that the other cultures differ from his own in countless ways, even if the ultimate essence of these differences eludes him or if, in spite of his best efforts, he can reach no more than an imperfect understanding of them" (*R&H*, 45). If one truly aspires to step out of the natural biases and ignorance of one's own culture into the regarding of "humanity," therefore, and if one wishes to truly belong to enlightenment, one must adopt the attitude Lévi-Strauss associates with anthropology: to observe and understand all the difference already in what there is, and engage in the "anticipation, understanding, and promotion of what is struggling into being" *(R&H, 49)*.

This little book spells the revival of Franz Boas and his school in postwar thought and cultural relativism's revenge upon the discourse of man. Lévi-Strauss's very short bibliography, ending the pamphlet, is conspicuous for the presence of Boas, Kroeber, and Melville Herskovits—the Boasian author, we have seen, of the American Anthropological Association statement about human rights declaration. Boasian "cultural wholes" and thoroughgoing cultural relativism had always sat oddly next to Boasian antiracism. The former contained a whole philosophy and worldview; the latter was a therapeutic or corrective campaign against a uniquely pernicious mistake. For Boas, the thesis of the unity of cognitive capability among *Homo sapiens* held the two arguments together: science first had to rid the world of a false idea of innate genetic differences in order for people to begin to think properly about cultural diversity. But the whole did not countenance the other unifications and homogenizations of humankind that Boas had to accept among his naive allies for the sake of the shared antiracist front. (Lévi-Strauss's opening gambit of the existence of histories for societies without writing is very much a Boasian argument; elsewhere, Lévi-Strauss sketched out the principles he honored from Boas, along with his rationale extending cross-cultural comparison and structural analysis far beyond the limits of "Boasian nominalism."[66]) Here, Lévi-Strauss—a great writer and rhetorician, as Boas never was—follows the argument out, decouples cultural relativism from agreeable certainties about race prejudice, and reanimates its skeptical power. It paints an Einsteinian moral: even the most indubitable Western superiority becomes just an observer effect amid cultural relativity.

This was also, of course, a bomb that Lévi-Strauss placed under a postwar consensus that newly believed in "international development" and "modernization" as a gift to humankind and a fulfillment of the promises of freedom from World War II. Truman had enunciated his famous Point Four in his inaugural address of 1949, speaking to Americans of the "underdeveloped areas" of the world as the place America must send its "preeminent . . . industrial and scientific techniques" and "capital investment."[67]

The "development" concept, as Gilbert Rist has argued, allowed the United States to speed the end of the colonial empires of England, France, and Belgium, while advancing "a new anti-colonial imperialism" of markets, export, and debt.[68] Lévi-Strauss's undermining of its moral basis would find an audience in the United States only a decade and a half later. In 1952, France was fighting a brutal colonial war in Vietnam against Ho Chi Minh to assert its dominion. That decade and a half later, the United States would be fighting the same war, against the same opponent, having taken over France's responsibilities of neocolonial hubris.

THE AMERICAN APPEAL OF STRUCTURALISM

Now something of the suite of ideas and principles that Lévi-Strauss and later structuralisms sent back to the United States of 1968 and after can be seen. There was systems thinking and the recovery of a "hermeneutic of suspicion" descended from Freud and Marx (the phrase itself, with a favorable implication, is attributed to Paul Ricoeur).[69] There was a linguistic turn and a new analytic method. Society-level analysis meant a dissolution of Man, phrased in fearsome ripostes to the midcentury discourse of man and subjectivist humanism, which had dishonestly pretended to be the only language of moral or scientific seriousness. Lévi-Straussian structuralism championed difference and differentiation as a structuring principle of thought and expression, but also praised it and valued its preservation socially, in the separate ethnographic constitution of difference as cultural "diversity," esteemed as the very core of human value. The relevant universality in structuralism *is* difference. Finally, the critique of ethnocentrism as a premier obstacle to true critical and humane thought gave strength to many of structuralism's American heirs: the anticentrisms (logocentrism, phallogocentrism), and the estranging maneuvers of anti-neocolonial and postcolonial critique. Lévi-Strauss helped restore the interpretation of symbols to the human sciences, along with cultural relativism.

Inevitably, a central term of the initial American reception of structuralism was the overthrowing of a constricting ideal of man. A phrase Lévi-Strauss coined in *The Savage Mind* to differentiate himself from Sartre and restate the antihumanist methodology of much classical social theory—"the ultimate goal of the human sciences is not to constitute, but to dissolve man"—was repeated frequently in the United States when structuralism was discussed in the late 1960s.[70] Though it had just appeared in 1966, and would not be translated for four years more, it was Foucault's essay in radically disjunctive historiography, *Les Mots et les Choses* (*The Order of Things*), that furnished many of the other most famous provocations Americans repeated in 1968. *The Order of Things*, a sensation in intellectual France, separated out the chronological but discontinuous modes of Western thought that Foucault called *epistemes*. Only the most recent had included Man as our "sciences of man" conceive him; this conception was neither eternal nor inevitable. "As the archeology of our thought easily shows, man is an invention of recent date. And one perhaps nearing its end"; Foucault foresaw new "arrangements" in which "man would be erased, like a face drawn in sand at the edge of the sea."[71]

Other such slogans were plentifully available in quotation, for example, from Lacan: "It is known that I have always felt a repugnance for the term *sciences humaines*, which seems to me a call to slavery itself."[72] "Man does not exist prior to language, either as a species or as an individual," Roland Barthes contributed, "it is language which teaches the definition of man, not the reverse."[73] Louis Althusser had been waging war in *For Marx* (1965) on the Marxist humanism that had become commonplace in the postwar era among those who turned to the writings of the rediscovered young Marx rather than the scientific antihumanism of *Capital*. Item one—quite literally—on Althusser's written list of things to abolish for a renewal of Marxism was "the notion of Man (the essence or nature of Man)."[74] He can be heard at his polemical best in conflicts surrounding the Parti Communiste Français in 1966–67:

> To put it plainly: we need to say once and for all to all those who . . . are constantly harping about man, men, we need to tell them once and for all that this idealist blackmail and unbearable, if not criminal, demagoguery have gone on long enough. . . . Our primary theoretical, ideological and political (I say political) duty today is to rid the domain of Marxist philosophy of all the "Humanist" rubbish that is brazenly being dumped into it. It is an offense to the thought of Marx and an insult to all revolutionary militants.[75]

Because of Lévi-Strauss's stature in France and his work's pure anthropological interest, his books had already been published in English translation starting in the early 1960s. *Tristes Tropiques* appeared in 1961 and was ignored. *Structural Anthropology* (a collection of programmatic scholarly papers), however, and *Totemism*, gained some notice in 1963. *Race and History* had been distributed in English by UNESCO without fanfare back in 1952, for anyone now curious enough to dig it up in the library. Susan Sontag advocated for *Structural Anthropology*, as we have seen, and soon began her long-standing championing of Roland Barthes.

Appreciation of Lévi-Strauss, and those he had inspired, truly began to come into its own in the period 1966 to 1968 as part of a desire to understand what structuralism meant and what purpose it served for America. The specialist journal *Yale French Studies*, having access to the necessary

Francophone networks of scholarship, did a "Structuralism" special issue in 1966. It would be a mark of interest in the new French philosophy that a few years later Anchor paperbacks took up that issue's text—lock, stock, and barrel—to relabel it as a mass-market volume just entitled *Structuralism* in 1970, seemingly the first such popularizing anthology on the movement.[76] The legendary American intellectual historian of modern Europe, H. Stuart Hughes, in his book *The Obstructed Path* (1968), wrote a remarkable chapter on Lévi-Strauss that went all the way up to 1966 ("broadly, the philosophical turning point [in France] of the 1960's could be defined as a concerted attempt at the liquidation of traditional humanism").[77] He treated the other structuralist successors as thinkers who must also soon be well known in America. As yet, however, they were not well known enough to prevent the publisher, or its copy editor, from promoting on the back cover the "exhilaration" of a history that went all the way to "Lévi-Strauss" and "a mention of the great structuralist names, Althusser, Lacan, and Doucault [*sic*]."[78]

In January 1968, the *New York Times Sunday Magazine* published a long and surprisingly sophisticated profile of Lévi-Strauss; it was titled, "There Are No Superior Societies," and it emphasized his cultural relativism and defense of diversity (and skepticism of Western "development" interventions in traditional societies).[79] The winter issue of *Partisan Review*, which likely came out about the same time, still a preeminent vehicle of intellect in America (though nearing the end of that authority), published a long explanation for its readers on the question "What is Structuralism?" The answer, by Peter Caws, teasingly noted the system-thinking capacities of the new French movement ("Nowhere is the preoccupation with system . . . more evident than in French intellectual life"), but became quite respectful of structuralism's movement away from man and traditional humanism. In part the admiration seemed misplaced, because Caws partially translated the Cartesian "subject" into a too-fixed and straitened conception of "the self" (a very American preoccupation)—if structuralism moved away from the self, then it was practical and unnarcissistic. Caws came closer to the point when he announced that structuralism did not attack man because structuralism was misanthropic but because its methodology for knowledge no longer derived from the individual knower, the central Cartesian subject:

And the structuralists have come to the conclusion that . . . a good deal of our trouble arises out of the invention of the self *as an object of study*, from the belief that man has a special kind of being, in short from the emergence of humanism. Structuralism is not a humanism, because it refuses to grant man any special status in the world. Obviously, it cannot deny that there are individual men who observe, think, write, and so on (although it does not encourage them in the narcissistic effort of "finding themselves," to use the popular jargon). Nor does it deny that there are more or less cohesive social groups with their own histories and cultures. Nothing concrete recognized or valued by the humanist is excluded, only the theoretical basis of humanism. In order to clarify this point it is necessary to consider the central question of structuralism, which comes to dominate all discussions of it, namely, the status of the *subject*.[80]

Caws saw structuralism as a way out of believing in the rational individualist fixity that American social science had applied to human beings. It reintroduced the complexities of social interpretation—an awareness of reflexivity, observer effects, and the true relevance of other people—all in a way that could inspire activism: "Structuralism, in effect, advocates an engagement with the world, an abandonment of too much self-examination in favor of participation in some significative activity, which in structuring the world will bring the subject into equilibrium with it."[81]

The personal-level transfer of French theory to American academia is customarily dated to a conference in 1966 at Johns Hopkins. This is not an uncontested origin. *Yale French Studies* had its rival claim to priority, in canvassing and trying to assimilate the new thought for the American academic scene, and scoring the first paperback anthology for general readers. In time, the French and Comparative Literature Departments at Yale (headed by Jacques Ehrmann, Paul de Man, and Geoffrey Hartman), eventually reinforced by young professors of English (J. Hillis Miller and Harold Bloom), would make the most of the new French resources to extend the New Criticism that had arrived at Yale in its dotage (not just with William Wimsatt but Cleanth Brooks and Robert Penn Warren, too, who had assumed Yale professorships in their sunset years). The eventual "Yale school" was a strictly literary-critical and rather arcane development, however. Hopkins professors and graduate students, likewise rooted in the literature department but tied also to an interdisciplinary humanities center, had a wider remit, plus Ford Foundation funding, to bring a variety of French structuralists across the ocean to Baltimore for a face-to-face exchange—with follow-up consultations over several years.

François Cusset has cannily shown how the mixed personnel of the Hopkins conference, convened under the unimpeachable title "The Languages of Criticism and the Sciences of Man," complicated the arrival of French theory in the American university.[82] A generational divide had begun emerging in structuralism, which led the Baltimore hosts to bring over critics and revisionists of the major originators, at the very moment the Americans present were trying to find out just what structuralism was as an original whole. Both Claude Lévi-Strauss and Fernand Braudel had been consulted about the conference, the organizers proudly announced, but neither attended.[83] Elsewhere in the first generation of structuralists, Lacan and Barthes did make the journey, but Althusser did not. Foucault, who would in time transition to the "revisionist" side of the generational divide, likewise stayed home. A new term, "poststructuralism," had to be coined quickly in the United States for the critics of the still largely unknown original undertaking, though it had no equivalent in France. For that matter, it was a habitual trait of many of the thinkers identified as structuralists to deny participation in any movement.

The surprise of the conference was the success of a younger philosopher, essentially unknown to the Americans, named Jacques Derrida. He had spent a year abroad at Harvard a decade earlier, however, and was comfortable in English.[84] Lacan, by contrast, the most eminent guest, proved both accentually and conceptually unintelligible. Derrida presented a long analysis of Lévi-Strauss that was to become a significant text in the American environment for many years to come: his "Structure, Sign, and Play in the Human Sciences." He offered an explication of Lévi-Strauss's procedure, which sought to identify systems of thought by their internal differentiating relations. Still, Derrida charged, Lévi-Strauss frequently found himself in danger of depending on some positive anchor to the world, some empirical determinant, a "center," an immediate "presence" not purely relational and deferred. That anchorage would spell the collapse of a truly radical project to get beyond all such nostalgias, presences, and essences, which Derrida insisted should be the real aim. What Lévi-Strauss ought to do to solve his predicament was affirm, with Derrida himself, the complete absence of any origin or ground or empirical link. This improved method "borrows from a heritage the resources necessary for the deconstruction of that heritage itself,"[85] without seeking to reground it in fundamentals. The proper stance "affirms freeplay and tries to pass beyond man and humanism, the name man being the name of that being who, throughout the history of metaphysics or of ontotheology—in other words, through the history of all of his history—has dreamed of full presence, the reassuring foundation, the origin and the end of the game."[86]

To an extent, the young Derrida's whole specialty was in picking these freewheeling battles with other thinkers on the basis of an instability he claimed to identify through close readings of their texts, while affirming "play" and undecidability as his own freedom from the nostalgia for foundations: it was a philosophical method rooted in school training, but also a not unfamiliar way of gaining notice in France. If the language of getting beyond "the history of metaphysics," passing "beyond man and humanism," escaping an illusion of "presence," and so forth sounds familiar, however, it is because Derrida was also deploying the language of Heidegger.

Heidegger had not died in World War II. Denazification proceedings led by US occupation authorities barred him from teaching for some time after the war. In 1946, though, when the French philosopher Jean Beaufret first solicited Heidegger's opinions on humanism and Sartrean existentialism, the philosopher of Being was found alive and well less than fifty miles from the French border, in the Black Forest, in Todtnauberg, and proved eager for a new audience. His reply, the "Letter on Humanism," inaugurated the long interweaving of a quietist and irrationalist Heideggerian antihumanism into postwar French thought that competed with the scientific antihumanism of Lévi-Strauss.[87] In the "Letter on Humanism," Heidegger could hardly advocate further frenzied human activity to make the world whole after World War II, when, on his new post-Nazi view, the activity of man as the all-powerful subject was precisely what had led to the current catastrophe. Nihilism had resulted from a scientific adherence to Man rather than silent obedience to deeper, primordial, premetaphysical Being. Thus, the German philosopher demanded a new, ever-more fundamental thinking about the human that would go into a dimension beyond the dangerous *ratio*, the abstract intellect, and prior to all philosophy as such. Heidegger's primordial Being would emerge not in philosophizing but in a form of "thinking" beyond the *ratio*. And if thinking emerged in language, that language would not be the *logos* anymore but a kind of poeticizing, involuntary utterance beneath it. "The thinking that is to come is no longer philosophy, because it thinks more originally than metaphysics. . . . Thinking is on the descent to the poverty of its provisional essence. Thinking gathers language into simple saying. In this way language is the language of Being, as clouds are the clouds of the sky."[88]

Derridean tics that were to become well known in America in the 1970s and 1980s could be found in Heidegger first. The "destruction of metaphysics" in Heidegger, most vividly, becomes their "deconstruction" in Derrida.[89] The crossed-out words ("under erasure") had been adopted by Heidegger in the 1920s. The Heideggerian neologisms and altered orthography ("existentiell," or "ontotheology," which Derrida uses here) inspired Derrida's keyword *différance*, where the misspelling signifies the conceptual twist. Derrida, as a matter of philosophical substance, radicalized Heidegger—or took Heidegger altogether at his word in overcoming metaphysics—because he, too, proposed to go behind the *logos* and the *ratio*, but not *to* anything. There was no primordial Being waiting; rather, polysemy, the play of the endlessly deferred and undecidable refoundation of meaning in language. Derrida would radicalize Lévi-Strauss's anticolonial project, too, by proving that not just every ethnocentrism, but every *cen-*

trism, indeed every center, failed to hold up when you poked and prodded it enough. Things were not one, and pairs did not resolve into a separable two, nor escape the need for some additional supplement. Derrida ran Saussure's and Jakobson's structural linguistics, with its dependence on differentiated phonemes, against Heidegger's insistence that some error of human thinking about Being obscured true reception of Being, so that Derrida could insist on his own account that *all* of Western thought labored under the illusion of a phonetic basis for writing, a nostalgia for the speaking presence—"logocentrism." Derrida promised a liberatory science of self-deconstructing systems of written signs, a "grammatology."

Thus, a structuralist antihumanism and a late Heideggerian antihumanism turning into "poststructuralism" started to circulate in the United States—where their philosophical anchors had been obscured beneath successive Atlantic passages—and they served assorted local needs.[90] Deconstruction briefly revivified the flagging fortunes of the New Criticism in literature departments in the 1970s by giving a new theoretical and avant-garde cast to postwar procedures of extremely close readings of small passages of text. Formerly, one discovered the condition of "paradox" in language; now, its decenteredness and undecidability.[91] The much more long-lasting value to deconstruction, however—and the thing that redeems it—was somewhat different. An extension of anti-ethnocentrism into a wider methodology, however arcane, of opposition to centrisms of other sorts (sexism, white privilege, heteronormativity), made deconstruction inspirational and useful to those who had to forge new philosophical underpinnings for the major intellectual projects of the era after the rise of the new social movements: feminist scholarship, queer scholarship, critical race scholarship, and a variety of discourses of social difference. Marx had been essential to that thought. Psychoanalysis had been essential. The rediscovery of Beauvoir's *The Second Sex* redeemed a strongly existentialist sense of the body's condition and situation, and the dialectic of self and Other, to root ideas of social construction in the weightiness of lived experience. Still, deconstruction added something. With deconstruction, one could think oppositions without simply choosing one option over another. One could think of fundamental structural paradox and deferral in disciplines whose lines of explanation, unlike literature's readings of poems, had previously eschewed it.

Still, the radical critical historicism of Foucault, who dug through archives to unmask the metamorphoses of techniques of domination, fit much more immediately into the explanatory schemes of social thought than did deconstruction, even when Foucault's proofs of the dominating functions of the human sciences and of "humane improvements" in psychiatry, penal reform, or sexual liberation were unwelcome. According to the citation- and article-counting done by the sociologist Michèle Lamont in the mid-1980s, Derrida's diffusion primarily occurred through specialist literature journals, while Foucault enjoyed a wider diffusion across the social sciences. Foucault, too, along with Roland Barthes, and the old guard of Lévi-Strauss and Sartre, received attention in the highbrow mass journals, from the *New York Times* to the *New York Review of Books* to the UK *Guardian*, where Derrida did not much figure.[92]

This is not to say that by the end of the sixties, these midcareer French figures were becoming the central authorities that young people, activists, and counterculturists, or even significant numbers of academics, looked to in explanation of their new world. That triumph was still a few years off. They were new. The familiar intellectual authorities by 1969 were still Marcuse, Marx and Engels, Mao, Castro, Sartre, possibly Fanon, and perhaps also the more humanistic social scientists of the US fifties and sixties—the post-Freudian psychologists and analysts especially, Maslow and Fromm, Horney and Klein. But with the exceptions of Marx and Engels (and Fanon, for black power and third worldist perspectives), the value of those authorities was already on the wane, and events had outpaced humanist certainties. The complex of ideas that Americans began to call "French theory" allowed some sectors of US thought at the end of the 1960s and moving into the 1970s to lay the first piers for a cathedral ceiling over a grand new discourse.

Likewise, the personal presence of so many living French figures shouldn't obscure a parallel edifice that helped to make "Theory," as a capitalized whole spectrum of new thought, gain life beyond poststructuralism. This was German "critical theory," synonymous with the practice of Frankfurt school thinkers, which we have seen intersect with the original discourse of the crisis of man. The initial step back onto the bridge to this tradition was not difficult. Younger American thinkers simply had to follow the footnotes and biographical references from Herbert Marcuse to the colleagues and comrades he frequently invoked: Max Horkheimer and Theodor Adorno. The martyr Walter Benjamin had been kept alive in US memory by Arendt, who edited and introduced an English selection from his *Illuminations* in 1968. A young professor at Yale, Fredric Jameson, looked back to open up the significance of Marcuse, Adorno, and Benjamin, with Ernst Bloch and Georg Lukàcs beyond them, in *Marxism and Form* (1971), while a dissertation-writing graduate student historian, Martin Jay, traveled to Frankfurt to consult the archives and interview the living principals, producing a sourcebook on the Institute for Social Research for generations of American students entitled *The Dialectical Imagination* (1973). The German New Left was critically engaged with these thinkers, too, though in a different context. The Frankfurt school were those anti-Nazi authority figures who had returned under American auspices after the war, but now, in the person of Adorno (the youngest original member, left in charge of the institute after Horkheimer's retirement), proved altogether too conservative for the younger militants, calling the police down on them.[93] The *Dialectic of Enlightenment* was finally republished in German in 1969, however, then translated into English for the first time in 1972, creating its extraordinary influence for the future.

The essential thing is the greater conjuncture. At the end of the sixties, Theory gained intellectual and critical grandeur by helping to give meaning to the end, death, and dissolution of the sealed, self-sustaining Man that the earlier discourse of the crisis of man had tried to conceive. The "death of man," the "end(s) of man," the "death of the subject," the "author [who] has disappeared," the "death of the author": each of these phrases had a discrete meaning in a particular argument.[94] But all shared a will in the 1960s and 1970s to free the experience of *reading* the record of the past, and writing the artifacts of the present and future, from a constricted viewpoint that had come to be associated with the emphasis on Man. The end of man, if you scrape beneath the exhortations, really seems to spell the birth of a new kind of audience and receiver. To outsiders, the liturgy of ends and deaths sounded like nihilism or fanciful conceptual homicide. To those inside the arguments, this rhetoric marked the quest for new means of analysis to match the new sensibility the sixties had engendered. This work of demolition made more plausible the new ways of life that the liberation movements had promised. A previous era had made the human closed, for safety's sake, for the sake of "his" own protection. The lattice was made, again, open.

THE END OF THE DISCOURSE OF MAN AS SALVATION OR LOSS?

To one who has followed the crisis of man discourse from its significant origins in the 1930s to its exhaustion thirty or forty years later, the initial breakup of a vulgarized universal man can also look like the discourse's salvation or fulfillment. There should be no regrets for the decomposition if it contributed to renewed sixties demands of liberation. The question that remains is how much of the original discourse survived in the transformation of the crisis of man's critical energies for new fundamental investigations into the details of American life across the "sixties" divide.

If the real connection between the discourse of the crisis of man and the sixties as a period of social tumult is to be understood, it will not be explicable only in the usual terms of causal continuity or discontinuity. It will depend, rather, on what I have insisted on at the beginning: the significance of a discourse that could not fulfill itself in its own scientific terms but worked by authorizing participants to tell others that it *must* be fulfilled; the consequences of a discourse that established urgency and authority and left it available to be transferred to other practical workers—activists and creative writers—who inevitably found inside it forms of contradiction, overgeneralization, and deception. We must observe the power of an orienting discourse that turned back briefly to the abstraction of man, even when this seemed empty, to rebuild an anthropological tradition that a subsequent generation would sublate and surpass.

What has proven difficult for subsequent decades to redeem, however, is the degree to which the legacy of earlier crisis of man discourse may have produced two separate and purportedly incompatible philosophical projects of justice and liberation. Neither represents an unbroken descent from an earlier phase nor a privileged inheritor. Each was a new project, recast in the postwar period and subtly reworked year by year. One was universal analytic philosophy in its ethical and legalist projects; the other was antihumanist continental theory. When they spoke to each other, they seemed victims of divergent evolution and speciation, as if mockingbirds were courting finches. Perhaps this illusion could have been overcome, especially to the degree that, if they had spoken to each other continuously, they might have found their common histories, unexpected crossovers of personnel in the prewar period, and shared ancestors, not to mention common goals. Yet they didn't speak to each other long enough or frequently enough even to disagree. An institutional history will have to be written someday to establish just how it was possible that two great philosophical lines managed to operate with covered eyes, as if one were taught in the Arctic and the other in Antarctica while, in universities in the United States through the end of the twentieth century, these conversations were actually occurring in classrooms on opposite sides of a hallway. This blind antinomy—unresolvable still, though I have tried to give it a history—will be meditated in my conclusion.

We can end with one very rare, but extremely famous, face-to-face debate that took place between Michel Foucault and Noam Chomsky on Dutch television in 1971, taking up the subject of human nature.[95] No one will question Foucault's appropriateness as a representative of critique or continental thought. Chomsky may seem surprising as a representative of universalism and analytic philosophy. In fact, he is the ideal counterpart to Foucault from the Anglo-American side. His achievements in linguistics and philosophy of language and mind were already of worldwide significance. But these had occurred within a tighter biographical connection to postwar analytic philosophy than most readers might guess. Chomsky, too, was formed intellectually by some of the most idealistic universalist dimensions of the midcentury discourse of the crisis of man. We are now in a position to understand those elements, and what they stood for. Yet it is primarily because Chomsky is so radical a political critic, and has been so ardent a critic of state power (though following an opposite direction from the political radicalism and critique of power of Foucault), that the confrontation is symbolic.

Chomsky had drawn an unusual track through the intellectual world of his time.[96] The son of a Hebrew teacher and linguist in Pennsylvania, from a Jewish family richly aware of the thirties' and forties' worlds of radical politics, social justice, and Zionism, his orientation in life was always to the minor, the marginal, the forgotten, and the unjustly suppressed. On daytrips to New York City to linger with his uncle, a hunchbacked news vendor with a street-corner salon of émigré amateur politicians (as if in an episode from *The Adventures of Augie March*), Chomsky became an anarchist along the lines of Dwight Macdonald, profoundly influenced by Macdonald's journal *Politics* and its contributors. As a precocious student at the University of Pennsylvania, he resumed the study of linguistics he had first encountered at home, apprenticing with the great American structural linguistics leader Zellig Harris, and at the same time studied the new analytic philosophy of language under future pillars of the Harvard philosophical ascendancy, including Nelson Goodman. He moved to Harvard and its Society of Fellows, both then dominated by Quine.

Chomsky seems to have found Harvard pretentious, Quine somewhat trivial, and structural linguistics a dead end. Most important, he did not believe the reigning empiricist-behaviorist thesis, that every child in the world learned language by hearing individual statements spoken, and internalizing and linking each and every statement. Clearly, children who learned language came to understand the meaning of new individual statements they had never heard before. They could generate vastly more linguistically correct and meaningful statements than the number they had heard already. And the way in which they learned and made systematic errors and corrected them was developmentally routinized for human children and not dependent on each specific language and culture. At least, so Chomsky believed—although this put him in the company of discredited Enlightenment and Cartesian rationalists, who had assumed the mind had schemas of thought, language, and perception already inside it at birth.[97] (For Chomsky, such innate ideas were simply the consequence of Darwinian evolution, just like the rest of the features of the body: if our eye had evolved with the brain, why shouldn't our language have evolved with the brain?) Thus, Chomsky retrieved the notion of a Universal Grammar, awakened in every human mind by the ordinary stimulation of child development (touch, care, and companionship, as well as exposure to human speech).

This belief could only be decisive, however, if he could offer a formal or mathematized account of the structure of such a "deep" or "generative" grammar, and then the rules of simple "transformation" that could let such a structure generate all possible meaningful statements in the surface level of all human languages. And it would only become scientific if this account suggested particular features of the real process of language acquisition, mistakes, correction, and surface utterance that could be proven true or false by empirical research and experiment. By his midtwenties, this was the account Chomsky claimed to be able to give, and to have written out formally. Its transformation of linguistic debates, acceptance and rejection, appearance in different formulations and publications, and later improvements and changes occupied the rest of his strictly linguistic and scientific career.[98]

Chomsky's political and mass-intellectual career was only beginning at the time he was making his major linguistic discoveries. As a libertarian anarchist in the tradition of Thoreau, he would have been regularly arrested for nonviolent civil disobedience against unjust US laws, no matter what. The escalation of the Vietnam War, however, combined with Chomsky's sudden explosion of prestige for having invented a revolutionary "generative grammar" or "transformational grammar," meant that he was invited to get arrested at increasingly large and prominent demonstrations—which he felt obliged to do. (Chomsky plays a role in Norman Mailer's account of the protest at the Pentagon in *The Armies of the Night*; he slept next to Mailer in jail but is unmemorable in Mailer's eyes because he was seemingly completely indifferent to all publicity and drama.)

In the debate between Foucault and Chomsky, the two master thinkers reached the nub of their philosophical and political differences, even as they understood each other well on their respective positions.

> *FOUCAULT:* It seems to me that the real political task in a society such as ours is to criticize the working of institutions, which appear to be both neutral and independent; to criticize and attack them in such a manner that the political violence which has always exercised itself obscurely through them will be unmasked, so that one can fight against them.

> *CHOMSKY:* [T]here are two intellectual tasks. . . . [T]he one that I was discussing, is to try to create the vision of a future just society; that is to create, if you like, a humanistic social theory that is based, if possible, on some firm and humane concept of the human essence or human nature. That's one task. Another task is to understand very clearly the nature of power and oppression and terror and destruction in our own society.

> *FOUCAULT:* [D]oesn't one risk defining this human nature—which is at the same time ideal and real, and has been hidden and repressed until

now—in terms borrowed from our society, from our civilization, from our culture? . . . [T]he proletariat doesn't wage war against the ruling class because it considers such a war to be just. The proletariat makes war with the ruling class because, for the first time in history, it wants to take power. And because it will overthrow the power of the ruling class, it considers such a war to be just.

CHOMSKY: Yeah, I don't agree.

FOUCAULT: One makes war to win, not because it is just.

CHOMSKY: I don't, personally, agree with that.[99]

One can summarize these positions. Foucault's task is critique, to reveal the secret violent power that sustains a ruling class. The war against the rulers requires no justification beyond itself. Subordinate classes fight to win, to destroy the ruling class and take power themselves. The attempt to take the measure of human nature inevitably fails because it cannot conceive humanity outside of its present constitution. The tools it would use to study and describe human nature are determined by that constitution. Change the order of the world and you will learn what else human nature might be. Chomsky admits the existence of violent power and its secrets. His task, however, is justice, and adherence to a true standard of moral order, serving people's rational needs, revealed by their universal human nature, which scientific reason can discern. Good people defend justice in defiance of what the state or ruling class believes. The reference of struggle is always to a known normative order, a better justice for all, which is anticipated as the conflict's consequence.

Here were two moral and intellectual heroes of the late century. They had the whole twentieth century behind them. They differed on points of first philosophy. To many who have followed them, the divisions seemed insurmountable. Coming one or two generations later, we have to ask what difference their differences should make.

CONCLUSION

Moral History and the Twentieth Century

What should be the starting point for twenty-first-century thought?

A friend, older than I, who had been educated in the 1980s and 1990s, once usefully clarified for me that he believed the intellectual tragedy of his generation had been a division between equally attractive camps. On one side, human rights and humanitarianism defended the human individual. On the other, the critique of the subject and the discovery of difference exposed the all-too-human coercions that kept the individual from true liberation. Each camp thought the other naive.

I came to this division as it was losing force at the turn of this century, though no new formation has wholly displaced it even now. The duality belonged to the university, but it also rules in political and moral life, in spheres of policy, activism, charity, and law. Universalism or difference, human rights or political liberation, law or critique, normativity or the struggle for power and representation—between these poles the thinker is often asked to choose a whole temperament and style of life. Different sets of authors and texts and cardinal references follow, different styles of argument, practice, and writing, almost different cultures of thought. The partition of the thinkable stood out most starkly at an abstract but also deep and disturbing level in an antagonism between "philosophy" (analytic or Anglo-American) and "theory." I found it hard to see this as anything but a folly.

Those who allied themselves with the Enlightenment and reason against what was called theory, and those who spoke the language of theory without a practical sense for how to liberate their imprisoned subjects, were equally well intentioned. But both risked depriving themselves reciprocally of resources for struggle and of the most complex formulations of truth. Humanitarianism vowed to protect the free soul in the face of the most extreme violence and tyranny, but always somewhere else than here. The ugliness and venality of real politics were denied, and the certainties of human rights—rights for someone else—were never risked, never put at stake. And theory sought to free the political subject from chains inside the core of civilization and its deceptive consensus, right here. But it struggled to find large public constituencies willing to be thus freed—it missed the drive to universalize, even in the quest by the different *for* power.

Power always holds the capacity to make the universal more attractive than difference, and the allure of joining the powerful superior to the satisfactions of being undeceived and critical (and struggling always from the margins). The most universal aspiration of the oppressed under such conditions may be a will to join the oppressors as soon as possible, and of many of the different to rationalize themselves as mainstream.

The universal, in its legitimate and even tyrannical institutions (law, the state, the nation, rights) hides trapdoors, tunnels, and tools installed by previous liberation struggles for its inner dismantling and reformation. Universalism turns out to be monolithic and exclusionary until the instant it suddenly shows itself to be fragile and alterable—desperate for new inclusions and relegitimation. Power may not be lying in the streets but it might be lying in the halls of power, not yet used up by tyrants. Sheep might have to put on wolves' clothes, to fight as wolves do; of course, the innocent may risk bloodying their own jaws—captured by discourses they should have known were predatory.

These antinomies turn round and round, until they resemble a pinwheel, exerting a hypnotic attraction. The needful thing, it seemed to me, would be to arrest the ceaseless spin, anatomize the parts, and see the construction as a whole.

My hope for the foregoing pages is that they answer a set of mysteries, and that these can now be recognized not as mysteries of arbitrary interest (or specialist fascinations, or effluences of one lone strand of historical inquiry) but as peepholes upon particular obstacles and stoppages that issued from the end of one century and now block thought in another.

In many books the author's motivations appear at the beginning. In this book I place them at the end. Without providing the example of an alternative construction of mid-twentieth-century thought, I could not assume that readers would know if such a reconceptualization was possible or desirable. In seeking my own starting point for twenty-first-century thought, it has seemed obvious to me that opposed projects passed on to us by preceding generations belong together, in a comprehensive analysis and defense of "the subject," both *here* and *there*, against obvious threats and recondite perils. Yet the means of unification, like the real structures of division, are never obvious.

Hence, the significance of my mysteries and solutions. In reverse chronological sequence: Why did theory succeed (in disciplines of literature, anthropology, and one side of political theory and historical study but not in philosophy, economics, and the other side of political science and historical study)? Because it furnished activist thought in the 1960s with depictions of grand systems, operating by nonhuman and nonindividualistic interactions of authorities and rules, structured through differentiation but capable of being disrupted by true difference, that matched the sense of official reason's absurdity and irrationality, yet valued the disjunctive possibilities the new protagonists of social movements represented. Why did the critique of the human subject succeed? Because in the perennial balancing act between explanations by individual action and those by social structure, the crisis of man, lasting too long, had come to weigh too heavily on the side of a sentimental and methodological individualism, and required a correction. Why had an analytic or Anglo-American line diverged? Because Austrian and German émigrés' insurgent efforts—against fascism and anti-Semitism—to purge language of irrationality and mysticism had been adopted by young figures in America and England with a different will: to emulate natural science and join the triumphant postwar preeminence of the "behavioral sciences." This new research program combined wartime engineering approaches to social research with an expansion of funding by the state—adding up to rigorization, and purification of the study of human cultures and beliefs from the side of the winners, the powerful. And yet the divergent line of philosophy found itself, when its activist and reforming personnel responded to the social transformations of the sixties, in possession of a crucial tributary of that earlier, antifascist and universalizing project—the rebirth of human rights. Why had human rights been reborn? Because world government had proven impossible, true internationalism had failed, and hopes fell back upon the solitary individual as the only ground on which an ideology and philosophy of resistance to the predations of states had been articulated. Moreover, it was an ideology phrased in the language of rights, treaties, and governance, which states might actually honor; or, if not "honor," then seize to use against other states, seeking to gain by exposing their rivals' flaws, thus inadvertently benefiting the oppressed in each country.

The paths by which I thought I might follow human rights and the discourse of the crisis of man directly to equal rights for African Americans and American women proved to be obstructed. They were blocked by racism, government hostility, and the demands of the Cold War. They required, rather, some further metamorphoses and reapplications or inversions of discourse, such that the crisis of man, which helped issue in human rights as one outcome, would also issue in others. Toward 1960, why could the crisis of man be reconstructed as domestic? Because totalitarianism abroad had inspired a rhetoric of total responsibility at home, a free-floating responsibility encouraged by moralists, activists, and the government, too. As the post-Nazi decades wore on, and the external threat of the Soviets seemed less threatening, an ethos of total responsibility did find itself more plausibly engaged at home. How could African Americans and women, in that moment, reemerge despite and through a public discourse of man that had excluded them? Because the discourse had become both mature and tiresome, allowing a new advocacy art of "punning," multiplying references and standpoints within the discourse of crisis, advancing and retracting claims to universality and to difference. How did white repudiation of whiteness emerge, which served to advance the claims of recognition on behalf of difference by the late 1960s? In part because of a displacement of fears of tyranny from the enemies of "universal man" onto that universal man himself—in the Pentagon making war, in the White House, in the squad car—no longer humanity as a whole but a tyrant mannequin, the Man. Franz Boas's commitment that "the world must be made safe for differences," as Ruth Benedict had once glossed his cultural relativism in the language of Wilsonian liberalism,[1] could be radicalized by Lévi-Strauss, in the era of decolonization, to make the only visible universal of mankind "ethnocentrism," and true humanism, as a scientific and philosophical attitude, the recognition and admiration of difference: "Humanity is forever involved in two conflicting currents, the one tending toward unification, and the other towards the maintenance or restoration of diversity. . . . [T]he true contribution of a culture consists, not in the list of inventions which it has personally produced, but in its difference from others."[2] His campaign against those who insisted the different must "advance" to the stature of the universal was compressed, as we have seen, into an aphorism: "The barbarian is, first and foremost, the man who believes in barbarism."[3]

The fact that so much rethinking of universality and difference transpired in "disciplines of the concrete," such as literature and anthropology (rather than philosophy), encouraged me to return to some postwar mysteries about the novel (available from my own training and experience as a critic of literature). The novel was briefly a space in which the new authority of unmarked, universal man could be borrowed and spread, and yet where its contradictions and gaps would come into relief. Why? Because, from one direction, it had been elevated, in the absence of religious and social unanimity and authority, to a prose art that could still sermonize, prophesize, and preach of ultimate things; because, from another direction, the transforming university and its generations of scholar-intellectuals in a nationalist project had coffered the past of American literature into Old and New Testaments, asserting the legitimacy of US culture as a rival to European cultures—and insisting new novels must keep up this high office of art and prophecy; and yet, by recalcitrant habit, because novels were still composed from below, requiring the depiction of plausible, generally lower-class American characters, who spoke vernacular language and embodied vernacular conflicts. There, high philosophical obligations must intersect the ordinary.

Behind all of this, once we enter the zone of midcentury and penetrate its dusky nebulae—Cold War, world war, the thirties—we face mysteries attributable to the long sweep of twentieth-century thought. Surprising as it is at this late date, I think we really don't know everything that we should of what underlies various movements and conflicts that have persisted from 1933, 1938, or 1945 to now. In my preface I spoke of the elemental chaos from which galaxies of thought and discourse are generated. In our cosmology of the twentieth century, once the early-century movements of pragmatism and progressivism are not the only or predominant US streams of thought in view, our science becomes boxed in with an astonishing rigidity by political polarities and taxonomies—of (political) liberal, conservative, socialist, anti-Communist, Cold War, New Right, Old Left, New Left—not only in the bygone polemical conflicts of our sources and documents but in historiography, still. There is a chronological hole in anyone's effort to read through the last century, even between the definite, authoritative intellectual history of James Kloppenberg's *Uncertain Victory* concerning Progressivism, or Louis Menand's popular *The Metaphysical Club* about pragmatism, and the piecemeal story picked up in Daniel Rodgers's *Age of Fracture* (in the 1970s and 1980s), or Howard Brick's *Age of Contradiction* in the 1960s and 1970s—nor need the accounting of the second half of the century abandon underlying syntheses as these last books seem to do even in their titles.[4]

Why do we have this hole in the historiography? In part, this book has suggested, because we haven't tracked the seemingly baffling and unpromising but actually underlying and discernible processes of constitution of the human subject as the subject of human nature, history, technology, and faith, not at the apodictic but the maieutic level—in negotiations and articulations of man and the human. Yet for my own wider purposes, this opens a still larger mystery than anything reducible to lacunae in historiography of the twentieth century. What are we really to do in the face of those projects that do come back multiply across modernity (as well as, perhaps differently, in premodern periods), not necessarily serving the same function in each return, nor even addressed to the intentions each instance promises or proclaims upon its surface? A prime example is the sort of anthropological inclination or quest that I have traced. Countless scholarly sources can show us convincingly that such reorientations occurred in the moments we think of as most "modern" or modernizing and may be almost constitutive of modernity ever since the first breach with the Middle Ages. If I take up the book I've been reading as I write this conclusion, an eminent Italian scholar of the Renaissance declares that in the fundamental change that marks the Renaissance, "scholastic distinctions and divisions were rejected, the very conception of philosophy was changing because its

chief object was now man—man was at the centre of every inquiry ...
[when] the direct appeal to classical models demanded the rejection of
traditional epistemological methods. ... In this process philosophy was
stripped of its ahistorical character and swept up in the transience and
mutability of human existence ... Throughout this period, however, the
dominant philosophical theme was the centrality of man."[5]

———

There is something moving underneath. This is the epochal consciousness
of advancing time, *Neuzeit*, modernity—time reborn as Renaissance,
shadows clarified in the Enlightenment. The new schemas of history, new
conceptions of technics, new faiths of the period since *it* happened—whatever it was, whatever we choose to call it—reflect the break with the medieval, the start of the clock of secular progress rather than patient waiting
for a Second Coming, the entry into our world of thought. "Our world"—
whose world? That of someone at the center—man, human, subject, individual—defining the ground of authority and hope. The specifics and contingencies of discrete historical moments keep revisiting this question of
the subject reconstructed against some underlying, mutable, but lawful
background (whether one considers it a fantasy of history or a truth of social development) of the modern.

I do not introduce this underlying feature of the conceptualization of
historical time to defend or legitimate it—after all that I have said about
its indeterminacies and yet its consequences for thought in a limited, quite
narrow period, 1933–73, which I have tried to make concrete. Rather,
these concepts of time bequeath us as scholars either a deeper etiology to
confront or else an undiagnosed syndrome, a kind of repetition compulsion in the domain of high intellect and our efforts to grasp our own era
in thought. This professional deformation has to do with the sinking of
"posts." The "postmodern," the "posthistorical," and recently the "posthuman" have arrived as paradigms for thinking through the meaningful
points of the contemporary trajectory of the West. But their virtue must
not be that they are disconnected one from the other, or delusively accepted as true breaks with predecessors rather than mutations, assimila-
ble to our thought only within a common frame. The frame is the issue,
not these bumps or corners.

Begin with the postmodern. The year 1973 is not a bad or unpopular date
for the opening of this new era as it is commonly conceived. And powerful
diagnoses of the break with the previous era of the modern began arriving
by the end of the decade of the 1970s. Jencks's *The Language of Post-
Modern Architecture* appeared in 1977. Fredric Jameson delivered his

Whitney Museum lecture, "Postmodernism, or the Cultural Logic of Late Capitalism," in 1982. Jean-François Lyotard's *The Postmodern Condition: A Report on Knowledge* was presented to the government of Quebec in 1979, then appeared in English in 1984—moving the postmodernism debate into the American gardens of French theory. David Harvey's *The Condition of Postmodernity*, shifting it further into theory's idea of economics and social theory, arrived in 1990.

Perry Anderson, in *The Origins of Postmodernity*, an intellectual history of postmodernism intended to honor Frederic Jameson's ingenuity, notes important early uses of both the postmodern word and concept shortly after World War II. Anderson singles out, for example, the ambitious program of the poet and intellectual Charles Olson to develop new modes of thought and life that would supersede the merely modern. The founder of projective verse wished to acknowledge his own era as "postmodern"—and to push it there, beyond the limits of the tradition of the modern West.[6]

But Olson's intervention at the start of the 1950s was not as sui generis as it might seem. As a professor and then rector at Black Mountain College, a cauldron of the avant-garde, he was linked to the likes of Robert Rauschenberg, Josef Albers, John Cage, and Merce Cunningham, figures who Susan Sontag would proclaim as avatars of the new sensibility in the sixties. Olson was the bearer to them of significant strains of the crisis of man. As a PhD student at Harvard he had participated in the Melville revival under F. O. Matthiessen. His wartime career had been spent at the Office of War Information (OWI), cauldron of New Deal–era artists and reconstructors of postwar Americanism from Arthur Schlesinger Jr. to Malcolm Cowley. He undertook personally to organize an "Institute of the New Sciences of Man" at Black Mountain in 1952, addressing "the totality of the problem of the phenomenon of man."[7] But high intellectual debate on the crisis of man had already been proceeding for some time at Black Mountain; none other than Erich Kahler, author of *Man the Measure* (and a protagonist of the émigré discourse in chapter 2), had delivered his series of influential lectures on "the evolution and transformation of the human form and of human consciousness" there in 1947, which in the 1950s became *Man the Measure*'s "sequel."[8] A voluntaristic dimension of the "postmodern," one must begin to see, is already woven into the later century diagnoses of "postmodernity," post-1973, as an unanticipated and undesired breaching of history. Most important, what Olson actually called for, in full, as his ambitions for the new world of man, was to "put men forward into the post-modern, the post-humanist, the post-historic."[9] And these three terms and concepts *together* formed the basis of a variety of manifestations discoverable from 1945 forward, rediscovered later by theorists as if they were analytic novelties rather than part of a preexisting intellectual narrative of chronology. Postmodernism, posthumanism, and the end of history are all parts of the same thing.

Try, next, the posthistoric. "The end of history" attained popular intellectual prominence at the fall of the Berlin Wall in 1989.[10] Francis Fukuyama's *The End of History and the Last Man* spelled out a case that is often remembered as mere liberal democratic or United States triumphalism, an opportunistic response to events.[11] Its epitome was this: With the dissolution of the Soviet Union, no alternative constitution of the state remained to rival the superiority of representative democracies whose true metabolism was free market capitalism. As Fukuyama actually unfolded his quite careful argument, however, he was consecutive in his steps and wholly honest about his sources. His theoretical structure was not his own, but Alexandre Kojève's, who, in Paris in the 1930s, had laid out the conditions for the end state of the West as a fulfillment of Hegel's schematization of Enlightenment universal history. That revision, publicized and sustained in the United States by Leo Strauss and his disciples at the University of Chicago (where Fukuyama found it), preserved the crisis structures of thought into the later fin de siècle.[12] Alongside triumphalism, Fukuyama retained the other dimension of the traditional argument, too— that a final state of convenience, peace, and administered satisfaction would, by evolving a technical structure to complete the conquest by science of outer and inner nature, make man, as a creature of passions and spirit, cease to exist. It would then unmoor criteria for preferring this end state (as fulfillment of the dreams of historical mankind) or guiding its long-term management. And besides the reference of Nietzsche's "last man" for this possibility, Fukuyama had recourse to none other than C. S. Lewis and his 1943 *Abolition of Man*, and Lewis's crisis-era "men without chests," human animals without human spirit.[13]

The German intellectual historian Lutz Niethammer, also in 1989, produced an account of posthistory (in German, it is, paradoxically, *das Posthistoire*, "which sounds like a French neologism, [but] does not actually exist in French"[14]) in which he identified more instances, going back to 1945 and even to the nineteenth century, with brilliant analytic insights into posthistory's components and core. In one strain of posthistory, there was essentially "a technocratic programme for the overcoming of history, which is understood as a lengthy epoch of chaotic conflicts. . . . [H]istory is identified as a process of subjective, meaning-oriented disputes, and posthistory refers to a condition where world civilization functions as a huge, scientifically trained apparatus and culture becomes petrified into a natural phenomenon." In the other strain, "the idea [is] that history is over, and that life will now continue in more or less animal form"; "the picture that

looms for theorists of posthistory is of a mortal life lived without any seriousness or struggle, in the regulated boredom of a perpetual reproduction
of modernity on a world scale. The problematic of posthistory is not the
end of the world but the end of meaning."[15] We can thus see how posthistory, putting aside the various evaluative positions of for and against, political Right and political Left, integrates dimensions of posthuman championing (the "becoming animal" of first-world humans, so dear to our early
twenty-first century); also, of postmodern critique (a similarity even more
evident elsewhere in Niethammer's analysis—"the focus on posthistory
or *Posthistoire*, with its arbitrary simulation of fragments of the past, belongs to an 'as if' aesthetic, a game with signs which, though quoted out
of context and no longer 'in force,' still seem to retain their power of
attraction"[16]).

In France and Germany, Niethammer convincingly locates "the formative stage of the post-history thesis, amid the radical changes that took
place before and after the Second World War."[17] If one has the wartime
and postwar United States as one's research area, it becomes possible to
add examples from this country: Roderick Seidenberg's *Post-historic Man*
(1950), for one. Eccentric but far from unknown, the book won guarded
praise from both Reinhold Niebuhr and Lewis Mumford because, though
each shared and appreciated Seidenberg's diagnosis, he (analogously with
Charles Olson) welcomed the coming of the completely integrated, machinic,
posthistoric and posthuman age the traditionalists sought to forestall.[18]

The posthuman is, of course, the newest break with modernity, the restrictive Enlightenment, the Cartesian subject—at least, the newest catchphrase to inspire thinkers at the turn of the twenty-first century and since.
"Posthuman*ism*" is admitted to be an older and more continuous affair, a
break with many of the same sorts of naive humanism that antihumanism
opposed in the era of French theory. But "the posthuman" itself, also sometimes identified as the "more than human," the "beyond the human," the
"becoming animal" and "cyborg," is proffered as if it constituted a reconceptualization. There is something reasonable in this, of course—to the
degree that practices, technics, events, and the mind-sets that accompany
them do change, and changes of degree eventually constitute changes of
kind. Historical novelty does exist, and it is analytically essential. But
"posthumanism" (old-style) possessed much more of "the posthuman" (new-
style) than one might expect. More important, "the posthuman" is inbuilt
to the chronologies and irresistible schemas of conceptualizing the modern; one must not miss how the category and its attributes had already
been programmed for its present "discoverers," and the degree to which it
is already partly contained and constituted by the postmodern and posthistorical (themselves analytic epiphenomena of the same background

historical schemas). Asserting that the posthuman furnishes everyone the means for a *voluntary* psychic break with the Enlightenment or the anthropocentrism of the past, meanwhile, is an unanalytic wrinkle more like the antique, maieutic advocacy of the crisis of man and its promises of re-enlightenment.

Suppose we just take up the late New York Intellectuals, a restrictive and imposing but hardly unique or particular foresightful grouping. Susan Sontag could speak dismissively of the supposed "'post-humanist' era now upon us" already in 1966 because it was already a part of the critical discourse on history, technology, and humanity developing since the war.[19] She was answering Leslie Fiedler, who had one year earlier taken up "the end of man . . . the transcendence or transformation of the human—the prospect of the radical transformation (under the impact of advanced technology and the transfer of traditional human functions to machines) of *Homo sapiens* into something else: the emergence—to use the language of Science Fiction itself—of 'mutants' among us."[20] Fiedler unequivocally declared: "the post-human future is now, and if not we, at least our children, are what it would be comfortable to pretend we still only foresee."[21] Chronologically, this change inevitably framed itself as the sudden fulfillment or mutation of a process that Fiedler found had been inaugurated by the Enlightenment, as 1776, 1789, or 1800; yet he felt "we may have reached a second critical point right now."[22] Six years earlier, in the same journal, Irving Howe was speaking of the "postmodern" and pulling out familiar prospects of the posthuman and posthistorical. "Let us assume for a moment that we have reached the end of one of those recurrent periods of cultural unrest, innovation and excitement that we call 'modern.'"[23] Howe's interest was largely in the novel. The "postmodern" was a category of literary-intellectual classification first. But his interest in the novel came down to its revelation of society's future. "The more serious of the 'postmodern' novelists . . . [have] begun to envisage that we may be on the threshold of enormous changes in human history."[24] What did those changes add up to? Nothing less than posthistory, in one of its central guises (an essential strain of the "end of history" thesis): "[T]he human creature, no longer a Quixote or a Faust, will become a docile attendant to an automated civilization. . . . [and] the 'aura of the human' will be replaced by the nihilism of satiety."[25]

My point is not that nothing is new under the sun. Nor am I trying to move any marker of intellectual priority backward in time. The point, again, to insist upon is that the postmodern, the posthistoric (or "end of history"), and the posthuman (not only the posthumanist) are essentially one complex. Pick up any of these appendages and you may miss seeing the sunken torso, but you will make the other limbs quiver. It is remarkable how one always finds traces of the others, in each account apparently re-stricted to one "post." The complex itself is a Frankenstein put together of spare parts cast off by modernity or the Enlightenment. We lengthen its life when we put energy into it at any part, any extremity, in sympathy *or* hostility—just as the thinker who hails reason and enlightenment does when he tries overtly to preserve the unfinished project of modernity.

We have not solved the problems of time and progress that the thinkers of wartime and midcentury tried to fix in re-enlightenment. We do achieve something in critique and analysis—and then fall back, in efforts to be-come morally superior to this past, autotherapeutically. The domains of the questionable legacy of the Enlightenment that they sought to shore up under pressure of war and fascism are translated, in the present weight-lessness, into illusory fractures and endings and revolutions, as if these old problems had one day just floated free. The four domains of re-enlightenment thought are continuous with the later, putative breaks and "posts." The problem of technics in the era of the crisis of man becomes in large measure the problematic we call the postmodern. The problem of history and progress generates posthistory. The problem of man and fun-damental anthropology translates into posthumanism and then "the post-human." The most mysterious and multiple of the earlier domains—what I called "faith" following the crisis of man usage, as a category that included both worries about secular ideology and about the inheritance of religion and theology—may seem to lack a clear opposite number in what comes after the end, excluded from the holy trinity of the postmodern, posthis-toric, and posthumanist. Of course, this isn't so. One only needs to dip into the current discourses of "the postpolitical" and "the postsecular" to find more compulsive repetition and illusory escape in the disguise of critical thinking. We insist that we come just after the moment of break or fracture with normalcy and tradition, that we are the first to discover a new muta-tion just coming into being—more Columbuses of the near at hand, to paraphrase Bellow. Perhaps we could show the true dimensions in which this is so—if we would just focus on the practical and concrete. But our ways of situating these revelations of our condition are not so practical, and therefore *not* new—the abstract belatedness came long ago, and was itself constituted by the chronology of newness, beginnings, and progress, and *it scripts our novelties for us*. Is modernity a bit like the weather—ev-eryone complains, but no one will do anything about it? Surely, though, it is a dereliction of thought to suppose, whenever one arrives *after* some-thing, that the plunge into darkness and unknownness must have just oc-curred, and the flash of dawn have just been seen on the horizon.

If we wanted to seek the new, to break through the complex of repeti-tions, it would require confronting modernity, *Neuzeit*, as the cage of our conceptions, and returning to the basic concrete project of taking apart and exhibiting our underlying notions of sequence, record-keeping, causation, explanation, obligation, necessity, objects, and subjects.

———

When I began the research for this book in 2003 and 2004, liberal intellectuals of a sort that I thought might be interested in the questions I hoped to plumb—of universalism and critique in the last century, human rights and political struggle—were busy preparing the justification of the US invasion of Iraq, somehow in connection with a response to the September 11 attacks, and on the basis of a renewed anthropological vision of "who we are" (in the West) against a new "they" figured as totalitarian.[26] I felt each day in the library that I was enmeshed, as a researcher, reading crisis of man discourse, in ideas these thinkers must have heard when young and now were disastrously repeating. Thus, the dead generations weigh on the brains of the living. Perhaps if I could lay bare the limitations of the earlier discourse, I consoled myself, false foundations and certainties could be discouraged in future moments of error. So I felt I had something relevant to pursue.

As I finish these last revisions (and type this conclusion) in 2014, a different set of progressive intellectuals whose interests and motivations I also hope my work might intersect—reformers and activists, say, who have a stake in both alternatives of normativity and difference—have been embarking on invocations of "the Anthropocene" as part of a reaction to the failure, thus far, to create political means to forestall global warming and catastrophic climate change. The parties concerned in this discourse point out that modernity constitutes an age in which industry, modern science, and technics, and thus *Anthropos*, humanity as a whole, dramatically changed the composition and behavior of Earth's land, atmosphere, animal species, and vegetation, to the point where the human species is now the force most recognizable in traditional geological samples used for scientific research. The renaming of our geological age—if we exit the Holocene and enter the Anthropocene—occurs with the hope of motivating a new research program across the social sciences and humanities. Its urgency now feels to me a bit like a public relations effort, motivated by the maddening presence of climate-change deniers in society and the wish to win over bystanders by some new conceptualization that "we" are doing this, or "we are all in this together, as humanity." Yet this discourse of the Anthropocene, like other environment- and "thing"-oriented intellectual projects of our moment, strikes me even more forcefully as another kind of work done by thinkers upon themselves, with little either of analytic signif-

icance or useful activism likely to come out of it, but guaranteeing an obligation for mental, rhetorical, or spiritual participation by neighbors and
colleagues in every field of inquiry, regardless of anything determinatively
argumentative or truth-finding at stake.

One begins to read, with disarming frequency, that a "key challenge for
social sciences and the humanities is thus to explore the extent to which
the human condition . . . has changed in the Anthropocene era and the nature of this change. This presents a real challenge to the humanities and
social sciences: does our conception of the human have to change?"[27] "Species may indeed be the name of a placeholder for an emergent, new universal history of humans that flashes up in the moment of the danger that is
climate change. . . . [C]limate change poses for us a question of a human
collectivity, an us, pointing to a figure of the universal that escapes our
capacity to experience. . . . It is more like a universal that arises from a
shared sense of a catastrophe. We may provisionally call it a 'negative universal history.' "[28]

The re-enlightenment that faced the "shared sense of catastrophe" in
Europe proposed exactly the same. And one recalls the maieutic coercions, and unpredictability of implication, of an earlier moment when
scholars on all sides were obligated to speak of "man." So a frustrating
sense of repetition without insight persists.

Speaking as a layperson, or a contemporary, a mind within the flow of
time and decision—in simplest terms, *outside* the guise of scholar—my
feeling from investigating the efforts of the mid-twentieth century to re-
open a fundamental philosophical anthropology, bearing upon the most
urgent crises, under the question "What is man?," is that, for my own time,
I want to tell my contemporaries: Stop! Anytime your inquiries lead you to
say, "At this moment we must ask and decide *who we fundamentally are*,
our solution and salvation must lie in a new picture of ourselves and humanity, this is our profound responsibility and a new opportunity"—just
stop. You have begun asking the wrong analytic questions for your moment. Your answers will be preprogrammed in ways you can't even begin
to imagine or see, which the future will unhappily exhume. Answer, rather,
the practical matters, concrete questions of value not requiring "who we
are" distinct from what we say and do, and find the immediate actions necessary to achieve an aim. Important investigations of "who we are" can
exist and are conceivable, but you can be sure that they transpire somewhere else than here in our sermonizing about responsibility, urgency, and
hapless prescription. The consequence of such questions in *this* context
will be a maieutic discourse of the background politics to rule and regulate what is thinkable, what must be spoken of and genuflected to, collect-

ing participants and legitimacy rather than accomplishing consequential thought.

Speaking as a scholar and historian, of course, who has tried to see and show all that the maieutic does *other* than investigate in the ordinary way—who can afford to be without judgment, because his sight is purely retrospective; who watches how thought and action develop by unexpected paths, and how seeming closure in one place inspires an opening in another—I can say nothing of this sort, and am embarrassed to have revealed the contemporary person's outraged instinct. How could I tell anyone to desist? How can the dispassionate analyst ever discourage even what seems to him to be folly? Persist in folly! Without folly, how would we have history?

———

In each line of work I pursue, in this book and elsewhere, I understand the overarching project to be the attempt to constitute a history of morals, understood as the history of the construal of necessity and obligation, a study that must be, at its starting point and ending point, *amoral.*

The fundamental question of morals, the element that makes any inquiry moral and that draws the boundaries to an incipient history of morality, is the appearance of an *ought.* An obligation and constraint of some kind, with certain sorts of emotions attached to it, certain cognitions, characteristic declarations of urgency and necessity, also perhaps feelings of rectitude that exceed the practical, instrumental, or sensuous—this describes the raised flag that calls the historian of morality to pursuit. However, it should be a virtue in a history of morality not to guess in advance what any of the relevant emotions, thoughts, declarations, and surpassing feelings are—or where in society the meaningful constraints and *oughts* will be found.

In truth, when I began this project, I was pursuing an altogether different element of the history of morals through its twentieth- and twenty-first-century development. This was the question of the attribution of obligations, moral status, or standing, to categories of beings that were *not* adult men and women. Children, animals, wilderness, nature, environment, fetuses, biological materials, cultural artifacts, technical creations—in the majority of cases, subjects and objects that were not human. That will now require another book.

What interrupted as of increasing importance, until I had to put the original inquiry aside, was the way in which Man and the constitution of the human subject crowded out those other subjects of obligation, in a particular time and across many milieus in the mid-twentieth century, but with the languages, urgencies, and feelings of that other kind of militant reform. Man must be reawakened, rethought—here was a different kind of ought, a different constraint and necessity—in ways that slipped out of the grasp of the argumentative, and out of the realm of narrow determinations, into an unknown order of fears and sentiments, in much the way that radical reform does. So I focused on the anomaly in the historical sequence I was developing—this period of fundamental concentration, explicitly, on man and the human, the universal subject and the supposed core, beginning in the era of totalitarian threat—rather than on the expansion of moral significance to others.

This raised the pursuit of the maieutic and maieutic discourse, as I have defined it in the preface, which of course constitutes another dimension of the history of morals as I anticipate it. Maieutics, as a branch of study, historicizes the discourses and "sciences" of the should, too—and the second-order production of discourses that require people to undertake those first-order discourses. What must we think about, what must we talk about, for the sake of—"humankind"?

No doubt an author sees his subject wherever he looks. Yet I feel we are entering another confused and ignorant moment when it comes to the construction of our fundamental subject, whatever, whoever "he" or "she" may be. And I—all of us—face it, as we must, enmeshed in the stupidity and mediocrity of our own time. "They" seem to be putting up a giant face again, made of words and warnings, manifestos and credos, papers of declaration and prophecy, objurgations and reverences; the face of the subject (of history, of humanity), the face of "us," with new "discoveries," "revolutions," and urgencies; installing it somewhere in the City, demanding our assent (or acquiescence), a mask filled, perhaps, with confetti—

The old debate returns, whether to try to live in one's moment and let it be or accept Ahab's madness to see what is in back of it: "To be enraged with a dumb thing, Captain Ahab, seems blasphemous." "Hark ye yet again— . . . If man will strike, strike through the mask! How can the prisoner reach outside except by thrusting through the wall?"[29]

NOTES

CHAPTER 1
INTRODUCTION

1. The United States Declaration of Independence (1776), France's Declaration of the Rights of Man and of the Citizen (1789).

2. Will Herberg, *Judaism and Modern Man: An Interpretation of Jewish Religion* (New York: Farrar, Straus and Young, 1951), 3.

3. Reinhold Niebuhr, *The Nature and Destiny of Man: A Christian Interpretation*, vol. 1, *Human Nature* (1941; Louisville, KY: Westminster John Knox Press, 1996), 1. Niebuhr likely delivered these lines originally in 1938 or 1939 in lectures in Scotland, discussed further in chapter 2. On the route by which Niebuhr became mentor to the ex-Communist Herberg, encouraging him to return to his Jewish faith for new foundations when he was considering conversion to Christianity, see James T. Fisher, "American Religion since 1945," in *A Companion to Post-1945 America*, ed. Jean-Christophe Agnew and Roy Rosenzweig (Malden, MA: Blackwell, 2002), 49.

4. E. J. Hobsbawm, *The Age of Extremes: A History of the World, 1914–1991* (New York: Vintage, 1994), 22.

5. Edward Hallett Carr, *The Twenty Years' Crisis, 1919–1939: An Introduction to the Study of International Relations* (London: Macmillan, 1939), ix.

6. Hannah Arendt, *The Origins of Totalitarianism*, 1st ed. (New York: Harcourt, Brace, 1951), vii.

7. For the history of early uses of "totalitarianism," see Abbott Gleason, *Totalitarianism: The Inner History of the Cold War* (New York: Oxford University Press, 1995).

8. From *Time*'s "Year in Books," December 14, 1941, 108, quoted in Gleason, *Totalitarianism*, 51.

9. On the "new man" in the transatlantic avant-garde leading up to this period, one finds exemplary statements, for example, in Eugene Jolas's editorial writings in *transition*, as when he commits the journal to "the attempt to define the new man in relation to his primal consciousness; the revolution of the world." Eugene Jolas, "Literature and the New Man," *transition* 19–20 (Spring–Summer 1930): 15. Adumbrations of the new man can be found throughout modernist reactions to the machine going back be-

fore the turn of the century, as in Henry Adams in the United States; a scholarly starting point on modernism and the new man is Michael Hollington, "The Rehumanization of Art: Modernism, Technology, and the Crisis of Humanism," in Paul Sheehan, ed., *Becoming Human: New Perspectives on the Inhuman Condition* (Westport, CT: Praeger, 2003), 29–41. On new man origins in early twentieth-century thought and among the post–World War I "front generation" in Germany, especially with reference to Ernst Jünger and the "conservative revolutionaries," see Jeffrey Herf, *Reactionary Modernism: Technology, Culture, and Politics in Weimar and the Third Reich* (Cambridge, UK: Cambridge University Press, 1984),15 and elsewhere, and Robert Wohl, *The Generation of 1914* (Cambridge, MA: Harvard University Press, 1979), 59, and elsewhere, which contains additional attention to pan-European comparisons and connections. For the important comparison between the Nazi and Soviet new man, tracing both genealogies backward to World War I and Bolshevik Revolution and forward to the annihilative warfare of the 1940s, see Peter Fritzsche and Jochen Hellbeck, "The New Man in Stalinist Russia and Nazi Germany," in *Beyond Totalitarianism: Stalinism and Nazism Compared*, ed. Michael Geyer and Sheila Fitzpatrick (Cambridge, UK: Cambridge University Press, 2009), 302–41.

10. Hermann Rauschning, *The Voice of Destruction* (New York: Putnam, 1940), 246.

11. The most compelling recent emphasis on new man ideology in fascism comes from Roger Griffin, *The Nature of Fascism* (London: Pinter, 1991); the best current review of the literature is now Michael Mann, *Fascists* (New York: Cambridge University Press, 2004), which concurs despite Mann's different emphasis on "transcendent nationalism."

12. Joachim C. Fest, *The Face of the Third Reich: Portraits of the Nazi Leadership*, trans. Michael Bullock (1963; London: Weidenfeld and Nicolson, 1970), 292.

13. See, for example, Kenneth Burke's analysis of the mobilizing rhetoric of *Mein Kampf*—taking issue with the contemporary superfluity of more superficial or dismissive reviews and descriptions of Hitler's book—in "The Rhetoric of Hitler's 'Battle,'" *Southern Review* (January 1939): 1–21, later integrated into his *The Philosophy of Literary Form: Studies in Symbolic Action* (Baton Rouge: Louisiana State University Press, 1941).

14. Quoted in Fest, *The Face of the Third Reich*, 95.

15. Ibid., 292.

16. Quoted by Fest, in his footnotes, from Poliakov and Wulf, *Das Dritte Reich und die Juden*. Fest, *The Face of the Third Reich*, 382. The tract has been translated into English and made available online at http://www.holocaustresearchproject.org/holoprelude/deruntermensch.html.

17. George L. Mosse, *The Fascist Revolution: Toward a General Theory of Fascism* (New York: Howard Fertig, 1999), 49.

18. Ibid., 32; Robert O. Paxton, *The Anatomy of Fascism* (New York: Knopf, 2004), 166.

19. Quoted in Rauschning, *Voice of Destruction*, 251–52.

20. "The Heart of the Problem: Without Vision of Deep Purpose We Shall Perish," *Fortune*, February 1942, n.p.

21. William Ernest Hocking, "What Man Can Make of Man," *Fortune*, February 1942, 91.

22. Jacques Maritain, "Christian Humanism: Life with Meaning and Direction," *Fortune*, April 1942, 164.

23. John W. Dodds, "The Place of the Humanities in a World of War: 'Feel Justly'—'Think Clearly,'" *Vital Speeches of the Day*, March 1, 1943, 311–12. The speech had been delivered in December 1942.

24. "What is man, that thou shouldest magnify him? and that thou shouldest set thine heart upon him?" Job says mournfully, addressing a God who will not give him peace (Job 7:17); "What is man that thou art mindful of him?" the psalmist asks more gratefully, thanking a generous God, "For thou hast made him a little lower than the angels, and hast crowned him with glory and honour" (Psalm 8:4–5).

25. Immanuel Kant, *Logic*, trans. Robert S. Hartman and Wolfgang Schwarz (1800; New York: Dover, 1974), 29.

26. Ernst Cassirer, *An Essay on Man: An Introduction to the Philosophy of Human Culture* (New Haven, CT: Yale University Press, 1944).

27. Lewis Mumford, *The Condition of Man* (New York: Harcourt, Brace, 1944), 3.

28. Martin Buber, "What is Man?" (1938), in *Between Man and Man*, trans. Ronald Gregor Smith (New York: Macmillan, 1948). Maurice Friedman specifies the degree to which "What is Man?" emerged in Buber's work, specifically in reference to "[t]he crisis of Nazism," in *Encounter on the Narrow Ridge: A Life of Martin Buber* (New York: Paragon House, 1991), 244.

29. R. G. Collingwood, *The New Leviathan; Or, Man, Society, Civilization, and Barbarism*, ed. David Boucher, rev. ed. (1942; Oxford, UK: Oxford University Press, 1992), 1.

30. Ibid.

31. Reinhold Niebuhr, *The Nature and Destiny of Man: A Christian Interpretation*, 2 vols. (1941–43; Louisville, KY: Westminster John Knox Press, 1996); Buber, *Between Man and Man*; Cassirer, *Essay on Man*; Julian Huxley, *Man in the Modern World* (London: Chatto and Windus, 1947), 150, 153; Erich Fromm, *Man for Himself: An Inquiry into the Psychology of Ethics* (New York: Rinehart, 1947), 7; Collingwood, *New Leviathan*; Her-

berg, *Judaism and Modern Man*; C. S. Lewis, *The Abolition of Man: Or, Reflections on Education with Special Reference to the Teaching of English in the Upper Forms of Schools* (1943; New York: Macmillan, 1947); Jean-Paul Sartre, *Existentialism*, trans. Bernard Frechtman (New York: Philosophical Library, 1947), 18–20. The more widely available translation today of Sartre's book *L'existentialisme est un humanisme* is the contemporaneous but slightly different British translation, *Existentialism and Humanism*, trans. Philip Mairet (1948; Brooklyn, NY: Haskell House, 1977), 28.

32. For a contemporary discussion, see Herschel Baker's intellectual history from 1947—but note that his account ends on the threshold of the modern era, unable to go further. Herschel Baker, *The Dignity of Man: Studies in the Persistence of an Idea* (Cambridge, MA: Harvard University Press, 1947). On the meaning and value of "dignity" in Catholic doctrine at midcentury, however, and in Catholic intellectual efforts to square a traditionalist communitarianism with modern human rights, see recent work by Samuel Moyn on Jacques Maritain. Samuel Moyn, "Jacques Maritain, Christian New Order, and the Birth of Human Rights," SSRN Working Paper (May 1, 2008), http://ssrn.com/abstract=1134345.

33. J. L. Austin, *How to Do Things with Words* (Cambridge, MA: Harvard University Press, 1962).

34. Herbert Agar, Frank Aydelotte, G. A. Borgese, et al., *City of Man: A Declaration on World Democracy* (New York: Viking, 1940), 27–28, 33–34.

35. Ruth Nanda Anshen, "Man as an Element of Every Experiment," in *Science and Man*, ed. Ruth Nanda Anshen (New York: Harcourt, Brace, 1942), 12.

36. Newton Arvin, contribution to "Religion and the Intellectuals: A Symposium," *Partisan Review* (February 1950): 117.

37. Delmore Schwartz, "The Grapes of Crisis," *Partisan Review* (January–February 1951): 12, 14.

38. Church Peace Union, *The Nature of Man: His World, His Spiritual Resources, His Destiny*, ed. A. William Loos (New York: Church Peace Union and the World Alliance for International Friendship Through Religion, 1950), 93–94.

39. Thus, William Graebner sees two halves split around 1945, divided between the wartime and late-radical "culture of the whole" and a postwar individualistic "turning-inward." Richard Pells positions his liberal intellectuals of the later 1940s and 1950s as a generation that "shared a disenchantment with the political and cultural radicalism of the 1930s" even when they had been active in the 1930s: "[T]heir work was suffused with the conviction that the troubles of the postwar years were very different from those of the past." William Graebner, *The Age of Doubt: American*

Thought and Culture in the 1940s (Boston: Twayne, 1991), 1, xi; Richard H. Pells, *The Liberal Mind in a Conservative Age: American Intellectuals in the 1940s and 1950s* (New York: Harper & Row, 1985), viii.

40. Purcell's analysis turns specifically to the consequences of wartime changes in thought for the theory of democracy, and looks exclusively at the meaning of the intellectual crisis for university academics and social scientists (x), and "[c]onspicuous[ly]" away from "literary figures, artists, and radical or Marxist intellectuals" (ix). Edward A. Purcell Jr.'s *The Crisis of Democratic Theory: Scientific Naturalism and the Problem of Value* (Lexington: University Press of Kentucky, 1973).

41. Michael Leja, *Reframing Abstract Expressionism: Subjectivity and Painting in the 1940s* (New Haven, CT: Yale University Press, 1993).

42. Irving Howe, "Intellectuals' Flight from Politics: A Discussion of Contemporary Trend [*sic*]," *New International: A Monthly Organ of Revolutionary Marxism*, October 1947, 241–42; emphasis in original.

43. The influential advocate for this position in an earlier generation of scholarship was Alan M. Wald. See his *The New York Intellectuals: The Rise and Decline of the Anti-Stalinist Left from the 1930s to the 1980s* (Chapel Hill: University of North Carolina Press, 1987), 227 and following. Within the history of the left, points about the limitation or decline of late 1930s and 1940s social protest are no doubt true, but they possess more pragmatic political determinations that need not be read back into the earlier thinkers as evaluative claims of cowardice, withdrawal, or obscurantism. A convincing account has been given by Howard Brick, who attributes "deradicalization" to an impasse and compromise between a weakened American socialism and a postwar capitalism that had to partially integrate organized labor. This compromise came into being between the moderating auspices of the New Deal welfare state and the persecutions of the Left by anti-Communist and revived probusiness forces. See Howard Brick, *Daniel Bell and the Decline of Intellectual Radicalism: Social Theory and Political Reconciliation in the 1940s* (Madison: University of Wisconsin Press, 1986), 8–10. A later phase of historiography, such as Gregory Sumner's work in the mid-1990s on Dwight Macdonald, has questioned the omnipresence of the "deradicalization" hypothesis on alternative lines, by taking stock of other kinds of "challenges to the status quo" as underrecognized political radicalism. See Gregory Sumner, *Dwight Macdonald and the "Politics" Circle: The Challenge of Cosmopolitan Democracy* (Ithaca, NY: Cornell University Press, 1996), 4–5.

44. Hollinger's contribution has been influential, and I have learned from it. As a parallel account to my own, I would argue that after 1920 it transpires within a somewhat separate domain of actors: in order to maintain the continuity of "inclusion" as a predominant concern for elite intel-

lectuals from the 1920s up through the 1950s, Hollinger must increasingly encapsulate his account within the circles of Deweyans and Boasians who were marginalized in debates on crisis and the human (because they saw nothing in them), and then in a postwar reconstruction by scholars largely limited to the academy and who were not well known outside it. For relevant passages on his protagonists and scope, see David A. Hollinger, *In the American Province: Studies in the History and Historiography of Ideas* (1985; Baltimore, MD: Johns Hopkins University Press, 1989), 59, and chapter 4; *Science, Jews, and Secular Culture: Studies in Mid-Twentieth-Century American Intellectual History* (Princeton, NJ: Princeton University Press, 1996), 160; *Cosmopolitanism and Solidarity: Studies in Ethnoracial, Religious, and Professional Affiliation in the United States* (Madison: University of Wisconsin Press, 2006), 131–32.

45. See David A. Hollinger, "How Wide the Circle of the 'We'? American Intellectuals and the Problem of the Ethnos since World War II," *American Historical Review* 98:2 (April 1993): 318; integrated into the popular polemic, David A. Hollinger, *Postethnic America: Beyond Multiculturalism* (New York: Basic Books, 1995), chapter 3.

46. See, for example, Ira Katznelson, *Desolation and Enlightenment: Political Knowledge after Total War, Totalitarianism, and the Holocaust* (New York: Columbia University Press, 2003), on postwar political science and the "political studies enlightenment" (xiii).

47. See, for example, Wendy L. Wall, *Inventing the "American Way": The Politics of Consensus from the New Deal to the Civil Rights Movement* (Oxford, UK: Oxford University Press, 2008).

48. On postwar antiprejudice campaigns, principally those of interfaith and ecumenical religious movements defending Catholics and Jews but including such wider public campaigns as "National Brotherhood Week" and white preparation for the civil rights movement, see, most recently, Kevin M. Schultz, *Tri-Faith America: How Catholics and Jews Held America to Its Protestant Promise* (New York: Oxford University Press, 2011).

49. Hans Kohn, *World Order in Historical Perspective* (Cambridge, MA: Harvard University Press, 1942), n.p.

50. Hans Kohn, *Revolutions and Dictatorships: Essays in Contemporary History* (Cambridge, MA: Harvard University Press, 1938), n.p.

51. Glenda Sluga, "René Cassin: *Les droits de l'homme* and the Universality of Human Rights, 1945–1966," in Stefan-Ludwig Hoffman, ed., *Human Rights in the Twentieth Century* (Cambridge, UK: Cambridge University Press, 2011), 115.

52. Kirsten Sellars, *The Rise and Rise of Human Rights: Human Rights and Modern War* (Stroud, UK: Sutton, 2002), 13. See also the account of the same events in Mary Ann Glendon, *A World Made New: Eleanor Roose-*

velt and the Universal Declaration of Human Rights (New York: Random House, 2001), 90. Glendon notes that the "representatives of the UN Commission on the Status of Women" were "present as observers."

53. Sluga, "René Cassin," 117.

54. Ruth Nanda Anshen, "Origin and Aim," in *Freedom: Its Meaning*, ed. Ruth Nanda Anshen (New York: Harcourt, Brace, 1940), 3, 8. The two later volumes are Anshen, ed., *Science and Man* and Anshen, ed., *Beyond Victory* (New York: Harcourt, Brace, 1943).

55. The occasional usage of "Man," capitalized, in her English text seems to have been an imposition of the 1952 English translation—as "Mankind" is, also, in her English subtitle. Simone Weil, *The Need for Roots: Prelude to a Declaration of Duties towards Mankind*, trans. A. F. Wills (1952; London: Routledge, 1978); in the original, *L'Enracinement: Prélude à une déclaration des devoirs envers l'être humain* (Paris: Gallimard, 1949).

56. Simone de Beauvoir, *The Ethics of Ambiguity*, trans. Bernard Frechtman (1946, 1948; New York: Citadel, 1976), 70, 71.

57. Simone de Beauvoir, *The Second Sex*, trans. H. M. Parshley (1953; New York: Vintage, 1989), 728.

58. Ibid., 732; emphasis added.

59. See Penny M. Von Eschen, *Race against Empire: Black Americans and Anticolonialism, 1937–1957* (Ithaca, NY: Cornell University Press, 1997), and Carol Anderson, *Eyes Off the Prize: The United Nations and the African American Struggle for Human Rights, 1944–1955* (Cambridge, UK: Cambridge University Press, 2003).

60. A synthetic account of the most important black nationalist and internationalist cross-currents is Nikil Pal Singh, *Black Is a Country: Race and the Unfinished Struggle for Democracy* (Cambridge, MA: Harvard University Press, 2004). On US government actions and compromises to stem international outrage about abuses in the Jim Crow South, see Mary L. Dudziak, *Cold War Civil Rights: Race and the Image of American Democracy* (Princeton, NJ: Princeton University Press, 2000).

61. Von Eschen, *Race Against Empire*, 183.

62. Anderson, *Eyes Off the Prize*; on Eleanor Roosevelt, 112.

63. Robert Duncan, "The Homosexual in Society," *Politics* (August 1944): 210–11.

64. Fromm, *Man for Himself*, 5.

65. Erich Kahler, *Man the Measure: A New Approach to History* (1943; New York: George Braziller, 1956), 640.

66. Hans Frank, *Technik Des Staates* (Berlin: Deutscher Rechtsverlag, 1942), quoted in Hannah Arendt, *Eichmann in Jerusalem*. One must not blame this on Kant. Though Arendt discovered the association of other

high Nazis with further perversions of Kantianism, she protested that this misuse of philosophy "was outrageous, on the face of it, and also incomprehensible, since Kant's moral philosophy is so closely bound up with man's faculty of judgment, which rules out blind obedience. Rather, the "distortion agrees with what [Adolf Eichmann, architect of the Nazi genocide] himself called the version of Kant 'for the household use of the little man,'" a recognizable and important feature, Arendt felt, of popular intellectual life in Hitler's Germany. Hannah Arendt, *Eichmann in Jerusalem: A Report on the Banality of Evil*, rev. ed. (1963/1965; New York: Penguin, 1994), 135–36.

67. Plato, *Theaetetus*, 150b, trans. M. J. Levett, rev. Myles Burnyeat, in Plato, *Complete Works*, ed. John M. Cooper (Indianapolis, IN: Hackett, 1997), 167.

68. Ibid., 150d, in Plato, *Complete Works*, 167.

CHAPTER 2
CURRENTS THROUGH THE WAR

1. See Robert B. Westbrook, *John Dewey and American Democracy* (Ithaca, NY: Cornell University Press, 1991); Richard Wightman Fox, *Reinhold Niebuhr: A Biography* (1985; Ithaca, NY: Cornell University Press, 1996); Casey Nelson Blake, *Beloved Community: The Cultural Criticism of Randolph Bourne, Van Wyck Brooks, Waldo Frank, and Lewis Mumford* (Chapel Hill: University of North Carolina Press, 1990); less celebrated but useful are Harry S. Ashmore, *Unseasonable Truths: The Life of Robert Maynard Hutchins* (Boston: Little, Brown, 1989), and Donald L. Miller, *Lewis Mumford: A Life* (New York: Grove, 1989); also useful is the remarkable collective volume containing contributions by Westbrook, Fox, Blake, and Miller, especially relevant for Fox's article "Tragedy, Responsibility, and the American Intellectual, 1925–1950," in *Lewis Mumford: Public Intellectual*, ed. Thomas P. Hughes and Agatha C. Hughes (New York: Oxford University Press, 1990).

2. Sidney Hook, *Out of Step: An Unquiet Life in the 20th Century* (New York: Harper & Row, 1987); Mortimer J. Adler, *Philosopher at Large: An Intellectual Autobiography* (New York: Macmillan, 1977). Reevaluations of Hook are Christopher Phelps, *Young Sidney Hook: Marxist and Pragmatist* (Ithaca, NY: Cornell University Press, 1997), which addresses the period before Hook renounced Marxism and ceased to be "a frankly revolutionary intellectual" (179) by the end of the 1930s, and the essays collected in Matthew J. Cotter, ed., *Sidney Hook Reconsidered* (Amherst, NY: Prometheus, 2004). Adler and the Adler-Hutchins relationship receive exemplary attention in two recent dissertations (Thomas's remarkable study

has been especially useful to me): Tim Lacy, "Making a Democratic Culture: The Great Books Idea, Mortimer J. Adler, and Twentieth-Century America" (PhD diss., Loyola University Chicago, 2006) and Robert S. Thomas, "Enlightenment and Authority: The Committee on Social Thought and the Ideology of Postwar Conservatism, 1927–1950" (PhD diss., Columbia University, 2010).

3. See John Dewey, *Human Nature and Conduct: An Introduction to Social Psychology* (New York: Holt, 1922).

4. For Dewey's anti-interventionist views on the European war through the 1930s, see Westbrook, *John Dewey*, 510–13.

5. John Dewey, "Does Human Nature Change?" (1938), in *Problems of Men* (New York: Philosophical Library, 1946), 184.

6. Reinhold Niebuhr, *The Nature and Destiny of Man: A Christian Interpretation*, vol. 1, *Human Nature* (1941; Louisville, KY: Westminster John Knox Press, 1996), 23. Subsequent citations are cited parenthetically in the text, including the volume number of this two-volume set of books, followed by the respective page number(s); a new footnote will mark the initial appearance of volume 2.

7. Fox, *Reinhold Niebuhr*, 191.

8. Purcell, *Crisis of Democratic Theory*, 218.

9. Mortimer J. Adler, "God and the Professors: Our Education Cannot Support Democracy," *Vital Speeches of the Day*, December 1, 1940, 99, 100, 98, 102. For Hook's version of the incident, see Hook, *Out of Step*, 336–37. The episode is also recounted in Westbrook, *John Dewey*, 519–20, and in Edward Shapiro, "Sidney Hook, Higher Education, and the New Failure of Nerve," in Cotter, *Sidney Hook Reconsidered*, 189.

10. On Adler's speech appearing in the "Hearst papers" for a national audience, see Mortimer Adler, "The Chicago School," *Harper's*, June 1, 1941, 385; Sidney Hook, "The New Medievalism," *New Republic*, October 28, 1940, 602–6; for Hook's memories of the episode, see Hook, *Out of Step*, 336–37.

11. This is a point Purcell makes in *Crisis of Democratic Theory*, 225–27.

12. Robert M. Hutchins, "Toward a Durable Society," *Fortune*, June 1943, 201 (emphasis added), 159.

13. Adler, "God and the Professors"; James B. Conant, "A Statement of Faith: 'What Is Man That Thou Art Mindful of Him?,'" *Vital Speeches of the Day*, July 15, 1942, 586; Hook, "The New Medievalism," 606.

14. See Tom Ambrose, *Hitler's Loss: What Britain and America Gained from Europe's Cultural Exiles* (London: Peter Owen, 2001), 23, and Anthony Heilbut, *Exiled in Paradise: German Refugee Artists and Intellectuals in America, from the 1930s to the Present* (New York: Viking, 1983), 23–25.

15. David Kettler and Volker Meja, *Karl Mannheim and the Crisis of Liberalism: The Secret of These New Times* (New Brunswick, NJ: Transaction, 1995), 4–6.

16. Karl Mannheim, *Man and Society in an Age of Reconstruction: Studies in Modern Social Structure* (1940; New York: Harcourt, Brace, 1949), 11.

17. Ibid., 39.

18. Karl Mannheim, *Diagnosis of Our Time: Wartime Essays of a Sociologist* (London: Kegan Paul, 1943), 11.

19. See part 5 of *Man and Society* and *Diagnosis of Our Time*. The best explication of Mannheim's projected combination of democracy and social control, integrating techniques of elite steering, universal education, and parliamentary politics, is Colin Loader, *The Intellectual Development of Karl Mannheim: Culture, Politics, and Planning* (Cambridge, UK: Cambridge University Press, 1985).

20. On the integration of psychology and anthropology into government war work, see Ellen Herman, *The Romance of American Psychology: Political Culture in the Age of Experts, 1940–1970* (Berkeley: University of California Press, 1995), esp. chapter 3, and Peter Mandler, *Return from the Natives: How Margaret Mead Won the Second World War and Lost the Cold War* (New Haven, CT: Yale University Press, 2013).

21. For indications of the influence that Mannheim's writing had on thinkers in America, both native-born and refugee—and a sense of the range of forms this influence could take—see such disparate documents as a commencement speech by the Harvard geography professor Kirtley F. Mather, with the somewhat misleading title "Oil for the Lamps of Freedom: Neither Democracy Nor Christianity Has Yet Failed" (Mather means that neither system has yet been adequately tried, in a properly planned society); *Vital Speeches of the Day*, August 15, 1941, 665–67; and an article by the crisis theologian Paul Tillich, at this time Reinhold Niebuhr's colleague at Union Theological Seminary, drawing its terms and analysis from Mannheim; Paul Tillich, "Freedom in the Period of Transformation," in Anshen, *Freedom: Its Meaning*, 123–44.

22. For Rauschning's political testament and his family's experience, see Hermann Rauschning, *The Conservative Revolution* (New York: Putnam, 1941), and Anna Rauschning, *No Retreat* (Indianapolis, IN: Bobbs-Merrill, 1942). Recent scholarship is in Jürgen Hensel and Pia Nordblom, eds., *Hermann Rauschning: Materialien und Beiträge zu einer politischen Biographie* (Osnabrück: Fibre, 2003), which includes a photograph of the two Rauschnings beaming in kerchiefs and overalls on their Oregon farmstead after the war, 96.

23. Hermann Rauschning, *The Revolution of Nihilism: Warning to the West*, trans. E. W. Dickes (New York: Alliance, 1939), 41.

24. Hermann Rauschning, *The Voice of Destruction* (New York: Putnam, 1940), 245–46, 252.

25. Rauschning, *Revolution of Nihilism*, 41.

26. Ibid., 48.

27. Harold Rosenberg, "Notes on Fascism and Bohemia," *Partisan Review* (Spring 1944): 177.

28. Indications of Rauschning's reception and influence are widespread in the discourse of the crisis of man but not always conspicuous. Uncredited quotations from Rauschning's book of conversations with Hitler open and frame the group manifesto *City of Man*; Herbert Agar, Frank Aydelotte, G. A. Borgese, et al., *City of Man: A Declaration on World Democracy* (New York: Viking, 1940), 11, 73. The émigré philosopher Leo Strauss delivered a lecture inspired by Rauschning's *Revolution of Nihilism* on the occasion of the General Seminar of the New School for Social Research, taking up Rauschning's book as its shared reading; other participants included Horace Kallen (the American philosopher credited with the theory of "cultural pluralism"), Kurt Riezler (the Weimar statesman), and Hans Kohn. See Susan Shell, " 'To Spare the Vanquished and Crush the Arrogant': Leo Strauss's Lecture on German Nihilism," in *The Cambridge Companion to Leo Strauss*, ed. Stephen B. Smith (New York: Cambridge University Press, 2009), 171–92. Thomas Mann, then the leading voice of the anti-Nazi exile in the United States, included Rauschning among a select group of authors—along with himself, his brother Heinrich, and the likes of Stefan Zweig, Paul Tillich, and Erwin Schrödinger—who he hoped would write pamphlets to smuggle back into Germany so its citizens would hear the voice of "intellectual Germany on the outside." He outlines the plan in a letter to Heinrich Mann of May 14, 1939, in Hans Wysling, ed., *Letters of Heinrich and Thomas Mann, 1900–1949*, ed. and trans. Don Reneau (Berkeley: University of California Press, 1998), 223–24.

29. In the earlier work *Moral Man and Immoral Society*, Niebuhr had already undertaken an assault on Dewey and characterized man the individual against his political representation in the mass. Yet that book, in context, belonged to an earlier thirties radical debate about liberal gradualism against what would today be called "direct action," with Niebuhr favoring the latter; it belongs to the phase that was broken with the run-up to World War II and had surprisingly little effect on the midcentury discourse of man. Reinhold Niebuhr, *Moral Man and Immoral Society: A Study in Ethics and Politics* (New York: C. Scribner's Sons, 1932).

30. Reinhold Niebuhr, *The Nature and Destiny of Man: A Christian*

Interpretation, vol. 2, *Human Destiny* (1943; Louisville, KY: Westminster John Knox Press, 1996), 207, 206; subsequent references are cited parenthetically in the text by volume and page numbers.

31. Sidney Hook, "The New Failure of Nerve," *Partisan Review* (January–February 1943): 15.

32. See Mark Hulsether, *Building a Protestant Left: "Christianity and Crisis" Magazine, 1941–1993* (Knoxville: University of Tennessee Press, 1999).

33. The historian of American Protestantism Gary Dorrien writes:

> Niebuhr's dialectical realism defined for much of his theological generation what the 'realities' of politics and ethics were. . . . In the foreign policy arena Niebuhr taught Christian ethicists to view the world as a theater of perpetual struggles for power among competing interests. Realism had a moral dimension for him, but its object was to secure a balance of power among existing regimes and a stable correlation of forces.

"Christian Realism: Reinhold Niebuhr's Theology, Ethics, and Politics," in *Reinhold Niebuhr Revisited: Engagements with an American Original*, ed. Daniel F. Rice (Grand Rapids, MI: Eerdmans, 2009), 22–23.

34. Adler eventually converted to Catholicism in the late 1990s, in the ninth decade of his life. See Mortimer J. Adler, *A Second Look in the Rearview Mirror: Further Autobiographical Reflections of a Philosopher at Large* (New York: Macmillan, 1992), esp. the chapter entitled "A Philosopher's Religious Faith."

35. Adler was also belligerent and independent enough, in his own way, to finally do the unforgivable among the Catholic philosophers who had become his friends—to argue that on close analysis, Saint Thomas Aquinas had not proven the existence of God when he thought he had, but that he, Adler, could at least make some improvements to the proof. See Mortimer J. Adler, "The Demonstration of God's Existence," *Thomist*, January 1943, 188–218; for Adler's explanation of this episode, Adler, *Philosopher at Large*, 310.

36. Ashmore, *Unseasonable Truths*, 90–91.

37. Shapiro, "Sidney Hook," 185.

38. Adler, *Philosopher at Large*, 64–65.

39. William McNeill and Edward Purcell draw the same interpretation. See William Hardy McNeill, *Hutchins' University: A Memoir of the University of Chicago, 1929–1950* (Chicago: University of Chicago Press, 1991), 34, and Purcell, *Crisis of Democratic Theory*, 143–44.

40. Robert M. Hutchins, *The Higher Learning in America* (New Haven, CT: Yale University Press, 1936); Ashmore, *Unseasonable Truths*, 157; Adler, *Philosopher at Large*, 163.

41. Sidney Hook, "Planning—and Freedom," review of *Man and Society in an Age of Reconstruction* by Karl Mannheim, *Nation* (October 26, 1940), 399.

42. John Dewey, "The Techniques of Reconstruction," review of *Man and Society in an Age of Reconstruction* by Karl Mannheim, *Saturday Review of Literature* 22 (August 31, 1940): 10, in *John Dewey: The Later Works, 1925–1953*, vol. 14, ed. Jo Ann Boydston (Carbondale: Southern Illinois University Press, 2008), 294.

43. Stefan Collini, "Clerisy or Undesirables: T. S. Eliot," in *Absent Minds: Intellectuals in Britain* (Oxford, UK: Oxford University Press, 2006), 316.

44. Keith Clements, ed., *The Moot Papers: Faith, Freedom and Society, 1938–1947* (London: T & T Clark, 2010), 10–11.

45. Alec R. Vidler, *Scenes from a Clerical Life: An Autobiography* (London: Collins, 1977), 119.

46. Hayek took up the faculty position in 1950. The details of the Chicago economics project, the funding of Hayek's position by Kansas City anti–New Deal businessmen, and the complicated inner politics of the university and of the birth of neoliberal Chicago school economics, are anatomized in Rob Van Horn and Philip Mirowski, "The Rise of the Chicago School of Economics and the Birth of Neoliberalism," in *The Road from Mont Pèlerin: The Making of the Neoliberal Thought Collective*, ed. Philip Mirowski and Dieter Plehwe (Cambridge, MA: Harvard University Press, 2009), 139–78.

47. See Leo Strauss, *Natural Right and History* (1950; Chicago: University of Chicago Press, 1953).

48. Leo Strauss, *Persecution and the Art of Writing* (Glencoe, IL: Free Press, 1952).

49. For the history of "Dewey's bulldog" in print—and Hook's adoption of it—see Michael Eldridge, "Dewey's Bulldog and the Eclipse of Pragmatism," in Cotter, ed., *Sidney Hook Reconsidered*, 131. The bulldog nomenclature of the nineteenth and twentieth centuries, incidentally, was an improvement over the eighteenth-century tradition; the publicist for Rousseau, Louis-Sébastien Mercier, was awarded the epithet "Jean-Jacques's Monkey."

50. Eldridge, "Dewey's Bulldog," 131.

51. Mary McCarthy, from a 1982 interview, quoted in Gregory D. Sumner, *Dwight Macdonald and the "Politics" Circle: The Challenge of Cosmopolitan Democracy* (Ithaca, NY: Cornell University Press, 1996), 206.

52. Lewis Mumford, *The Golden Day: A Study in American Experience and Culture* (New York: Boni and Liveright, 1926), 255.

53. Sidney Hook, "Some Memories of John Dewey, 1859–1952," *Commentary* (September 1952): 249.

54. Hook, "New Failure," 2–3.

55. Robert M. Hutchins, *Education for Freedom* (Baton Rouge: Louisiana State University Press, 1943), 14.

56. Sidney Hook, *Education for Modern Man* (New York: Dial Press, 1946), 25.

57. For Boas's contribution of the model of "cultural wholes" and his critique of "evolutionism" among societies, see Franz Boas, *A Franz Boas Reader: The Shaping of American Anthropology, 1883–1911*, ed. George W. Stocking Jr. (Chicago: University of Chicago Press, 1974).

58. Nor was Benedict shy about it: relativism meant there could be no weighing or hierarchy of cultures, including no superiority of the West. "Social thinking at the present time has no more important task before it than that of taking adequate account of cultural relativity," she wrote and frequently repeated. Ruth Benedict, *Patterns of Culture* (1934; Boston: Houghton Mifflin, 1959), 3, 278.

59. The best history of these developments, as well as the developing positions of Boas and Benedict through the 1930s and 1940s, is George W. Stocking Jr., "Ideas and Institutions in American Anthropology: Thoughts Toward the History of the Interwar Years," in *The Ethnographer's Magic and Other Essays in the History of Anthropology* (Madison: University of Wisconsin Press, 1992).

60. Forward to Ralph Linton, ed., *The Science of Man in the World Crisis* (New York: Columbia University Press), 1945, vii. See Judith Schachter Modell, *Ruth Benedict: Patterns of a Life* (Philadelphia: University of Pennsylvania Press, 1983), 257.

61. For Benedict's struggles at Columbia, and her wartime career and its complexities, see Margaret M. Caffrey, *Ruth Benedict: Stranger in this Land* (Austin: University of Texas Press, 1989), chapter 13, and Modell, *Ruth Benedict*, chapters 10 and 11.

62. Ruth Benedict, "Human Nature is Not a Trap," *Partisan Review* (March–April 1943): 163.

63. Edward Purcell argues on the contrary that the opposition of camps like those of Niebuhr and Hutchins (which he terms "absolutist") ultimately led to a new "relativist" synthesis in wartime and postwar American academic thought, which retained more of Dewey than it rejected, even if Dewey had been personally eclipsed.

64. Morton White, *Social Thought in America: The Revolt against Formalism*, new ed. (1949; London: Oxford University Press, 1976), 3.

65. Westbrook, *John Dewey*, 537. Westbrook cites the linguistic turn and professionalization of postwar American philosophy, however, as marginalizing Dewey's contributions still more than the "growing influence" (532) of the successful challenge from Niebuhr and his ilk.

66. Sidney Hook, contribution to "Religion and the Intellectuals II," *Partisan Review* (March 1950): 225.

67. Peter E. Gordon, *Continental Divide: Heidegger, Cassirer, Davos* (Cambridge, MA: Harvard University Press, 2010), 11.

68. Ernst Cassirer, *An Essay on Man: An Introduction to a Philosophy of Human Culture* (New Haven, CT: Yale University Press, 1944), 9, table of contents, 4.

69. See Thomas Mann and Erich Kahler, *An Exceptional Friendship: The Correspondence of Thomas Mann and Erich Kahler*, trans. Richard and Clara Winston (Ithaca, NY: Cornell University Press, 1975), 47.

70. Erich Kahler, *Man the Measure: A New Approach to History* (1943; New York: George Braziller, 1956), 5, 6.

71. Ibid., 640, 3.

72. Ibid., 3.

73. See the "Translator's Introduction" and the lectures and writings in Edmund Husserl, *The Crisis of European Sciences and Transcendental Phenomenology: An Introduction to Phenomenological Philosophy*, trans. David Carr (Evanston, IL: Northwestern University Press, 1970).

74. Schlick was often identified by anti-Semitic opponents as Jewish or an advocate for "Jewry"; his family protested after his murder against imputations that they were Jewish. For contemporary documentation from the Schlick murder and its cultural situation, see Friedrich Stadler, *The Vienna Circle: Studies in the Origins, Development, and Influence of Logical Empiricism* (Vienna: Springer, 2001), 866–909.

75. For German associations of technics with government, German usage of "technics," and consequences of the technics-politics debate, see John P. McCormick, *Carl Schmitt's Critique of Liberalism: Against Politics as Technology* (Cambridge, UK: Cambridge University Press, 1997), esp. introduction.

76. Mikael Hård, "German Regulation: The Integration of Modern Technology into National Culture," in *The Intellectual Appropriation of Technology: Discourses on Modernity, 1900–1939*, ed. Mikael Hård and Andrew Jamison (Cambridge, MA: MIT Press, 1998), 39–41.

77. Bernhard Rieger, *Technology and the Culture of Modernity in Britain and Germany, 1890–1945* (Cambridge, UK: Cambridge University Press, 2005).

78. Walther Rathenau, *Kritik der Zeit* (Berlin: Fischer, 1912).

79. Jeffrey Herf, *Reactionary Modernism: Technology, Culture, and Politics in Weimar and the Third Reich* (Cambridge, UK: Cambridge University Press, 1984).

80. Thus *Man and Technics* is often included, quite plausibly, in other treatments of technology as a major *anti*-technological work, as in Lang-

don Winner's *Autonomous Technology: Technics-out-of-Control as a Theme in Political Thought* (Cambridge, MA: MIT Press, 1977), 174. Herbert Marcuse, reading it in wartime, seems to have drawn the same conclusion; see Herbert Marcuse, "Some Social Implications of Modern Technology" (1941), in *Technology, War, and Fascism: Collected Papers of Herbert Marcuse*, vol. 1, ed. Douglas Kellner (London: Routledge, 1998), 63n40. Herf's biographical and contemporary information is convincing, however; Herf, *Reactionary Modernism*, 64–67.

81. Oswald Spengler, *Man and Technics: A Contribution to the Philosophy of Life*, trans. Charles Francis Atkinson (New York: Knopf, 1932), 42. The order of the last two quotations is reversed. Spengler eventually turned against the Nazis, and they against him—their opportunistic revolution did not match his particular conservatism—but not before he had bestowed on the world these sanguinary foretastes of the Nazi mood. See H. Stuart Hughes, *Oswald Spengler: A Critical Estimate*, rev. ed. (1952; New York: Scribner's, 1962), 101.

82. Spengler, *Man and Technics*, 44.

83. Ibid., 90.

84. The anthropologist Ralph Linton was one US figure who picked up this cautionary fantasy of technics dying out in the West (where they were linked to philosophical bases in the Enlightenment)—but surviving in the underdeveloped world—and turned it into a dream of how technology could be reintegrated with traditional culture if the West destroyed itself. See Ralph Linton, "The Scope and Aims of Anthropology," in *The Science of Man in the World Crisis*, ed. Ralph Linton (New York: Columbia University Press, 1945), 221.

85. Karl Jaspers, *Man in the Modern Age*, trans. Eden Paul and Cedar Paul (New York: Holt, 1933), 22.

86. Ibid., 63.

87. Leo Strauss, *On Tyranny: Corrected and Expanded Edition*, ed. Victor Gourevitch and Michael S. Roth (1948; Chicago: University of Chicago Press, 2013), 23, 27.

88. C. S. Lewis, *The Abolition of Man; Or, Reflections on Education with Special Reference to the Teaching of English in the Upper Forms of Schools* (1943; New York: Macmillan, 1947), 38, 40.

89. Peter F. Drucker, *The End of Economic Man: A Study of the New Totalitarianism* (New York: John Day, 1939), 23, 268.

90. G. A. Borgese, *Goliath: The March of Fascism* (New York: Viking, 1937); Franz Neumann, *Behemoth: The Structure and Practice of National Socialism* (New York: Oxford University Press, 1942).

91. The major account of historicism by one of its self-conscious practitioners (who considered it "one of the greatest intellectual revolutions that

has ever taken place in Western thought" [liv]) is Friedrich Meinecke, *Historism: The Rise of a New Historical Outlook*, trans. J. E. Anderson (1934, 1959; London: Routledge and K. Paul, 1972).

92. Quoted in Meinecke, *Historism*, 506.

93. This point about the impulse to "historicize" is suggested by a discussion by Frederick C. Beiser, *The German Historicist Tradition* (Oxford, UK: Oxford University Press, 2011), 2.

94. See Karl Mannheim, "Historicism" (1924), in his *Essays on the Sociology of Knowledge*, ed. Paul Kecskemeti (London: Routledge, 1952).

95. Peter Novick, *That Noble Dream: The "Objectivity Question" and the American Historical Profession* (New York: Cambridge University Press, 1988), 26–31. Novick suggests Ranke's passionate, spiritualized historicism was simply, and incorrectly, naturalized in America as a form of scientific empiricism.

96. See the classic account in H. Stuart Hughes, *Consciousness and Society: The Reorientation of European Social Thought, 1890–1930* (New York: Vintage, 1958), 232–48.

97. In fact, Troeltsch himself had used "crisis" language for the situation of historicism already in 1921 in an article précis he published in *Die Neue Rundschau* as "Die Krise des Historismus"; Beiser, *German Historicist Tradition*, 23. Karl Heussi explicitly attributed the confusion into which the word "historicism" had fallen through the whole of the 1920s to a crisis of history writing that accompanied the German social and intellectual crises of 1920–30 after World War I, but he laid a particular charge against relativist and modernist currents: "Aestheticism, skepticism, relativism in the sense of the relativization of all values, here threateningly raised their heads, held history in the framework of bare appearance, and robbed it of every strong effect." Karl Heussi, *Die Krisis des Historismus* (Tübingen: J.C.B. Mohr, 1932), 7.

98. Peter Gay, *The Enlightenment: An Interpretation*, vol. 1, *The Rise of Modern Paganism* (1966; New York: Norton, 1977), 34, 35. Historiography of the Enlightenment has of course progressed since Gay's two-volume opus, passing through revisionary decades of multiple "Enlightenments" of distinct national or social-historical character, as well as the present significant challenge of Jonathan Israel's "radical Enlightenment" derived from Spinoza. I remain with Gay because he is adequate, accurate, and relevant (though subsequent) to the re-enlightenment project of the older émigré generation, without being shackled to it or compromised by it.

99. Before this, "Universal History" had stood for the proof of a static Christian picture, as in Bossuet. After this time, in Hegel, it would become a dialectical progress, through conflict, to accomplish a unity already con-

tained in the Absolute. Between the two, Herder is the generative figure. He is often ignored precisely because he inspires both the Enlightenment conception of species-level progress and the Romantic historicist reaction, which understood different peoples and cultures as individual unities, each with its own development; as Isaiah Berlin quipped, "Herder is one of those not very many thinkers in the world who really do absolutely adore things for being what they are, and do not condemn them for not being something else. For Herder everything is delightful." See the useful introductory material to Hans Adler and Ernest A. Menze's selection in Gottfried Herder, *On World History: An Anthology*, trans. Ernest A. Menze and Michael Palma (Armonk, NY: M. E. Sharpe, 1996); Isaiah Berlin, *The Roots of Romanticism*, 2nd ed., ed. Henry Hardy (1999; Princeton, NJ: Princeton University Press, 2013), 74.

100. Immanuel Kant, "Idea for a Universal History with a Cosmopolitan Purpose" (1784), in *Political Writings*, 2nd ed., ed. Hans Reiss, trans. H. B. Nisbet (Cambridge, UK: Cambridge University Press, 1991), 50.

101. Kahler, *Man the Measure*, 25.

102. Ibid., 3–4.

103. Mann and Kahler, *Exceptional Friendship*, 68.

104. Thus, for Kohn, "The age of nationalism represents the first period of universal history" (vii). Hans Kohn, *The Idea of Nationalism* (1967; New York: Collier Books, 1944).

105. Lewis Mumford, *The Condition of Man* (New York: Harcourt, Brace, 1944), 3, 13.

106. Arnold J. Toynbee, *A Study of History: Abridgement of Vol. I–VI*, by D. C. Somervell (New York: Oxford University Press, 1946).

107. " 'Challenge and Response': What Are American Civilization's Chances of Survival? It's Up to Us," *Fortune*, July 1943, 104–5.

108. Hans Kohn, "This Century of Betrayal: Can America Lead a New Struggle for Independence?" *Commentary* (September 1946): 201.

109. Ibid., 203.

110. Compare Gay's analysis of the periods into which Enlightenment historians persistently divided the past, and from which this re-enlightenment schema has been critically altered:

> The Enlightenment's conception of history as a continuing struggle between two types of mentality implies a general scheme of periodization. The philosophes divided the past, roughly, into four great epochs: the great river civilizations of the Near East; ancient Greece and Rome; the Christian millennium; and modern times, beginning with the "revival of letters." These four epochs were rhythmically related to each other: the first and third were paired off as ages of

myth, belief, and superstition, while the second and fourth were ages of rationality, science, and enlightenment.

In re-enlightenment history, the worst age, the third, has been made the best.

Gay, *The Enlightenment,* 1:34.

111. T. J. Jackson Lears, *No Place of Grace: Antimodernism and the Transformation of American Culture, 1880–1920* (1981; Chicago: University of Chicago Press, 1994), 142.

112. Maritain's *Humanisme Intégral,* published in English in 1938 in both New York and London as *True Humanism* (later translations return to *Integral Humanism,* the title by which it is best known today), was both an important location for Catholic and medieval Thomist integralism for the transatlantic crisis of man, and, it must be remembered, a crucial intervention in its original publication against protofascist affiliations of Catholicism in France before the war—its title seems designed to contrast specifically with Charles Maurras's *Nationalisme Intégral.* For another presentation, within the literature of the wartime discourse of man, directly from French neo-Thomism, see Étienne Gilson, "Medieval Universalism and Its Present Value in the Concept of Freedom," in Anshen, ed., *Freedom: Its Meaning,* 152–72.

113. Notably, Fromm's schema allowed Jewish intellectuals to take up and examine the "medieval synthesis" vision of history without the baggage of Christianity. See, for example, William Phillips's contribution to "Mr. Eliot and Notions of Culture: A Discussion," *Partisan Review* (Summer 1944): 307, 309, and Nathan Glazer, "The 'Alienation' of Modern Man: Some Diagnoses of the Malady," *Commentary* (April 1947): 378–85.

114. Lawrence J. Friedman, *The Lives of Erich Fromm: Love's Prophet* (New York: Columbia University Press, 2013), 104.

115. Hermann Broch, "History as Ethical Anthropology: Erich Kahler's Scienza Nuova," in *Erich Kahler,* ed. Eleanor L. Wolff and Herbert Steiner (New York: Privately printed, 1951).

116. "Broch demanded a resurrection of universality, without which humanity would plunge into what he called *Massenwahn*—mass insanity. Broch presented his readers with a simple choice: either reconstruction of a centralized value system that reconnects every man and woman to the social totality, or the war of all against all; either a politically prescribed universalism or mass insanity." Stefan Jonsson, "The Ideology of Universalism," *New Left Review* 63 (May–June 2010): 119.

117. Jürgen Habermas has suggested from personal experience, against this history of delayed effects, that "[c]opies of the first [Amsterdam 1947] edition were available for almost twenty years," and that "[t]he impact of

350 | NOTES TO PAGES 58–62

this book . . . stands in a curious relation to the number of its purchasers," such that it "exercised a special influence upon the intellectual development of the Federal Republic of Germany, especially in its first two decades." The judgment may be influenced, however, by Habermas's special position of study with Adorno and eventual accession to Horkheimer's chair and the directorship of the Institute for Social Research in Frankfurt. Jürgen Habermas, *The Philosophical Discourse of Modernity: Twelve Lectures*, trans. Frederick Lawrence (1985; Cambridge, MA: MIT Press, 1990,) 106–7.

118. For the émigrés' sense of California, see Heilbut, *Exiled in Paradise*, 54.

119. This edition was in mimeographed typescript and bore the title *Philosophical Fragments*. Rolf Wiggershaus, *The Frankfurt School: Its History, Theories, and Political Significance*, trans. Michael Robertson (Cambridge, MA: MIT Press, 1995), 325; Stefan Müller-Doohm, *Adorno: A Biography*, trans. Rodney Livingstone (Cambridge, UK: Polity, 2005), 282.

120. Max Horkheimer and Theodor W. Adorno, *Dialectic of Enlightenment*, trans. John Cumming (1944; New York: Continuum, 1972), xiii, 6; subsequent references are cited by page number parenthetically in the text.

121. Mumford, *Condition of Man*, 393.

122. Habermas, *Philosophical Discourse of Modernity*, 106.

123. Lewis Mumford, *Technics and Civilization* (New York: Harcourt Brace, 1934); on the change in view within the book, and its possible division into two halves, see Thomas P. Hughes and Agatha C. Hughes, "General Introduction: Mumford's Modern World," in *Lewis Mumford: Public Intellectual*, 5.

124. Mumford, *Condition of Man*, 376.

CHAPTER 3
THE END OF THE WAR AND AFTER

1. Paul S. Boyer, *By the Bomb's Early Light: American Thought and Culture at the Dawn of the Atomic Age* (1985; Chapel Hill: University of North Carolina Press, 1994), 12.

2. Boyer, *Bomb's Early Light*; for sources on the reception of the Holocaust in America, see note 7 below.

3. Lewis Mumford, *Programme for Survival* (London: Secker and Warburg, 1946), 2–3.

4. Ibid., 5.

5. Norman Cousins, "Modern Man Is Obsolete: An Editorial," *Saturday Review of Literature* (August 18, 1945): 5.

6. Cousins, "Modern Man Is Obsolete," 6.

7. Early works that documented American Holocaust indifference include David S. Wyman, *The Abandonment of the Jews: America and the Holocaust, 1941–1945* (New York: Pantheon Books, 1984), and Deborah E. Lipstadt, *Beyond Belief: The American Press and the Coming of the Holocaust, 1933–1945* (New York: Free Press, 1986). An interesting analysis of the degree to which the New York Intellectuals addressed the Holocaust is Robert B. Westbrook, "The Responsibility of Peoples: Dwight Macdonald and the Holocaust" (1983), in *Why We Fought: Forging American Obligations in World War II* (Washington, DC: Smithsonian Books, 2004), esp. 93–104. The idea of a traumatic delay in camp survivors' testimonies is a folk mistake that somehow came to be mixed up with the revival of psychoanalytic theories of Holocaust "testimony" in the 1980s, associated with a misprision of the Freudian model, which assumes a latency period between trauma and expression. Researchers on the historical side, however, should always have been aware that first-person accounts of the camps appeared as literature, reportage, and personal interviews immediately after the war, including such books as David Rousset's *L'Univers concentrationnaire* (1946) about Jews in Buchenwald (published in English as *The Other Kingdom* [1947]) or Olga Lengyel's *Five Chimneys* (1947) about Auschwitz (Lengyel was not Jewish, but detailed the systematic murder of Jews witnessed in her time as an inmate).

8. This is a partial summary of Mark Greif, *The American Transformation of the Holocaust, 1945–1965* (AB thesis, Harvard University, 1997). The part left out as a matter of continuing controversy—the dating and reasons for the reemergence—represents the substance of the rest of that study. Peter Novick's influential book *The Holocaust in American Life* (Boston: Houghton Mifflin, 1999) has contributed to the recent change in thought on the history of American Holocaust reception. Where Novick places the reemergence of the Holocaust in its modern form in the late 1960s, attributing it to activism by an organized Jewish community in support of Israel, I found that the Nazi murder of the Jews reemerged in its recognizable present form in years before and after 1960, not because of "organized Jewry" but first through creative figures in intellectual life and the arts.

9. Cited in D. D. Guttenplan, *The Holocaust on Trial: History, Justice and the David Irving Libel Case* (London: Granta, 2001), 188. The numbers for the quantities of human goods from Jews found at Birkenau in Auschwitz, recorded by the Red Army, are reported by the historian of Auschwitz, Robert Jan van Pelt. The Nazi collecting of goods from the dead and soon-to-be murdered had been intimated in scattered form in press accounts from the discovery of the camps in 1945. The most recent and

reliable historical accounting of what was exploited by the Nazis from Jewish bodies appears in Andrzej Strzelecki, "The Plunder of Victims and Their Corpses," in *Anatomy of the Auschwitz Death Camp*, ed. Yisrael Gutman and Michael Berenbaum (Bloomington: United States Holocaust Memorial Museum/Indiana University Press, 1994), 246–66. In addition to leather goods, personal effects, and gold pulled from the teeth of corpses, a reliable trail exists to prove the extensive use of human hair in German industry. "There is no doubt that hair from the victims of Auschwitz and other camps was used to manufacture felt, yarn (threads), fabric (haircloth), stockings, and socks. Testimonies, memoirs, research analyses, and some court rulings indicate that human hair was used in the ignition mechanism of bombs with delayed ignitions, ropes and cords (on ships), and mattresses and clothing" (261). Ashes were indeed exploited locally for fertilizer and possibly for construction and repair, but rendered human fat seems only to have been used as fuel for the cremation of more victims.

10. Dwight Macdonald, "The Responsibility of Peoples," *Politics*, March 1945, 82–93; the quote appears on p. 83.

11. Abraham Joshua Heschel, *Who Is Man?* (Stanford, CA: Stanford University Press, 1965), 24.

12. In a pivotal scene of Wouk's Pulitzer Prize winner for fiction, and longtime best seller, Greenwald, the Jewish American lawyer who has gained acquittal for the USS *Caine*'s righteous mutineers, turns the moral tables and gives a folksy speech on the importance of the US Navy and military, right or wrong, to protect the weak—turning the assimilated Jew into a figure of generalized, and sentimental, vulnerability, all around "soap":

> I'm a Jew, guess most of you know that. . . . Well, sure, you guys all have mothers, but they wouldn't be in the same bad shape mine would if we'd of lost this war. . . . See, the Germans aren't kidding about the Jews. They're cooking us down to soap over there. They think we're vermin and should be 'sterminated [*sic*] and our corpses turned into something useful. . . . But I just can't cotton to the idea of my mom melted down into a bar of soap. I had an uncle and an aunt in Cracow, who are soap now, but that's different, I never saw my uncle and aunt, just saw letters in Jewish from them, ever since I was a kid, but never could read them. Jew, but I can't read Jewish.

Herman Wouk, *The Caine Mutiny* (1951; New York: Back Bay, 1992), 481.

13. Quoted in Terry A. Cooney, *The Rise of the New York Intellectuals: "Partisan Review" and Its Circle* (Madison: University of Wisconsin Press, 1986), 4.

14. Editors' advertisement in *Partisan Review* (September–October 1942): n.p.

15. The opening of Hook's eventual contribution to "The New Failure of Nerve" strongly echoes the editors' advertisement for the "special issue"; whether this was because Hook drew from their prospectus or because the editors drew from a preexisting draft by Hook, it is impossible to say. Hook was, for this brief moment, the closest thing *Partisan Review* had to an official philosopher apart from Trotsky and Marx. He had taught William Phillips and Delmore Schwartz as students (Christopher Phelps, *Young Sidney Hook: Marxist and Pragmatist* [Ithaca, NY: Cornell University Press, 1997], 168–69). But Hook's predominance was short lived, though he continued to write for the magazine, especially on anti-Communist and Cold War issues. The existentialist turn is part of what replaced him, as well as the way in which William Barrett, who later became *Partisan Review*'s in-house philosophy professor when he joined the editorial board, synthesized a longer tradition of existentialism even after the editors had become frustrated with their actual French contacts.

16. T. S. Eliot, "Notes Towards a Definition of Culture," *Partisan Review* (Spring 1944): 138–44. It was republished from the *New English Weekly* (January–February 1943). At this point, *Partisan Review* had suffered its major internal conflict and split over opposition to the war; the editorial board now included only Rahv, Phillips, and Delmore Schwartz.

17. Richard Chase, "The Armed Obscurantist" (review of Lewis Mumford, *The Condition of Man*), *Partisan Review* 11, 3 (Summer 1944): 346–47.

18. See, for example, Alan M. Wald, *The New York Intellectuals: The Rise and Decline of the Anti-Stalinist Left from the 1930s to the 1980s* (Chapel Hill: University of North Carolina Press, 1987), 217.

19. H. J. Kaplan, "Paris Letter," *Partisan Review* (Fall 1945): 474.

20. Annie Cohen-Solal, *Sartre: A Life*, trans. Anna Cancogni (New York: Pantheon Books, 1987), 276; George Cotkin, *Existential America* (Baltimore, MD: Johns Hopkins University Press, 2003), 112–13.

21. Cotkin, *Existential America*, 116.

22. See Mary McCarthy, "America the Beautiful: The Humanist in the Bathtub" (1947), in *A Bolt from the Blue and Other Essays*, ed. A. O. Scott (New York: New York Review Books, 2002), 225–38. *Partisan Review* reported on Beauvoir's animosity toward itself (as evidenced in Beauvoir's diary of her US trip in the December 1947 *Les Temps Modernes*) by May 1948. Louis Clair [Lewis Coser], "French Periodicals," *Partisan Review* (May 1948): 605. In the same issue, however, and in subsequent issues, *Partisan Review* ran more long articles by Sartre. Personal assessments of existentialists other than Camus generally headed downhill all through these years, even while "existentialism" itself held its ground. (The New York Intellectuals never lost their affection for Camus.) The final salvo

against Beauvoir in particular, bookending McCarthy's impressions, was William Phillips's review in 1953 of Beauvoir's eventual book collection on America, *America Day by Day*, including his own recollection of her 1947 visit. William Phillips, "A French Lady on the Dark Continent," *Commentary* (July 1953): 25–28.

23. "New French Writing" was the spring 1946 *Partisan Review* issue. Merleau-Ponty appeared in *Partisan Review* in September–October 1946.

24. On anti-Communist liberals' distaste for Truman despite their campaigns against his third-party opponent, Henry Wallace, see Stephen Gillon's study of Americans for Democratic Action. Steven M. Gillon, *Politics and Vision: The ADA and American Liberalism, 1947–1985* (New York: Oxford University Press), 1987.

25. The degree to which the Resistance moment remained a lasting exemplary episode of a special kind of political action, even among the most unsentimental of thinkers, can be measured by its treatment at the start of Hannah Arendt, *Between Past and Future: Eight Exercises in Political Thought* (enlarged ed., 1961/1968; New York: Penguin, 1993), 3–4.

26. Ralph Harper, *Existentialism: A Theory of Man* (Cambridge, MA: Harvard University Press, 1938); the second quotation is Marjorie Grene, *Dreadful Freedom: A Critique of Existentialism* (Chicago: University of Chicago Press, 1948), 14, quoted in Cotkin, *Existential America*, 139.

27. William Barrett, "Talent and Career of Jean-Paul Sartre," *Partisan Review* (Spring 1946): 239, 238. In his later *Irrational Man* (1958), Barrett defended instead an existentialism that had turned away from Sartre (as a philosophically shallow epigone) to a German- and Russian-language tradition. Hints of this suspicious genealogy are apparent in the early reception of existentialism, even when *Partisan Review* seemed most enthusiastic, as in the publications by Barrett and by Arendt (Hannah Arendt, "What is Existenz Philosophy?" *Partisan Review* [Winter 1946]: 34–56).

28. Anna Boschetti, in her analysis of Sartre's rise to dominance of two separate fields in France—literature and philosophy—has likewise noted that Sartre first had an identity as a litterateur, then, through his new connection to the Resistance, combined with institutional ties to academic legitimation (via his École Normale Supérieure education), managed to become prominent as a philosopher. She shows this progress in France; one can begin to sketch a much more rapid progress toward the same end in America. Anna Boschetti, *The Intellectual Enterprise: Sartre and "Les Temps Modernes,"* trans. Richard McCleary (Chicago: Northwestern University Press, 1987).

29. Cotkin, *Existential America*, 94–96.

30. Cohen-Solal, *Sartre: A Life*, 275.

31. Arendt, "What is Existenz Philosophy?," 46n. The essay is reprinted

in different form in Hannah Arendt, *Essays in Understanding 1930–1954*, ed. Jerome Kohn (New York: Harcourt, 1994), 163–87, in a new translation from a 1948 German publication that expunged the factual details of the Heidegger footnote. Her editor, Kohn, restores the missing portion of the American footnote in brackets (187), preserving both Arendt's presumed ideal text in German and an important part of the historical record of her relationship to Heidegger. I have discussed the contradictions of Arendt's behavior toward Heidegger in Mark Greif, "Arendt's Judgment," *Dissent*, Spring 2004, 98–103.

32. F. Duras, "Heidegger's Record," *Partisan Review* (November 1948): 1262.

33. According to historian Anne Fulton, summarizing eyewitness accounts by the French philosopher Jean Wahl and the American Richard McKeon, there were only three groups remaining in postwar French philosophy: "the Catholics (dominated by the neo-Thomists who were the official spokespeople for Catholic thought), the Communists, and the existentialists." While these battled—each with a practical orientation, an impulse to moralism and action—the scientific and "value neutral" alternatives were left on the sidelines, Fulton says: "Idealistic, nominalistic, and naturalistic thought had virtually disappeared from French philosophical discourse during this period and the analytic tradition was almost nonexistent"; Ann Fulton, *Apostles of Sartre: Existentialism in America, 1945–1963* (Evanston, IL: Northwestern University Press, 1999), 18.

34. As elaborated also in *Being and Nothingness*—a book most Americans were unable to read until it appeared in translation more than ten years later—Sartre's doctrine was a set of themes around an antiessentialist position on human life. Man made himself, actual existence preceded essence, God was absent, and phenomenology (the Husserlian-Heideggerian approach to analysis of things as they appear) was an appropriate approach to "philosophical ontology." Jean-Paul Sartre, *Being and Nothingness: An Essay on Phenomenological Ontology*, trans. Hazel E. Barnes (New York: Philosophical Library, 1956).

35. Jean-Paul Sartre, *Existentialism*, trans. Bernard Frechtman (New York: Philosophical Library, 1947), 18–20, 27–28.

36. Phillip Rahv, contribution to "The Jewish Writer and the English Literary Tradition: A Symposium; Part II," *Commentary* (October 1949): 361.

37. The standard biography of Macdonald is Michael Wreszin, *A Rebel in Defense of Tradition: The Life and Politics of Dwight Macdonald* (New York: Basic Books, 1994). Wreszin discusses the Trotsky quotation on 82–83. A short intellectual biography is Stephen J. Whitfield, *A Critical American: The Politics of Dwight Macdonald* (Hamden, CT: Archon Books, 1984). The most important critical study for the crisis of man phase

of Macdonald's activity in the 1940s is Gregory D. Sumner, *Dwight Macdonald and the "Politics" Circle: The Challenge of Cosmopolitan Democracy* (Ithaca, NY: Cornell University Press, 1996). An earlier, brief analysis of the same period is Westbrook, "Responsibility of Peoples."

38. Dwight Macdonald, "The Root is Man: Part Two," *Politics*, July 1946, 194; subsequent references are cited by page number parenthetically in the text.

39. For example, Boyer, *Bomb's Early Light*, 225–26. He cites John Hersey as another rare writer who addressed both. One could add Lewis Mumford to this select list. The best interpretation of Macdonald's address to the Holocaust in his "The Responsibility of Peoples" is still Westbrook, "The Responsibility of Peoples," 108–23.

40. Different portions of the Office of War Information (OWI) and also the Office of Strategic Services (OSS) during the war included an impressive and eccentric range of European intellectuals and young native-born academics. A factional battle within the OWI led to the departure of key American leftists by 1942, but among the disparate group recruited in 1942 or after were still such figures as André Breton, French founder of surrealism in the 1920s (who mostly read prepared text for French radio broadcasts), the French anthropologist and philosopher Claude Lévi-Strauss, and the actor Yul Brynner. The historiography of the OWI has tended to emphasize the conflicts within the organization between Archibald MacLeish and his group of American-born writers and artists, and a Madison Avenue business faction that was brought in later in 1942 and 1943 to minimize political friction for President Roosevelt. For Breton, see Mark Polizzotti, *Revolution of the Mind: The Life of André Breton* (New York: Farrar, Straus and Giroux, 1995), 509–10; for the eclectic new hires after 1942, see Clayton D. Laurie, "Ideology and American Propaganda: The Psychological Warfare Campaign against Nazi Germany, 1941–1945" (PhD diss., American University, 1990), 279–80; for an account of the "writer's revolt" in 1942–43, see Sydney Weinberg, "What to Tell America: The Writers' Quarrel in the Office of War Information," *Journal of American History* 55 (June 1968): 73–89. The standard institutional history of the OWI and its antecedent organizations, which does not deal with the role of the European émigrés (except to note some mistrust of the 493 foreign "aliens" employed by the Overseas Branch in New York [44]), is Allan M. Winkler, *The Politics of Propaganda: The Office of War Information, 1942–1945* (New Haven, CT: Yale University Press, 1978).

41. Sumner, *Dwight Macdonald*, 27.

42. The resulting press accounts on Dachau and Buchenwald as the models of "concentration camps" helped to confuse the earliest American understandings of the progress of the Jewish genocide. The best organized

killing had been accomplished at death camps in the East, several of them destroyed by the Nazis before they were captured by the Red Army. Belsen, however, which was liberated by the British, was heavily Jewish at the end of the war only because of an influx of prisoners from decommissioned Auschwitz.

43. Dwight Macdonald, "The Responsibility of Peoples," 89. The question of personal responsibility in Macdonald's well-known essay is ultimately confusing. Temperamentally, Macdonald was not one to blame himself. "We, Too, Are Guilty," Macdonald could write, but he meant first that Churchill and FDR were guilty, just like Hitler and Stalin. His essay should be compared to his friend Hannah Arendt's 1945 essay "German Guilt," which Macdonald quotes at the end of his own effort: "In political terms, the idea of humanity, excluding no people and assigning a monopoly of guilt to no one, is the only guarantee that one 'superior race' after another may not feel obligated to follow the 'natural law' of the right of the powerful." Arendt, "Organized Guilt and Universal Responsibility," in *Essays in Understanding*, 131.

44. Macdonald, "The Responsibility of Peoples," 87.

45. This was not Haskell's main argument, but it seems a fair subargument to draw from him. His essays concerned the relation of antislavery to capitalism. He saw antislavery as a consequence of market capitalism, as new markets causally connected economic actors to slaves and thus made certain capitalists (principally Quakers) responsible (and subsequently activist) for their rescue. Thomas Haskell, "Capitalism and the Origins of the Humanitarian Sensibility, Part 1 and Part 2" (1985), in *The Antislavery Debate: Capitalism and Abolitionism as a Problem in Historical Interpretation*, ed. Thomas Bender (Berkeley: University of California Press, 1992), 107–60. From a different disciplinary formation, the sociology of social movements and mobilization offers comparable arguments with more richly developed mechanisms and diverse historical cases, introducing such terms as "repertoires," "mobilizing technologies," and "scripts." A much more sophisticated sociological expansion of a Haskell-like argument, drawing upon both historical and social movement sociology, can now be found in Peter Stamatov, *The Origins of Global Humanitarianism: Religion, Empires, and Advocacy* (Cambridge, UK: Cambridge University Press, 2013).

46. William L. Bird Jr. and Harry R. Rubenstein, *Design for Victory: World War II Posters on the American Home Front* (New York: Princeton Architectural Press, 1998). A study of the means by which different aspects of "public culture" (presidential speeches, newspaper editorials, newsreels, and opinion polls) kept these feelings of global responsibility alive in the 1945–50 transition from world war to Cold War is John Fousek,

To Lead the Free World: American Nationalism and the Cultural Roots of the Cold War (Chapel Hill: University of North Carolina Press, 2000); see especially chapter 3, "The Meaning of Global Responsibility."

47. James Agee, contribution to "Religion and the Intellectuals: A Symposium," *Partisan Review* (February 1950): 108.

48. A provisional answer: In the two decades that followed 1945, the recipes for foreign intervention, singularly hard to activate for private citizens, were as likely to turn into domestic recipes—applying the same norms and fears from the international situation to the discovery of similar problems in the United States and in one's own state and community (the concentration camp in the kitchen, the hidden starving refugees in America, etc.). This line of thought is pursued in Greif, *American Transformation of the Holocaust*, chapter 3. In the international arena, one also sees a new self-awareness in the subsequent period of the ability of nongovernmental organizations (NGOs) to work outside of state frameworks.

49. Letter of November 11, 1946, in *Hannah Arendt/Karl Jaspers: Correspondence, 1926–1969*, ed. Lotte Kohler and Hans Saner, trans. Robert and Rita Kimber (New York: Harcourt, 1992), 66.

50. Nicola Chiaromonte, "Paris Letter," *Partisan Review* (September–October 1950): 711–12.

51. Albert Camus, "The Human Crisis," trans. Lionel Abel, *Twice a Year* (Fall–Winter 1946–47): 28.

52. Justin O'Brien, quoted from his *The French Literary Horizon* (1967), in Herbert R. Lottman, *Albert Camus: A Biography* (Garden City, NY: Doubleday, 1979), 381.

53. Camus, "Human Crisis," 29.

54. Sumner gives an account of the New York activities of the Europe-America Groups, initiated by Macdonald and Chiaromonte with Mary McCarthy as prime mover and chairman, including their battles with the more narrowly anti-Communist *Partisan Review* intellectuals, as well as the groups' failure to connect successfully with their European opposite numbers. Sumner, *Dwight Macdonald*, 203–11. Lottman, in *Albert Camus*, describes the *Groupes de Liaison Internationale* from the French side and claims a more robust connection to the New York–based Europe-America Groups—crediting the creation of the groups to Chiaromonte, McCarthy, and Alfred Kazin, and only tangentially involving Macdonald. Lottman says the groups provided real financial help to refugees in Paris through their fund-raising for the French *Groupes de Liaison*; Lottman, *Albert Camus*, 458–63.

55. Camus, "The Human Crisis," 29.

56. Erich Kahler, *Man the Measure: A New Approach to History* (1943; New York: George Braziller, 1956), 626.

57. Mumford, *Programme for Survival*, 31; emphasis in original.

58. Harry S. Ashmore, *Unseasonable Truths: The Life of Robert Maynard Hutchins* (Boston: Little, Brown, 1989), 270.

59. Reinhold Niebuhr, *The Children of Light and the Children of Darkness: A Vindication of Democracy and a Critique of Its Traditional Defense* (1944; New York: Scribner's, 1949), 187, 189.

60. "A Proposal to History," *Saturday Review of Literature* (April 3, 1948): 6.

61. William Graebner, *The Age of Doubt: American Thought and Culture in the 1940s* (Boston: Twayne, 1991), 72. The ups and downs of Garry Davis through the 1940s chart the changing fortunes of the world government or "world federation" dream. Most striking in Davis's 1961 autobiography is the number of other individuals and organizations interested in renouncing national citizenships, identifying pieces of earth belonging to no nation (so that they could swear allegiance to them), or making stateless humanity a *positive* juridical category within the bureaucratic maze of refugee statelessness of the immediate postwar era. Garry Davis, *The World Is My Country: The Autobiography of Garry Davis* (New York: Putnam, 1961).

62. An embittered Lewis Mumford called the United Nations an "institution . . . already twenty years out of date when it was formed: the very terms of the Dumbarton Oaks proposals show how little the politicians and the diplomats and the so-called experts had been awakened"; *Programme for Survival*, 42. In Stephen C. Schlesinger's purely diplomatic history of the San Francisco conference, one can hear in passing the disappointed voices of world government advocate E. B. White of the *New Yorker* ("It would be deluding the people to imply that [international] controversies, from now on, will be settled in accordance with 'principles of justice'") and of twenty-seven-year-old journalist and future president John F. Kennedy. Schlesinger, *Act of Creation: The Founding of the United Nations* (Boulder, CO: Westview, 2003), 156; the historian himself finally acknowledges some of the new institution's weaknesses and the "paralyzing" "effect" of the veto in the Security Council "for forty-five years during the Cold War," 284–86.

63. Elizabeth Borgwardt, *A New Deal for the World: America's Vision for Human Rights* (Cambridge, MA: Harvard University Press, 2005), 53.

64. Ibid., *New Deal*, 20–21; A. W. Brian Simpson, *Human Rights and the End of Empire: Britain and the Genesis of the European Convention* (Oxford, UK: Oxford University Press, 2001), 172–85; Kirsten Sellars, *The Rise and Rise of Human Rights: Human Rights and Modern War* (Stroud, UK: Sutton, 2002), x.

65. Borgwardt, *New Deal*, 21.

66. See Robert B. Westbrook, "Fighting for the American Family: Private Interests and Political Obligations in World War II," in *The Power of Culture: Critical Essays in American History*, ed. Richard Wightman Fox and T. J. Jackson Lears (Chicago: University of Chicago Press, 1993), 195–222.

67. Borgwardt, *New Deal*, 20–21.

68. The US Office of War Information turned them into a 1942 pamphlet, for worldwide propaganda, that made the Four Freedoms the purpose (from the American point of view) of the fight of all the Allied countries: *The United Nations Fight for the Four Freedoms*. See Simpson, *Human Rights*, 185n134.

69. Sumner, *Dwight Macdonald*, 45.

70. Percy E. Corbett, "Next Steps after the Charter: An Approach to the Enforcement of Human Rights," *Commentary* (November 1945): 24.

71. Paul Gordon Lauren, *The Evolution of International Human Rights: Visions Seen* (Philadelphia: University of Pennsylvania Press, 1998), 185.

72. Ibid., 184.

73. Ibid., 185.

74. Borgwardt, *New Deal*, 189.

75. The longest retelling of the meeting is in William Korey, *NGOs and the Universal Declaration of Human Rights: A Curious Grapevine* (New York: St. Martin's Press, 1998), chapter 1; the most reliable and factual is probably Mary Ann Glendon, *A World Made New: Eleanor Roosevelt and the Universal Declaration of Human Rights* (New York: Random House, 2001), 17. A provocative, detailed, and hostile revisionist account that depicts the NGOs as dupes of US policy is Sellars, *Rise and Rise*, 1–3.

76. Mark Mazower, "The Strange Triumph of Human Rights, 1933–1950," *Historical Journal* 47, 2 (2004): 385–86.

77. For the human rights language woven throughout the United Nations Charter from preamble to ending, see Simpson, *Human Rights and the End of Empire*, 263.

78. See Harry Truman, speech of June 26, 1945, reprinted as an appendix to Schlesinger, *Act of Creation*, 293.

79. Editors' introduction to Corbett, "Next Steps," 21.

80. Editors of *Commentary*, "The Crisis of the Individual: A Series," *Commentary* (December 1945): 1.

81. Editors of *Commentary*, "The Crisis of the Individual: The Second Article in a Series," *Commentary* (January 1946): 1.

82. Editors' introduction to Hans Kohn, "This Century of Betrayal: Can America Lead a New Struggle for Independence?" *Commentary* (September 1946): 201.

83. Elliot E. Cohen, "The Intellectuals and the Jewish Community: The Hope for Our Heritage in America," *Commentary* (July 1949): 23.

84. The UNESCO constitution is available in numerous forms, including on the UNESCO website at www.unesco.org.

85. *On Living in a Revolution* contains the more significant essays, though the two were reprinted together in Julian Huxley, *Man in the Modern World* (London: Chatto and Windus, 1947).

86. Ashmore, *Unseasonable Truths*, 302.

87. Stephen Spender, "United Nations: Cultural Division; Unesco's Program and Problems," *Commentary* (April 1947): 338.

88. Julian Huxley, *UNESCO: Its Purpose and Its Philosophy* (1946; Washington, DC: Public Affairs Press, 1947), 13.

89. Glendon, *World Made New*, 38–39; Lauren, *Evolution of Human Rights*, 220–21.

90. Quoted in Glendon, *World Made New*, 51.

91. Quotations about the project are from UNESCO, ed., *Human Rights: Comments and Interpretations* (New York: Columbia University Press, 1949), 7; see also Lauren, *Evolution of Human Rights*, 223, and Glendon, *World Made New*, 51.

92. The most compelling evidence on the origins and progress of the statement appears in Mark Goodale, "Toward a Critical Anthropology of Human Rights," *Current Anthropology* 47:3 (June 2006): especially at 486n3. The evidence for collaboration comes from research done by Wilcomb Washburn in "Cultural Relativism, Human Rights, and the AAA," *American Anthropologist*, New Series, 89:4 (December 1987): 940.

93. The Executive Board, American Anthropological Association, "Statement on Human Rights," *American Anthropologist*, New Series, 49:1 (October–December 1947): 541–42.

94. Ibid., 540.

95. Ibid., 542, 541.

96. Karen Engle, "From Skepticism to Embrace: Human Rights and the American Anthropological Association from 1947–1999," *Human Rights Quarterly* 23 (2001): 536–59.

97. Mark Goodale, "Ethical Theory as Social Practice," *American Anthropologist* 108: 1 (March 2006): 25.

98. See Mark Goodale, "Introduction to 'Anthropology and Human Rights in a New Key,'" *American Anthropologist* 108: 1 (March 2006): 1–8, and Goodale, "Ethical Theory," 25–37.

99. Lauren, *Evolution of Human Rights*, 224.

100. Glendon, who has closely studied the records of the commission, thinks they did ignore it. See *World Made New*, 83. Lauren presents contrary evidence that at least René Cassin and Charles Malik had read the

UNESCO report and felt it had an influence, based on their separate personal testimonies; *Evolution of Human Rights*, 224n.

101. *Universal Declaration of Human Rights*. These quotations come from the first two paragraphs of the preamble and the first article of the enumeration of proclaimed principles. Glendon has an excellent history of how the odd word "conscience" came in—where, admittedly, it points also in other languages to "consciousness" or a certain inalienable rational status, but was originally intended by a Chinese delegate, P. C. Chang, to point to conceptions of compassion, fellow-feeling, and mutual obligation, and suffered a bad translation. Glendon, *World Made New*, 67.

102. Jacques Maritain, introduction to UNESCO, ed., *Human Rights*, 9.

103. Anthony Heilbut, *Exiled in Paradise: German Refugee Artists and Intellectuals in America, from the 1930s to the Present* (New York: Viking Press, 1983), 35.

104. Elisabeth Young-Bruehl, *Hannah Arendt: For Love of the World* (New Haven, CT: Yale University Press, 1982), 105; Hannah Arendt, "Preface to Part Three: Antisemitism" [1966], in *The Origins of Totalitarianism*, new ed. (San Diego, CA: Harcourt, 1968), xxiii.

105. An account of the genesis and structure of *The Origins of Totalitarianism*, which has influenced me here, is Margaret Canovan, *Hannah Arendt: A Reinterpretation of Her Political Thought* (Cambridge, UK: Cambridge University Press, 1992).

106. Hannah Arendt, *The Origins of Totalitarianism*, 1st ed. (New York: Harcourt, Brace, 1951). The new edition (1968) discards important material from the first edition, but the first edition is not easily available. Therefore I will cite all quotations unique to the first edition as "1st," and all quotations shared with the new edition as "New." Page numbers and editions will be cited parenthetically in the text.

107. According to Arendt's account of modern anti-Semitism, the Jews had gained some safety in Europe by early alliance with the state as bankers or with high society as "exceptions"—sticking to privilege and pardon rather than the political assertions of right. But this made them targets of others' rage: the Jews represented Europe, in their cosmopolitan role in the balance of power, to those who aspired to dominate Europe as a whole, and represented "the state" to rival groups who could not attack state power directly but could attack the Jews. As the imperialisms came back to roost in Europe in the "pan-movements"—pan-Slavism, pan-Germanism, a racist imperialism for the European continent rather than Africa—the Jews found themselves the hapless opponents of all those who hated the state, needed new subjects for imported racism, or envied the supposed shadow-control and Europe-wide conspiratorial power imputed to the Jews.

108. For an acknowledgment of the centrality of this one chapter for

many different thinkers, see Ian Balfour and Eduardo Cadava, "The Claims of Human Rights: An Introduction," *South Atlantic Quarterly* 103 (Spring/Summer 2004): 280.

109. See Stephen J. Whitfield, *Into the Dark: Hannah Arendt and Totalitarianism* (Philadelphia: Temple University Press, 1980), 111.

110. See Canovan, *Hannah Arendt*, 27.

111. As Arendt commented, to the disillusion the enthusiasts

> one must add the confusion created by the many recent attempts to frame a new bill of human rights, which have demonstrated that no one seems able to define with any assurance what these general human rights, as distinguished from the rights of citizens, really are. Although everyone seems to agree that the plight of these people consists precisely in their loss of the Rights of Man, no one seems to know which rights they lost when they lost these human rights" (*Origins of Totalitarianism* [new ed., 293]).

112. Lincoln Reis, "An Old-School Testament," review of *The Measure of Man*, by Joseph Wood Krutch, *Commentary* (December 1954): 581.

113. Gerald Weales, "Middle Way as Metaphysics," review of *The Dignity of Man*, by Russell W. Davenport, *Commentary* (November 1955): 488–89.

114. Quoted in Hilton Kramer, "Exhibiting the Family of Man: 'The World's Most Talked About Photographs,'" *Commentary* (October 1955): 365.

115. Erik J. Sandeen, *Picturing an Exhibition: "The Family of Man" and 1950s America* (Albuquerque: University of New Mexico Press, 1995), 2.

116. Ibid., 46.

117. Kramer, "Exhibiting the Family of Man," 364. Sandeen indicates—against Kramer's claim that the 250,000 copies sold in three weeks—that the book was actually first published in May.

118. Roland Barthes, "The Great Family of Man," in *Mythologies*, trans. Annette Lavers (1957; New York: Hill and Wang, 1972), 101, 102.

119. Edward Steichen, introduction to *The Family of Man* by Edward Steichen and the Museum of Modern Art ([New York]: Published for the Museum of Modern Art by Simon and Schuster, 1955), n.p.

120. Sandeen, *Picturing an Exhibition*, 48.

121. Ibid., 138.

CHAPTER 4
CRITICISM AND THE LITERARY CRISIS OF MAN

1. Malcolm Cowley, "Humanizing Society," in *The Critique of Humanism: A Symposium*, ed. C. Hartley Grattan (New York: Brewer and Warren, 1930), 63.

2. Peter Sloterdijk, *Regeln für den Menschenpark: Ein Antwortschreiben zu Heideggers Brief über den Humanismus* (Frankfurt am Main: Suhrkamp, 1999). In his polemic, the German philosopher Sloterdijk is skeptical of the power of humanism to succeed in any culture (like that of the contemporary West) whose media have moved beyond the book. He interestingly identifies the post-1945 period of literature and education in Germany as a time of militant attempts to recover a book-based humanism—exactly paralleling the demands I am chronicling in the United States—to overcome Germany's wartime inhumanity. For a comparable view on the necessary connection between humanism and "written culture" and the "age of print"—followed by its late twentieth-century complications in a period of rival media—see Terry Cochran, *Twilight of the Literary: Figures of Thought in the Age of Print* (Cambridge, MA: Harvard University Press, 2001).

3. This book, *The Critique of Humanism* (1930), consisted of the then-younger generation of critics—including Cowley, Edmund Wilson, Kenneth Burke, R. P. Blackmur, and Yvor Winters—disposing of the remains of the New Humanism, such that, by the time of the era of the crisis of man starting in the late 1930s, "humanism" did not necessarily recall the Babbitt-More era.

4. In 1948 specifically it was reprinted in an important summary volume: T. S. Eliot, "Ulysses, Order, and Myth," in *Forms of Modern Fiction: Essays in Honor of Joseph Warren Beach*, ed. Walter Van O'Connor (Minneapolis: University of Minnesota Press, 1948), 123.

5. Lionel Trilling, "Art and Fortune," *Partisan Review* (December 1948): 1271; subsequent references are cited by page number parenthetically in the text.

6. José Ortega y Gasset, *The Dehumanization of Art and Notes on the Novel*, trans. Helen Weyl (1925; Princeton, NJ: Princeton University Press, 1948).

7. It is possible to see this thesis revive with different fears for the death of the novel in the sixties and beyond, once the concern with man had been undermined. For an influential example, see John Barth, "The Literature of Exhaustion" (1967), in *The American Novel since World War II*, ed. Marcus Klein (Greenwich, CT: Fawcett, 1969).

8. For the theory that the English novel depended on the rising middle classes of the eighteenth century, Trilling had the tradition of Leslie Stephen, for example, to draw upon; Leslie Stephen, *English Literature and Society in the Eighteenth Century* (London: Duckworth, 1904). A decade after Trilling, Ian Watt traced the complete genealogy of such views (while rearticulating them in classic form) all the way to Madame de Staël and the Vicomte de Bonald in the first decade of the nineteenth century; Ian P.

Watt, *The Rise of the Novel: Studies in Defoe, Richardson, and Fielding* (Berkeley: University of California Press, 1957), 300.

9. *Partisan Review* had begun translating selections from Sartre's *What Is Literature?* in January 1948, with further installments appearing during that year. The whole appeared in book form in the United States in 1949. Jean-Paul Sartre, *What Is Literature?*, trans. Bernard Frechtman (New York: Philosophical Library, 1949).

10. On the cultural significance of Trilling's Columbia promotion, and the resistance to it, see David A. Hollinger, *Science, Jews, and Secular Culture: Studies in Mid-Twentieth-Century American Intellectual History* (Princeton, NJ: Princeton University Press, 1996), 159. Diana Trilling recounts the precise details in *The Beginning of the Journey: The Marriage of Diana and Lionel Trilling* (New York: Harcourt Brace, 1993), chapter 10.

11. Arthur Krystal, ed., *A Company of Readers: Uncollected Writings of W. H. Auden, Jacques Barzun, and Lionel Trilling from the Readers' Subscription and Mid-Century Book Clubs* (New York: Free Press, 2001).

12. "The Great American Novel," *Nation*, January 9, 1868, in *The Idea of an American Novel*, ed. Louis D. Rubin Jr. and John Rees Moore (New York: Thomas Y. Crowell, 1961).

13. Hannah Arendt, "Franz Kafka: A Reevaluation," *Partisan Review* (Fall 1944): 420.

14. Clifton Fadiman, "The Decline of Attention," *Saturday Review of Literature* (August 6, 1949): 20.

15. Harrison Smith, "Chaos, Fear and the Modern Novel," *Saturday Review of Literature* (June 3, 1950): 22.

16. "Fiction in the U.S.: We Need a Novelist to Re-Create American Values Instead of Wallowing in the Literary Slums," *Life*, August 16, 1948, 24. The editorial inveighed specifically against Norman Mailer's *The Naked and the Dead*, then notorious for what was considered its crudeness and profanity.

17. Lionel Trilling, "Manners, Morals, and the Novel" (1948), in Trilling, *The Liberal Imagination: Essays on Literature and Society* (New York: Viking, 1950), 222. The essay originally appeared in *Kenyon Review*.

18. The history of the disciplinary rise of English departments is told in Gerald Graff, *Professing Literature: An Institutional History* (Chicago: University of Chicago Press, 1987).

19. Kermit Vanderbilt, *American Literature and the Academy: The Roots, Growth, and Maturity of a Profession* (Philadelphia: University of Pennsylvania Press, 1986), 85, 257.

20. David R. Shumway, *Creating American Civilization: A Genealogy*

of American Literature as an Academic Discipline (Minneapolis: University of Minnesota Press, 1994), 192.

21. F. O. Matthiessen, *American Renaissance: Art and Expression in the Age of Emerson and Whitman* (London: Oxford University Press, 1941).

22. This canon of American literature had been preceded by a canon created, not in colleges and universities, but in the public schools, where selections from Hawthorne and Emerson contributed to the making of young citizens in elementary and secondary education, beginning in the 1850s and 1860s and lasting through the turn of the century. See Richard H. Brodhead, *The School of Hawthorne* (Oxford, UK: Oxford University Press, 1986).

23. Robert E. Spiller, Willard Thorp, Thomas H. Johnson, Henry Seidel Canby, *Literary History of the United States*, 2 vols. (New York: Macmillan, 1948).

24. One may take this with a small grain of historical salt; it comes from the authors' long contribution to the new *Cambridge History of American Literature*, in eight volumes, the major attempt in the 1990s to replace the Spiller project with the revisionary wisdom of the late twentieth century. Evan Carton and Gerald Graff, "Criticism since 1940," in *The Cambridge History of American Literature*, vol. 8, *Poetry and Criticism*, ed. Sacvan Bercovitch (Cambridge, UK: Cambridge University Press, 1996), 308.

25. See Brian Higgins and Hershel Parker, introduction to *Critical Essays on Herman Melville's "Moby-Dick,"* ed. Brian Higgins and Hershel Parker (New York: G. K. Hall, 1992), 15.

26. Lewis Mumford, *Herman Melville: A Study of His Life and Vision*, rev. ed. (1929; New York: Harcourt, Brace & World, 1962), xv, 107.

27. The unsigned but credited author of this quotation was the prolific Malcolm Cowley. "American Books Abroad," in *Literary History of the United States*, 2:1374.

28. Ibid., 2:1391.

29. Harrison Smith, "Standards of Criticism," *Saturday Review of Literature* 33 (November 4, 1950): 20.

30. For details of how this transpired, see Malcolm Cowley, "The Fitzgerald Revival: 1941–1953," in *Fitzgerald/Hemingway Annual 1974*, ed. Matthew J. Bruccoli and C. E. Frazer Clark (Englewood, CO: Microcard Editions Books, 1975), 11–13.

31. This discussion of an American modernist canon leaves implicit the parallel and preceding work by US critics and scholars to create a canon of British and European modernist authors and legitimate it as material for university instruction. This history is addressed in David A. Hollinger, "The

Canon and Its Keepers: Modernism and Mid-Twentieth-Century American Intellectuals," in *In the American Province: Studies in the History and Historiography of Ideas* (1985; Baltimore, MD: Johns Hopkins University Press, 1989), 74–91.

32. The term was revived for study of American literature by the Harvard scholar Perry Miller in his writings on Roger Williams, the Puritan apostate, and later by Miller's antagonist and successor Sacvan Bercovitch, during the retrieval of American Puritanism for literature in the postwar period. The post-Miller reconstruction of typology can be found in Sacvan Bercovitch, *The American Jeremiad* (Madison: University of Wisconsin Press, 1978). A good assessment of the extended controversy over typology can be found in James P. Byrd, *The Challenge of Roger Williams: Religious Liberty, Violent Persecution, and the Bible* (Macon, GA: Mercer University Press, 2002), 41–48.

33. Ellipses in original in second quotation. Gore Vidal, "A Note on the Novel," in *United States: Essays, 1952–1992* (New York: Random House, 1993), 24, 23. Originally published in the *New York Times Book Review*, August 5, 1956.

34. William Phillips, "Portrait of the Artist as a Middle-Aged Man," *Partisan Review* (Winter 1944): 119–22.

35. Louis Bromfield, "A Case of Literary Sickness," *Saturday Review of Literature* (September 13, 1947): 7.

36. John Crowe Ransom, contribution to "The State of American Writing, 1948," *Partisan Review* (August 1948): 880.

37. John Berryman, contribution to "The State of American Writing, 1948," *Partisan Review* (August 1948): 858.

38. The *Saturday Review of Literature* statement is editorial text in a special twenty-fifth anniversary issue, summarizing and agreeing with a pessimistic overview article by editor Henry Seidel Canby, "Footnotes to 1949," *Saturday Review of Literature* (August 6, 1949): 17–19, 175ff.

39. "Personal & Otherwise," *Harper's*, November 1951, 8.

40. C. Hartley Grattan, "The Trouble with Books Today," *Harper's*, November 1951, 36.

41. John W. Aldridge, *After the Lost Generation: A Critical Study of the Writers of Two Wars* (1951; New York: Noonday, 1958), 142.

42. Aldridge, *After the Lost Generation*, 87. The same statement appears in an earlier version of his argument published not long after Trilling's "Art and Fortune" essay. John W. Aldridge, "America's Young Novelists: Uneasy Inheritors of a Revolution," *Saturday Review of Literature* (February 12, 1949): 6.

43. Aldridge, *After the Lost Generation*, 90.

44. William Barrett, "American Fiction and American Values," *Partisan Review* (November–December 1951): 682.

45. Lawrence H. Schwartz, *Creating Faulkner's Reputation: The Politics of Modern Literary Criticism* (Knoxville: University of Tennessee Press, 1988), 1.

46. Quoted in Schwartz, *Creating Faulkner's Reputation*, 9.

47. "When the Dam Breaks," *Time*, January 23, 1939, 45–48.

48. Editor's introduction to the section "Modern Times," in William Faulkner, *The Portable Faulkner*, ed. Malcolm Cowley (New York: Viking Press, 1946), 651.

49. Robert Penn Warren, "William Faulkner" (1946–50), in *Selected Essays* (New York: Random House, 1958), 65.

50. Ibid., 65–66, 67–68.

51. Ibid., 78–79.

52. Schwartz, *Creating Faulkner's Reputation*, 29.

53. The Nobel Prize speech was made the last section of the revised and expanded edition of the *Portable* released in 1967 and in all subsequent printings. William Faulkner, "Address upon Receiving the Nobel Prize for Literature," in *The Portable Faulkner*, ed. Malcolm Cowley, rev. and expanded ed. (New York: Viking Press, 1967), 723–24. It had been widely publicized in its own time, too, as we will see.

54. William Faulkner, "I Decline to Accept the End of Man," *Perspectives USA*, Pilot Issue (January 1952): 5–6.

55. "Trade Winds," *Saturday Review of Literature* (February 3, 1951): 4.

56. For the situation of *Perspectives USA* within the Ford Foundation's wider mission of intellectual-sponsorship-as-propaganda, and the magazine's connection to the CIA-funded pro-American intellectual journals in Europe, including *Encounter* in England, *Preuves* in France, and *Der Monat* in Germany, see Frances Stonor Saunders, *The Cultural Cold War: The CIA and the World of Arts and Letters* (New York: New Press, 1999).

57. In addition to Adler for Chicago, the board included Delmore Schwartz and Alfred Kazin for the New York Intellectuals; Allen Tate, Cleanth Brooks, and Robert Penn Warren for Southerners and proto-New Critics; Jacques Barzun from Columbia and Harry Levin and Perry Miller from Harvard, for academics; John Crowe Ransom; W. H. Auden; James T. Farrell; James Agee; Robert Motherwell for painters; Aaron Copland for composers; Eero Saarinen for architects; Tennessee Williams for playwrights— and the historian and establishment liberal Arthur Schlesinger Jr. for good measure.

58. This raises the question of the degree to which one can already see

a coded Cold War rhetoric of man, in which man himself was supposed to be somehow antitotalitarian, as a creeping patriotic vulgarization of lines of thought expressed, for example, in Arendt's *Origins of Totalitarianism*, or in Dwight Macdonald's writings, or other intellectual projects discussed in chapter 3, above. *Perspectives USA*, Pilot Issue (January 1952); *Perspectives USA* 1 (Fall 1952).

59. Michael S. Reynolds, *Hemingway: The Final Years* (New York: W. W. Norton, 1999), 153–54.

60. Philip Rahv, "Into the Trees and Out of Sight," review of *Across the River and Into the Trees*, by Ernest Hemingway, *Commentary* (October 1950): 400–402.

61. Reynolds, *Hemingway*, 154.

62. The exchange with Breit is in Reynolds, *Hemingway*, 252–53; I am responsible for this interpretation.

63. I am grateful to John Plotz for bringing this to my attention.

64. "A Great American Storyteller," *Life*, September 1, 1952, 20.

65. "From Ernest Hemingway to the Editors of *Life*," *Life*, August 25, 1952, 124.

66. Reynolds, *Hemingway*, 258.

67. Ernest Hemingway, *The Old Man and the Sea* (New York: Scribner's, 1952); subsequent references are cited by page number parenthetically in the text.

68. Maxwell Geismar, "Decline of the Classic Moderns" (1955), collected in *American Moderns: From Rebellion to Conformity* (New York: Hill and Wang, 1958), 12.

69. For a stimulating reading of *A Fable* as a fable of the bureaucracy of war, see James Dawes, *The Language of War: Literature and Culture in the U.S. from the Civil War through World War II* (Cambridge, MA: Harvard University Press, 2002), chapter 5.

70. William Faulkner, *A Fable* (New York: Random House, 1954), 123, emphasis added; subsequent references are cited by page number parenthetically in the text.

71. Jay Parini, *One Matchless Time: A Life of William Faulkner* (New York: HarperCollins, 2004), 365.

72. Faulkner's first positive letter to Cowley about the critic's writings resuscitating his reputation was dated November 1944, with Faulkner jokingly hinting he would want to "collaborate" in the process if Cowley showed him more such writings before publication. By August 1945, Cowley had arranged the *Portable Faulkner* and they were indeed collaborating (under Cowley's direction) on its contents. See Malcolm Cowley, *The Faulkner-Cowley File: Letters and Memories, 1944–1962* (New York: Viking Press, 1966), 14, 20–27.

73. Parini says *A Fable* took Faulkner the longest of any of his books to write; it seems to have become a nightmare and duty by the end, though his collapses and hospitalizations while writing it (through 1953 and 1954) were, of course, also the product of alcoholism and alcoholic depression. On the composition of *A Fable*, including binges, psychiatry, and electroshock treatments, see Parini, *One Matchless Time*, 350–57. The best and most thorough biography of Faulkner remains Joseph Leo Blotner, *Faulkner: A Biography*, 2 vols. (New York: Random House, 1974).

74. Richard Wright, *The Outsider* (1953), in *Later Works* (New York: Library of America, 1991); subsequent references are cited by page number parenthetically in the text.

75. "Mr. Eliot," *Time*, March 6, 1950, 22–23, 25.

76. Randall Stewart, "Poetically the Most Accurate Man Alive," *Modern Age* 6 (1962), quoted in Schwartz, *Creating Faulkner's Reputation*, 10.

77. Norman Mailer, contribution to "Our Country and Our Culture," *Partisan Review* (May–June 1952): 299.

78. Saul Bellow, "Man Underground," review of *Invisible Man*, by Ralph Ellison, *Commentary* (June 1952): 609.

79. Granville Hicks, foreword to *The Living Novel: A Symposium*, ed. Granville Hicks (New York: Macmillan, 1957), viii.

80. Saul Bellow, "Distractions of a Fiction Writer," in Hicks, *The Living Novel*, 16.

81. Hicks, *Living Novel*, x.

82. Flannery O'Connor, "The Fiction Writer and His Country," in Hicks, *The Living Novel*, 158; also included in O'Connor, *Collected Works* (New York: Library of America, 1988), 801.

83. Ralph Ellison, "Society, Morality, and the Novel," in Hicks, *The Living Novel*, 87, 89.

84. James Burnham, "Observations on Kafka," *Partisan Review* (March–April 1947): 193.

85. Paul Goodman, *Kafka's Prayer* (New York: Vanguard, 1947).

86. John Kelly, "Franz Kafka's *Trial* and the Theology of Crisis," *Southern Review* (Spring 1940): 748.

87. Angel Flores, ed., *The Kafka Problem* (New York: New Directions, 1946). The Flores volume contains the best 1940s bibliography of the international publication of Kafka and development of the Czech writer's reputation since his death in 1924.

88. Arendt, "Franz Kafka," 416.

89. Burnham, "Observations on Kafka," 193.

90. Heinz Politzer, "From Mendelssohn to Kafka: The Jewish Man of Letters in Germany," *Commentary* (April 1947): 350. Politzer had collaborated with Max Brod in 1935 on the original German edition of Kafka's complete works.

91. F. W. Dupee, "The Fabulous and the Familiar," review of *The Trial*, by Franz Kafka, *Partisan Review* (December 1937): 66–68; "specially translated" is from the back cover of *Partisan Review* (March 1938); "characteristic Kafkian art" is in the editors' introduction to Max Brod, "Kafka: Father and Son," *Partisan Review* (May 1938): 19–29.

92. Editors' advertisement, *Partisan Review* (August–September 1938): n.p.

93. One practical development was Schocken's publication of the *Gesammelte Schriften* in Berlin between 1935 and 1937 and the republication of the collection later in New York, where the Jewish publisher was forced to move his operations under pressure from the Nazis (Salman Schocken himself emigrated first to Palestine in 1934, and to New York only in 1940).

94. The later 1940s publication events for Kafka can also be periodized. They came after war's end, and they reflected, first, a moment of still avantgarde or coterie publication and criticism, then, second, and very quickly, the beginning of academic admission. At the end of the war, Vanguard leaped in with a translation of *The Metamorphosis* (1946); New Directions with *Amerika* (1946) (in their New Classics series); and Schocken followed up with an English-language story compilation, *The Great Wall of China* (1946) (with notes by Philip Rahv of *Partisan Review*) and the translation of Max Brod's biography of Kafka (1947). The academic moment arrived in 1948, as university presses entered the field; in that year alone, Oxford brought out Charles Neider's *The Frozen Sea: A Study of Kafka*, Yale translated the German scholar Herbert Tauber's early book on Kafka's complete oeuvre (*Franz Kafka: An Interpretation of His Work*), and the University of Chicago released the New Critic Austin Warren's *Rage for Order*, including a prominent chapter on Kafka. Also, by 1948, the individual essays on Kafka in quarterlies were increasingly scholastic, and they had spread to the provinces: in *Accent*, a quarterly put out by the University of Illinois, Urbana, one critic's explication of "The Hunger Artist" now existed in a maze of obligations to other criticism: "a critic of *The Castle* points out . . . ," "One critic of *The Burrow* describes that story as . . ."; Robert W. Stallman, "Kafka's Cage," *Accent* (Winter 1948): 117. By 1949, when the nonbohemian, non-avant-garde publisher Rinehart anthologized "Short Novels of the Masters," they advertised only "Henry James, Thomas Mann, Kafka, and others." No first name was needed for this newest "master."

95. Irving Howe, "The Value of Taste," review of *Classics and Commercials*, by Edmund Wilson, *Partisan Review* (January–February 1951): 128; John Berryman, contribution to "The State of American Writing, 1948: A Symposium," *Partisan Review* (August 1948): 858; Heinz Politzer, "Messenger of the King," review of *The Diaries of Franz Kafka* by Max Brod; *Franz Kafkas Glauben und Lehre* by Max Brod; *Franz Kafka: An Interpretation of His Works* by Herbert Tauber, *Commentary* (July 1949): 95;

and Elliot E. Cohen, "The Intellectuals and the Jewish Community: The Hope for Our Heritage in America," *Commentary* (July 1949): 25.

96. Anatole Broyard, *Kafka Was the Rage: A Greenwich Village Memoir* (1993; New York: Vintage, 1997).

97. Edmund Wilson, "A Dissenting Opinion on Kafka," in *Classics and Commercials: A Literary Chronicle of the Forties* (New York: Farrar, Straus, 1950), 383. The date of original publication is given as July 26, 1947.

98. Ibid., 385.

99. Ibid., 384.

100. Ibid., 388.

101. Philip Rahv, "Notes on the Decline of Naturalism," in *Image and Idea: Fourteen Essays on Literary Themes* (New York: New Directions, 1949), 130.

102. Randall Jarrell, "In All Directions," review of *New Directions, 1941, Partisan Review* (July–August 1942): 346.

103. Rahv, "Notes on the Decline," 130; italics in original.

104. Isaac Rosenfeld, "Ubiquitous Oblique," review of *The Body* by William Sansom and *Two Worlds and Their Ways* by Ivy Compton-Burnett, *Partisan Review* (September 1949): 950–52.

105. William Phillips, "Dostoevsky's Underground Man," *Partisan Review* (November–December 1946): 558.

106. William Phillips, "The Great Wall of Criticism," *Commentary* (June 1947): 596.

107. William Barrett, "What Existentialism Offers Modern Man: A Philosophy of Fundamental Human Realities," *Commentary* (July 1951): 17–23.

108. Caroline Gordon, "Letter to Flannery O'Connor" (November 13, 1951), in *Letters to a Fiction Writer*, ed. Frederick Busch (New York: W. W. Norton, 1999), 265.

109. Lawrence Jackson, *Ralph Ellison: Emergence of Genius* (New York: Wiley, 2002), 421.

110. See Thomas Pynchon, introduction to *Slow Learner: Early Stories* (Boston: Little, Brown, 1984), 20.

CHAPTER 5
SAUL BELLOW AND RALPH ELLISON

1. David Remnick, "Visible Man," in *The Devil Problem and Other True Stories* (New York: Random House, 1996), 239.

2. The next US writer to receive the Nobel Prize in Literature was Toni Morrison in 1993, the last American to date.

3. Isaac Bashevis Singer, "Gimpel the Fool," trans. Saul Bellow, *Partisan Review* (May–June 1953): 300–313.

4. Saul Bellow, "Ralph Ellison in Tivoli," *Partisan Review* (Fall 1998): 524.

5. James Atlas, *Bellow: A Biography* (New York: Random House, 2000), 89.

6. Lawrence Jackson, *Ralph Ellison: Emergence of Genius* (New York: Wiley, 2002), 296–300; Atlas, *Bellow*, 101.

7. Saul Bellow, "Man Underground," review of *Invisible Man*, by Ralph Ellison, *Commentary* (June 1952): 608.

8. Albert Murray and John F. Callahan, eds., *Trading Twelves: The Selected Letters of Ralph Ellison and Albert Murray* (New York: Modern Library, 2000), 25.

9. Gloria L. Cronin and Ben Siegel, *Conversations with Saul Bellow* (Jackson: University Press of Mississippi, 1994), 280.

10. The two men's relationship and the similarities in their work have not been much studied by critics. An exception is Kasia Boddy, "The White Boy Looks at the Black Boy, the Black Boy Looks at the White Boy: Saul Bellow, Ralph Ellison, and the Great Omni-American Novel," *Saul Bellow Journal* 16–17 (Summer and Fall 2000/Winter 2001): 51–73.

11. Bellow, "Ralph Ellison in Tivoli," 525.

12. Atlas, *Bellow*, 260.

13. Ellison made the lifelong promise of a second novel and worked on its text until the year of his death. His literary editor published a portion of it as *Juneteenth* in 1999, while the bulk of the manuscript appeared in 2010 as *Six Days after the Shooting*. Ellison's essays and ideas, however, in hindsight, seem equally capable of being approached as the necessary "second half" of his total achievement.

14. Saul Bellow, *Dangling Man* (1944; New York: Penguin/Plume, 1988), 9; subsequent references are cited by page number parenthetically in the text.

15. Lionel Trilling, "Art and Fortune," *Partisan Review* (December 1948): 1280, 1271. See chapter 4 for the full passages that contain these quotations.

16. Saul Bellow, "Notes of a Dangling Man," *Partisan Review* (September–October 1943): 402–9, 429–38. I will continue citing quotations parenthetically according to the book's pagination; only where the journal text differs significantly will I cite its page number.

17. James Atlas says the book is modeled on Rilke's *Notebooks*, which it does not much resemble; the *Columbia Literary History of the United States* (ed. Emory Elliott [New York: Columbia University Press, 1988]), somewhat anachronistically adds Sartre's *Nausea*, which New Directions published in English only in 1949. Bellow could conceivably have read it in French, but before 1945 and Sartre's discovery by New York, he might have

had little reason to do so. Atlas, *Bellow*, 97; "Neorealist Fiction," in *Columbia Literary History of the United States*, 1136.

18. Later we learn that "Myron Adler [said] . . . his agency had decided to hire women to make the survey; there is less possibility of their being taken away, leaving things in mid-air" (58). Not only do women, and their homes, phones, and phonographs (as we'll see) represent everything that drives Joseph wild with anger and disgust, they're less likely to dangle, too.

19. This appears on page 25 in the published book, 405 in the *Partisan Review* excerpt. The wording differs very slightly between the two, but without differences significant to this reading.

20. Saul Bellow, "Distractions of a Fiction Writer," in *The Living Novel: A Symposium*, ed. Granville Hicks (New York: Macmillan, 1957), 19.

21. Lionel Trilling, "The Sense of the Past," *Partisan Review* (May–June 1942): 229–41. This same issue with Trilling's essay, in fact, included the publication of Bellow's second story, "The Mexican General," two years earlier than "Notes of a Dangling Man"; there is every likelihood that Bellow was familiar with Trilling's text.

22. James Atlas, *Bellow*, 84. Atlas's citation is from a letter to Kazin in the Berg Collection, New York Public Library.

23. Robert M. Hutchins, "Toward a Durable Society," *Fortune*, June 1943, 201; see citation in chapter 2 above.

24. Emily Miller Budick, *Blacks and Jews in Literary Conversation* (Cambridge, UK: Cambridge University Press, 1998), 9–10.

25. Karen Brodkin, *How Jews Became White Folks and What that Says about Race in America* (New Brunswick, NJ: Rutgers University Press, 1998). Brodkin's title and argument are derivative of other books in the 1990s-era field of whiteness studies: Noel Ignatiev's *How the Irish Became White* (1996) and the earlier landmark books by David Roediger (*The Wages of Whiteness* [1991]) and Theodore Allen (*The Invention of the White Race* [two volumes, 1994 and 1997]). The best interethnic account and idealized case for our purposes may come from Matthew Frye Jacobson's *Whiteness of a Different Color* (1998), where Jacobson demonstrates through a complex web of evidence that the 1940s were the decade of distinct attention to the "race" of Jewishness, in order to move Jews out of a separate racial category and into the newer, more capacious framework of the Caucasian. This occurred at the same moment that American political and cultural life came to be structured around the single racial division between Negro and Caucasian while adding a new range of virtuous white "ethnicities." It is hard to do justice to Jacobson's argument in a short summary, but his periodization is significant. In his view, for Jews "World War II will present a . . . turning point . . . in the final transformation toward

Caucasian whiteness," yet it was "precisely that post-Nazi moment" at which " 'racial' Jewishness was still a live, yet a newly intolerable, conception" (176). Matthew Frye Jacobson, *Whiteness of a Different Color: European Immigrants and the Alchemy of Race* (Cambridge, MA: Harvard University Press, 1998), especially chapter 3, "Becoming Caucasian," and chapter 5, "Looking Jewish, Seeing Jews." A decade and a half later, the more schematic accounts of whiteness or nonwhiteness for various groups have been complicated by additional specialist research; see especially Eric L. Goldstein, *The Price of Whiteness: Jews, Race, and American Identity* (Princeton, NJ: Princeton University Press, 2006).

26. See Budick's pages on *Commentary*, with a different emphasis; *Blacks and Jews*, 62–63.

27. James Baldwin, "The Harlem Ghetto: Winter 1948; The Vicious Circle of Frustration and Prejudice," *Commentary* (February 1948): 165–70; "Previous Condition: A Story," *Commentary* (October 1948): 334–42.

28. Anatole Broyard, "Portrait of the Inauthentic Negro: How Prejudice Distorts the Victim's Personality," *Commentary* (July 1950): 56–64. Broyard had not yet made his now well-known choice to pass as white as a book critic of the *New York Times*; for that history, see Henry Louis Gates Jr., "The Passing of Anatole Broyard," in *Thirteen Ways of Looking at a Black Man* (New York: Random House, 1997).

29. Donald Paneth, "The Bergmans' Queenie: 'Pick Yourself Up; Do the Best You Can,' " *Commentary* (September 1951): 260–68.

30. Saul Bellow, "Looking for Mr. Green: A Story," *Commentary* (March 1951): 251–61; subsequent references are cited by page number parenthetically in the text. The story was first collected with some very slight later revisions of wording (which do not affect my interpretation) in Saul Bellow, "Looking for Mr. Green," in *Seize the Day, with Three Short Stories and a One-Act Play* (New York: Viking, 1956), 135–60.

31. Quoted in Adam Zachary Newton, *Facing Black and Jew: Literature as Public Space in Twentieth-Century America* (Cambridge, UK: Cambridge University Press, 1999), xi.

32. Or so Ellison's publishers quote Lewis on the cover of the paperback edition (Vintage, 1989). I haven't found the correct source, though Lewis wrote glowingly on *Invisible Man* at the end of his influential book *The American Adam: Innocence, Tragedy, and Tradition in the Nineteenth Century* (Chicago: University of Chicago Press, 1955).

33. Described in John Corry, "An American Novelist Who Sometimes Teaches," *New York Times Magazine*, November 20, 1966, reprinted in Maryemma Graham and Amritjit Singh, eds., *Conversations with Ralph Ellison* (Jackson: University Press of Mississippi, 1995), 99.

34. "Professor's Choice," *Wilson Quarterly* 2 (Winter 1978): 136–37.

35. Raymond Mazurek, "Courses and Canons: The Post-1945 U.S. Novel," *Critique* 31 (Spring 1990): 149.

36. Seymour Krim, "Two Communications: The Fiction of Fiction; A Critical Nudger," *Partisan Review* (May–June 1952): 353.

37. Ralph Ellison, *Invisible Man* (1952; New York: Vintage, 1989), 51; subsequent references are cited by page number parenthetically in the text.

38. Jackson, *Ralph Ellison*, esp. chapters 7 and 8. On Ellison and the Communist Party, see also Barbara Foley, *Wrestling with the Left: The Making of Ralph Ellison's Invisible Man* (Durham, NC: Duke University Press, 2010).

39. From a letter to Langston Hughes, quoted by Jackson, *Ralph Ellison*, 167.

40. Jackson, *Ralph Ellison*, 185.

41. The simple account of the lord-bondsman dialectic that follows, which in other hands, and in popular memory, has taken on the character of an elaborate myth, is drawn from the relevant sections 178 to 196, in G.W.F. Hegel, *Phenomenology of Spirit*, trans. A. V. Miller (1807; Oxford, UK: Oxford University Press, 1977), 111–19; subsequent references are cited by page number parenthetically in the text.

42. Alexandre Kojève, *Introduction to the Reading of Hegel: Lectures on the "Phenomenology of Spirit,"* ed. Raymond Queneau and Allan Bloom, trans. James H. Nichols Jr. (1947/1969; Ithaca, NY: Cornell University Press, 1980).

43. For Hobbes's views on the inability to surrender one's life, see *Leviathan*, chapter 14 (199). C. B. Macpherson, editor of the Penguin edition, also cites (39) a stronger formulation in Hobbes's *Philosophical Rudiments Concerning Government and Society*, chap. 1, sec. 7, Hobbes's English translation of his own *De Cive*. For Hobbes on slavery, see *Leviathan*, chap. 20 (255–66). Thomas Hobbes, *Leviathan*, ed. C. B. Macpherson (1651; London: Penguin, 1985). For Locke on slavery, see the *Second Treatise of Government*, chap. 4, sec. 23–24, in John Locke, *Two Treatises of Government*, ed. Peter Laslett (1689; Cambridge, UK: Cambridge University Press, 1988), 284–85. David Brion Davis, *The Problem of Slavery in Western Culture* (1966; New York: Oxford University Press, 1988), 116–120, analyzes Hobbes and Locke on these points; while the epilogue to David Brion Davis, *The Problem of Slavery in the Age of Revolution, 1770–1823* (1975; New York: Oxford University Press, 1999) places them in contrast to Hegel, who represents "the apex of a changing ethical consciousness" (559) because Hegel, in effect, usefully added the problem of recognition to the philosophical discourse of slavery. Davis also places Hegel's slave dialectic, intellectually, in the context of the conflict between Napoleon and Toussaint L'Ouverture, though not by direct influence as Susan Buck-Morss has in *Hegel, Haiti, and Universal History* (Pittsburgh: University

of Pittsburgh Press, 2009). Notably, Davis's interpretation of Hegel is also quite openly an interpretation of Hegel through Alexandre Kojève. Paul Gilroy, too, returns to Davis and Kojève to reconsider the place of Hegel's dialectic of lord and bondsman in the philosophy of modernity and its development between Europe and America (including the Caribbean) in the geo-intellectual province of thought he has termed the Black Atlantic; Paul Gilroy, *The Black Atlantic: Modernity and Double Consciousness* (Cambridge, MA: Harvard University Press, 1993), 50–63.

44. Jackson, *Ralph Ellison*, 229. These words are the biographer's.

45. This is from a letter Ellison wrote to Wright on April 22, 1940, quoted in Jackson, *Ralph Ellison*, 229.

46. Buck-Morss, *Hegel, Haiti, and Universal History*.

47. From Hegel's preface to *Hegel's Philosophy of Right*, ed. T. M. Knox (1820; Oxford, UK: Clarendon Press, 1942), 13.

48. Alfred Chester and Vilma Howard, "The Art of Fiction: An Interview" (1954/1955), in Graham and Singh, *Conversations with Ralph Ellison*, 15.

49. Frederick Douglass, *My Bondage and My Freedom* (1855), in *Autobiographies* (New York: Library of America, 1994), 283–87.

50. On Hegel and Douglass, see also Gilroy, *The Black Atlantic*, 60.

51. See, for example, Kojève, *Introduction to the Reading of Hegel*, 22.

52. Ellison's ambivalence about violence comes from his sense that it is self-destructive, when it can seize only objects near at hand rather than distant causes (in geography, in history)—all the more so if, as we will see, we acknowledge his view that "white" America is ineradicably, already, black. If black violence targets white artifacts or culture, it risks rejecting or striking back at elements of its own achievements, things it has built. The positive temptation of violence for his black characters exists simply to prove that they can *do* it, because of a doubt that blacks have the courage or strength to destroy anything, even as white society claims they are the source of violence and destruction—and to this form of self-discovery, *Invisible Man* is more sympathetic. "On each floor . . . smoke and flame arose," the narrator says, during the book's final black riot in Harlem. "And now I was seized with a fierce sense of exaltation. They've done it, I thought. They organized it and carried it through alone. . . . Capable of their own action" (548).

CHAPTER 6
RALPH ELLISON AND SAUL BELLOW

1. Ralph Ellison, *Invisible Man* (1952; New York: Vintage, 1989), 553; subsequent references are cited by page number parenthetically in the text.

2. I discuss Lawrence Jackson's similar assessment below, but Henry Louis Gates has also identified these ideas as part of a wider common project between Ellison and his longtime friend Albert Murray, author of *The Omni-Americans*. See Henry Louis Gates, "King of Cats," in *Thirteen Ways of Looking at a Black Man* (New York: Random House, 1997).

3. Leslie Fiedler, "Come Back to the Raft Ag'in, Huck Honey!," *Partisan Review* (June 1948): 664–71; Fiedler's original essay also opened with an implicit attack on both the censuring of "underground" homosexuality and overt racism toward blacks, equating or analogizing the two in a way that (though now it seems progressive) was unfamiliar for the time and may help explain Ellison's frustration with Fiedler, and the teasing Mr. Emerson episode. The phrase "[s]ociological significance" is from Leslie Fiedler, *Love and Death in the American Novel*, rev. ed. (1960; New York: Stein and Day, 1966), 366.

4. Lawrence Jackson, *Ralph Ellison: Emergence of Genius* (New York: Wiley, 2002), 344.

5. Ibid., 385–87.

6. Roderick A. Ferguson, *Aberrations in Black: Toward a Queer of Color Critique* (Minneapolis: University of Minnesota Press, 2004), 58–65. See also Barbara Foley, *Wrestling with the Left: The Making of Ralph Ellison's Invisible Man* (Durham, NC: Duke University Press, 2010), 164–68. On Mr. Emerson, the best discussion is currently Michael Trask, *Camp Sites: Sex, Politics, and Academic Style in Postwar America* (Stanford, CA: Stanford University Press, 2013), 43–46.

7. Toni Morrison, *Playing in the Dark: Whiteness and the Literary Imagination* (1992; New York: Vintage, 1993), 37.

8. The classic reading of *The Deerslayer*, which extended this line, belongs to Philip Fisher in *Hard Facts* (New York: Oxford University Press, 1985).

9. Delmore Schwartz, "Fiction Chronicle: The Wrongs of Innocence and Experience," *Partisan Review* (May–June 1952): 358–59. I have reordered these quotations from their sequence in the original.

10. Saul Bellow, "Man Underground," review of *Invisible Man*, by Ralph Ellison, *Commentary* (June 1952): 609, emphasis added.

11. Jackson, *Ralph Ellison*, 442, confirmed by personal communication with Rebecca Keith, National Book Foundation, February 28, 2007. The five judges were Saul Bellow, Martha Foley, Irving Howe, Howard Mumford Jones, and Alfred Kazin.

12. Details about the unpublished letter to Wright come from Jackson, *Ralph Ellison*, 442–44. There is some confusion in the literature about the dating of this letter to Wright. Kasia Boddy cites it as having been written in 1945 and pertaining to *Dangling Man*, which would fit oddly with the

chronology of Bellow and Ellison's friendship and codevelopment. Her assumption can be traced to an editing error, however, in the article by Michael Fabre, "From *Native Son* to *Invisible Man*: Some Notes on Ralph Ellison's Evolution in the 1950s," in *Speaking for You: The Vision of Ralph Ellison*, ed. Kimberly W. Benston (Washington, DC: Howard University Press), 215, from which Boddy is working. Fabre seems to make clear that Ellison's comment on Bellow's book was added to an account Ellison sent to Wright of his own National Book Award speech, delivered in January 1953. However, by a misplaced "Ibid.," Fabre points backward to the previous citation of a different letter from August 1945.

13. Leon Trotsky, "Celine and Poincare: Novelist and Politician" (1935), in *Leon Trotsky on Literature and Art*, ed. Paul N. Siegel (New York: Pathfinder Press, 1970), 191. My thanks to Aaron Matz and Morris Dickstein for knowledge of this quotation.

14. From an interview in 1953: "The great pleasure of the book was that it came easily. All I had to do was be there with buckets to catch it. That's why the form is loose." Harvey Breit, "A Talk with Saul Bellow," *New York Times Book Review*, September 20, 1953, 22, reprinted in Gloria L. Cronin and Ben Siegel, eds., *Conversations with Saul Bellow* (Jackson: University Press of Mississippi, 1994), 4. See also the account Bellow gave to Philip Roth in Philip Roth, "I Got a Scheme!" *New Yorker*, April 25, 2005.

15. Saul Bellow, *The Adventures of Augie March* (1953; New York: Penguin, 1996), 129; subsequent references are cited by page number parenthetically in the text.

16. Maxwell Geismar, "Saul Bellow, Novelist of the Intellectuals" (1958), in Irving Malin, ed., *Saul Bellow and the Critics* (New York: New York University Press, 1967), 17.

17. Mortimer J. Adler, ed., *The Great Ideas: A Synopticon of Great Books of the Western World*, vol. 1 (1952; Chicago: Encyclopaedia Britannica, 1971), n.p.

18. James Atlas, *Bellow: A Biography* (New York: Random House, 2000), 92.

19. Robert M. Hutchins, *The Great Conversation: The Substance of a Liberal Education*, vol. 1 of *Great Books of the Western World* (Chicago: Encyclopaedia Britannica, 1952), 8–9.

20. Atlas, *Bellow*, 93.

21. Hannah Arendt, *The Human Condition*, 2nd ed. (1958; Chicago: University of Chicago Press, 1998).

22. For Fanny Ellison's weekend visits, see, for example, Ellison's letter to Albert Murray of August 1959, in Albert Murray and John F. Callahan, eds., *Trading Twelves: The Selected Letters of Ralph Ellison and Albert Murray* (New York: Modern Library, 2000), 218. Bellow did include Elli-

son's wife in his second account of arrangements in Tivoli, mentioned in the next paragraph. This alternate account is the 1995 preface to Ellison's *Collected Essays*, published just one year after Ellison's death. Bellow writes there: "Toward the end of the fifties, the Ellisons and the Bellows lived together in a spooky Dutchess County house. . . . My children spent their holidays with me, and occasionally my Aunt Jennie came up from New York. Fanny [Ellison] arrived regularly on Friday evening and returned on Sunday afternoon." Saul Bellow, preface to *The Collected Essays of Ralph Ellison*, rev. ed., ed. John F. Callahan (1995; New York: Modern Library, 2003), x.

23. Saul Bellow, "Ralph Ellison in Tivoli," *Partisan Review* (Fall 1998): 524; subsequent references are cited by page number parenthetically in the text.

24. Ralph Ellison, "The World and the Jug" (1963), in *The Collected Essays of Ralph Ellison*, 173.

CHAPTER 7
FLANNERY O'CONNOR AND FAITH

1. James T. Fisher, "American Religion since 1945," in *A Companion to Post-1945 America*, ed. Jean-Christophe Agnew and Roy Rosenzweig (Malden, MA: Blackwell, 2002), 45.

2. Flannery O'Connor, *Collected Works* (New York: Library of America, 1988), 215–16. All citations of O'Connor's fiction and essays will be indicated parenthetically from this edition, except where the Library of America volume omits essays included in the collection *Mystery and Manners*. These will be cited separately in notes.

3. Ibid., 897.

4. Letter to A., August 9, 1955, in O'Connor, *Collected Works*, 945.

5. Letter to Dr. T. R. Spivey, November 30, 1959, in O'Connor, *Collected Works*, 1113.

6. Letter to A., September 15, 1955, in O'Connor, *Collected Works*, 955–56.

7. Letter to Dr. T. R. Spivey, October 19, 1958, in O'Connor, *Collected Works*, 1077.

8. Letter to A., November 22, 1958, in O'Connor, *Collected Works*, 1082.

9. Letter to Beverly Brunson, September 13, 1954, in O'Connor, *Collected Works*, 925.

10. Martin Woessner, *Heidegger in America* (New York: Cambridge University Press, 2011), 95.

11. See Robert S. Thomas, "Enlightenment and Authority: The Commit-

tee on Social Thought and the Ideology of Postwar Conservatism, 1927–1950" (PhD diss. Columbia University, 2010), 612.

12. The extensive summary materials were written by Werner Brock. Martin Heidegger, *Existence and Time* (Chicago: Regnery, 1949).

13. Letter to A., August 2, 1955, in O'Connor, *Collected Works*, 943.

14. Ibid., 949.

15. Ibid., 942.

16. Extreme versions of the social science critique were also shared by conservative figures among the "Southern Agrarians," including Allen Tate, the spouse of O'Connor's mentor Caroline Gordon, as in his *Reason in Madness: Critical Essays* (New York: Putnam, 1941)

17. Letter to A., August 28, 1955, in O'Connor, *Collected Works*, 950.

18. Letter to A., October 20, 1955, in O'Connor, *Collected Works*, 964.

19. Flannery O'Connor, "Writing Short Stories," in *Mystery and Manners: Occasional Prose*, ed. Sally and Robert Fitzgerald (New York: Farrar, Straus and Giroux, 1969), 99.

20. Robert A. Orsi, "'Mildred, Is It Fun to Be a Cripple?': The Culture of Suffering in Mid-Twentieth Century American Catholicism," *South Atlantic Quarterly* 93 (1994): 547–90. Reprinted in his *Between Heaven and Earth: The Religious Worlds People Make and the Scholars Who Study Them* (Princeton, NJ: Princeton University Press, 1995).

21. Alice Walker, "Beyond the Peacock: The Reconstruction of Flannery O'Connor" (1975), in *In Search of Our Mothers' Gardens: Womanist Prose* (San Diego, CA: Harcourt Brace Jovanovich, 1983), 42–59. Walker writes that "*essential* O'Connor is not about race at all, which is why it is so refreshing, coming, as it does, out of such a *racial* culture" (53; italics in original); that "O'Connor caused white women to look ridiculous on pedestals, and she approached her black characters—as a mature artist—with unusual humility and restraint" (59), and also takes O'Connor's late stories about black rage and violence to show "that *she* believed in justice for the individual" because she "added . . . rage" but "waited until she saw it *exhibited* by black people before she recorded it." At the same time, Walker was disturbed by one of Robert Fitzgerald's published allusions to O'Connor's untroubled use of the word "niggers" in then-unpublished correspondence. Had she been able to read the quantity of O'Connor's correspondence now available, she might have responded to the fiction very differently.

22. See Sally Fitzgerald's "Chronology," in O'Connor, *Collected Works*, 1247.

23. Letter to A., September 6, 1955, in O'Connor, *Collected Works*, 954.

24. Letter to Maryat Lee, April 25, 1959, in O'Connor, *Collected Works*, 1094–95.

25. Letter to Maryat Lee, May 21, 1964, in O'Connor, *Collected Works*, 1208–9.

CHAPTER 8
THOMAS PYNCHON AND TECHNOLOGY

1. Thomas Pynchon, *The Crying of Lot 49* (1966; New York: Perennial Library, 1990), 24; subsequent references are cited parenthetically in the text as *CL49* followed by the page number.

2. Thomas Pynchon, *V.* (1963; New York: Perennial Library, 1986), 359; subsequent references are cited parenthetically in the text as *V.* followed by the page number.

3. See Rick Perlstein, *Before the Storm: Barry Goldwater and the Unmaking of the American Consensus* (New York: Hill and Wang, 2001).

4. Only the careful Reader of *V.* will know the true history of Yoyodyne Corporation when it subsequently plays its role as the aerospace arms manufacturer in *The Crying of Lot 49*; Pynchon, *V.*, 227.

5. See Thomas Pynchon, introduction to *Slow Learner: Early Stories* (Boston: Little, Brown, 1984), 13.

6. Norbert Wiener, *The Human Use of Human Beings: Cybernetics and Society* (Boston: Houghton Mifflin, 1950), 37.

7. Michael Bérubé, *Marginal Forces/Cultural Centers: Tolson, Pynchon, and the Politics of the Canon* (Ithaca, NY: Cornell University Press, 1992).

8. Dwight Macdonald, "The Responsibilty of Peoples," *Politics*, March 1945, 87.

9. What we finally know of V's explicit meaning, as nearly as Stencil can make her purpose out, is that she was there wherever imperial power "tossed sparks in search of a fuse" (*V.*, 386), though it was not the war itself that she wanted. Something different, "something monstrous had been building. Not the War, nor the socialist tide which brought us Soviet Russia. Those were symptoms, that's all" (*V.*, 387). What they were symptoms of, we can supply as readers—of the growing "inanimacy." World War II was then an episode of its culmination, "a war [V had] not started but whose etiology was also her own" (*V.*, 387), says Stencil. And it is her fulfillment and death.

10. Dwight Macdonald, "The Responsibility of Peoples," 83. Quoted in chapter 3.

11. It is also characteristic of Pynchon to create continuity in the fictional world described by his books, so that all of them are linked in a single story or satire: that slightly juvenile joke of the Vivaldi Kazoo Concerto had last appeared in the late pages of *V.*, as "the lost Vivaldi Kazoo

Concerto," lost because of "its theft from a monastery by certain Fascist music-lovers" (*V.*, 419). Like so many other things turning up in Pynchon's Southern California, somehow it has moved, transmitted by forgotten fascists, to take up residence in America.

12. In this sense, a core echoic text of social criticism for *The Crying of Lot 49*, which, as far as I know, is never mentioned in Pynchon criticism, is Vance Packard's *The Waste Makers* (1960), the book that introduced "planned obsolescence" to the American vernacular and warned about the junking of still-usable stuff in a great American heap.

13. Entropy has been of so much interest to Pynchon critics because it seems to appear in so many of his works (in the early short story "Entropy," here in *Lot 49*, and maybe as an aspect of the apocalyptic inanimacy of the universe in *V.*) and because it links him to both scientific thinkers (like Norbert Wiener and Claude Shannon) and historical thinkers (like Henry Adams). The classic writings on these issues are Anne Mangel, "Maxwell's Demon, Entropy, Information: *The Crying of Lot 49*," in *Mindful Pleasures: Essays on Thomas Pynchon*, ed. George Levine and David Leverenz (Boston: Little, Brown, 1976), 87–100, and on entropy more generally, Tony Tanner, *City of Words: American Fiction, 1950–1970* (London: Jonathan Cape, 1971), 153–80.

14. See, for example, Edward Mendelson, "The Sacred, the Profane, and *The Crying of Lot 49*," in *Pynchon: A Collection of Critical Essays*, ed. Edward Mendelson (Englewood Cliffs, NJ: Prentice-Hall, 1978), 135. Mendelson's essay is the best written on many of the details of the book, despite my disagreement with the essential orientation (that *"religious meaning is itself the central issue of the plot"* [120; emphasis in original]). Equally, this numerological overdetail is an example of one way in which I think Pynchon criticism can go awry. The number does not really help us, and neither do interpretations that try to make use of this level of game playing. This is why Pynchon creates so much difficulty when perceived as a puzzle writer. He seems alive to intelligible echoes in all his decisions, but this can land the critic him- or herself in an echo chamber or, as in Mendelson's case, within an overreliance on a single arbitrary determination of one (say, religious) purpose. Yet the religious purpose is not thereby invalidated; nor can it be neglected. For the role of Pentecost (and revivification) as an alternative to inanimacy in *V.*, for example, see also W. T. Lhamon Jr., "Pentecost, Promiscuity, and Pynchon's *V.*: From the Scaffold to the Impulsive," in *Mindful Pleasures*, 69–86.

15. A bilingual friend put it to me that "Mucho Maas," Oedipa's husband's name, is most naturally translated "a lot more," rather than through the English cognate "much more": so "lot" and "lots" recovers its emphasis on

sheer plenty, a quantity of stuff, even in this most central pun of the book. "Oedipa Maas," then, would be something like the searcher and sufferer of the Sphinx's riddle and ancient Thebes—but facing, now, more.

CHAPTER 9
THE SIXTIES AS BIG BANG

1. José Ortega Y Gasset, *Man and Crisis*, trans. Mildred Adams (New York: W. W. Norton, 1958).

2. David Lodge, *The British Museum Is Falling Down* (1965; New York: Penguin, 1981), 61.

3. Wallace W. Douglas, "Souls among Masterpieces: The Solemn Style of Modern Critics," *American Scholar* (Winter 1953–54): 44.

4. Arthur M. Schlesinger Jr., *The Vital Center: The Politics of Freedom* (1949; New Brunswick, NJ: Transaction, 1998), 56–57.

5. Hannah Arendt, *The Human Condition*, 2nd ed. (1958; Chicago: University of Chicago Press, 1998). Arendt introduced the material of *The Human Condition* originally as lectures at the University of Chicago in 1956.

6. Herbert Marcuse, *One-Dimensional Man: Studies in the Ideology of Advanced Industrial Society*, 2nd ed. (1964; Boston: Beacon Press, 1991), 9; subsequent references are cited by page number parenthetically in the text.

7. Herbert Marcuse, "Introduction to the First Edition," in *One-Dimensional Man*, xlix. For Vance Packard, and his dramatization of a transition from a "producer ethic" to a consumer ethic in American life, see Daniel Horowitz, *Vance Packard and American Social Criticism* (Chapel Hill: University of North Carolina Press, 1994).

8. Margaret Canovan, *Hannah Arendt: A Reinterpretation of Her Political Thought* (Cambridge, UK: Cambridge University Press, 1992), 63 and chapter 3 as a whole. See also Margaret Canovan, introduction to Arendt, *Human Condition*, 2nd ed.

9. Thomas Wheatland, *The Frankfurt School in Exile* (Minneapolis: University of Minnesota Press, 2009), 285.

10. Arendt, *Human Condition*, 60.

11. Douglas Kellner, introduction to *One-Dimensional Man*, 2nd ed., xvii–xviii, and "Technology, War, and Fascism: Marcuse in the 1940s," in Herbert Marcuse, *Technology, War, and Fascism: Collected Papers of Herbert Marcuse*, vol. 1, ed. Douglas Kellner (London: Routledge, 1998), 15–16.

12. Abbott Gleason, *Totalitarianism: The Inner History of the Cold War* (New York: Oxford University Press, 1995), 34–35.

13. Orwell's famous quotation is from *Nineteen Eighty-Four* (1949), certainly one of the key fictional allegories of the earlier "totalitarian" vision of the crisis of man in the '40s from the British side. Orwell had originally intended to title his dystopian novel *The Last Man in Europe*—one more "man" novel.

14. James Baldwin, "The Dangerous Road before Martin Luther King," originally published in *Harper's*, February 1961; reprinted in Baldwin, *Collected Essays* (New York: Library of America, 1998), 642.

15. Malcolm X, "Black Man's History," in *The End of White World Supremacy: Four Speeches* (New York: Arcade, 1971), 24.

16. Malcolm X, "The Old Negro and the New Negro," in *The End of White World Supremacy*, 82, 95–96.

17. Malcolm X, "God's Judgment of White America," in *The End of White World Supremacy*, 130.

18. Malcolm X, "The Ballot or the Bullet." This line is discussed in Samuel Moyn, *The Last Utopia: Human Rights in History* (Cambridge, MA: Harvard University Press, 2010), 105.

19. Martin Luther King Jr., *Stride toward Freedom: The Montgomery Story* (New York: Harper, 1958), 95.

20. Martin Luther King Jr., "The Theology of Reinhold Niebuhr" (1954), in *The Papers of Martin Luther King*, vol. 2, ed. Ralph E. Luker, Penny A. Russell, and Peter Holloran (Berkeley: University of California Press, 1994), 278.

21. Fredrik Sunnemark, *Ring Out Freedom! The Voice of Martin Luther King, Jr. and the Making of the Civil Rights Movement* (Bloomington: Indiana University Press, 2004), 31–32.

22. "What is Man?," quoted in Sunnemark, *Ring Out Freedom!*, 32. The sermon was delivered in 1959 and originally published in Martin Luther King Jr., *The Measure of a Man* (Philadelphia: Christian Education Press, 1959). Sunnemark quotes the version republished in Martin Luther King Jr., *Strength to Love* (New York: Harper & Row, 1963); he also cites an unpublished manuscript sermon under the same title from 1958 (Sunnemark, *Ring Out Freedom!*, 263).

23. Quoted in Sunnemark, *Ring Out Freedom!*, 33.

24. Moyn, *The Last Utopia*, 105, citing Thomas F. Jackson, *From Civil Rights to Human Rights: Martin Luther King, Jr. and the Struggle for Economic Justice* (Philadelphia, 2007).

25. Students for a Democratic Society, "Port Huron Statement," in Judith Clavir Albert and Stewart Edward Albert, ed., *The Sixties Papers: Docu-*

ments of a Rebellious Decade (New York: Praeger, 1984), 180; emphasis in original.

26. Todd Gitlin, afterword to C. Wright Mills, *The Sociological Imagination* (1959; New York: Oxford University Press, 2000), 230.

27. C. Wright Mills, *The Causes of World War Three* (New York: Simon & Schuster, 1958), 171.

28. Joan Wallach Scott, *Only Paradoxes to Offer: French Feminists and the Rights of Man* (Cambridge, MA: Harvard University Press, 1996), 3–4.

29. Betty Friedan, *The Feminine Mystique* (1963; New York: Dell, 1984), 43.

30. Ibid., 67.

31. Ibid., 77.

32. Alice Echols has attempted to get to the bottom of the bra-burning question:

> They tossed "instruments of torture to women"—high-heeled shoes, bras, girdles, typing books, curlers, false eyelashes, and copies of *Playboy, Cosmopolitan,* and *Ladies Home Journal*—into a "Freedom Trash Can." . . . Although it was widely reported in the mainstream media that the women burned a bra during the protest, there was, in fact, no bra-burning. Most feminist accounts of the protest suggest that the media invented the bra-burning to discredit the movement. But at least one of the organizers of the protest reportedly leaked word of the bra-burning to the press to stimulate media interest in the action.

Alice Echols, *Daring to Be Bad: Radical Feminism in America, 1967–1975* (Minneapolis: University of Minnesota Press, 1989), 93–94.

33. Shulamith Firestone, *The Dialectic of Sex: The Case for Feminist Revolution* (New York: Morrow, 1970), 19.

34. Ibid., 167.

35. Ibid., 105.

36. Robin Morgan, introduction to *Sisterhood Is Powerful: An Anthology of Writings from the Women's Liberation Movement*, ed. Robin Morgan (New York: Random House, 1970), xxxv.

37. *Womankind* (1971), Chicago, Illinois.

38. Robin Lakoff, "Language and Woman's Place," *Language in Society* 2:1 (April 1973): 45–80. It was expanded into book form as *Language and Woman's Place* (New York: Harper and Row, 1975).

39. Ibid., 73–75.

40. Alma Graham, "The Making of a Nonsexist Dictionary," originally published in *Ms.*, December 1973, 12–14, 16; reprinted in Barrie Thorne and

Nancy Henley, ed., *Language and Sex: Difference and Dominance* (Rowley, MA: Newbury House, 1975). The quotation is on page 62.

41. Ibid., 63 (from the reprint copy).

42. Mike Silverstein, "An Open Letter to Tennessee Williams," *[People's] Gay Sunshine*, October 1971, in Karla Jay and Allen Young, *Out of the Closets: Voices of Gay Liberation*, 2nd ed. (1972; New York: New York University Press, 1992), 69–70.

43. Clarence Major, *Dictionary of Afro-American Slang* (New York: International, 1970), 80, 81, 82.

44. Harold Wentworth and Stuart Berg Flexner, *Dictionary of American Slang* (New York: Thomas Crowell, 1960). The white musician Roy Orbison had an early rock-and-roll success with "Working for the Man" in 1962. But this was a bizarre pastiche of rueful African American songs about the boss or master (including, in the background, the hammer blows of prison or work-gang hollers), which ended with the white protagonist's plan to marry the boss's daughter and become "the Man" or overseer himself. Roy Orbison, "Working for the Man," Monument MO 467, August 1962.

45. James Baldwin, *The Fire Next Time*, in *Collected Essays* (1963; New York: Library of America, 1998), 298. The dating of the issue is in "Chronology," in Baldwin, *Collected Essays*, 851.

46. August Meier and Elliott Rudwick, *CORE: A Study in the Civil Rights Movement, 1942–1968* (New York: Oxford University Press, 1973), 300–302.

47. J. E. Lighter, ed., *Random House Historical Dictionary of American Slang*, vol. 2 (New York: Random House, 1997).

48. Thomas A. Johnson, "The US Negro in Vietnam," *New York Times*, April 29, 1968, in *Reporting Vietnam: American Journalism, 1959–1975* (New York: Library of America, 2000), 358–59.

49. Stokely Carmichael, excerpt from "What We Want" (1966), in Albert and Albert, *Sixties Papers*, 141–42.

50. I have been influenced here by Michael Szalay's superb analyses in Michael Szalay, *Hip Figures: A Literary History of the Democratic Party* (Stanford, CA: Stanford University Press, 2012), 234–35.

51. Baldwin, *Fire Next Time*, 341.

52. Ibid., 311.

53. See Norbert Elias, "Informalization and the Civilizing Process" (1989), in *The Norbert Elias Reader: A Biographical Selection*, ed. Johan Goudsblom and Stephen Mennell (Oxford, UK: Blackwell, 1998), 235–45.

54. Sam Binkley, *Getting Loose: Lifestyle Consumption in the 1970s* (Durham, NC: Duke University Press, 2007), 4.

55. Baldwin, *Fire Next Time*, 311.

56. For the progress of the "brown vs. white" metaphor—manifested

most importantly in bread and rice—within the sixties "food counterculture," see Warren James Belasco, *Appetite for Change: How the Counterculture Took on the Food Industry*, 2nd updated ed. (1989; Ithaca, NY: Cornell University Press, 2007), 48–50.

57. Norman Mailer, *The Armies of the Night: History as a Novel, the Novel as History* (1968; New York: Plume, 1994), 60–62.

58. The best current study of the post-1960s shift within white American mores to idealization of loosened and lengthened hair, "relaxation," "letting it all hang out," and opposition to the tight, fixed, formal, and closed, is Binkley, *Getting Loose*.

59. Jerry Rubin, *We Are Everywhere* (New York: Harper & Row, 1971), 42–43. I have reversed the order of the quotations.

60. Crosby, Stills, Nash, and Young, "Almost Cut My Hair," on *Déjà Vu*, Atlantic SD-7200, March 1970.

61. Bob Seger, "Turn the Page," on *Back in '72*, Palladium/Reprise MS-2126, January 1973.

62. Free [Abbie Hoffman], *Revolution for the Hell of It* (1968; New York: Thunder's Mouth Press, 2005), 29.

63. This is quoted from Joe McGinniss, *The Selling of the President, 1968* (New York: Trident, 1969), in Michael Szalay, *Hip Figures*, 230.

64. This last quotation is from Hunter S. Thompson, quoted in Szalay, *Hip Figures*, 230.

65. Andrew Ross, "Hip, and the Long Front of Color," in *No Respect: Intellectuals and Popular Culture* (London: Routledge, 1989), 96.

66. Renata Adler, "Fly Trans-Love Airlines" (1967), *Toward a Radical Middle: Fourteen Pieces of Reporting and Criticism* (New York: Random House, 1969), 50.

67. The 1968 advertisement is quoted in Thomas Frank, *The Conquest of Cool: Business Culture, Counterculture, and the Rise of Hip Consumerism* (Chicago: University of Chicago Press, 1997), 7.

68. Susan Sontag, contribution to "What's Happening to America (A Symposium)," *Partisan Review* (Winter 1967): 51–58.

69. Ibid.

70. Susan Sontag, "Against Interpretation" (1964), in *Against Interpretation* (1966; New York: Picador, 2001), 7, 8.

71. Susan Sontag, "One Culture and the New Sensibility" (1965), in *Against Interpretation*, 297.

72. Susan Sontag, "Freak Show," *New York Review of Books*, November 15, 1973, integrated into Susan Sontag, *On Photography* (1977; New York: Picador, 2001), 34. If you place Barthes's English text side by side with Sontag, you see that Sontag is in effect quoting or recalling Barthes without saying so. Barthes: "[F]rom this pluralism, a type of unity is magically

produced: *man is born, works, laughs and dies everywhere in the same way*" (100; emphasis added). "Everything here . . . aims *to suppress the determining weight of History* . . . prevented precisely by sentimentality from penetrating into this ulterior zone of human behaviour where historical alienation introduces some *'differences' which we shall here quite simply call 'injustices'*" (101; emphasis added). Barthes's book had appeared in English in the previous year. Roland Barthes, "The Great Family of Man," in *Mythologies*, trans. Annette Lavers (1957; New York: Hill and Wang, 1972), 101, 102.

73. Sontag, "Freak Show," *New York Review of Books*, and *On Photography*, 33–34.

CHAPTER 10
UNIVERSAL PHILOSOPHY AND ANTIHUMANIST THEORY

1. Paul Potter, "Speech to the April 17, 1965 March on Washington," in *The Sixties Papers: Documents of a Rebellious Decade*, ed. Judith Clavir Albert and Stewart Edward Albert (New York: Praeger, 1984), 223.

2. Jeremy Varon, *Bringing the War Home: The Weather Underground, the Red Army Faction, and Revolutionary Violence in the Sixties and Seventies* (Berkeley: University of California Press, 2004), 24.

3. Susan Sontag, *On Photography* (1977; New York: Picador, 2001), 19–20.

4. Susan Sontag, *Reborn: Journals and Notebooks, 1947–1963*, ed. David Rieff (New York: Farrar, Straus and Giroux, 2008), 34.

5. Ibid., 28.

6. Sontag speaks of "the disgusting company of Allan Bloom" in *Reborn*, 186. The publication that posthumously revealed Allan Bloom's sexuality and acknowledged Bloom's death of AIDS (a fact previously hidden) was a lightly fictionalized memoir by Saul Bellow, his close friend in Chicago toward the end of his life. Saul Bellow, *Ravelstein* (New York: Viking, 2000).

7. "Chronology," in Susan Sontag, *Essays of the 1960s and 70s*, ed. David Rieff (New York: Library of America, 2013), 816.

8. Sontag, *Reborn*, 174.

9. Ibid., 158.

10. Susan Sontag, "Notes on Camp" (1964), in *Essays of the 1960s and 70s*, 272–73.

11. Sontag, "The Third World of Women" (1973), in ibid., 774–75, 797.

12. Sontag, "What's Happening in America (1966)," as reprinted in her collection *Styles of Radical Will*, in *Essays of the 1960s and 70s*, 459–60. This was the book publication of the contribution to the *Partisan Review* symposium cited in chapter 9, under the magazine's title "What's Happen-

ing to America (A Symposium)." Sontag is quoting and disagreeing with the older New York Intellectual figure Leslie Fiedler here.

13. Susan Sontag, "The Anthropologist as Hero" (1963), in *Against Interpretation and Other Essays* (New York: Farrar, Straus and Giroux, 1966). The review appeared originally in the *New York Review of Books* as "A Hero of Our Time," November 28, 1963.

14. Robert Silvers, personal communication, December 2013.

15. Howard met Barthes in 1957 and translated his *On Racine* (New York: Hill and Wang, 1964). The next year he translated Foucault's *Madness and Civilization: A History of Insanity in the Age of Reason* (New York: Pantheon, 1965).

16. The best contribution is François Cusset's *French Theory*, first published in French in 2003 (then published in the United States in 2008 by University of Minnesota Press). It explains the progress of the main French thinkers in America, but it is outside its purview to establish why Theory found a systematic place in American thinking beyond the short-term needs of individual disciplines, university departments, or single personalities. François Cusset, *French Theory: How Foucault, Derrida, Deleuze, & Co. Transformed the Intellectual Life of the United States*, trans. Jeff Fort (Minneapolis: University of Minnesota Press, 2008). Other recent meditations at the macrolevel include Ian Hunter, "The History of Theory," *Critical Inquiry*, 33:1 (Autumn 2006): 78–112; Fredric Jameson, "How Not to Historicize Theory," *Critical Inquiry*, 34:3 (Spring 2008): 563–82; and Warren Breckman, "Times of Theory: On Writing the History of French Theory," *Journal of the History of Ideas*, 71:3 (July 2010): 339–61. My first consideration of these matters was Mark Greif, "Life after Theory," *American Prospect*, July 2004, 62–65. A cause for optimism is the careful microhistories of individual French thinkers in a growing new literature on post-1945 European intellectual history, many individual contributions to which I have profited from and cite below.

17. This is the term wisely chosen and explained, however, in the best recent account of the earlier twentieth-century philosophical tradition in France, which prepared the ground, largely before World War II, for the distinctive forms of antihumanism that would become regnant in the 1950s: Stefanos Geroulanos, *An Atheism that Is Not Humanist Emerges in French Thought* (Stanford, CA: Stanford University Press, 2010).

18. For a careful reconstruction of the humanist requirements upon all positions in the French philosophical field in the immediate postwar period and a French discourse of man, see historian Edward Baring's chapter entitled "Humanist Pretensions: Catholics, Communists, and Sartre's Struggle for Existentialism in Postwar France," in his *The Young Derrida*

and French Philosophy, 1945–1968 (Cambridge, UK: Cambridge University Press, 2011).

19. Foucault, "Interview de Michel Foucault" (1981), in *Dits et Écrits*, Vol. 2, *1976–1988* (1994; Paris: Gallimard Quarto, 2001), 1485.

20. "'Fieldwork in Philosophy,' interview with A. Honneth, H. Kocyba and B. Scwibs, April 1985," in Pierre Bourdieu, *In Other Words: Essays Towards a Reflexive Sociology*, trans. Matthew Adamson (Stanford, CA: Stanford University Press, 1990), 4–5.

21. Morton White, *Science and Sentiment in America: Philosophical Thought from Jonathan Edwards to John Dewey* (New York: Oxford University Press, 1972), 301.

22. Rudolf Carnap, "The Elimination of Metaphysics through Logical Analysis of Language," trans. Arthur Pap, in A. J. Ayer, ed., *Logical Positivism* (New York: Free Press, 1959), 69. The original German title of this 1932 article, importantly, is actually "Überwindung der Metaphysik durch Logische Analyse der Sprache"—"overcoming" of metaphysics, not "elimination"—when overcoming metaphysics is precisely what Heidegger promised to do himself in his *Being and Time* (1929), and matches language Heidegger adopted in the late 1930s, as in the text entitled "Überwindung der Metaphysik," published finally in 1954. Michael Friedman, *A Parting of the Ways: Carnap, Cassirer, and Heidegger* (Chicago: Open Court, 2000), 23n29.

23. Friedman, *A Parting of the Ways*, 8.

24. Richard Rorty, *The Linguistic Turn: Recent Essays in Philosophical Method* (Chicago: University of Chicago Press, 1967).

25. In addition to Michael Friedman's work, see A. W. Carus, *Carnap and Twentieth-Century Thought: Explication as Enlightenment* (Cambridge, UK: Cambridge University Press, 2007).

26. Friedman, *A Parting of the Ways*, 153n210.

27. Rudolf Carnap, "Intellectual Autobiography," in *The Philosophy of Rudolf Carnap*, ed. Paul Arthur Schilpp (LaSalle, IL: Open Court, 1963), 69.

28. George A. Reisch, *How the Cold War Transformed Philosophy of Science: To the Icy Slopes of Logic* (New York: Cambridge University Press, 2005).

29. See Joel Isaac, "W. V. Quine and the Origins of Analytic Philosophy in the United States," *Modern Intellectual History* 2:2 (2005): 205–34, partly integrated into his *Working Knowledge: Making the Human Sciences from Parsons to Kuhn* (Cambridge, MA: Harvard University Press, 2012).

30. On the social success of *Language, Truth and Logic*, see "No True

Answers: A. J. Ayer," in Stefan Collini, *Absent Minds: Intellectuals in Britain* (Oxford, UK: Oxford University Press, 2006), 399–401.

31. Carnap, "Elimination of Metaphysics," 80.

32. On the Harvard and Princeton departments, see Bruce Kuklick, "Philosophy and Inclusion in the United States, 1929–2001," in David A. Hollinger, ed., *The Humanities and the Dynamics of Inclusion since World War II* (Baltimore, MD: Johns Hopkins University Press, 2006), 159–88.

33. W.V.O. Quine, *The Time of My Life* (Cambridge, MA: MIT Press, 1985), 194.

34. A. J. Ayer, "The Claims of Philosophy," in *Reflections on Our Age: Lectures Delivered at the Opening Session of UNESCO* (London, 1948), 51–66.

35. W.V.O. Quine, *Word and Object* (Cambridge, MA: MIT Press, 1960), 133.

36. See Andrew Jewett, "Canonizing Dewey: Naturalism, Logical Empiricism, and the Idea of American Philosophy," *Modern Intellectual History* 8:1 (2011): 91–125.

37. On the repudiation of the original analytic project, see Richard Rorty, introduction to Wilfrid Sellars, *Empiricism and the Philosophy of Mind* (Cambridge, MA: Harvard University Press, 1997), 1–6.

38. On the precise dating of the moment that "analytic" philosophy becomes hegemonic and the many alternatives become outliers, I am most impressed by the retrospection of Hilary Putnam, traveling on the Harvard-Princeton axis and to other places in between, who puts it definitively no earlier than 1953 (based on his own biography); this would be consistent, too, with Stanley Cavell's autobiographical recollections of those years. Hilary Putnam, "A Half Century of Philosophy, Viewed from Within," in *American Academic Culture in Transformation: Fifty Years, Four Disciplines*, ed. Thomas Bender and Carl E. Schorske (Princeton, NJ: Princeton University Press, 1998); and Stanley Cavell, *Little Did I Know: Excerpts from Memory* (Stanford, CA: Stanford University Press, 2010).

39. Quine, *Time of My Life*, 352.

40. Herbert Marcuse, *One-Dimensional Man: Studies in the Ideology of Advanced Industrial Society*, 2nd ed. (1964; Boston: Beacon Press, 1991), 216, 149n2.

41. See William Ruddick, "Philosophy and Public Affairs," *Social Research* 47:4 (Winter 1980): 734–48.

42. The primary biography of Lévi-Strauss in English is now Patrick Wilcken, *Claude Lévi-Strauss: The Poet in the Laboratory* (New York: Penguin, 2010).

43. Peter M. Rutkoff and William B. Scott, *New School: A History of the New School for Social Research* (New York: Free Press, 1986), 157.

44. Wilcken, *Claude Lévi-Strauss*, 123.

45. Rutkoff and Scott, *New School*, 153, 170.

46. See Claude Lévi-Strauss, "The Lessons of Linguistics," in *The View from Afar*, trans. Joachim Neugroschel and Phoebe Hoss (1983; New York: Basic Books, 1985), 138–47.

47. Claude Lévi-Strauss, "New York in 1941," in *The View from Afar*, 266; Wilcken, *Claude Lévi-Strauss*, 141.

48. Lévi-Strauss's presentation of his background and intellectual debts comes in *Tristes Tropiques*, trans. John and Doreen Weightman (1955; New York: Picador, 1973), 70–71. The French original, published in 1955, also received a different, abridged translation by John Russell that first appeared in the United States in 1961 under the more academic title *Tristes Tropiques: Anthropological Studies of Primitive Society in Brazil* and in the United Kingdom as *A World on the Wane*.

49. Christopher Johnson, *Claude Lévi-Strauss: The Formative Years* (Cambridge, UK: Cambridge University Press, 2003), 9–10.

50. Lévi-Strauss complained about it himself, and responded in *Tristes Tropiques*, where, interestingly, his defense was to insist that Boasianism ("the authors to whom I willingly proclaim my debt, Lowie, Kroeber, and Boas") was "as far removed as possible" from Anglo-American philosophies which either he, or his French adversaries, would truly find objectionable: the pragmatism of "James or Dewey" and "what is now called logical positivism" (73).

51. Rutkoff and Scott, *New School*, 170.

52. Wilcken, *Claude Lévi-Strauss*, 161. The sixth section of the École Pratique eventually became independent as the École des Hautes Études en Sciences Sociales (EHESS), the central institution of present-day university social science in France.

53. A rare book that acknowledges the history and implications of both linguistic turns, and gestures toward a third (the "linguistic relativism" advocated by Franz Boas's student Edward Sapir and Sapir's student Benjamin Whorf, better known as the "Sapir-Whorf hypothesis," which can "be considered a ruling paradigm in the contemporary social sciences" [2]) is Michael Losonsky, *Linguistic Turns in Modern Philosophy* (Cambridge, UK: Cambridge University Press, 2006). See also Judith Surkis, "When Was the Linguistic Turn? A Genealogy," *American Historical Review* 117:3 (June 2012): 700–722.

54. Indeed, though Carnap was among a very few students even to attend Frege's courses—and he participated in three of them—it was not by this personal instruction that he understood the implications of Frege's

doctrines, he claimed: "Only much later, after the first world war, when I read Frege's and Russell's books with greater attention, did I recognize the value of Frege's work not only for the foundations of mathematics, but for philosophy in general." Rudolf Carnap, "Intellectual Autobiography," in Paul Arthur Schilpp, ed., *The Philosophy of Rudolf Carnap* (La Salle, IL: Open Court, 1963), 6.

55. Carl E. Schorske, "The New Rigorism in the Human Sciences, 1940–1960," in *American Academic Culture in Transformation: Fifty Years, Four Disciplines*, ed. Thomas Bender and Carl E. Schorske (Princeton, NJ: Princeton University Press, 1997), 309–29. Schorske notes regretfully that "most of the academic culture [of this new rigorism] . . . fell back in the 1950s on its Anglo-Saxon heritage and built, almost unwittingly, a kind of Atlantic wall against continental thought" (328). A recent tour d'horizon that draws similar conclusions about postwar social science transformations is Hamilton Cravens, "Column Right, March! Nationalism, Scientific Positivism, and the Conservative Turn of the American Social Sciences in the Cold War Era," in *Cold War Social Science: Knowledge Production, Liberal Democracy, and Human Nature*, ed. Mark Solovey and Hamilton Cravens (New York: Palgrave Macmillan, 2012), 117–36.

56. Wilcken, *Claude Lévi-Strauss*, 11.

57. See Randall Collins, *Four Sociological Traditions* (Oxford, UK: Oxford University Press, 1994), 198–203 and 239n7; Collins traces the structural functionalism of Parsons and Robert Merton back to the Durkheimian tradition.

58. Johnson, *Claude Lévi-Strauss: The Formative Years*, 92 and 91–103 as a whole. On the history of the Macy Conferences, which began in 1942, see Jean-Pierre Dupuy, *The Mechanization of the Mind: On the Origins of Cognitive Science*, trans. M. B. DeBevoise (Princeton, NJ: Princeton University Press, 2000), chapter 3, and Katherine Hayles, *How We Became Posthuman: Virtual Bodies in Cybernetics, Literature, and Informatics* (Chicago: University of Chicago Press, 1999), esp. chapter 3.

59. See Bernard Dionysius Geoghegan, "From Information Theory to French Theory: Jakobson, Lévi-Strauss, and the Scientific Apparatus," *Critical Inquiry* 38 (Autumn 2011): 96–126.

60. Quine, *Time of My Life*, 228. The finished *Word and Object* appeared in 1960.

61. Anthony Q. Hazard Jr., *Postwar Anti-Racism: The United States, UNESCO, and "Race," 1945–1968* (New York: Palgrave Macmillan, 2012), 35.

62. Claude Lévi-Strauss, *Race and History* (Paris: UNESCO, 1952), 5–7; subsequent references are cited in the text as *R&H* followed by the page number.

63. This theme of true enlightenment as the ethnographic admiration for diversity is spelled out further in Lévi-Strauss, "The Three Humanisms" (1956), integrated into the chapter "Answers to Some Investigations," in *Structural Anthropology*, vol. 2, trans. Monique Layton (Chicago: University of Chicago Press, 1983), 271–74.

64. Claude Lévi-Strauss, *Race et Histoire* (1952; Paris: Denoël, 1987), 19; *R&H*, 11.

65. Lévi-Strauss, *The Savage Mind* (1962, 1966; Oxford, UK: Oxford University Press, 1996), 16.

66. Claude Lévi-Strauss, "Introduction: History and Anthropology," in *Structural Anthropology*, vol. 1, trans. Claire Jacobson and Brooke Grundfest Schoepf (1958; New York: Basic Books, 1963), 6–11; "Boasian nominalism" appears on 10.

67. Gilbert Rist, *The History of Development: From Western Origins to Global Faith*, new ed., trans. Patrick Camiller (2001; London: Zed Books, 2002), 67.

68. Ibid., 75.

69. The famous phrase is a condensation of Ricoeur's discussion of ways to situate Freud in relation to different interpretive traditions including "the whole stream of hermeneutics which we shall . . . place under the heading of 'suspicion'"; Paul Ricoeur, *Freud and Philosophy: An Essay on Interpretation*, trans. Denis Savage (New Haven, CT: Yale University Press, 1970), 30.

70. Claude Lévi-Strauss, *The Savage Mind*, 246–47.

71. Michel Foucault, *The Order of Things: An Archaeology of the Human Sciences* (1966; New York: Pantheon Books, 1971), 387.

72. Quoted in Caws, "What is Structuralism?," *Partisan Review* 35:1 (Winter 1968): 82, 86.

73. Roland Barthes, "To Write: An Intransitive Verb?," in *The Languages of Criticism and the Sciences of Man: The Structuralist Controversy*, ed. Richard Macksey and Eugenio Donato (Baltimore, MD: Johns Hopkins University Press, 1970), 135.

74. Louis Althusser, "The Humanist Controversy" (1967), in his *The Humanist Controversy and Other Writings*, ed. François Matheron, trans. G. M. Goshgarian (London: Verso, 2003), 273.

75. Ibid., 265, 266.

76. "Structuralism," Special Issue, *Yale French Studies* 36–37 (1966); Jacques Ehrmann, ed., *Structuralism* (New York: Anchor-Doubleday, 1970).

77. H. Stuart Hughes, *The Obstructed Path: French Social Thought in the Years of Desperation, 1930–1960* (New York: Harper, 1968), 290, back cover of the HarperTorchbooks paperback edition.

78. Ibid.

79. Sanche de Gramont, "There Are No Superior Societies," *New York Times Magazine*, January 28, 1968. Reprinted in E. Nelson Hayes and Tanya Hayes, eds., *Claude Lévi-Strauss: The Anthropologist as Hero* (Cambridge, MA: MIT Press), 1970.

80. Caws, "What is Structuralism?," *Partisan Review* 35:1 (Winter 1968): 82.

81. Ibid., 87.

82. François Cusset, *French Theory*, 29–32.

83. Preface to Macksey and Donato, eds., *The Languages of Criticism and the Sciences of Man*, xi.

84. Baring, *Young Derrida*, 109.

85. Jacques Derrida, "Structure, Sign, and Play in the Discourse of the Human Sciences," in Macksey and Donato, eds., *The Languages of Criticism and the Sciences of Man*, 252.

86. Ibid., 264–65.

87. For Heidegger's extensive pre–and post–World War II successes in France, see Ethan Kleinberg, *Generation Existential: Heidegger's Philosophy in France, 1927–1961* (Ithaca, NY: Cornell University Press, 2005).

88. Martin Heidegger, "Letter on Humanism" (1947), trans. Frank A. Capuzzi and J. Glenn Gray, in *Basic Writings*, 2nd ed., ed. David Farrell Krell (New York: HarperCollins, 1993), 265.

89. See Peter Eli Gordon, "Hammer without a Master: French Phenomenology and the Origins of Deconstruction (Or, How Derrida Read Heidegger)," in *Histories of Postmodernism*, ed. Mark Bevir, Jill Hargus, and Sara Rushing (New York: Routledge, 2007), 103–30.

90. This may be the place to answer why Heidegger, despite his Nazism, his postwar impenitence and dismissal of the Nazi Holocaust of Europe's Jews, and the quasi-mysticism of his late work, continued to be indispensable to philosophers in the postwar period and remains so today. To make the question more challenging, we can acknowledge and put to one side the vital advances in phenomenology made by *Being and Time* (1929), ideas about being-in-the-world, which will always be valuable but require no contribution from Heidegger after 1933. Likewise, we can sequester the pre-1933 personal ties and tutelage that sustained Heidegger's influence for so many famous former students and auditors, including, among the Jewish refugees to America, Hannah Arendt, Herbert Marcuse, and Leo Strauss. In the terms of the discourse of the crisis of man as I have reconstructed it, Heidegger's indispensable value, which persisted in his "late" writings from the 1940s through the 1960s, is that he knew and articulated the same analysis of the crises of modernity that had animated re-enlightenment thought, admitted the shared challenge that only negative

reconstructions of these fundamental pieces of the modern project might undo the crisis, and then—unlike most everyone else—dove in at the darkest point, embracing passivity, fatalism, speechlessness or poeticizing, mysticism, and the insecurity of rational protection of humanity or any preservation of civilization. In chapter 2, we could see that chastened, logical demands for a universal history without progress, a philosophical anthropology without superiority or self-protection, science without technical mastery, and faith without object or belief could be recognized but hardly accommodated by re-enlightenment thinkers who wanted finally to preserve action, philosophy, reason, and civilization. So Heidegger is preserved as the black sheep in the family of re-enlightenment thinking, and needed as its essential alter ego: facing a path no one wanted to take, he took it and never ceased praising it in different sets of metaphors. The late Frankfurt school of Adorno may have come closest to philosophical solutions commensurate with Heideggerian fatalism when it followed the wartime *Dialectic of Enlightenment* with the pursuit, well into the 1960s, of a "negative dialectic." Adorno tried to repel the rival Heideggerian project of existentialist negativity in *The Jargon of Authenticity*, which originally formed a part of the growing manuscript that became *Negative Dialectics*; see "Author's Note" (1967) to Theodor W. Adorno, *The Jargon of Authenticity*, trans. Knut Tarnowski and Frederic Will (1964; Evanston, IL: Northwestern University Press, 1973), xix–xx.

91. The best account remains Art Berman, *From the New Criticism to Deconstruction: The Reception of Structuralism and Post-Structuralism* (Urbana: University of Illinois Press, 1988).

92. Michèle Lamont, "How to Become a Dominant French Philosopher: The Case of Jacques Derrida," *American Journal of Sociology* 93:3 (November 1987): 612.

93. This was the "farce," in Rolf Wiggershaus's description, in which in January 1969, fearing that a large meeting of students in the Institute building secretly foreshadowed a longer-term occupation, Adorno and his colleagues had them all arrested. Wiggershaus, *The Frankfurt School*, 633.

94. "Death of man": Michel Foucault, "L'homme, est-il mort?" (1966) in *Dits et Écrits*, vol. 1, 1954–1975, (1994; Paris: Gallimard Quarto, 2001), 568–72; "Ends of man": Jacques Derrida, "The Ends of Man" (1968), in *Margins of Philosophy*, trans. Alan Bass (1972; Chicago: University of Chicago Press, 1982), 109–36; "the author has disappeared": Michel Foucault, "What is an Author?" (1969), trans. Josué V. Harari, in *Aesthetics, Method, and Epistemology*, vol. 2, *Essential Works of Foucault, 1954–1984* (New York: New Press, 1998), 205–22; "death of the author": Roland Barthes, "The Death of the Author," trans. Richard Howard, *Aspen*, 5–6 (Fall–Winter 1967): n.p.; and "death of literature": Jacques Ehrmann, "The Death of Lit-

erature," *New Literary History* 3:1 (Autumn 1971): 31–47. I have not been able to ascertain when "death of the subject" comes into use initially, except to note that by the 1980s it stands as a hyperbolic and dismissive formulation used to denominate a fashionable but already clichéd critique of the Cartesian or bourgeois subject. Prominent uses appear in Fredric Jameson, "Postmodernism, Or the Cultural Logic of Late Capitalism," *New Left Review* 1:146 (July/August 1984): 63; and Donna Haraway, "Situated Knowledges: The Science Question in Feminism and the Privilege of Partial Perspective," *Feminist Studies* 14:3 (Autumn 1988): 585.

95. The transcript appears as Noam Chomsky and Michel Foucault, "Human Nature: Justice vs. Power" (1971), in *The Chomsky-Foucault Debate: On Human Nature* (New York: New Press, 2006).

96. All biographical information on Chomsky comes from Robert F. Barsky, *Noam Chomsky: A Life of Dissent* (Cambridge, MA: MIT Press, 1997).

97. See Noam Chomsky, *Cartesian Linguistics: A Chapter in the History of Rationalist Thought*, 3rd ed. (1966; Cambridge, UK: Cambridge University Press, 2009).

98. For Chomsky's presentation of his ideas and theories to a general audience in the 1960s, see Noam Chomsky, *Language and Mind*, enlarged ed. (1968; New York: Harcourt Brace Jovanovich, 1972).

99. Chomsky and Foucault, "Human Nature," 41–43, 51–52, 55.

CONCLUSION
MORAL HISTORY AND THE TWENTIETH CENTURY

1. Ruth Benedict, "Franz Boas: An Obituary," *Nation*, January 2, 1943, 15.

2. Claude Lévi-Strauss, *Race and History* (Paris: UNESCO, 1952), 49 and 45.

3. Ibid., 12.

4. James T. Kloppenberg, *Uncertain Victory: Social Democracy and Progressivism in European and American Thought, 1870–1920* (New York: Oxford University Press, 1986); Louis Menand, *The Metaphysical Club* (New York: Farrar, Straus & Giroux, 2001); Howard Brick, *Age of Contradiction: American Thought and Culture in the 1960s* (New York: Twayne, 1998); Daniel T. Rodgers, *Age of Fracture* (Cambridge, MA: Harvard University Press, 2011). Meanwhile, Brick has in fact produced a model of a new kind of synthetic history for the period in a book on "post-capitalist visions," and Rodgers authored a history of Progressivism as estimable as Kloppenberg's though different in approach. Howard Brick, *Transcending Capitalism: Visions of a New Society in Modern Ameri-*

can Thought (Ithaca, NY: Cornell University Press, 2006); Daniel T. Rodgers, *Atlantic Crossings: Social Politics in a Progressive Age* (Cambridge, MA: Harvard University Press, 1998).

5. Cesare Vasoli, "The Renaissance Concept of Philosophy," in *The Cambridge History of Renaissance Philosophy*, ed. Charles B. Schmitt and Quentin Skinner (Cambridge, UK: Cambridge University Press, 1988), 61–62.

6. Perry Anderson, *The Origins of Postmodernity* (London: Verso, 1998), 7–12.

7. Olson quoted in Tom Clark, *Charles Olson: The Allegory of a Poet's Life* (New York: Norton, 1991), 233.

8. Erich Kahler, *The Tower and the Abyss: An Inquiry into the Transformation of the Individual* (New York: George Braziller, 1957). Quotations are from the preface, xi.

9. Charles Olson, "The Present is Prologue" (1952), in *Collected Prose*, ed. Donald Allen and Benjamin Friedlander (Berkeley: University of California Press, 1997), 207. Perry Anderson quotes a comparable statement, which may well be the same text produced by a different chain of sources— an autobiographical entry "set down" "[o]n 4 November 1952" and published in *Twentieth Century Authors—First Supplement* (1955). Anderson, *Origins of Postmodernity*, 7 and 7n10.

10. For an essay on all varieties of "end of history" and posthistorical thinking, see Perry Anderson, "The Ends of History" (1992), in Perry Anderson, *A Zone of Engagement* (London: Verso, 1992).

11. Fukuyama's initial article, "The End of History?" appeared promptly in the *National Interest* in 1989. His influential book came out in 1992.

12. Thus the English translation of Kojève's courses (delivered in French in the 1930s, assembled by Raymond Queneau and published in France in 1947) was edited and published in the United States by Leo Strauss's successor, Allan Bloom. Alexandre Kojève, *Introduction to the Reading of Hegel: Lectures on the Phenomenology of Spirit*, ed. Raymond Queneau and Allan Bloom, trans. James H. Nichols Jr. (1947; New York: Basic Books, 1969).

13. Francis Fukuyama, *The End of History and the Last Man* (1992; New York: Free Press, 2006), 188.

14. Lutz Niethammer, *Posthistoire: Has History Come to an End?*, trans. Patrick Camiller (1989; London: Verso), 2.

15. Ibid., 2–3.

16. Ibid., 1.

17. Ibid., 4.

18. The endorsements from Niebuhr and Mumford appear on the front and back of the jacket of the original hardcover publication. Roderick Se-

idenberg, *Post-historic Man: An Inquiry* (Chapel Hill: University of North Carolina Press, 1950), n.p. The book was later issued as a paperback by Beacon Press (publishers of Herbert Marcuse) in 1957, and by Viking in 1974, ascending the ladder of publishing prestige with each reissue. Niethammer mentions Seidenberg, who he groups with Teilhard de Chardin, in Lutz Niethammer, "Afterthoughts on Posthistoire," *History and Memory* 1:1 (Spring–Summer 1989), 28.

19. Susan Sontag, "What's Happening in America (1966)," in *Essays of the 1960s and 70s,* ed. David Rieff (New York: Library of America, 2013), 457.

20. Leslie Fiedler, "The New Mutants," *Partisan Review* (Fall 1965): 508.

21. Ibid., 505.

22. Ibid.

23. Irving Howe, "Mass Society and Post-Modern Fiction," *Partisan Review* (Summer 1959): 422.

24. Ibid., 436.

25. Ibid.

26. An important anthology (a form very meaningful to the earlier discourse) was George Packer, ed., *The Fight Is for Democracy: Winning the War of Ideas in America and the World* (New York: HarperPerennial, 2003).

27. Gisli Palsson, et al., "Reconceptualizing the 'Anthropos' in the Anthropocene: Integrating the Social Sciences and Humanities in Global Environmental Change Research," *Environmental Science & Policy* 28 (April 2013): 8.

28. Dipesh Chakrabarty, "The Climate of History: Four Theses," *Critical Inquiry* 35:2 (January 2009): 221–22.

29. Herman Melville, *Moby-Dick* (1851; New York: Library of America, 2010), 197.

ACKNOWLEDGMENTS

The compensation for being such a slow writer is that one accumulates debts to so many people. Each name recalls a contribution of kindness, conversation, or tutelage that is a pleasure to remember.

For training in the fields of this study, I am grateful to Philip Fisher, Elaine Scarry, John McGreevy, Thomas Augst, the late Donald Fleming, and John Plotz at Harvard; Tom Paulin, John Kelly, Christopher Butler, Valentine Cunningham, and Hermione Lee at Oxford; and David Bromwich, Michael Trask, Michael Denning, Nigel Alderman, Elizabeth Dillon, Peter Brooks, David Brion Davis, Jon Butler, Harry Stout, the late Frank Turner, and Nancy Cott at Yale.

This book began as a dissertation, and I am profoundly grateful to my advisers, the historian Jean-Christophe Agnew and the literary scholar Wai Chee Dimock, for their patience and the pressure of their thought.

I have had another occasion to express my debt to Stanley Cavell. I may not have another chance as suitable as this one to say what I owe to Philip Fisher. I have encountered in no other circumstance a lecturer as great, a mind as serious and profound, or a standard of intellectual commitment as admirable. Without perhaps acquiring anything he intended, I trace my orientations as a critic to what I learned and took from him.

Long ago in college and ever since, I have been especially grateful for the friendship, conversation, and ideas of Trieu Truong, Jace Clayton, Elizabeth Anne Davis, Benjamin Kunkel, Akash Kapur, Elizabeth Harman, and Jason Disterhoft. In England, I was grateful for the companionship and camaraderie of Matthew Creasy, Aravind Adiga, Jerome DeGroot, Sharon Rustin, Robert MacFarlane, Joyelle McSweeney, Julie Suk, Rupert Cousens, Helen Enchelmeier, and Heather Stewart. From graduate school, I am grateful to Isaac Reed, Lucia Trimbur, Eric Lindstrom, Lara Cohen, Rebecca Berne, Megan Quigley, Nick Salvato, Kamran Javadizadeh, Amy Reading, Mark Krotov, Sandy Zipp, Johannes Türk, Tobias Boes, Aaron Matz, and Marco Roth.

At *n+1*, I am especially grateful to Keith Gessen, for his friendship and profound influence during the time we worked together. But I am grateful also for the influence and collaboration of Benjamin Kunkel, Marco Roth, Allison Lorentzen, Chad Harbach, Isaac Scarborough, Carla Blumenkranz, Nikil Saval, Christian Lorentzen, Sabine Rogers, Elif Batuman, Alexandra Heifetz, Dan O. Williams, Kathleen Ross, Dayna Tortorici, Charles Petersen, Elizabeth Gumport, Christopher Glazek, Richard Beck, Martha Sharpe, and Jo-ey Tang.

In Boston, New York, Toronto, and assorted locales, I am grateful to J. D. Daniels, Susanna Kaysen, Alexander Star, Mary Karr, Gerald Howard, Melissa Flashman, Christine Smallwood, Gemma Sieff, Astra Taylor, Chris Parris-Lamb, Rachel Rosenfelt, Molly Young, Nika Mavrody, Erin Sheehy, Sam Stark, Deborah Friedell, Peter Terzian, Caleb Crain, Lorin Stein, Robin Kirman, Joel Pava, Daniel Menaker, Andrea Graham, Maura Kelly, Ceridwen Dovey, Laura Kipnis, Helen DeWitt, Kristin Dombek, Claire Jarvis, Donnan Steele, Gideon Lewis-Kraus, Guy Walter, Cédric Duroux, Heinrich Geiselberger, Margaux Williamson, Misha Glouberman, Sheila Heti, Lucas Rebick, Jessica Johnson, Adam Thirlwell, Lawrence Jackson, the late André Schiffrin, and Leina Schiffrin.

At the New School I have benefited from the collegiality and conversation of Laura Frost, Noah Isenberg, Alexandra Chasin, Robin Mookerjee, Inessa Medzhebovskaya, Albert Mobilio, Elizabeth Kendall, Margo Jefferson, Siddhartha Deb, Wendy Walters, Julie Napolin, Val Vinokur, Rose Réjouis, Ann Snitow, Zishan Ugurlu, McKenzie Wark, James Miller, and Nancy Fraser. I am especially grateful for the encouragement of former Dean Neil Gordon and the support of Dean Stephanie Browner, both of Eugene Lang College. Three research assistants, Nika Mavrody, Anne Schult, and Emily Johnson, have my utmost gratitude and friendship.

I am grateful to Walter Benn Michaels for championing this book and to Peter Brooks for helping it find its way to publication, and to Bruce Robbins, Mark McGurl, Susie Linfield, Ross Posnock, Casey Nelson Blake, Lindsay Waters, William Flesch, David Hollinger, Morris Dickstein, Sean McCann, Paul Bové, Amy Hungerford, Paul Fry, and Robert Silvers.

At a critical moment, James Wood's belief in the project and encouragement was essential to my morale. In a chance meeting in the college library Adam Kirsch invoked the name of Erich Kahler—an essential piece of intellectual help. Julie Mehretu generously gave her permission for the cover and worked to improve the design.

At the Institute for Advanced Study in Princeton, I am grateful to Kirstie Venanzi and Marcia Tucker of the HS-SS library for assistance that, it is no exaggeration to say, helped to transform and deepen the book. I thank Michael Walzer for the loan of books, Danielle Allen for help with Greek, and Didier Fassin for talk about Claude Lévi-Strauss and moral anthropology. Nothing I can say can adequately acknowledge the debt I owe to Joan Wallach Scott, whose brilliance and responsiveness encountering the whole manuscript at a late stage was a further gift of my year at the Institute and her unique generosity. I gained particular insight from two colleagues in the School of Social Science, Svërker Sörlin and Joseph Masco.

Emily Ascher has been a true friend over many years. My two oldest and most trusted friends, Dushko Petrovich and Daniel Trutt, as well as Victoria Solan, are beloved to me.

At Princeton University Press, I am grateful to Anne Savarese, Alison MacKeen, Hanne Winarsky, Claudia Acevedo, Juliana Fidler, Debbie Tegarden, the incomparable Cathy Slovensky, Julia Haav, Jessica Pellien, Jason Alejandro, and Tom Broughton-Willett, as well as the three readers for the press.

Much of the book was written in the Snow Public Library, Orleans, Massachusetts, and I am grateful to its librarians and patrons.

Alan Greif, Gabrielle Jackson, Keith Gessen, Marco Roth, Dayna Tortorici, Dushko Petrovich, Elizabeth Anne Davis, Jason Disterhoft, Alex Star, Charles Petersen, and Yael Goldstein all gave comments.

The book's dedication is to my parents, Alan Greif and Esther Blank Greif. It is an inadequate tribute for a lifetime of thoughtfulness, help, and love.

The person to whom I owe everything, joyfully, today and for the last fourteen years, is Gabrielle Benette Jackson. With the recent arrival of Simone Petal, who likes to play with books as much as she likes them read to her, our replacement is here. Working on a book doesn't compare to the joy of raising a bright-eyed little person—but that, too, like everything, is for Gabrielle.

INDEX